Clinical Legal Education: Theory and Practice

Clinical Legal Education: Theory and Practice

Jacqueline Kinghan
Amir Paz-Fuchs
Lucy Yeatman

OXFORD
UNIVERSITY PRESS

OXFORD
UNIVERSITY PRESS

Great Clarendon Street, Oxford, OX2 6DP,
United Kingdom

Oxford University Press is a department of the University of Oxford.
It furthers the University's objective of excellence in research, scholarship,
and education by publishing worldwide. Oxford is a registered trade mark of
Oxford University Press in the UK and in certain other countries.

Published in the United States of America by Oxford University Press
198 Madison Avenue, New York, NY 10016, United States of America

British Library Cataloguing in Publication Data
Data available

Library of Congress Control Number: 2025946734

ISBN 9780198878407

Printed and bound by CPI Group (UK) Ltd., Croydon, CR0 4YY

The manufacturer's authorized representative in the EU for product safety is
Oxford University Press España S.A. of Parque Empresarial San Fernando de Henares,
Avenida de Castilla, 2 – 28830 Madrid (www.oup.es/en or product.safety@oup.com).
OUP España S.A. also acts as importer into Spain of products made by the manufacturer.

MIX
Paper | Supporting
responsible forestry
FSC® C013604

Acknowledgement

The authors would like to thank colleagues who contributed insights to the 'View from Clinical Practice' sections in each chapter and, more generally, for the valuable support of the clinical legal education community in being so willing to share reflections on best practice in the field. We also extend our thanks to the anonymous reviewers and to Professors Steven Vaughan and Tim Casey for helpful review comments; and to Cameron Dunleavy for his assistance with the study in Chapter 12. Any errors or omissions are of course our own.

Finally, we would like to dedicate this textbook to the late Professor William Twining, who sadly passed away during the final stages of its preparation. William was an inspirational colleague whose commitment to understanding, and promoting, both the theory and practice of legal education leaves a lasting legacy.

Brief contents

Detailed contents

SECTION ONE **Clinical Legal Education and Access to Justice**

Guide to Using this Book

Clinical Legal Education: Theory and Practice provides a reflective learning experience in which the issues and concepts underpinning clinical legal practice are set against the realistic context of clinical casework and related projects. Readers are encouraged to reflect on their own experiences of clinical legal education as they move through the textbook. That said, chapters do not have to be read sequentially and many can be consulted in a standalone way with reference to issues that might arise on an ad hoc basis during clinical practice (for example, an ethical problem, exposure to legal aid or a technological innovation) and/or reading assigned as part of clinical courses as part of the law school curriculum.

The key features included in the book are outlined here to ensure that you understand each topic and that you can consider, and reflect upon, theoretical issues in light of practical experience.

> **Chapter Overview**
>
> This chapter will introduce you to legal aid provision and i
> legal education. It explores the way in which legal aid in th
> **years and the impact of those changes on those who cann**
> advice and/or representation in relation to their legal prob
> By the end of this chapter, you should be able to:
>
> - Understand the history and background to legal aid pro

Learning Objectives

The Learning Objectives at the start of each chapter set out what you will learn by the end of reading the chapter. Together with the Chapter Overview, these objectives should also acquaint you with content of each chapter and help you to navigate through different sections.

> **REFLECTION POINT**
>
> Consider the factors above that might weigh in favour of an entit
> representation funded by legal aid for those accused and charge
>
> - Do you consider the criteria to be too wide or narrow?
> - What do you think might constitute 'any other reasons' weighi
> ment to a lawyer in the interests of justice?

Reflection Points

At different points throughout each chapter you will be encouraged to reflect on issues discussed, particularly in light of your own clinical experience. As explored throughout the book, reflection is an integral part of clinical legal education and most law schools adopt some form of reflective assessment. The Reflection Points therefore help to prepare you for reflective discussion you will have as part of your clinical course provision, as well as for your written assessments.

Practical Exercises

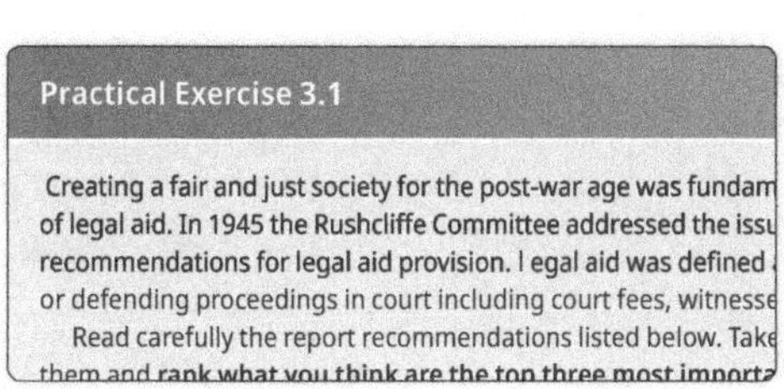
Practical Exercise 3.1

Creating a fair and just society for the post-war age was fundam
of legal aid. In 1945 the Rushcliffe Committee addressed the issu
recommendations for legal aid provision. l egal aid was defined
or defending proceedings in court including court fees, witness
Read carefully the report recommendations listed below. Take
them and rank what you think are the top three most importa

Each chapter has Practical Exercises relevant to the chapter content. These help to situate the 'theory' of book in the 'practice' of clinical legal education. You can complete these practical exercises independently, or, you may wish to do them with other students from your course in order to hear different perspectives on issues that arise.

A View From Clinical Practice

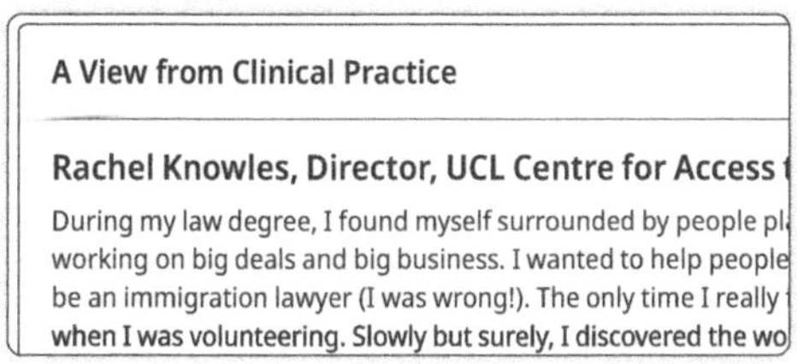
A View from Clinical Practice

Rachel Knowles, Director, UCL Centre for Access
During my law degree, I found myself surrounded by people pl
working on big deals and big business. I wanted to help people
be an immigration lawyer (I was wrong!). The only time I really
when I was volunteering. Slowly but surely, I discovered the wo

Clinical legal educators, and other colleagues involved in the management or delivery of clinical legal education, bring rich experience to each chapter through sections entitled 'A View from Clinical Practice'. Some of these sections contain tips to help you on your own education journey and others give insights based on experience to inform your understanding of how theoretical issues might arise in practice. You may wish to consult these sections and discuss them with your own lecturers or supervising lawyers in clinic.

Taking Stock

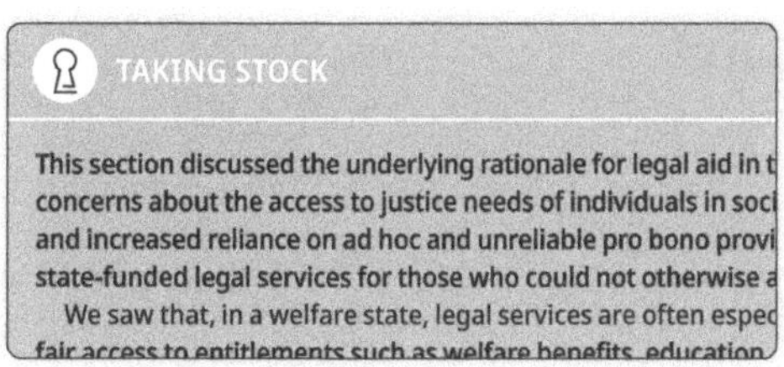
TAKING STOCK

This section discussed the underlying rationale for legal aid in t
concerns about the access to justice needs of individuals in soci
and increased reliance on ad hoc and unreliable pro bono provi
state-funded legal services for those who could not otherwise a
We saw that, in a welfare state, legal services are often espec
fair access to entitlements such as welfare benefits, education

Each chapter is divided into three or four sections. At the end of some sections there is a 'Taking Stock' box. This provides a brief summary of the key themes covered in that section of the chapter, providing a helpful point for you to pause and review your own understanding of the material before moving on.

Take Your Learning Further

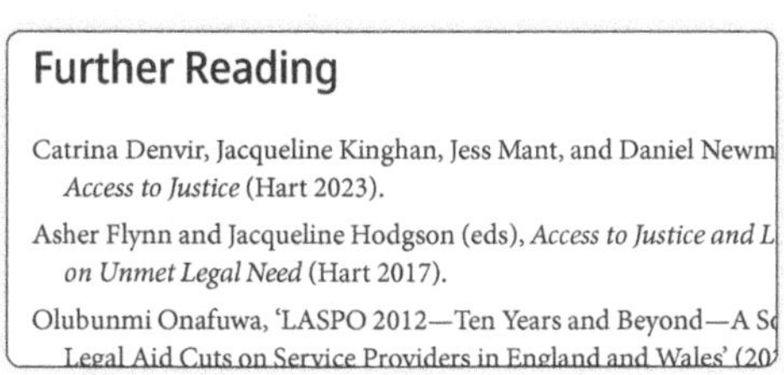
Further Reading

Catrina Denvir, Jacqueline Kinghan, Jess Mant, and Daniel Newm
Access to Justice (Hart 2023).
Asher Flynn and Jacqueline Hodgson (eds), *Access to Justice and L
on Unmet Legal Need* (Hart 2017).
Olubunmi Onafuwa, 'LASPO 2012—Ten Years and Beyond—A S
Legal Aid Cuts on Service Providers in England and Wales' (20

The further reading sections at the end of each chapter provide a useful list of books and journal articles as a jumping-off point for further research.

SECTION ONE

Clinical Legal Education and Access to Justice

Introduction 1

Writing a textbook on clinical legal education (CLE) is no small task. Textbooks on more traditional modules come with their own challenges, but they usually benefit from an agreed list of essential topics and a rough sense of how to approach them (through the discussion of cases, legislation, examples, texts, and so forth). In contrast, CLE is much more than a single module: first, it aims to offer a paradigm shift in legal education, with relevance across the curriculum;[1] second, and relatedly, it is highly theoretical, seeking to justify its place within law schools as a pedagogy and as a form of ethical teaching. But, third, and confusingly, it also claims to be far more aligned with the practice of law and with the demands of the profession. Fourth, and finally, CLE also relates, of course, directly to the work of law clinics. These clinics vary wildly: some are part of a module, others are linked more loosely to the curriculum, and others still are entirely extra-curricular. Their operation also differs: some involve partnership with charities, others rely on external practitioners for support, and yet others are supervised by academic members of staff, whether practising or not. How can all the issues raised by those clinics, and moreover by all those strands of theory and practice, be addressed within one textbook? That is the challenge in this book.

We begin with the view that this challenge can and should be addressed. Clinical legal education has come of age and deserves comprehensive and meaningful treatment. We do not aim to simplify its contribution—quite the contrary. As we discuss extensively in Chapter 5, the case method has been the paradigm pedagogy through which students across different jurisdictions have studied law for more than 150 years. During this time, the introduction of clinical legal education 'was to prove the most important'[2] contribution to legal education. Moreover, we are inclined to say that if, 25 years ago, two American academics observed that clinical legal education is 'so often called the most significant change in how the law is taught that it now sounds trite',[3] then this is now increasingly true beyond the United States.

According to LawWorks, a charity that supports and develops a network of free legal advice clinics across England and Wales, there were almost 300 clinics within the network

[1] Jonny Hall and Kevin Kerrigan, 'Clinic and the Wider Law Curriculum' (2011) 15 International Journal of Clinical Legal Education 25.

[2] Robert Stevens, *Law School: Legal Education in America from the 1850s to the 1980s* (University of North Carolina Press 1983) 211.

[3] Philip Schrag and Michael Meltsner, *Reflections on Clinical Legal Education* (Northeastern University Press 1998) 5.

in October 2024, with nearly half based in law schools.[4] This figure represents an increase of more than 70 per cent on the 175 clinics which were registered in the network in 2014. Through top-down decisions and grassroots initiatives, CLE is changing and reshaping how legal education is delivered in the UK.

1.1 **What Is CLE?**

Committing to a definition of any subject matter can risk creating more disagreement than consensus. This is partly because any definition is necessarily exclusionary. This matter is, perhaps, even more problematic in a field such as (higher) education, in which those engaged in a particular practice understandably feel committed to it, to the particular way they understand and implement it, and to the view that their endeavours fall under the broader aims of clinical legal education. And yet, offering a working definition of CLE is necessary if one wishes to understand its history, and work towards developing its aims, objectives, rationales, challenges, and prospects for the future. One can do so while simultaneously being aware of a family of projects that support CLE and are supported by it, such as client interviewing competitions, work experience schemes, final-year modules focused on ethics and professional responsibility, and so forth.

The definition we adopt here is heavily indebted to those suggested by Boone, Jeeves, and Macfarlane[5] and Bleasdale et al,[6] though not identical to either. Boone, Jeeves, and Macfarlane identify five requirements which they found to be constitutive of CLE. In what follows, we replace one of their five features, which we found unconvincing, with two drawn from Bleasdale et al that we believe are central to CLE.[7] The features we identify are: first, active participation; second, interaction 'in role'; third, the dynamic nature of the problem; fourth, the embeddedness of CLE within a planned curriculum; fifth, the incorporation of reflective practices as part of the process, and ideally as part of the assessment; and sixth, attention to the way law operates in everyday life, how it is experienced, and the way it advances or hinders social justice.

It will be useful to elaborate somewhat on each of these features. But first, it is worth explaining how we identified them. Any definition, particularly if it relates to an institution that operates in 'real life', could be viewed as arbitrary if it is not linked to that institution's goals. In this case, then, before listing the features that we think constitute CLE, we should explain what CLE is *for*. What are its *goals and aims*? Only once these goals are clear can we identify the features of CLE that best support them.

[4] LawWorks, *LawWorks Clinics Network Report January 2023–December 2023* (October 2024) 3, 5. https://www.lawworks.org.uk/sites/default/files/files/LW-ClinicsReport2023-web.pdf (last accessed 5 December 2024).

[5] Andrew Boone, Michael Jeeves, and Julie Macfarlane, 'Clinical Anatomy: Towards a Working Definition of Clinical Legal Education' (1987) 21 The Law Teacher 61.

[6] Lydia Bleasdale et al, 'Law Clinics: What, Why and How' in Linden Thomas and Nicholas Johnson (eds), *The Clinical Legal Education Handbook* (University of London Press 2020) https://press.uchicago.edu/ucp/books/book/distributed/C/bo52584691.html (last accessed 25 February 2022).

[7] In particular, we replaced the requirement that students be 'responsible for the outcome' with the study of the effect of law on society and the need for reflection as an inherent part of the process.

1.1.1 The Goals of CLE

The most widely accepted goal of CLE is to 'link theory and practice'. But even if there is broad agreement on this idea, it is not always clear what 'practice' means in this context. For example, some describe the goal of CLE as teaching the students 'practising ethical lawyering' and 'developing critical thinking'.[8] Others argue that while 'practice' is necessary, it is not sufficient. For them, the 'primary goal of clinical legal education is to teach students how to learn from experience'.[9] We explore this further in Chapter 6. Although these aspects of legal thinking—and, from the teacher's perspective, legal pedagogy—are centrally tied to law, they form part of a broader approach often called 'experiential learning'. CLE is, clearly, a natural setting for experiential learning. Students meet real (as opposed to simulated) clients, handle live cases, and face unpredictable challenges. In doing so, students develop a wide range of skills—legal, personal, and interpersonal, which we address in detail in Chapters 9, 10, 11, and 12—and deepen their legal knowledge. To summarize, the goals of CLE can be described as:

1. Linking theory with practice.
2. Learning through experience.
3. Developing lawyering skills.
4. Understanding, embedding, and applying legal ethics.
5. Appreciating the complex role of law and lawyers in the justice system and in society.

Clearly, different law clinics may emphasize some goals more than others, but these aims are widely shared. So we can ask: are these aims too ambitious for any one clinic to achieve? Jane Aiken reflects on this near-impossible mission of law clinics:

> We want our students to come away from the clinic with a more varied understanding of what it means to be a lawyer serving a client, with strong lawyering skills including negotiation, counselling, interviewing, and fact investigation. We hope to give them opportunities to develop their trial preparation and presentation of evidence skills and to gain an understanding of effective legal writing. On top of this, we want to expose our students to the deep injustices of poverty and abuse of power. We want to instil in them an abiding desire to use their legal skills to remedy these injustices and the wisdom to know the limitations of the legal system in effectuating comprehensive change in the conditions within which they operate. Needless to say, this is a set-up for failure.[10]

[8] William Berman, 'When Will They Ever Learn? Learning and Teaching from Mistakes in the Clinical Context' (2007) 13 Clinical Law Review 115, 118.

[9] Kenneth Kreiling, 'Clinical Education and Lawyer Competency: The Process of Learning to Learn from Experience through Properly Structured Clinical Supervision' (1981) 40 Maryland Law Review 284, 286; Justine Dunlap and Peter Joy, 'Reflection-in-Action: Designing New Clinical Teacher Training by Using Lessons Learned from New Clinicians' (2005) 11 Clinical Law Review 49, 52–53.

[10] Jane Aiken, 'Provocateurs for Justice' (2001) Georgetown Law Faculty Publications and Other Works 304, https://scholarship.law.georgetown.edu/facpub/304

REFLECTION POINT

Do you agree with Professor Aiken? Are clinics trying to do too much?

What is your experience?

Do you think that your clinic, and perhaps others that you're familiar with, get the balance right?

If that is not enough, a further proposed goal suggests that CLE should 'expose students to social injustices and to the potential (and limits) of the law and lawyers in addressing those injustices'.[11] We note immediately that this aim differs from the stronger claim that clinical legal education should *directly advance* 'social justice'. Law clinics clearly offer a valuable opportunity to explore how law and social justice interact and to reflect on the role of lawyers and the legal profession in that regard. Consider, for instance, the role of lawyers in the Post Office scandal, now widely regarded as the greatest miscarriage of justice in UK legal history. Richard Moorhead has been especially vocal in arguing that the Post Office scandal is not an isolated event, but the most extreme example of deeper, systemic concerns about lawyers' powers and responsibility in society. In the first of his three Hamlyn Lectures, he refers to lawyers as 'unreliable gods' and notes:

> The Post Office Scandal is emblematic of how ethical and system failure can lead to profound injustice. And I think it speaks to a significant problem of honesty and responsibility in political, commercial, and legal life.
>
> That problem is encapsulated in broader concerns about a cover-up culture but also a sense, amongst so many scandal victims, that there is one law for them and another for the powerful: two-tier legality driven by, what I am going to define as, aggressive lawyering. I will argue that the Post Office but also other cases are emblematic of three things:
>
> 1. . . . How unreliable gods (self-regarding, unaccountable lawyers) with fearless logics are vulnerable to wrongdoing. How their logics spring from conventional but unbalanced ideas about professional partisanship. How those logics are structured by money, secrecy, and moral sophistry. How they are amplified by human frailties—psychological dispositions—that magnify the chances of failure.
> 2. The second lecture looks at how amoral, unreliable lawyering combines with unbalanced organisations. How irresponsible legal orthodoxies can drive cover-ups, 'deliberate concealment', 'a lack of candour', 'the retelling of half-truths' and the massaging of risk.

[11] Stephen Wizner, 'Is Social Justice Still Relevant?' (2012) 32 Boston College Journal of Law & Social Justice 345, 351.

3. The third will consider reform and suggest legal ethics is not solely a problem of individual lawyers, or unbalanced organisations, or legal and regulatory failure. Ethics is both an individual *and* a systemic problem requiring change in corporate governance, court practice, legal education, professional leadership, and better regulation.[12]

This is why legal ethics and professional identity are explored in depth in Chapters 7 and 8, respectively, in this book. Indeed, in both the US and the UK, law clinics are viewed by clinicians 'as a partial antidote to diminished ethicality during law school'.[13] Whether they succeed in this role, however, is a matter of debate.[14]

One argument for including the 'advancement of social justice' as a core part of CLE draws on its historical roots. As Steve Wizner explains, students and teachers in American law schools of the 1960s were exposed to and participated in political action supporting civil rights, the war on poverty, and social justice movements domestically and globally. The impact was significant. The Chair of the Association of American Law Schools' special committee wrote that 'to many people, the relationship between clinical programs and the justice mission of American law schools is so clear as to be self-evident . . . Indeed, for many law students, the law clinic may be the *only* place in which concerns about justice are discussed and, at least sometimes, acted upon'.[15] These advocates argued that the traditional law school curriculum upholds the status quo by ignoring, and thereby becoming complicit in, social injustice, and they called for its reform.[16]

Even if one rejects the claim that parts of the law school curriculum ignore questions of social justice, it is still clear that CLE has long been associated with advancing such goals. Some have even argued, unapologetically, that CLE should 'forge warriors to justice'.[17] Proponents of this position associate 'justice' with the protection of rights and interests of individuals who are in poverty, are members of marginalized communities, or otherwise face serious obstacles accessing justice. However, as may be expected, this interpretation has been contested. As we discuss in Chapter 5, advocates of conservative, business-oriented and majoritarian interests have proposed, and established, law clinics under *their* understanding of 'justice' and also interpret the term 'public interest law' in this way. Should such clinics fall outside the definition of CLE? The answer to this question rests on a more basic

[12] Richard Moorhead, 'What Drives Ethical Failure? Unreliable Gods and Their Fearless Logics' in *Frail Professionalism: Lawyers' Ethics after the Post Office and Other Cases* (The Hamlyn Lectures 2024), https://richardmoorhead.substack.com/p/what-drives-ethical-failure-unreliable

[13] Richard Moorhead et al, 'The Ethical Identity of Law Students' (2016) 23 International Journal of the Legal Profession 235, 238.

[14] See, eg, Sally Maresh, 'The Impact of Clinical Legal Education on Decisions of Law Students to Practice Public Interest Law' in Jeremy Cooper and Louise Trubek (eds), *Educating for Justice* (Routledge 1997) 154 [finding that 32 of 46 students who had no intention of engaging in public interest careers changed their mind after law clinic participation]; but *cf* Rebecca Sandefur and Jeffrey Selbin, 'The Clinic Effect' (2009) 16 Clinical Law Review 57, 92 [finding no such effect for CLE].

[15] Robert Dinerstein, 'Clinical Scholarship and the Justice Mission' (1992) 40 Cleveland State Law Review 469, 469.

[16] Ibid 347.

[17] Donald Nicolson, 'Legal Education, Ethics and Access to Justice: Forging Warriors for Justice in a Neo-Liberal World' (2015) 22 International Journal of the Legal Profession 51.

one: to what extent should the aim of 'advancing social justice' be included in the definition of CLE? Interestingly, Wizner, quoted above, identified four core 'tenets' of clinical pedagogy, none of which include the pursuit of social justice (though he does emphasize the importance of teaching about law's effects on social justice).[18] For example, some argue that students in 'business' or 'transactional' law clinics encounter 'practice and ethical issues' that are not present 'in clinics for the poor', even when serving 'medium or even high income' clients.[19]

While we are sympathetic to the idea that law clinics, and law schools and universities more generally, *should* advance social justice, we do not believe that clinics with a different focus should be excluded from the CLE definition. Clinics are part of law schools which, in turn, are part of the universities, institutions whose primary role is to educate, not to promote a particular agenda.

Perhaps one way to resolve this tension is to suggest—borrowing from Plato—that there exists an 'ideal form' of the clinic,[20] one in which students not only develop professional skills, but also engage in public interest work and serve the community. And yet, there are also other clinics, which do not rise to that ideal. Moreover, even this position can be challenged. The reason, to which we have already alluded, is that social justice, as a subset of ideals of morality and justice more broadly, is heavily contested. McKeown and Hall argue:[21]

> Some legal clinics adopt a policy that they will only represent tenants. If the landlord is seeking possession because the tenant has complained about the condition of the property, or the landlord is merely seeking to increase the rent with new tenants, then it is arguable that it is unjust to recover possession of the tenant's home. However, if the reason for seeking possession was the antisocial behaviour of the tenant such as loud noise, harassment of neighbour and even criminal activity within the property [then the] question could legitimately be posed as to whether it is still unjust to seek possession of the tenant's home? . . .
>
> The world is not black and white, and indeed, there is a significant grey area when we consider cases within a clinical setting. Therefore, we must be cautious as to the imposition of our own moral perspective on our students. Notions of what is just and unjust will often be determined by an individual's moral positioning. Because

[18] According to Wizner (n 11) the four tenets of clinical pedagogy are: (1) teaching students to employ legal knowledge, theory, and skills to meet individual and social needs; (2) exposing students to the ways in which the law (and lawyers) can both advance and subvert the achievement of social justice and public welfare; (3) instilling in students good professional values; and (4) providing supervised opportunities for students—acting in the role of lawyers—to learn to exercise judgement in a professionally competent, ethical, and socially responsible manner.

[19] Elaine Campbell, 'Recognising the Social and Economic Value of Transactional Law Clinics: A View from the United Kingdom' (2016) 65 Journal of Legal Education 580, 590–591.

[20] Plato, *Phaedo*, in JM Cooper (ed), *Plato: Complete Works* (Hackett 1997) 64c–69e; Richard Kraut, 'Plato's Ethics' (*Stanford Encyclopedia of Philosophy*, Summer 2022 Edition) https://plato.stanford.edu/entries/plato-ethics/ accessed 30 September 2025.

[21] Paul McKeown and Elaine Hall, 'If We Could Instil Social Justice Values through Clinical Legal Education, Should We?' (2018) 143 Journal of International and Comparative Law 5; David Barnizer, 'The University Ideal and Clinical Legal Education' (1990) 35 NY Law School Law Review 87, 112: 'the point is not to proselytize law students into accepting the law teacher's personal view of justice but to assist students, in fact to demand that student become aware of their responsibility to do justice and the need to develop their own reflective system of justice.'

our students may adopt a different moral position to ourselves does not mean they are morally wrong. Therefore, what can we do?

Our role is to provide the students with the framework to critique the world in which they live and strive to develop their own moral position. . . .

As Barnhizer suggested, clinicians must be prepared to have the legitimacy of their own beliefs called into question, thus enabling the exploration of competing interests and concepts of justice. In adopting such an approach, we inculcate in our students the ability to think rather than what to think.

It is not the place of [clinicians] to prescribe what [students] ought to consider virtuous. But surely [clinics] should do whatever they can to prepare their students to arrive at thoughtful judgments of their own.

Therefore, while clinics can, and perhaps should, advance public interest goals, they should not be excluded if they do not do so.

1.1.2 **The Features of CLE**

After identifying the goals of CLE, we now turn to a brief overview of its features, which derive from and support those goals. Both the features and the goals will be discussed in greater depth in this book.

First, Active Participation. Even in 1987, Boone et al were aware that 'some teaching methods permit student participation, and others positively encourage it'.[22] Against that background, one might argue that in the current age of 'flipped classrooms', emphasizing active participation seems anachronistic. However, two things may be added in this regard. First, that a feature is identified as integral to CLE does not mean that it cannot also be found in other contexts. Indeed, if active participation is valued as 'good pedagogy', it should be a matter for celebration, not confusion, if it becomes a feature of other, more traditional, modules. Second, CLE is likely unique in that it not only encourages participation, but 'requires and relies'[23] on it. Engagement with 'real' partners and clients shifts the educational emphasis: if a student or team fails to engage with a designated task or follow instructions, the consequences affect not only the student's grade but also the client, other students, relationships with external partners, and the reputation of the law school and the university.

Second, 'Interaction in Role'. This refers to students adopting professional roles, such as giving advice or representing a client, which differ markedly from the passive role of a student.[24] Gary Bellow describes role adjustment as the 'central feature of the clinical method', noting that adopting a professional role changes how one views the world, with 'sensation, perception, intuition, feeling, cognition [which] necessarily combine to produce "new knowledge" at different levels of awareness, complexity, particularity, and immediacy'.[25] He continues to explain that whereas in traditional law school teaching, 'the case provides the

[22] Boone, Jeeves and Macfarlane (n 5) 65. [23] Id 66. [24] Kreiling (n 9) 287.

[25] Gary Bellow, 'On Teaching the Teachers: Some Reflections on Clinical Education as Methodology, in Clinical Legal Education for the Law Student', CLEPR conference, June 1973, 380–82; cited ibid and in Carolyn Grose, 'Beyond Skills Training, Revisited: The clinical legal education spiral' (2013) 19 Clinical Law Review 489, 499.

raw material from which the meanings are drawn . . . In clinical teaching, the . . . decisions [of students as lawyers] in a variety of roles and contexts are the central sources of meaning; the diverse ways of examining and evaluating problem-solving experience provide the basic models of explanation'.[26]

Third, the Dynamic Nature of the Problem. This may be the most distinctive feature of CLE pedagogy. In the traditional format, legal education relies on problem questions or 'scenarios' on which students are asked to 'apply the law' during the course of seminars and as part of their assessments. These scenarios are often carefully tailored and, indeed, teachers regularly emphasize that every 'fact' in the scenario has 'legal meaning'. The clinical experience differs markedly in several respects. Primarily, the student is not presented with a neat set of facts but rather is tasked with engaging with the client. During or after the interview, the student must distinguish 'relevant' from 'irrelevant' facts: is it 'relevant' that the client was black? That they were an immigrant? That they had a disability? and so on. This skill, which is often cited by professional lawyers as crucially important, is side-stepped in non-clinical modules. Moreover, engaging with this question opens a discussion that relates to the *criteria* for determining which facts are, or should be, relevant, including the client's age, sex, race, migration status, dis/ability, employment history, and criminal record. Indeed, some of the contestation between the parties may concern whether these background facts should be deemed legally relevant. And, finally, while a student in a non-clinical module can often identify the precise chapter within a textbook to which the relevant 'facts' relate, the student on a clinical module will not, necessarily, be sure which textbook to pick up: is this a consumer law issue or an employment law matter, for example? Should the main focus be public law or criminal law? And so forth.

Fourth, and perhaps most controversially, is the insistence that the clinical experience should 'exist within the context of a *Planned Curriculum* as part of a strategy to achieve pre-determined and stated learning goals'.[27] This does not necessarily mean that clinical education needs to be part of an assessed module. The difference between education and experience is that there are clear goals for student development and space for feedback, reflection, and theory if it is to fall within the definition of clinical legal *education*. Within the UK, Donald Nicolson is perhaps the most prominent advocate for the extra-curricular clinic. In a series of articles,[28] Nicolson argues that extra-curricular (hereafter EC) clinics have a number of advantages over clinics that are embedded in the curriculum. First, EC clinics do not need to balance social justice imperatives of serving the community with pedagogical principles, such as the educational benefits (or lack thereof) attributed to a particular case. Second, relying on student-volunteers increases clinic capacity. This feature, in turns, may expand the range of potential assistance that may be offered. Third, ethically, Nicolson cites cases in which students 'benefit' from a poor interview, without worrying about their mark, because it is an important 'learning experience'.

[26] Bellow, cited in Marc Feldman, 'On the Margins of Legal Education' (1984) 13 New York University Review of Law & Social Change 607.

[27] Boone, Jeeves, and Macfarlane (n 1) 67.

[28] Donald Nicolson, '"Education, Education, Education": Legal, Moral and Clinical' (2008) 42 Law Teacher 145; Donald Nicolson, 'Legal Education or Community Service? The Extra-curricular Student Law Clinic' (2006) The Web Journal of Current Legal Issues.

We agree that there can be clear pedagogical benefits to extra-curricular clinical education. Removing the pressure of assessment—'how do I get a first?'—and replacing it with a focus on 'how do I write a good letter?' or 'how can I improve my client interviews?' can create a rich learning environment where students feel free to engage with their own development and understanding of the messiness of law in the real world.

And yet, notwithstanding the obvious importance that can be derived from pro bono and voluntary experience, both for the recipient and for the volunteer, 'clinical *experience* is not the same thing as clinical [legal] *education*'.[29] Education requires theorizing, extrapolating particular experiences, conceptualizing and framing them, understanding them as part of a general structure, and trying again on the basis of that understanding.[30] It should thus be clear that there is no hierarchy implied in this delineation: it could well be that 'pure', extra-curricular, pro bono, voluntary work is more valuable to the community, enhances social justice to greater effect, and leads to greater individual satisfaction for those involved. But without time and support to reflect and develop it, such activity could not be included within the remit of legal education. The processes needed to transform law clinics from experience to education can take place in an extra-curricular environment or within an assessed module. There are benefits and drawbacks to both models, but what distinguishes clinical legal education from clinical legal experience must be that space is created for theorizing, reflecting, and making sense of experience before trying again.

This leads us nicely to the *fifth* feature of CLE: the central role of *Reflection* within clinical pedagogy. Legal education has long resisted incorporating reflection into its pedagogy, making it an outlier among professionally oriented disciplines in higher education. In university departments such as medicine, public health, social work, and education, reflection is a routine part of many, if not most, modules. Its importance is understood to lie in its power to guide 'students' extraction of theory from practice, and the application of practice to theory; and it pushes students to generalize from the specific and transfer their learning beyond that specific'.[31] As indicated in the previous discussion, part of the reflective process, which we will discuss at length in Chapter 6, requires conceptualizing the experience, activities, and techniques to facilitate greater understanding of the dynamics that took place. For now, we only note the general process and purpose of reflection within clinical legal education, namely to go beyond 'doing' and 'acting', and to 'be an observer of [one's] own thought processes and actual behaviour in the system in which she is participating'.[32]

Sixth, and finally, is *Access to Justice*. While the previous five features sit comfortably within the realm of pedagogy, this final component addresses the substance of CLE. After all, if CLE is to find its place within a law school's curriculum, surely there must be essential, substantive elements that will facilitate contextualizing, theorizing, and, eventually, the critical thinking on which universities pride themselves. In the same way that modules on contract, tort, or crime must have their own components without which one could justifiably say 'this isn't a real Contract Law module', CLE has now matured sufficiently to articulate its

[29] Kevin Kerrigan, 'What Is Clinical Legal Education and Pro Bono?' in Kevin Kerrigan and Victoria Murray (eds), *A Student Guide to Clinical Legal Education and Pro Bono* (Palgrave Macmillan 2011) 7.

[30] Linden Thomas, Steven Vaughan, and Bharat Malkani, 'Clinical Legal Education Reimagined' in Linden Thomas and others (eds), *Reimagining Clinical Legal Education* (Hart Publishing 2018).

[31] Grose (n 25) 500. [32] Feldman (n 26) 616.

contribution to the research and education within the law school curriculum. In particular, CLE is uniquely positioned to encourage students to reflect not only on their experience with clients (see above) but also on the client's experience with the legal system, and to contextualize, theorize, and criticize this experience, thus gaining a deeper understanding of legal doctrine, legal theory, and the complex relationship of law and justice in practice.[33] As we discuss in Chapters 2 and 8, focusing on these real challenges, namely the obstacles facing an individual's access to justice, provides exceptional material to teach and learn 'the ways in which the law (and lawyers) can both advance and subvert the achievement of social justice and public welfare'.[34] It is this content, and not particular goals or aims, which elevates CLE 'beyond skills training'.[35]

1.2 A Brief History of (Clinical) Legal Education

The history of CLE cannot be separated from the longer and more chequered story of legal education in England.

1.2.1 Legal Education in England and Wales until the 1970s: 'a dreary procession of disappointments and missed opportunities'

For more than five centuries, the study of law took place within the Inns of Court—effectively an apprenticeship model, where students observed practice, took notes, and absorbed the profession's norms. The idea of organized university legal education was even banned in 1234 by King Henry III, perhaps to protect the universities of Oxford and Cambridge,[36] or perhaps to ensure that students did not develop and spread 'opinion about the law'.[37] Instead, in the Inns,[38] their training, to the extent that it existed, was executed solely through 'doing'. A less charitable description of the students' qualification at the time suggests that a student was assessed by his 'ability to eat and drink and to sign one's name and to learn to tell a plain story in very unintelligible language'.[39] Another account suggests that the Inns 'flourished as finishing schools for the sons of the upper classes'.[40]

However, criticism began to spread. William Blackstone wrote that 'obscure and illiterate men' were being given the tools to interpret and enforce the law and that this was

[33] Stephen Wizner, 'The Law School Clinic: Legal Education in the Interests of Justice Colloquium: What Does It Mean to Practice Law in the Interests of Justice in the Twenty-First Century' (2001) 70 Fordham Law Review 1929.

[34] Wizner, 'Is Social Justice Still Relevant?' (n 9) 345.

[35] *Cf* Stephen Wizner, 'Beyond Skills Training' (2001) 7 Clinical Law Review 327.

[36] Andrew Boon and Julian Webb, 'Legal Education and Training in England and Wales: Back to the Future?' (2008) 58 Journal of Legal Education 79, 82.

[37] Gary Slapper, 'The History of Legal Education' (2011) 8 Journal of Commonwealth Law and Legal Education 9, 10.

[38] Boon and Webb (n 36) 83.

[39] LCB Gower, 'English Legal Training' (1950) 13 The Modern Law Review 137, 139.

[40] Judith Maute, 'Alice's Adventures in Wonderland: Preliminary Reflections on the History of the Split English Legal Profession and the Fusion Debate (1000–1900 AD)' (2003) 71 Fordham Law Review 1357, 1368.

'a matter of very public concern'.[41] Blackstone suggested that the only remedy would be 'by making academical education a previous step to the profession of the common law, and at the same time making the rudiments of the law a part of academical education'.[42]

A similar approach was taken by the 1846 Report by a Parliamentary Select Committee, which recognized that 'the present state of legal education, both professional and unprofessional, is extremely unsatisfactory and incomplete and in striking contrast and inferiority to such education in all the more civilised States of Europe and America' and that 'No legal education worthy of the name is at the moment to be had in either England or Ireland'.[43] Its primary recommendation was the establishment of a university that would include a School of Law, which would hold lectures and examinations.

This approach, however, was met by opposition. A prominent voice of resistance came from one of the most esteemed law professors of his generation, AV Dicey, whose inaugural lecture as Vinerian Chair at All Souls College, Oxford in 1883 was entitled 'Can English Law be Taught at the Universities?' Dicey argued, essentially, for a division of labour between the two institutions: courts and chambers should teach the practice of law, whereas at university the law would be 'taught as a whole' and include 'what from the nature of things can never be learnt in chambers—the habit of analysing and defining legal conceptions'.[44]

This and other similar suggestions proposed by prominent legal scholars over the course of more than a century did not lead to significant (if any) change in the mindset, let alone pedagogical reform. In sum, 'the story of institutionalisation of the discipline of law in England is generally presented as a *dreary procession of disappointments and missed opportunities* . . . the study of English Law can be traced back over several centuries; its *failure* to become established or accepted in universities is the general theme'.[45]

1.2.2 Choosing between Pericles and the Plumber: The Battle for the Purpose of Legal Education

There is a sound reason why, in the UK, '"the study of law [became] concerned with the professional training of barristers and solicitors" and lagged behind other countries in considering the wider social implications of the subject'.[46] Unlike subjects such as medicine, social work, or engineering, which embrace their vocational focus, legal scholarship and teaching constantly tries to straddle two aims: to provide an education suited to the arts, humanities, or social sciences departments, while also pleasing (or at least trying to please) the legal professions.

To an extent, the tension between these two ideals is not new; nor is it unique to law. As William Twining puts it, 'How to reconcile the liberal tradition with the demands of the

[41] William Blackstone, 'On the Study of Law' in *Commentaries on the Laws of England* 6, 33 (5th ed, 1773) [emphasis added].

[42] Ibid.

[43] Select Committee on Legal Education (No. 686, 1846) BPP Vol. X; see Gower (n 39) 141.

[44] Cited in Slapper (n 37) 16.

[45] William Twining, *Blackstone's Tower: The English Law School* (The Hamlyn Lectures, Sweet & Maxwell 1994); see also Gower (n 39).

[46] Twining (n 45) 32, citing the *Report of the Committee on Social Studies* (Heyworth Committee) (1965) Cmnd 2660, para 38.

world of affairs is one of the perennial problems of university education'.[47] But, he continues, law faces this dilemma 'in its most acute form'.[48] This is because teaching law as a vocation cannot simply be supplemented with theory, in the way that engineering can with particle physics, or medicine with molecular biology. Theoretical approaches to law involve a critical lens that can clash with the authoritative nature of law as a vocation. If you study law with the aim of training as a practitioner, you are expected to accept the hierarchy of norms (in legislation or case law), to uphold the doctrine of precedent, and to apply rules of interpretation to resolve conflicts. Most generally, to operate within the system, you are expected, at *some* level, to have faith in it. In contrast, academics thrive by identifying inconsistencies in the law, systematic biases in the legal system, and, more broadly, the gap between the law as it is and the law as it should be.[49]

Twining captured this tension as a choice between 'Pericles and the Plumber'.[50] The plumber is a master of technical skill, uninterested in the philosophy of plumbing, history in ancient Rome, or comparative plumbing in other jurisdictions. Such learning is wasteful at best, and confusing and harmful at worst. This is the vocational approach to legal education: practical, skills-based, and employability-focused. Pericles, by contrast, represents the lawgiver and enlightened policy maker. He is the critical thinker, interested in asking why the law is as it is, what it could be, and how we can make it better.

We saw that, initially, legal training in the UK was firmly based on the 'Plumber' approach, and that law schools seemed adamant that legal education should be the preserve of Pericles: thoughtful, theoretical, and critical. However, in the first half of the twentieth century, developments in legal education in England started to track those in the US, understanding that education in universities could and should contribute to the profession—thus bringing the Plumber into the house of Pericles, if you will.

REFLECTION POINT

A well-known example offered to first year law students is the juxtaposition of *R v Brown* [1993], in which five men were convicted of consensual sadomasochistic acts, and *R v Wilson* [1996], in which a husband and wife were acquitted from committing assault on each other because 'consensual activity in a matrimonial home is not a proper matter for criminal investigation or prosecution'.

How would a practitioner (plumber) approach the gap between the two cases? And what would be an example of a 'Periclian', critical, academic explanation?

In 1966, the Wilson Report on Legal Education tried to square the circle by concluding that 'law degree courses should be designed with a liberal education and to train him to think like a lawyer rather than to give him a vocational training'.[51] It is striking that this seminal

[47] William Twining, *Law in Context: Enlarging a Discipline* (OUP 1997); originally published as 'Pericles and the Plumber' (1967) 83 LQR 65.

[48] Ibid. [49] See eg John Griffiths, *The Politics of the Judiciary* (Fontana 1997). [50] Twining (n 47).

[51] JF Wilson, 'A Survey of Legal Education in the United Kingdom' (1966) 9 Journal of the Society of Public Teachers of the Law 1, 92.

report drew such a clear contrast between 'thinking like a lawyer' and 'vocational training'. Confused? You're not alone.

Gower observed that this very tension causes UK law schools to 'fall between two stools and to be in part schools of theoretical instruction and in part vocational training establishments'.[52] Decades later, Gerald Lopez wryly commented that 'at the end of three years of education, law students . . . [are] neither very theoretical nor very skilful. They are consumed by doctrine, much as they have been made to consume it'.[53]

REFLECTION POINT

The critics were clearly right that law schools cannot effectively train lawyers to become practitioners without engaging them in the day-to-day experience of practical law.

However, they *assumed* that this is what law schools should be doing. In contrast, one could argue that law school should not be about training for practice, but for teaching law as an academic, intellectual phenomenon, its philosophical underpinnings, and its relation to society.

But is your law school doing *that*?

Or is it caught between the two models, managing not to perfect either?

It was not until the 1970s that a more deliberate attempt to reshape legal education gained traction. Pioneering university-based law clinics emerged first as marginal, often extra-curricular efforts, then increasingly as part of broader pedagogic reform. Even so, law schools were slow to embrace CLE, particularly in the UK, where the tradition of doctrinal, lecture-based teaching remained dominant.

The dramatic effort to organize the chaos occurred following the publication of the Ormrod Committee Report of 1971.[54] This report recommended that, in England and Wales, academic qualification will take place in universities; that professional qualifications be set by the Bar (for barristers) or the Law Society (for solicitors); and that the profession will have only a limited impact on the law degree, by prescribing six required subjects. It established that law should be a graduate profession and that law degrees should involve 'academic' studies and not only practical training. It also allowed, in a manner uncommon in other jurisdictions, for lawyers to qualify having not studied law at university. In 1975, the International Legal Center reflected on the value of studying law, stating:

> 90. . . . Typically, the discipline of law is regarded as part of the humanities. This is so because:
>
> (a) law covers so many human activities and relationships; but
>
> (b) it also deals with much of the same phenomena as the social sciences, and is increasingly informed by them; and

[52] Gower (n 39) 155.

[53] Gerald López, 'Training Future Lawyers to Work with the Politically and Socially Subordinated: Anti-Generic Legal Education' (1989) 91 West Virginia Law Review 305, 326.

[54] *The Committee on Legal Education* (Cmd 4595, the Ormrod Report, 1971).

(c) it is intellectually demanding—requiring abilities to draw from a variety of sources in analyzing problems, evidence and arguments to make careful distinctions and to handle abstract concepts; and

(d) it is directly related to the world of concrete practical problems; and

(e) it is concerned, as perhaps no other subject is concerned, with the practical operation of processes and procedures; and

(f) it has a rich heritage of literature, philosophy and historical experience.

91. While none of these elements is, on its own, peculiar to law, perhaps no other discipline combines them in quite the same way or to the same degree. The study of law can be

(a) as intellectually exacting as philosophy, but more down to earth;

(b) as concerned with contemporary, real-life problems as medicine or engineering, but with a greater diversity of concerns and with closer links to the humanities;

(c) as concerned with power and decision-making as political science, but more concerned with the processes and practicalities of wielding power and, indeed, often more concerned with the limits and abuses of power and the importance of accountability to processes which are seen to be fair.

The result was that, when compared to the past, and to other countries, law schools in the UK enjoyed much greater freedom 'to define their role, interpret their subject and choose their clientele'.[55] Correspondingly, the impact on the growth of law schools was explosive: as late as 1940, there were only about 130 legal academics teaching about 2,000 students in England, of which two-thirds were in Oxford, Cambridge and the University of London, with the rest spread across ten other institutions.[56] By 1960 these numbers rose slowly to 250 academics and 3,000 students. Following the Ormrod Report, by 1980, about 1,200 were teaching more than 12,000 students at 58 law schools; and a decade later the corresponding numbers were 2,000 and 20,000, respectively. It is fair to say that the 'scientific and systematic study of law' is no longer 'scorned or deprecated'. In fact, law as an academic discipline is held in high esteem and is consistently one of the most popular undergraduate disciplines in the United Kingdom.[57] It has managed to distance itself from the training orientation that took place within the Inns and garner prestige and disciplinary independence.

Bringing us closer to the present day, the Legal Education and Training Review (LETR), launched in 2011 and concluded in 2013, marked the most significant review of legal education and training in England and Wales for more than two decades. Commissioned jointly by the Solicitors Regulation Authority (SRA), the Bar Standards Board (BSB), and

[55] Twining (n 45) 985.

[56] John Henry Schlegel, 'Talkin' Dirty: Twining's Tower and Kalman's Strange Career' (1996) 21 Law & Social Inquiry 981.

[57] HESA, 'What Do HE Students Study' (12 September 2024) https://www.hesa.ac.uk/data-and-analysis/students/what-study accessed 5 December 2024.

ILEX Professional Standards (IPS), the LETR aimed to assess whether the legal education system was fit for purpose in a rapidly changing legal services market. It acknowledged increasing globalization, the rise of technology and legal process outsourcing, and a growing awareness of issues around access to justice and social mobility. One of the review's key findings was that the existing system placed too much emphasis on narrow doctrinal learning and too little on skills development, ethical awareness, and understanding law in its broader social context. Although the review fell short of proposing a radical overhaul, it encouraged a shift towards outcomes-focused education and called for greater flexibility in qualification pathways.

For clinical legal education, the implications were significant, even if indirect. While LETR did not recommend a universal integration of CLE into the curriculum, it highlighted the importance of experiential and reflective learning and questioned the traditional divide between academic and vocational stages of legal education. It is against this background that CLE gained increased legitimacy as a means of helping students develop not only technical legal knowledge, but also the broader skills and ethical sensibilities required for modern legal practice. The LETR arguably paved the way for further reforms, including the eventual development of the Solicitors Qualifying Examination (SQE) in England and Wales, which explicitly recognized the value of Qualifying Work Experience (QWE), a category into which supervised clinical work often falls. As we explore in later chapters, these regulatory changes offer both opportunities and challenges for CLE, particularly in negotiating its dual commitments to pedagogy and professionalism.

Together, LETR and the SQE reflect a growing acknowledgement, by regulators as well as educators, that CLE is not an optional enrichment but a vital part of preparing lawyers for practice. These reforms also force a renewed debate about the pedagogic role of law schools: not just to teach black-letter law, but to foster reflection, professionalism, and critical engagement with justice in action.

In sum, the question is: Is it possible to reconcile, and even integrate, doctrine (which still has a place, even according to critics of the current approach), skills, *and* theory? Curiously, some have found that while this is, indeed, a formidable challenge, clinical legal education is the 'most obvious site to do so'.[58] Others have even described the 'essence' of clinical legal education in linking theory and practice.[59]

1.2.3 The Development of Clinical Legal Education as a Holistic Response?

It has been suggested that the genesis of the clinical legal education movement can be traced to Jerome Frank's critique of traditional legal education in 1933, captured in his article aptly titled 'Why Not a Clinical Lawyer School?'[60] As we see in more detail below, Frank poured

[58] AJ Goldsmith, 'An Unruly Conjunction? Social Thought and Legal Action in Clinical Legal Education' (1993) 43 Journal of Legal Education 415.

[59] Brenda Bratton Blom, 'Finding Your Balance on the Tightrope: Reflections from a Clinical Life' (2004) 4 University of Maryland Law Journal of Race, Religion, Gender and Class 273.

[60] Jerome Frank, 'Why Not a Clinical Lawyer-School?' (1933) 81 University of Pennsylvania Law Review and American Law Register 907. See McKeown and Hall (n 21).

scorn on the existing system for being significantly disconnected from practice. Interestingly, and linked to our choice of definition for CLE above, he did not view CLE as inherently about serving only those who cannot afford legal advice. He wrote that legal clinics

> would not confine their activities to such as are now undertaken by the Legal Aid Society. They could take on important work for governmental agencies or other quasi-public bodies. The professional work they would do would include virtually every kind of service rendered by law offices.[61]

We now know that Frank's vision was never fully realized. Law clinics grew, motivated by the desire to enhance access to justice. They were driven by the high-minded ideal of forging 'warriors for justice'.[62] However, first in the US and then in the UK, the urgency for their development was driven at least as much by the slightly more mundane rules of supply and demand. As we will see in upcoming chapters, the seminal US Supreme Court case of *Gideon*[63] expanded the understanding of access to justice in a manner that led to a serious, and somewhat unexpected, problem: there simply were not enough lawyers to handle the sudden influx of work that was required to serve indigent individuals who faced criminal prosecution. As the Dean and Associate Dean of one American Law School candidly wrote at the time:

> Now that the access to legal services for all economic levels is recognized as essential, the demand for lawyer time has increased so greatly that it is nearly impossible for government agencies to handle their caseloads with their present attorney and staff allotments . . . Law students provide a manpower resource to augment overworked and understaffed offices.[64]

The process that led to the (later) development of law clinics in the UK was different in some way from the US, but shaped by similar forces. As students became aware of the experience enjoyed by their American counterparts in law clinics, and the ability to enhance legal skills in that context, pressure began to build on universities to establish clinics. As early as 1950, British academics mused about the idea of developing partnerships between law firms and barristers' chambers, on the one hand, and the 'Poor Man's Lawyer Centres' (notwithstanding the outdated and unfortunate title!) that existed at the time, on the other. But the combination of generous legal aid and widespread neighbourhood law centres removed the urgency for law clinics in universities to fill in any gaps. So while many academics of the time found the idea of incorporating partnerships with legal advice centres too radical for the UK, they recognized the need to enhance legal training, in a manner similar to law clinics in America.[65]

Law clinics in the UK were initiated by academics inspired by the American experience, first at the University of Kent in 1973 (efforts that folded within a few years) and then in

[61] Frank (n 60) 918. [62] Nicolson (n 28). [63] *Gideon v Wainwright*, 372 US 335 (1963).

[64] Marvin Anderson and Guy Kornblum, 'Clinical Legal Education: A Growing Reform' (1971) 57 American Bar Association J 591, 592.

[65] Gower (n 39).

the universities of Warwick, Birmingham, London Southbank, and Northumbria.[66] At that stage, and for the next 20 years, it is difficult to say that anything resembling a clinical legal education 'movement' existed in the UK, with only eight universities running a clinical programme.[67]

It was only when legal aid was cut dramatically—by more than 50 per cent in real terms,[68] leading to the closure of over half of community legal advice centres in England and Wales[69]—that, somewhat paradoxically, the positive development of law clinics became a reality.[70] As we note in Chapter 3, the percentage of the population eligible for legal aid dropped from 79 per cent in the 1980s to 29 per cent in 2007 (a consequence of the removal of a number of areas from scope as a result of the *Access to Justice Act* 1999)[71] and even further following the implementation of the *Legal Aid, Sentencing and Punishment of Offenders Act* 2012.[72] As the sector adapted, the 'natural consequence' of the reduction in the scope of legal aid has been the reduction in the number of firms providing legal aid services.[73] Some have called for clinical legal education to assist in bridging, or plugging, the access to justice gap.[74] The most recent survey of law clinic activity managed to get responses from 78 UK law schools, of which all but one reported involvement in some CLE or pro bono activity. This figure translates to more than 70 per cent of all UK law schools, engaging more than 3,000 students.[75]

This isn't necessarily a bad thing. Rather, it would suggest that 'serving social justice' is akin to, or at least significantly overlaps with, serving those who are less resourceful in the immediate community. And so, clinical legal education has its foundations in serving the poor. As such, it has a valuable purpose, as we noted: providing necessary assistance, while

[66] Richard Grimes, Joel Klaff, and Colleen Smith, 'Legal Skills and Clinical Legal Education—A Survey of Undergraduate Law School Practice' (1996) 30 The Law Teacher 44.

[67] Ibid.

[68] National Audit Office, *Government's Management of Legal Aid* (Legal Aid Agency, Ministry of Justice, Session 2023–24, HC 514, February 2024) https://www.nao.org.uk/wp-content/uploads/2024/02/governments-management-of-legal-aid.pdf

[69] Owen Bowcott, 'Legal Advice Centres in England and Wales Halved since 2013–14' *The Guardian* (15 July 2019) https://www.theguardian.com/law/2019/jul/15/legal-advice-centres-in-england-and-wales-halved-since-2013-14

[70] McKeown and Hall (n 21) 147. The authors also note that the development of law clinics coincided with, and probably supported by, deeper social movements, such as 'social and political upheaval . . . the civil rights movement, the fall of communism and apartheid. In the United Kingdom and Australia, clinical legal education was adopted during a period of educational reform with "new universities" adopting the method and thus differentiating themselves from the Establishment'—ibid 154.

[71] Henry Brooke, 'The History of Legal Aid 1945–2010' (Bach Commission on Access to Justice—Appendix 6, 2017) 23 https://fabians.org.uk/wp-content/uploads/2017/09/Bach-Commission-Appendix-6-F-1-1.pdf

[72] National Audit Office (n 68); Christopher Bellamy, *Independent Review of Criminal Legal Aid* (November 2021) [1.24] https://assets.publishing.service.gov.uk/government/uploads/system/uploads/attachment_data/file/1041117/clar-independent-review-report-2021.pdf

[73] National Audit Office (n 68) [2.15].

[74] Victoria Murray, 'The Rise and Fall of Social Justice within Clinical Legal Education' in Chris Ashford and Paul McKeown (eds), *Social Justice and Legal Education* (Cambridge Scholars Publishing 2019).

[75] James Sandbach and Richard Grimes, *Law School Pro Bono and Clinic Report 2020* (LawWorks and CLEO 2021) https://www.lawworks.org.uk/sites/default/files/files/LawWorks%20Law%20Schools%20Report%202020_1.pdf

simultaneously expanding the experience of students and raising awareness about the legal problems affecting disadvantaged communities and the wider access to justice gap.

And yet, some have referred to this focus as simultaneously important and 'destructive'.[76] This is so for a number of reasons. One challenge, as McKweon and Hall note, is that:

> If clinical programmes are going to provide their students with a real-life experience, they need a source [for] that experience. At the risk of sounding cynical, the poor and disadvantaged in society are a source of clients as they are unlikely to receive assistance elsewhere. Whether the educational mission or the social justice mission primarily motivates a clinical programme, it is likely that the poor and disadvantaged will provide the client base of the programme. As a consequence, an epistemic system belief has emerged in relation to the notion of social justice and public service, inextricably fusing the concepts within the very fabric of clinical legal education. So much so that for many, it has become a part of the definition of clinical legal education.[77]

The uncomfortable suggestion at the heart of this quote is that the idealistic and the cynical can operate simultaneously: we (students, academics, practitioner-supervisors) can be motivated by the desire to help members of the community who face a significant access to justice gap (the idealistic), while simultaneously being aware that we 'need clients' so students can get the necessary 'experience', training, development, and, in the case of curricular clinics, even assessment.

A second concern is that, given their limited resources, the advice and support given in clinics will never match the quality provided by law firms. Specifically, concerns were raised regarding the lack of supervision (some clinics are run almost exclusively by students, as a matter of ideology and pride[78]) and, consequently perhaps, the quality of provision ('poor service for poor people').[79]

Third, a related challenge concerns the quality and breadth of educational benefit to the students. This was seen as relegated to 'secondary', while 'community service was the main objective'.[80] Juxtaposed against the two previous concerns, we may conclude that clinics are caught in a zero-sum situation, in which they're damned if they focus on students (at the expense of clients) and damned if they focus on clients (at the expense of students). A reasonable response could be, perhaps: does it *have* to be 'zero-sum'? Or can it be 'win–win'?

These critiques are compounded by the sceptical approach to law in general, and to the application of law to marginalized and disenfranchised groups. This approach is quite common within the clinics' critical approach, which we referred to earlier.[81] Closely linked,

[76] Richard Wilson, *The Global Evolution of Clinical Legal Education: More than a Method* (Cambridge University Press 2015) 142.

[77] McKeown and Hall (n 21) 155.

[78] Nicolson (n 17).

[79] Robert Holmes, 'Use of Clinic Students' Extant Talents: Negative Exploitation or a Peek at the Future of Legal Education' (2013) 66 Rutgers Law Review 685.

[80] George Grossman, 'Clinical Legal Education: History and Diagnosis' (1973) 26 Journal of Legal Education 162, 174; Nicolson (n 17) 63.

[81] See text to n 51*ff*.

however, is a common and pragmatic view held by many clinicians, explicitly or implicitly. This is the 'realization' that law clinics may not lead to social change, as clinicians have found 'less faith in the legal system to provide justice'.[82]

By stepping outside of academia, engaging with clients, supervisors, and the legal system more broadly, law clinics thus navigate contradictory tensions. They do so to the best of their ability, sometimes extremely successfully. However, with the realization that many of these forces are beyond their control, clinics gradually develop a new focus: to transform legal education through clinics.[83] What is embedded in this approach is that, as a matter of pedagogy, law clinics not only add the ability to enhance practical skills, such as client interviewing or drafting letters of advice; they also help students build 'soft skills', such as reflecting on their experience, analysing their effects, and planning for future action. Finally, clinics also contribute to legal skills which the generalist modules often sidestep: we noted above the ability to identify 'relevant' from 'irrelevant' facts in a client's story; to categorize those facts as 'helpful' to the client or to the opposing party; to isolate the relevant field, or fields, of law that may be affected by the case and if there are more than one, to strategize which would be the most useful.

REFLECTION POINT

Anthony Bradney has written in opposition to the vocational trends in British law schools in strong terms, encouraging them to 'raise the drawbridge'. He argued, first, that only half of law students become lawyers. But more principally:

> [U]niversities exist to educate students not workers . . . Universities seek to provide their students with the intellectual means to make better choices about their lives. This includes the means to select and pursue the occupation which best suits their talents and their aspirations. It should, however, go far wider than this occupational aim. . . . It is not the function of the university law school to encourage anybody to become lawyers or to pursue any other particular occupation . . . A law degree might properly be taught with little reference to either barristers or solicitors. What reference there is need not persuade people either to become or not to become lawyers. University law schools concern themselves with the study of law not lawyers.[84]

Do you agree with this position? To what extent does it impact on the justification for CLE? And, turning to your self-reflection: what motivated you to study law: the pursuit of a career, intellectual development, a bit of both, or perhaps something else?

[82] Jane Aiken, 'Walking the Clinical Tightrope: Embracing the Role of Teacher' (2004) 4 University of Maryland Law Journal of Race, Religion, Gender and Class 267.

[83] Grossman (n 80) 186.

[84] Anthony Bradney, 'Raising the Drawbridge: Defending University Law Schools' (1995) 1 Web Journal of Current Legal Issues. Available at https://www.bailii.org/uk/other/journals/WebJCLI/1995/issue1/bradney1.html

1.3 **The Structure and Features of This Book**

We now turn to the structure of the book and its key features. The book includes three main sections. Section 1—*Clinical Legal Education and Access to Justice*—sets out the theoretical, historical, and institutional framework for clinical legal education, and therefore for the book as a whole. Section 2—*Clinical Legal Education and Legal Professionalism*—explores the pedagogical, social, and institutional dimensions of CLE. It examines the role of lawyers in society, their responsibilities and commitments, and how they might navigate them. Finally, Section 3—*Practical Legal Skills for Clinical Legal Education*—covers key professional and legal skills such as client interviewing, time management, and legal writing. It provides practical tips and insights into the method behind the madness of clinical work. We note that the final section differs in style from the earlier ones, which focus more closely on relevant scholarship and theory.

Before turning to the chapters in detail, we would like to highlight some of the book's more original or non-traditional features. First, in an effort to practise what we preach, we have included 'Reflection Point' boxes throughout each chapter. These will encourage you to pause, take a moment, and think about what you just read. When used well, these prompts shift your reading from a mostly passive activity to active and critical engagement with the material. For example, you might ask yourself whether you agree with the point that you just read; whether you can think of relevant examples from your experience, clinical or otherwise; or, perhaps, how you would apply the theoretical insights in the future. A second feature—one we're especially excited about—includes tips and insights from CLE colleagues across the sector, mostly in the UK but also beyond, who are experts in the relevant areas. This initiative reflects our recognition that CLE is a thriving and energetic community, with hundreds—and, globally, thousands—of academics and practitioners who bring vast experience to their work. We are humbled by and grateful to those who agreed to take part, read the chapters, and send in their contributions.

And now, to the chapters themselves.

Section 1 contains three chapters. Chapter 2, *Access to Justice*, will introduce you to some of the principles underpinning access to justice and explore how they are related to wider questions of social justice. The chapter breaks down the concept of Access to Justice by asking first 'What Is Access' and then 'What Is Justice', and suggests that there are three common responses to each of these questions. It then examines key barriers to accessing justice, including cost, lack of knowledge, disadvantage and exclusion, and weaknesses in justice infrastructure.

Chapter 3, *Legal Aid and the Changing Landscape of Access to Justice*, moves from theory to practice, tracing the institutional history and development of legal aid and access to justice. It maps different models of legal aid provision, with a particular focus on UK developments. It outlines the changes introduced by the *Legal Aid, Sentencing and Punishment of Offenders Act* 2012 (LASPO) in England and Wales, alongside commentary on their impact. It also considers more generally the relationship between legal aid provision and third sector legal advice provision (ie by charities, law centres, and NGOs). Discussion of the changing landscape includes consideration of literature on litigants in person in the courts and other legislative reforms relevant to access to justice.

Chapter 4 looks ahead to the future of access to justice. Its particular focus can be gleaned from the title: *Technology and the Future of Access to Justice*. The chapter deals with the evolving role of technology in shaping the future of access to justice. While the 'technology revolution' is placed alongside its predecessors—the agricultural and industrial revolutions—some argue that this revolution, which we are in, is 'something different'. In this revolution, technology doesn't just help us work more efficiently—it is reshaping what we do, how we do it, and even how we think about the law itself. For this reason it is rightly described as a 'great disrupter'. The chapter thus looks at a number of relevant legal sectors. In the public justice system, the chapter examines how technology has affected users and stakeholders, especially through the rise of online courts. In the private sector, the chapter offers some 'tasters' of the central areas in which legal practice has embraced legal tech. And, finally, within higher education, we ask how law schools in general, and clinical legal education in particular, should respond to the changing and emerging landscape. Throughout, the chapter engages with the positive and negative impact that technology has had, and continues to have, on access to justice.

Section 2 focuses on clinical legal education and contains four chapters. Chapter 5, *The Theory of the Practice: The Intellectual Background to Clinical Legal Education*, explores the history and development of CLE and its relationship to more traditional forms of legal education. It considers CLE's theoretical underpinnings, which are rooted in Legal Realism. As the chapter shows, Legal Realism developed 'a theory of the practice': it called for honesty in how we discuss and teach the law, and for alignment between how law operates in real life and how it is taught in law schools. CLE is, perhaps unsurprisingly, a natural and almost ideal link between law school and legal practice. Indeed, Legal Realists were not only early advocates of CLE but also called for a more comprehensive and radical overhaul of legal education.

Chapter 6, *Reflection*, explores the core principles of reflective learning and models for developing reflective legal practice. It begins by explaining the reasons *why* reflection is valuable in CLE, in education more broadly, and in professional life. The chapter then explores different forms of reflection—journal entry writing, portfolios, reflective essays—to identify its key characteristics and ask: *What* is reflection? *How* should one reflect? The chapter introduces four different models of reflection, each with its own strengths and limitations. These models matter because, unlike free-flowing journal writing, structured reflection grounded in established frameworks offers more scope for personal and professional growth through concrete, realistic action plans.

Chapter 7, *Professional Legal Ethics*, outlines the ethical theories that guide legal practice across jurisdictions. We are informed by the regulatory frameworks which underpin the practice of solicitors in England and Wales; however, the principles discussed in this chapter have wide relevance. This includes consideration of confidentiality, privilege, duties to the court, the fair administration of justice, and wider professional conduct issues, as well as consideration of what happens in the event of breach. It also engages with emerging scholarship on the way law school clinics can foster students' ethical awareness, offering questions and exercises for reflection.

Chapter 8, *Lawyers and Social Justice*, explores the different types of social justice lawyering connected to CLE, including, but not limited to, cause lawyering and community lawyering. It explores the extent to which lawyers might achieve social change and the tools they use for this purpose, including policy advocacy, campaigning, and strategic litigation. The chapter encourages students to critically engage with these approaches and ask: 'What type of lawyer do I want to be?' It builds on the access to justice themes introduced in Chapters 2 and 3, and links to the discussion of reflective practice.

The chapters in Section 3 offer practical guidance on key skills needed in law clinics. University law clinics vary in the experiences they offer to students, but some core skills—such as client interviewing, practical legal research, advice, and letter writing—are common across most settings. The chapters in this final section offer tips and practical exercises, linking back to the earlier chapters on reflection, professionalism, and access to justice. The skills covered in these chapters are based on skills listed in the Statement of Solicitor Competence for England and Wales. We recognize that this framework is designed specifically for solicitors in England and Wales, and that not all law students using this book wish or intend to practise as solicitors in England and Wales. However, the skills outlined are transferable and relevant not only to the legal professions across many jurisdictions and areas of legal practice, but in many cases also to other jobs or professions. We have used the SRA Statement of Solicitor Competence to underpin the structure of these chapters because law students who wish to qualify as solicitors can count time spent in a university law clinic setting as one of the four placements that make up their qualifying work experience. To do so, students must show that their placement gave them opportunities to develop the skills listed in the Statement of Solicitor Competence. The legal skills chapters therefore aim to help students reflect on and record the skills required to qualify as solicitors in England and Wales, while also providing broader guidance on transferable skills that can support students in any clinic setting, regardless of their future career path.

Chapter 9, *Core Skills—Getting Started in a Clinical Legal Setting*, introduces the core skills that underpin all the work that students are likely to undertake in a law clinic setting. We begin with communication skills, which are the foundation on which the legal skills of interviewing, drafting, negotiation, and advocacy are built. The second part of the chapter explores the need for case management systems, both with respect to the practicalities of organizing files (whether electronically or paper-based) and to the reasons why case management supports clear communication with colleagues and supervisors. It links back to Chapter 7 and the ethical framework that makes good case management systems a professional necessity. Finally we turn to broader time management skills. Not only is the pace and nature of the work in a student law clinic setting likely to be very different to that of a more traditional university course, thus necessitating a change of habit and study pattern for many students, but keeping to deadlines and managing workloads are identified by the SRA as essential skills for practising lawyers in the Statement of Solicitor Competence.

Chapter 10, *Working with Others*, begins by looking at the growing recognition that law students and legal professionals are at risk of stress and burnout and explores ways in which a law clinic setting can support law students to build relationships of trust with peers and supervisors that will support their mental well-being and empower them to ask for help if needed. Group work or team work often plays a key role in CLE, and we consider some of the benefits of group work for students while recognizing that working with others can be fraught with challenges. The chapter considers some of the reasons why students may resist group work and provides tips and guidance on how to make groups work. The final section of the chapter turns to the important relationship between a lawyer and their client. How to conduct a client interview is explored in detail in Chapter 11, so this chapter lays the foundations for communicating with a client, including an exploration of the ways in which vulnerability of clients and students may impact on communication and ways in which a relationship may develop.

Chapter 11, *Interviewing and Advising*, focuses on the key practical skills involved in interviewing and advising clients. It covers fact analysis, interviewing techniques, legal research, and writing letters of advice. The chapter includes practical exercises and builds on the core skills set out in the previous two chapters, placing the need to understand the client and build a relationship based on trust at the heart of the practical guidance on how to carry out these key legal tasks.

Chapter 12, *Representing Your Client*, focuses on the practical legal skills needed to represent clients. This includes drafting legal documents such as statements, applications, or contracts, negotiation, and advocacy. In line with the previous skills chapters, this chapter features practical exercises and reflection points, and builds on the core skills explored in Chapters 9 and 10.

2 Access to Justice

Chapter Overview

This chapter introduces the background context of clinical legal education with respect to access to justice. In doing so, it aims to show how both 'access' and 'justice', and hence 'access to justice', may be understood differently by different people. In particular, while our interest here is mainly in access to justice insofar as it relates to legal disputes, these should not be understood as limited to 'access to courts' or even 'access to lawyers'. While those are both vital, 'access to justice', and consequently the barriers to access to justice, should be viewed as much broader.

By the end of this chapter you should be able to:

- Explain the different layers of 'access' and 'justice'
- Analyse the different interpretations of the term 'access to justice'
- Examine policy issues regarding funding of legal services
- Reflect on the barriers to justice that people encounter when trying to access justice.

Introduction

One of the main aims of law clinics, if not *the* main aim, is to support, facilitate, and aid access to justice. Once you become sufficiently aware of the issue, you will start to notice problems of access to justice in much of your work, perhaps with every client you meet. At a basic level, clients often seek free legal advice because they can't afford to pay for it—though of course this is not always the case. That alone is an 'access to justice' issue. But access issues go beyond costs: clients may come because they don't know their rights, because they don't trust the justice system, or because of other barriers.

Law clinics therefore aim to advance access to justice—a goal that, at face value, seems uncontroversial. After all, who isn't in favour of 'access to justice'? As Americans might say, it's like 'motherhood and apple pie': so basic and good that no one would claim to be against it. In that sense, it resembles another core constitutional norm—that of the *rule of law*, which requires that everyone follow the law, that rights work in practice, and that state power is accountable and restrained. Given how fundamental the rule of law is, it is striking that the

Bach Report on *The Right to Justice* opened with the following statement, linking it directly to 'access to justice':

> We live at a time when the rule of law is under attack. Too many powerful institutions pay lip service to the concept of access to justice without having sufficient regard for what it actually means. It is, after all, fairly simple: unless everybody can get some access to the legal system at the time in their lives when they need it, trust in our institutions and in the rule of law breaks down. When that happens, society breaks down.[1]

Similarly, TH Marshall saw access to justice as a core part of the welfare state, and therefore argued that the *right* to access to justice should be guaranteed alongside civil, political, social, and economic rights.[2] Access to justice is therefore a foundational right: without it, other rights risk becoming hollow or unenforceable.[3] Moreover, this right matters especially for marginalized groups, because 'poor people are more likely to get into trouble with the law, come into contact with state agencies, suffer violence and abuse, experience precarious and sometimes dangerous employment, live in poor quality housing and be exploited by, for instance, private landlords'.[4]

Notwithstanding the force of rhetoric, access to justice may not be, as the Bach Report suggested, 'fairly simple'. While there is a compelling case for its importance, we should ask: what exactly are we agreeing to when we say that we support access to justice? Without clarity on what 'basic access to justice' entails, how can we confidently assert, as the Report does, that 'more and more people are unable to exercise their basic right to justice'?[5]

Let us take up the challenge of unpacking this phrase. 'Access to justice' brings together two elements: one procedural, and one substantive. The procedural element—*access*—refers to the 'right or opportunity to benefit from or use a system or service'.[6] This is compelling because it seems self-evident: if a system or service exists, and guarantees you a right, clearly you should be able to benefit from it? Otherwise, what would be the point of the system?

The substantive element of the concept—*justice*—is powerful for a different reason. It has captured the public imagination for centuries, inspiring struggles, sacrifices, and iconic phrases such as Martin Luther King's 'The arc of the moral universe is long, but it bends towards justice'. It is carved into buildings and embedded in constitutional ideals ('liberty and justice for all'). But this broad appeal is also a weakness: justice is a term claimed by all sides, often in support of very different positions.

[1] The Bach Commission, *The Right to Justice: The Final Report of the Bach Commission* (Fabian Society 2017) 5.

[2] TH Marshall, *Citizenship and Social Class* (Cambridge University Press 1950) 10–11.

[3] Hilary Sommerlad, 'Reflections on the Reconfiguration of Access to Justice' (2008) 15 International Journal of the Legal Profession 179, 180; Jess Mant, 'Neoliberalism, Family Law and the Cost of Access to Justice' (2017) 39 Journal of Social Welfare and Family Law 246, 249.

[4] Peter Sanderson and Hilary Sommerlad, 'Colonising Law for the Poor: Access to Justice in the New Regulatory State' in Valerie Bryson and Pamela Fisher (eds), *Redefining Social Justice: New Labour Rhetoric and Reality* (Manchester University Press 2011) 179.

[5] Ibid 11. [6] Oxford English Dictionary.

So, as we move forward, we consider each element in turn: first, the history and construction of 'access', and then the idea of 'justice', within the phrase 'access to justice'. However, we should acknowledge that the distinction between 'access' and 'justice' is partly artificial and made here for analytical clarity. In practice, the two are closely connected. For example, if the claim for 'justice' is, in effect, a claim for a fair process in a disciplinary hearing before an employer, the 'access' will be viewed very differently when compared to 'justice' involved in a trial that involves the death penalty, for example. Where the stakes for 'perversion of justice' are lower, we may be willing to satisfy ourselves with a more limited version of access, and vice versa.

And yet, especially in law clinics, it can be useful to tease apart the components of a client's 'access to justice' problem: is the issue one of access, or one of justice? For example, court fees or the cost of legal advice are typically seen as access barriers—they presume that the justice system itself is sound, but hard to reach. But how should we think about the three-month time limit to bring an employment discrimination claim before a tribunal?[7] And when law clinics and law centres seek justice for, for example, victims of the Grenfell Tower fire (in this case, the North Kensington Law Centre), are they addressing issues of access, or of justice?[8] This is more than a theoretical debate—it has real-world implications. For instance, if students aim to support Grenfell survivors, how should they identify the main 'access to justice' problem? Is it the matter of ensuring that they receive compensation within the existing system (access);[9] or should they address the housing, including safety, situation that allowed such a tragedy to occur (access/justice), or perhaps the hostile environment that governs the situation of many of the residents, which prevents them from coming forward with a wide range of claims (justice)?[10]

This chapter consists of three main sections. The first section explores how we understand 'access', and the second turns to the concept of 'justice', both within the wider idea of 'access to justice'. Finally, because law operates in the real world, we consider the practical barriers that can stand in the way of fully achieving this aspiration.

2.1 The Procedural Question: What Is Access?

Even in its legal form, and even within the Anglo-American tradition, access to justice is not a modern idea. One of its most celebrated early statements appears in Magna Carta of 1215. In Clause 40, it declares: 'To no one will we sell, to no one will we deny or delay, right or justice.' The meaning of 'To no one will we sell' may not be immediately obvious, but over time it has come to be understood as a promise that justice should be available to all, *regardless of financial means.*

[7] Equality Act 2010, s 123(1).

[8] Jon Robins, 'Underfunded and overstretched: the lawyers seeking justice for Grenfell' *The Guardian* (24 July 2017) https://www.theguardian.com/inequality/2017/jul/24/underfunded-and-overstretched-the-lawyers-seeking-justice-for-grenfell-tower-fire

[9] Ibid.

[10] Richard Warren, 'Grenfell Tower and the Hostile Environment' *Countercurrents: Critical Law at Kent* (3 July 2017) https://blogs.kent.ac.uk/countercurrents/2017/07/03/grenfell-tower-and-the-hostile-environment/

Figure 2.1 What is access?

Jeremy Bentham strongly supported this interpretation, famously arguing that any requirement to pay for legal redress could result in a denial of justice. In typically sharp language, he wrote: 'The statesman who contributes to put justice out of reach, the financier who comes into the house with a law-tax in his hand, is an accessory after the fact to every crime; every villain may hail him brother, every malefactor may boast of him as an accomplice.'[11]

But what does Bentham mean by putting justice 'out of reach'? We can think of three interpretations—or levels—of 'access' that help us unpack the idea. As you can see from Figure 2.1 above, these are: (1) the right to approach the court; (2) the right to receive legal assistance; and (3) the right to have the state cover the cost of that assistance. Let's consider each in turn.

2.1.1 Access as the Right to Approach the Court

In Bentham's approach we find, therefore, our **first interpretation** of 'access'—that there be a formal (as opposed to 'effective'[12]), *uninhibited*, right to issue proceedings and lodge a claim before the court. This narrow approach is also reflected in the writings of Edward Coke, who interpreted Clause 40 of Magna Carta as demanding that justice be '*free*, because nothing is more iniquitous than saleable justice; *full*, because justice ought not to limp; and *speedy*, because delay is in effect a denial.'[13] This triplet—free, full, and speedy—outlines the classical ideals of access to justice in its most basic procedural form.

Indeed, we can find explicit pronouncements along those lines. For example, the Court of Appeal has stated that 'It is a principle of our law that every citizen has a right of unimpeded access to a court.'[14] And yet, even this basic principle was never accepted literally as such. Because if it was, then the access should be completely free, and tribunal and court fees, for example, would not be permitted as a condition for pursuing a claim and issuing proceedings.[15]

Some of you may now be thinking: who cares what eighteenth-century philosophers thought about a thirteenth-century document? Well, you'd be surprised: Bentham's ghost, or

[11] Jeremy Bentham, *A Protest Against Law Taxes* (1795) 574.

[12] Bryant Garth and Mauro Cappelletti, 'Access to Justice: The Newest Wave in the Worldwide Movement to Make Rights Effective' (1978) Buffalo Law Review 113.

[13] Coke, Institutes of the Laws of England (1809 ed) 56. But cf Lord Sumption's claim that Coke was responsible for 'inventing the myth of Magna Carta' which, according to Sumption, did not intend to carry the weight that we now, thanks to Coke, ascribe to it: Jonathan Sumption, 'Magna Carta Then and Now' *Address to the Friends of the British Library* (9 March 2015) https://www.supremecourt.uk/docs/speech-150309.pdf (accessed 16 March 2020).

[14] *Home Office v Leech No 2* [1993] EWCA Civ 12, per LJ Steyn.

[15] *Lightfoot v the Lord Chancellor* [1999] EWCA Civ 3025; Lord Thomas of Cwmgiedd, *The Legacy of Magna Carta: Justice in the 21st Century* (Speech to the Legal Research Foundation, 25 September 2015) https://www.judiciary.uk/wp-content/uploads/2015/10/the-legacy-of-magna-carta-lcj.pdf

spirit, has carried through the ages. Just over 800 years after Magna Carta was promulgated, the UK Supreme Court had the opportunity, in the case of *Unison*, to refer to the document, and to echo Bentham's concern. It explained that the premise should be that 'people must in principle have unimpeded access to [the courts]'.[16] Referring to Magna Carta, the Court explained that the words of Clause 40 'are not a prohibition on the charging of court fees, but they are a guarantee of access to courts which administer justice promptly and fairly'.[17] In other words, the Court acknowledged that while some level of fees might be acceptable, they must not be set at a level that would deter ordinary people from bringing claims. Thus, the idea that courts must be available to all remains not only a historical principle but also a living doctrine with contemporary force.

Key Case *R (on the application of Unison) v Lord Chancellor* (2017) UK Supreme Court

Facts: An increase in fees for the Employment Tribunal was introduced by the Lord Chancellor using statutory powers. Applicants had to pay an issue fee and a hearing fee, which were £600 for uncomplicated cases and £1200 for cases such as unfair dismissal and employment discrimination. Following the increase in fees, applications to the Tribunal fell by approximately 70 per cent.

Legal Issue: Whether the fees charged under the Employment Tribunals and Employment Appeals Tribunal Order 2013 were unlawful.

Judgment: The Supreme Court found that the fees were unlawful because they had hindered access to the court, which is a constitutional right that is inherent in the rule of law and of benefit to the whole of society, and not just to individuals bringing the claim. A change of this nature had to be approved by Parliament. The fees also led to a real risk that people would be prevented from having access to justice. This could be seen in the dramatic drop in the number of cases brought following the introduction of the fees. Affordability had to be considered in a practical way and if middle- to low-income families could not afford the fees without sacrificing expenditure required to maintain a reasonable standard of living, they could not be said to be affordable.

Looking slightly beyond the domestic UK context, we find further endorsement of this principle in European jurisprudence. The Advocate General of the Court of Justice of the European Union (CJEU) clarified that while charging a court fee is not, in itself, a violation of the right to access the courts, 'it may be incompatible with Article 47 of the Charter [which guarantees a right to effective remedy and a fair trial] to levy several and cumulative courts fees in judicial proceedings, at least if these cumulative fees have a *dissuasive effect* and are *disproportionate*'.[18]

[16] *Unison v Lord Chancellor* [2017] UKSC 51 [68]. [17] Ibid [74].

[18] Opinion of Mr Advocate General Jääskinen in Case C-61/14 *Orrizonte Salute—Studio Infermieristico Associato v Azienda Pubblica di Servizi alla persona 'San Valentino'* (7 May 2015) [54, emphasis added].

REFLECTION POINT

Bentham and Coke seemed to think that the process to issue proceedings before the court should be completely free. In contrast, there is a tendency in modern times to see public services as services for which users need to pay. This is the case, for example, when we renew our passport or driving licence. The government's argument is that citizens who use the service need to pay for the cost of running it.

However, the Unison case suggests that this approach can lead to fees that are disproportionate, and while they may come closer to covering the true cost of the service, they also discourage individuals from pursuing their claims. Think of cases that you've encountered and consider which approach would you advocate for: completely free, nominal fee, or a fee that covers the true cost of the service?

2.1.2 Access as the Right to Legal Assistance

A **second interpretation** of access to justice refers to an individual's right to seek assistance when making their case, most prominently before the courts. It may seem difficult to imagine, but for hundreds of years, English law required claimants—even defendants in criminal cases—to represent themselves in court, even when they could afford counsel. Curiously, the only exception to this rule was made for the crime of treason, introduced in 1695 by Members of Parliament concerned that they might, if political tides shifted, face such charges themselves.[19] It was only in 1791 in the United States (through the Sixth Amendment) and in 1836 in Britain that all defendants in criminal cases gained the right to assistance of counsel. If this historical state of affairs seems peculiar to you now, it is because the legal context has changed dramatically over the past two centuries. At the time, the society, the economy, and, consequently, the law were far less complex, and individuals could often competently represent themselves or seek non-professional advice.[20] As these contexts evolved, those without access to a lawyer were at a considerable disadvantage. You may wish to pause here and consider: where does the responsibility lie for the current state of affairs? Why do so many people now require legal assistance in matters such as housing, family disputes, and interaction with neighbours and local councils, when in the past they could manage on their own? Is this because society and economy just *became* more complex; or have lawyers contributed to that complexity, rendering their own services indispensable? Or perhaps it is a bit of both?

Another argument against restrictions on legal representation comes not from the side of the claimants or defendants, but from that of the lawyers. Their own freedom to work, and freedom to contract for work, were arguably unlawfully limited by these restrictions.

[19] Deborah Rhode, *Access to Justice* (OUP 2004) 82.

[20] Ibid 81; Lawrence Friedman, 'Access to Justice: Some Historical Comments' (2010) 37 Fordham Urban Law Journal 3; Garth and Cappelletti (n 12) 184.

Unsurprisingly, this second argument was not as persuasive, and the celebrated cases that established the right to legal counsel, such as the US Supreme Court case of *Powell v Alabama*,[21] naturally focused on the serious implications of denying defendants access to legal counsel at a crucial point in the process.

In that case, the US Supreme Court made a strong case for the right to be assisted by legal counsel in a serious legal matter: nine young, black men were convicted of raping two white women and, apart from the 13-year-old Roy Wright, were sentenced to death in a series of one-day trials. They were told that they could not hire a lawyer to plan their defence until shortly before the trial. The court explained the importance of the right to legal counsel as the basis for a fair trial, and thus for other rights in the legal process:

> The right to be heard would be, in many cases, of little avail if it did not comprehend the right to be heard by counsel. Even the intelligent and educated layman has small and sometimes no skill in the science of law. If charged with crime, he is incapable, generally, of determining for himself whether the indictment is good or bad. He is unfamiliar with the rules of evidence. Left without the aid of counsel, he may be put on trial without a proper charge, and convicted upon incompetent evidence, or evidence irrelevant to the issue or otherwise inadmissible. He lacks both the skill and knowledge adequately to prepare his defense, even though he may have a perfect one. He requires the guiding hand of counsel at every step in the proceedings against him. Without it, though he be not guilty, he faces the danger of conviction because he does not know how to establish his innocence . . .
>
> In the light of the . . . ignorance and illiteracy of the defendants, their youth, the circumstances of public hostility, the imprisonment and the close surveillance of the defendants by the military forces . . . under the circumstances just stated, the necessity of counsel was so vital and imperative that the failure of the trial court to make an effective appointment of counsel was likewise a denial of due process within the meaning of the Fourteenth Amendment.[22]

However, the US Supreme Court refrained from stating whether its ruling would apply in less extreme circumstances, which did not involve the death penalty or defendants who were so vulnerable. And this raises the question: Who is 'vulnerable' enough to require legal assistance from the state? Many of us tend to think of a person's vulnerability as an objective reality, that is related to their economic situation, their race or ethnicity, their dis/ability, their migration status, and so on. But perhaps we should think of it as contextual, that is: all of us may become vulnerable in particular situations, for example when navigating the law and the legal system. If that is the case, what should our expectations be about the role of the state in mitigating those vulnerabilities?[23]

21 287 US 45 (1932). 22 Ibid 68–69, 71.

23 Martha Fineman, 'The Vulnerable Subject: Anchoring Equality in the Human Condition' (2008) Yale Journal of Law and Feminism 1; Martha Fineman, 'Vulnerability and Inevitable Equality' (2017) 4 Oslo Law Review 133, 134; Naomi Cruetzfeldt et al, *Access to Justice, Digitalization and Vulnerability* (Bristol University Press 2024) 22–35.

REFLECTION POINT

Today, it is inconceivable that criminal defendants, or even parties to a serious civil case, would not be allowed to avail themselves of legal assistance. And yet, there are proceedings, such as employment disciplinary hearings and mediation sessions, in which the parties cannot be accompanied by legal representatives. Can you think of reasons for this approach? What do you think of it?

2.1.3 Access as the Right that the State Pay for Legal Assistance

The **third**, and final, **interpretation** of 'access' requires a more active role on the part of the state. If we use familiar distinctions from the discourse on social and economic rights, the first two interpretations correspond to 'negative' obligations: duties on the state to *respect* a right by refraining from interference. To be clear: *negative* here does not imply something undesirable, but simply a duty not to act. In contrast, this third, more ambitious, interpretation refers to the 'positive' manifestation of the right, that is: the demand that the state protect, or even realize, the right by *taking action*. In this case, that duty may fall on the courts to ensure that legal representation is provided, and may imply an individual right to have counsel appointed free of charge.

A well-known historical reference point is the Law of Henry VII, enacted in 1495, which allowed courts to appoint counsel for poor individuals. The statute directed Justices to 'assign to the same poor Person . . . Counsel learned, by their Discretions, which shall give their Counsels, taking nothing for the same'.[24] While this marked a symbolic commitment to access, the measure was used only sparingly and could not bridge the growing gap in legal needs—especially as the law became more complex and the population expanded. A further step was taken with the Poor Prisoners' Defence Act 1903, which authorized English judges to appoint compensated counsel where justice demanded it 'by reason of the gravity of the charges' or other 'exceptional' circumstances.[25]

Meaningful reform came with the Legal Aid and Advice Act 1949. This Act established a more generous compensation structure and shifted the judicial default position—encouraging judges, when in doubt, to appoint counsel. The 1949 Act laid the foundations for the modern system of legal aid, which we explore further in chapters that follow. But for now, we can say, briefly, that legal aid refers to the provision of publicly funded legal assistance to those who need it but cannot afford it. In England and Wales, legal aid is available in certain areas of law, provided that: (1) the individual passes a *means* test (relating to income and capital); (2) the case meets a *merits* test (eg likelihood of success); and (3) the issue falls within the defined *scope* for legal aid funding. Does that mean that all legal needs are covered today? Many would say that this is far from the case. Indeed, a novel legal needs survey was conducted in England and Wales in 2019. Among its key findings are that 64 per cent of adults experienced

[24] 11 Hen 7, c12; Rhode (n 19) 79; and by the Supreme Court of Canada's decision in *Trial Lawyers Association of British Columbia v British Columbia (Attorney General)* 2014 SCC 59 [48].

[25] Rhode (n 19) 83.

a legal issue during the previous four years and 3 in 10 had an unmet legal need, either because they did not receive any help or because they required further assistance.[26]

In the US, it was only in 1963, in the celebrated *Gideon v Wainwright*,[27] that the Supreme Court declared not only that the 'noble ideal' of 'fair trials before impartial tribunals in which every defendant stands equal before the law . . . cannot be realized if the poor man charged with crime has to face his accusers without a lawyer to assist him'. The Court went further, and addressed the fact that this ideal may be hindered by an individual's means. In such a case, 'reason and reflection require us to recognize that in our adversary system of criminal justice, any person hauled into court, who is too poor to hire a lawyer, cannot be assured a fair trial unless counsel is provided for him'.[28]

REFLECTION POINT

The point made in *Gideon v Wainwright*, that without representation a fair trial was not possible, related to criminal trials. In England and Wales thousands of people represent themselves in courts and tribunals. Think about your own clinical legal experience and the clients you have worked with. Do you think that your clients are able to get a fair hearing without representation? What different issues are raised by civil and criminal proceedings? Do you think the above quote from *Gideon v Wainwright* could apply to the people that you have advised or assisted?

TAKING STOCK

This section focused on the first half of the phrase 'access to justice', by asking 'what is access'? In particular, it was suggested that we can identify three layers of access, with increasing degrees of generosity. These are: the right to approach the court; the right to receive legal assistance (at one's own expense); and the right to receive state-provided legal assistance, known in the UK as 'legal aid'.

Hopefully, you will have seen that the brief historical overview in each section suggested that, in principle, nothing is new under the sun. However, positing the present against the background of the past also shows the new form and the new challenges of each layer. For example, costs are a very real, and modern, obstacle to approaching the court; a range of proceedings do not allow a claimant to be accompanied by a legal representative; and legal aid has been cut dramatically.

Finally, while acknowledging this section's focus on 'access', we clarified that there is a strong relationship between the way we understand 'access' and the way we understand 'justice'. Different types of 'access' naturally correspond to different understandings of 'justice'. With that in mind, we turn now to the second half of the phrase, thus asking: 'access to what'?

[26] The Law Society, *Legal Needs of Individuals in England and Wales: Summary Report* (London: Law Society 2019/20) https://www.lawsociety.org.uk/topics/research/legal-needs-of-individuals-in-england-and-wales-report

[27] 372 US 335 (1963). [28] Ibid 344.

2.2 The Conceptual Question: Access to What?

The previous section addressed the question of *what constitutes access*: does it mean free, unimpeded entry to legal processes on one's own? The ability to secure the assistance of a legal representative? Or even a positive duty on the state to actively facilitate, fund, and realize that access? In pursuing these questions, however, we left aside a deeper question: *access to what*, exactly? The implicit assumption in much of the previous discussion was that the focus was on access to the courts. But courts are not necessarily the only, or even the most important, sites of justice. The focus on judicial mechanisms partly reflects the fact that lawyers—including academic lawyers and judges—tend to engage in a fair bit of institutional introspection (or, more charitably, efforts to improve their own professional domain) by concentrating their reform efforts close to home.

Before we turn to the substantive question—access to what?—it is helpful to recall an earlier observation from this chapter. We analytically separated the phrase *access to justice* into two parts to examine each more clearly. But in practice, these elements are closely interwoven. For example, we tend to insist on strong and meaningful access in criminal trials because the stakes—such as loss of liberty or life—are so high. By contrast, we may be willing to accept more modest forms of access where the outcomes are less severe, such as in regulatory or disciplinary contexts. Thus, the strength of our commitment to 'access' may depend on what kind of 'justice' is at stake.

With this in mind, the discussion that follows explores a spectrum of interpretations of the term 'justice' within the phrase *access to justice*. As illustrated by Figure 2.2 below, we begin with the narrowest conception: 'access to justice' as little more than 'access to courts' (often bundled with access to legal counsel). From there, we expand outward to consider 'access to law' as a broader principle. Finally, we turn to the more elusive idea of 'access to justice' as . . . 'access to justice'—a phrase that demands deeper unpacking and invites more critical scrutiny.

2.2.1 Access to Courts

You would not be blamed if you were to conclude, based on a quick overview of the literature on access to justice, that the phrase 'access to justice' is synonymous with 'access to courts'. This view is supported by popular understandings of the phrase 'criminal justice system' or

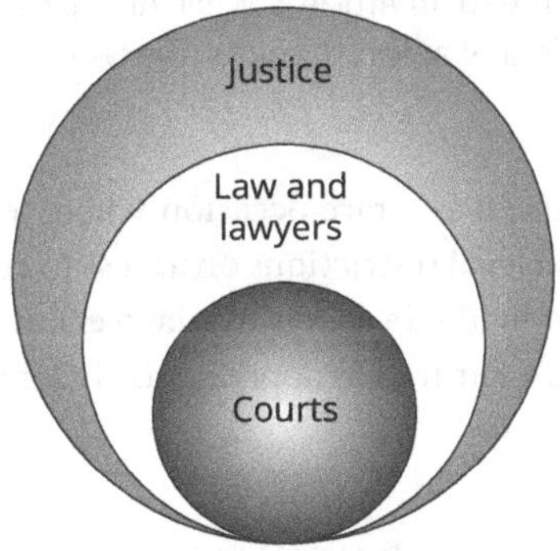

Figure 2.2 Access to what?

'civil justice system', which are typically taken to refer to the legal systems administered by the courts. This framing is also common in formal legal instruments. For example, Title VI of the European Union Charter of Fundamental Rights is titled 'Justice'. Yet the provisions it contains are not abstract philosophical musings on the nature of justice; rather, they focus—reasonably and predictably—on procedural guarantees, ensuring 'an effective remedy', 'a fair and public hearing', and legal aid 'to those who lack sufficient resources'.

A trio of important cases show the expanding interpretation of the 'right of access to courts'. In all these cases, the courts moved fluidly between 'access to courts' and 'access to lawyers', underlining a key insight: as the law becomes more complex, formal access without effective assistance is of little practical value. Indeed, if a litigant is unable to understand or frame the legal issues, or to present relevant facts and arguments, then access in theory may amount to exclusion in practice. It serves no one—the claimant, the judge, or the system—if a person appears in court unable to participate meaningfully. For that reason, the cases below reveal how tightly linked *access to courts* and *access to representation* have become.

The first case, *Golder v UK*,[29] offers an interesting bridge between criminal and civil proceedings. While access rights are more commonly associated with criminal trials, *Golder* confirmed that civil proceedings also fall within the scope of Article 6 of the European Convention on Human Rights.

Key Case: *Golder v UK* (1975) ECHR

Facts: The applicant was a prisoner who was wrongfully accused by a prison guard of participating in a prison riot. Conscious of the effects that such an accusation would have on, inter alia, his likelihood in succeeding in future parole proceedings, he sought to claim damages against the guard for libel. However, under the Prison Rules 1964, prisoners were not able to communicate with any person outside the prison without the leave of the Home Secretary. Employing that power, the Home Secretary denied Golder the opportunity to consult a solicitor.

Legal Issue: Is Article 6 limited to guaranteeing the right to a fair trial in legal proceedings which are already pending, or does it also secure a right of access to the courts for those wishing to commence an action?

Judgment: There had been a breach of Article 6. While Article 6 mentions the right to a fair trial, and not, explicitly, the right of access to courts, the two 'stem from the same basic idea'.

This case is interesting because it is a rare occasion where, even in the second half of the twentieth century, we find real legal restrictions on access to courts in the '*negative*' sense (ie the state's restriction on an individual's access to a lawyer). It is also important because the Court interpreted the right to a fair trial as applying to civil, not just criminal, cases. Finally,

[29] [1975] ECHR 1.

it is interesting because the Court anchors its understanding in the rule of law. As noted at the start of this chapter, 'access to justice' is closely tied to the rule of law. The Court affirmed this link, stating at [34] that 'in civil matters one can scarcely conceive of the rule of law without there being a possibility of having access to the courts'. This view is echoed in Lord Neuberger's lecture, where he stated: 'Access to legal advice and representation is of course a fundamental ingredient of the rule of law.'[30]

However, the Court also clarified that, like many rights, the right to access courts is not absolute.[31] Legitimate restrictions may exist, for instance for minors or individuals of 'unsound mind'.[32] However, in the current circumstances, the Home Secretary failed to respect Golder's right to have his issue determined by an independent and impartial court.

While *Golder* demonstrates that restrictions on the negative right to access courts (that is, the state's duty *not to act* to impede access) still occur, they are relatively rare, with one glaring exception: tribunal and court fees. By setting such fees, the state essentially places a financial condition on access, relating to the ability to pay. If the fees are too high, individuals who have a right to access the court in theory may be unable to use it in practice.

As discussed earlier, Jeremy Bentham interpreted Clause 40 to mean that *any* fee constituted a denial of justice. In *Unison*, the UK Supreme Court revisited Clause 40 and its underlying principles in a challenge to Employment Tribunal fees. One claimant exclaimed: 'Well as far as I'm concerned, for me, there is no law or legal system . . . as far it is me getting justice, you know. You've got to pay for justice. What sort of justice is that?'[33] After accepting that fees might be justified to help fund the system, the Court nevertheless held that it 'follows from the authorities cited that the Fees Order will be ultra vires if there is a real risk that persons will effectively be prevented from having access to justice'.[34] It concluded that this was indeed the case and struck down the fees. However, it is worth noting that this decision was made possible, at least in part, because the fees were set to a level that had extreme consequences.

Following the introduction of fees in 2013, single-claimant cases dropped by 68 per cent, and group claims by 75 per cent.[35] Analysis by Jeremias Prassl and Abi Adams suggested that, due to the fees, 20 per cent of claimants in *successful* unfair dismissal cases (where the fees were £1200) were expected to lose money, as their awards would be lower than the fees. In low-value cases such as unlawful deduction of wages, where fees were £600, 45 per cent of claimants were expected to be financially worse off.[36]

[30] Neuberger, 'Access to Justice: Welcome Address to the Australian Bar Association Biennial Conference' (2017) https://supremecourt.uk/uploads/speech_170703_2dfb0de76f.pdf

[31] Ibid [38]. [32] Ibid [39].

[33] Quoted in Nicole Busby, 'The Costs of Justice: Barriers and Challenges to Accessing the Employment Tribunal System' in Samuel Kirwan (ed), *Advising in Austerity: Reflections on Challenging Times for Advice Agencies* (Bristol University Press 2017) 79, 86.

[34] *Unison* (n 16) [87].

[35] Doug Pyper, Feargal McGuiness, and Jennifer Brown, *Employment Tribunal Fees* (House of Commons Briefing Paper 7081 2017).

[36] Abi Adams and Jeremias Prassl, 'Vexatious Claims: Challenging the Case for Employment Tribunal Fees' (2017) 80 Modern Law Review 412.

These figures were instrumental in persuading the Court to strike down the fees. Indeed, an earlier challenge to the same fees, in 2015, was not successful. In that case, known as *Unison I*, the Court of Appeal had found the fees proportionate and concluded that there was no evidence they rendered access to justice 'unaffordable'. According to Underhill LJ, we simply cannot know, without further information, how claimants organized their finances. For some, fees might be prohibitively high; for others, they may be worth the cost. He concluded that 'there is simply no safe basis for an untutored intuition about claimant behaviour or therefore for an inference that the decline cannot consist entirely of cases where potential claimants could realistically have afforded to bring proceedings but have made a *choice* not to'.[37]

However, as Michael Ford KC notes, the distinction between claimants' inability and unwillingness to pay is 'elusive if not to say nonexistent'.[38] This framing also shifts the conception of court access from a public good to a consumer product. Indeed, the *principal aim* of the introduction of Employment Tribunal fees in the UK, in 2012, was 'to transfer part of the cost burden of the tribunals *from taxpayers to users* of their services'.[39] Claimants were to assess the cost–benefit of bringing a case as they might assess the value of a restaurant meal. Under this logic, we can never know what goes through an individual claimant's mind, and when a particular fee would be 'too high' and necessitate court intervention. This approach sets an unrealistically high bar before the claimants to prove that the fees denied them effective access to justice. If the test is that claimants must show they *could not possibly* afford the fee without, for example, selling a car, taking out a loan, or asking friends or family for help, then almost no one can meet it. At what point, then, can we say that someone has been denied 'access to courts'?

Ultimately, to establish such a claim would require empirical data, which can only be gathered after the fact. The few studies that have investigated barriers to bringing legal claims have consistently found that the costs of proceedings—including but not limited to fees—are among the most prominent obstacles to legal action.[40] This evidence is vital. But it also reveals a stark fact: many potential claimants had already been excluded from courts, and thus from justice, by the time those findings emerged.

So far, we have explored the legitimacy and legality of restrictions on the 'negative' right of access, in which the state erects direct barriers. A few years after *Golder*, the European Court of Human Rights in *Airey* expanded its interpretation of Article 6 beyond its previous holding, asking whether the state has a *positive* duty to assist those who cannot afford legal representation.[41]

[37] *Unison* (n 16) [68] (emphasis added).

[38] Michael Ford, 'A Reflection on Case Study Two: Laura and the Effects of Fees' in Samuel Kirwan (ed), *Advising in Austerity: Reflections on Challenging Times for Advice Agencies* (Bristol University Press 2017) 69, 75.

[39] *Unison* (n 16) [56] (emphasis added).

[40] Richard Craven and Sue Arrowsmith, 'Public Procurement and Access to Justice: A Legal and Empirical Study of the UK System' (2016) 6 Public Procurement Law Review 227.

[41] *Airey v Ireland* [1979] ECHR 3.

Key Case: *Airey v Ireland* (1979) ECHR

Facts: Mrs Airey suffered from domestic abuse and violence at the hands of her husband. Under Irish law at the time, divorce was not legal, and married couples were obliged to cohabit. However, it was possible to seek a 'decree of judicial separation' from the High Court. Legal aid was not available for civil matters in Ireland, and these include judicial separation proceedings.

Legal Issue: Article 6(3)(c) explicitly mandates the provision of legal aid only in criminal proceedings. Should it be interpreted to demand such provision in civil proceedings as well?

Judgment: There had been a breach of Article 6. Despite the absence of a similar clause for civil litigation, Article 6 may compel the State to provide for the assistance of a lawyer when such assistance proves indispensable for effective access to court, for example because of the complexity of the procedure or the case.

Unsurprisingly, the Irish government in *Airey* sought to distinguish this case from *Golder* by claiming that while *Golder* involved a demand that the government *not intervene* (and thus, a 'negative' obligation), here the government is required *to intervene* (a 'positive' obligation). This interpretation, they claimed, was a step too far. The Court rejected this distinction, stating that 'fulfilment of a duty under the Convention on occasion necessitates some positive action on the part of the State; in such circumstances, the State cannot simply remain passive and "there is . . . no room to distinguish between acts and omissions" '.[42]

Interestingly, the Court in this case expressed a sentiment that is similar to the approach taken in the US Supreme Court's analysis in *Powell*, noted above. In both cases, the courts recognized that access to justice must consider the *complexity* of the legal process in relation to the *capacities* of the individual. The ECtHR noted that proceedings before the High Court—'the least accessible court' in Ireland—were especially complex. This was particularly true for separation cases, evidenced by the fact that in all 255 such cases between 1972 and 1978, petitioners were legally represented. It was 'not realistic', the Court concluded, for an applicant who 'comes from a humble background' to 'effectively conduct her own case'.

Finally, the UK case of *Steel and Morris* took this principle a step further. While *Airey* affirmed the importance of legal aid in civil matters, the UK government maintained that it could legitimately determine which types of civil cases merited such aid. In its view, grave family matters might justify state-funded assistance, but defamation claims did not meet that threshold. The European Court of Human Rights partly accepted this differentiation but placed crucial weight on the *circumstances* of the case. It was not Ms Steel and Mr Morris who chose to litigate. Rather, they were sued by a multinational corporation: McDonald's. The Court observed that in this context, 'the inequality of arms could not have been greater'.[43]

[42] Ibid [25].

[43] *Steel and Morris v UK* [2005] ECHR 103 at [50].

McDonald's had global sales of $30 billion in 1995. In contrast, David Morris earned £65 per week from part-time work and Helen Steel was an unwaged single parent. The Court reiterated that while the right of access to courts is not absolute and may be subject to restrictions, those restrictions must pursue a legitimate aim and remain proportionate.

Key Case: *Steel and Morris v UK* (2005) ECHR

Facts: Steel and Morris were environmental campaigners who handed out leaflets outside a branch of McDonald's claiming that McDonald's endangered health and was responsible for cruelty to animals, unfair labour practices, and endangering the health of its patrons.

McDonald's sued them for defamation. Legal aid was not available for defamation cases, but the Legal Services Commission could have granted discretionary 'exceptional funding'. It declined to do so, so Steel and Morris had to represent themselves. The case ran for nine years—the longest case, civil or criminal, in English legal history.

Legal Issue: Did the refusal to grant legal aid breach the right to a fair trial under Art 6 of the European Convention of Human Rights because of the inequality of arms?

Judgment: There had been a breach of Article 6 (as well as the applicants' right to freedom of expression, under Article 10). The question of whether legal aid was necessary to enable a fair trial would depend on the facts and circumstances of each case, but in this case the disparity between the parties, the complexity of the issues, the impact on the two appellants, and the length of the proceedings all gave rise to unfairness.

The Court found that the *inequality of arms* between the parties in *Steel and Morris* constituted a breach of Article 6 ECHR. This interpretation of access to justice 'denotes the general subject of the extent to which citizens are able to gain access to the legal services necessary to protect and vindicate their legal rights'.[44] However, it does not go as far as some would like.

For example, Tom Cornford argues that 'the ideal of *equal access* is the core normative meaning of access to justice';[45] Geoffrey Bindman similarly insists that 'Justice demands a level playing field';[46] and the Bach Report suggests that 'if you recognise your problem has a legal remedy but don't have the means to access the justice system on a *fair footing* with your adversary, then the outcome that is reached is unlikely to be just'.[47] Even the US Supreme Court declared that 'there can be no equal justice where the kind of trial a man gets depends on the amount of money he has'.[48]

Yet to what extent is this notion of 'equal justice' reflected in practice? Cynics may lean toward the famously wry observation, often attributed to Irish judge Sir James Mathew, that

[44] Tom Cornford, 'The Meaning of Access to Justice' in E Palmer et al (eds), *Access to Justice: Beyond the Policies and Politics of Austerity* (Hart 2016) 28.

[45] Ibid 36 [emphasis added].

[46] Geoffrey Bindman, 'The Legal Aid Challenge' (2016) 166 NLJ 7727.

[47] Bach Commission (n 1) 11 [emphasis added].

[48] *Griffin v Illinois* 351 US 12 (1956).

justice in England 'is open to all, just like the Ritz hotel'. The basic truth behind this quip is that financial resources matter. The more money a litigant has, the more legal expertise and advocacy they can afford. This reality sits uneasily alongside the principle of 'equality before the law'.

As a result, while the Court is willing to intervene where the *inequality of arms* is so extreme as to deny one party a fair trial, it refrains from requiring the State to ensure true equality of resources. Instead, the test becomes whether 'each side is afforded a reasonable opportunity to present his or her case under conditions that do not place him or her at a substantial disadvantage vis-à-vis the adversary'.[49] This limited commitment to equal justice draws sharp criticism from scholars such as Geoffrey Hazard:

> Hence, when we say that everyone is equal before the law, we must mean that everyone is, so far as practicable, entitled in legal process to essentially equal treatment. Or we are simply mouthing comforting phrases. Or simply being hypocrites. Or some combination of all of the above.[50]

So we conclude this subsection with an intriguing thought: that access to courts is incomplete without access to lawyers; that access to lawyers is insufficient without state funding for legal representation; and that legal representation alone is not enough if it does not secure equality of arms and a level playing field.

REFLECTION POINT

Think about your own clinical legal experience and the clients you have worked with. How ambitious do you think we should be in our demand to realize access to courts and lawyers:

- No limits on accessing courts?
- No limits on accessing lawyers?
- Funding for legal aid, and if so, in which areas of law, and in which cases?
- If funding is mandated, should it be at a level to negate any inequality of arms?

2.2.2 **Access to Lawyers**

Although courts, lawyers, and the law are often closely associated, legal process extends beyond the courtroom. A broader definition of access to justice suggests that 'the concept of access to justice . . . embodies the ideal that everybody, regardless of his or her capabilities, should have the chance to enjoy the protection and enforcement of his or her rights by the use of law and the legal system'.[51] Lawyers provide 'access to law': knowledge of the law,

[49] *Steel and Morris* (n 43) at [62].

[50] Geoffrey Hazard, 'After Legal Aid Is Abolished' (1999) 2 Journal of the Institute for the Study of Legal Ethics 375.

[51] Stefan Wrbka, Steven van Utysel, and Mathias Siems, 'Access to Justice and Collective Actions' in Stefan Wrbka, Steven van Utysel, and Mathias Siems (eds), *Collective Actions: Enhancing Access to Justice and Reconciling Multilayer Interests?* (Cambridge University Press 2012) 1, 2.

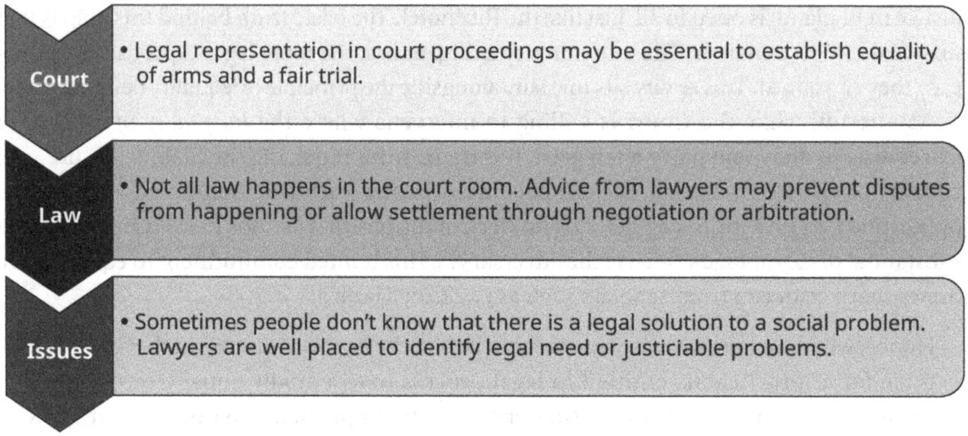

Figure 2.3 Access to law/yers

including avenues to protect oneself and claim a remedy, alternatives to the law and the limits and constraints of the law.[52] The Bach Commission stated clearly: 'Access to the courts and access to justice are not synonymous', explaining that 'reasonable legal assistance includes the full spectrum of public legal education, information, advice and representation'.[53]

These elements—public legal education, information, and advice—often matter well before a case ever reaches court, if it reaches court at all. As illustrated by Figure 2.3, access to law involves a continuum: from public legal education and rights awareness, to early informal advice, to formal legal consultation, through to dispute resolution options such as mediation or arbitration, and, finally, to courtroom representation. With an eye towards the chapters that follow, we can now start thinking about the role of legal education and, particularly, clinical legal education, with this understanding of 'access to justice' in mind. In other words, if law clinics, and law schools more generally, wish to support and enhance access to justice, what role should they play in improving public legal knowledge, offering accessible legal advice, and supporting early stage interventions that empower individuals, irrespective of courtroom confrontation?[54]

Indeed, in a number of cases, the court engaged with a wide array of scenarios in which the claimant asserted that they could not realize their rights without legal representation, even though their case was not before a court. For instance, in the US case of *Lassiter*,[55] the claimant argued that the Department of Social Services should not be able to terminate her parental rights without granting her legal counsel. Her claim, however, was rejected by the US Supreme Court. Similarly, in *Goss v Lopez*,[56] the same court denied students facing a ten-day suspension the right to legal representation during school disciplinary proceedings.

52 Stephen Pepper, 'Access to What' (1999) 2 Journal of the Institute for the Study of Legal Ethics 269, 270–271.
53 Bach Commission (n 1) 16.
54 Donald Nicolson, 'Legal Education, Ethics and Access to Justice: Forging Warriors for Justice in a Neo-Liberal World' (2015) 22 International Journal of the Legal Profession 51.
55 *Lassiter v Department of Social Services* 452 US 18 (1981).
56 419 US 565 (1975).

The position, which essentially equates 'access to justice' with 'access to law', has deep historical roots. Early on, the terms 'justice' and 'law' were synonymous. This is somewhat unsurprising, as '*jus*' means law.[57] Natural law theorists developed this idea into the enduring claim that an 'unjust law is not law'.[58]

From this perspective, access to lawyers becomes a logical extension of the assumption that legal knowledge and legal assistance are necessary to realize justice. While this might be seen as a somewhat self-serving view promoted by the legal profession, there is a more charitable interpretation. One's right to legal representation reflects the deeper ideal of **equality before the law**. Even outside the criminal context, it is easy to imagine how power imbalances, such as where a child is facing expulsion, a social worker is accused of 'gross misconduct' and subject to a risk of losing her licence to practice,[59] or a tenant is threatened with eviction, can have life-altering consequences. In such situations, legal procedures can be used to inflict significant harm, and the ability to respond with legal assistance may be essential to redressing the imbalance.

But how does a lawyer, or a law clinic for that matter, assist? We often think of them becoming relevant at a stage where the client comes with a problem—I've been deducted pay; my ex-wife won't let me see my kids; I'm being evicted—which implies that the client already *knows*, or at least *assumes*, that their problem has a legal angle, and therefore that the law could, perhaps, assist them in their predicament. But this isn't always, or perhaps even usually, the case.

As Abel, Felstiner, and Sarat showed, in an immediate-classic piece of sociology of law, very few grievances turn into claims, and very few claims turn into trials.[60] In a major contribution to what is known as the 'dispute perspective in legal studies', they introduced the process as *Naming, Blaming, and Claiming*. First, people must recognize, or *name*, that something injurious has happened to them—a shift from what the authors call an 'unPerceived Injurious Experience' (unPIE) to a 'Perceived Injurious Experience' (PIE). Then, they must identify someone or something to *blame*. Only after this can they proceed to *claim*, formally invoking the law to seek redress. This process—naming, blaming, and claiming—is not straightforward. Many legal injuries—such as exposure to asbestos, experiences of sexual harassment, or exploitative loan agreements—went unrecognized for years. It was only when lawyers and legal advocates brought the law into the picture that these harms were named and addressed. In this respect, lawyering is not just about defending rights in court, but about **making legal consciousness possible** in the first place.

As Hazel Genn notes, '*social problems or social needs can become legal needs* when the law provides a right or benefit that would alleviate or attenuate the social need, but the law cannot be mobilized, for example, because of lack of knowledge or opportunity to take advantage

[57] Thomas Kearns and Austin Sarat, *Legal Justice and Injustice: Towards a Situated Perspective* (University of Michigan Press 1996) 2.

[58] For recent formulations see: Robert George, *Natural Law Theory: Contemporary Essays* (OUP 1993); John Finnis, *Natural Law and Natural Rights* (OUP 1980).

[59] As in the English case of *Gogay v Hertfordshire County Council* [2000] EWCA 228 (the case presented such a situation, although the question of the right to counsel was not raised).

[60] William Felstiner, Richard Abel, and Austin Sarat, 'The Emergence and Transformation of Disputes: Naming, Blaming, Claiming . . . ' (1980) 15 Law & Society Review 631.

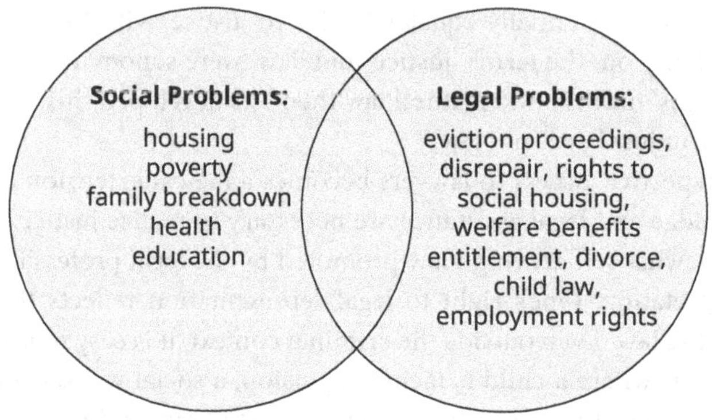

Figure 2.4 Social and legal problems

of a legal process or remedy'.[61] The partial overlap between social and legal problems is illustrated by Figure 2.4 above. Genn coined the term 'justiciable problem' to describe any form of dispute that might have a legal remedy.[62] It helped shift the focus from courts to the wider array of everyday issues—housing, employment, family breakdown, consumer rights—that could, in principle, be addressed through legal means. Lawyers, in turn, are uniquely positioned to identify such issues. They serve as translators, converting social needs into legal claims, and highlighting the often hidden legal dimensions of disputes.

So is moving from naming to blaming to claiming *always* a good thing? Not so fast. Abel, Felstiner, and Sarat explained how identifying access to justice with access to courts may actually do more harm than good. This is because promoting access to justice where disputes become lawsuits 'may accentuate the effects of inequality at the earlier, less visible stages, where it is harder to detect, diagnose, and correct'.[63] Actors such as governments and multinational corporations are 'repeat players'. They know how to plan legal risks in advance, shape the rules in their favour, and use the system tactically.[64]

Sally Engle Merry's ethnographic study of working-class litigants in lower courts offers some cautionary insights into the development of legal consciousness.[65] She found that, contrary to the idea of law as an all-powerful or imperialistic force, courts were often reluctant to engage with low-level, interpersonal disputes, which they viewed as moral or social pathologies:

> To the people who work in the lower courts—the judges, prosecutors, and clerks—interpersonal cases are unwelcome. Court officials do not feel that they can refuse these requests for intervention, yet they also feel that these cases are not really 'crimes', not

[61] Hazel Genn, 'When Law Is Good for Your Health: Mitigating the Social Determinants of Health through Access to Justice' (2019) 72 Current Legal Problems 159, 164 [emphasis in original]; see also Bach Commission (n 1) 11.

[62] Hazel Genn, *Paths to Justice: What People Do and Think About Going to Law* (Hart Publishing 1999).

[63] Felstiner, Abel, and Sarat (n 60) 637.

[64] Marc Galanter, 'Why the Haves Come Out Ahead: Speculations on the Limit of Legal Change' (1974) 9 Law and Society Review 95, esp 98–103; Gillian Hadfield, 'Higher Demand, Lower Supply? A Comparative Assessment of the Legal Resource Landscape for Ordinary Americans' (2010) Fordham Urban Law Journal 129, 132, 151; Craven and Arrowsmith (n 40).

[65] Sally Engle Merry, *Getting Justice and Getting Even: Legal Consciousness among Working-Class Americans* (2nd ed, University of Chicago Press 1990).

> 'real legal problems'. They call them 'garbage cases', 'junk cases', 'shit cases', and so forth. The cases are seen as difficult, troublesome, and often frivolous. Many say that people are simply 'using' the court to fight with each other. To clerks and prosecutors, the existence of ongoing relations and mutual accusations, revealed by crosscomplaints, are markers of garbage cases. Court officials recognize that plaintiffs seek a form of help—better treatment from spouses; protection from angry jilted lovers; more consideration from family, neighbors, and friends; more money to pay bills—which is hard for the court to provide. Ensuring that the husband stops hitting his wife, that the neighbor turns off his music at 10:00 p.m., that the teenager treats his parents with respect seems impossible. 'It doesn't belong here' is another way of saying 'We can't handle it here'.[66]

More generally, most of the scholarship, and perhaps all of the advocacy, concerning access to justice assumes that the problem is one of scarcity: that people lack sufficient access, and that this gap needs to be closed. Yet this view may conflict with the position that the person on the street would take if asked whether 'enough' people go to court. In fact, they would probably say that far too many people go to court, far too often, for far too many issues that could and should be resolved without resorting to law. How would we explain this clash in perspective?

First, some may say that the person on the street is simply misinformed. They are influenced by the media's delight in reporting 'loony litigation', Deborah Rhode's term for cases such as the following, all of which are real:

> football fans who sue referees; beauty contestants who sue each other; prison inmates who want chunky rather than smooth peanut butter; mothers who ask a court to resolve a playground shoving match between their three-year-olds; fathers unhappy about their fifteen-year-old's position on high school athletic team or their fifth-grader's failure to make the cheerleading squad; and a purchaser of cracker jacks who demands damages for a missing prize.[67]

There are three obvious problems with the tendency to extract an overarching conclusion regarding the state of access to justice based on such examples. First, the media representation of these cases is often unfair and sensationalist, caricaturing a serious tort, family, or public law issue to provoke reader eye-rolling. Second, claims that seem absurd at first may later prove pathbreaking. As Abel, Felstiner, and Sarat explained, individuals do not automatically perceive their grievances as legal injuries to be named, blamed, and claimed. Watch a few episodes of *Mad Men* and the everyday sexual harassment of that era becomes clear—yet early sexual harassment cases were often dismissed by the media as ludicrous.[68] A similar story may be told about, for example, claims for emotional injury which once seemed outlandish but are now routinely litigated. Finally, it bears mentioning that even if they are true, and truly ludicrous, these cases are clearly anecdotal, and not representative. We all know this, and yet it is difficult to extract them from our mind when we think of the everyday, often quite routine and boring, work of lawyers and courts. By way of example, in 2018, Magistrates' Courts in the UK received 1.5 million cases; Crown Courts dealt with

[66] Ibid 14. [67] Rhode (n 19) 47. [68] Abel, Felstiner, and Sarat (n 23).

103,000 cases; County Courts received 2.1 million claims; Family Courts received 263,000 cases; and tribunals received 449,000. What we need, then, is an 'antidote to anecdote'.[69]

Still, these statistics invite a serious question: even if the extreme examples are unrepresentative, do they not support the claim that we have *too much* access to justice—at least in the sense of access to courts and law? The answer may be that we have both too much *and* too little, law and lawyers. US President Jimmy Carter once put it starkly: 'no resource of talent and training . . . is more wastefully or unfairly distributed than legal skills. Ninety percent of our lawyers serve ten percent of our people. We are overlawyered and underrepresented.'[70] The problem, in other words, is not a uniform scarcity of access, but one marked by deep social and economic inequality. Just as with food, housing, or medicine, there is no general shortage: some have far more than they need, while others have none at all.

Yet this insight is not enough. It rests on an assumption that deserves scrutiny: that for those with too little access to law, the solution is simply *more* law. Earlier we explored the conceptual distinction between access to law and access to justice. Here, we must question the practical implications of equating them. Even among access to justice advocates, there is growing awareness that law and courts are not always the best mechanisms for resolving disputes. As Lawrence Friedman writes:

> Let us try to imagine a world in which everyone who had any claim whatsoever could get a hearing, had inexpensive and convenient access to counsel, and presumably could get his claim resolved in his favor. Would this be a good society? It could be an Orwellian nightmare. . . .
>
> Suppose you live in a large apartment building. You play music, a bit loud maybe, until ten o'clock at night. A neighbor, who goes to bed at nine, complains and asks you to please stop. You politely refuse, which ends the matter most of the time. Suppose the neighbor could easily, without cost or fuss, bring you before some sort of apartment tribunal . . . this is not likely to make for a better society. There are times and places where complexities such as cost and fuss have virtues, such as preventing outbursts of small, annoying claims and disputes that would be better off forgotten.[71]

Curiously, Marc Galanter recounts cases in which residents of (now former) Yugoslavia and the Philippines engage in very similar practices, suing each other as a matter of course, for extremely minor instances, such as a 'nasty look' at one's dog or a bent fence.[72] These cases illustrate a legal culture in which the invocation of formal mechanisms becomes routine, even for grievances that might be better resolved through informal channels. The lesson here is not that law should be avoided altogether, but that more law does not always equal more justice and that access to justice requires a more careful balance between formal and informal, legal and social, individual and collective solutions.

[69] Georgina Sturge, *Court Statistics for England and Wales* (Briefing Paper 8372, House of Commons Library, December 2019) 3.

[70] Anon, 'Excerpts from Carter's Speech to the Bar Association' *NY Times* (5 May 1978, A5) https://www.nytimes.com/1978/05/05/archives/excerpts-from-carters-speech-to-the-bar-association-overlawyered.html (accessed 30 March 2020).

[71] Friedman (n 20) 7.

[72] Galanter (n 64) 104–05 fn 22.

REFLECTION POINT

Think about your own clinical legal experience and the clients you have worked with. What type of access do you provide: Access to court through representation and better equality of arms; access to legal knowledge through advice and/mediation; or gateway access to identifying legal need and referral to the most appropriate services for advice and representation?

2.2.3 **Access to . . . Justice**

On the occasion of President Barack Obama's inauguration, the young poet Amanda Gorman read from her poem 'The Hill We Climb', which included the following two lines:

We've learned that quiet isn't always peace,

and the norms and notions of what 'just' is isn't always justice

What if 'access to justice' actually means access to . . . *justice*? Not 'justice' as in 'courts', or 'justice' as in 'law', but rather 'justice' in the everyday, and yet majestic, sense of the word. Traditionally, the term 'access to justice' was associated with a formal, institutional system and profession, which concerns dispute processing and resolution.[73] The idea that 'access to justice' would refer to ideas of fairness, merit, equality, and the like seemed, and perhaps to some still seems, quite foreign. This modest interpretation of the phrase is partly a result of a pragmatic compromise: an implicit admission that while we may be unable to agree on what true justice entails, we can at least work toward improving access to the legal process.

But perhaps the times are a-changing. In 2021, justice ministers from 16 countries wrote to the Secretary General of the United Nations in support of his call for a 'new social contract'. They referred repeatedly to 'justice problems' and 'justice systems', but offered a strikingly people-centred vision of access to justice: 'Access to justice is best understood as the ability of people to resolve their justice problems, and to use justice as a platform to participate in their economies and societies.'[74] Note how their articulation of access to justice makes no mention of law or lawyers.

But most people *do* have a particular view of what 'justice' means for them, and those correspond to some idea of fairness, desert, need, participation, or equality.[75] Yet that interpretation—whatever it may be—seems quite distinct from their understanding of 'access to justice', which is usually associated, somehow, with courts, law, and lawyers.

[73] Estelle Hurter, 'Access to Justice: To Dream the Impossible Dream?' (2011) 44 Comparative and International Law Journal of Southern Africa 408, 409.

[74] Pathfinders for Peaceful, Just and Inclusive Societies, 'Reimagining Social Contracts: A Call to Put People at the Centre of Justice' (14 April 2021), https://www.sdg16.plus/wp-content/uploads/sites/3/2023/09/EN-Joint-Letter-to-the-UNSG-on-Common-Agenda-2021.pdf

[75] David Miller, *Principles of Social Justice* (Harvard University Press 1999); Trevor Farrow, 'What Is Access to Justice?' (2014) 51 Osgoode Hall Law Journal 957.

In her fieldwork, Eleanor Kirk interviewed clients who approached Citizens Advice Bureaux (CABx) and found that most clients assumed that the law aligns with their idea of justice. They 'adopt a position in which egregious experiences "must be illegal" and seek advice regarding the validity of this supposition'.[76] For example, she notes the case of Jack, who 'was unaware that there was a two year qualifying period of service for unfair dismissal but suspected that his employer could not just dismiss him so easily'.[77] Similarly, Nicole Busby quoted a client who was dismayed that zero-hour contracts, in which employers do not have to commit to offer regular work and pay, are legal. Her frustration was clear: 'Nobody can get a mortgage on a zero-hour contract. Nobody can get a car insurance on a zero-hour contract.'[78]

Moreover, Kirk notes that many clients sought remedies that were well beyond what courts, or even the law, can offer. For example, many clients 'wanted to "clear their names", and being called a liar by their employer in the course of the dispute had been a sticking-point for them',[79] and were frustrated that the law offered no route to vindication. This gap could place advisers, including student advisers in clinics, in a very difficult position:

> The tears in people's eyes when you tell them that the law is no good to them . . . 'But that's not fair'. You're darn right it's not! . . . a lot of my conversations to do with employment law are negative . . . it's not my job to mislead people, so you have to tell them what the hurdles are going to be.[80]

So what would happen if we insist on bridging that divide, and remind ourselves (and others) that 'access to justice' should mean, in effect, access to *justice*? Deborah Rhode sees promise in this approach. She argues that the legal profession has an interest in framing the access to justice problem as a shortage of lawyers whereas in reality, what people seek is 'more justice, not necessarily more lawyering'.[81] Moreover, even the CABx clients, mentioned earlier, who seemed to have a broader idea of 'justice', still insisted on pursuing justice through legal means, refusing a settlement offer so as not to allow employers off the hook.[82]

If that is the case, then what type of 'justice' should we aim for? A common approach is to distinguish between procedural and substantive 'families' of justice, as you can see from Figure 2.5 below.

As the Figure illustrates, it is clear that agreeing on the terms of 'procedural justice' is easier than agreeing on the content of 'substantive justice'. Perhaps that explains why procedural justice principles are considered to be foundational, constitutive elements of any legal and administrative system.[83] The classic principles of 'natural justice'—the rule against bias, the right to a fair hearing, and the right to reasoned decisions[84]—are *procedural* norms familiar to most law students. Reasonable people may disagree about whether the death penalty should ever be imposed, but most would agree that if it is imposed it must follow a

[76] Eleanor Kirk, 'Justice and Legal Remedies in Employment Disputes: Adviser and Advisee Perspectives' in Samuel Kirwan (ed), *Advising in Austerity: Reflections on Challenging Times for Advice Agencies* (Bristol University Press 2017) 91, 93.

[77] Ibid 98. [78] Quoted in Busby (n 33) 87. [79] Kirk (n 76) 94. [80] Ibid 97.

[81] Rhode (n 19) 129. [82] Kirk (n 76) 95. [83] Friedman (n 20) 4.

[84] David Phillip Jones and Anne de Villars, *Principles of Administrative Law* (5th ed, Carswell 2009) 209.

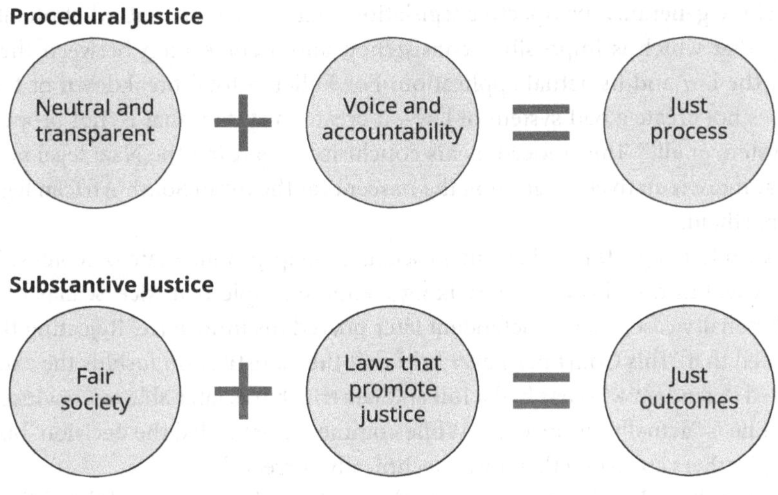

Figure 2.5 Procedural and substantive justice

fair trial. This is why procedural justice plays a central role in public trust and institutional legitimacy.[85] People care deeply about how they are treated and how their complaints are handled, regardless of the outcome. When they are dissatisfied with the *process*, they lose trust in the institution, and the institution gradually loses its legitimacy. This is because of the 'fundamental importance of fairness—many individuals . . . value being treated fairly and respectfully by power-holders they encounter'.[86]

As the example of the death penalty shows, procedural justice often overlaps with the narrower conception of access to justice as access to courts and lawyers. We expect courts to be open and transparent, judges to be unbiased, and claimants to be given their 'day in court', ideally with legal representation. As Kearns and Sarat suggest, 'procedural justice is inextricably tied to law itself'.[87] But this connection is not inevitable.

First, procedural justice can apply outside the courtroom. It is relevant in workplace disciplinary procedures, alternative dispute resolution (ADR) settings from commercial relationships to family disputes, and even peer-to-peer conflict resolution amongst peers and neighbours.

The second reason is more complex. The law is said to be 'neutral', in the sense that it can be used for good or bad ends: it can promote equality or require racial segregation; it can require transfer of money from the rich to the poor, or from the poor to the rich. Justice, by contrast, is normative: we evaluate law as just or unjust. This raises a question about procedural justice, which focuses on process. Would following fair procedures *necessarily* lead to just results?

Some thinkers believe so. In his book *The Morality of Law*, Lon Fuller lists eight conditions of natural procedural law which distinguish a legal system from an arbitrary system of power.[88]

[85] Cruetzfeldt et al (n 23) 43. [86] Ibid 47. [87] Kearns and Sarat (n 57) 7.
[88] Lon Fuller, *The Morality of Law* (Yale University Press, Revised ed 1969) 33–38.

These include generality, prospective legislation, clarity, lack of contradiction, absence of requiring that which is impossible, consistency, and a correlation between the requirements of the law and its actual application. For Fuller, a total breakdown of these principles does not create a bad system of law—it creates a system that is 'not properly called a legal system at all'.[89] This, indeed, is his conclusion regarding the Nazi legal system and, somewhat more tentatively, regarding the nascent (at the time) South African legal system under Apartheid.

Fuller's underlying idea is that fair procedures help produce fair outcomes. This may often be true, but not always. One striking counterexample is Justice Scalia's dissent in a US death penalty case where a defendant later proved his innocence. Rejecting the appeal, Scalia stated that 'This Court has *never* held that the Constitution forbids the execution of a convicted defendant who has had a full and fair trial but is later able to convince a habeas court that he is "actually" innocent'.[90] While commentators called the decision 'bizarre' and 'revolting',[91] others conceded that it was 'technically correct'.[92]

More generally, HLA Hart rejected Fuller's broader claim. He argued that following procedural principles might ensure sound legal craft, but this has little to do with morality. It's no more the 'morality of law', he said, than the techniques of avoiding vomiting are the 'morality of poisoning'.[93]

If that is indeed the case, should access to justice be understood as access to *substantive* justice? After all, 'if the legal rules and practices are set against you, due process is not much help'.[94] If so, then perhaps the call for 'access to justice' should be more ambitious, such as aiming to eliminate poverty, eradicate sexism and racism in society, and promote equal opportunities for all? As Amartya Sen has argued, 'When people across the world agitate to get more global justice ... they are not clamouring for some kind of "minimal humanitarianism" '.[95]

This broader vision could require converting, or translating, *more* social needs and interests into legal needs, in a manner already discussed above.[96] Importantly, what we classify as social needs and interests may, and does, shift. Marc Galanter justifiably notes that 'What was seen as fate may come to be seen as the product of inappropriate policy. Advances in human capability and rising expectations result in a moving frontier of injustice'.[97] For example, if having an incurable disease was once viewed as inalterable misfortune, developments in science, technology, and care can now dictate, in far more cases, who will live and who will die. So if a new treatment can now save me, can I now argue that *justice* requires that it be given to me, perhaps even free of charge? Can I say that I have a legal right to the treatment? These expectations do not relate only to science and technology. Social norms evolve

[89] Fuller (n 88) 39. [90] *In re Davis*, 130 S. Ct. 1, 3 (2009). [91] Friedman (n 20) 4.

[92] Joshua Lott, 'The End of Innocence? Federal Habeas Corpus Law After *In Re Davis*' 27 Georgia State University Law Review (2010) 443, 443.

[93] HLA Hart, 'Book Review: The Morality of Law' (1965) 78 Harvard Law Review 1281, 1287.

[94] Friedman (n 20) 4. [95] Amartya Sen, *The Idea of Justice* (Harvard University Press 2008) 341.

[96] See text to nn 23–24 above.

[97] Marc Galanter, 'Access to Justice in a World of Expanding Social Capability' (2010) 37 Fordham Urban Law Journal 115, 125.

too. Less than 50 years ago, few people would have thought that denying same-sex couples the right to marry is an injustice. As values shift, so do our understandings of justice and injustice. This is why 'justice/injustice is not a zero-sum game, rather both grow together'.[98]

If law and substantive justice do not always align, perhaps we should explore ways of resolving disputes outside both courts and the legal system altogether. That is, in essence, the approach taken by advocates of alternative dispute resolution (ADR)—at least in some contexts. We will return to these methods later in the book, but for now it is worth noting that ADR includes a broad range of mechanisms. Some are closely connected to the legal system, while others operate entirely outside it. For example, courts may refer parties to mediation as part of litigation, with the case returning to court if the mediation fails. In other cases, parties within religious or business communities, for example, may decide to opt out completely from the legal system, whether to avoid the publicity of the dispute, to resolve it with speed, or because they wish to apply different rules or settle the dispute based on a different set of values by which the legal system is bound.[99]

In many cases, ADR can clearly offer better access to justice than the traditional legal system. As we will see in Chapter 4, which looks at the role of technology, platforms such as eBay and Amazon already operate extra-legal arbitration systems that handle hundreds of millions of consumer disputes daily—with remarkable efficiency. In addition, mediation has the potential to soften the adversarial nature of legal processes. It can allow neighbours, colleagues, and family members to preserve their relationships, through a procedure that is far less costly and time-consuming.

If you're thinking at this point 'surely ADR can't be all good', then you're absolutely correct. While ADR processes have many advantages in enhancing access to justice, they are not immune to problems. Like any system, they can also be open to abuse:

> A steady diet of the anabolic steroids of corporate and governmental support has made ADR not only far larger than its siblings, but increasingly distant from them. As indicated by the fierce contention over the legitimacy and effects of mandatory arbitration and by concerns about court-imposed mediation, ADR no longer enjoys the assumption of facilitating Access to Justice. Rather, it has become an object of suspicion, and in some cases, a direct rival to access-to-justice programs.[100]

Carrie Menkel-Meadow similarly observes that the 'Haves'—repeat players such as employers, private health providers, corporations, and banks—have found ADR forums highly advantageous. Many now use standard-form contracts to require that any future disputes be resolved through arbitration, where they hold a clear upper hand.[101] For example, businesses often require workers or consumers (in financial contracts, mobile phone agreements, nursing home admissions, and so on) to sign contracts that waive their right to go to court or tribunal.[102] In these arbitration proceedings, workers may not have a right to legal

[98] Ibid 126. [99] Galanter (n 64) 124–135. [100] Galanter (n 97) 121.

[101] Carrie Menkel-Meadow, 'Do the Haves Come Out Ahead in Alternative Justice Systems? Repeat Players in ADR' (1999) 15 Ohio State Journal on Dispute Resolution 19, 32–33.

[102] Alexander Colvin, 'The Metastization of Mandatory Arbitration' (2019) 94 Chicago-Kent Law Review 3.

representation, the hearings are private, and there is often no genuine right of appeal. Ironically, and regrettably, in our pursuit of a more just system, we may find ourselves circling back to undermine some of the most basic principles of access to justice.

This has been a complex section, so let us conclude with a summary. As we've seen, once we move beyond the secure confines of the formal 'justice' system, matters become more hazy and murky. Procedural justice may be limited in ambition, but it offers a 'big tent', a common foundation to agree on *some* form of justice. By contrast, the more ideologically ambitious forms of justice—abolish the death penalty! equality for all! amnesty for asylum seekers!—risk excluding, and even alienating, those who disagree with that particular vision.

How does this tension relate to the ambition of law clinics to promote access to justice? Consider the rise of Business Law clinics. More than 140 such clinics now operate in the United States, and interest is growing in the UK.[103] Should such clinics be viewed as limiting the 'potential of the clinic in furthering the social justice mission', assuming that they should be doing that?[104] After all, 'businesses' are often the very parties clinics traditionally oppose when representing workers, tenants, or consumers. And yet, some argue that these clinics still serve social and economic justice. It is worth noting that small businesses include 'caterers, retail clothing stores, restaurants, antique dealers and consignment shops, computer consultants, barbers, massage therapists, beauticians [and] book publishers'.[105] Helping them could align with a broader, more inclusive view of justice that benefits both students and communities.

But how far can we stretch the idea of 'justice' before it becomes so broad that it simply means 'interests'? One provocative answer came in 2019, when the Harvard Federalist Society wrote to the Law School Dean demanding the creation of clinics that supported causes such as 'Pro Life', Second Amendment rights (gun ownership), and First Amendment claims (including the right to discriminate on the basis of sex or sexual orientation).[106] Notwithstanding the specious nature of the demand (Harvard already has a number of similar clinics of that nature),[107] it has already proved persuasive in other law schools, which have set up clinical programmes explicitly orientated towards conservative causes.[108]

[103] Elaine Campbell, 'A Dangerous Method? Defending the Rise of Business Law Clinics in the UK' (2015) 49 The Law Teacher 165.

[104] Antoinette Sedillo Lopez, 'Learning through Service in a Clinical Setting: The Effect of Specialization on Social Justice and Skills Training' (2001) 7 Clinical Law Review 307, 317.

[105] Susan Jones, 'Promoting Social and Economic Justice Through Interdisciplinary Work in Transactional Law' (2004) 14 Washington University Journal of Law and Policy 249, 267–68.

[106] Jacob Carrel, 'Purpose: What FedSoc Got Wrong about Clinics, and How Students Can Learn from Their Mistake?' Harvard Civil Rights—Civil Liberties Law Review (18 November 2019) https://harvardcrcl.org/purpose-what-fedsoc-got-wrong-about-clinics-and-how-students-can-learn-from-their-mistake/ (accessed 26 March 2020).

[107] Elie Mystal, 'Harvard FedSoc demands right-wing clinics, 'cause i guess helping poor people is liberal?' *Above the Law* (28 October 2019) https://abovethelaw.com/2019/10/harvard-fedsoc-demands-right-wing-clinics-cause-i-guess-helping-poor-people-is-liberal/

[108] Ann Southworth, *Lawyers of the Right: Professionalizing the Conservative Coalition* (University of Chicago Press 2008) 171.

REFLECTION POINT

Think about your own clinical legal experience and the clients you have worked with. What does justice look like to your clients? What kind of justice do you think law clinics should advance—procedural and/or substantive? If substantive, should clinics have a clear philosophical, or even political, orientation? Has your clinical experience changed how you think about justice?

TAKING STOCK

This section focused on the second half of the phrase 'access to justice', by asking 'access to what'? Once again, we identified three such layers, this time with increasing degrees of ambition. The first layer focuses on what is perhaps the common understanding of the object of 'access to justice', namely courts and lawyers, and in that respect provides a helpful bridge from the previous section. With the second and third layers, however, we move beyond the traditional legal institutions. The second layer concerns the very real problem of access to justice that comes in the form of 'access to law'. By this we refer to the problem that claimants don't always know if their problem is actually a *legal* problem, that has a legal remedy. Law clinics, of course, have an important role in addressing this gap. Finally, with the third layer, we look well beyond the law, and to 'justice', as it is understood by philosophers and by individual claimants. The gap between law and justice here is important for those involved in law clinics in at least two respects: first, how can that gap be narrowed; but second, what impact the gap may have on the experience, including the morale, of those engaged with members of the community and committed to assist them.

A View from Clinical Practice

Alice Stevens, Pro Bono Coordinator and Supervising Solicitor, The University of Law

If you asked me to describe myself as a lawyer, social justice and human rights would feature heavily along with my time as a law clinic student. I began my career working in the Liverpool Law Clinic at the University of Liverpool. Within the law clinic, I was fortunate to be able to work on an innovative project supporting Broudie Jackson Canter with their work representing families bereaved by the Hillsborough Disaster on 15 April 1989. The project allowed students to immerse themselves in a current, significant case of immense importance to the local community of Liverpool and to engage with human rights law in action. Students attended the clinic in person as often as they could to complete the work required and were supervised by solicitors from the external law firm and the law clinic.

As a result of this project, I was able to apply for a summer placement working on the Hillsborough Inquest and subsequently worked at Broudie Jackson Canter full time. I can still say with confidence that working alongside the Hillsborough families for those few years is one of the greatest privileges of my life so far, and it shaped my career moving forwards.

At the core of my career and the work I've been lucky enough to do has always been the work I completed at Liverpool Law Clinic. It enabled me to gain experience and insight into a type of lawyer I didn't know existed, but am eternally grateful I have been able to become. I was able to work alongside some of the best human rights lawyers in the country, arguably in the world, and understand what a career as a human rights and social justice lawyer might entail. I was able to work with incredible clients and meet likeminded people who also believed in using the law to empower others. It was, quite frankly, a revelation.

In my view, law clinic work is invaluable for aspiring social justice lawyers. It is a safe space to gain experience and knowledge; it provides crucial networking opportunities; it inspires and encourages students; it can include life-changing work and can lead to exceptional careers. For me, it forged the pathway for my career and my passion for social justice and systemic change.

Tips for clinic students and aspiring social justice lawyers:

1. Treat clinic work with the same dignity, respect, and dedication as you would treat a paid role. Do not treat the work as simply a means to an end. For the clients you are working with, their case is likely to be one of the most important things in their life.
2. Reflect on the clinic work you have completed: What could you have done better? What went well? What did or didn't you enjoy? What further training would you like to do to improve your skills?
3. Make sure you update your CV with the new skills you've gained through clinic work and remember to include ethical skills, like understanding confidentiality and client care.
4. Consider approaching lawyers you have worked with in clinics to ask for advice or mentoring; most will be aware of how difficult it can be to start out as a social justice lawyer and will be happy to help.

2.3 Barriers to Access to Justice

Our initial exploration has shown where the concept of access to justice is relatively clear and where it becomes elusive and open-ended. While often discussed in relation to courts and lawyers, its boundaries become more difficult to define when we shift from 'access to law' to 'access to justice'. Even within the more familiar domains—access to courts and to legal representation—reasonable people may disagree about whether a particular scenario constitutes an illegitimate barrier. We have already touched on several such barriers; this final section brings them together in a more structured way.

Before we do so, it is worth noting that mapping these barriers is not as simple as it might appear. Many of them intersect, overlap, and reinforce one another. The most famous literary account of this phenomenon is probably Kafka's untitled parable *The Trial*. Here, a gatekeeper guards access to the law and says he cannot grant the old man, who has travelled from the country, entry 'at the moment'. The gate is open, enticing the old man, but his entry is deferred to some unknown point in the future:

> At the moment the gate to the law stands open, as always, and the gatekeeper walks to the side, so the man bends over in order to see through the gate into the inside. When the gatekeeper notices that, he laughs and says: 'If it tempts you so much, try it in spite of my prohibition. But take note: I am powerful. And I am only the most lowly gatekeeper. But from room to room stand gatekeepers, each more powerful than the other. I can't endure even one glimpse of the third'.
>
> The man from the country has not expected such difficulties: the law should always be accessible for everyone but as he now looks more closely at the gatekeeper in his fur coat . . . he decides that it would be better to wait until he gets permission to go inside. The gatekeeper gives him a stool and allows him to sit down at the side in front of the gate. There he sits for days and years.[109]

In the end, the old man dies waiting for entry to the law. Despite the entrance being 'assigned only to [him]', his own lack of knowledge and will, set against the gatekeeper's authority, rendered his pursuit of the law futile. This short parable, published in 1915, captured some of the most enduring barriers to access to justice: geographic distance, lack of financial means, lack of awareness of rights, disadvantage and exclusion. The promise of justice at some point in the future only deepens the harm caused by the inaccessible system. In analysing Kafka's parable, Jacques Derrida found that it raised fundamental questions about the boundaries of legal knowledge and the nature of legal language.[110] The boundary of the law is reinforced simply by being so unknown and the countryman comes to the law with beliefs that only serve to make it more inaccessible.[111] Empirical research on access to justice confirms this point: perception matters. People's sense of how accessible the legal system is depends on their exposure to it. Second-hand or anecdotal accounts—as opposed to direct experience—can strongly shape whether one views the system as fair and approachable.[112]

A View from Clinical Legal Practice

Professor Martha Minow, 300th Anniversary University Professor, Harvard Law School

In Franz Kafka's parable, the gatekeeper closes the door to law. Now, the writer's name connotes inaccessible courts and nightmarish bureaucracies, like the workers' accident

[109] Nahum Glatzer (ed), 'Before the Law' (trans by Willa and Edwin Muir) in *Franz Kafka: the Complete Stories* (Schocken Books 1971) 3–4.

[110] Jacques Derrida, 'Before the Law' in Derek Attridge (ed), *Acts of Literature* (Routledge 1992) 183–220.

[111] William Conklin, 'Derrida's Kafka and the Imagined Boundary of Legal Knowledge' (2016) Law, Culture and Humanities 1, 4.

[112] Nigel Balmer et al, *Law . . . What Is It Good For? How People See the Law, Lawyers and Courts in Australia* (Victoria Law Foundation 2019) 35.

insurance operation employing him in turn-of-the-twentieth century Prague.[113] Filing fees, lawyers' bills, inscrutable language, and vexing forms bar entry to courthouses. Too many do not know their rights to battle crushing debt, homelessness, and intimate violence. Those most disadvantaged suffer adversities directly, but unenforced rights injure everyone. Repercussions of unaddressed legal harms cascade into mounting pain and costs. For want of legal help, a tenant becomes homeless, loses custody of her children, and is assaulted in a shelter. Because the law does not by itself enforce rights against unfair and illegal contract terms, scores of individuals endure mistreatment. Broken promises of equality before the law destroy basic trust in institutions and other people and invite disinvestment, violence, and disorder. Meanwhile, justice requires even more than enforcement of often inadequate existing laws.

Changes can and do happen. 'Civilization advances when what was perceived as misfortune is perceived as injustice.'[114] Innovations leverage digital technologies, law students and faculties, practicing and retired lawyers, bar associations—and also libraries and businesses—with inventive ways to help tenants stay in their homes, obtain services for which they qualify, keep their children in school, and enjoy rights that the law says they have. Reforms can undo punishments for nonlawyers who offer legal help.[115]

An Alaskan village lacking courthouses and local police now has community justice workers, partnering with health workers addressing incidents of domestic violence.[116] Mobile law offices bring people, computers, and internet access to rural communities in Tennessee.[117] In Utah, judges and justice workers come by canoe and bicycle to reach homeless people.[118] Libraries and courthouses offer access to chatbots using Artificial Intelligence to answer legal questions and also to complete and file legal forms. An international organization named Namati trains people to serve as community paralegals in countries from Sierra Leone to Bangladesh.[119]

Money spent to provide legal help to people who cannot afford it yields financial benefits to communities while improving daily lives of those immediately involved. Military veterans with legal help succeed with claims when they get legal assistance—though removing

[113] Ashfaq G Chowdhury, 'Franz Kafka: Enemy of the Kafkaesque' (19 December 2024) https://www.dailyjournal.com/articles/382561-franz-kafka-enemy-of-the-kafkaesque

[114] Judith N Shklar, *The Faces of Injustice* (Yale University Press 1990), quoted in Harvard Law School Human Rights Program, 'Economic and social rights and the right to health: An interdisciplinary discussion held at Harvard Law School in September 1993'. See also Alicia Ely Yamin, *When Misfortune Becomes Injustice: Evolving Human Rights Struggles for Health and Social Equality* (Stanford University Press 2023).

[115] Rebecca L Sandefur and Lucy Ricca, 'Outside the Box: How States are Increasing Access to Justice through Evidence-Based Regulation of the Practice of Law' (2024) 108(1) *Judicature*. Available at: https://judicature.duke.edu/articles/outside-the-box-how-states-are-increasing-access-to-justice-through-evidence-based-regulation-of-the-practice-of-law/

[116] Stacey Marz, Mara Kimmel, and Miguel Willis, 'Alaska's Justice Ecosystem: Building a Partnership of Providers,' Alaska Court System Access to Justice Committee (22 December 2017). Available at: https://courts.alaska.gov/jfa/docs/plan.pdf; Community Justice Worker Program—Alaska Legal Services Corporation, https://www.alsc-law.org/cjw/

[117] Academy of Arts and Sciences, 'Achieving Civil Justice' (December 2024). Available at: https://www.amacad.org/publication/achieving-civil-justice

[118] Taylor Stevens, '"Kayak Court" Brings the Justice System to Salt Lake City's Homeless on the Banks of the Jordan River,' *Salt Lake Tribune*, 27 July 2021 (reporting on an interview with Salt Lake City Justice Court Judge Jeanne Robison, who proposed the idea and serves as a Kayak Court judge).

[119] See Namati, 'What We Do'. Available at: www.namati.org

obstacles government creates requires deeper reform.[120] Justice should centre on the people in need, not systems designed for lawyers—or designed to deny benefits.

Some may think of access to justice as a lawyers' problem. Others may think the topic is too small to tackle oppressive structures. Yet when people forfeit their rights simply due to absence of help, we all suffer. Rights need laws to be enforceable; laws when enforced produce stability and undergird security for entire nations. A sturdy rule of law strengthens the climate for businesses and serves workers, families, and consumers. No community thrives when people are homeless, children are out of school, corrupt companies bilk customers, or families experience violence. Justice Thurgood Marshall once said, 'In recognizing the humanity of our fellow beings, we pay ourselves the highest tribute.'[121] That is what access to justice should entail.

The concept of *legal empowerment* is important in this context. It refers to 'the use of law and rights specifically to help increase disadvantaged populations' control over their lives'.[122] As we explore further in Chapter 8, legal empowerment can relate to a variety of activities and strategies ranging from legal rights awareness (StreetLaw is a good example) to legal aid provision and public interest litigation. Its importance lies in the central aim of increasing power and control for the relatively powerless in society so that their rights and interests might be advanced. The lack of power, and related lack of legal capability, comes from the experience of, often, multiple and significant barriers to access to justice. Against this background, we set out in this section four main barriers and consider how they might be overcome. They are: financial barriers; disadvantage and social exclusion; lack of legal knowledge; and poor justice infrastructure (Figure 2.6).

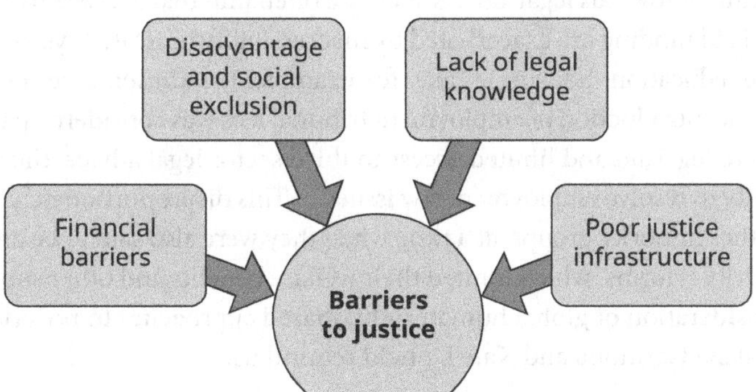

Figure 2.6 Barriers to justice

[120] National Organization of Veterans' Advocates, *Why Professional Advocacy is the Veterans' Best Option*. Available at: https://www.vetadvocates.org/cpages/why-professional-advocacy

[121] *Powerful Quotes by Thurgood Marshall*. Available at: https://www.biography.com/legal-figures/thurgood-marshall-quotes

[122] Stephen Golub, 'Beyond Rule of Law Orthodoxy: The Legal Empowerment Alternative', Working Paper No 41, Rule of Law Series (Carnegie Endowment for International Peace 2003) 15.

2.3.1 **Financial Barriers**

We discussed earlier the problem of financial inequality between parties in court, and how this creates an 'inequality of arms'. Globally, the scale of economic barriers to justice is vast. In 2008, the UN Commission on Legal Empowerment of the Poor estimated that 4 billion people were excluded from the rule of law. For many individuals, even the early stages of resolving legal issues are out of reach due to the high cost of legal advice. Indirect costs—such as transport, childcare, or taking time off work—can also be significant. On top of that, court fees, charges for submitting legal documents, and the risk of having to pay the other side's legal costs if the case is lost (known as adverse costs) can all add to the burden. Those unable to pay for legal services from their own pocket may turn to conditional fee agreements (such as 'no win, no fee'), third party litigation funding, crowdfunding or pro bono legal service provision. However, as we consider in later chapters, these avenues are often not widely available.

As noted, for those without means, state-funded legal aid provision might provide assistance. Over the past two decades, however, the areas for which legal aid is made available have been considerably curtailed in the UK, especially in areas such as social welfare, family, immigration, and housing. It is interesting to note, by way of comparison, that the funding restrictions brought about by the Legal Aid, Sentencing and Punishment of Offenders Act 2012 (LASPO) and the Criminal Justice and Courts Act 2015 in England and Wales mirrored congressional restrictions enacted in the US in 1996. Those restrictions similarly sought to limit the provision of US Legal Services Corporation funding in welfare provision, housing and immigration, as well as funding given to organizations that might also engage in lobbying, class actions, or public interest litigation.[123]

As we saw, it seems that the provision of legal aid in many jurisdictions across the globe tends to mirror the political will at the time, with attitudes to welfare provision often similarly reflected in attitudes towards legal aid. As such, we often find that barriers that result from inaccessible legal aid funding are exacerbated by inaccessibility in related systems (for example, health, welfare, education, housing). Take, for example, the *Unison* case mentioned above. The impact of the introduction of employment tribunal fees was considered particularly acute alongside cuts to legal aid and limited access to third sector legal advice, thus compounding people's inability to resolve employment law issues.[124] This disproportionately impacted upon women and other minority groups, at a time when they were also said to be affected by wider so-called austerity reforms, which limited their welfare benefits and other support.[125]

In their consideration of global human rights-based approaches to poverty and access to justice, Magdalena Carmona and Kate Donald remind us:

> The poor also suffer most when justice mechanisms are corrupt, ineffective or out of reach, as they can least afford the bribes demanded or withstand the lengthy delays.

[123] Scott Cummings, 'The Politics of Pro Bono' (2004) 52 UCLA Law Review 1, 22.

[124] James Organ and Jennifer Sigafoos, *The Impact of LASPO on Routes to Justice* (Equality and Human Rights Commission 2018) 47.

[125] Karen Grayson, 'Response of the Equality and Human Rights Commission to the Review of the Introduction of Employment Fees' (Equality and Human Rights Commission, 20 March 2017); Amnesty International, *Cuts that Hurt: The Impact of Legal Aid Cuts in England on Access to Justice* (Amnesty 2016).

> The unnecessary complexity and formal requirements of judicial processes also impact disproportionately on them, due to their lack of information and knowledge about the law and their rights. They may even be entirely invisible in the eyes of law; nearly 230 million children under the age of five have never been registered and therefore lack legal identities—a problem that will follow the majority of them well into adulthood.[126]

Access to justice barriers are therefore complex and multifaceted and often rest at the intersection of economic, cultural, social, and structural issues. As Philip Alston, the UN Special Rapporteur on Human Rights and Extreme Poverty, made clear on his visit to the UK in 2018, such barriers can still be experienced in wealthy nations where legal aid provision is inadequate:

> Legal aid has been dramatically reduced in England and Wales . . . As a result, many poor people are unable to effectively claim and enforce their rights, have lost access to critical support, and some have even reportedly lost custody of their children. Lack of access to legal aid also exacerbates extreme poverty, since justiciable problems that could have been resolved with legal representation go unaddressed.[127]

Indeed, Garth and Cappelletti view '*effective* access to justice' as no less than 'the most basic human right . . . [for] a modern, egalitarian legal system which proposes to guarantee, and not merely proclaim, legal rights for all'.[128]

To summarize this point: most people agree that access to justice is crucially important, and fundamental, in *theory*. But this right would be meaningless for many, in practice, if the state does not fund the service through taxation, without passing the cost of running it on to the users, through court and tribunal fees; and does not provide support for legal assistance, through legal aid. However, while the argument to keep fees at a level that is not overly burdensome has been relatively successful, at this stage the same cannot be said about the argument in favour of enhanced and expanded legal aid. Here, because of the reliance on general taxation, there is a constant struggle to keep legal aid at a level that is adequate. After all, it is often a challenge to convince the public that the recipients of legal aid are 'deserving' of public funds. As the Director of one American Legal Aid society quipped, 'the only thing less popular than a poor person these days is a poor person with a lawyer'.[129] And one may add: that is particularly the case when the poor person is accused of committing a crime, entering the country illegally or committing gross misconduct that led to their dismissal from work.

So now we're still talking about money, but not the money that claimants have to pay to access justice. Instead, here we refer to the money that the state must use to realize access to justice, through legal aid. This is an interesting area of law and politics, in which lofty ideas

[126] Magdelena Carmona and Kate Donald, 'Beyond Legal Empowerment: Improving Access to Justice from the Human Rights Perspective' (2015) 19 The International Journal of Human Rights 242, 243.

[127] Philip Alston, Visit to the United Kingdom of Great Britain and Northern Ireland: Report (Human Rights Council, 41st Session, 24 June–12 July 2019) 9.

[128] Garth and Cappelletti (n 12) 185.

[129] Robert Pear, 'As Welfare Overhaul Looms, Legal Aid for Poor Dwindles' *New York Times* (5 September 1995) Al.

Public good	Money spent on legal aid and access to justice contributes to the rule of law and a fair justice system, thus contributing to the public good.
Public trust	Widespread misunderstandings about the real cost of legal aid fuelled by inaccurate news stories of 'fat cat lawyers'.
Public benefits	Solving legal problems often solves social problems thus saving the state money in other areas such as health and welfare.

Figure 2.7 Justifications for legal aid

concerning rights meet the harsh reality of fiscal objections and popular sentiments.[130] This clash has led some authors to state that to talk about money as a barrier to rights seems 'an offense to polite manners'.[131]

How can advocates of legal aid persuade the public, and thus the government, to continue to provide adequate support? We find that this is often done by referring, primarily, not to the benefit for the claimant or defendant, but to the benefit to the public. In particular, we can identify three common justifications: public good; public trust; and public benefits, as you can see in Figure 2.7 above.

The first justification is already familiar by now, as it highlights the public value of access to justice and, in particular, its contribution to the rule of law.[132] As Nicole Busby writes, with respect to the imposition of fees in Employment Tribunals: 'Given that the ET performs such an important role with obvious implications for public health, workplace harmony and, consequently, economic prosperity, one might imagine that its successful operation would be a matter of the utmost priority for policy makers.'[133] Indeed, soon after, in the *Unison* case which referred to those fees, Lord Reed wrote: 'When Parliament passes laws creating employment rights, for example, it does so not merely in order to confer benefits on individual employees, but because it has decided that *it is in the public interest that those rights should be given effect*.'[134] Since everyone benefits from them, everyone should pay for them, through taxes, whether they acknowledge the benefits or not.

A second response suggests that the public has reservations about funding legal assistance not only because it is unaware of the benefits, but also because it is unaware of the costs.

[130] See, generally, Amir Paz-Fuchs, 'The Fiscal Objections to Social Welfare Rights: A Closer Look' in Gideon Sapir, Daphne Barak-Erez, and Aharon Barak (eds), *Israel Constitutional Law in the Making* (Hart 2014) 333.

[131] Stephen Holmes and Cass Sunstein, *The Cost of Rights: Why Liberty Depends on Taxes* (WW Norton 1999) 24.

[132] *Unison* (n 16) [68]; Mark Elliott, 'The Rule of Law and Access to Justice: Some Home Truths' (2018) 77 CLJ 5.

[133] Nicole Busby, 'The Costs of Justice: Barriers and Challenges to Accessing the Employment Tribunal System' in Samuel Kirwan (ed), *Advising in Austerity: Reflections on Challenging Times for Advice Agencies* (Bristol University Press 2017) 79, 81.

[134] *Unison* (n 16) [72] (emphasis added).

Thus, 80 per cent of Americans believe (incorrectly) that legal aid is available in civil cases.[135] In the UK, there is widespread, inadequate understanding of the cost of justice when compared to other jurisdictions. Some argue that legal aid overspending is a myth perpetuated by confusion between legal aid provision and the cost of the adversarial (as opposed to inquisitorial) justice system as a whole. While the legal aid budget appears high, its proponents are quick to point to the overall justice bill average being comparable with other European countries.[136]

A third response has been to stress the importance of access to justice as a cost-saving exercise. For example, Hazel Genn's landmark *Paths to Justice* study found that one in five people said that their health had suffered as a result of a failure to resolve their legal problem leading to knock-on costs in health service provision.[137] The insight that legal issues can 'cluster' means that there are ensuing economic impacts on, for example, the spheres of education, housing, and employment without early access to legal help and advice. Advocates of legal aid therefore suggest that its cost be considered against the background of the relative savings it provides.[138]

2.3.2 **Disadvantage and Exclusion**

Alongside lack of financial means, wider forms of disadvantage and exclusion unsurprisingly create barriers to access to justice. For example, research has shown that those with mental ill-health conditions often struggle to access and participate in the justice system effectively, both in terms of access to early advice and in litigation processes.[139] Likewise, children, the elderly, single parents, and those in minority ethnic groups are more likely to experience multiple barriers to justice. By way of example, to make their participation effective, children require specialized forms of legal support tailored to their levels of maturity and the opportunity, consistent with Article 12 of the United Nations Convention on the Rights of the Child, for their voices to be heard and listened to. All too often, however, lawyers receive little or no training in child-centred legal representation and the courts are unduly hostile environments for children. Against this background, the concept of *access to justice for children* has emerged in the past two decades at an international level as a means of empowering children and facilitating both procedures and remedies that are child-sensitive.[140]

[135] Deborah L Rhode, 'Access to Justice' (2000) 69 Fordham Law Review 1785.

[136] The Bach Commission on Access to Justice, *The Crisis in the Justice System in England and Wales* (Fabian Society 2016).

[137] Genn (n 62) 251.

[138] For discussion in the context of legal aid and judicial review see Maurice Sunkin et al, *The Value and Effects of Judicial Review: The Nature of Claims, Their Consequences and Outcomes* (The Public Law Project 2015).

[139] Pascoe Pleasence and Nigel Balmer, 'Mental Health and the Experience of Social Problems Involving Rights: Findings from the United Kingdom and New Zealand' (2009) 16 Psychology and Law 123.

[140] Ton Liefaard, 'Access to Justice for Children: Towards a Specific Research and Implementation Agenda' (2019) 27(2) The International Journal of Children's Rights 195.

REFLECTION POINT

Read the account from Jennifer, a student who took part in a welfare law clinic. The client asked that Jennifer

> send all important documentation to her cousin's home, not her own home, and requested that I do not show up at her home to have papers signed even though it would be much more convenient for her because, according to her, it would not [be] good if her landlord knew a 'black woman' was going through social security proceedings. I think she fears that her landlord will kick her out knowing that she has limited to no money.[141]

Think of this report in terms of exclusion and disadvantage. It is apparent that more than one layer of disadvantage is in operation. What are they, and how do they intersect and interact?

Organizations such as the OECD have also worked to draw attention to practices which exclude minority groups, noting, for example, that 'women, who often face multiple forms of discrimination, violence and sexual harassment, are particularly affected by legal exclusion.'[142] The OECD also highlighted the extent to which social relations within communities can impact access to justice. Where social interactions create feelings of shame or fear of stigmatization, people are less likely to seek legal help and advice in order to resolve legal problems. Finally, as we will see in Chapter 4, digital exclusion as a result of poor digital literacy and a lack of digital connectivity creates higher rates of legal exclusion, which can be exacerbated by a comparative inability to 'leverage connectivity in social networks'.[143]

2.3.3 Lack of Legal Knowledge

Individuals often fail to understand when they need legal support; nor do they know where to find it, if they lack legal knowledge and rights awareness. Lack of legal knowledge can intersect with other forms of legal exclusion, for example, poor language or literacy. Importantly, without some level of understanding of legal processes it is often hard to anticipate or avoid problems before it is too late:

> Enabled citizens are better equipped to take the sort of preventive action that avoids escalation and crises. They can avoid, for example, tribunal and court proceedings, leading to outcomes that are quicker, less stressful and less costly for both sides in a

[141] Jonel Newman and Donald Nicolson, 'A Tale of Two Clinics: Similarities and Differences in Evidence of the Clinic Effect on the Development of Law Students' Ethical and Altruistic Professional Identities' (2016) 35 Buffalo Public Interest Law Journal 1, 87.

[142] OECD, *Leveraging the SDGs for Inclusive Growth: Delivering Access to Justice for All* (OECD-Open Society Foundations 2016) 2.

[143] Ibid 8.

dispute. Also, relationships between parties can continue where otherwise these might break down. Earlier settlement of disputes, especially before formal stages are reached, is less consuming of resources overall.[144]

The term 'public legal education' therefore refers to enhancing knowledge and awareness of rights together with trying to raise the confidence and skills needed to assert legal rights at early stages. While, on the one hand, so-called loony litigation risks creating a compensation culture, on the other hand a failure to understand legal principles—for example, mistaken assumptions about 'common law marriage', lease agreements, or basic contracts of employment—can lead to disputes that also place a considerable economic burden on society. Proponents of public legal education therefore argue that it makes citizens more capable and empowered in resolving their own legal problems, thus saving the public purse considerable sums of money that would otherwise be spent as a result of increased debt, lost earnings, or relationship breakdown.[145] Awareness of legal rights also aims to improve misconceptions, or the 'perception problem', so that more people see the law as relevant and meaningful to issues in their own lives rather than something alienating or confusing. As we consider in later chapters, the provision of public legal education is a key component of clinical legal education provision across the globe given that law students are well placed with the knowledge, skills, and enthusiasm to deliver it.[146]

Another relevant barrier to legal knowledge and rights awareness relates to geography and location. In some jurisdictions, especially across Africa, the use of paralegals in rural communities serves to enhance legal skills at a local level or in particular environments such as, for example, the provision of advice to prisoners or educating community leaders about discriminatory practices. Paralegals can help to ensure familiarity with complex processes or that documents are filed in court on time.[147]

Finally, a lack of legal knowledge creates a considerable barrier to access to justice for litigants in person (or *pro se* litigants) in the courts and tribunals. Here too, the provision of legal information found in accessible guides, toolkits, explanatory court forms, lay representation (such as 'McKenzie Friends' in the UK), and the 'unbundling' of legal services into separate components (for example, support with document preparation) can help people to navigate otherwise intimidating and inaccessible court processes.

2.3.4 **Poor Justice System Infrastructure**

Both in the criminal and in the civil spheres, a poor justice system infrastructure can both create and sustain barriers to access to justice. Insufficient funding and resources lead to the poor functioning of justice systems. From crumbling court buildings and court closures to failures to embed effective case management systems, structural problems have considerable

[144] PLEAS Task Force, *Developing Capable Citizens: The Role of Public Legal Education* (PLEAS July 2007) 9.

[145] Ibid 8.

[146] David McQuoid Mason, 'Street Law as a Clinical Program: The South African Experience with Particular Reference to the University of KwaZulu-Natal' (2018) 17 Griffith Law Review 27.

[147] Carmona and Donald (n 126) 249.

knock-on impacts for people trying to effectively access and participate in the resolution of their legal problems.

Physical location and the inability to reach services pose challenges to those in remote areas.[148] Similarly, there is also the problem of 'legal advice deserts', which refer to particular geographic regions in which matters simply aren't covered by legal advice provision. For example, in the UK, cuts to legal aid have resulted in the closure of many local law centres and reduced incentives for private practitioners to take on legal aid work that is not financially viable. As such, some geographic areas are without lawyers in areas including housing, social care, and education law.[149] There are also challenges posed by staff retention issues and the lack of opportunities to train in social welfare-related legal service provision.[150]

Other infrastructure challenges include long waiting times and repeated referrals. Research shows that where people are referred from one service provider to another because of, for example, a lack of capacity or legal expertise to deal with the issue, they are more likely to give up on resolving their legal problem altogether. This is described in the literature as 'referral fatigue' and also relates to the 'clustering' of legal problems.[151] Take, for example, someone with an employment issue who is unable to access legal services for advice on unfair dismissal as a result of discrimination in the workplace. A failure to access legal advice results in loss of earnings which leads to a debt issue; this in turn may lead to an inability to pay rent, which may result in prospective homelessness and/or the possibility of family disruption or separation. The legal issues here (ie employment, debt, housing, family) all 'cluster' as a result of a structural failure to access early information and advice and resolve legal issues at an early stage.

REFLECTION POINT

Read the following accounts from students who took part in a number of law clinics.

Maria found that while the procedures and mechanisms relating to the welfare and disability infrastructure were supposedly 'designed for this population . . . they have too many systemic walls.'

Lynn commented:

> The agencies that we work with aren't always the easiest to manoeuvre and I cannot imagine most of my clients successfully meeting their goals. I feel that the populations [that] many of the policies and laws are set out to help are not afforded the proper guidance.

[148] Julinda Beqiraj and Lawrence McNamara, *International Access to Justice: Barriers and Solutions* (Bingham Centre for the Rule of Law 2014) 21.

[149] See for example, The Law Society of England and Wales, *Parliamentary Briefing: Housing Legal Aid Deserts* (The Law Society 2019); Jo Wilding, *No Access to Justice: How Legal Advice Deserts Fail Refugees, Migrants, Our Communities* (Refugees Action 2022).

[150] Emma Howard, 'Going into legal aid work is now career suicide' *The Guardian* (6 January 2016).

[151] Genn (n 62); Pascoe Pleasance et al, *Paths to Justice: A Past, Present and Future Roadmap* (The Nuffield Foundation 2013).

And, finally, John reflected on the fact that he

> never realized how tough it was to deal with the [Social Security Administration] and how unbelievable the premise is that clients should be able to represent themselves pro se.[152]

Can you think of the systemic, structural barriers that your clients have encountered?

Finally, we can think of the design of the law itself—its 'architecture', if you will—as creating barriers. The areas of benefit and debt are notoriously complex, and complaints in that area include 'finding the rules and regulations for benefits confusing and contradictory; being given partial, incorrect or conflicting information by officials; and not being told when changes to the benefits system were to be implemented'.[153] Clients couldn't help but notice this, intriguingly using a geographical metaphor even stronger than 'infrastructure' or 'barrier': 'You know it's a bit of a minefield, . . . if you have this benefit it can knock this benefit, but you may be able to get this benefit . . . so, just didn't know where I was like'.[154]

Indeed, the law, and the procedures involved, can be more or less complex. For example, Bolen documented the complexity of applications for benefits in America:

> The average length of an application is 12 pages, though it runs over twenty pages in ten states, and reaches thirty-six pages in Minnesota. In fact, the average food stamp application is six times longer than the federal application for a firearms permit and three times as long as the federal home mortgage loan application.[155]

The International Bar Association highlights three prevalent institutional barriers that exist in poorly resourced justice systems:

1. insufficient and unequal geographical distribution of justice institutions affects physical access to the delivery of justice;
2. failure to record the commencement of action (sometimes referred to as a failure to register complaints), which often affects the most vulnerable groups and has the consequence of validating impunity for offenders, while victims of injustices are either disregarded or mistreated; and
3. judiciaries may be inadequately trained or qualified, with the result that independence is compromised and decisions are poorly reasoned, inconsistent, or biased.[156]

[152] Jonel Newman and Donald Nicolson, 'A Tale of Two Clinics: Similarities and Differences in Evidence of the Clinic Effect on the Development of Law Students' Ethical and Altruistic Professional Identities' (2016) 35 Buffalo Public Interest Law Journal 1, 85, 90.

[153] Alison Kite, 'Power and Legality in Benefits Advice' in Samuel Kirwan (ed), *Advising in Austerity: Reflections on Challenging Times for Advice Agencies* (Bristol University Press 2017) 127, 128–29.

[154] Ibid 129.

[155] Ed Bolen, 'A Poor Measure of the Wrong Thing: The Food Stamp Program's Quality Control System Discourages Participation by Working Families' (2001) 53 Hastings Law Journal 213, 218; Amir Paz-Fuchs, *Welfare-to-Work: Conditional Rights in Social Policy* (OUP 2008) 111.

[156] Beqiraj and McNamara (n 148) 21.

The Association finds that where these barriers intersect with other cultural or social barriers, such as exclusion and disadvantage, there is a greater likelihood of adverse impacts. Its research points to a number of solutions that have been explored across different jurisdictions, including the use of technology to access to remote communities, 'pop-up' law clinics in remote areas, greater recourse to ADR, more comprehensive judicial training, greater transparency of justice system decision making, and improved case management systems.[157] To complicate matters further, some of these vulnerabilities—such as those that are cultural, social, economic, or mental health-related—may also be hidden, or even invisible, thus creating invisible barriers to access to justice.[158]

TAKING STOCK

This final section addressed the barriers to accessing justice. These include financial barriers; disadvantage and exclusion; lack of legal knowledge; and poor justice system infrastructure. While previous sections mentioned some of these issues during the course of the analysis, it is important to look at each category of barriers separately and identify the particular challenges, both long-term and in their more recent form.

Of those categories, financial barriers were probably those that were addressed most frequently in the chapter. But here we had the opportunity to engage not only with the financial difficulties that claimants face, but also with the possible reasons why governments are less inclined to fund the sector and provide support. The discussion of disadvantage and exclusion had the advantage of widening the perspective from the individual to the structure, and asked what *categories* of claimants suffer from identifiable barriers, why that is the case, and perhaps what can be done about that. Lack of legal knowledge was, again, a barrier that should have been familiar by this stage, so this was a good opportunity to understand it more broadly, even on a global scale, and identify possible mechanisms to address it. Finally, probably far less familiar is the barrier posed by the infrastructure, and even architecture, of the legal justice system, its complexity, and its (lack of) accessibility.

Conclusion

In this chapter we looked at different theories about access to justice and different ideas about how justice can be achieved. Hopefully, you will have seen that the very common phrase 'access to justice' is less clear and more contested than it may appear at first sight. What constitutes 'access' and what qualifies as 'justice' are both matters for serious debate which have troubled academics and courts for decades, if not centuries. Different social, economic, and

157 Ibid 22.

158 Naomi Cruetzfeldt et al (n 23) 200.

political contexts bring about different problems, or barriers, for realizing access to justice, and to complicate matters further, the ideal itself is not constant, but is something of a 'moving target'.

We began by looking at traditional understandings focused on formal legal processes, such as access to courts, lawyers, and legal aid. While these remain important, they tell only part of the story. Over the years, researchers, practitioners, and communities have developed broader ways of thinking about justice—ones that include how people recognize their legal needs, the support they can access, and whether outcomes feel fair in the context of their everyday lives.

We also considered the barriers that people face when trying to resolve legal problems. These may be financial, cultural, structural, or simply the result of how intimidating and complex the legal system can seem. In this sense, access to justice is about far more than the availability of legal services. It touches on questions of power, inequality, and the capacity of legal institutions to meet the needs of diverse communities.

Clinical legal education provides an important opportunity to think about these issues in a real-world context. As students working with clients or community partners, you may encounter individuals who have struggled to access the law, or who feel that the legal system has failed them. Understanding the wider debates around access to justice can help you make sense of these experiences—not just in terms of what the law says, but in terms of how justice is felt, delivered, or denied in practice.

It can also prompt reflection on your own role. Working in a clinic allows you to see the difference that legal support can make, but also to notice its limits. Clinics are not a complete solution to access to justice, and they operate within the same systems and constraints that shape the wider legal world. But they do offer a space to think critically, act ethically, and begin imagining what a more just legal system might look like.

In the next chapter we will look at legal aid as a potential way to help realize access to justice in society. We will also examine the current state of legal aid in England and Wales to explore the adverse impacts of funding restrictions more generally on justice systems.

Further Reading

Tom Cornford, 'The Meaning of Access to Justice' in E Palmer et al (eds), *Access to Justice: Beyond the Policies and Politics of Austerity* (Hart Publishing 2016).

Naomi Creutzfeldt et al, *Access to Justice, Digitalization and Vulnerability* (Bristol University Press 2024).

William Felstiner, Richard Abel, and Austin Sarat, 'The Emergence and Transformation of Disputes: Naming, Blaming, Claiming . . . ' (1980) 15 Law & Society Review 631.

Hazel Genn, 'Introduction' in *Judging Civil Justice* (Cambridge University Press 2009) 1.

Samuel Kirwan (ed), *Advising in Austerity* (Bristol University Press 2017).

Alan Paterson, 'Introduction: Determining the Public Good' in *Lawyers and The Public Good* (Cambridge University Press 2011) 1.

Stephen Pepper, 'Access to What' (1999) 2 Journal of the Institute for the Study of Legal Ethics 269.

3 Legal Aid and the Changing Landscape of Access to Justice

In England, justice is open to all, like the Ritz hotel.

Sir James Mathew

Chapter Overview

This chapter will introduce you to legal aid provision and its relationship to clinical legal education. It explores the way in which legal aid in the UK has changed in recent years and the impact of those changes on those who cannot otherwise afford legal advice and/or representation in relation to their legal problems.

By the end of this chapter, you should be able to:

- Understand the history and background to legal aid provision in the UK;
- Discuss the principles underpinning the legal aid system;
- Identify different types of legal aid in relation to both civil and criminal justice;
- Consider the factors that might determine whether someone is eligible for legal aid;
- Understand the differences between legal aid and pro bono provision.

Introduction

In the previous chapter, we discussed the different possible interpretations of access, of justice, and thus of access to justice. In this chapter we focus on what is arguably the most prominent of those interpretations, namely, the availability of legal aid and its role in shaping the access to justice landscape. Legal aid refers to the provision of assistance to people who cannot otherwise afford legal advice or representation. It has long been regarded as a central component of access to justice in view of its importance in ensuring equality before the law. The availability of legal aid affects whether individuals in society are able to, in reality, enforce their rights and access entitlements which they are owed. As we observed in the last chapter, whether access to justice is made real in practice is not impervious to social and economic inequalities. As Robert Egerton noted, 'the laws may be good, the courts may be impartial but if for any reason the law cannot be invoked, the machinery of justice is of no practical use'.[1] Legal aid is meant to address these concerns but, increasingly, there has been a 'justice gap' in society as legal aid becomes harder to access due to resource constraints. This gap refers to the shortfall between legal needs and legal services.[2] In the UK context, it has been used to describe the increasing number of people who are not eligible for state-funded legal aid advice or representation but nonetheless cannot afford to pay for a lawyer themselves.[3] As we have explored, empirical legal research has long shown that a failure to resolve a legal problem can lead to a 'clustering' of problems with knock-on adverse impacts on people's lives. State provision of early advice has therefore been deemed crucial in ensuring access to justice and equality before the law.

In this chapter we consider the history and background of legal aid and explore how the provision of state-funded legal services has changed over time. We set out what legal aid means in practice by exploring the different types of provision across both civil and criminal law. In particular, the chapter addresses the changes to civil legal aid in England and Wales to demonstrate how restrictions to state-funded provision might have an impact on different individuals and groups, as well as the equality and human rights issues a lack of provision raises.

Notably, the relationship between the state provision of legal aid and law school clinics can be complex. In the UK, at the time of writing, few law schools deliver legal aid services on behalf of the state. Legal aid work is typically carried out by legal aid law firms or not-for-profit civil society organizations. Notably, in some other countries, such as the US and parts of Africa and Latin America, it is much more common for law school clinics to deliver legal aid services.[4] Depending on the legal jurisdiction, opportunities for students to engage in clinical criminal legal casework may be especially limited. This can be for a variety of reasons, including the fact that state-funded legal aid tends to already fund qualified criminal lawyers for those unable to afford one and because of perceived risks associated with criminal casework. That said, there has been an increasing tendency for students, in the UK and elsewhere, to work on miscarriage of justice cases, for example within the Innocence Project, to support the exoneration of the wrongly convicted.[5] In any event, the question of whether the provision of legal services to those who cannot otherwise afford to pay should be funded by the state, or alternatively by lawyers or law students in a pro bono or clinical capacity, is an important one. We explore this further below in our consideration of arguments for and against legal aid.

[1] Robert Egerton, *Legal Aid* (Kegan Paul 1945) 1.

[2] James Sandman, 'The Role of the Legal Services Corporation in Improving Access to Justice' (2019) Daedalus 148(1) 113–19.

[3] Steve Hynes and Jon Robins, *The Justice Gap* (Legal Action Group 2009).

[4] See e.g. Richard Wilson, 'Legal Aid and Clinical Legal Education in Europe and the USA: Are They Compatible?' in Halvorsen Rønning and Ole Hammerslev (eds), *Outsourcing Legal Aid in the Nordic Welfare States* (Palgrave Macmillan 2018) 263–85.

[5] Jan Stiglitz, Justin Brooks, and Tara Shulman, 'The Hurricane Meets the Paper Chase: Innocence Projects New Emerging Role in Clinical Legal Education' (2002) 38 Californian Western Law Review 413; Daniel S. Medwed, 'Actual Innocents: Considerations in Selecting Cases for a New Innocence Project' (2003) 81 Nebraska Law Review 1097.

3.1 The Development of Legal Aid

Put simply, it is suggested that where people cannot afford to pay the cost of legal advice and representation there should be a right to the state provision of legal assistance, which has been broadly termed legal aid. Why is that the case? After all, if people cannot afford a car or a mobile phone, the state does not simply supply those. Of course, the state does assist (adequately or not) those in poverty through the welfare benefits system, but then beneficiaries use that money to buy clothes and food and pay for transportation costs, for example. And legal advice is readily available on the marketplace, like those products and services. So why should it be treated differently?[6]

The answer is that while legal advice may be acquired in the market, it is not perceived as a good or a service that should be *solely* in the market. In that respect it is similar to health and education, which may also be purchased, but most people wouldn't argue that a person with limited funds should choose whether she can afford to learn or eat or, in the now painfully familiar phrase, 'heat or eat'. Moreover, legal aid and wider social welfare provision tend to be closely related because there is a strong connection between legal aid and the practical realization of social, economic, and cultural rights. These might include, for example, the right to housing, education, healthcare, social security and social care, employment rights, and freedom from discrimination. Across these areas, where entitlements related to those rights have been denied or restricted, legal aid provides an important means of facilitating legal challenge for those individuals who cannot otherwise afford advice and representation. It has now been widely observed that legal aid does more than simply providing funding for legal services and that it has 'a purpose beyond facilitating individual disputes'.[7] Beyond the realisation of individual rights, it also supports the wider 'public good'.[8] Legal aid has been said to play a critical role as it 'underwrites the social contract in liberal democracies and helps to sustain order'.[9] It is not surprising therefore, first, that attitudes and socio-political perspectives towards social welfare provision tend to mirror those towards legal aid and, second, that welfare reform in western democracies has historically included the development and expansion of legal aid.

While the right of access to the courts has long been recognized, it is only in more recent times that a constitutional right to legal aid has been established in some jurisdictions.[10] Previously, legal aid arrangements were ad hoc or largely reliant on pro bono legal services. For example, the Poor Man's Lawyer movement in England and Wales was established at the end of the nineteenth century to provide pro bono advice and assistance to those living in charitable settlements. Other rights to access legal representation existed in statute; for example, the Poor Prisoners' Defence Act 1903 ensured the provision of legal aid services to those

[6] See eg *A Tool for Justice: The Cost Benefit Analysis of Legal Aid* (The World Bank 2019).

[7] Sarah Moore and Alex Newbury, *Legal Aid in Crisis: Assessing the Impact of Reform* (Policy Press 2017) 3.

[8] Alan Paterson, 'Resourcing Civil Justice' in Alan Paterson and Tamara Goriely (eds), *Resourcing Civil Justice* (OUP 1996) 3–12.

[9] Ibid 3.

[10] See eg Article 6, European Convention on Human Rights.

who had a defence to a criminal charge against them but no means of paying for a lawyer.[11] A number of schemes developed in the 1930s and 1940s to provide advice and assistance to those experiencing civil law problems, especially in the aftermath of the Second World War. As in many other jurisdictions internationally, such ad hoc types of voluntary and charitable service provision were somewhat unreliable and unevenly geographically spread.

And yet, these voluntary service provisions played an important role in identifying legal needs, which can be critical in ensuring that any system of legal service provision is fit for purpose. The political will for legal aid in western democracies was also strengthened from the turn of the twentieth century as the extent of legal needs, and the impact of a failure to resolve them, became more apparent. The importance of equality of arms, which we explored in Chapter 2, also began to gain greater recognition. In an address to the American Bar Association in 1922, Lord Shaw commented that 'society is rotten where one citizen as against another cannot overpower him or undermine him by law wielded with an uneven hand'.[12] In the UK, in 1945 the post-war Labour government accepted the proposals made by a Committee which sought to address the inadequacy of legal services for the poor and argued for widespread reorganization and expansion of legal aid provision. The seminal report of the Rushcliffe Committee recommended a comprehensive legal aid system available not only to those 'normally classed as poor' but also to those of 'small or moderate means'.[13]

A crucially important moment in the historical development of legal aid came at that time when, alongside the development of a national education system and the NHS, the Legal Aid and Advice Act 1949 made state-funded civil legal aid available in all courts and tribunals where lawyers would normally appear for private clients. There would be tests for both the 'merit' of the cases and 'means' (ie financial eligibility), and barristers and solicitors were to receive 'adequate remuneration' for their services. Reform to criminal legal aid followed but had to wait until the 1960s. It is also worth noting that the system that developed in the UK was a 'judicare' model, which means that clients have a degree of choice in selecting their lawyer who is then compensated by the state for providing those services,[14] and is contrasted with a 'salaried staff' model. In the latter model, familiar to many from American television shows, 'if you cannot afford an attorney, one will be appointed to you by the court'. However, the client has no choice in the matter. Indeed, the Rushcliffe Committee had proposed legal advice centres staffed by qualified lawyers, but this was resisted by the legal profession and a hybrid 'mixed model' (ie charitable and judicare) was not developed until 20 years later, with the arrival of law centres.[15] The term 'judicare' was first coined in the US with reference to 'Medicare', the federally funded programmes which provide free or low-cost services to

[11] Entitlements can be traced back much earlier; eg in Scotland there is some form of civil legal aid in legislation in 1424.

[12] Egerton (n 1) 3.

[13] Rushcliffe Committee, *Report of the Committee on Legal Aid and Legal Advice in England and Wales*, Cmd 6641 (HMSO 1945).

[14] See eg Alan Paterson, *Lawyers and the Public Good: Democracy in Action?* (Cambridge University Press 2011) 67; Arnold Schlossberg and William Weinberg, 'The Role of Judicare in the American Legal System' (1964) 54 American Bar Association Journal 1000.

[15] Paterson (n 14) 72.

those who cannot afford to pay. In the UK context another term used is a 'private practice' model of legal aid; however, there has been debate as to the suitability of this term given that services are being provided using public money and in the public interest.[16]

There has also been some debate over the retention of the judicare model in the UK, rather than adopting a salaried model of provision where lawyers are paid directly by the state. It is worth noting that some limited legal aid services operate discrete direct salaried funding models, for example, the Public Defence Solicitors' Office (PDSO) in Scotland and the Public Defenders Service (PDS) in Wales. However, when compared to directly paid NHS doctors, we can perhaps see how legal services have been treated differently to medical services over time.[17] Bindman observes that in the UK context there was early resistance to salaried employment. He comments that there were two practical arguments in favour of resisting such close association with the state. First, 'anatomy and physiology makes no distinctions between rich and poor and so the main work of the medical profession by and large can be justified in terms of a universal right to medical care'.[18] Second, he notes how much of a lawyer's work is 'partisan', and 'equal justice requires that the poor litigant be put as far as possible on the same level as the rich'.[19] It is deemed important in a system that upholds equality before the law for both rich and poor to receive the same access and quality of service so that they can approach the same lawyers (solicitors and barristers) under the judicare model of representation. Bindman concluded almost 20 years ago that the judicare model would likely need to be revisited: 'It cannot be expected that the law will escape the searching scrutiny to which all the other aspects of our social system are being submitted. The process has in fact already begun. Legal aid reform will come; it is only a question of how soon, and how thorough it will be.'[20]

Practical Exercise 3.1

Creating a fair and just society for the post-war age was fundamental to the development of legal aid. In 1945 the Rushcliffe Committee addressed the issue and laid down some recommendations for legal aid provision. Legal aid was defined as 'assistance in conducting or defending proceedings in court including court fees, witnesses and other expenses'.

Read carefully the report recommendations listed below. Take some time to consider them and **rank what you think are the top three most important recommendations, with reasons for your ranking.**

1. Legal aid should be available in all courts and in such manner as will enable persons in need to have access to the professional help they require.
2. This provision should not be limited to those who are normally classed as poor but should include a wider income group.

[16] Emma Cooke, 'Fat-cats versus "Church Mice": Unveiling Legal Aid Practice from Behind the Shadows of Private Legal Practice in England and Wales' (2024) 44(4) Legal Studies 573–90.

[17] Geoffrey Bindman, 'Richard Abel on Legal Aid' (2004) 11 International Journal of the Legal Profession 103.

[18] Ibid 103. [19] Ibid 104. [20] Ibid.

3. Those who cannot afford to pay anything for legal aid should receive this free of cost. There should be a scale of contributions for those who can pay something toward costs.
4. The cost of the legal aid scheme should be borne by the state, but the scheme should not be administered either as a department of state or by local authorities.
5. The legal profession should be responsible for the administration of the scheme.
6. Barristers and solicitors should receive adequate remuneration for their services.
7. The Law Society should be requested to frame a scheme on the lines outlined in the detailed recommendations providing for the establishment of Legal Aid Centres in appropriate towns and cities throughout the country.
8. The Law Society should be answerable to the Lord Chancellor for the administration of the scheme, and a central Advisory Committee should be appointed to advise him on matters of general policy.
9. The term 'poor person' should be discarded and the term 'assisted person' adopted.[21]

Legal aid similarly developed in other western democracies from this period onwards. It has been noted that the US legal profession, especially following the 1963 Supreme Court case of *Gideon v Wainwright*[22] discussed in Chapter 2, began to understand with 'startling suddenness' that 'a society can guarantee equal justice only by providing all citizens with effective access to the institutions by which justice is obtained' and that equal justice means access to lawyers 'in the broadest sense'.[23] To this end, a social welfare approach to legal aid was adopted by the Legal Services Programme of the Office of Economic Opportunity. Neighbourhood law offices offered services to those in poverty to resolve their legal issues, while also aiming to use legal tools generally as a form of community action to alleviate discrimination and disadvantage as part of the War on Poverty. Writing in 1966, Bamberger commented that the neighbourhood offices provided 'national recognition that the least affluent members of our society have at least as many legal problems as the rest of us, and probably more'.[24] He surmised that lawyers might play a transformative role by offering legal advice as a form of community action:

> These are facts of the lives of the poor—the city slum dweller, the mountaineer, the racial outcast—effects and causes of their destitution and the deprivation of that decency and dignity we find so casually in our daily lives. Lawyers can change this scene. They are already doing so in New York where the courts finally destroyed the odd administrative presumption, by which thousands had been denied public assistance, that a person coming to a city without employment must have come for the purpose of receiving welfare in violation of the statute ... This kind of service will become increasingly

[21] Rushcliffe Committee (n 13). [22] 372 US 335 (1963).

[23] Daniel Lowenstein and Michael Waggoner, 'Neighbourhood Law Offices: The New Wave in Legal Services for the Poor' (1967) 80(4) Harvard Law Review 805–50, 805.

[24] E Clinton Bamberger, 'The Legal Service Program of the Office of Economic Opportunity' (1966) 41 Notre Dame Law Review 847.

> commonplace as more and more community action programs add the skills of lawyers to their arsenals. Perhaps the arsenal image suggests something which cannot be emphasized enough, that we are engaged in giving arms, not alms, to the poor.[25]

As Bamberger predicted, this form of community legal advice became more commonplace and embedded in a range of community action programmes across the US. It also quickly spread to other jurisdictions and a similar movement of community law centres began in the UK in the 1970s, playing a critically important role both in frontline service provision in areas of social welfare law and in developing the strategic use of law to achieve social change.[26] These were important developments, not only for the relationship between law and social justice but also for shaping new forms of professional legal identity. We will return to these developments later in Chapter 8 when we address the theory and practice of 'community lawyering'.

3.2 **For and Against Legal Aid**

Many of the most persuasive arguments in relation to legal aid were documented by Mauro Cappelleti and others in 1975. They recognized, in a landmark study, the importance of making the legal system universally accessible regardless of different levels of income.[27] Hilary Sommerlad has also observed in the UK context how the establishment of legal aid provided a 'new stage in the relationship between law and society and was thus fundamental to the development of an inclusionary form of citizenship'.[28] It represented, in itself, a tool 'in the struggle against social exclusion'.[29] Sommerlad draws upon TH Marshall's conception of social citizenship, whose concern—reminiscent of our consideration in the last chapter of procedural and substantive approaches to access to justice—was with social justice rather than exclusively with formal legal justice:

> The civil element (of citizenship) is composed of the rights necessary for individual freedom—liberty of the person, freedom of speech, thought and faith, the right to own property and to conclude valid contracts, and the right to justice. The last is of a different order from the others, because it is the right to defend and assert all one's rights on terms of equality with others and by due process of law.[30]

Social citizenship demands that individuals can assert their rights equally. However, the role of legal aid in terms of being constitutive of social citizenship has the potential to move in different directions, both towards and away from positive models of social citizenship. The social contract can, in fact, be undermined where legal aid is not available to ensure that

[25] Ibid 848. [26] Jacqueline Kinghan, *Lawyers, Networks and Progressive Social Change* (Hart 2021) 10–11.

[27] Mauro Cappelletti, James Gordley, and Earl Johnson Jr, *Toward Equal Justice: A Comparative Study of Legal Aid in Modern Societies (Texts and Materials)* (Oceana Publications Inc 1975).

[28] Hilary Sommerlad, 'Some Reflections on the Relationship between Citizenship, Access to Justice, and the Reform of Legal Aid' (2004) 31 Journal of Law and Society 345, 348.

[29] Ibid 348. [30] TH Marshall, *Citizenship and Social Class* (Cambridge University Press 1950) 10–11.

social rights can be upheld,[31] as has been recently highlighted in the context of England and Wales and is explored further below. Restrictions to legal aid provision, including what Sommerlad terms 'management control', might also expressly be used as a way to limit access to justice for particular individuals and groups in the same way that welfare benefits might be available only to the so-called deserving poor.[32] This can undermine democratic citizenship and have potentially adverse consequences.

Related to this, and another argument in favour of legal aid, was noted by Egerton in 1945: that the 'absence of legal aid is one of the principal causes of industrial unrest'.[33] Genn has similarly highlighted how limiting legal aid generally has the potential to create 'unhealthy' democracies.[34] The UK Ministry of Justice boldly claimed in 2010 that civil legal aid was the 'hallmark of a civil society'[35] before proposing wide-ranging restrictions on the areas of advice that would fall within scope for provision. As Alan Paterson comments, by indicating that legal aid is available only for a restricted group it is 'as though the NHS were to say we believe in universal healthcare, but only the most needy, those of no or very low income with advanced cancer or a severe heart condition will be helped'.[36] The justice system could arguably therefore no longer be described as preventative given the reluctance to fund early legal advice and assistance.

In this context, the relationship between legal aid and human rights should not be overlooked. Access to justice will generally be better facilitated in environments that build capacity and raise awareness of human rights. International human rights law sets minimum standards for the resolution of rights issues and prescribes that processes should be timely, accessible, and affordable. Likewise, the outcome of the process (ie the remedy) should be adequate and effective, ensure non-repetition of any rights infringement, and help change poor practice relevant to systemic issues.[37] International bodies have also set out standards in relation to legal aid; for example, the European Committee for the Prevention of Torture and the UN Subcommittee on Prevention of Torture have both stressed the importance of legal aid as a fundamental safeguard against intimidation, ill-treatment, or torture.[38] These bodies have developed guidelines in relation to legal aid systems being fit for purpose, for example, by being adequately resourced, managed, and staffed.[39] Notably, simply appointing a lawyer is not enough to fulfil a State's obligation to provide effective legal assistance. The representation must be 'effective' and the State may be required to intervene where this

[31] Jennfier Sigafoos and James Organ, '"What About the Poor People's Rights?" The Dismantling of Social Citizenship through Access to Justice and Welfare Reform Policy' (2021) 48(3) Journal of Law and Society 362–85.

[32] Sommerlad (n 28).

[33] Egerton (n 1) 4.

[34] Hazel Genn, 'Why the Privatisation of Civil Justice is a Rule of Law Issue', 36th F A Mann Lecture, Lincoln's Inn (19 November 2012).

[35] Ministry of Justice, Proposals for the Reform of Legal Aid in England and Wales, Consultation Paper CP12/10, Cm 7967 (London: HMSO, November 2010), para 1.1.

[36] Paterson (n 14) 68.

[37] Scottish Human Rights Commission, *Adequate and Effective Remedies for Economic, Social and Cultural Rights: Background Briefing Paper for the National Taskforce on Human Rights Leadership* (December 2020).

[38] Open Society Justice Initiative, Legal Aid in Europe: Minimum Requirements under International Law (April 2015) 4. Available at https://www.justiceinitiative.org/uploads/d69e329c-6cb7-47ca-bdf0-07f8992a728b/ee-legal-aid-standards-20150427.pdf

[39] Ibid 13.

standard has not been met.[40] As such, legal aid plays an important role in fulfilling international human rights obligations.

On the other hand, some critics argue that the cost of legal aid is simply too high in many jurisdictions and that such expense should not be borne by the state. It might therefore be said that law school clinics are one way of keeping legal aid costs to a minimum. For example, a recent review of civil legal aid in England and Wales addressed law school clinics in Scotland as a potential model for efficiency and effectiveness.[41] However, this raises questions about whether clinics might potentially undermine legal aid provision by fulfilling obligations that should in fact be met by the state. As Wizner and Aiken note, 'the primary obligation to provide legal services to the poor resides with the government, and to a lesser extent with the legal profession, not with law schools'.[42]

Another argument therefore is that the private sector—including commercial lawyers providing pro bono services—should make a greater contribution to the cost. Notably, some jurisdictions allow for the recovery of expenses even where representation has been provided pro bono. This means that the unsuccessful litigant would pay the costs of the litigation and these can often be paid directly to a prescribed charity, which generally promotes access to justice.[43] In England and Wales, arguments have been made for contingency legal aid funds to be established by way of a levy on city law firms. Many practitioners are not receptive to this proposal and stress that they should not be responsible for the justice system simply because they have qualified into the justice system. They make comparisons with other professions, such as being a builder, tradesman, or plumber, and note that they are not required to provide pro bono services. One commentator notes in response:

> The problem with this line of argument . . . is that we solicitors spend most of our time arguing that we are not like other trades or professions, because we are part of the administration of justice and are bound to defend the public interest . . . Our clients have certain basic human rights, and we must defend them against governmental (and other) actions . . . It seems to me that we cannot have it both ways: on the one hand, argue that we are not to be treated like plumbers and builders . . . because we have higher duties within the justice system, and yet demand to be treated like plumbers, builders and accountants in relation to other aspects.[44]

These arguments, and the related ethical responsibilities for legal professionals, are considered further in Chapter 7.

[40] *Kamasinski v Austria*, ECtHR, judgment of 19 December 1989.

[41] UK Government, Review of Civil Legal Aid in England and Wales: Comparative Analysis of Legal Aid Systems (Open Innovation Team 2024). Available at https://assets.publishing.service.gov.uk/media/66461e94993111924d9d36ab/240516_-_RoCLA_Comparative_Analysis_of_Legal_Aid_Systems.pdf

[42] Stephen Wizner and Jane Aiken, 'Teaching and Doing: The Role of Law School Clinics in Enhancing Access to Justice' (2004) 73 Fordham Law Review 997–1011, 997.

[43] See eg Legal Aid, Sentencing and Punishment of Offenders Act 2012, s 61. The prescribed charity in this case is the Access to Justice Foundation.

[44] Jonathan Goldsmith, 'It's time to debate legal aid funding alternatives' *The Law Society Gazette* (16 July 2019). Available at https://www.lawgazette.co.uk/commentary-and-opinion/its-time-to-debate-legal-aid-funding-alternatives/5071007.article

Practical Exercise 3.2

Consider the following statement and think of at least five points either for or against the position:

> Legal aid is not charity stemming from private philanthropy but a right which the state has a duty to foster and protect. In the same way that the state must ensure the health of its citizens through adequate healthcare provision, legal aid must be comprehensively available to ensure access to justice.

TAKING STOCK

This section discussed the underlying rationale for legal aid in the UK. It identified that concerns about the access to justice needs of individuals in society without financial means, and increased reliance on ad hoc and unreliable pro bono provision, justified the need for state-funded legal services for those who could not otherwise afford it.

We saw that, in a welfare state, legal services are often especially relied upon to ensure fair access to entitlements such as welfare benefits, education, health, housing, and social care. While the legal aid model in the UK initially envisaged private services provided by law firms, law centres soon emerged in the 1970s as a way of providing legal aid-funded advice provision more rooted in local communities.

As legal aid spending has increased over time, the cost-effectiveness of legal aid has been the subject of much debate. Pro bono provision, and the work of law school clinics, has sometimes been identified as one way of reducing legal aid spending. This raises questions about the extent to which law schools can and should be required to bear the cost of delivering legal services, which should, some argue, be borne by the state or the legal profession.

3.3 Legal Aid—For What?

In a judicare model, legal aid can be used to fund legal services across a wide range of providers, including, for example, private law firms, law centres, charities and NGOs, the independent Bar, and law school clinics.[45] Other models of provision include public defender schemes, specialized services (eg to women, children, prisoners), or paralegal schemes. The UNODC Model Law on Legal Aid recognizes this diversity:

> Legal aid systems develop in the context of a State's legal and criminal justice systems, as well as its available resources and needs. Indeed, the adoption of a certain legal aid model is dependent on a number of factors, including the number and availability

[45] Kinghan (n 26) 51–53.

of lawyers, demand for legal aid services, vulnerability of potential beneficiaries and available financial resources. No matter what system is adopted, however, the institutional arrangements and funding mechanisms should ensure the independence of legal aid providers in the performance of their functions.[46]

In terms of services, aside from formal advice and representation, legal aid might fund, for example, public legal education, alternative forms of dispute resolution, and restorative justice.[47] It is important to delineate the different types of services available to clients and the distinctions between them. Legally aided work would differ depending on, for example, whether general legal information, rights awareness, or early general legal advice was being provided. As a step further, there are obvious distinctions between advising clients on the merits of their case or the next steps to take in a dispute with another party and more formal legal representation in the courts and tribunals. The complexity of issues, the merits or strength of the case, and the perceived need for representation are all factors that may be taken into account in determining whether someone is eligible for legal aid. In practical terms, then, what does (and what should) legal aid actually fund for a client? This will obviously vary across different legal jurisdictions; however, a spectrum, with informal legal information or rights awareness at the one end and more formal representation at the other, is clear. We can also identify distinctions between civil and criminal justice.

3.3.1 **Civil Justice**

Civil legal aid provision can be distinguished from criminal legal aid as it is more focused on the early resolution of legal issues and access to a range of different formal and informal mechanisms to do so. Areas of civil legal aid include family and child law, community and social care law, education, welfare benefits, housing, debt, immigration and asylum, consumer matters, personal injury, clinical negligence, and employment law. Empirical legal research on civil legal needs has played an instrumental role in shaping this approach across many jurisdictions. National legal needs surveys have been an important tool for measuring legal needs in society and therefore designing policies and services to best meet those needs. The data can also help to provide a picture of how legal problems are experienced by different demographic groups, as well as indicating which types of issues certain groups might be most vulnerable to. For example, research has shown that adults with mental health issues, those with long-term health conditions, racialized groups, the elderly, refugees and asylum seekers, Travellers, and lone parents are more likely to experience civil legal problems.[48]

It is important to note that some problems that engage legal issues may require legal 'advice' to resolve them, but many do not. The 'Paths to Justice' tradition developed by Hazel Genn and others appreciates that the law does not always provide the best solutions to legal problems. Since the 1990s, large-scale studies have sought to address problems across a

[46] United Nations Office on Drugs and Crime, Model Law for Legal Aid in Criminal Justice Systems, Commentary to Article 13 (2017). Available at https://www.unodc.org/documents/justice-and-prison-reform/LegalAid/Model_Law_on_Legal_Aid.pdf

[47] Ibid.

[48] Rosaline Sullivan, *The Legal Needs of Consumer Groups* (Legal Services Board 2011).

broad spectrum, from everyday problems that may not be understood as 'legal' to more formal legal interventions.[49] One Australian study in New South Wales demonstrated that half of Australian residents experience a legal problem every year.[50] For some, such as single parents, people with a disability, and the unemployed, the likelihood of experiencing a problem is significantly increased. Likewise, experiencing more than one type of disadvantage greatly increases the risk of experiencing a legal problem.[51] Such studies can therefore be illuminating in terms of helping us understand how people actually experience the law, whether they are conscious or not that the problem might be characterized as legal, and how legal aid services can be designed to realistically meet access to justice needs. A further comprehensive analysis of 26 large-scale national surveys since the 1990s across 15 separate jurisdictions demonstrated the following:

- Legal problems are generally associated with ill-health/disability, particularly mental ill-health
- Consumer problems are among the most reported, alongside problems concerning neighbours and money
- Employment problems are associated with working age
- Unemployment and family problems are most associated with mid-life
- Lone parenthood is mostly associated with being divorced
- Money problems are associated with lone parenthood.[52]

In terms of 'advice-seeking' behaviours, the following trends have been identified internationally:

- Inaction in relation to legal problems is more common with men and less common with age and higher levels of education
- Women are more likely than men to seek help for a legal problem and advice seeking rises with age and seriousness of the problem
- Advice is least often obtained in relation to consumer issues
- Legal advice is most often obtained for family breakdown, personal injury, employment, and issues related to owned housing.[53]

For some civil law problems, information and rights awareness can help equip individuals to resolve the problems themselves. The evidence also demonstrates, however, that for others a 'self-help' approach is simply not viable for a variety of reasons, as, for example, where there may be communication issues or for litigants in person experiencing specific vulnerabilities.

[49] Hazel Genn, *Paths to Justice* (Hart 1999).

[50] Christine Coumarelos et al, *Legal Australia-Wide Survey: Legal Needs in Australia. In Access to Justice and Legal Needs* (Law and Justice Foundation of New South Wales 2012).

[51] Ibid.

[52] Pascoe Pleasence et al, *Paths to Justice: A Past, Present and Future Roadmap* (Nuffield Foundation 2013) iv.

[53] Ibid.

In practical terms, civil legal aid can ensure the delivery of some, or all, of the following services, depending on the nature of the issue.

Public Legal Education (PLE)

PLE is largely concerned with raising awareness of law, legal rules, and the justice system, and aims to help people to identify the legal dimensions of issues so that they are better able to resolve them. It can include having increased awareness of when and where to go to find legal help and might also be described as 'community legal education' or 'community legal information'. While legal aid funding may be available to fund PLE initiatives, in many jurisdictions PLE is also funded by charitable sources or undertaken by lawyers as part of their pro bono activities (see further discussion in Chapter 8). It is extremely common for law students to deliver PLE either as an extra-curricular pro bono project or as an integrated part of a clinical legal education programme.[54] There is considerable divergence in the field as to what constitutes PLE and efforts to define it have been problematic such that it is often defined by what it is not (ie legal advice or representation). Importantly, it is not aimed at answering specific legal questions but rather at raising 'legal capability', which is 'the ability of individuals to recognise and deal with law-related issues they might face.'[55] With different individual capabilities in mind, it is widely recognized that diversity in the provision of PLE is important:

> Legal education and information can be provided in a variety of ways that may involve passive or active engagement—through face-to-face contact, via social media, by telephone or via leaflets and other written material. Diverse methods of delivery are needed to reflect the fact that people receive and understand information in a number of ways, something that may be determined by their level of education or even by their cultural or community background. Interactive approaches, properly resourced, can be particularly effective.[56]

Examples of public legal education initiatives include subject-specific workshops with schools or community groups (eg debt, housing, employment), online information in relation to legal rights (eg a step-by-step online guide to support disabled people to challenge discrimination in the workplace), or awareness-raising campaigns (eg a government campaign to raise awareness of changes to tax rules).

Legal 'Help'

Legal help can be thought of as tailored support towards diagnosing a legal problem. Usually delivered by lawyers or trained advisers, it might involve some early investigation of issues and helps clients to try to ensure timely resolution. In some cases, this might include

[54] See Richard Grimes et al, 'Street Law and Social Justice Education' in Frank S Bloch, *The Global Clinical Movement: Educating Lawyers for Social Justice* (OUP 2010).

[55] Sharon Collard et al, *Public Legal Education: Evaluation Framework* (University of Bristol Personal Finance Research Centre 2011) 7. See also Frances Ridout and Linden Thomas, *Street Law: Theory and Practice* (Hart 2023).

[56] Advice Services Alliance, *Towards a National Strategy for Public Legal Education* (Citizenship Foundation & ASA 2004) 4.

providing written or oral advice, drafting letters, advising on small claims proceedings, obtaining information from third parties and negotiating with them, or helping individuals to understand what evidence they might need to gather in support of their case (eg medical reports or written statements). Should the matter be deemed serious enough or further legal advice and representation be required, a lawyer might work towards securing further legal aid funding for full representation to act on a client's behalf when appropriate. The distinction therefore between legal 'help' and more formal advice is not always clear and it is important to recognize the interrelationship between them. This is especially the case in view of ethical obligations, where it is imperative that those providing such services do not hold themselves out as lawyers giving advice if they are not qualified, and regulated, to do so. These ethical obligations are explored further in Chapter 7.

Help at Court

Legal aid at court is often available to support clients (who would otherwise be 'litigants in person' or 'pro se' litigants) in relation to court hearings. For example, where an individual does not have someone to represent them in a court hearing, legal aid may provide some help to support that person in presenting issues before the court or to advise them on the relevant procedures. In the UK context, this person can usually speak on a client's behalf in court but does not formally act as a representative in the proceedings or on court records. Other rules may apply in different jurisdictions when determining the point at which someone providing help at court can be said to be formally providing legal representation. State-funded help at court in civil matters is most common in areas where the court hearing itself might lead to an immediate adverse outcome for a client (eg housing eviction proceedings leading to homelessness, a debt matter leading to bankruptcy, family proceedings with potential custody issues).

Legal Advice and Representation

The type of legal advice and representation available will vary depending on the area of civil law and the applicable rules and procedures. Some jurisdictions use the term 'ABWOR' (assistance by way of representation) to distinguish representation and advice and there are often different approval or eligibility mechanisms in place for formal representation. This is usually done to control spending so that cases with no likelihood of success are not funded, mindful of the fact that formal legal representation in relation to instituting, conducting, or defending legal proceedings tends to be the most expensive type of legal service provision. In any event, confidential legal advice is aimed at determining the legal issues in relation to a matter and identifying the potential avenues for resolution. Legally aided advice and representation might include investigating the matter, conducting legal research, drafting correspondence, collating evidence, making formal applications to the court or otherwise preparing documents (eg witness statements, agreements, statements of claim, skeleton arguments), and liaising with opposing parties and their representatives.

Alternative Forms of Dispute Resolution (ADR)

The most common form of ADR is mediation, which involves the use of an independent third party to help resolve an issue in a way that is fair to both sides. It is particularly common in family law. In some jurisdictions, legal aid might be available for other forms of ADR, such as arbitration or negotiation. Particularly in employment matters, personal injury claims, or small business disputes, ADR can be a quicker and more cost-effective way of resolving matters. If the complaint involves a public body, another alternative to going to court is through an Ombudsman scheme. Some advice agencies may support individuals with a complaint to the relevant Ombudsman, which may result in an apology, compensation, or an express recommendation that practices and procedures be followed in future.

3.3.2 **Criminal Justice**

There is usually a requirement that criminal legal aid be provided in the interests of justice. In Chapter 2, we noted that the right to a fair trial is set out in Article 6 ECHR. Article 6 states that where a suspect or defendant lacks 'sufficient means', legal aid must be provided. Article 14(3)(d) of the International Covenant on Civil and Political Rights (ICCPR) also prescribes that everyone is entitled to a fair and impartial hearing when charged with a criminal offence. Factors such as the seriousness of the offence, the severity of the sentence, or the complexity of the case would particularly weigh in favour of legal aid provision.[57] For example, in the case of *Benham v the United Kingdom*,[58] the applicant had been charged with non-payment of a debt and faced a possible maximum three-month prison sentence. The European Court of Human Rights (ECtHR) held that this potential sentence was severe enough that the interests of justice demanded that the applicant should have had the benefit of legal aid. In practice, courts usually have the power to appoint a legal aid lawyer when an accused faces a prison sentence and is otherwise unrepresented. The jurisprudence of the ECtHR has also established that anyone in police custody has the right to consult a lawyer at their first interrogation by the police if they choose, unless there are compelling reasons to restrict such a right.[59]

Police Station Advice

It is important that a person's choice to exercise a right to legal advice be made before being questioned, and that the advice itself is independent of the police. In the UK, for example, advice upon arrest and before being questioned is funded by legal aid and provided free of charge to all detainees. There are some exceptions to the exercise of the right; for example, where it is necessary in the interests of an investigation or for the prevention of crime or the apprehension of offenders. In most circumstances, however, a police interview cannot begin without a lawyer being present unless the suspect waives his or her right to representation.

[57] *Benham v UK* (1996) 22 EHRR 293; *Granger v UK* (1990) 12 EHRR 469.
[58] Ibid.
[59] *Salduz v Turkey* [2008] ECHR 1542.

In many legal jurisdictions, a lawyer or other 'appropriate adult' must *always* be present during police interview when a child is being interviewed or the suspect appears to be unable to understand sufficiently by reason of mental disorder and/or cannot communicate effectively.[60]

Legal Advice and Representation

When accused of a criminal charge and facing trial, legal representation can be of crucial importance to ensure equality of arms. The provision of criminal legal aid is usually subject to a test of financial eligibility as well as consideration of the interests of justice. As set out above, the more serious the charge or its consequences, the more likely it is that legal aid will be provided. The factors to be considered were first set out by the Widgery Committee in 1966.[61] Known as the 'Widgery criteria', they are instructive in this context (considered from the client's perspective):

- It's likely I'll lose my liberty
- I've been given a sentence that's suspended or non-custodial: if I break this, the court may be able to deal with me for the original offence
- It's likely that I'll lose my livelihood
- It's likely that I'll suffer serious damage to my reputation
- A substantial question of law may be involved
- I may not be able to understand the court proceedings or present my own case
- I may need witnesses to be traced or interviewed on my behalf
- The proceedings may involve expert cross-examination of a prosecution witness
- It's in the interests of another person that I'm represented
- Any other reasons.[62]

The case law of the ECtHR has reflected some aspects of the criteria. For example, in the case of *Barsom and Varli v Sweden*, the court found that the denial of legal aid was appropriate because the legal issues in the case were straightforward. The case concerned whether or not the applicant had submitted an incorrect tax return.[63] In the case of *Quaranta v Switzerland*, the ECtHR held that the legal issues were particularly complicated given the applicant's personal situation, some of which might fall with 'any other reasons' in the Widgery criteria set out above: 'a young adult of foreign origin from an underprivileged background, he had no real

[60] See eg Police and Criminal Evidence Act 1984, Code C 3.21A(d): 'If they are a juvenile or vulnerable and do not want legal advice, their appropriate adult has the right to ask for a solicitor to attend if this would be in their best interests and the appropriate adult must be so informed. In this case, action to secure the provision of advice if so requested by their appropriate adult will be taken without delay in the same way as if requested by the person . . . '

[61] Hon Mr Justice Widgery, *Report of the Departmental Committee on Legal Aid in Criminal Legal Proceedings* (Cmnd 2934, 1966).

[62] Legal Aid Agency, *Guidance on the Consideration of Defence Order Representation Applications* (November 2021) 4. Available at https://assets.publishing.service.gov.uk/government/uploads/system/uploads/attachment_data/file/1032881/Interests_of_justice_desktop_aid_2018_v3_.pdf

[63] *Barsom and Varli v Sweden*, ECtHR, Decision of 4 January 2008.

occupational training and a long criminal record. He had taken drugs since 1975, almost daily since 1983, and, at the material time, was living with his family on social security benefit.'[64]

REFLECTION POINT

Consider the factors above that might weigh in favour of an entitlement to advice and representation funded by legal aid for those accused and charged with a crime.

- Do you consider the criteria to be too wide or narrow?
- What do you think might constitute 'any other reasons' weighing in favour of an entitlement to a lawyer in the interests of justice?

Now imagine a defendant in court charged with assault. He is unrepresented and does not have enough money to pay for a lawyer. His case did not pass the interests of justice test as it was considered that he should be able to present his own case. However, the defendant struggles with alcohol and substance misuse and is often disruptive in court. Do you think 'any other reasons' should apply in his case?

Restorative Justice

Restorative justice has been described as 'a process whereby all the parties with a stake in a particular offence come together to resolve collectively how to deal with the aftermath of the offence and its implications for the future.'[65] There is considerable divergence globally in the extent to which states might fund restorative justice initiatives as well as their willingness to experiment with different restorative approaches. In some jurisdictions, such as the US, Canada, and Australia, specific provision might be made for the use of 'problem-solving courts' that prioritize the rehabilitation of offenders and aim to address the underlying causes of criminal behaviour.[66] In Rwanda, the Gacaca courts were widely relied upon after the genocide as an indigenous form of post-conflict restorative justice.[67] The UK has also experimented with 'drug courts', which are specifically designed to provide an alternative to traditional sentencing to include more holistic forms of treatment and supervision. However, they have not tended to have the same longevity in the UK as in other jurisdictions.[68] Other examples of restorative justice include victim–offender mediation, sentencing or 'peacemaking' circles, and family group conferencing.[69]

[64] *Quaranta v Switzerland*, ECtHR, Decision of 24 May 1991, at para 35.

[65] United Nations Working Group on Restorative Justice, 1996 cited in Don Clairmont, *Restorative Justice: From the Margins to the Mainstream* (Atlantic Institute of Criminology 1999) 1.

[66] Richard Weiner and Eve Brank, *Problem Solving Courts: Social Science and Legal Perspectives* (Springer 2013).

[67] Max Rettig, 'Gacaca: Truth, Justice and Reconciliation in Post Conflict Rwanda' (2008) African Studies Review 51(3) 25–50.

[68] See eg Anna Grace Kawalek, *Problem-Solving Court, Criminal Justice, and the International Gold Standard: Reframing the English and Welsh Drug Courts* (Routledge 2021).

[69] See eg Mark Umbreit and Marilyn Armour, *Restorative Justice Dialogue: An Essential Guide for Research and Practice* (Springer 2010).

A View from Clinical Practice

Rachel Knowles, Director, UCL Centre for Access to Justice

During my law degree, I found myself surrounded by people planning to work in the city, working on big deals and big business. I wanted to help people and I thought I wanted to be an immigration lawyer (I was wrong!). The only time I really felt like I found my place was when I was volunteering. Slowly but surely, I discovered the world of legal aid. I was lucky enough to secure a training contract with a large legal aid firm and there I discovered a wonderful world of camaraderie and support, a sense of community and working together for a greater purpose. I learned from some brilliant lawyers and saw how they were able to achieve great results for clients and change the law.

Even before the Legal Aid, Sentencing and Punishment of Offenders Act (LASPO) 2012 was enacted, the evidence of pressure on the business due to cuts to legal aid was evident. On qualifying as a solicitor, I moved into the not-for-profit sector. There, I experienced the pleasure of being able to prioritize the needs of my client over the need for a business to make money. However, I missed the benefits of being able to offer legal aid services to clients and secured a legal aid contract for the charity I worked at.

I later moved into clinical legal education and am now the Director of the UCL Centre for Access to Justice in London. When setting up the UCL Integrated Legal Advice Clinic in East London, I was passionate about bringing the spirit and camaraderie of legal aid to our student community. I wanted students who might have felt out of place like I did to find a home in legal aid practice. I wanted them to experience the power of legal aid and see first-hand how it can truly change people's lives. I have tried to build this community with our clinic solicitors, working alongside our students as a team.

Having a legal aid contract means that we can provide a full service to our clients. Without any cost risk to them, we can litigate for them rather than risking referral fatigue or them giving up on the resolution of their legal issue. With legal aid, we can bring county court proceedings and judicial review proceedings as required, giving students the opportunity to experience the full spectrum of the different ways that the law is used in practice to challenge injustice or unlawful public decision making. In fact, topics that may seem nebulous in public law are brought to life through the legal aid work of the clinic.

Students also get to experience the challenges of the administration of legal aid of completing controlled work forms or applications on client and cost management systems. They also get to experience what time recording under a legal aid contract looks like compared to what it may look like in privately paid work.

Most importantly, working on legal aid cases in law school helps students to learn that legal aid does still exist and does still help some people despite the constraints and pressures in the field. I hope to help students see legal aid practice as a viable career path, as I worry about the dwindling number of students pursuing this career path and what this will mean for legal aid in the long term.

There's no doubt that managing a legal aid contract can bring challenges and, especially within a university context, can feel like fitting a square peg into a round hole. However, I believe that it's worth it to make our service as effective as possible for the local community and as meaningful as possible for our students. I am fortunate enough to work for an institution that agrees and supports this endeavour.

3.4 The Expansion and Decline of Legal Aid

Across the globe, legal aid provision has tended to come in waves and can be facilitated or constrained by a range of factors. Provision can be especially vulnerable to changing perceptions and politics depending on the policy positions of the government in power. For example, the creation of new criminal offences may come with an increased need for legal research and preparation, and thus more time-consuming and costly legal representation. Similarly, the passing of legislation could create new rights or duties resulting in increased need for legal advice and representation. Further, the failure of government agencies to fulfil their legal obligations can impact on legal aid spending given the need to fund those bringing claims against the state by way of judicial review.[70] Scholars and policymakers have long grappled with trying to understand the factors weighing upon changes in legal aid spending, often through comparison of different jurisdictions to determine the ways in which expansion or decline is necessitated, or indeed justified. However, it can be challenging to comparatively capture legal aid frameworks for a number of reasons, as explained below:

> comparing legal aid programmes is difficult: in part, this is because the available data is often incomplete; and also because of differences between jurisdictions. For example, there may be differences in the definition of what they consider to be justiciable problems, differences in substantive law and legal process, how cases are processed, the definition and ambit of legal aid, the presence and scale of generalist and specialist advice services, and in the take up and scope of legal expenses insurance and third-party service provision, for example by trade unions.[71]

Cyrus Tata similarly argues that it is impossible to even accurately define what a legal 'case' is. As such, comparisons should look at a range of explanations and behaviours to explain patterns of expansion or decline rather than simply the units of work.[72] In this section, legal aid reforms in England and Wales are analysed in order to illustrate how changes in provision can impact more widely upon the access to justice landscape. As we have discussed, the legal aid system had historically rested upon the Rushcliffe principles and had aimed to ensure early resolution of legal problems. In the decades after the establishment of legal aid there was said to be a 'golden age' period where provision expanded quite rapidly, which led to backlash as public spending increased. The legal aid reforms brought about by the LASPO Act 2012 were arguably so profound that they shifted 'just in case' entitlement to 'just in time'. Notably, before the changes were enacted, Alan Paterson had noted:

> Indeed, the indications are that the Ministry of Justice intends that the access to justice priorities of the public are to be determined, not from the mass of solid research evidence available to the [Ministry of Justice], but on a philosophy that rejects early intervention by lawyers and favours the avoidance of courts at almost any cost.[73]

[70] Paterson (n 14) 75.

[71] Martyn Evans, *Rethinking Legal Aid: An Independent Strategic Review* (Scottish Legal Aid Board 2018) 18.

[72] Cyrus Tata, 'The Construction of "Comparison" in Legal Aid Spending: The Promise and Perils of a Jurisdiction-Centred Approach to (International) Legal Aid Research' in Franic Regan et al (eds), *The Transformation of Legal Aid: Historical and Comparative Studies* (OUP 1999).

[73] Paterson (n 14) 63.

Table 3.1 Example areas of civil legal aid provision in England and Wales pre-LASPO 2012

Family—Divorce	Child Arrangement Orders
Welfare Benefits	Employment Disputes
Debt	Education
Discrimination	Immigration (asylum)
Immigration (non-asylum)	Housing

Table 3.2 Example areas removed from scope of legal aid provision in England and Wales by LASPO 2012

Family—Divorce (unless domestic violence proven)	Child Arrangement Orders (unless domestic violence proven)
Welfare Benefits (unless appealing a point of law to Upper Tribunal)	Employment Disputes (yes for discrimination)
Debt (by telephone gateway, only if bankrupt or losing home)	Education (by telephone gateway, only Special Educational Needs)
Discrimination	Immigration (asylum)
Immigration (non-asylum)	Housing (only certain types of cases eg prospectively homeless)

This is illustrated by the tables above:[74] Table 3.1 outlines areas in which legal aid had previously been available prior to the enactment of LASPO and Table 3.2 sets out the 2012 changes to civil legal aid brought about by the new legislation. In Table 3.2, those areas highlighted in dark grey are no longer in scope for legal aid unless limited exceptions apply (ie welfare benefits, divorce, child arrangement orders, employment, non-asylum immigration); those in mid grey show legal aid only being available via the (then) so-called telephone gateway or in limited cases (ie education, debt, discrimination, and housing). As shown, of these areas, only asylum immigration cases remained unchanged.

In practice, for example, this meant that separating couples could not obtain legal advice in relation to divorce or custody arrangements (unless domestic violence was proven). Similarly, legal aid was no longer available for those experiencing poor housing conditions, welfare benefits issues, or unfair dismissal from employment. Face-to-face provision was extremely limited, posing difficulties for those with communication difficulties, for example those who did not speak English as a first language. While a new framework for 'exceptional cases'[75] was introduced to ensure that there could still be access to a lawyer even outside of these areas where it might otherwise breach Article 6 ECHR, applications to that scheme have been extremely low, with the system proving difficult to navigate. The dramatic changes to provision

[74] The authors express their thanks to Rachel Knowles for contributing these tables.

[75] Legal Aid, Sentencing and Punishment of Offenders Act 2012, s 10.

therefore reveal a number of issues of importance in the access to justice landscape. We focus on three in particular: the impact of unresolved legal issues on individuals and groups; the rise in litigants in person in the courts; and the creation of so-called advice deserts and droughts.

3.4.1 The Impact of Unresolved Legal Issues

Following the changes outlined above, the number of civil legal aid cases significantly declined, particularly in relation to legal help. This led to adverse impacts disproportionately experienced by particular individuals and groups, as demonstrated by research undertaken by Amnesty International (UK):

> Every day, ordinary people face legal problems where they need to be able to get the right advice and support as soon as possible. Be it a parent trying to secure contact with their child, a disabled person who has had her benefits wrongly cut, or an 18-year-old born in the UK who is trying to regularise his immigration status or claim her entitlement to British citizenship. Without that advice and support the consequences can be profound: they could face being made homeless, falling deeply into debt, being prevented from seeing their children, or being separated from their families. This has a significant human cost for the individuals themselves and their families, and a wider cost to society as other services have to take the strain of supporting people whose problems have spiralled out of control.[76]

Amnesty's report concluded that cuts to legal aid together with wider so-called austerity cuts (eg to welfare benefits or housing allocation) were impacting three groups in particular: children and vulnerable young people, migrants and refugees, and those with specific vulnerabilities. People with 'mental health conditions, learning disabilities, low numeracy and literacy levels, language problems, medical conditions such as terminal illness, and alcohol and drug dependency' were unable to effectively advocate for themselves and claim their rights.[77] Many people had to wait until crisis point before they were able to access help or advice, leading to further knock-on adverse impacts (for example, falling into debt, experiencing homelessness, or losing access to their children).

These findings were borne out in other research studies and inquiries. For example, Grainne McKeever and others found that the changes exacerbated extreme poverty due to a failure to resolve issues at an early stage.[78] The Bach Commission, which reported in 2017, found that there was 'an urgent need to bring some areas of civil law back into scope' and to 'refocus on early legal help in order to help prevent problems escalating'.[79] The primary recommendation of the Bach Commission was a new statutory 'right to justice' set out in a Right to Justice Act. This right would codify and serve to supplement rights that already existed, for example, as set out in Magna Carta and the Human Rights Act 1998. The Commission

[76] *Cuts that Hurt: The Impact of Legal Aid Cuts in England on Access to Justice* (Amnesty International UK 2016) 3.
[77] Ibid 4.
[78] Grainne McKeever et al, *Destitution and Paths to Justice* (Joseph Rowntree Foundation 2018).
[79] Fabian Society, *The Right to Justice: The Final Report of the Bach Commission* (September 2017) 5.

also proposed a new right for individuals to receive reasonable legal assistance.[80] These recommendations have been endorsed elsewhere but have yet to be implemented.[81]

Professor Philip Alston, in his capacity as the UN Special Rapporteur for Extreme Poverty and Human Rights, also visited the UK in 2018 and reported on the impact of austerity measures alongside the cuts to legal aid provision. He noted that the lack of availability of legal aid had 'overwhelmingly affected the poor and people with disabilities' and that they had lost their 'safety net'.[82] It was a damning report and yet, as Moore and Newbury noted, the adverse impacts of legal aid cuts that were highlighted were barely mentioned in news coverage at the time. They comment that this was 'no accidental omission'.[83] Some argue that there is a culture of complacency in the wider public sphere in relation to legal aid which, when considered alongside negative 'fat cat' and 'activist' lawyer tropes, not only can inhibit the resolution of systemic issues but also has a damaging effect on well-being and on lawyers' self-perceptions of their own work.[84]

There have been consecutive reviews into the impact of changes. A government-led review of the implementation of LASPO in 2019 made a number of observations about concerns raised during the review process:

- Limitations on the scope of legal aid limit the availability of early advice which means that problems escalate before they can be addressed
- Many people who need legal aid cannot access it
- Exceptional case funding does not work
- The fees are inadequate
- There has been a rise in the number of litigants in person and
- There are advice deserts, where people cannot access advice.[85]

While this review made some limited changes, such as abolishing the telephone advice gateway, they were not comprehensive enough to address the problems outlined. This was expressly noted by the 2021 Justice Committee inquiry on the *Future of Legal Aid*. The Committee further observed that the civil legal aid system in England and Wales was 'in a difficult place' and that 'a much smaller proportion of the population' are now able to access civil legal aid.[86] A subsequent Westminster Commission inquiry similarly found that 'the sector as a

80 Ibid 14–18.

81 Jon Robins and Daniel Newman, *Justice in a Time of Austerity: Stories from a System in Crisis* (Bristol University Press 2021).

82 United National Human Rights Office of the High Commissioner, *Report of the Visit of Professor Philip Alston to the UK* (UN OHCHR, July 2019). Available at https://undocs.org/A/HRC/41/39/Add.1

83 Sarah Moore and Alex Newbury, *Legal Aid in Crisis: Assessing the Impact of Reform* (Bristol University Press 2017) 1.

84 Hilary Sommerlad, '"I've lost the plot": An Everyday Story of Legal Aid Lawyers' (2001) 28(3) Journal of Law and Society 335–60; Catrina Denvir, Jacqueline Kinghan et al, *We Are Legal Aid: Report of the Legal Aid Census Findings* 2021 (Legal Aid Practitioners Group 2022).

85 Ministry of Justice, Post-Implementation Review of Part 1 of the Legal Aid, Sentencing and Punishment of Offenders Act 2012, (2019) para 1165.

86 Justice Committee, *Future of Legal Aid Report* (2021) para 81.

whole is in desperate need of revitalisation and investment if it is to meet public demand in the years to come'.[87]

3.4.2 **The Rise of Litigants in Person**

Following cuts to legal aid funding, the rise in unrepresented litigants in the family courts was particularly acute. For example, in the family courts some 47 per cent of litigants in 2020 had representation, as compared to 62 per cent in 2011.[88] There has been a considerable impact on vulnerable litigants but also more widely on the justice system. For example, hearings take longer because the arguments are not as focused and it is challenging for judges to ensure that proceedings are fair.[89] This was a recurring theme in the *Future of Legal Aid* report: that the fairness of the justice system was at risk because of the fundamental changes to the system.

Likewise, litigants in person may struggle to find information relevant to their case and to communicate such information to the court. It is also challenging where proceedings are essentially adversarial in nature, meaning that parties in a dispute may be required to cross-examine one another where they are not represented. In a 2014 study of litigants in person in the family courts, Trinder et al found that almost all 'had difficulties with court procedures and the legal issues involved in their case, and around half were personally vulnerable in some way'.[90] This meant that litigants in person found 'negotiation of the legal and procedural requirements of self-representation more difficult'.[91] Wider problems created by the rise in litigants in person included a refusal to engage with proceedings, and, less commonly, aggressive and disruptive behaviour.[92]

Finally, it is worth noting that the *Future of Legal Aid* report made a number of recommendations based around five key themes. These are reminiscent, to some extent, of the Rushcliffe principles drafted more than 70 years earlier:

1. The legal aid system should be designed around the needs of those who use it.
2. The regulation of the legal aid system should prioritise the quality of the work provided and should ensure that the public are supplied with the right legal work at the right time.
3. The legal aid framework should enable the Government to act strategically and target support in areas where it is needed most and where it can improve the effectiveness of the courts and the justice system.
4. Legal aid should be regarded as a public service, which benefits all of society.
5. Legal aid is critical to the fairness of the justice system, enabling those without sufficient financial means to participate on equal terms with those that can afford representation.[93]

[87] Westminster Commission on Legal Aid, *Inquiry into the Sustainability and Recovery of the Legal Aid Sector in England and Wales* (APPG on Legal Aid 2024) 7. Available at https://lapg.co.uk/wp-content/uploads/The-Westminster-Commission-on-Legal-Aid_WEB.pdf

[88] Ibid para 102. [89] Ibid para 103.

[90] Liz Trinder et al, *Litigants in Person in Private Family Cases* (Ministry of Justice Analytical Series 2014) 11.

[91] Ibid. [92] Ibid.

[93] Justice Committee, *Legal Aid Needs Urgent Reform* (4 October 2021). Available at https://ukparliament.shorthandstories.com/justice-future-of-legal-aid/index.html

REFLECTION POINT

Consider the five key themes of the Future of Legal Aid report referenced above. Which of these themes do you consider to be most important? How does this compare to the top three Rushcliffe principles you selected above?

3.4.3 Legal Advice Deserts and Droughts

A further issue raised by the reduction of legal aid provision is the creation of so-called legal advice deserts and droughts. An advice desert is a geographic area that has no legal aid provision for particular areas of law such that people cannot access any face-to-face legal advice. Advice deserts are particularly common in community care and housing law in England and Wales.[94] Advice droughts, on the other hand, describe areas that have legal aid provision, but there is so much pressure on those providers in terms of supply and demand that not everyone is able to access advice. Research shows that legal aid droughts are particularly common in immigration and asylum law.[95] The existence of legal aid deserts and droughts is also useful in considering 'justice gaps' in society, that is, where people do not qualify for legal aid but are nonetheless unable to pay for legal services. For some areas of law, there is a greater likelihood of a justice gap where there are simply not enough qualified lawyers providing services in some areas of law. It is a challenge where legal aid work, often due to comparatively lower rates of pay or the complexity of bureaucratic procedures, is unattractive to private practitioners and therefore places an additional burden on not-for-profit providers. Law school clinics will often work to keep these considerations in mind when designing clinical programmes.

REFLECTION POINT

Advice deserts are especially likely to exist in remote and rural areas. Let us consider a young girl who has been excluded from school for behavioural issues. Her parents believe she has an undiagnosed learning disability but the school refuses to conduct an assessment of her educational needs. The school has also said there is no appeal process available in respect of the exclusion decision. The child's parent wants to speak to a lawyer but does not have the means to pay. There are no legal aid providers locally who provide education law advice. Imagine you are the child's parent and you are trying to find out more about how to deal with the issue. Consider the following questions:

1. What types of legal information and/or advice might help you in this situation?
2. In the absence of local legal aid provision, where might you go to find help?
3. Can you find any examples of innovative projects (pro bono, charitable, or law school clinic provision) or resources that might assist you?

[94] Law Society of England and Wales, *Legal Aid Deserts* (Law Society, 27 September 2021). Available at https://www.lawsociety.org.uk/en/campaigns/legal-aid-deserts

[95] Jo Wilding, *The Legal Aid Market: Challenges for Publicly Funded Immigration and Asylum Legal Representation* (Bristol University Press 2021).

Conclusion

The provision of legal information, advice, or representation to members of the local community who cannot otherwise afford it has a vital role to play in the access to justice landscape. Some individuals may not be eligible for legal aid and others may have found it difficult to access provision either because of reduced provision or because their issue doesn't fall within scope for funding. For them, pro bono has a critical role to play, which we explore further in Chapter 8. This chapter has sought to highlight the arguments for and against state-funded legal aid provision, the different types of provision available, and the impacts that limiting legal aid can have on individuals and groups in terms of deepening disadvantage. It is important to interrogate the extent to which legal aid should be considered an entitlement which the state has a duty to provide. As we have explored in this chapter, there are critical questions in relation to the extent to which pro bono work, including the free provision of legal services by students in law school clinics, might serve to undermine or threaten the fulfilment of the state's obligations to make legal services available to those who cannot afford to pay.

Further Reading

Catrina Denvir, Jacqueline Kinghan, Jess Mant, and Daniel Newman, *Legal Aid and the Future of Access to Justice* (Hart 2023).

Asher Flynn and Jacqueline Hodgson (eds), *Access to Justice and Legal Aid: Comparative Perspectives on Unmet Legal Need* (Hart 2017).

Olubunmi Onafuwa, 'LASPO 2012—Ten Years and Beyond—A Socio-legal Study of the Impact of Legal Aid Cuts on Service Providers in England and Wales' (2024) 27(1) Legal Ethics 45–62.

Jon Robins and Daniel Newman, *Justice in a Time of Austerity: Stories from a System in Crisis* (Bristol University Press 2021).

Technology and the Future of Access to Justice

4

Prediction is very difficult, especially about the future.

Niels Bohr

Chapter Overview

This chapter will introduce you to the ways in which technology has changed, and is expected to continue to change, legal practice and legal education. The aim of the chapter is to introduce you to the way technology is disrupting how we practise, and perhaps even understand, law itself. In particular, the chapter provides an overview of the most fundamental areas in which legal practice has embraced technological opportunities.

By the end of this chapter, you should be able to

- examine the technological reforms, planned and implemented, within the public justice system, and the effects these have had on the users of the system, both positive and challenging
- have a strong understanding of the positive and negative impacts that technology has had, to date, on access to justice, across a number of axes
- understand the way technology has already impacted legal education and clinical legal education, and highlight the potential for future developments in those realms

Introduction

In the musical *Hamilton*, Lin-Manuel Miranda wrote 'In the eye of the storm, there is quiet'. And there is a good chance that many, as they're reading this, will not be aware of the significant turbulence around them, upending all that was familiar. We refer, in this case, to the momentous impact of technology on, well, everything, including (but clearly not limited to) communications, relationships, associations, concepts, and perceptions. Historian Yuval Noah Harari identifies this moment—which he calls the information revolution—as the third major revolution since the dawn of civilization 70,000 years ago, following the agrarian and the industrial.[1] Klaus Schwab refers to it as the Fourth Industrial Revolution by reference to the materials and systems that were used in the production: first, water; second,

[1] Yuval Noah Harrari, *Sapiens*.

electric power; third, electronics and IT; and now, artificial intelligence (AI), nanotechnology, and biotechnology.[2] While previous revolutions upended social and labour relations, this current revolution is far more dramatic. The numbers bear witness to this claim: if humans created five exabytes of information up to 2003, now we create that amount every hour or so.[3] The change, in other words, is 'exponentially faster than in preceding revolutions'.[4]

It is not as if that amount of information creates more certainty. Indeed, it is probably the opposite. Harari notes, for example, that 'We are in a unique situation in human history when, for the first time, we have no idea what the job market will look like in 20 or 30 years. That was never before the case in history.' The reference to the job market is important, relating, among other things, to the fear that 'robots will take our jobs' as well as to the changes in the way work is done (remotely? under digital surveillance? and so on). We return to this aspect, insofar as it relates to the legal sector, later in this chapter, but for now we should note that, as dramatic as this change will be, the impact of this information revolution on the 'business of justice' and the legal system goes well beyond the operational delivery of justice. Moreover, the gap between what technology offers and how law responds is likely to widen further. Consider this observation, written more than 30 years ago and still relevant today:

> Law adapts by continuous increments and at a pace second only to geology in its stateliness. Technology advances in . . . lunging jerks, like the punctuation of biological evolution grotesquely accelerated. Real world conditions will continue to change at a blinding pace, and *the law will get further behind*, more profoundly confused. *This mismatch is permanent*.[5]

It would seem that technology provides not only the opportunity but, perhaps, even the necessity to rethink the basic understandings, premises, and practices underpinning the justice system that have remained in place for centuries. The change is not merely about quantity—of data, of information, of speed—but also, and perhaps most importantly, a conceptual and qualitative shift. It is often referred to as a moment of 'disruption' for law, legal practice, and indeed legal reasoning.[6] It requires thinking about the fit of 'old law' to new objects: are cryptocurrencies 'property'? Are smart contracts—discussed further below—'contracts'?[7] Should society deal with new problems created by technology, such as motor-assisted bikes, drastic measures of surveillance,[8] and prevalence of cell phones, for example,

[2] Klaus Schwab, The Fourth Industrial Revolution: What it means, how to respond (2016) https://www.weforum.org/agenda/2016/01/the-fourth-industrial-revolution-what-it-means-and-how-to-respond/

[3] Richard Susskind, *Online Courts and the Future of Justice* (OUP 2019) 37.

[4] Hazel Genn, 'Online Courts and the Future of Justice' (UCL Birkenhead Lecture 2017, Gray's Inn). https://www.ucl.ac.uk/laws/sites/laws/files/birkenhead_lecture_2017_professor_dame_hazel_genn_final_version.pdf

[5] John Perry Barlow, 'The Economy of Ideas: Selling Wine without Bottles on the Global Net' Wired (March 1994) https://www.wired.com/1994/03/economy-ideas/

[6] See eg Roger Brownsword, *Law 3.0* (Routledge 2021) 13–47.

[7] Ibid 3; a Law Commission Report says 'yes': Law Commission, *Smart Legal Contracts* (Law Com No 401, CP 563, November 2021) https://s3-eu-west-2.amazonaws.com/cloud-platform-e218f50a4812967ba1215eaecede923f/uploads/sites/30/2021/11/Smart-legal-contracts-accessible.pdf

[8] Daniel Boffey, 'Police to be able to run face recognition searches on 50m driving licence holders' *The Guardian* (20 December 2023) https://www.theguardian.com/technology/2023/dec/20/police-to-be-able-to-run-face-recognition-searches-on-50m-driving-licence-holders

through more rules (licensing requirements; enhanced data protection rights; fining or confiscating inappropriate use of phones used at school or theatres), or through technology (eg manufacturers limit the bikes' speed; cameras do not store photos for more than 24 hours; reception-blocking technology)? Roger Brownsword refers to the blend of *ex post* (after the fact) legal rules with *ex ante* (preventative) technology as Law 3.0.[9] On the face of it, technology seems like a perfect regulatory tool to add to law: instead of the imperfect, and inefficient, chasing of rule-violators, why not just make it impossible to violate the rule? For instance, instead of pursuing shoplifters, why not design a system where the door simply won't open unless all items have been paid for?

Seems simple enough. But Evgeny Morozov raises a very interesting reservation: if we scale up technological regulation, we may eliminate not only the infractions we genuinely wish to prevent but also acts of civil disobedience that are central to our understanding of democracy and justice. If, for example, Rosa Parks could only board the bus with a card granting her access exclusively to the back section—and no passage was physically possible between the two sections—history might have unfolded very differently. He explains:

> Will this new transportation system be convenient? Sure. Will it give us Rosa Parks? Probably not, because she would never have gotten to the front of the bus to begin with. The odds are that a perfectly efficient seat-distribution system—abetted by ubiquitous technology, sensors and facial recognition—would have robbed us of one of the proudest moments in American history. Laws that are enforced by appealing to our moral or prudential registers leave just enough space for friction; friction breeds tension, tension creates conflict, and conflict produces change. In contrast, when laws are enforced through the technological register, there's little space for friction and tension—and quite likely for change.[10]

Brownsword acknowledges that 'we need to beware civilisations and technocrats that are "committed to the quest for continually improved means to carelessly examined ends"'.[11] In other words, the fact that we *can* do something technologically is a necessary but not a sufficient reason to do it. He suggests that today's practices of dataveillance, much like the surveillance imagined in Orwell's *1984*, 'may be doing less to deter destructive acts than [slowly to narrow] the range of tolerable thought and behaviour'.[12] Technology may close doors as well as open them. Indeed, technological regulation is a very effective use of power, all the more so because it is often the least visible, and thus not subject to scrutiny.[13]

This opening charts the parameters of this chapter and thus what it is *not* about. We cannot, and do not intend to, address the wide variety of intersections of law and technology. These would include areas such as intellectual property, privacy and security, employment and discrimination, free speech and defamation, criminal liability in the virtual world, and much

[9] Brownsword (n 6).

[10] Evgeny Morozov, *To Save Everything, Click Here*, 205. Copyright 2013 Allen Lane.

[11] Brownsword (n 6) 71, quoting Robert Merton, 'Foreword' in Jacques Ellul, *The Technological Society* (1964) vi.

[12] Ibid 74, quoting Frank Pasquale, *The Black Box Society* (Harvard University Press 2015) 52.

[13] Steven Lukes, *Power: A Radical View* (2nd ed, Palgrave Macmillan 2005) 1.

more. It is important to clarify that questions raised in these areas are not for some distant future. Technology has expanded dramatically both the number and the nature of disputes in which people are involved, often making current systems inadequate.[14] And so, at the very least, it is easy to agree that 'new forms of resolving and preventing disputes will move us even further away from the idea that the legal system is at the centre of the dispute resolution solar system.'[15]

This chapter addresses developments that have been taking place in the legal system, and the legal sector, as a whole, exploring their implications for access to justice as well as for speed and efficiency. In addition, it considers the changes in the legal sector and in legal education. This chapter's focus, then, is on the present and the future of law as an institution, a profession, and an ideal. In doing so, it tries to address the question posed by Hazel Genn: 'What can all of this technology do for the justice system?'[16] Genn, for her part, answers:

> There is probably no limit, but at the moment the following are already happening in our own jurisdiction and elsewhere:
>
> - Technology can help to reach out—communication/information;
> - It can speed up processes—e-filing, online procedures; document handling;
> - It can simplify processes for LiPs—by embedding procedural rules within online forms and processes. You don't need to know the rule if the system prompts you to do things and explains why;
> - It can facilitate the sharing of complex information instantaneously;
> - It can allow people to congregate without the need for physical presence;
> - It can facilitate online resolution;
> - Ultimately it could support or replace human decision-making through automated processes;
> - Finally, data bases of the subject matter, duration and outcome of disputes could help dispute prevention and early resolution.

This chapter will address all of those areas.[17] In terms of structure, it will explore the intersection of law and technology across four axes. First, from the perspective of legal institutions—predominantly the courts—which are undergoing a radical overhaul. Second, from the perspective of users, considering the potential for technology to enhance access to justice on the one hand and the risks it poses to open justice on the other. Third, from the perspective of the profession, outlining developments in law firms that change how lawyers do research, assess, and provide advice. And fourth, it will conclude with an introspective look at how technology can, and should, transform legal education in general, and clinical legal education in particular.

[14] Ethan Katsh and Orna Rabinovich-Einy, *Digital Justice* (OUP 2017) 44.

[15] Ibid 20. [16] Genn (n 4).

[17] It will not, however, engage with other, related issues, which are fascinating but are not immediately relevant to the intersection of law, technology and access to justice. These include, for example, the potential and risks of automated decision making, and the ethics of automated advice. See, eg James E. Cabral et al, 'Using Technology to Enhance Access to Justice' (2012) 26 Harvard Journal of Law and Technology 241, 302, 317–22.

4.1 The Future of Online Courts

In 2018, the Chief Executive of HMCTS did not mince words when describing the dire state of the existing court and tribunal system:[18]

- Labour-intensive, paper-based systems which create error, duplication, inefficiency and overstretch, and also drive over-reliance on physical presence even to administer and move cases forward.
- Many buildings are not fit for purpose.
- Arcane processes that are hard to administer and even harder to navigate; few modern, swift routes available even for simpler things.
- Resource and time allocation do not reflect the work being done.

It should be acknowledged that the wretched state of the justice system, outlined above only in bullet points, is the result of years of austerity, financial cuts, and neglect. Although we cannot expand on this context here, it is crucially important because, for many, a motivating factor for incorporating technology into the court and tribunal system is the need to 'do more with less' and to 'deliver justice in the age of austerity'.[19] While it is true that the motivations for reform need not determine how we assess them, recognizing these motivations may invite caution when considering other stated rationales, such as the enhancement of access to justice, as discussed below.

4.1.1 The Long Road towards Online Courts in the UK and Beyond

The focus on the physical foundations of a 'court' as a building was also evident in a report authored by the Lord Chancellor, the Lord Chief Justice, and the Senior President of Tribunals. The report provided a similarly bleak portrayal of the state of affairs in HMCTS and also indicated the intended direction of travel:

> We currently have over 400 court and tribunal buildings, many of them old, small, inefficient, yet expensive to maintain. In 2014–15, around half (48%) of courts and tribunals were used for less than half of the time. Many will be closed over the next four years to fund investment in fewer, more modern buildings that can better serve people's needs.[20]

To clarify: the intention underlying this statement was not simply to invest in more modern buildings that would host the same number of claimants, lawyers, and hearings. Instead,

[18] Susan Acland-Hood, 'Modernising the Courts and Tribunals Service: Future of Justice Conference' (14 May 2018). https://www.ucl.ac.uk/laws/sites/laws/files/ucl_foj_01_03_acland-hood.pdf

[19] Linda Mulcahy and Emma Rowden, *The Democratic Courthouse* (2020) 308–09.

Lord Thomas, *Reshaping Justice* (Speech to *Justice*, 3 March 2014) https://www.judiciary.gov.uk/wp-content/uploads/JCO/Documents/Speeches/lcj-speech-reshaping-justice.pdf

[20] Lord Chancellor, Lord Chief Justice and Senior President of Tribunals, *Transforming our Justice System* (Ministry of Justice 2016) 7. https://assets.publishing.service.gov.uk/government/uploads/system/uploads/attachment_data/file/553261/joint-vision-statement.pdf

as a number of reports during that same period made clear, technology was expected to be deployed in a way that would render these buildings redundant by moving disputes online. Accordingly, the Online Dispute Resolution Advisory Group recommended establishing a new internet-based court service, to be known as HM Online Court. Specifically, it recommended establishing an Online Dispute Resolution (ODR) process for civil disputes valued under £25,000.[21] A year later, the Civil Courts Structure Review,[22] chaired by Lord Briggs, made a similar proposal for an 'Online Solutions Court' for cases of comparable value. Both reports emphasized that, while important, the use of technology will not be limited to improving the existing system so it can operate in the same way (for example, by going paperless or conducting hearings via video conferencing). Instead, they asked to reimagine the way disputes are organized, processed, and resolved. As the Senior President of the Tribunals noted:

> To serve the needs of a 21st Century society, the justice system must be *digital by default* and design ... The creation of online justice cannot therefore simply be a matter of digitising what might be called the frontline processes. It must go further than that. It must properly embrace what is described as Online Dispute Resolution.[23]

Indeed, technology itself has provided inspiration, as we see from the fact that one of the central models referred to in the reports is the dispute resolution procedure conducted by eBay, which oversees 60 million disputes between buyers and sellers each year.[24] It was observed that if 'this were a small claims court, it would be the largest court in the world'.[25] And while it is not operated directly by public authorities, this form of dispute resolution carries legal force, through contractual mechanisms that are backed by courts and tribunals.

The mention of the eBay resolution system should not suggest that there are no other, more traditional, public, judicial systems that have already embraced technology. Indeed, that of England and Wales was credited as being among the first to do so: since 2006, claimants have been able to claim up to £100,000 via Money Claim Online. While impressive in that respect, 'technology' has a role only at the start of the process, whereas the remainder of the judicial proceedings continues in the traditional, familiar format (ie with a judge, in person, etc). In contrast, public justice systems in other countries have moved further and faster in developing end-to-end digitization.[26]

The first such online tribunal system is the Civil Resolution Tribunal (CRT), launched in 2015 in British Columbia, Canada, under the Civil Resolution Tribunal Act. The Netherlands

[21] Online Dispute Resolution Advisory Group, *Online Dispute Resolution for Low Value Civil Claims* (Civil Justice Council, February 2015) https://www.judiciary.uk/wp-content/uploads/2015/02/Online-Dispute-Resolution-Final-Web-Version1.pdf

[22] Lord Justice Briggs, *Civil Courts Structure Review: Final Report* (Judiciary of England and Wales, July 2016) https://www.judiciary.uk/wp-content/uploads/2016/07/civil-courts-structure-review-final-report-jul-16-final-1.pdf

[23] Sir Ernst Ryder, *The Modernisation of Access to Justice in Times of Austerity* (5th Annual Ryder Lecture 2016) 8.

[24] Online Dispute Resolution Advisory Group (n 21) [4.2].

[25] Katsh and Rabinovich-Einy (n 14) 4.

[26] Catrina Denvir and Amanda Darshini Selvarajah, 'Safeguarding Access to Justice in the Age of Online Courts' (2022) 85 Modern Law Review 25, 27.

and New South Wales, Australia, also have advanced online systems in place.[27] Shannon Salter, who led the CRT at the time, explained the working rationale for the online tribunal:

> In Canada—and these figures are the same in the US, in England and Australia—we know that, **for every 100 people who go down to a courthouse and file a civil claim, only two of those will go to trial**. But we have oriented our entire civil justice system in the common-law world around this idea of a day in court—that we know doesn't come 98 per cent of the time. And we know that about half of those 98 per cent of people don't settle their claim: they just give up because they run out of time and money and energy.
>
> We have tried to flip that model. We assume that you're not going to have your day in court: the equivalent, for us, is a day in front of a tribunal member. We assume that, with the right support and help, you can reach a consensual agreement. And we have built the tribunal around that notion.[28]

REFLECTION POINT

Pause and think about this quote. We highlighted the fact that only 2 per cent of people who file a claim actually end up going to trial. Think, then, about the extent to which you agree with Shannon Salter's observation that our system is oriented towards the court, and that many people just give up en route, lacking resources, time, or energy. To what extent does the way your clinic operates follow that paradigm, and to what extent does it offer an alternative to it?

In an effort to keep up, HMCTS announced in 2016 a £1bn court reform programme that is 'the most ambitious in the world' in terms of scope and pace.[29] Within two years, that figure rose to £1.3bn, but let's not pinch pennies. The programme was due to encompass 44 projects across five streams: crime; civil and family courts and tribunals; property; and two cross-cutting streams (eg video conferencing). Unsurprisingly, the move to online proceedings was accelerated when lockdowns were imposed in response to the Covid-19 outbreak. Pilots and expansions were rolled out rapidly across civil, family, and criminal courts and tribunals.[30] The effect of this expansion on access to justice will be discussed in the next section.

To a large extent, the recommendations relied on the Canadian model, proposing three 'tiers' in handling the dispute. The first tier—sometimes referred to as 'triage'—guides the user through a series of questions to explore the issue. In the CRT, this is referred to as the 'Solution Explorer'. The process is anonymous, and includes questions such as: Do

[27] JUSTICE, *Delivering Justice in an Age of Austerity* (2015) 35–37.

[28] Joshua Rozenberg, '*The Online Court: Will IT Work*,' from The Legal Education Foundation. https://long-reads.thelegaleducationfoundation.org/the-worlds-first-online-court/ [emphasis added].

[29] Acland-Hood (n 18); Transforming our Justice System (n 20).

[30] Justice Committee, *Coronavirus (COVID-19): The Impact on Courts* (HC 519, 30 July 2020) 16.

you have an issue with something you sold or bought? When did the purchase take place? What was the cost of the item? And so forth. This is an interesting phase because it is not, as one of the reports suggests, designed exactly as 'dispute avoidance'.[31] Rather, and here we can refer to our discussion of access to justice in Chapter 2, it can help users understand if their grievance has a legal basis at all, if it is not limited by procedural requirements (eg statute of limitations), and what type of remedies the user can expect. This stage can be designed, or informed, by charities, law firms, and/or academics in the field. In his report, Lord Justice Briggs gives an example:

> Suppose that A has a dispute with her builder B relating to works carried out at her house. After entering the common Court Service Portal and selecting the OC as the appropriate court (if necessary with online guidance), and after providing her name and contact details, A would be asked to identify the object of her grievance by reference to a series of tick boxes which might include her bank, her holiday company, her next door neighbour and her builder. Having ticked 'Builder' the software would present new questions designed to elicit the essential nature of the dispute, for example whether it was about the quality of the work, the amount charged or delays in completion. Ticking (or clicking) the appropriate box would reveal further successive pages, including a page requiring A to identify B and provide his (or if a company, its) contact details, to state whether the building works were covered by an agreement and, if in writing.[32]

The second tier—facilitation—involves trained mediators who help the parties in their negotiation. A similar method is employed by the Financial Ombudsman Service, which resolves 90 per cent of cases at this stage, leaving only a small minority to be considered by the Ombudsmen themselves.[33]

After this filtering process, only at the third tier are judges involved. And even here, the traditional model gives way to judges who work online. This means that the process is asynchronous: in other words, the parties and the judge do not need to be in the same room—even if a virtual room—at the same time. Instead, documents are sent electronically, one in reply to the other, until the judge is satisfied that they have the information required to deliver a decision, which is binding and enforceable.

Despite the laudable aims and ambitious plans, reality proved far more complicated than expected. The original four-year deadlines were repeatedly extended and although more than £1.1bn of the budget was spent, only 24 of the 44 projects have been completed at the time of writing. Moreover, HMCTS's approach was criticized by the House of Commons' Public Accounts Committee as

> detached from the needs of those who use the courts system. For example, court staff such as legal advisers, have had to deal with common platform technical and functionality issues in an already stressful court environment. It has not done enough to listen

[31] Online Dispute Resolution Advisory Group (n 21) [5.3].

[32] Lord Justice Briggs, 'Civil Courts Structure Review: Interim Report The Online Court' 77, [6.8]. December 2015 Judiciary of England and Wales.

[33] Online Dispute Resolution Advisory Group (n 21) [6.3].

and respond to users' concerns, leaving staff and courts to suffer the consequences. HMCTS's lack of data and research means that it has a limited understanding of whether reformed services are delivering the expected benefits, the total cost of its reforms to the taxpayer, or the impact on other services. Its research so far is insufficient and the evidence that does exist is concerning. The common platform has already placed an unacceptable additional burden on the courts, and HMCTS clearly has a lot to do to make it a success.[34]

4.1.2 **Online Courts: The Good and the Controversial**

So far, then, we have outlined the direction of travel in practice, and the obstacles en route. But let us pause here to take a broader theoretical and critical perspective. We can start with a deceptively simple question: 'What is a court?' Is it a building or a service?[35] And if it is, as most would probably answer, a service within a dedicated building, is the latter necessary for the former? Or could we imagine the service existing without the shelter of a building?[36]

At least in the current context, those asking this particular question do so as if it were rhetorical: *of course* the building is irrelevant and the service is the be-all and end-all. After all, one rarely hears a client declaring that their aims from a legal process include any reference to a room, furniture, and hallways. Our busy lives and increasingly outcome-oriented outlook also direct us towards a preference for a streamlined process, eliminating commuting, waiting times, and costs. So why *wouldn't* we opt to replace the current system with one which involves simply clicking, uploading, and submitting documents, from the comfort of our home (or office) at a time that suits us?

This juxtaposition of the old and the new has merit, and truth, to it.[37] However, it also flattens the user's experience of the existing process, much of which is rooted in the courtroom and is valuable.

First, there is the non-quantifiable, and perhaps even non-observable to the naked eye, 'feel' of the courtroom, and the implications of that feeling. In other words, we need to tackle the question of 'the court as a service or a building' head on. It appears that the rhetorical tone in which that question was presented above is unjustified, and somewhat facetious. Court proceedings are processes that can have very serious consequences for the participants. For this reason, courtrooms were built in a manner which emulates places of worship: high ceilings, grand foyers, an elevated 'bench' for judges. Similarly, judges often wear robes, like priests, and are referred to in a manner that is highly formal and respectful.

[34] Public Accounts Committee, *Progress on the Courts and Tribunals Reform Programme* (HC 1002, House of Commons Committee on Public Accounts 2023) 3.

[35] Civil Justice Council, *Online Dispute Resolution for Low Value Civil Claims* (2015) 5. https://www.judiciary.uk/wp-content/uploads/2015/02/Online-Dispute-Resolution-Final-Web-Version1.pdf

[36] Lord Chancellor, Lord Chief Justice and Senior President of Tribunals, *Transforming Our Justice System* (Ministry of Justice 2016) 6. https://assets.publishing.service.gov.uk/government/uploads/system/uploads/attachment_data/file/553261/joint-vision-statement.pdf

[37] See further, in the criminal context: M Rossner and D Tait, 'Presence and Participation in a Virtual Court' (2023) Criminology and Criminal Justice 135; Susan Bandes and Neal Feigenson, 'Virtual Trials: Necessity, Invention, and the Evolution of the Courtroom' (2020) 68 Buffalo Law Review 1275.

A word often used in this context is 'solemnity', and it is the same word that is used to describe what is missing in online hearing.[38] As Emma Rowden explains, courts 'operate simultaneously on a symbolic, a structural and an embodied level, and in combination they contribute to our collective notions of justice'.[39] Robert Ferguson observed that courtrooms aim to create 'an aura, a mystique of authenticity and legitimacy'.[40] Courthouses as public buildings, in accessible venues, have been viewed as symbols of inclusiveness, in which every litigant and witness is recognized 'as worthy of equal dignity and respect',[41] and where justice is not only done, but also seen to be done. By contrast, in the remote setting 'the importance of architecture and design is marginalised if not completely denied',[42] and there is a risk that 'the "majesty of the law" is also being depersonalized due to the informal nature of remote tribunal proceedings'.[43]

Now, one could argue that revisiting—or even completely abandoning—existing architectural ideals and structures of justice would be a positive move. First, many courthouses and courtrooms fall far below the ideal described above. Many are antiquated, overcrowded, and cold, offer poor acoustics, and are humiliating spaces for defendants.[44] Second, where courtrooms *do* create a sense of awe and respect, they also hold the 'potential to create insiders and outsiders; empowered and disempowered'.[45] Thus, some lay users of the courts, including clients in law clinics, may feel intimidated and stressed by the formal character of the proceedings, and the online courtroom may allow them to feel more relaxed.[46] For example, a Special Educational Needs and Disability (SEND) judge explained:

> We're supposed to be an informal tribunal, so the parties were coming in, especially parents, who were feeling more relaxed, they didn't have to find childcare for their child if they're home educated. We could hear from the child or young person if they wanted to . . . Because we wouldn't see them in court generally, we wouldn't want them to be in court, we don't want them to hear what can seem quite negative, for a whole day . . . So it's nice that they can come in, come out, come say hello to us, give us their views, tell us something.[47]

While these principled observations should not be neglected, it has also been noted that online proceedings can be detrimental to claimants and defendants who are unaware of the

[38] Vanessa Long, 'Online Courts: Re-Assessing Inequality in the "Remote" Courtroom' (2021) 11 Excursions 77, 84, 93.

[39] Emma Rowden, 'Virtual Courts and Putting "Summary" back into "Summary Justice": Merely Brief, or Unjust?' in J Simon, N Temple, and R Tobe (eds), *Architecture and Justice* (Routledge 2013) 101, 105.

[40] Cited in Susan Bandes and Neal Feigenson, 'Virtual Trials: Necessity, Invention and the Evolution of the Courtroom' (2020) 68 Buffalo Law Review 1275, 1281.

[41] Bandes and Feigenson (n 37) 1312.

[42] Linda Mulcahy, 'The Unbearable Lightness of Being? Shifts Towards the Virtual Trial' (2008) 35 Journal of Law and Society 464, 480.

[43] Naomi Creutzfeldt et al, *Access to Justice, Digitalization and Vulnerability* (Routledge 2024) 161.

[44] Bandes and Feigenson (n 37) 1312; Linda Mulcahy and Emma Rowden, *The Democratic Courthouse* (2020) 15.

[45] Linda Mulcahy, *Legal Architecture: Justice, Due Process and the Place of Law* (Routledge 2011) 1.

[46] Bandes and Feigenson (n 37) 1313.

[47] Cited in Creutzfeldt et al (n 43) 154.

implications and fail to treat them with the necessary seriousness. Vanessa Long observed in her fieldwork that

> These include speaking out of turn, having their hoods up, visibly smoking on camera and slumping in their chairs. One example included a male defendant appearing in an online hearing 'bare chested' and visibly drinking a takeaway coffee, prompting his representative to have to tell him to put a top on.[48]

Others have offered similar examples, of 'public users joining the hearing from locations that were not considered appropriate, such as parks, walking down a street, driving up a motorway, in a public phone box and on a plane'.[49] Discussing another study, which focused on the use of video technology in US deportation cases, Hazel Genn concludes that 'Litigants separated from the traditional courtroom setting simply disengaged from the entire process'.[50]

In general, many users 'were confused and uncertain about what exactly it was that they were taking part in'.[51] Reviewing extensive evidence on this issue, Judith Townend and Lucy Welsh note that users of online courts often 'had not understood they were formally appearing in a court at all' and that 'Participants in these studies felt that such incidents undermined the solemnity, disciplining, and deterrent effect of experiencing criminal proceedings, therefore undermining some of the functions of the criminal process'.[52] Clearly, such behaviour risked defendants in online criminal cases being 'viewed unfavourably by the court'.[53]

In the civil arena, a Property Chamber barrister noted that

> the unrepresented parties didn't take it quite as seriously when it was online and it's a slightly weird thing to say because often you're fighting about their home and money and such like, but what I mean by that is, when you're all in the room there's that slightly greater sense of decorum because you can pick up on the body language.[54]

And from a user's perspective, Tiana Clark wrote of her experience of getting her divorce over Zoom:

> My virtual divorce felt dreamlike—weeks later, I sometimes wonder whether it really happened. So much of dreaming feels like you're trying to grab the hem of something that dissipates right in front of you. Videoconferencing has the same effect, inducing an exhausting sense of placelessness. I wanted the courtroom iconography (eagles, maybe?), a backdrop of dark mahogany. I wanted the formalities, the trappings. Instead, I had my lawyer's voice hovering in my speakers—her camera wasn't working . . . Perhaps

[48] Long (n 38) 92.

[49] Janet Clark, *HMCTS Evaluation* of *Remote Hearing during the Covid-19 Pandemic: Research Report* (HMCTS 2021) 29. https://www.gov.uk/government/publications/hmcts-remote-hearing-evaluation

[50] Genn (n 4) 13.

[51] Rowden (n 39) 101, 103.

[52] Judith Townend and Lucy Welsh, *Observing Justice: Digital Transparency, Openness and Accountability in Criminal Courts* (Bristol University Press 2023).

[53] Clark (n 49) 29.

[54] Cited in Creutzfeldt et al (n 43) 164.

> I craved the physicality of a courtroom because I wanted something to lend gravity to the proceedings. Instead, my online divorce felt like I was watching a simulacrum of myself in a YouTube clip.[55]

So we can ask, to summarize this point: Is Ms Clark's experience representative? Have your clients mentioned either satisfaction or frustration with the role that technology now plays in legal proceedings? To what extent does 'solemnity' really matter? And even if it does matter, is that a price worth paying?

A second concern arises with the move to remote proceedings. Critics of the remote-working trend note that informal dynamics are lost when meetings are held online and confined to the designated time. For example, a report on the Video Enabled Justice Programme observed that 'informal "corridor conversations" between legal professionals and court staff in-between hearings and, as a consequence, communication and interaction between the parties involved in hearings, could become "disjointed"'.[56] Users of the Programme noted that the loss of non-verbal communication limited the practitioners' ability to pick up cues, such as the client wanting to speak with them, which made the process feel more 'detached' and 'impersonal'.[57] A Special Educational Needs (SEND) Adviser described her experience from an online tribunal hearing, in which a parent had an emotional reaction which the participants failed to pick up:

> the parent was asked a question that ended up upsetting them during this virtual hearing and the other participants on the hearing, including the adviser supporter who's sitting at another computer somewhere else in the country, didn't pick up on how upset they were because that sort of thing was, sort of, lost on the screen when we're these little windows ... And their advocate, their legal advocate, wasn't there in person so they weren't even able to pick up that that had happened. And that's a real difference where you would hope that if you were in the same room in a tribunal hearing situation that it would be obvious and it wouldn't have, you know, ended up going that kind of way.[58]

Legal representatives, for their part, reported that not being in the same room with their clients meant that 'it is much harder to take instructions from clients, harder to judge if a client is upset and harder to manage situations where the client is talking too much or behaving inappropriately'.[59] The format also had an undesirable effect on the ability to facilitate

[55] Tiana Clark, 'The Surreal Anticlimax of Getting Divorced over Videoconference' *Washington Post*. Copyright June 23 2020 *The Washington Post*. https://www.washingtonpost.com/outlook/2020/06/23/surreal-anticlimax-getting-divorced-over-videoconference/

[56] Nigel Fielding et al, *Video Enabled Justice Programme: University of Surrey Independent Evaluation* (2020) 94. https://www.sussex-pcc.gov.uk/our-priorities/access-to-justice/video-enabled-justice-vej/video-enabled-justice-programme-university-of-surrey-independent-evaluation/

[57] Ibid 64. See also examples in Vanessa Long, 'Online Courts: Re-Assessing Inequality in the "Remote" Courtroom' (2021) 11 Excursions 77, 90; also Michael Legg and Anthony Song, 'The Courts, the Remote Hearing the Pandemic: From Action to Reflection' 44 University of New South Wales Law Journal 126, 138–9.

[58] Cited in Cruetzfeldt et al (n 43) 167.

[59] Clark (n 49) 28–9.

communication between two parties to the proceedings. For example, it has been noted, within the criminal context, that

> Face-to-face contact helped to bolster professional working relationships. The building of trust and rapport, particularly between the prosecution and defence, is an important asset when working to resolve complex issues. Communication inside the courtroom involved an element of 'give and take' between the different parties . . . and reduced face-to-face contact made it difficult for prosecutors and advocates to engage in informal communication about sensitive matters relating to hearings e.g., around the plea.[60]

Third, despite the seemingly obvious practical benefits and cost-effectiveness of virtual hearings, there are also practical disadvantages. Experience to date suggests that tasks previously handled seamlessly, 'such as completing paperwork or case management', have become 'more challenging . . . as participants were unable to physically pass documentation one to another'.[61] Another important concern relates to the principle of transparent and open justice. The ability of members of the public, including the media, students, and others, to walk into most courtrooms and observe a session has been, traditionally, a proud hallmark of judicial systems. Experience during the Covid-19 lockdown suggests that access to virtual courts was 'patchy' and lacked sufficient planning or priority.[62] Moreover, and somewhat surprisingly, after asserting that transparency is one of the seven principles of justice, Richard Susskind dismisses its denial in the context of online courts, reasoning that as only one of seven principles, it is not significant enough to hinder progress.[63]

Arguably, a more constructive approach would be to take the educational and public values of transparency seriously, ensuring that the move to virtual courts would be accompanied by more, rather than less, transparency. This was the intention taken by the insertion of section 85A to the Courts Act 2003, which empowers the Lord Chancellor to publish regulations facilitating greater public access to courts, including virtual courts.[64] After all, virtual accessibility can be far more effective in terms of the number of people who can attend, the costs involved, and the practical obstacles of being present in a specific court at a specific time. Publicly advertising links to proceedings and maintaining robust systems to enable access would enhance transparency, turning it into an added benefit of reform rather than a seemingly unavoidable cost.

REFLECTION POINT

This section outlined arguments for and against the move from physical to online courts. Which arguments persuaded you most? Do you think that the current reservations about online courts are resolvable, and will be resolved, in the future, through technology, education, and experience? Do you think that some are inherently serious and cannot be resolved? Think about your experience with clients: have any had positive or negative experience with online courts? If not, how would you envisage them handling that change?

[60] Fielding (n 56) 95 [references omitted]. [61] Ibid 96. [62] Townend and Welsh (n 52).
[63] Susskind (n 3) 196–197. [64] See discussion in Townend and Welsh (n 52).

4.1.3 **The Final Frontier: The AI Judge?**

While some of the measures discussed as part of the reforms towards Online Courts may seem far-reaching, they still preserve one core aspect of the traditional approach: judicial decisions are made by human judges. However, an alternative approach is already emerging. We mentioned, above, the systems that companies such as eBay and Amazon already have in place, which are highly reliant on technology. What we did not mention was that those systems rely on algorithmic mediators to resolve vast numbers of disputes without human intervention.[65]

But what about the public judicial system? If AI continues to improve and efficiently replace the work of lawyers, would it also be able to replace judges? And if it could, *should* it? The advantages of this approach are relatively clear. Adrian Zuckerman explains:

> The use of AI in adjudication would have certain advantages over human judges: machines are able to avoid mistakes of reasoning and unconscious bias. Unconscious bias in adjudication is both widespread and virtually impossible to overcome. Machine processing power is superior; machines can scan and analyse vast amounts of data and therefore ensure greater compatibility with principle and precedent. Accordingly, AI adjudication would have far greater capacity to analyse and synthesise than humans. Machines would be capable of depths of reasoning which are beyond the reach of individuals or even teams of expert lawyers. AI would have instant access to the entire body of legal sources: legislation in all its varieties, databases of all decisions that have ever been made in all the courts and tribunals, and to the entire body of books and learned articles that have ever been written. Legal research that might take humans hundreds of hours could be done much more comprehensively and in minutes by machines, and at a fraction of the present cost. AI adjudication could reach levels of consistency unimaginable today.[66]

REFLECTION POINT

Interestingly, technology has essentially caught up with legal theory. In 1986, one of the great legal philosophers of the twentieth century, Ronald Dworkin, sought to ground his theory of 'Law as Integrity' by asking his readers to imagine a 'judge of superhuman intellectual power and patience'.[67] Such a judge—which Dworkin referred to as Hercules—will manage to unearth the deep structure of the law as a 'coherent set of principles about justice and fairness and procedural due process'[68] and apply those standards to the case before them.

[65] Melissa Perry, 'idecide: Administrative Decision-Making in The Digital World, Administrative Law' (2017) 91 Australian Law Journal 29, 48.

[66] Adrian Zuckerman, 'Artificial Intelligence in the Administration of Justice,' Andrew Higgins (ed), *The Civil Procedure Rules at 20* (OUP 2020) 291. Eugene Volokh, 'Chief Justice Robots' (2016) Duke Law Journal 1135.

[67] Ronald Dworkin, *Law's Empire* (Fontanta 1986, Hart 1999) 239.

[68] Ibid 243.

At the time, it was clear that no such judge exists, or even can exist. Indeed, one of the objections that Dworkin deals with is that Hercules is 'a myth'.[69] His response acknowledges, of course, that Hercules is more of an intellectual exercise, an ideal form of what the judge should aspire to, but is important in that sense.

Closing the circle now, we can ask: What if Hercules is no longer a myth? Wouldn't the advancement of the law's 'integrity', in both senses of the term (first, as an integration into a whole; second, as an institution that fosters trust and reliability) benefit from decisions that apply general principles to the current case in a manner that is consistent?

Moreover, should it not matter that this AI judge is not only consistent but incredibly *effective*, in two respects: first, of course, in the speed of decision-making; but second, in its ability to take into account the foreseeable risks and benefits of every decision on future consequences?[70]

As always, there are counterarguments. In a manner that chimes with the discussion concerning the move to online courts in general, removing the human interlocutor—who can express empathy and consider concerns beyond quantifiable data—may worry many people. In addition, it is not clear that algorithms are less prone to bias than humans. Indeed, there is concern that some algorithms already used in both the private and in the public sector have biases 'built in'.[71] As one early journalistic exposé declared: 'There's software used across the country to predict future criminals. And it's biased against blacks [sic]'.[72] Awareness of bias is crucial, as identifying the problem is necessary for resolving it, and one can only hope that future algorithms will prove more resistant to such flaws. However, it could also be that problems with reliance on algorithms occur in a manner that is not necessarily related to such flagrant bias. A notable example is Sarah Wysocki, a fifth-grade teacher highlighted in the book *Weapons of Math Destruction*,[73] who was dismissed based on a decision by a performance evaluation tool, IMPACT, used in Washington DC. The algorithm failed to account for the fact that other teachers inflated their grades, which made Wysocki's 'performance' appear low by comparison. The high regard in which she was held was not enough to challenge her dismissal.

When considering the prospect of an AI judge, observers increasingly look to China for a glimpse of the future. There, investment in the field has eclipsed any other country in the world. In 2019, a court in Hangzhou, south of Shanghai, began using AI to resolve financial disputes, traffic accidents, and even criminal cases. The system analyses more than 100 million available cases, thus putatively ensuring consistency across similar cases. However, ethical issues have been raised, partly because corporate giants such as Alibaba have been involved in the development of the tool.[74]

69 Ibid 264–5. 70 According to Brownsword (n 6), these criteria for law underpin Law 2.0.

71 Sandra Mayson, 'Bias in, Bias Out' (2019) 128 Yale Law Journal 2218.

72 Julia Angwin et al, 'Machine Bias' ProPublica (23 May 2016) https://www.propublica.org/article/machine-bias-risk-assessments-in-criminal-sentencing

73 Cathy O'Neil, *Weapons of Math Destruction* (Penguin 2017).

74 Alina Zhabina, 'How China's AI is automating the legal system' DW (20 January 2023) https://www.dw.com/en/how-chinas-ai-is-automating-the-legal-system/a-64465988

TAKING STOCK

This section identified the plans for the technological reforms in courts in England and Wales and the UK tribunal system, and their implementation in other jurisdictions. It also raised arguments for and against the move towards online, and virtual, methods of dispute resolution.

For:

1. Savings on public infrastructure, including buildings
2. More accessible to many clients with respect to time and resources
3. Less intimidating than the public courtroom
4. Geared more towards conciliation, less adversarial process.

Against:

1. Risk that users will not understand the process and take it seriously
2. Undermining the opportunity to build and act on relations during the process
3. Potential for algorithmic bias.

4.2 Technology and Access to Justice

Almost every proposal or report for court reform pledges that 'access to justice must be improved and not reduced',[75] and that 'its aim [that is: *the* aim of Online Dispute Resolution] is to broaden access to justice'.[76] In other words, while cost saving and ease of use are acknowledged, the broader implications of technological transformation for access to justice are central. One could argue that such reforms should be judged primarily by their impact on access to justice. But how can the impact of institutional reform on such a notoriously nebulous concept—which has both normative and legal foundations—be measured? Chapter 2 of this book provides helpful background for assessing the agendas set out in these proposals and reforms. Understandably, this agenda often interprets 'access to justice' as synonymous with 'access to *courts*'. As we saw in Chapter 2, this is a distinctly narrow understanding of the concept. For example, access to justice should include improving public understanding of the law through public legal education. It should also address forms of injustice not yet recognized by the law, such as discrimination on grounds not covered by existing protected characteristics, structural injustices that do not trigger legal action, or substantive legal rights blocked by procedural obstacles, such as strict time limits or evidential requirements.

In contrast, the technical focus on online courts in the reports discussed earlier sometimes frames access to justice in ways that seem like an unnatural extension of the concept.

[75] For example: Senior President of Tribunals, *The Modernisation of Tribunals 2018: A Report by the Senior President of Tribunals* (2018) 10 https://www.judiciary.uk/wp-content/uploads/2019/01/SupplementarySPT-report-Dec-2018_final.pdf

[76] Online Dispute Resolution Advisory Group (n 21), Foreword from the Rt Hon Lord Dyson.

This occurs, for example, when 'containment'—reducing the number of cases before courts and increasing plea bargains—is presented as a reason to advance online courts under the banner of access to justice.[77] In fact, the fact that plea bargaining (which, of course, diverts a case away from the court) is so pervasive in the US criminal justice system, for example, is often seen as a *problem* of access to justice, rather than evidence of its advancement. This critique is perhaps best captured by the Law Society's evidence, which stated that current reforms 'provided access to process, rather than access to justice'.[78]

So, the first question is: What 'access to justice' problems can the incorporation of technology actually address?

4.2.1 How Technology Could Promote Access to Justice

First, technology can enhance legal knowledge by making information more easily accessible, thereby improving public legal education. Indeed, technology has played this role in relation to law for decades.[79] At a basic level, this could apply to one's own case. For example, victims of violent and sexual crimes seeking court hearing transcripts were recently quoted sums of up to £7,500.[80] Enter technology: a barrister set up a social enterprise aiming to cut these costs by half—and in some cases by up to 90 per cent—using voice recognition software.[81] As a result, individuals can now search online for similar cases and basic advice.

In practice, however, matters are not always so straightforward. As we noted in Chapter 2, knowing whether a 'grievance' is actionable is a necessary precondition for bringing a claim, making lack of legal knowledge a significant obstacle to justice.[82] And yet, 'most justiciable issues that arise in society never get as far as consultation with a lawyer, let alone reach the courts'.[83] We discussed the barriers to 'naming', 'blaming', and 'claiming'.[84] These could be addressed without requiring access to courts, or even to a lawyer.[85] Apps, for example, can guide users through their situation, asking questions such as: Were you dismissed? Did you have an employment contract? When were you hired? Do you believe you suffered discrimination? In doing so, they help clarify the client's legal position.

Second, technological tools already assist, and could further assist, people in exercising legal powers. For example, you don't have to make a will, but the law gives you the *power* to

[77] Online Dispute Resolution Advisory Group (n 21), [5.2]–[5.7].

[78] Public Accounts Committee (n 34) 13.

[79] Ayelet Sela, 'Streamlining Justice: How Online Courts Can Resolve the Challenges of Pro Se Litigation' (2016) 26 Cornell Journal of Law and Public Policy 331, 333.

[80] Sima Kotecha, 'Court Transcripts are Exploitative – Victims' BBC (24 October 2023) https://www.bbc.co.uk/news/uk-67123893

[81] Michael Cross, 'New Tech to "halve" transcripts costs' Law Gazette (1 April 2019) https://www.lawgazette.co.uk/news/new-tech-to-halve-transcript-costs/5069820.article

[82] See further: Pascoe Pleasence, Nigel Balmer, and Catrina Denvir, 'Wrong about Rights: Public Knowledge of Key Areas of Consumer, Housing and Employment Law in England and Wales' (2017) 80 Modern Law Review 836.

[83] Amy Schmitz, 'Measuring Access to Justice in the Rush to Digitize' (2020) 88 Fordham Law Review 2381, 2393.

[84] William Felstiner, Richard Abel, and Austin Sarat, 'The Emergence and Transformation of Disputes: Naming, Blaming, Claiming . . . ' (1980) 15 Law & Society Review 631.

[85] Drew Shimshaw, 'Access to AI Justice: Avoiding an Inequitable Two Tiered System of Legal Services' (2022) Yale Journal of Law and Technology 150, 165.

do so. However, such a document will be valid, and thus granted legal force, only if it satisfies certain conditions.[86] This could include the requirement for a signature or witnesses. Software can draft the will, prevent finalization if formal conditions aren't met, and alert users to potential issues.

Third, current court operations themselves pose access to justice problems that technology could help address. Hazel Genn notes that

> The access to justice problem which online processes are said to address is that the courts are too slow, expensive, and complicated for people to use without help, and that for most people help is either unaffordable or unavailable ... A relatively swift, cheap, fair, online service, accessed from the comfort of home or even on a hand-held device which engages both parties in the process and incorporates the possibility of ODR should be attractive for certain cases. Literate, educated individuals and small businesses, who cannot afford lawyers, will be likely to benefit. Those who previously might have paid for legal advice may feel that that is no longer necessary and can navigate a new system without advice.[87]

The transition to ODR allows litigants to take their time, refine their submission, and eventually file their claim from their kitchen table, without the hassle of losing a day's work, finding parking, or arranging childcare—obstacles long recognized as barriers towards accessing justice.[88] This is not merely theoretical. An employee of the Independent Provider of Special Education Advice (IPSEA) described their experience with online SEND hearings:

> a remote hearing was the only viable option for this family because the child ... had complex needs including complex health needs that meant that arranging care for them if they were to physically have to travel to a tribunal venue would have been incredibly difficult. They had nursing support and there were risks that ... realistically ... [s]he couldn't envisage how it could have been done face-to-face in person.[89]

Beyond these practicalities, observers of court proceedings have long documented the imbalance of power between parties, particularly when one party is not represented. Litigants in person often 'fail to conform to the expected formal strictures'[90] of court proceedings, and fall into narratives that are viewed as 'an uneconomic, rambling mode of communication, and as an inappropriate means for raising or demonstrating cognizable legal claims on which legal relief may be given'.[91] As a result, the structural dynamics of the traditional process have been argued to effectively 'silence' litigants in person.[92] If technology restricts the role of lawyers to the background (for example, assisting drafting submissions), and replaces court theatrics with online practicalities, these dynamics are greatly diminished. This would suggest that the incorporation of technology improves access to justice not merely

[86] Roger Brownsword, *Rethinking Law, Regulation and Technology* (Elgar 2022) 110. [87] Genn (n 4).
[88] Katsch and Rabinovich-Einy (n 14) 41–42. [89] Cited in Cruetzfeldt et al (n 43) 167.
[90] Sela (n 48) 338.
[91] Paris Baldacci, 'Assuring Access to Justice: The Role of the Judge in Assisting Pro Se Litigants in Litigating Their Cases in New York City's Housing Court' (2006) 3 Cardozo Public Law, Policy and Ethics Journal 659, 664.
[92] Sela (n 79) 359.

when people can 'access the online system' but also when they 'participate effectively and feel they have done so, and achieve substantively just outcomes'.[93] Similarly, strong evidence suggests that vulnerable witnesses, such as victims in criminal trials, children, or those who have been intimidated, 'were significantly less unhappy, more audible and more forthcoming, or less likely to cry, report fear or describe the trial as unfair' when taking part in online processes.[94]

4.2.2 How Technology Could Create Barriers to Access to Justice

While technology has the potential to enhance access to justice, it will not automatically do so. Indeed, technology may limit access to justice, at least in some cases and for some groups.[95] Despite their clear promise and potential, 'increased reliance on and legitimization of these technologies could increase inequities—widening, rather than closing, the justice gap'.[96]

When assessing this risk, a key question concerns the motivation for reforms: are they genuinely driven by admirable aims or, as some commentators suggest, are they 'primarily driven by the 40% Ministry of Justice budget reduction, rather than any genuine desire to improve access to justice or the service provided'?[97] This view has led some to conclude that

> Reform both implemented and proposed is having a *negative impact on access to justice in all jurisdictions*. It will not improve or even maintain access to justice but will continue a worrying trend over the last six years that has resulted in a two-tier justice system; one for the rich and one for the poor.[98]

While reflecting on the 'true' motivations behind the reforms is important, it is difficult to assess them with certainty. Instead, it may be more useful to focus on objective realities: what new barriers are created by the incorporation of technology for access to justice?

The first, and most obvious, concern refers to the digital divide. Reliance on technology to enhance access to justice assumes that everyone has access to it. But what do we mean by 'access to technology'? It often conflates two distinct issues: physical (ideally high-speed) internet access and, separately, digital skills. Let us address them in turn.

Recent figures suggest that the proportion of those excluded from internet access ranges from 6 per cent to 10 per cent.[99] This could be a concerningly high figure for some or an acceptable price to pay, and less of an issue, for others. The latter tend to suggest that any assessment of these figures is necessarily a snapshot, quickly rendered outdated by rapid change.[100] For example, more than 98 per cent of young adults are internet users, and by the time ODR is fully rolled out to replace existing structures, similar levels of use may be seen across the wider population.[101] Moreover, the physical–digital divide is being addressed by increasing connectivity, particularly in rural areas. While it is possible that residents in these

[93] Ibid 14. [94] Legg and Song (n 57) 131.
[95] Denvir and Selvarajah (n 26) 28. [96] Shimshaw (n 85) 170.
[97] Public and Commercial Services Union, 'Written Evidence from Public and Commercial Services Union (CTS0010)' (House of Commons 2019) [5].
[98] Ibid [13] (emphasis added). [99] Denvir and Selvarajah (n 26) 45.
[100] Susskind (n 3) 215–19. [101] Denvir and Selvarajah (n 26) 45.

areas bear the brunt of the digital divide, it should be acknowledged that they already face significant travel times and costs, alongside difficulties in accessing legal aid offices due to staff shortages in those areas.[102] For those individuals, therefore, technology 'helps mitigate large geographical distances'.[103] Moreover, it is important to note that the asynchronous nature of the process reduces the reliance on high-speed and highly reliable access. In other words, if users are expected to submit information and forms, rather than participate in online meetings and hearings, this could take place over standard (not high-speed) bandwidth and at times convenient for the user.

However, breaking down these headlines reveals a more complex, and troubling, picture. A survey of more than 10,000 people revealed that close to 15 per cent of those between the ages of 65 and 74 are predicted to lack access to the internet, and the figure increases to 26.5 per cent for those over 75.[104] The same survey also found significant differences based on income: among those earning over £60,000, only 3.8 per cent are predicted to lack access, compared with 14.7 per cent for those earning less than £15,000. Finally, those without formal educational qualifications are twice as likely to lack internet access as those with qualifications.[105] This would mean that the poor and the elderly are much more likely to suffer from a lack of digital access (to justice).

Matters become even more complicated when we move from quantity to quality. What we mean by this is that your client may have access to the internet, and be very happy to shop, post on social media, and view videos on their smartphone; but how useful is a smartphone when navigating thousands of pages in a complex legal bundle? This is an issue of access to justice in a straightforward matter, and the challenge becomes more serious when overlaid with issues surrounding traditional legal representation, as this quote, from a Property Chamber barrister, makes clear:

> It is plainly much much harder for unrepresented parties to manage online cases. I did a significant proportion of my cases where I was against someone who didn't have a lawyer and they'd be doing it on their phone and you can just imagine the difficulty of trying to manage even a modest bundle of a couple of hundred pages on your phone, but if we get into bundles of, I've got one down here that runs to 20,000 pages, doing that on your phone is absurd. That's unusual but not completely out of kilter for what this tribunal does and the difference between the represented parties and the unrepresented parties there is enormous. It's relatively easy for me to buy a second screen so I can have one for the bundle and one for the thing, it's relatively easy for me to just buy a headset. The divide between represented and unrepresented parties got much much greater.[106]

Finally, it is important to note that, while likely to improve over time, the courts' current physical infrastructure is far from ideal. A report by the Magistrates Association highlighted

[102] James Cabral et al, 'Using Technology to Enhance Access to Justice' (2012) 26 Harvard Journal of Law and Technology 241, 261.
[103] Legg and Song (n 57) 132. [104] Denvir and Selvarajah (n 26) 45.
[105] Id 47. [106] Cited in Creutzfeldt et al (n 43) 164.

poor infrastructure that created 'pervasive'[107] technical barriers to 'communication, participation and the quality of justice'.[108]

Turning to the digital skills divide, we find that while 99 per cent of the population were online in 2022 (up from 89 per cent in 2016), 14 million people (27 per cent) still have the lowest digital capability. This means that many people are online and may access news and videos but still struggle to manage online services, leaving them 'at risk of being left behind'.[109] As with internet access, it is unsurprising that digital skills are unevenly distributed and align with identifiable characteristics. Indeed, age continues to be the largest correlating factor, with those aged 18–24 three times as likely to have basic foundational skills compared to those aged 75+ (94 per cent versus 31 per cent).[110] Similarly, an inverse correlation was found with respect to income: those earning under £15,000 are three times less likely to have basic digital skills than those earning over £60,000.[111]

With this in mind, a report by the Legal Education Foundation recommended assessing the impact of proposed reforms on specific groups. As is shown in Table 4.1 below, it took a socio-legal and critical approach extending beyond groups protected under the Equality Act to include characteristics identified in court practice directions as linked to vulnerability, as well as those normatively associated with digital exclusion.[112]

While the table below is informative, two notable omissions stand out. First, as a category, the straightforward issue of 'digital (il)literacy'—it does not reflect the importance of digital illiteracy or the lack of necessary skills. Second, as a legal measure, the European Convention on Human Rights, which remains relevant to UK jurisprudence. Interestingly, both the category and the measure featured in *Bishop*, a 2013 Tax Tribunal case concerning the legality of requiring tax returns to be filed via HMRC's online system. The Tribunal held that it

> was not convinced that under the Convention it would be lawful in all cases to discriminate against a person on the grounds, say, that they were illiterate (ie unable to read and write). And if illiteracy was a protected status, then I could see no reason why computer illiteracy would not be a protected status.[113]

Concerns about digital exclusion could be mitigated by insisting on 'channel plurality'[114] or, in simple terms, with assurances, given by senior officials and judges, that 'no one unable to engage digitally with the court and tribunal system will have to do so'.[115] And yet it

[107] Magistrates Association, *Magistrates Courts and Covid-19* (2022) 17. [108] Townend and Welsh (n 52).

[109] Lloyds Bank, *2022 Consumer Digital Index: The UK's Largest Study of Digital and Financial Lives* (2022) 9. https://www.ipsos.com/sites/default/files/ct/publication/documents/2022-11/221103-lloyds-consumer-digital-index-2022-report.pdf

[110] Id 40. [111] Denvir and Selvarajah (n 26) 51.

[112] Natalie Byrom, *Digital Justice: HMCTS Data Strategy and Delivering Access to Justice: Report and Recommendations* (The Legal Education Foundation 2019) 5.

[113] *L H Bishop Electric Co Ltd A F Sheldon (t/a Aztec Distributors) v Revenue & Customs* (2013) UKFTT 522 (TC) (unpublished).

[114] Denvir and Selvarajah (n 26). [115] Justice Committee (n 30) 20.

Table 4.1 Data required to measure vulnerability

#	Individual attributes to be captured	Data in practice directions used to identify vulnerability?	Data related to digital exclusion?	Data needed to monitor duties under the Equality Act 2010?
1	Age	✓	✓	X
2	Disability[11]	✓	✓	✓
3	Employment status/income	✓	✓	X
4	English as a foreign language	✓	X	X
5	Gender reassignment	X	X	✓
6	Highest level of education (proxy for literacy)	✓	✓	X
7	Postcode (permanent address, to identify whether in a care home, homeless, in an area of low internet coverage, etc)	✓	✓	X
8	Pregnancy and maternity	X	X	✓
9	Race	X	X	✓
10	Religion or belief	X	X	✓
11	Sex	X	X	✓
12	Sexual orientation	X	X	✓
13	Fear or distress connected with the case, eg domestic violence/abuse, in detention, survivor of trafficking/trauma	✓	X	X

appears that, as reliance on technology has become much more prevalent since *Bishop*, the bar for a justification to opt out of the online procedures is also raised. Tellingly, the current mindset has been captured via the paradox according to which such requests to opt out of remote participation must be submitted via email or the court's e-filing system.[116] Needless to say, this is hardly feasible if the very reason for the request is a lack of access to technology.

[116] Denvir and Selvarajah (n 26) 36–7, 54–6.

REFLECTION POINT

Consider one characteristic that is protected under the Equality Act 2010 (for example: disability) and one characteristic that is not (for example: limited English proficiency). How, and to what extent, do you think that technology could address barriers to access that are associated with these characteristics?

Turning to the second concern, it is important to note that current online court models do not aim to replicate the physical experience in virtual form through, for example, remote participation. Instead, much of the deliberation and determination of the outcome will be based on the submission of documents, in an asynchronous fashion (ie first one party submits, then another responds, and so on). The immediate casualty will be, of course, the culturally celebrated moment of a party's 'day in court'. That 'day' is now deprived: the opportunity to accuse, or to face the accuser, or to look the (lawyer of the) big, bad corporation in the eye is gone. But beyond the Hollywood-driven myth of this moment, how many people truly want it? How many would prefer not to lose a day's work to sit in a grey building simply to give testimony that could just as easily have been drafted and submitted on paper? It is clear that the myth is a reality for some claimants (in this case, from the Brighton Housing Trust) who said that remote hearings conducted during the pandemic 'robbed [them] of their day in court. There might never be a feeling that procedures were conducted fairly and openly.'[117] If prevalent, then it is a crucial concern. But *is* it prevalent? This is not a rhetorical question but a fundamental one, the answer to which is unknown. If this 'day in court' is important, then it is important to note that it will get increasingly withdrawn.

A third, closely related but more tangible, concern arises here. What happens if two claimants with identical cases appear before a tribunal, but one has their case decided solely on written submissions while the other has an oral hearing? If you're thinking 'I guess we'll never know', then you'd be wrong. Cheryl Thomas and Hazel Genn designed a study to test this very question.[118] They drafted a simulated case concerning Disability Living Allowance (DLA)—a social security benefit—and involved 66 panels with 198 members across three regions of the UK. Some of the panels decided the case only by paper; others engaged with paper submissions and an oral hearing. The results? 60 per cent of the claimants who had an oral hearing had their claim allowed, compared to 24 per cent who had a 'paper only' case. Moreover, the study suggested that the disparity was partly explained by the fact that claimants were rated more favourably when they were seen and heard in person. In a real-life, criminal context, studies have found that virtual trials have been linked to higher rates of

[117] Natalie Byrom, Sarah Beardon, and Abby Kendrick, 'The Impact of Covid-19 Measures on the Civil Justice System' (Research Resport, Civil Justice Council, 202) 62 [6.6].

[118] Cheryl Thomas and Hazel Genn, *Understanding Tribunal Decision-Making: A Foundational Study* (Nuffield Foundation 2013) https://www.nuffieldfoundation.org/sites/default/files/files/NUFJ0000_Tribunal)decision_making_27_03_14.pdf

custodial sentences and more costly bail bonds.[119] The explanations are attributed to the lack of opportunity to build trust and rapport between prosecution and defence, which we noted above, and to limited ability to engage with the defendants and their families.

Conversely, another study suggests the opposite effect.[120] Recognizing the longstanding, and well-documented, judicial bias and its effect on protected groups, the study finds that 'the shift from traditional in-person judicial proceedings to online . . . proceedings *reduces* measured age- and race-based disparities in litigation outcomes'.[121] In other words, while the group identity (race, sex, age, disability, etc) of the parties plays a significant role in judges' decision-making in traditional proceedings, online proceedings put in place, quite inadvertently, 'debiasing' mechanisms. They do so in several ways. First, as mentioned, by reducing reliance on oral testimony, they remove the face-to-face element and 'effectively *shield* judges'.[122] Second, by limiting judicial discretion over proceedings, the software inherently becomes more neutral and less prone to bias.

So where does all of this leave us regarding the implications of incorporating more technology into access to justice? If you're feeling somewhat confused, you're not alone. The aforementioned report by the Public Accounts Committee expressed concern that HMCTS 'does not yet fully understand how reforms are impacting court users, victims, or the public's access to justice'.[123] Indeed, much remains to be studied about how technology affects access to justice. First, of course, 'technology' covers a broad and expanding range, from video conferencing and document serving to full dispute resolution processes. Second, as this section suggested, reforms may affect different vulnerable groups—such as those defined by age, disability, or language skills—in different ways. Third, technology may have varying effects on different types depending on the type of case, whether debt, family, employment, or criminal.

REFLECTION POINT

In their book *Digital Justice*, Ethan Katsh and Orna Rabinovich-Einy ask and suggest:

> Will parties who participate in these processes feel that they have received their 'day in court' and have been 'heard'? Will users perceive these processes as fair? Will judges sustain their neutrality and authority, and will courts, relying on algorithms, maintain their legitimacy? . . . Indeed, there is promise for transforming our very understanding of the meaning of *justice*. (pp 162–3)

How would you feel about having your own case handled in such new conditions? How would you think you would feel about handling a client's case?

[119] Cited in Legg and Song (n 57) 143–144.

[120] Avital Mentovich, JJ Prescott, and Orna Rabinovich-Einy, 'Are Litigation Outcome Disparities Inevitable? Courts, Technology, and the Future of Impartiality' (2020) 71 Alabama Law Review 893.

[121] Id 898 (emphasis added). [122] Id 925. [123] Public Accounts Committee (n 34) 6, 12–13.

4.2.3 **The Final Frontier: The AI Lawyer?**

We've made it this far without mentioning ChatGPT (or Microsoft Copilot)! These tools are collectively known as Large Language Models (confusingly, for law students: LLMs) as they process, summarize, and 'understand' vast datasets to predict new content.

Well, it seems that we can no longer ignore these LLM 'assistants', in this chapter as in the world at large. They are likely to become, for better or worse, one of the most significant disruptors within legal proceedings, used by the public at large, by lawyers, and by students (among other things, in legal clinics). We will discuss developments in the legal sector as part of the next section, so LLMs sit nicely here, bridging the discussion of access to justice and the legal profession.

First, with respect to access to justice: David Freeman Engstrom, an authority on legal tech and the future of civil justice (indeed, that's the title of his recent book[124]), didn't think, until recently, that AI 'was powerful enough to move the dial on access to justice'.[125] But ChatGPT was, for him, a 'lightning-bolt moment'. Now, to an extent, a wide range of topic-specific apps worldwide—GetAid for legal aid, DoNotPay for parking fines, JusticeBot for landlord–tenant disputes, and LawBot for victims of crime—already use machine learning technologies. What makes ChatGPT and similar LLMs unique is their popularity, their familiarity, and the fact that they're not designed by subject-specific experts. So how can members of the public use these tools? As a first port of call, they serve to supply individuals with legal information so they can understand their situation. Second, individuals can ask the tool for advice, whether legal (would a person in my situation be classified as a worker under current tests?),[126] strategic (what are the pros and cons of settling?), tactical (how do I appeal this decision?), or technical (they can use the tool to draft their application).

So how optimistic or pessimistic should we be about these tools' ability to narrow the justice gap, even slightly? Given how rapidly this technology evolves, the answer at the time this is written may differ from the answer by the time you read this. That said, a relatively recent study from Montreal's Cyberjustice Laboratory compared and evaluated JusticeBot and ChatGPT's performance across these criteria:[127]

- Language Comprehension: Effective communication to a layperson.
- Accuracy: Correct, reliable, consistent with legal sources.
- Completeness: Provides necessary context and guidance.
- Trustworthiness: Does not provide misleading, wrong, or incomplete information.
- Harmless: Does not generate toxic or offensive statements, and does not favourite specific individuals or interests.
- User-friendly: Easy to use.

[124] David Freeman Engstrom (ed), *Legal Tech and the Future of Civil Justice* (Cambridge University Press 2023).

[125] Thomas Weber, 'Artificial Intelligence and the Law' 109 Stanford Lawyer (5 December 2023) https://law.stanford.edu/stanford-lawyer/articles/artificial-intelligence-and-the-law/

[126] The example discussed by Benjamin Alarie, 'The Path of the Law: Toward a Legal Singularity' (2016) 66 University of Toronto Law Journal 443, 445.

[127] Jinzhe Tan, Hannes Westermann, and Karim Beyekhlef, 'ChatGPT as an Artificial Lawyer' *Proceedings of the ICAIL 2023 Workshop on Artificial Intelligence for Access to Justice* (ICAIL 2023).

The study found that while ChatGPT performs well in language comprehension, it lacks in information accuracy, completeness, and trustworthiness, areas in which JusticeBot performs well. In contrast, JusticeBot is more limited in its ability to make sense of typos and confusion inserted by users, and therefore is more dependent on the user's ability to provide a good description of their situation. While those are clear limitations, the most serious shortcoming of ChatGPT is its accuracy. Indeed, there have already been well-documented examples of ChatGPT simply making up answers to legal questions, and grounding its response in sources (case law, report, legislation) that simply do not exist.

In 2023, a litigant in person, Ms Harber, challenged an HMRC penalty for 'failure to notify' a property disposal that incurred capital gains tax.[128] She produced a response that seemed to support her argument for a 'reasonable excuse', citing nine relevant authorities. However, the response was generated by AI and unfortunately none of the cited authorities were genuine. The Tribunal refers to a recent report from the Solicitors' Regulation Authority, which states:

> All computers can make mistakes. AI language models such as ChatGPT, however, can be more prone to this. That is because they work by anticipating the text that should follow the input they are given, but do not have a concept of 'reality'. The result is known as 'hallucination', where a system produces highly plausible but incorrect results.[129]

In another case, the High Court recently found that a solicitor and a barrister presented it with fake citations generated by AI.[130] It concluded that 'there was a lamentable failure to comply with the basic requirement to check the accuracy of material that is put before the court . . . It is the lawyer's professional responsibility to ensure the accuracy of such material.'[131] In the US, a court fined two lawyers and their firm for submitting a court filing which included 'hallucinated' authorities generated by ChatGPT.[132] The strong words of the judge in the US case are cited by the Tribunal in *Harber*, and are worth repeating here as a warning about the intersection of AI and professional ethics (see further in Chapter 7):

> Many harms flow from the submission of fake opinions. The opposing party wastes time and money in exposing the deception. The Court's time is taken from other important endeavors. The client may be deprived of arguments based on authentic judicial precedents. There is potential harm to the reputation of judges and courts whose names are falsely invoked as authors of the bogus opinions and to the reputation of a party attributed with fictional conduct. It promotes cynicism about the legal profession and the . . . judicial system. And a future litigant may be tempted to defy a judicial ruling by disingenuously claiming doubt about its authenticity.[133]

[128] *Harber v Commissioners for His Majesty's Revenue & Customs* [2023] UKFTT 01007 (TC).

[129] Solicitors' Regulation Authority, *Risk Outlook Report: The Use of Artificial Intelligence in the Legal Market* (20 November 2023) https://www.sra.org.uk/sra/research-publications/artificial-intelligence-legal-market/

[130] *Ayinde v London Bureau of Haringey* [2025] EWHC 1383 (Admin).

[131] Ibid [81].

[132] Dan Milmo, 'Two US Lawyers Fined for Submitting Fake Court Citations from ChatGPT' *The Guardian* (23 June 2023) https://www.theguardian.com/technology/2023/jun/23/two-us-lawyers-fined-submitting-fake-court-citations-chatgpt

[133] *Harber* (n 128) [23].

TAKING STOCK

This section provided a critical overview of the impact of technology on access to justice. You will have seen that there are strong suggestions that technology has increased access to justice, alongside arguments that it has made matters worse. It is important to note that both can happen at the same time. Many people can benefit from easier access, flexible methods of application and engagement, and guidance along the way. At the same time, those who relied on in-person support may find that their situation has worsened significantly. The fact that this latter group is 'vulnerable' in many respects makes the overarching assessment more challenging.

4.3 The Legal Sector: What Are Law Firms Doing?

Until now, we have focused on measures implemented in the public sector—primarily, the courts—and their implications for access to justice. We now turn to the private operators of the legal system: lawyers and law firms. As noted earlier, the vast majority of cases never reach a courtroom. Therefore, the implications of technology for the legal profession cannot be observed solely by reference to courts. Moreover, the private sector is far better resourced than the public sector, meaning that technology has been adopted there more swiftly and on a broader scale.

In 2020, Lord Hodge, then Deputy President of the UK Supreme Court, warned that the legal profession was 'on the brink of unprecedented upheaval'.[134] He noted that

> in Coca-Cola's legal department, AI tools have streamlined the drafting process for many contractual documents, reducing the time that lawyers had been spending on review from as much as 10 hours to about 15 minutes. Not only does this improve efficiency, observers say, it also results in more consistent agreements while freeing up the legal team for more strategic tasks. Similarly, JP Morgan Chase invested in its own proprietary AI platform—COIN (short for Contract Intelligence)—to review commercial loan agreements. The financial giant estimates that this automation has saved 360,000 hours of work by lawyers and loan officers annually, and it has expanded this platform to more complex matters, including credit default swaps and custody agreements.[135]

If that was 'the brink' at the time, it seems that we have now moved beyond it. Alongside top-down initiatives, such as those described above, the rise of technology has encouraged—or perhaps forced—law firms to abandon practices that have endured for decades, even

[134] Lord Hodge, 'Technology and the Law' Dover House Lecture (10 March 2020) https://www.supremecourt.uk/docs/speech-200310.pdf, referring to Richard Susskind and Daniel Susskind, *The Future of the Professions: How Technology Will Transform the Work of Human Experts* (OUP 2015) 67.

[135] Ibid 12–13 (references omitted).

centuries. For example, as we explain below, firms have introduced technological innovations not only to complete tasks and deliver services more efficiently, but also with wider effects: increasing the use of fixed costs, unbundling legal services, and expanding online dispute resolution.[136] Major law firms are also building capacity by offering dedicated training contracts focused solely on law and technology, selecting applicants for their ability to 'think differently'.[137]

It is fair to say that the legal profession is entering the most significant transition in its centuries-long history. But why are these changes unique? This question matters: if students do not understand the 'why', then mastering digital skills risks 'simply becomes one more hoop, through which a student must jump to gain their qualifications'.[138] After all, technological innovations have shaped the legal realm for centuries, from the printing press to copy machines, word processors, and legal databases. So why are today's developments any different?

> The key differences are two. First, the technology is now beginning to substitute for core legal skills, unlike copying and transcription. The physical acts of writing and copying were not core legal skills. Indeed, lawyers generally depended on copyists or secretaries to complete these tasks. But now machines are climbing the value-added ladder, encroaching on the domain of lawyers. Second, the rate at which machines are improving, and thus substituting for lawyers, is faster than ever before.[139]

There are several push-and-pull factors driving firms to adapt, and those forces will only intensify over time. First, drawing on various reports, the Law Society estimates that 30 to 40 per cent of legal sector jobs will soon be automated.[140] This is because 30 to 50 per cent of tasks once handled by junior lawyers—such as document review and due diligence—can now be completed far faster and more accurately by machines. Second, there are clear cost implications: if some firms can complete discovery or due diligence in a fraction of the time with far greater accuracy, others must explain to clients why they still rely on junior lawyers, who cost more to perform repetitive tasks less efficiently than a computer programme. Third, the easy dissemination of information online allows many people to gain basic legal knowledge without consulting a professional, increasing pressure to make legal services more affordable.[141] This has fuelled the growing popularity of 'unbundling' legal services, so clients pay only for specific aspects of a matter—for example, advice on applying for a planning permission exemption—rather than the full suite of services involved in buying or selling a property.

[136] Alan Cunningham et al, *Disruptive Technologies and Legal Service Provision in the UK: A Preliminary Study* (2018) 5, 26.

[137] Francine Ryan, 'Rage Against the Machine? Incorporating Legal Tech into Legal Education' (2021) 55 The Law Teacher 392.

[138] Ryan Murray and Helen Edwards, 'Legal Tech and Sustainability' in Ann Thanaraj and Kris Gledhill (eds), *Teaching Legal Education in the Digital Age* (Routledge 2022) 108.

[139] John McGinnis and Russell Pearce, 'The Great Disruption: How Machine Intelligence Will Transform the Role of Lawyers in the Delivery of Legal Services' (2014) 82 Fordham Law Review 3041, 3056.

[140] The Law Society, *Future Skills for Law* (2018).

[141] Richard Susskind and Daniel Susskind, *The Future of the Professions: How Technology Will Transform the Work of Human Experts* (OUP 2015).

Notably, this surge in demand from law firms has been matched by a surge in legal tech startups. Since 2022, LegalGeek has tracked legal tech startups monthly across categories such as People and Resources, Finance and Operations, Clients, Knowledge, Risk, Rights Management, Documents and Contracts, Litigation, Transactions, and Consumer Services.[142] A report by LawTechUK concludes that 'conservative estimates indicate that potential annual demand for lawtech products and services, excluding regulatory compliance products, could be worth £7bn to £22bn', and that employment in these companies will grow to between 8,000 to 12,000 employees.[143]

Against this backdrop, key questions arise: who will these employees be, what backgrounds will they have, and how will this shape our understanding of what law is and what it means to 'do law'? Richard Susskind argued that much of the work in these startups was driven by computer scientists with only a superficial grasp of law and jurisprudence.[144] Thirty years later, observers noted that 'the legal profession is becoming a subset of a larger legal industry that is increasingly populated by nonlawyers, technologists and entrepreneurs'.[145] If that is the case, will the absence of meaningful lawyer input cause technology to reduce law to a purely 'technical' endeavour—one that can be 'broken down into its component parts, re-engineered, [and] streamlined'?[146]

In what follows, this section continues with an overview of existing, and some future, developments in the field.[147] As you read through them, take time to reflect.

4.3.1 **Document Review and eDiscovery towards Litigation**

Gone are the days when paralegals and junior lawyers sifted through mountains of paper documents, correspondence, and other materials in the discovery phase of civil litigation. To explain: In civil litigation, parties are required to disclose all relevant documents, including electronic files, to the opposing side.[148] Sifting through boxes of documents has always been extremely laborious, time consuming, and expensive. One academic recalled spending two months, six days a week, reviewing thousands of documents as a junior associate, costing a client more than 500 billable hours. Today, the same task can be completed in days by a computer, with only minimal oversight from a single legal assistant.[149] But if discovery in the past was challenging, today it would have been unmanageable without the use of technology. This is because individuals, corporations, and public bodies now communicate and

[142] https://www.legalgeek.co/startup-map/#startups-map-section

[143] Frontier Economics, *The Contribution of Lawtech to the UK Economy* (Lawtech UK 2021) 4–5.

[144] Richard Susskind, 'Expert Systems in Law: A Jurisprudential Approach to Artificial Intelligence and Legal Reasoning' (1986) 49 Modern Law Review 168; and the response from Philip Leith, 'The Emperor's New Expert System' (1987) 50 Modern Law Review 128.

[145] William Henderson, 'A Blueprint for Change' (2013) 40 Pepperdine Law Review 461, 462.

[146] Ibid 463.

[147] For a different arrangement of these developments, as '*enabling*, *support process* and *substantive tech solutions*' see Cunningham et al (n 136) 40.

[148] Part 31 of the Civil Procedure Rules (CPR).

[149] Michele Pistone, 'Law Schools and Technology: Where We Are and Where We Are Heading' (2015) 64 Journal of Legal Education 586, 590.

store vast amounts of data electronically, producing huge volumes of electronically stored information (ESI).[150] So technology, in a sense, created (or exacerbated) the problem, and technology has provided the solution. Technology assisted review (TAR) is now the standard, at least in large firms, and is accepted as not only faster and cheaper, but also more accurate and efficient.[151] As information is increasingly stored electronically, this process, known as eDiscovery or predictive coding, refers to the process of identifying, collecting, and reviewing ESI.

REFLECTION POINT

An ongoing debate is taking place, which is quite philosophical in its orientation: to what extent can legal strategy, legal processes, 'thinking like a lawyer', be broken down in a manner that could be replicated, and indeed improved, by computers?

In the first UK case approving its use,[152] the court allowed predictive coding due to the sheer volume of documents: 17.6 million, reduced to 3.1 million after de-duplication. The court noted that the 'overriding objective' of dispute resolution includes handling cases in a way that is 'proportionate'.[153] The judgment then helpfully explains the process in detail, which is reproduced below. When reading through the technical overview, note that while the technology is central, there is also an important role for the lawyers' discretion, to make judgements at critical junctures:

> 19. . . . First of all, the parties will settle a predictive coding protocol, setting out the process in more detail, including definition of the data set, sample size, batches, control set, reviewers, confidence level and margin of error. Then criteria (perhaps agreed, perhaps unilateral) must be decided upon for inclusion of documents in the process. . . .
>
> 20. Then a representative sample of the 'included' documents is used to 'train' the software. In the present case, Mr Spencer suggests that it will comprise 1600–1800 documents . . . A person who would otherwise be making the decisions as to relevance for the whole document set (ie a lawyer involved in the litigation) considers and makes a decision for each of the documents in the sample, and each such document is categorised accordingly. It is essential that the criteria for relevance be consistently applied at this stage. So the best practice would be for a single, senior lawyer who has mastered the issues in the case to consider the whole sample . . . Based on the training that the software has received, it then reviews and categorises each individual document in the whole document set as either relevant or not.

150 *Goodale v Ministry of Justice* [2009] EWHC B41 (QB) [1]–[2].
151 McGinnis and Pearce (n 139) 3047–8.
152 *Pyrrho Investments Ltd v MWB Property Ltd* [2016] EWHC 256 (Ch).
153 Rule 1.1 of the CPR.

21. The results of this categorisation exercise are then validated through a number of quality assurance exercises. These are based on statistical sampling . . .
22. The samples selected are (blind) reviewed by a human for relevance. The software creates a report of software decisions overturned by humans. The overturns are themselves reviewed by a senior reviewer. Where the human decision is adjudged correct, it is fed back into the system for further learning. (It analyses the correctly overturned documents just as the originals were analysed.) Where not correct, the document is removed from the overturns. Where the relevance of the original document was incorrectly assessed at the first stage, that is changed and all the documents depending on it will have to be re-assessed.
23. The process of sampling is repeated as many times as required to bring the overturns to a level within agreed tolerances, and so as to achieve a stability pattern . . .
24. Although the number of documents that have to be manually reviewed in a predictive coding process may be high in absolute numbers, it will be only a small proportion of the total that need to be reviewed in the present case.

As the court notes, predictive coding 'is not a case of machine replacing humans: it is the process used and the interaction of man and machine'.[154] This interaction, and its reasonableness in light of the resources involved when comparing manual and electronic processes, remain subject to the court's review.

4.3.2 Client Delivery: Expert Advice and Document Generation

Most of us are now familiar—sometimes overly so—with the rise of 'bots' on customer service platforms. Some, of course, are more effective than others. In the legal services sector, these platforms provide 24/7 automated delivery of services within specific legal fields. For example, the American Data Centre market in the field of Mergers and Acquisitions exceeded $48bn in 2021.[155] AI tools are trained to develop expertise in specific fields, handling an estimated 80 per cent of client needs. The remaining 20 per cent—typically more complex issues—are handled by a lawyer, who therefore has more time for higher-value, often more satisfying work. From the client's perspective, costs can be significantly reduced through 'unbundling', which we have mentioned, allowing them to choose how much to rely on cheaper automated services versus more costly human input.

This form of 'low end disruptive innovation',[156] sometimes referred to as 'low bono',[157] could also, potentially, expand access to justice, albeit not necessarily to the clients who rely on legal aid and on free legal advice. Like low-cost airlines offering simple, affordable

[154] Ibid [25] citing *Moore v Publicis Groupe* [2012] 11 Civ 1279 (Southern District of New York), perhaps the first case to authorize predictive coding.

[155] Dan Roe, 'Akerman Debuts Data Center and Digital Infrastructure Practice With Bryan Cave Leighton Paisner Laterals' American Lawyer (7 July 2022) https://www.akerman.com/a/web/tsQNd48tqPbAYfsEdFYd4h/amlaw-data-centers-akerman.pdf

[156] Cunningham et al (n 136) 12.

[157] Raymond Brescia et al, 'Embracing Disruption: How Technological Change in the Delivery of Legal Services Can Improve Access to Justice' (2015) 78 Albany Law Review 553, 554.

services, these legal tools can give small businesses access to good-quality legal expertise at a reasonable price. Indeed, by using basic technology such as text messages and chatbots, assisting clients to identify legal problems, and then streamlining automation by creating legal documents and filling out legal forms through AI-driven projects, these tools are predicted to bring about the 'true disruption' in the legal services market.[158] One of the leaders in the market, *LegalZoom*, was set up in 2001 to help clients create legal documents—particularly wills and living trusts—without having to hire a lawyer. Since then, it expanded its offering to business formation documents and intellectual property (trademark and copyright applications). When LegalZoom went public in 2001, it was valued at $7.35bn, and its CEO estimated the wider legal tech market at $50bn.[159]

A related and rapidly growing area in legal tech is document generation. Legal tech companies now offer user-friendly apps that guide users through questions about their situation and, where appropriate, generate relevant legal documents. For example, Valla, a UK-based employment law-focused app,[160] takes the user through a series of questions:

- Was there discrimination?
- If so, on what basis?
- Can you provide a timeline (what happened when)? Do you have a document to support each part of the timeline?
- What is the remedy that you are after? [offering these options: compensation for past losses; compensation for future losses; basic award for unfair dismissal; injury to feelings for discrimination; unpaid wages, holiday pay, redundancy pay; reinstatement or re-engagement; etc]
- What are the respondent's details?

Based on the user's responses, the system generates an Employment Tribunal Claim form (ET1), which can, for a fee, be reviewed by a team member.

This process is considered a form of 'simple' document generation.[161] At the other end of the spectrum is a growing interest in 'smart' documents, that is, 'documents which have an active, practical existence . . . which in a sense monitors its own legal life, arguably challeng[ing] a large part of what it is a lawyer is expected to do'.[162] The most notable example in this category is probably 'smart contracts', which the Law Commission defines as 'a legally binding contract in which some or all of the contractual obligations are defined in and/or performed *automatically* by a computer program'.[163] To some extent, this is familiar territory: after all, direct debits or standing orders already follow rules of automatic execution. However, the range of activities can be far more complex. For example, a code can trigger

[158] Ibid.

[159] Pia Singh, 'LegalZoom shares jump 35% in market debut; CEO sees further opportunity in online legal service' CNBC (30 June 2021) https://www.cnbc.com/2021/06/30/legalzoom-debuted-up-30percent-ceo-sells-further-push-into-digital-market.html

[160] valla.uk [161] Cunningham et al (n 136) 35. [162] Ibid. [163] Law Commission (n 7) 1.

a series of actions—such as transferring title in an asset sale—once payment is received. Although lawyers may draft the contract, no human intervention is required for its performance. Smart contracts can go further, with all contractual terms encoded rather than written in natural language. Between these extremes are 'hybrid' smart contracts, where some terms are expressed in code and others in traditional legal language.[164]

4.3.3 **Contract Review and Analysis**

Many law firms consider this tool as 'one of the most useful'.[165] It uses an AI engine to analyse contracts against relevant legislation and compliance rules, ensuring the client is not exposed to risks or liabilities. The CEO of a UK-based company which developed one of the more successful tools in this field explained:

> This is about day-to-day contract management but we think that compliance is going to be more and more strict, and it's going to be much more difficult—there are so many new regulations, about [the Modern] Slavery Act, about GDPR, MiFid II [Markets in Financial Instruments Directive] and so many other compliances that [with] all this accumulated risk analysis from your contracts, we think it's not possible to be viable for humans anymore—you need to bring the robots.[166]

This quote highlights both the benefits and the limits of such software: at this stage, they are *not* intended, nor are they able, to replace experienced legal professionals in crafting sophisticated documents. What they can do, however, is provide rapid and precise cross-checking of language, saving hours of human labour and significant costs. A similar principle applies to the next set of tools, which are used in a different legal context.

4.3.4 **Practical Legal Research**

Supporting client cases often requires finding the relevant law—legislation, case law, or guidance—or arguments (for example, a mortgage not being registered in time) that strengthen the case and pre-empt the opposing party's arguments. When successful, this can be very rewarding, but it can also involve an extremely laborious process. As expected, tools have been developed to automate the process, where AI-based technology reviews and categorizes the documents. In 2021 the global law firm Linklaters rolled out its *Atticus* document verification system (hopefully named after one of the most iconic fictional lawyers), designed to reduce risk and increase efficiency. For example,

> if a law firm is working on a stock market listing, the prospectus for the IPO needs to contain plenty of information, from financial data, to claims about the business, to statements about its corporate profile. All this needs to be verified and the law firms involved have to ensure it's all correct.

[164] Ibid 22–3. [165] Cunningham et al (n 136) 31.
[166] Natasha Lomas, 'Cognitiv+ is Using AI for Contract Analysis and Tracking' (8 March 2017) https://techcrunch.com/2017/03/08/cognitiv-is-using-ai-for-contract-analysis-and-tracking/?guccounter=1

The realm of legal research captured in the quote above focuses on the automation of simple or repetitive tasks. A more sophisticated, AI-driven version of legal research draws on the insight from Oliver Wendell Holmes, one of the prophets of Legal Realism, who declared, in 1897, that 'the prophecies of what the courts will do in fact, and nothing more pretentious, is what I mean by the law'.[167] What if there were tools capable of accurately predicting how certain judges might rule in specific cases? Lawyers, including the present authors, are familiar with the phenomenon: some judges simply 'dislike' certain arguments—whether on bail, property dissolution, or eviction. Such knowledge would be extremely valuable in designing strategy: selecting the most persuasive precedents for a given fact pattern, deciding whether a case is strong enough to pursue or better settled,[168] and even considering a change of jurisdiction ('forum shopping'). Here, the relevant technology—machine learning—refers to 'a set of methods that can automatically detect patterns in data, and then use the uncovered patterns to predict future data, or to perform other kinds of decision-making under uncertainty (such as planning how to collect more data)'.[169] This type of practical knowledge and decision-making is, as mentioned, already common in discrete areas of law for some lawyers, but, through the use of machine learning and data science, may be available at a far more precise level, on a global scale.[170]

TAKING STOCK

This section provided an overview of technological developments in the legal profession. They include:

1. **Document review and eDiscovery as part of the preparation towards litigation.**
2. **Engagement with clients and the development of 'low bono' services, or app-based production of legal documents.**
3. **Contract review and analysis.**
4. **Legal research that incorporates semantic analysis of court decisions to assist practitioners in the construction of the right argument in the right forum.**

But apart from an overview of the fast-paced innovations, it also raises some broader issues, or perhaps concerns: it is clear that 'machines' will take at least some lawyers' jobs. That is already happening. At the moment, many lawyers are learning to work with machines, on the job. To what extent should this change the way we understand what we mean by 'the law'? And to what extent should it change the way we teach law?

[167] Oliver Wendell Holmes, 'The Path of Law' (1897) 10 Harvard Law Review 460, 461.
[168] McGinnis and Pearce (n 139) 3049, 3052–3.
[169] Kevin Murphy, *Machine Learning: A Probabilistic Perspective* (MIT Press 2012) 1.
[170] This was the expertise of LexPredict, a company acquired in 2018 by Elevate: 'Elevate acquires LexPredict, Expanding Capabilities in Artificial Intelligence and Data Science' https://elevate.law/news/elevate-acquires-lexpredict/

4.4 Technology and (Clinical) Legal Education

By this point, it has hopefully become clear that the legal sector—encompassing both public institutions (such as courts) and private actors (such as law firms)—is undergoing unprecedented disruption driven by technology. It is unsurprising that these changes have, and should have, implications for legal education in general, and clinical legal education (CLE) in particular. Indeed, it has been forcefully argued that 'The legal academy can no longer afford to give [advanced information] systems as little attention as it presently does. Lawyers can no longer afford to have as little understandings of algorithms, ontologies, and other computational concepts as they do.'[171] It is worth noting that this sharp assessment was written more than a decade ago. In the United States, the American Bar Association responded by amending its Model Rules of Professional Conduct in 2012 to clarify that technological understanding is an essential element of professional competence. Comment 8 to Rule 1.1 now states:

> [8] To maintain the requisite knowledge and skill, a lawyer should keep abreast of changes in the law and its practice, *including the benefits and risks associated with relevant technology*, engage in continuing study and education and comply with all continuing legal education requirements to which the lawyer is subject.[172]

So how should legal education evolve to prepare students for the new employment reality? And how should CLE not only prepare students but also evolve to make the most of technological opportunities while enhancing access to justice? For those who are still sceptical about the need to do so, Andy Unger provides a warning, or perhaps the motivation.

A View from Clinical Practice

Andy Unger, Head of Law, London South Bank University

If you are considering a career in law, it is no longer optional to understand and work with technology—it is essential. The legal landscape is rapidly evolving, and the integration of LawTech into legal services, courts, and education is reshaping what it means to be a lawyer. Increasingly, employers are seeking graduates who can demonstrate technological fluency alongside legal knowledge. In fact, lawyers with LawTech skills are not only more employable, but also more likely to secure higher salaries.

If you already possess strong LawTech capabilities, you are ahead of the curve—well done. If not, this is the ideal moment to begin developing them. A simple yet powerful starting point is to experiment with free Generative AI tools such as Microsoft Copilot or the basic version of ChatGPT. Using these tools regularly—even for just a few minutes a day—will

[171] Ronald Staudt and Marc Lauritsen, 'Introduction: Justice, Lawyering and Legal Education in the Digital Age' (2013) 88 Chicago-Kent Law Review 687, 687.

[172] Model Rules of Professional Conduct Rule 1.1 (ABA 2021) [emphasis added].

help you build both your technical confidence and your prompting skills, which are quickly becoming essential legal competencies.

Here is your challenge: engage with a Generative AI tool this week, and explore what it can (and cannot) do. Here are some mini-activities to spark your thinking:

- **Start with curiosity**: Ask the AI how it works. Then ask it to predict what technological innovations might shape legal services in the next five years.
- **Make it personal**: Ask how technology is likely to impact your future legal career. Be specific—tell it where you're studying and the area of law that interests you.
- **Dig deeper**: Ask what challenges emerging technologies pose for the rule of law. Use follow-up questions to probe issues around transparency, accountability, and bias.
- **Turn it into a tutor**: Ask the AI to generate multiple-choice questions on a topic you're revising. Request explanations for both the correct and incorrect answers to reinforce your understanding.
- **Enter into dialogue**: Ask the AI to adopt the persona of a law professor and engage you in a Socratic dialogue on a complex issue, such as the ethics and legality of physician-assisted suicide.
- **Practice applied learning**: If you volunteer in a law clinic or advice centre, ask the AI to draft a list of eligibility questions for areas like legal aid, employment rights, or welfare benefits. Always remember: AI tools can 'hallucinate'—that is, generate inaccurate or fabricated information—so your critical judgement remains essential.

This isn't just about acquiring a new skill—it's about future-proofing your legal career. As the saying goes: *lawyers won't be replaced by technology, but those who fail to use it will be replaced by those who do.*

So take up the challenge. Be curious, be critical, and above all, be creative. The future of law isn't waiting.

4.4.1 Technology and Legal Education

At the outset, we should clarify that the interdisciplinary approach to law and technology here is not concerned with form, such as using technology to engage students through distance learning, polling, or surveys; nor simply with how technology can modernize legal education by encouraging interactive learning, group activities, and problem-solving.[173] Those could apply, of course, to any subject matter (eg history, art, maths, etc). The challenge, in other words, for future generations of lawyers is 'not only need to be aware of emerging technologies but also to have an understanding of how technology works to appreciate the impact that technology has on the practice of law'.[174] We provided an overview of the 'what' (is happening) in the previous section, discussing the range of technological innovations

[173] Les McCrimmon, Ros Vickers, and Ken Parish, 'Online Clinical Legal Education: Challenging the Traditional Model' (2016) 23 International Journal of Clinical Legal Education 33, 55–6.

[174] Emma Jones et al, 'Introduction: Defining Digital Lawyering' in Emma Jones et al (eds), *Digital Lawyering Technology and Legal Practice in the 21st Century* (Routledge 2022) 1.

reshaping the legal profession and practice more broadly. We conclude this chapter by exploring how to teach the subject matter often referred to as 'legal tech'.

The importance of enriching legal education with a clear understanding of technology was tragically highlighted when details of the 'Post Office Scandal' dominated headlines in early 2024. In truth, the scandal—described as one of the greatest miscarriages of justice in UK legal history—had been rumbling for at least 15 years, and at its core lay a damaging mismatch between law and technology. This mismatch led to more than 900 subpostmasters being wrongly convicted of theft, fraud, and false accounting due to failures in the Horizon accounting system. Professor John Naughton, from the Centre for Technology and Democracy at the University of Cambridge, concluded that 'at the root of the problem was the blind faith of a corporation in technology that it had expensively purchased'.[175] In that sense, it echoes the case of fourth-grade teacher Sarah Wysocki mentioned earlier.[176] Roger Brownsword noted that 'where there is confidence (and, in some cases, over-confidence) in the technology, it is for those who contest the scores to come up with compelling counter-evidence and . . . this was something that Wysocki could not do'.[177]

A similar sentiment could apply to the legal system—prosecutors and courts—which advanced and convicted (reminder: beyond reasonable doubt) hundreds of innocent individuals without questioning the technology that underpinned the evidence. Indeed, the aforementioned SRA Report on AI in the legal market[178] refers to research which suggests that people (including lawyers and judges!) tend to trust computers more than humans, 'especially if a task becomes challenging'.[179]

Some suggest that teaching legal tech should include 'proper' computer science skills, such as coding, within the law school curriculum. As may be expected, American universities are at the forefront of legal innovation that incorporates technology. A couple of prominent examples may be noted. Stanford University's Center for Legal Informatics is CodeX:

> At CodeX, researchers, lawyers, entrepreneurs and technologists work side-by-side to advance the frontier of legal technology, bringing new levels of legal efficiency, transparency, and access to legal systems around the world. CodeX's emphasis is on the research and development of computational law (complaw)—the branch of legal informatics concerned with the mechanization of legal reasoning.[180]

Georgetown's Institute for Technology, Law and Policy

> . . . is a hub for policymakers, academics, advocates, and technologists to study and discuss how to center humans and the social good, using technology as a tool. We train the next generation of lawyers and lawmakers with deep expertise

[175] John Naughton, 'Horrified by Horizon? Then Get Ready to be Totally Appalled by AI' *The Guardian* (13 January 2024) https://www.theguardian.com/uk-news/2024/jan/13/horrified-by-horizon-then-get-ready-to-be-totally-appalled-by-ai

[176] See text near n 70. [177] Brownsword (n 86) 113. [178] SRA (n 117).

[179] Science News, 'People may trust computers more than humans' *ScienceDaily* (13 April 2021) https://www.sciencedaily.com/releases/2021/04/210413114040.htm

[180] https://law.stanford.edu/codex-the-stanford-center-for-legal-informatics/

> in technology law and policy and provide non-partisan insights to policymakers on issues relating to new and emerging technologies ... we also foster interdisciplinary approaches to solving complex technology law and policy problems. The Tech Institute also identifies and creates opportunities for technology to improve access to justice.[181]

For example, students at Georgetown developed the 'Same Sex Adviser app', which informs users if they can get married in a particular US state and explains the implications of marriage or cohabitation for their rights.[182]

Developments in the UK are less advanced but clearly emerging. Two examples are the University of Oxford's LawTech Education programme, a joint initiative of the Law Faculty, the Computer Science Department, and industry partners; and the Legal Innovation at the University of Ulster, a collaboration between the School of Law and the School of Computing and Intelligent Systems.[183]

As these examples illustrate, interdisciplinary collaboration is central to these initiatives. Yet it goes beyond that. It has been argued that the disruptive force of technology on legal education results in looking at legal education and, by extension, law itself through a different prism. Problems are visualized differently, for example, in less linear and more decision-tree formats; the interdisciplinary nature demands collaboration in teams with diverse skills and approaches, which is a valuable skill in itself; and the new opportunities create greater scope for innovation and creativity.

All of these developments are as exciting as they are challenging, in at least three ways: first, what are the boundaries of creativity and innovation? In other words, when is innovation simply a result of ignorance—going out on a limb without a clear understanding of the subject matter—and when is it genuinely useful and even ground-breaking? Second, how can such skills be taught in a meaningful and lasting way? Third, while these programmes develop and refine crucial skills, they often overlook the underlying normative issues. These involve critical engagement with the 'moral and ethical questions raised by applications of technology', including 'how law is being mediated by technology'.[184]

REFLECTION POINT

It is very easy, and even natural, to be enraged with the ease with which individuals, including legal professionals, involved in the Post Office did not question the underlying technology. But now try to place yourself in their shoes: if you were a prosecutor, or a judge, who was presented with printouts that pointed to fraud, what would it take for you to ask for more information? Can you see yourself, or others, becoming more sceptical about technologically generated evidence? If so, is that only a good thing, or is it also risky?

181 https://www.law.georgetown.edu/tech-institute/

182 Tanina Rostain, Roger Skalbeck, and Kevin Mulcahy, 'Thinking Like a Lawyer, Designing Like an Architect: Preparing Students for the 21st Century Practice' (2013) 88 Chicago-Kent Law Review 743.

183 https://www.ulster.ac.uk/legalinnovation/about

184 Ryan (n 137).

4.4.2 Technology and Clinical Legal Education

Arguably, CLE is a 'uniquely fertile environment to develop pedagogies that develop the capacity for students to thrive in a technologically transformed and transforming legal landscape'[185] and 'the very project of clinical education lends itself to the task of teaching technology'.[186]

This claim is convincing for three reasons. First, CLE bridges theory and practice and relies on ongoing collaboration between academics and practitioners—an approach that is essential for integrating law and technology.[187] Second, one of the central motivations of the CLE movement was, and remains, to challenge the existing law school curriculum, suggesting that it does not prepare students for the intellectual and professional challenges of the workplace. Advocates for incorporating technology into the curriculum could easily make the same argument.[188] Third, Lawtech enthusiasts, particularly in academia and policy, often share with clinical educators at least a rhetorical—and sometimes a deep—commitment to enhancing access to justice.[189]

In the CLE sphere, technology is relevant across three main streams. First, there is the use of technology in the delivery of clinic services. In this respect, clinics emulate legal practice, albeit within their sometimes limited resources. Here we refer, particularly in the post-Covid environment, to conducting client meetings, casework, and supervision remotely or via hybrid methods; using cloud-based case management systems; and employing collaborative tools for client intake, document management, and conflict checking.[190] The engagement with these tools clearly requires training that relates to technical skills, but, in the spirit of critical engagement, also raises questions concerning data security, client confidentiality (including across social media), and wider ethical issues, all of which offer grounds for fruitful conversation in a clinical context.

In addition, the clinic offers a perfect setting to experience, train, reflect, and assess the transformation of legal services in the digital age. We noted above the ambivalence expressed with respect to the effect of digital engagement on the relationship between the lawyer (or, generally, adviser) and the client; between the two parties; and between the parties and the judge. Indeed, 'there is something of a paradox in that, while law is increasingly looking towards technologically-based solutions for dispute resolution, at the same time the fundamentally relational nature of legal practice is also being more widely acknowledged'.[191] So can the reinvention of legal settings, supported by technology, provide 'a form of antidote to

[185] Francine Ryan and Hugh McFaul, 'Innovative Technologies in UK Legal Education' in Emma Jones and Fiona Cownie (eds), *Key Directions In Legal Education: National and International Perspectives* (Routledge 2020) 67, 71.

[186] Sarah Boonin and Luz Herrera, 'From Pandemic to Pedagogy: Teaching the Technology of Lawyering in Law Clinics' (2022) 68 Washington University Journal of Law and Policy 109, 120.

[187] Jacqueline Weinberg and Ross Hyams, 'The Law Tech Clinic: Leading the Way in Entrepreneurial Law Clinics' (2023) International Journal of Clinical Legal Education 34, 44–7.

[188] Ronald Staudt and Andrew Medeiros, 'Access to Justice and Technology Clinics: A 4% Solution' (2013) 88 Chicago-Kent Law Review 695, 697–8.

[189] Ibid 699. [190] Boonin and Herrera (n 186) 125–30.

[191] Emma Jones, Hugh Mcfaul, and Francine Ryan, 'Clinical Legal Education in the United Kingdom: Origins, Growth and the Technological Innovations and Challenges of Its Future' (2017) 4 German Journal of Legal Education 107, 124.

the adversarialism of common law jurisdictions and position lawyers as creative, emotionally intelligent problem-solvers'?[192]

Second, there is the engagement with the legal implications of technology, and technological developments. Clinics focusing on intellectual property would be natural candidates for such endeavours, and unsurprisingly, their number has surged over the past two decades.[193] However, technology-related clinics also engage with other 'cyberlaw' subjects such as employment, immigration, corporate governance (eg supporting tech startups), and tort law. These clinics support local businesses, independent artists and musicians, and charities.[194] Moreover, within this strand of legal implications, clinics could deploy legal tools to challenge inequities created by or through technology. We referred to some of these initiatives earlier in this chapter, so it is possible to mention them briefly here.[195] First, we can think of the effects that the digital divide has, not only on access to legal services (discussed above), but also on access to education, health, and other services. Second, clinics can take on cases that challenge algorithms that embed biased decision-making (for example, in employment, housing and education) and present these decisions as 'neutral'. Third, technology has raised concerns regarding privacy and surveillance particularly, but not solely, in the employment realm. Competent lawyering in these fields cannot be advanced without a keen understanding of the technologies that are in place 'under the hood'.

The third stream connecting CLE and technology involves improving access to justice within the existing ('traditional') judicial system, including broadening access to information and assisting users in managing it in a helpful way.[196] Thus, at the Chicago-Kent's Center for Access to Justice & Technology,[197] students are trained to use, and help clients use, A2J Author,[198] a system co-developed by Chicago-Kent which has been adopted on a national scale.[199] The software guides individuals to assemble documents, complete forms, and send in claims. The *Lawyering in the Digital Age Law Clinic* at Columbia Law School partnered with a Manhattan legal services organization to develop an automated rent calculator.[200]

In the UK, a number of law schools have lawtech modules in which law and computing students learn to design 'access to justice apps'.[201] For example, at the Law and Technology Hub at the University of Surrey School of Law,

> students, academics, business leaders and legal practitioners forge close links to work on complex digital transformation and law related research topics. The Hub provides opportunities for collaboration with partners from both in and outside the university,

[192] Ibid 125.

[193] Cynthia Dahl and Victoria Phillips, 'Innovation and Tradition: A Survey of Intellectual Property and Technology Legal Clinics' (2018) 25 Clinical Law Review 95, 99.

[194] Dahl and Phillips (n 193).

[195] See further: Laura Moy, 'Tech Support: Wiring Technology Law Clinics to Serve Racial Justice' (2023) Clinical Law Review 205, 208–12.

[196] Boonin and Herrera (n 186) 118–19.

[197] https://www.kentlaw.iit.edu/institutes-centers/center-for-access-to-justiceand-technology

[198] https://www.a2jauthor.org

[199] Pistone (n 149) 599.

[200] Lawyering in the Digital Age: Using Technology to Win Tenants' Rights, Columbia Law School, https://www.law.columbia.edu/academics/experiential/clinics/lawyering-digital-age-clinic

[201] Legal Cheek, 'Three More Unis Launch Lawtech Modules' (2018) https://www.legalcheek.com/2018/10/three-more-unis-launch-lawtech-modules/

aiding digital legal education, academic research, local business and community support, and, ultimately, career development for students.[202]

At London South Bank University, the Law and Computer Science Divisions offer a joint practical module on law and technology, where students collaborate 'to design and develop resources for real clients drawn from the local legal community, with an emphasis on using LawTech to support access to justice'.[203]

Clearly, law clinics are leading the way with respect to the incorporation of technology into legal education, and will likely continue to do so in the years ahead.

TAKING STOCK

This section provided an account of the ways in which technology could be incorporated into the delivery and understanding of legal education in general, and clinical legal education in particular. Against the background of the previous sections, it is the role of legal educators to prepare students to an environment that truly grasps the interdisciplinary nature of 'legal tech'. In the clinical context, beyond training in technical skills of future practice, there is an opportunity to engage with soft skills (such as relationality that overcomes digital barriers) alongside ethical and normative questions more broadly.

Conclusion

There are a number of conclusions that should be evident from this chapter. First, the impact of technology on the legal system, like the impact of technology on our life in general, is immense. This is true in the public sector as well as in private practice. Law firms have been quick to invest significant resources in technologies that deliver legal services faster and more efficiently than ever before. In contrast, judicial reform has advanced in a way that could be described, to coin a phrase, as one step forward and one step sideways. This is to say that significant advancements have been followed by stagnation, hesitation, and inadequate investment. Indeed, this point is crucial: is the main rationale for investing in judicial technology to improve service and enhance access to justice, or is it primarily to cut costs by reducing spending on court buildings and judges' salaries? Each approach would lead to very different developments and consequences.

Combining both the public and private sector developments, we also asked if technology improves or creates more barriers with respect to access to justice. The answer, at this stage, seems to be that the jury is out, or: it depends. It is clear that for some, and at some junctures, technology enhances access to justice significantly. Individuals can now access

[202] https://surreylawtech.org/

[203] Luica Otoyo et al, 'Legal Education Meets Computer Science: An Interdisciplinary Approach to Teaching LawTech' in Ann Thanaraj and Kris Gledhill (eds), *Teaching Legal Education in the Digital Age* (Routledge 2022) 131.

legal information and advice online and use apps or 'low bono' law firm services, and these are all significant and welcome developments. The ability to access the court system from the comfort of one's home, without the need to travel and arrange for caring responsibilities, is also a positive development. However, for many, technology itself becomes a barrier; for them, a traditional 'day in court' remains vital, and the loss of in-person communication can have serious consequences.

Finally, we considered how teachers and students should address these developments, both in law schools generally and in clinics in particular. Clearly, we must ensure that technology works for, not against, clients in need. To that end, we need a deeper understanding of technology, both 'under the hood' by developing lawtech tools, and in terms of its broader consequences.

Further Reading

Abdi Aidid and Benjamin Alarie, The Legal Singularity: *How Artificial Intelligence Can Make Law Radically Better* (University of Toronto Press 2023).

Naomi Cruetzfeldt et al, *Access to Justice, Digitalisation and Vulnerability: Exploring Trust in Justice* (Bristol University Press 2024).

David Freeman Engstrom (ed), *Legal Tech and the Future of Civil Justice* (Cambridge University Press 2023).

Richard Susskind, *Online Courts and the Future of Justice* (OUP 2019).

Richard Susskind (with Daniel Susskind), *The Future of the Professions* (OUP 2015).

SECTION TWO

Clinical Legal Education and Legal Professionalism

The Theory of the Practice

5

The Intellectual Background to Clinical Legal Education

There is nothing so practical as a good theory.

Kurt Lewin

Chapter Overview

This chapter will present you with the intellectual background of clinical legal education. In essence, this is the 'theory' behind the 'practice'. As the epigraph to this chapter, above, suggests, we will be better practitioners by having a strong understanding of *why* we do things, what challenges are real, what structures we're not seeing, and where we focus our attention and efforts on the wrong things. In particular, the chapter introduces the basic features of legal realism which, from its inception more than 100 years ago, has been crucial to the development of clinical legal education, sometimes explicitly, sometimes implicitly.

By the end of this chapter you should be able to:

- Have a good understanding of the traditional way in which law is currently taught.
- Appreciate the critique that advocates of legal realism offer against the current method of legal education.
- Explain the links between the theoretical approach of legal realism and the practical implications to legal practice and legal education.
- Reflect on the way clinical legal education has developed as a result of those insights, and what further developments should entail.

Introduction

This chapter explores the intellectual history and development of clinical legal education and its relationship to more traditional forms of legal education. It considers the theoretical underpinnings of clinical legal education, which rest on two layers. First, clinical legal education embraces an approach to *law* that is distinct from most mainstream modules.

The second layer concerns legal *education*, and the particular contribution that clinical legal education offers in that regard.

Some of you may think, initially, that such a chapter seems too theoretical and thus 'out of place' in a book about practice. In that case, consider two quotes that help answer this concern. The first is attributed to the famed philosopher Immanuel Kant: 'theory without practice is empty; practice without theory is blind.' Of course, we need not worry about the first part of the quote, since much of the work in CLE is practical. The second part chimes nicely with this lovely turn of phrase from the psychologist Kurt Lewin, which we chose as the epigraph for this chapter: 'There is nothing so practical as a good theory.' These quotes suggest how important it is, sometimes, to take a step back and see what we're doing within a wider context. Without such reflection, how can we understand why we're doing it, whether we're doing it the right way, and how to improve? But it goes further. In this chapter, the theory behind the practice will help you gain more than just practical skills. It situates your work within a broader understanding of law, creating a feedback loop where clinical work and legal education enrich one another.

In particular, we investigate the impact that legal realism had on legal education and, probably more obviously, on the development of clinical legal education. Legal realism gained traction by rejecting the entrenched case study approach developed by the Dean of Harvard Law School, Christopher Columbus Langdell, in the late nineteenth century. It continued, with the help of CLE, by proposing a pedagogy that highlights 'learning through doing', which embraces the study of the practice of lawyering as a skill and an art. Yet the practical focus of CLE—emphasizing employability in the twenty-first century—sits uneasily alongside the social justice aims that clinicians and Realists have historically embraced. In what follows, you will see how legal realism contributes to our understanding of legal practice and has made an enduring contribution to legal education in general, and to clinical legal education in particular.[1] At the same time, Realists were also interested in expanding the social perspective of legal education by introducing the social sciences—including psychology, sociology, economics, and politics—into the law curriculum.[2] Finally, as noted, Realists also had an ideological, and even political, agenda, which included striving towards justice in general, and social justice and access to justice in particular, as an integral part of the legal curriculum. That seems quite a bit for one approach. Can all these diverse aims be reconciled?

This chapter, therefore, opens the door to reflection on the way law is taught in 'traditional' modules, but also to the motivations that drive this module itself: is it concerned with a new, different, and perhaps better way of teaching law? Is it motivated by the desire to understand the needs of those deprived of legal assistance? Or, finally, is it dominated by the instrumental concern to improve students' prospects of gaining a foothold in an increasingly competitive job market?

One final word before we embark: when assessing the debates over legal theory and legal education in the first half of the twentieth century, you may note that more attention

[1] Neil Duxbury, 'Jerome Frank and the Legacy of Legal Realism' (1991) 18 Journal of Law and Society 175, 187.

[2] Karl Llewellyn, 'On What Is Wrong with So-called Legal Education' (1935) 35 Columbia Law Review 651, 660.

will be given to those that occurred in the United States. This is because those vibrant and thoughtful debates were, sadly, in 'striking contrast' to the 'professional complacency' in the UK at the time.[3]

5.1 Legal Realism and the Critique of Legal Education

The American Supreme Court Justice Felix Frankfurter once wrote that 'the law and the lawyers are what law schools make them'.[4] That may work as a descriptive insight, but does the way law schools 'make' lawyers leave something to be desired? In the first half of the twentieth century, a group of academics, practitioners, and, somewhat surprisingly, even judges who can broadly be described as 'legal realists' began challenging how law is conceptualized, researched, and taught. They faced, and to some extent still face, serious opposition, but their impact cannot be ignored or minimized—so much so that it has become a cliché for legal scholars to say, 'We are all realists now'.[5]

To understand the contribution of legal realism to law in general, and to legal education in particular, we must first understand the paradigm that legal realism opposed and targeted with its criticism. In this book, we cannot do full justice (pun intended!) to the copious literature for and against legal realism or the various strands that developed, or even seriously discuss its central tenets.[6] Instead, this brief sketch of the contribution of legal realism is very pragmatically focused towards explaining how it serves as the ground for the establishment and development of clinical legal education.[7]

While you may naturally be interested, primarily, in the latter, it appears almost impossible to disentangle the realists' understanding of the law and of jurisprudence, on the one hand, and their ideas concerning legal education, on the other.[8] They argued that the law experienced by practitioners is very different from the law found in appellate decisions. For ordinary people—the neighbour, the parent, the tenant, the worker who walks into a law clinic or a Citizens' Advice office with a bag of documents—the law is lived in everyday disputes. In contrast, appellate courts focus on 'the most pathological phenomenon in the

[3] LCB Gower, 'English Legal Training: A Critical Survey' (1950) 13 Modern Law Review 137, 137.

[4] Cited in Stephen Wizner, 'The Law School Clinic: Legal Education in the Interests of Justice Colloquium: What Does It Mean to Practice Law in the Interests of Justice in the Twenty-First Century' (2001) 70 Fordham Law Review 1929.

[5] Joseph Singer, 'Legal Realism Now' (1988) 76 California Law Review 465, 467.

[6] In addition to the references noted below, those who are intrigued by some of the discussion here and would like to explore further may wish to explore some of these foundational texts: Oliver Wendell Holmes, 'The Path of the Law' (1897) 10 Harvard Law Review 457; Jerome Frank, *Law and the Modern Mind* (Brentano's 1930); Karl Llewellyn, 'Some Realism About Realism' (1931) 44 Harvard Law Review 1222; Robert Hale, 'Coercion and Distribution in a Supposedly Non-Coercive State' (1923) 38 Political Science Quarterly. And some of these more contemporary writings: Brian Leiter, 'American Legal Realism' in Martin Golding and William Edmundson (eds), *Blackwell Guide to the Philosophy of Law and Legal Theory* (Blackwell 2005); Brian Tamanaha, *Beyond the Formalist–Realist Divide: The Role of Politics in Judging* (Princeton University Press 2010).

[7] Elizabeth Mertz, 'New Legal Realism: Law and Social Science in the New Millennium' in Elizabeth Mertz, Stewart Macaulay, and Thomas Mitchel (eds), *The New Legal Realism* (Cambridge University Press 2016) 1, 7.

[8] William Twining, *Law in Context: Enlarging a Discipline* (OUP 1997).

body politic, the most serious diseases, and the leading cases are the worst, and least typical of all'.[9] If that is true of what law really *is*, then the way law is *taught* must also change. Law schools, they argued, wrongly emphasize appellate courts and ignore the day-to-day complexities of trial courts. Their solution was to bring law schools closer to the medical school model, creating legal 'clinics' that make legal education more vocational in orientation.[10]

5.1.1 The Langdell Case Method

It may be surprising to realize that the way most law schools across the Anglosphere still teach law can be traced back to a single individual: Christopher Columbus Langdell at Harvard University, around 1870. Since then, new disciplines have emerged, societies have transformed, and world wars have reshaped nations, yet legal education has largely remained anchored to Langdell's model.[11] It is true that we are now far more aware of law's relationship to class, race, gender, and so on, thanks to the burgeoning development of studies in law and society in general, and empirical legal studies in particular. And yet, Langdell's hold on the law school curriculum remains strong, and so it merits discussion.

Before doing so, it is worth referring to our discussion in the Introduction and reminding ourselves that Langdell's initiative revolutionized an Anglo-American system of teaching law that was largely based on apprenticeship. At the time, practitioners and scholars began to develop great treatises on 'the law of contracts', crime or tort, legal education, which consisted of memorizing these grand texts. As we noted in Chapter 2, this was possible then because the law was far more simple and far less diverse than it is today, thus making it more manageable to assert that, for example, '*this* is the law on offer and acceptance'.

The Industrial Revolution brought about rapid commercial expansion, increased mobility, and new forms of conflict, making the law increasingly complex. Courts had to deal with more matters, and they became increasingly more intricate. Enter Christopher Columbus Langdell. Langdell sought to move away from reliance on treatises and instead focused on appellate case law, which he saw as the best source for identifying legal principles. In that sense, one can suggest that he tried to move towards 'practice', to the way lawyers think and work, and thus 'from an emphasis on knowledge to an emphasis on skill'.[12] But what skills are involved here? Langdell's case method required that a student analyse each case, distinguishing between relevant and irrelevant facts and between the possible and actual grounds of a decision. After doing this, the students were asked: to what extent are the facts and grounds of this case similar or dissimilar to another case? In this way, the student learned to emulate the work of lawyers and, indeed, of judges.[13] For Langdell and some of his supporters, these were the skills that would serve a lawyer. However, this approach developed only a narrow

[9] Otto Kahn-Freund, 'Reflections on Legal Education' (1966) 29 Modern Law Review 121, 125.

[10] Llewellyn (n 2) 658.

[11] Mark Spiegel, 'Theory and Practice in Legal Education: An Essay on Clinical Education Symposium: Clinical Education' (1986) 34 UCLA Law Review 577.

[12] Twining (n 8) 72.

[13] Spiegel (n 11) 585; Edward Rubin, 'What's Wrong with Langdell's Method, and What to Do About It?' (2007) 60 Vanderbilt Law Review 609, 619.

subset of the skills lawyers need. It omitted crucial dimensions of practice, particularly those involving human interaction and client engagement.[14]

This method will sound familiar to any law student in the English-speaking world. From the first year, students are trained to extract the *ratio decidendi* from *obiter dicta*, to track how new tests replace old ones, and to analyse evolving concepts such as 'reasonableness' in public law or 'control' in employment law. For Langdell, a student can learn the law without ever leaving the library, setting foot in a law firm, arguing a case, or engaging with clients.[15]

But Langdell's approach to education was focused not only on 'teaching practice' and ensuring competence in lawyerly skills. It was, fundamentally, based on a theory of law as a science that consists of rules, principles, and doctrines that must be unearthed. The two—the theory of the law and the theory of legal education—merged nicely. According to Langdell,

> Law, considered as a science, consists of certain principles or doctrines. To have such a mastery of these as to be able to apply them with constant facility and certainty to the even tangled skein of human affairs is what constitutes a true lawyer; and hence to acquire that mastery should be the business of every earnest student of law. Each of these doctrines has arrived at its present state by slow degrees; in other words, it is a growth, extending in many cases through centuries. This growth is to be traced in the main through a series of cases; and much the shortest and best, if not the only, way of mastering the doctrine effectually is by studying the cases in which it is embodied.[16]

Langdell's approach to legal education only makes sense within the paradigm of legal formalism,[17] sometimes referred to as the 'doctrinal' approach to law.[18] It seems somewhat peculiar to explain here what is meant by legal formalism because, to an extent, there is a good chance you, as a law student, are already very familiar with it. But there is also some importance in taking a step back and observing the method that governs the teaching and practice of law, even if, to paraphrase Molière, you may have been 'speaking prose without knowing it' or, in this case, practicing formalism without realizing it[19]—swimming in it like a fish that does not know what water is.[20] But as these two examples suggest, sometimes it is necessary

[14] Richard Wilson, *The Global Evolution of Clinical Legal Education: More than a Method* (Cambridge University Press 2015) 135.

[15] Ibid.

[16] Christopher C Langdell, Preface to *A Selection of Cases on the Law of Contracts* (1871) viii, cited by Twining (n 8) 70.

[17] Brian Leiter, 'Legal Realism and Legal Positivism Reconsidered' (2001) 111 Ethics 278; Frederick Schauer, 'Foreword' in William Twining, *Karl Llewellyn and the Realist Movement* (2012) ix, x.

[18] William Twining, 'Legal R/realism and Jurisprudence: Ten Theses' in Elizabeth Mertz, Stewart Macaulay, and Thomas Mitchell (eds), *The New Legal Realism* (Vol 1, Cambridge University Press 2016) 121, 126.

[19] Molière, The Bourgeois Gentleman (1670):

Mr Jourdain: Oh, really? So when I say: 'Nicole bring me my slippers and fetch my nightcap,' is that prose?

Philosophy Master: Most clearly.

Mr Jourdain: Well, what do you know about that! These forty years now I've been speaking in prose without knowing it.

[20] David Foster Wallace, *This Is Water: Some Thoughts, Delivered on a Significant Occasion, About Living a Compassionate Life* (2009).

to take a step back and 'make the familiar strange', examining the assumptions that underpin what feels natural. So let's turn to do that now.

REFLECTION POINT

Based on work experience that you may have already gained, or on your understanding of the way law is practiced in the UK, to what extent do you think that the law in books, and the case method, help a legal practitioner to do their job well? What are the skills that you could build on? What would you have to learn 'on the job'? Are there even some aspects of your legal study that you think you will have to 'unlearn', because they are detrimental to work as a practitioner?

5.1.2 **What Is Law Made Of: Facts or Rules?**

Somewhat crudely, the essence of legal formalism is often captured in the syllogism: 'Rule x Fact = Decision.'[21] This assumes that a judge first identifies the relevant facts, then locates the applicable rules—whether statutory or from case law—and applies those rules to the facts to reach a legal conclusion. As we saw earlier, the case study method of *teaching* law rests on this same understanding of the judicial process. Whether labelled 'scenarios', 'problem questions', or—in American law schools—'hypos' (short for hypotheticals), the case method tests students' ability to apply the law to a given set of facts. The aim is to identify the legal issues that arise and determine how the law would resolve them.

This very basic paradigm, and the case method built upon it, provoked sharp criticism from legal realists. They rejected the syllogism that opened this section ('Decision = Facts × Rules') and replaced it with Oliver Wendell Holmes's seminal claim:

> The life of the law has not been logic: it has been experience. The felt necessities of the time, the prevalent moral and political theories, intuitions of public policy, avowed or unconscious, even the prejudices which judges share with their fellow men, have a good deal more to do than the syllogism in determining the rules by which men should be governed.[22]

And this alternative vision of law profoundly shaped the Realists' approach to legal education. Studying the *so-called* reasons given in appellate decisions, they argued, does little to predict what courts will actually do in future cases. Focusing narrowly on those opinions, therefore, misses the point entirely. As Jerome Frank observed:

> Students trained under the Langdell system are like future horticulturists confining their studies to cut flowers, like architects who study pictures of buildings and nothing else. They resemble prospective dog breeders who never see anything but stuffed dogs.

[21] Jerome Frank, 'Are Judges Human? Part 2: As Through a Glass Darkly' (1931) 80 University of Pennsylvania Law Review 233, 242.

[22] Oliver Wendell Holmes, *The Common Law* (1881) 1.

> And it is beginning to be suspected that there is some correlation between that kind of stuffed-dog study and the overproduction of stuffed shirts in the legal profession.[23]

We will return to the matter of the legal profession in more detail in Chapter 8. But for now, we must ask: is Frank right in his acerbic critique? And if so, what alternative vision of law do the Realists offer to challenge the one we are so accustomed to? After all, do lawyers not argue their cases by reference to precedents, and do judges not cite those same precedents as authoritative? They do, of course, the Realists conceded. But they insisted that 'judicial decisions are influenced by the manner in which the facts are *perceived* as much as by legal authorities; the good lawyer must be able to interpret the facts of his case in terms of the conditions and values of contemporary society'.[24] Notice how important the facts are for the Realists. This emphasis is in striking contrast to the way law schools often treat 'the law' as the decisive factor in the case. To illustrate this, Realists have invoked Chancellor Kent as an example of a great judge:

> in deciding cases his practice was first to make himself perfectly and accurately master of the facts. Then he says: 'I was master of the cause and ready to decide it. I saw where justice lay and the moral sense decided the cause half the time, and I then sat down to search the authorities until I had exhausted my books, and I might once in a while be embarrassed by a technical rule, but I most always found principles suited to my views of the case.'[25]

This is a uniquely relevant quote for our purposes here, for three reasons. First, because the focus on the facts of a case is so central to the work in law clinics, and in that sense is very different from the way law is taught in other modules. As LCB Gower explained, 'Law school training encourages the belief that the relevant facts, no more and no less, are presented neatly docketed to the lawyer, who merely has to apply the legal rules'.[26] Students often memorize the 'bottom line' of a case and the doctrinal tweak it adds, but they are rarely required to note so-called irrelevant facts, such as the claimant's age, race, or employment history; the size of their business; or the background to the proceedings. And yet, in the clinics (as in legal practice in general), a client comes in an unpolished, unvarnished, unrefined story, and it is the work of the students to structure a narrative of facts that will be most persuasive (while also pre-empting those facts that support the opposing party's case). Chancellor Kent suggests that it is ultimately the force of each party's narrative that will determine who wins the case.

The second reason this quote is relevant lies in its subtle placement of the word 'justice'. This suggests that the argument in favour of 'where justice lay' is not distinguished from the argument of 'where the law lay'. Consequently, it would mean that to argue the law is also to argue over justice (think, once again, about 'access to justice'), and that shifting public perceptions of justice inevitably shape professional understandings of law. Indeed, as you can imagine by now (and as we see below), legal realists had something to say about the link between law and justice.

[23] Jerome Frank, 'Why Not a Clinical Lawyer-School?' (1933) 81 University of Pennsylvania Law Review 907, 912.

[24] Twining (n 8) 32 [emphasis added]. [25] Cited in ibid. [26] Gower (n 3) 189.

This is fine in theory, you may be thinking, but how is the link between law and justice relevant in practice? One of the most famous examples in common law history is the Brandeis Brief, written by the future US Supreme Court Justice Louis Brandeis and his sister-in-law Josephine Goldmark. At the height of the *Lochner* era,[27] as the Supreme Court was striking down labour protections in the name of 'freedom of contract' and property rights, the Court was asked to assess the constitutionality of a law that prescribed the maximum hours for working women.[28] Defying convention, Brandeis submitted a brief 'containing two pages of legal argument and ninety-five pages of sociological and economic data about the conditions of working women's lives in the factories'.[29] The success of the brief was a rare victory within the *Lochner* era, and to this day serves as a shining example of the power of persuasive arguments to serve the cause of 'justice', whether they are considered 'legal' or 'extra-legal'. The Brandeis Brief cared very little about such a distinction. It sought to persuade the judges to do 'what's right', and trusted them to find the doctrinal concepts and formulations which would justify that decision. Brandeis was proven right.

Moreover, and this is the third point, Chancellor Kent unabashedly writes that he first decides where the justice lies, and then manages to find the law that would lead to that conclusion. This directly opposes the traditional view that we should 'follow the law' to whatever conclusion it leads us. Instead, it implies that the law can be steered towards whatever outcome we seek. We turn to this radical suggestion now.

5.1.3 **Law's Indeterminacy and the Link between Law and Justice**

It is clear, then, that legal realists rejected the formalist approach to law and judicial decision-making. In fact, they used harsh words to express their objection. They viewed legal formalism as central to the foundational myth of law. According to this myth, legal rules are clear and certain, and lower-court judges can—and routinely do—apply them straightforwardly. In contrast, they argued that tribunals and trial courts have considerable discretion to decide cases as they see fit. We saw this, at least implicitly, in the quote from Chancellor Kent above. Now we need to understand how that is the case. After all, this argument flies in the face of years of indoctrination about *stare decisis* (Latin for 'to stand by things decided'), the doctrine of precedent under which lower courts are legally bound to follow higher-court decisions.

Realists recognize the gravity of their claim. After all, they attacked what they saw as a foundational myth, summarized in the words of a popular legal podcast: '*stare decisis* is for suckers.'[30] By this they mean that courts follow precedents only when it suits them. Realists base this position on two central arguments: the inherent vagueness of language and the sheer complexity of the law. Both are significant issues, of course, but a very brief introduction will suffice for present purposes. First, it is widely acknowledged, even by formalists, that language is not always determinate. In one famous example, we know that we cannot

[27] Named after the case of *Lochner v New York* (1905). [28] *Muller v Oregon* (1908).

[29] Morton Horwitz, *The Transformation of American Law, 1870–1960: The Crisis of Legal Orthodoxy* (1992) 206.

[30] The phrase was popularized on the podcast Strict Scrutiny, hosted by Professors Leah Litman, Melissa Murray, and Kate Shaw.

drive an SUV on a park path marked 'no motor vehicles'; but does that prohibition apply to an electric wheelchair? An e-bike? An electric scooter?[31] There will always be 'core' instances of words, but around them 'penumbra' cases, where the conclusion is less obvious.

The second reason that leads to the indeterminacy of law relates to its complexity. Realists have noted a 'conspicuously wide range of norms'[32] governing almost every issue. Legal norms may be seen as 'hunting in pairs'[33] because 'for every legal principle there exist[s] a potential counter-principle'.[34] Therefore, a court may prefer freedom of speech over privacy, or vice versa; may view two previous cases as conflicting (thus giving itself leeway to choose between them) or reconcilable;[35] may draw on other jurisdictions or view them as irrelevant, and so on. If judges have broad discretion to choose the decision that they see fit, 'the predictive power of doctrinal analysis becomes suspect. As a theory of how the law operates *and* what the central tasks of being a lawyer are, legal doctrine is unimpressive.'[36]

Moreover, the indeterminacy of law also brings to light the legal system's commitment to justice (or lack thereof), which is also a central concern for (clinical) legal education. Realists emphasized that the myth according to which rules are determinative is not neutral, but rather serves a purpose, and contributes to *in*justice. Felix Cohen, for example, suggested that, as the victims of the judicial system are often those who are less well-off, traditional legal discourse operates as 'economic prejudice masquerading in the cloak of legal logic . . . to perpetuate class prejudices and uncritical assumptions which could not survive the sunlight of free ethical controversy'.[37] Pause for a moment: what exactly is Cohen suggesting here?

Note the stark contrast here between 'legal logic' and 'free ethical controversy'. 'Legal logic' suggests that the law is value-neutral, and therefore that legal education should be value-neutral. As Julian Webb notes, legal neutrality is a myth, and treating education as value-neutral is equally misguided.[38] In contrast, 'free ethical controversy' is often referred to by a different term: 'critical thinking': 'the courage to form and express a reasoned opinion without any fear of so-called "authority".'[39] While this is, presumably, a common tension in other fields as well, legal education is particularly notable for its effort to teach students to understand the law 'as it is' while simultaneously encouraging them to question it.[40] This is a difficult balancing act, and many law students struggle, particularly in their first year, to get it right.

[31] These are modern examples based on the famous hypothetical offered by HLA Hart, *The Concept of Law* (2nd ed, OUP 1994) 125–7.

[32] Mark Freedland, 'The Legal Structure of the Contract of Employment' in M. Freedland et al (eds), *The Contract of Employment* (OUP 2016) (referring to the contract of employment).

[33] Walter Wheeler Cook, Book Review (1929) 38 Yale Law Journal 405, 406 (reviewing B. Cardozo, *The Paradoxes of Legal Science* (1928)).

[34] GE White, 'The Inevitability of Critical Legal Studies' (1984) 36 Stanford Law Review 649, 651.

[35] For a closely related example see Alan Bogg, 'Sham Self Employment in the Supreme Court' (2012) 41 Independent Law Journal 328, 329.

[36] AJ Goldsmith, 'An Unruly Conjunction? Social Thought and Legal Action in Clinical Legal Education' (1993) 43 Journal of Legal Education 415.

[37] Felix Cohen, 'Transcendental Nonsense and the Functional Approach' (1935) 35 Columbia Law Review 809, 817, 840.

[38] Julian Webb, 'Taking Values Seriously: The Democratic Intellect and the Place of Values in the Law School Curriculum' in M Robertson, L Corbin, K Tranter, and F Bartlett (eds), *The Ethics Project in Legal Education* (Routledge 2010) 9, 11.

[39] Kahn-Freund (n 9) 123. [40] Ibid 124.

REFLECTION POINT

Initiatives such as the Feminist Judgments Project take real cases and rewrite them 'as if' a feminist judge were sitting on the bench and faced with the same facts and legal norms, reaching a different decision or the same decision but for different reasons.

Of the cases that you've read and studied, think of two that stand out as the most unjust in their result: they are seriously detrimental to a weak party, and perhaps even to a group to which that party is associated (poor people, minorities, migrants, and so on). How were those decisions justified in legal terms? Could you have written a decision with a different focus that reaches a different conclusion, still based on existing legal principles? How does that make you feel about these decisions, decisions like it, and the law in general?

The Realists went beyond simply critiquing law's role in entrenching injustice. Some suggested that it is up to those within the legal system to construct, shall we say, a *justice* system. Oliver Wendell Holmes, whom we mentioned earlier, wrote that law should serve individual and social ends, urging that 'we shall spend our energy on a study of the ends sought to attained and the reasons for desiring them'.[41] In England, ECS Wade dedicated his inaugural address at Cambridge Law School to the aims of legal education, warning that students risk losing sight of the fact that 'law is a great human institution serving social and economic needs . . . and does not develop in a vacuum apart from the political, social and economic environment of the people it exists to serve'.[42]

So how might we use clients' experiences to improve their interaction with justice? Donald Black, concerned with the system's failure to protect those facing structural disadvantage, proposed two approaches: de-socializing law and de-legalizing society. By de-socializing law, Black means to *reduce* the amount of information that the court may consider. In doing so, this approach recognizes that, rather than providing the 'whole picture', some information leads to bias which, in turn, creates injustice rather than justice.[43] While this approach may seem controversial, it is in effect already implemented. For example, in many jurisdictions the judge or jury cannot be made aware of past offences of the accused, or the sexual history of a victim of assault, so it does not cloud their judgement. In addition, although not strictly a legal process, a similar idea underpins anonymized job applications, where names, gender, and background are removed to avoid implicit bias.

By 'de-legalizing society', Black meant removing certain issues or conflicts from the immediate reach of law. Though this contrasts with the broader trend of 'juridification'—turning more social conflicts into legal ones—we see signs of this trend as well. Examples include limiting lawyers' rights to appear in small claims or disciplinary hearings, and promoting ADR.

[41] Oliver Wendell Holmes, *The Path of the Law* (1897, 2009 The Floating Press) 15.

[42] ECS Wade, 'The Aim of Legal Education' (1945–1947) 9 Cambridge Law Journal 286, 288. Strikingly, for his time, he also notes that the lawyer's training is not complete without an 'experience of law in action'.

[43] Donald Black, *Sociological Justice* (OUP 1989) 57–72.

In summary, Realists argued that students and practitioners must confront the impact of their decisions on workers, minorities, vulnerable individuals, and the broader 'downstream' effects of denying rights. A judicial focus on concepts, tests, and categories, therefore, is unpersuasive if it leads to injustice. Roscoe Pound wrote that 'as a means to an end, [law] must be judged by the results it achieves, not by the niceties of its internal structure'.[44] To do so, we must 'supersede the jurisprudence of conceptions' with 'jurisprudence of results'.[45] Wade argued that law should be taught 'not as an exercise in professional technique but in relation to its place in the world in which we live'.[46] Similarly, Otto Kahn-Freund, a 'founding figure' of British employment law, said that legal education is at its best when students address each case both in a 'rigidly dogmatic way and . . . as a social situation requiring the solution of a social problem'.[47]

5.1.4 **Towards a 21st-Century Version of Legal Education**

Before we move on to clinical legal education, we can identify three prongs to the critique of the case study method, each leading to its own suggestion for reform. First, critics were dissatisfied with the way legal education is broken down into courses, or modules, which claim to represent coherent areas of law. They argued that the current divisions—such as contract, tort, land/property, and crime—no longer reflect the way law is organized or experienced in modern society. Instead of clinging to categories established before the industrial revolution, we should ask: 'If law is to be classified in terms of the life which it affects, what aspects of that life shall be chosen as the bases of classification?'[48] Brainerd Currie developed this further by suggesting that

> the formal categories of the law, shaped by tradition and by accident, tend to obscure the social problems with which law deals, the purpose which is the vital element of principle, and the actual working of legal processes; they constitute a framework which forces artificiality in perspective and development; they must be revised along lines of correspondence with the types of human activity involved.[49]

Several English academics similarly recognized that the existing system encourages a student 'to keep his law in water-tight compartments labelled contract, tort, land law, etc',[50] while overlooking the social and economic reality that shapes those fields. For instance, principles of contract law often play out differently in a commercial setting than in an employment setting. If that is the case, why not design a course specifically around these contexts—commercial law, employment law, environmental law—focusing on the distinctive legal factual issues in each? These courses, which are now common, demonstrate the deep impact of the Realist agenda on the legal curriculum, as it was 'assimilated into law school culture and began to be taken for granted'.[51]

[44] Roscoe Pound, 'Mechanical Jurisprudence' (1908) 605. [45] Ibid 610.

[46] Wade (n 42) 9 Cambridge Law Journal 286.

[47] Kahn-Freund (n 9) 129; see similarly in Otto Kahn-Freund, 'Postscript' in R Lewis and J Clark, *Labour Law and Politics in the Weimar Republic* (OUP 1981) 199.

[48] Cited in William Twining, *Karl Llewellyn and the Realist Movement* (2nd ed, Cambridge University Press 2012) 48.

[49] Brainerd Currie, 'The Materials of Law Study' (1951) 3 Journal of Legal Education 331.

[50] Gower (n 3) 183. [51] Twining (n 8) 68.

However, the Realists' ambitions were even more radical. They proposed a fundamental transformation of the structure of the degree. Such a reform would require not just redrafting course titles, but rewriting teaching materials entirely. Indeed, during the 1950s, several innovative casebooks appeared, organized not by traditional categories but by 'situation types', such as 'surgical operations', 'keeping of animals', 'traffic and transportation', and so forth.[52]

REFLECTION POINT

Imagine yourself sitting on a Law School committee tasked with re-designing the curriculum. You have absolute authority to discard any modules and to replace them with new ones. Which modules would you keep, which would you remove, and which would you initiate? Think of precise situation types such as the ones suggested above (and we can add to that list others, such as 'disciplinary hearings' or 'family disputes'). But you may want to offer a bird's-eye view of these situations, under grand headings such as 'Law and Power' (which would include parts of criminal law, constitutional law, administrative law, tax law, parts of land law, etc) and 'Promises and the Law' (which would range from contract law through consumer law, equity, contract, etc). Which model would you prefer, and why?

A second proposed reform was to 'open up' the legal curriculum to the social sciences.[53] Holmes memorably captured this approach: 'For the rational study of the law the blackletter man may be the man of the present, but the man of the future is the man of statistics and the master of economics.'[54] Currie, again, articulated this idea in more detail:

> Since law is a means of social control, it ought to be studied as such. Solutions to the problems of a changing social order are not implicit in the rules and principles which are formally elaborated on the basis of past decisions, to be evoked by merely formal logical processes; and effective legal education cannot proceed in disregard of this fact. . . . an understanding of the social structure in which law operates can no longer be taken for granted or regarded as irrelevant; law students—and hence law teachers—must acquire that understanding, and must somehow learn to take into account the contributions which other disciplines and sciences can make to the solution of social problems.[55]

This approach was familiar to English legal scholars of the time. In a 1933 lecture at King's College London, Lord Atkin described law as a 'great science', but not in the sense of 'modern

[52] Brian Leiter, 'Legal Realism and Legal Positivism Reconsidered' (2001) 111 Ethics 278, 282; Stewart Macaulay, 'The New versus the Old Legal Realism: "Things Ain't What They Used to be"' (2005) Wisconsin Law Review 365, 374–5.

[53] George Grossman, 'Clinical Legal Education: History and Diagnosis' (1973) 26 Journal of Legal Education 162; Spiegel (n 11) 586.

[54] Holmes (n 6) 11–12. The passage continues, also quite memorably, in a manner that further highlights the realists' focus on the future, rather than the past: 'It is revolting to have no better reason for a rule of law than that so it was laid down in the time of Henry IV. It is still more revolting if the grounds upon which it was laid down have vanished long since, and the rule simply persists from blind imitation of the past'—ibid 12.

[55] Currie (n 49) 334.

physical sciences', but as a discipline concerned with matters of 'immense human interest' and 'one that does more to quicken and invigorate the understanding than all the other kinds of learning put together'.[56] He thus suggested that law should be taught alongside history, morality, and economics, creating a single degree that helps students understand the wider context of social interactions, patterns, and rules. A year later, the Lord Chancellor noted that 'Law joins hands as never before with problems in economics, problems in political science, problems in the technique of administration. It is important that the curricula of our law schools should send out lawyers trained to appreciate the meaning of these relationships.'[57] This interdisciplinary view has a long history in England. William Blackstone famously wrote that 'Sciences are of a sociable disposition, and flourish best in the neighbourhood of each other'.[58] These academics, judges, and politicians made a simple but powerful point: law is not a 'science' that can be studied in isolation from social reality. Law is made by people, it is interpreted by people, and it affects people. In striving for the best version of 'the law', we should ask which version creates the best society. Is that really so controversial?

However, while this approach took hold in the United States, it barely made ripples across the UK. Gower quoted Lon Fuller, of Harvard Law School, who said: 'For about twenty years now . . . American professors of law have been agreeing with one another that we ought to do something about the integration of law with the other social sciences'. Gower then sighed: 'England could not say as much. At most we might perhaps claim that for the last two or three years we have been disagreeing with each other on whether we ought to do something about it.'[59]

The third prong of reform is related to the other two, but also stands apart, and it is the most relevant for present purposes. For Langdell, the *library* was the perfect laboratory for legal studies; for the Realists it was the *law firm*. And if that's the case, they argued, the best way to study law is 'to have such laboratories inside the law school'[60] and to teach students 'what it means to be a lawyer, help them advance and acquire lawyering skills'.[61] And what are these 'laboratories within law schools' if not law clinics? But deciding to set up a clinic is just the start of the journey. After they have been set up, what should the focus be?

REFLECTION POINT

The Realists were clearly right that law schools cannot effectively train lawyers to become practitioners without engaging them in the day-to-day experience of practical law.

However, they *assumed* that this is what law schools should be doing. In contrast, one could argue that law school should not be about training for practice, but for teaching law as an academic, intellectual phenomenon, its philosophical underpinnings, and its relation to society.

What is *your* law school doing? Has it found the right balance, or is it caught between the two models, managing not to perfect either?

[56] Lord Atkin, 'Law as an Educational Subject' (1932) Journal of the Society of Public Teachers of Law 27, 29.

[57] WPM Kennedy, 'Legal Subjects in the Universities of Canada' (1933) Journal of the Society of Public Teachers of Law 23.

[58] Cited in Kahn-Freund (n 9) 128.

[59] Gower (n 3) 172.

[60] Jerome Frank, 'A Plea for Lawyer-Schools' (1947) 56 Yale Law Journal 1303, 1329.

[61] Katherine Kruse, 'Getting Real about Legal Realism, New Legal Realism, and Clinical Legal Education' (2011) 56 New York Law School Law Review 659, 682.

We turn, then, to the engagement of theory and practice within CLE, beginning with the question: What, at the end of the day, is the purpose of CLE?

5.2 So What Now? The Plan for Clinical Legal Education

William Twining framed the core question of legal education, and perhaps for education more broadly, as: 'For what purpose should what be taught by whom using what methods in what milieux with what resources?'[62]

Here, we focus specifically on clinical legal education (CLE), while recognizing that it sits within the broader debate on legal education. In this section we start by addressing the first part of Twining's question: *For what purpose* should CLE be taught? The next subsection will look at *what* should be taught, and the third and final subsection in this chapter will address the *how*, or in Twining's version 'using what methods'.

5.2.1 What Is the Overriding Purpose of CLE?

From the extensive scholarship on CLE, three aims consistently emerge as the main motivations: developing practical skills, advancing social justice in both the community and the profession, and improving the overall quality of legal education.

We begin, then, with the claim that clinical legal education is justified as a means to develop students' practical and professional skills and, consequently, their employability. The argument begins with an obvious parallel: medical students learn how to take a patient's history because gathering a complete picture is essential for accurate diagnosis and advice, and retrieving that information is rarely straightforward. So why shouldn't law students be trained in the same way? They need skills at both the micro and macro levels. At the micro level, this includes interviewing clients, conducting investigations, offering advice, assessing strategies, and negotiating with the opposing party. At the macro level, it involves understanding the lawyer's broader role in society: 'an instrument of dispute resolution, an agent of social change, a medium for greater democratic participation, and as a mechanism of social control and symbol of stylized ritual.'[63]

Many law schools that embrace clinical projects do so because they recognize the need for students to develop proficiency at both these micro and macro levels. Indeed, when a law school committee seeks to expand 'skills training' as part of a curriculum review, it often does so by strengthening and expanding its clinical offerings.[64] Pragmatic concerns about employability have also fuelled the popularity of law clinics among university leaders, students, and practitioners, who see them as valuable training grounds.[65] Yet many

[62] Twining (n 8) 64.

[63] Carrie Menkel-Meadow, 'The Legacy of Clinical Education: Theories about Lawyering' (1980) 29 Cleveland State Law Review 555, 557.

[64] Spiegel (n 11) 603.

[65] Wizner (n 4) 332; Spiegel (n 11) 605–06; Donald Nicolson, 'Legal Education, Ethics and Access to Justice: Forging Warriors for Justice in a Neo-Liberal World' (2015) 22 International Journal of the Legal Profession 51, 53.

clinicians view this support with mixed feelings. While they embrace experiential learning as a core pedagogical approach (see below), they do not see skills training as the sole or ultimate purpose of CLE.

Again, they can, and indeed have, drawn on the insights of legal realists. Karl Llewllyn memorably, and poignantly, wrote: 'Ideals without technique are a mess. But technique without ideals is a menace.'[66] He added that finding *a* path is not the same as finding the *right* one, since 'To train, we must know what we are training for'.[67] You can probably sense that we are moving towards the second aim mentioned earlier: social justice. Steve Wizner brings the point into focus when he argues that clinical teaching

> must go beyond skills training . . . We need to profess a social, political and moral agenda in our teaching, an agenda that exposes students to the maldistribution of wealth, power and rights in society, and that seeks to inculcate in them a sense of their own ability and responsibility for using law to challenge injustice by assisting the poor and the powerless.[68]

Jane Aiken makes the case even more forcefully:

> If all I can do in law school is to teach students skills ungrounded in a sense of justice then at best there is no meaning to my work, and at worst, I am contributing to the distress in the world. I am sending more people into the community armed with legal training but without a sense of responsibility for others or for the delivery of justice in our society.[69]

In the Introduction to this book, we noted that social justice was a key driver in the development of CLE. We also saw that social justice has become a source of heated debate, with conservative, religious, and business-oriented students calling for clinics that reflect their own agendas. Here, however, we shift focus to a different divide: not right versus left, but rather those *interested* in the public or community versus those *not interested*. With this in mind, Jane Aiken's earlier quote can be read, in part, as a corrective.

In the US there is a well-documented trend of 'public interest drift':[70] students enter law school 'full of idealism' and leave, 'almost all of them, for large firms'. In contrast, UK studies on the change in students' idealism are very limited—two focused mainly on ethical values rather than social justice itself, and two other studies were limited in scope [71] So, for now, let us begin with the American case, simply because it is better documented.

Who is to blame for this shift, where students move from idealism to a more instrumental mindset? Some reasons lie outside law schools and may be uniquely American. For example,

[66] Llewellyn (n 6) 662. [67] Ibid 667.

[68] Steve Wizner, 'Beyond Skills Training' (2001) 7 Clinical Law Review 327, 332.

[69] Jane Aiken, 'Striving to Teach "Justice, Fairness and Morality"' (1997) 4 Clinical Law Review 1, 6 n 10.

[70] Alexi Freeman and Katie Steefel, 'Uniting the Head, Hands, and Heart: How Specialty Externships Can Combat Public Interest Drift' (2018) 25 Clinical Law Review 325, 327.

[71] Jonel Newman and Donald Nicolson, 'A Tale of Two Clinics: Similarities and Differences in Evidence of the Clinic Effect on the Development of Law Students' Ethical and Altruistic Professional Identities' (2016) 35 Buffalo Public Interest Law Journal 1 [which does address matters of access to justice as part of 'ethics']; Richard Moorehead et al, 'The Ethical Identity of Law Students' (2016) 23 International Journal of the Legal Profession 235.

American graduates often leave with six-figure debts and face a job market where private sector salaries are 2.5 times higher than public interest roles. These figures are not unique, but are likely less extreme in the UK. Some reasons lie outside law schools but still affect countries such as the UK, including the prestige of 'magic circle' firms and the limited availability of public interest jobs, which may be even scarcer in the UK.

Yet, at least partly, legal academics have blamed law schools themselves, noting that 'students do come to law school filled with passion, with morality, with a sense of justice, and we spend, the generic we, the law school itself, spends three years doing our best to crush them.'[72] A slightly less self-critical version, aligned with legal realist thinking, argues that law teachers 'strip law of its political content, framing moral commitments as antithetical to good lawyering,'[73] thereby fostering, even demanding, a passive classroom experience and a detached view of the legal system.[74] As noted earlier, the belief in law's neutrality creates a value-neutral approach to teaching it.[75] In other words, the belief is that the CLE approach, if embraced not only locally but across the curriculum, has the potential to improve the quality of legal education, and thus the legal profession.

Some view CLE as significant for fostering 'the belief that law school can serve an important role in producing lawyers who will go on to change the nature and function of legal practice in the interests of more humane social values, and the advancement of the poor and the disadvantaged.'[76] When this was written, in 1997, the authors highlighted the UK's 'general reluctance to embrace CLE', leaving law schools without 'a crucial element in educating students in social justice.'[77] Today, this statement simply highlights how much has changed.

REFLECTION POINT

Anthony Bradney has written in opposition to the vocational trends in British Law Schools in strong terms, encouraging them to 'raise the drawbridge'. He argued, first, that only half of law students become lawyers. But more principally:

> [U]niversities exist to educate students not workers . . . Universities seek to provide their students with the intellectual means to make better choices about their lives. This includes the means to select and pursue the occupation which best suits their talents and their aspirations. It should, however, go far wider than this occupational aim . . . It is not the function of the university law school to encourage anybody to become lawyers or to pursue any other particular occupation . . . A law degree might properly be taught with

[72] Robert Solomon, 'Teaching Morality' (1992) 42 Cleveland State Law Review 508.

[73] Catherine Albiston, Scott Cummings, and Richard Abel, 'Making Public Interest Lawyers in a Time of Crisis: An Evidence-Based Approach' (2020) 34 Georgetown Journal of Legal Ethics 223.

[74] Duncan Kennedy, 'Legal Education as Training for Hierarchy' in D Kairys (ed), *The Politics of Law: A Progressive Critique* (2010) 54.

[75] See text to n 38.

[76] Jeremy Cooper and Louise C Trubek, *Educating for Justice* (Routledge 1997, republished 2018).

[77] Ibid.

little reference to either barristers or solicitors. What reference there is need not persuade people either to become or not to become lawyers. University law schools concern themselves with the study of law, not lawyers.[78]

Do you agree with this position? To what extent does it impact on the justification for CLE?

5.2.2 **Law in Action, Not (Only) Law in Books**

Turning to Twining's question of *what should be taught* in CLE, it is helpful to note that a core tenet of legal realism is the focus on *law in action* rather than simply *law in books*. The appeal of this shift is clear: it shows that law matters because of its *real-life* consequences, which cannot be fully understood by simply reading statutes or court decisions—even from the Supreme Court.

But this distinction is based on the idea that there is a significant gap between the two. Specifically, this refers to the gap between the written rules and how agencies—such as tax authorities, police, or immigration officials—actually apply them.[79] One way to see this gap is through the myth that 'changing the words used in a legal opinion can automatically cause real change on the ground', a view that, it seems, 'everyone knows to be fiction'.[80] Karl Llewellyn called the rules found in statutes and case law 'paper rules', distinguishing them from 'working' or 'real' rules.[81] Paper rules often emerge by taking phrases from a specific social context, generalizing them, and then misapplying them to very different cases in time, place, and context.[82] This is the more theoretical problem with relying on paper rules. But it is made worse by ignoring the actual impact—or lack of impact—of legal decisions in real life.

For example, imagine learning about restraint of trade clauses in employment contracts (eg a rule that prevents a former employee from working in the legal sector for five years) through a case where the court said such clauses are enforceable if reasonable.[83] However, while this is the *paper rule* on restrictive covenants, in reality the employee easily avoided the injunction by opening the new business under his wife's name.[84] Shouldn't this—the way people can avoid the law—be part of the way we address, learn, and teach the law? Similarly, we often act as if 'passing a law to protect consumers would in fact protect them . . . [but] we cannot just assume that words on paper have little legs so that they can wiggle down off the page and enforce themselves'.[85] For example, in 2021, the UK Justice Secretary admitted that

[78] Anthony Bradney, 'Raising the Drawbridge: Defending University Law Schools' (1995) 1 Web Journal of Current Legal Issues. Available at https://www.bailii.org/uk/other/journals/WebJCLI/1995/issue1/bradney1.html

[79] Roscoe Pound, 'Law in Books and Law in Action' (1910) 44 American Law Review 12.

[80] Elizabeth Mertz, 'New Legal Realism: Law and Social Science in the New Millenium' in *The New Legal Realism* (n 7) 1, 2.

[81] Karl Llewellyn, 'A Realistic Jurisprudence—The Next Step' (1930) 30 Columbia Law Review 431.

[82] Robert Gordon, 'Legal Storytelling as a Variety of Legal Realism' in *The New Legal Realism* (n 7) 169, 171.

[83] *Harcus Sinclair LLP v Your Lawyers Ltd* [2021] UKSC 32.

[84] Gordon (n 82) 173.

[85] Stuart Macaulay, 'A New Legal Realism: Elegant Models and the Messy Law in Action' in *The New Legal Realism* (n 7) 29, 36–7.

budget cuts were partly to blame for 'record low' conviction rates for rape cases.[86] Even more starkly, early legal realist Robert Hale noted that even when state law supposedly protected black Americans and criminalized lynching, lynchers were 'rarely, if ever, punished'.[87] He argued further that the systematic failure to prosecute lynchers effectively amounted to 'a formal withdrawal of penalties for such crimes'.[88]

Legal rules cannot enforce themselves. For them to have real effects, officials must know about the changes, set up procedures, and receive proper funding for implementation and enforcement. It is *unrealistic* to expect lawyers, or anyone else for that matter, to ignore this reality and pretend that law is only about rules and logic. By contrast, CLE's focus on serving the client's best interests offers a more realistic and holistic understanding of problems and solutions, some found in legal rules, others in the wider social context. Awareness of *law in action* may help narrow the gap, bringing the *law in books* closer to how law works in real life. Alternatively, it could bring more modesty among teachers, lawyers, and judges, and more realistic expectations for clients, who may need to hear that even with the law on their side, 'you may spend a lot of money with little to show for your trouble'.[89]

This does not mean, to be clear, that the need for theory is discarded. On the contrary, as this chapter's introduction explains, a strong theory can be immensely valuable for practice, even if it remains highly 'theoretical'. Moreover, it has been argued that 'the only knowledge of permanent value is theoretical knowledge; and the broader it is, the greater the chance it will prove useful in practice'.[90] As noted earlier, this new theory opened the door for integrating empirical studies into law, drawing insights from economics (initially the most prominent), psychology, politics, criminology, and other fields. This approach encourages law students to 'see it as it works', to ask 'what is it for?' and 'how has it been working?'[91] This serves the broader aim identified earlier: 'the use of social sciences in legal education can—and should—go hand in hand with heightened attention to achieving justice.'[92]

Practical Exercise 5.1

Think of two cases/instances in your clinical work in which the law does not live up to its promise, where the rule as dictated by legislation or case has not led to the expected result, or perhaps has led to the opposite result. Now try to find reports or academic articles that suggest how to address those gaps. Do you think the gaps you found are the rule or the exception? Are you satisfied with the suggestions for reform?

[86] BBC News, 'Priti Patel and Robert Buckland "deeply ashamed" of rape conviction rates' BBC (19 June 2021) https://www.bbc.co.uk/news/uk-politics-57511425

[87] Quoted in Note, 'Legal Realism and the Race Question: Some Realism about Realism on Race Relations' (1995) 108 Harvard Law Review 1607, 1615.

[88] Ibid. [89] Gordon (n 82) 173.

[90] Daniel Bell, *The Reforming of General Education* (Routledge 1966) 108 quoted in Phyllis Goldfarb, 'A Theory–Practice Spiral: The Ethics of Feminism and Clinical Education' (1990) 75 Minnesota Law Review 1599.

[91] Karl Llewellyn, *The Common Law Tradition: Deciding Appeals* (Little, Brown 1960) 510; on this 'pragmatic' approach see Brian Leiter, 'Rethinking Legal Realism: Toward a Naturalized Jurisprudence' (1997) 76 Texas Law Review 267, 275.

[92] Mertz (n 7) 13.

5.2.3 **Experiential Learning**

In addressing Twining's question 'by what methods', you may think that we are entering the realm of form, and departing from the world of substance and theory. Nothing could be further from reality. Indeed, Richard Wilson goes so far as to declare that

> The unifying theory of clinical legal education has more to do with education—how law is taught ... than lawyering—what lawyers do ... The unifying theory of clinic lies in the concept and principles of experiential learning itself, a subset of educational theory ... which was—and is—revolutionary in its approach to learning and teaching, at least within legal education.[93]

You may recall that, according to Christopher Columbus Langdell, 'the library is the proper workshop of [law] professors and students alike ... it is to us all that the laboratories of the university are to the chemists and physicists, the museum of natural history to the zoologists, the botanical garden to the botanists'.[94] We also noted the critique of this view, which suggested that 'life of law' is one of experience rather than logic. It is no coincidence that, in offering this critique, Realists proposed not only a new way to understand and study law, but also a radically different pedagogy. In doing so, they followed an approach advanced at the time by John Dewey, who is often described as 'the most influential educator of the twentieth century'.[95]

Dewey rejected the prevailing view of education as a process in which the student remains detached from the subject matter and merely absorbs passively. Instead, he argued that education is a developmental process requiring *interaction* between the student and the subject matter. He stated that 'it is only in experience that any theory has vital and verifiable significance ... a theory apart from an experience cannot be grasped even as theory'.[96] Dewey's influence on the Realists of the time is immediately clear. Jerome Frank echoed Dewey, stating that 'An interest in the practical should not preclude, on the contrary it should invite, a lively interest in theory. For practices unavoidably blossom into theories, and most theories induce practices, good or bad.'[97]

As Dewey later explained more explicitly,[98] 'traditional' education is not education at all, because it denies students the opportunity to study the world and understand its meanings and values. In a 'traditional' setting, teachers act as external repositories of knowledge and skills while students' attitude is expected to be one of 'docility, receptivity and obedience'.[99] Learning in the traditional setting means acquiring *static* knowledge presented as a finished product, with little room for exploration.

In contrast, what Dewey viewed as 'progressive' education rests on the idea that there is 'an intimate and necessary relation between the processes of actual experience and education'.[100] This is not to say that all experience is inherently valuable and positive. Experience

[93] Wilson (n 14) 127 [emphasis added].

[94] Christopher Langdell, 'Harvard Celebration Speeches' (1887) 3 Law Quarterly Review 123, 124.

[95] Richard Wilson, *The Global Evolution of Clinical Legal Education: More than a Method* (Cambridge University Press 2015) 128.

[96] John Dewey, *Democracy and Education: An Introduction to the Philosophy of Education* (1916) 169.

[97] Frank (n 21) 1321.

[98] John Dewey, *Experience and Education* (Simon and Schuster 1938).

[99] Ibid 19.

[100] Ibid 20.

may be wasteful, or even harmful and mis-educative, if not guided and structured to facilitate growth and development through meaningful interaction.

We can almost hear Dewey joining the debate over the true 'legal laboratory'—whether the library, as Langdell claimed, or the law firm, as Frank and the Realists preferred. He criticized traditional education for failing to 'demand that the teacher should become intimately acquainted with the conditions of the local community, physical, historical, economic, occupational, etc. in order to utilize them as educational resources . . . There is no such thing as educational value in the abstract'.[101] Traditional legal education makes no distinction between studying in Birmingham, Alabama and in Birmingham in the West Midlands, or between Aberdeen, Scotland and Aberdeen, South Africa. The progressive approach insists that students be aware of the issues affecting their local community and that law teachers use these issues as resources to deepen understanding of how law operates 'in action'. Wilson cites the idea that 'knowledge and the environment are not fixed' and continues to say that 'No statement better theorizes the justification, indeed the necessity, for experiential learning through clinical education'.[102]

It is common to hear senior legal practitioners gently tell academics that graduates must 'unlearn' much of what they were taught in law school. Dewey predicted this outcome whenever subjects are learned in isolation, sealed in a 'water-tight compartment'.[103] Even the practice of reflection, which is often introduced in law schools through CLE and explored further in Chapter 6, was central to Dewey's philosophy. He explained that the phrase 'stop and think' is truly sound, psychologically. It enhances informed judgement and facilitates a 'more comprehensive and coherent plan of act[ion]'.[104]

Dewey's approach has been widely accepted and integrated into educational theory and pedagogy throughout the twentieth century. Thankfully, primary and secondary schools in the UK and elsewhere have moved away from the old model where students sat in rows listening to teachers for hours on end. Teachers have moved from being 'the sage on the stage' to 'the guide on the side'. Even in Higher Education, disciplines such as social work, medicine, education, public health, and business now recognize that meaningful learning must include experiential elements. Against this backdrop, legal education remains a notable outlier, prompting Rubin to exclaim that

> To rely on a model of education that was designed in the 1870s, therefore, as the traditional approach to legal education does, denies us the benefit of the entire range of modern thought about the educational process and of the entire field of modern psychology that informs this area . . .
>
> [T]he Langdellian notion of education treats its subject matter as a pre-established set of rules or methodologies that exists 'out there' in a passive realm separate from and independent of the students. This notion is entirely inconsistent with the now generally accepted fact that what law schools teach is a human product, something that is socially constructed. Even more importantly for present purposes, this notion is inconsistent

[101] Ibid 40, 46. [102] Wilson (n 95) 132; also Nicolson (n 65) 57. [103] Dewey (n 98) 47.
[104] Ibid 64.

> with the learning process, which, as Dewey noted, is primarily experiential. A basic understanding of legal practice and even legal theory can be achieved only by actually performing legal tasks or observing legal behaviors. Students who have never tried to draft a contract, or who have never seen one being negotiated, have not merely failed to receive training in a particular skill; they will not be able to understand what a contract means, what purposes it serves, or how it should be read by either the parties or an adjudicator . . . The self-contained, rule-based Langdellian curriculum has closed them off from the twentieth-century insight that learning comes from experience, and is itself an experience.[105]

Notwithstanding the above, Realists and other critics did not see the case method as unnecessary for legal education. On the contrary, they regarded the 'technical skills' emphasized by Langdell as 'the necessary foundation'[106] for legal training and 'at the heart of successful clinical instruction'.[107] These skills include reading and interpreting cases, analysing and applying doctrine, and developing logical reasoning and critical thinking.[108] However, while they acknowledged the value of these skills, some argued they could be mastered in just six months, after which 'boredom sets in'.[109] In the English context, critics point out that if a one-year conversion course equips non-law graduates with the same legal knowledge, it questions the need for a three-year undergraduate law degree.[110]

After all, the case method does not teach many essential practical skills, such as client interviewing, hands-on legal research, fact gathering, negotiation, or broader social, professional, and ethical responsibilities.[111] Llewellyn suggested that law schools should complement traditional skills with others, including statutory interpretation, advocacy, drafting, counselling, and policy decision-making. Amsterdam, for his part, offered a more abstract list, which included: ends–means thinking; hypothesis formulation and testing information gathering; and decision-making under uncertainty and varying degrees of risk.[112] You might now ask yourself: to what extent am I learning these skills in my clinical legal education module? Or in any other module?

Incorporating these suggestions into the curriculum would show students that law is far less certain and far more subjective than case law suggests. The 'factual matrix' of a case may vary, due to 'the faulty memory of witnesses, the bias of witnesses, the perjury of witnesses'; the 'effects of fatigue, alertness, political pull, graft, laziness, conscientiousness, patience, impatience, prejudice and open-mindedness of judges'; and the craft used in negotiation and drafting documents.[113]

[105] Rubin (n 13).
[106] Karl Llewellyn, *Jurisprudence: Realism in Theory and Practice* (University of Chicago Press 1962) 377.
[107] Wilson (n 14) 146.
[108] Anthony Amsterdam, 'Clinical Legal Education—A 21st Century Perspective' (1984) 34 Journal of Legal Education 612, 613.
[109] George Grossman, 'Clinical Legal Education: History and Diagnosis' (1973) 26 Journal of Legal Education 162, 166.
[110] Bradney (n 78).
[111] Grossman (n 109) 166, 188.
[112] Amsterdam (n 108) 612.
[113] Frank (n 21) 918.

TAKING STOCK

This section moved from the legal realist approach to law to a clearer focus on legal education in general, and clinical legal education in particular. Perhaps one of the most important insights developed by Realists lies in identifying the gap between 'law in books' and 'law in action'. They understood that even if the law is clear, stable, and well understood (and it rarely is), it could be made irrelevant because of lack of enforcement, due to negligence, lack of willingness, lack of funding, and so on. From this insight flows the understanding that the only way to become knowledgeable in a profession is to engage in it, in the front line or at the coal face. Along with John Dewey, Realists helped to develop a programme to integrate theory and skills, and even the theory of skills. They did not seek to undermine the case method wholesale, but rather to build on it and add on a range of skills that are partly vocational and partly theoretical.

Conclusion

More than 25 years ago, the UK's Advisory Committee on Legal Education and Conduct (ACLEC) concluded that

> A liberal and humane legal education implies that students are engaged in active rather than passive learning, and are enabled to develop intellectually by means of significant study in depth of issues and problems as part of a coherent and integrated course, and that the teaching of appropriate and defined skills is undertaken in a way which combines practical knowledge with theoretical understanding . . .
>
> The freedom of universities to decide what, whom and how they teach, has to be reconciled with the duty of the professional bodies to maintain and improve the educational standards and qualifications of entrants and practitioners; if greater flexibility, variety, diversity and intellectual rigour are to be achieved, as well as a liberalisation of the law degree, universities will need greater freedom of manoeuvre and institutional autonomy; at the same time the rigid demarcation between the 'academic' and 'vocational' stages needs to disappear; what is required is a new partnership between the universities and the professional bodies at all stages of legal education and training.[114]

Throughout this chapter, we have identified several concerns raised about legal education. If you are reading this and thinking 'this is depressing; have I wasted the last three years studying law?', we have two responses: First, spare a thought for those of us writing this book, who have spent decades *teaching* law. Second, and more seriously, the answer is clear: no, you have not been wasting your time. When pointing out the shortcomings of any institution,

[114] Lord Chancellor's Advisory Committee on Legal Education and Conduct (April 1996) [2.2].

including legal education, it can seem as though the critic sees no redeeming features at all. It is important to clarify that not all is wrong with legal education, or even with the case method. Legal skills are real and valuable. Law students should be able to identify a ratio, compare and distinguish cases, and understand the language in which the law is practised. However, this chapter suggests that while the case method is necessary, it is not sufficient for fully understanding the law or for becoming a truly effective lawyer. Therefore, 150 years after Langdell's revolution, legal education is primed for a second one.

What form should this revolution take? Clinical legal education has been waiting in the wings for almost a century. Whether inspired by the legal realists, who urged a focus on *law in action* rather than just *law in books*, or by education scholars such as John Dewey, who stressed that learning must include an element of *doing*, clinical legal education offers a new framework for thinking about both the law and legal education.

This chapter does not suggest a one-size-fits-all model for clinical legal education any more than there is a single 'right' framework for legal education generally. Different clinics may strike different balances between theory and practice, social justice and employability, or the roles of academics and practitioners. This debate will continue, and should continue.

Further Reading

- On legal education

William Twining, *Law in Context: Enlarging a Discipline* (OUP 1997).

- On legal realism and clinical legal education:

Jerome Frank, 'Why Not a Clinical Lawyer School' (1932) 81 University of Pennsylvania Law Review and American Law Register 907.

KR Kruse, 'Getting Real about Legal Realism, New Legal Realism, and Clinical Legal Education I. Clinical Theory Workshop' (2011) 56 New York Law School Law Review 659.

- On the aims and ends of clinical legal education

Donald Nicolson, 'Legal Education, Ethics and Access to Justice: Forging Warriors for Justice in a Neo-Liberal World' (2015) 22 International Journal of the Legal Profession 51.

Richard J Wilson, *The Global Evolution of Clinical Legal Education: More than a Method* (Cambridge University Press 2017).

6 Reflection

The irony of life is that it is lived forward but understood backward.

Soren Kierkegaard

By three methods we may learn wisdom: first, by reflection, which is the noblest; second, by imitation, which is easiest; and third, by experience, which is the bitterest.

Confucius

Chapter Overview

This chapter will introduce you to the concept and practice of reflective practice, the different types and models of reflection, and the challenges to the practice and the ideal of reflection.

The aim of the chapter is to:

- introduce you to the various definitions and features of reflection
- explain the benefits and value of reflection in clinical legal education
- provide an overview of a number of reflection models, which assist, in a structured way, with the practice of 'how to reflect'
- explore some of the common barriers to reflection
- identify a number of ethical and practical critiques of reflection.

Introduction

One of the more striking, and perhaps unfortunate, aspects of legal education is the lack of attention and resources devoted to reflection and to the theory that supports its role. This is regrettable because, although 'learning through doing' is better than passively receiving information, it is still not enough. John Dewey, as we saw in Chapter 5, was an early advocate of this approach and argued that there is an 'organic connection between education and personal experience'.[1] His belief that education relies on experience also has an illustrious

[1] John Dewey, *Education and Experience* (Simon and Schuster 1938) 25.

intellectual lineage. In 1689, John Locke asked: 'Whence has it all the materials of reason and knowledge?' and answered: '. . . in one word, from experience. In that all our knowledge is founded, and from that it ultimately derives itself . . . Experience here must teach me what reason cannot'.[2] But Dewey also noted that experience is not enough, since 'we do not learn from experience . . . we learn from reflecting on experience'.[3] Or, to use the old saying: reflection is the difference between 20 years of experience and one year of experience repeated 20 times.[4]

If we are serious, for example, about 'lifelong learning' (a strategic goal across the EU since 2007), then *learning to reflect* is a necessary part of that process. Since law graduates often move into roles that involve practice (whether in law or elsewhere), learning to reflect on their work clearly strengthens their professional abilities. We mentioned in Chapter 5 that in comparable professions such as social work, health, and education, reflection has been an integral part of training and assessment since at least the 1980s.

Against this background, it should be unsurprising that Clinical Legal Education has led the way in incorporating reflection into legal education. Within law schools, CLE was the first to recognize the importance of reflection, not only for meeting clear competencies such as legal knowledge, client care, and ethics but also for developing thoughtful, critically minded professionals. To that end, CLE places strong emphasis on teaching students how to reflect by introducing different models of reflection and encouraging them to choose the one that best suits their experience and preferences. Indeed, it has been suggested that teaching law students how to learn from experience is the goal of CLE,[5] and that the 'mantra of clinical legal pedagogy [is] reflect, reflect, reflect'.[6] Moreover, the introduction to reflective practice is not approached as an abstract exercise. Many CLE programmes and modules even assess students on the basis of their reflection—a decision that, as we will see, is not beyond controversy. Thus, while the experience and the thoughts it generates may be personal and subjective, the reflective process still involves objective criteria. There are, dare we say, right and wrong ways to reflect, which students can be assessed on. Hopefully, this provides sufficient motivation to read on, with attention.

6.1 Why Reflect?

The introduction above began to answer this question. However, a more structured inquiry reveals three key motivations: meaningful learning, dynamic learning, and critical learning.

[2] John Locke, *An Essay Concerning Human Understanding* (38th ed, 1689, William Tegg, Book II, chapter 1).

[3] John Dewey, *How We Think* (Dover 2003) 78.

[4] Quoted in, eg, David Kolb, *Experiential Learning: Experience as the Source of Learning and Development* (2nd ed, Pearson 2015) 46; Julian Webb, 'Where the Action Is: Developing Artistry in Legal Education' (1995) 2 International Journal of the Legal Profession 187; Liz Beaty, *Developing Your Teaching through Reflective Practice* (SEDA 1997) 8.

[5] Anthony G Amsterdam, 'Clinical Legal Education—A 21st Century Perspective' (1984) 34 Journal of Legal Education 612.

[6] Abbe Smith, 'Carrying On in Criminal Court: When Criminal Defence Is Not So Sexy and Other Grievances' (1995) 1 Clinical Law Review 723, 728.

6.1.1 **Meaningful Learning**

If we care about learning—and we do—then we should care about reflection. 'Learning' is 'the process whereby knowledge is created through the transformation of experience'[7] and 'occurs not in the doing but in the reflection and conceptualization that takes place during and after the event'.[8] The futurist Alvin Toffler famously declared that 'The illiterates of the 21st century will not be those who cannot read and write, but those who cannot learn, unlearn, and relearn'. In relation to legal education, it has been argued that 'developing lifelong learning skills', that is, helping students learn from experience, 'may be the most important goal of legal education'.[9] More broadly, Paolo Freire, the Brazilian philosopher, educator, and liberation theologist, connected the themes of theory ('words'), experience ('action'), and reflection, noting:

> Liberation is a praxis: the action and reflection of men upon their world in order to transform it. When a word is deprived of its dimension of action, reflection automatically suffers as well; and the work is changed into idle chatter, into verbalism, into an alienated and alienating 'blah'. On the other hand, if action is emphasised exclusively, to the detriment of reflection, the word is converted into activism . . . Men are not built in silence, but in words, in work, in action-reflection.[10]

This insight seems profound, or abstract. Let us try to make it more concrete. Freire suggests that reflection bridges how we think about the world in the abstract with how we engage and experience it. We might believe that people are generally selfish and competitive, only to encounter the unsolicited kindness of strangers. Or we might naively assume that racism and sexism have disappeared, only to face them in a harsh and ugly encounter. We could, of course, ignore these experiences and stick to our convictions, insisting: 'my mind's made up—don't confuse me with the facts.'

Alternatively, we can pause to reflect on the gap between our vision of the world and the reality we have encountered. In doing so, we may uncover important truths previously hidden by our biases and assumptions. Stephen Brookfield identifies three assumptions that we carry around with us: paradigmatic, prescriptive, and causal.[11] Briefly, paradigmatic assumptions are 'the structuring assumptions we use to order the world into fundamental categories'.[12] Prescriptive assumptions are 'assumptions about what we *think* ought to be happening in a particular situation'.[13] And causal assumptions concern 'how different parts

[7] Kolb (n 4) 49.

[8] Hugh Brayne, Nigel Duncan, and Richard Grimes, *Clinical Legal Education: Active Learning in Your Law School* (Blackstone Press 1998) 47.

[9] Roy Stuckey et al, *Best Practices for Legal Education: A Vision and a Road Map* (Clinical Legal Education Association 2007) 126.

[10] Paulo Freire, *Pedagogy of the Oppressed* (Seabury Press 1973) 66, 75–6.

[11] Stephen Brookfield, *Becoming a Critically Reflective Teacher* (2nd ed, Wiley 2017).

[12] Ibid 5. [13] Ibid 6.

of the world work and about the conditions under which these can be changed'.[14] Jane Aiken helpfully applies these insights to the Clinical Legal Education setting:[15]

> Paradigmatic assumptions are perhaps the most difficult to pin down because they are the very structural assumptions we use to put our experience into fundamental categories. Many times we see these assumptions as merely facts, the way things are. For example, students often believe that if a person is actually innocent, he cannot be legally held in prison. Clinics that do post-conviction work provide eye-opening experiences for students who learn that actual innocence often is not a ground for a habeas petition. Grappling with that offers students the opportunity to explore how the criminal justice system works and the degree to which a defendant's lack of resources at trial is treated as irrelevant in an assessment of post-conviction remedies . . .
>
> Prescriptive assumptions are what we think ought to be happening in a given situation. For example, if you take for granted that people are always able to make it on time to pre-arranged appointments if they are sufficiently organized, then you may believe that a client is disorganized and unmotivated if she fails to arrive on time . . . Bryant and Peters describe a very effective method for getting at these kinds of assumptions by challenging the students to imagine parallel universes. The teacher asks the student to generate alternative interpretations of a client's behavior. This process allows the student to understand how little the student knows about the client's life, helps forestall a rush to judgment and fosters open-mindedness . . .
>
> The third kind of assumption is causal. These assumptions help us understand how the world works and how we can effectuate change . . . For example, a clinical student acted as guardian *ad litem* representing a child whose mother was drug addicted. In a supervision session, the student proposed that we should recommend to the court that the mother's visitation should be conditioned on her active participation in a drug treatment program. If she dropped out, she lost visitation. The student justified this proposal by stating that the mother needed the incentive, and it was in the best interest of the child to have a drug-free mother. No drug treatment, no visits . . . By exploring the underlying assumptions about the causal connection between being a drug addict and being a bad parent, the student understood how little she actually knew about the cause of the mother's instability.
>
> (references omitted)

[14] Ibid 7.

[15] Jane H Aiken, 'Provocateurs for Justice' (2001) Georgetown Law Faculty Publications and Other Works 304. https://scholarship.law.georgetown.edu/facpub/304

REFLECTION POINT

Assumptions: Paradigmatic, Prescriptive, and Causal

Here are some additional examples of assumptions from 'traditional' clinical areas:

Paradigmatic: 'Unemployed people are lazy.'

Prescriptive: 'People shouldn't confess to a crime that they didn't commit.'

Causal: 'People don't lose visitation rights to their children because of legal technicalities. They're probably bad parents.'

Can you think of assumptions relevant to your clinic? Perhaps try to think of assumptions that you held in the past, but no longer hold.

Although it may seem obvious, challenging assumptions is essential for learning in general, but particularly important for adult learning ('andragogy', as distinct from 'pedagogy', which refers to children's learning). Adults' prior experience can be both a strength and a weakness. It is a strength when it provides a solid basis for learning, building, and expanding on prior knowledge. But it can also be a hindrance if experience breeds inflexibility and leads to assumptions that limit the ability to absorb and process new knowledge. Being set in our ways can dull our awareness of our surroundings and inhibit our ability to recognize the significance of what has just happened.[16]

This is why Clinical Legal Education is considered 'andragogically sound':[17] it aligns closely with theories and insights of adult education. On the importance of challenging prior assumptions, Fran Quigley highlights the process in adult learning theory that begins with the 'disorienting moment'.[18] This is 'when the learner confronts an experience that is disorienting or even disturbing because the experience cannot be easily explained by reference to the learner's prior understanding—referred to in learning theory as "meaning schemes"—of how the world works'.[19] It is here that reflection is key, the 'magic ingredient which converts legal experience into education':[20]

> Reflection . . . allows the learner to contrast the lessons of the disorienting moment with the learner's existing meaning schemes and determine what part of his or her meaning schemes must be amended to account for the surprising information provided in the disorienting moment.[21]

[16] David Boud and David Walker, 'Barriers to Reflection on Experience' in David Boud, Ruth Cohen, and David Walker (eds), *Using Experience For Learning* (Society for Research Into Higher Education 1993) 80.

[17] Frank S Bloch, 'The Andragogical Basis of Clinical Legal Education' (1982) 35 Vanderbilt Law Review 321.

[18] Fran Quigley, 'Seizing the Disorienting Moment: Adult Learning Theory and the Teaching of Social Justice in Law School Clinics' (1995) 2 Clinical Law Review 37.

[19] Ibid 51.

[20] Georgina Ledvinka, 'Reflection and Assessment in Clinical Legal Education: Do You See What I See?' (2006) 9 International Journal of Clinical Legal Education, 29, 29–30.

[21] Quigley (n 18) 55.

6.1.2 **Dynamic Learning**

As we will see when reviewing the different models for reflection below, they are often shown graphically in a circular format, such as the one in Figure 6.1. The implication would be that the output of one stage of reflection constitutes the input of the next stage. So, if a particular reflection model has four phases, the graphic illustration might look like this:

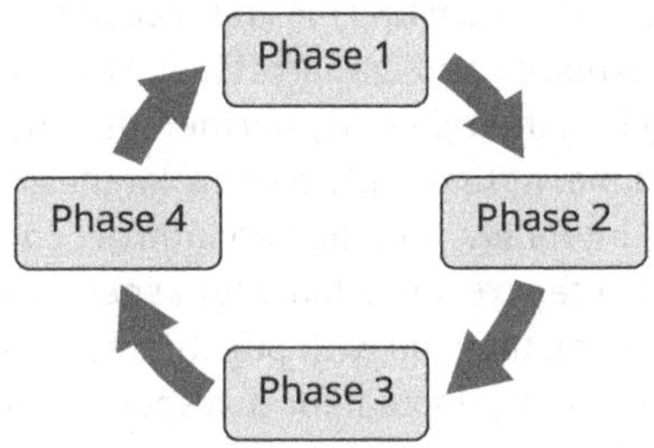

Figure 6.1 Generic reflection model

A key insight about this aspect of the reflective process is that it relies on a view of reality, and of how we understand it, that sharply contrasts with the Langdellian vision of law as a fixed science. Reflection is not linear, nor is it like solving a single puzzle and then moving on to the next, unrelated one. It is also not meant to capture an objective, standalone truth that, once reached, lets us simply 'move on' to other issues. In other words, it is not a simple 'reflection' such as the one we face in the mirror. Instead, it is more like an ongoing 'conversation with the situation'. When developing the need for and design of experiential learning, its proponents 'were responding to the general phenomena—the idea that knowledge and the environment are not fixed'.[22] Richard Wilson concludes that the dynamic nature of the social and legal environment, together with the development of personal and collective knowledge, fully supports 'the justification, indeed the necessity, for experiential learning through clinical legal education'.[23]

Jonel Newman and Donald Nicolson explain further that

> reflection may lead to the adoption of new, or the adaptation of existing, theories about how to handle issues (including moral issues), which can then be put into practice when similar situations arise. This new experience provides the material for further reflection, theory adaption, and theory testing, and so on. Moreover, it seems obvious that the more opportunities for experience and reflection students confront, the more sophisticated their theories will become, and the more habitual the resultant behavior will be.[24]

[22] Kenneth Ludmerer, cited in Richard Wilson, *The Global Evolution of Clinical Legal Education: More Than a Method* (Cambridge University Press 2017) 132.

[23] Ibid.

[24] Jonel Newman and Donald Nicolson, 'A Tale of Two Clinics: Similarities and Differences in Evidence of the Clinic Effect on the Development of Law Students' Ethical and Altruistic Professional Identities' [2016] Buffalo Public Interest Law Journal 35.

A Conversation with the Situation

Read the (real) reflection from a student about the development of their skills. Can you see how the situatiown challenged not only their skills, but also what they thought of their skills, and what they can do about it?

My partner and I struggled to find a quiet room to conduct the interview after the seminar; when we did, we struggled with IT issues, causing us to be 20 minutes late for the client interview. I was stressed and embarrassed, especially because I was the lead interviewer, and it was my first interview. My partner also showed signs of panic, which further demoralized me. At first, I blamed my lateness on the CLE seminar that ended just before the interview, and the bad internet connection. However, in retrospect, I realize I must accept responsibility for aspects that I could have avoided. I accepted that I had a poor relationship with punctuality prior to beginning my CLE role, and that telling myself to be punctual for this specific meeting did not mean I would automatically transform into a punctual person without taking active steps. Despite this, I was able to use positive skillsets by communicating the complications with my client and supervisor via email, assuring them that I would try to start the meeting as soon as possible. My supervising solicitor also provided feedback, stating that I was pleasant and polite. This is significant to me because I did not realize I could work through high-pressure situations while remaining calm . . . To stay organized, I would suggest to my partner that we set our own deadline and complete all necessary tasks before any actual deadlines . . .

Initially, my partner and I decided to work as a team and share the tasks equally . . . The situation involved a very complicated employment issue that I was unfamiliar with . . . I was hesitant to contact the supervising solicitor for assistance or guidance because I did not want to be bothersome, and I did not ask my partner for help with the advice letter because I did not want to appear incapable after having a difficult interview. In retrospect, I realised that I may be afraid of asking for help, and that this will impede my development and the quality of my work. This has required me to accept and be confident in my weaknesses to understand that seeking assistance will only strengthen areas or skills that are underdeveloped. Furthermore, I was disappointed that my partner only requested to outline the advice letter, such as the date and address, leaving me to form the advice; however, I should have communicated my needs and requested that we work as a team. I didn't mind covering a large portion of the advice letter, but I would have preferred not to do it all because it made me feel like I was working alone. Alternatively, this situation could be viewed more positively, as I learned to be resourceful and conduct independent research, though this took longer than necessary due to my fears and lack of communication.

On reflection, I have realized that I can communicate client matters and research problems effectively with my partner, but I cannot communicate when something bothers me or when I'm having difficulty to avoid conflict . . . I should have communicated with my partner by suggesting that we split the tasks . . . I can now embrace the collaborative process because it is a trial and error process that must be tailored to different individuals and needs.

6.1.3 **Critical Learning in and towards a Role**

As mentioned above, reflection carries added weight and significance when the learning involves a professional role, such as education, health, social work, or law.[25] Why is that the case? As seen in Timothy Casey's model of reflection (discussed in detail below), professional roles require meeting objective standards of competence.[26] How do you prepare for a case? How should you treat a client? What are your duties regarding confidentiality and conflicts of interest? These are vital questions, and it is essential to have a clear grasp of the answers. However, *understanding* the 'objective standard' of the profession is only the first step before critically appraising those standards and expectations. After all, we must know what we are critiquing before we can critique it meaningfully.

Thus, 'the reflective process amplif[ies] the knowledge, skill and values related to professional identity'.[27] This may involve ethical considerations, personal biases and preferences, the biases and traits of others involved, and broader 'systemic power dynamics, political and social realities, and economic forces that affect their decisions'.[28]

The latter aspect of reflection—which engages the political, social, and economic realities—helps build 'critical consciousness', which takes the student or practitioner away from strict objective standards and even challenges the desire for 'certainty'. This is an important issue and worth exploring in more detail.

The issue of certainty, or uncertainty, is relevant because of the very different approaches taken by law schools, on the one hand, and advocates of learning through practice and reflection, on the other. It is quite common, for example, for students in general, and law students in particular, to write academic essays proposing reforms aimed at promoting 'certainty'.[29] But, while chaos and anarchy are clearly not an aspiration, a mindset that seeks certainty 'does not generate the flexibly enquiring attitude required by learning'. Moreover, the flaw lies not only in the desire for certainty but also in the effort to frame situations as if they are fixed, refusing to see alternative explanations or possible ways forward. Schön observes that some people are 'virtuosos in avoiding uncertainty'[30] by choosing not to pay attention to it. David Kolb quotes Hegel, who stated that 'Any experience that does not violate expectation is not worthy of the name experience'.[31]

What does Hegel (as quoted by Kolb) mean by that provocative claim? Surely, we can gain experience simply by engaging in practice, day in, day out, without encountering the

[25] See also Quigley (n 18) 50.

[26] Timothy Casey, 'Reflective Practice in Legal Education: The Stages of Reflection' (2014) 20 Clinical Law Review 317.

[27] Ibid. [28] Ibid 344.

[29] As an aside, it should be noted that this phenomenon is not limited to students. Moreover, they may solely be emulating the fact that uncertainty and lack of clarity are often identified as the true source of structural problems (even when the source often lies elsewhere). See, for example, the government-commissioned *Good Work—The Taylor Review of Modern Work Practices*, which identified three main areas on which to focus interest, of which one was 'increasing clarity in the law'. https://assets.publishing.service.gov.uk/government/uploads/system/uploads/attachment_data/file/627671/good-work-taylor-review-modern-working-practices-rg.pdf

And see the critique of the 'preoccupation with clarity' in Katie Bales, Alan Bogg, and Tonia Novitz, '"Voice" and "Choice" in Modern Working Practices: Problems With the Taylor Review' (2018) 47 Industrial Law Journal 46.

[30] Cited in Neil Kibble, 'Reflection and Supervision in Clinical Legal Education: Do Work Placements Have a Role in Undergraduate Legal Education?' (1998) 5 International Journal of the Legal Profession 83, 99.

[31] Kolb (n 4) 39.

unexpected. However, a surprise encounter has a different quality because it catches us unprepared. The experience gains even greater value if we recognize it as unexpected, acknowledge our unpreparedness, and later revisit both the event and our response to it. Those who think this reaction is obvious or easy should recall Schön's point about people who are 'virtuosos in avoiding uncertainty'. Think of those you know who, frustratingly, dismiss shocking, disturbing, or exciting events by shrugging them off with, 'of course that's what happened! What else could have happened?'

Returning to higher education, the following was written about business school students but could easily apply to law students: 'the ability to face, frame and build solutions to ambiguous highly uncertain situations is [essential] in rapidly evolving and globalizing business settings . . . Yet our finding showed that reflection is the least taught skill in business schools . . . and the most challenging for students.'[32] This is unfortunate because, in education, 'working towards habits of uncertainty and puzzlement is need[ed] . . . [In fact,] certainty goes down as experiential learning goes up.'[33] Employers and governments repeatedly stress the importance of *flexibility* as a mindset for navigating an uncertain world. Now consider the curious etymological link between flexibility and reflexibility, the latter often used as a synonym for reflection. Is that a coincidence? Or perhaps reflection increases 'acceptance of, and confidence with, the essential complexity, uncertainty and perspectival nature of professional life'.[34]

This lack of certainty ties in nicely to our discussion in Chapter 5. We noted there the need to recognize the discretion that decision-makers, such as administrators and judges, hold, despite our reverence for the principle of *stare decisis*. That principle suggests a level of certainty far greater than what the legal world actually exhibits in practice. This nuanced understanding of binding precedent may be necessary for students to become 'aware of what it means to think about their role in the delivery of justice'.[35] It also supports and enhances students' capacity for 'decisionmaking in situations where options involve . . . uncertain degrees of risk'.[36]

To summarize, much can be gained by suspending the need to find for certainty, as a famous traveller discovered:

> 'Would you tell me, please, which way I ought to go from here?'
>
> 'That depends a good deal where you want to get to' said the Cheshire Cat.
>
> 'I don't much care where . . .' said Alice.
>
> 'Then it doesn't matter which way you go', said the Cat.
>
> 'So long as I get somewhere', Alice added as an explanation.
>
> 'Oh, you're sure to do that', said the Cat, 'if you only walk long enough'.

[32] Syeda Inamdar and Malu Roldan, 'The MBA Capstone Course: Building Theoretical, Practical, Applied and Reflective Skills' (2013) 37 Journal of Management Education 747, 766. And Casey (n 26) 330 does just that, stating, with respect to law students, that they 'should have experience in solving "unstructured problems" that require the student to confront indeterminacy and uncertainty'.

[33] Joann Phillion and F Michael Connelly, 'Narrative, Diversity and Teacher Education' (2004) 20 Teaching and Teacher Education 457, 468.

[34] Gillie Bolton and Russell Delderfield, *Reflective Practice: Writing and Professional Development* (5th ed, Sage 2017) 8.

[35] Aiken (n 15) 295.

[36] Amsterdam (n 5) 614.

6.1.4 **Reflection to Develop Resilience and Support Lifelong Learning**

We identified the dominant approach to legal education as heavily reliant on the Langdellian, scientific view of law. Almost by necessity, this scientific approach suppresses emotion and prioritizes logic and reason. In the next section, we will explore how reflection combines the intellectual and emotional (or affective) sides of learning to create a more meaningful result.[37] Before doing so, we conclude this section by emphasizing that ignoring the emotional—and therefore reflective—side to learning is costly for the student experience. Scott Turrow's memoir *One L* describes law school at Harvard as a transformative experience, and not in a positive way. He recalls students saying that

> they were limited, harmed, by the education, forced to substitute dry reason for emotion, to cultivate opinions which were 'rational' but which had no roots in experience, the life they'd had before. They were being cut away from themselves.[38]

Moving beyond the realm of (non)fiction, Duncan Kennedy, in his seminal polemic, makes a very similar point about the first-year experience, concluding that 'emoting will only isolate and incapacitate you'.[39] More broadly, academic studies have noted that law students 'feel a sense of loss' during their studies, and that report 'declining happiness and well-being'[40] along with higher levels of stress, anxiety, and depression than university students in other disciplines.[41] None of this paints a tempting picture of student experience.

Against this backdrop, it is worth noting that reflection during university studies may serve as an antidote—even if not a cure—for some of these issues. A study which followed first-year students who were encouraged to keep diaries found that

> Those students who used diaries tended to find that they helped them to deal with concerns which are commonly found during transition to university. Identifiable themes emerged, showing that diaries helped many students in this sample group to settle in, evaluate their experiences, develop new learning strategies, encouraged self-reliance and prompted them to become more aware of their developing confidence so promoting self-belief.[42]

Within CLE, it has been concluded that 'the reflective dimension of clinical legal education can address this problem [of isolation] by inculcating a sense of belonging through

[37] Alan Lerner, 'From Socrates to Damasio, from Langdell to Kandel: The Role of Emotion in Modern Legal Education' in Paul Maharg and Caroline Maughan (eds), *Affect and Legal Education: Emotion in Learning and Teaching the Law* (Ashgate Publishing 2011) 151.

[38] Cited in James Elkins, 'Rites de Passage: Law Students "Telling Their Lives"' (1985) 35 Journal of Legal Education 27, 31.

[39] Duncan Kennedy, 'Legal Education and the Reproduction of Hierarchy' (1982) 32 Journal of Legal Education 591, 595.

[40] Kennon Sheldon and Lawrence Krieger, 'Does Legal Education Have Undermining Effects on Law Students? Evaluating Changes in Motivation, Values, and Well-being' (2004) 22 Behavioral Sciences and the Law 261, 275.

[41] Natalie Skread and Shane Rogers, 'Stress, Anxiety and Depression in Law Students: How Student Behaviours Affect Student Wellbeing' (2014) 30 Monash University Law Review 564 at 566; Ben Gibson, 'How Law Students Can Cope: A Student's View' (2010) 60 Journal of Legal Education 140.

[42] Simon Brooman and Sue Darwent, 'A Positive View of First-year Undergraduate Reflective Diaries: Focusing on What Students *Can* Do' (2012) 13 Reflective Practice 517, 526.

involvement, engagement and connectedness'.[43] Moreover, given the growing struggles that students—especially law students—face with mental health and anxiety, reflection offers a vital, lifelong tool for building resilience. It achieves this by offering 'a structure and a process'[44] that helps students make sense of their experiences, perspectives, and professional context. Reflection is empowering because it encourages learners and practitioners to 'step back and critique the structures in which they find themselves operating, rather than feel powerless and be swept along by them'.[45] Furthermore, when reflections are read by a tutor, they open additional channels of communication between students and teachers.[46]

In addition, developing capacity, competencies, and resilience is crucial for building the soft skills that support future employability. Therefore, 'Legal education should prepare students for the emotional dimensions of lawyering. We fail our students if we fail to prepare them for the impact of their emotional lives, as well as those of their clients, on the practice of law'.[47] By contrast, and to end this section on a positive note, a law school that heavily integrated reflective practices into the curriculum found that alumni 'carried with them the benefits of reflective practice. As stated by one, by learning early on that keeping tabs on what you are doing well and what you could do better makes you both better in your job and also better at life generally'.[48]

TAKING STOCK

This section answered the question 'why should we reflect' by explaining that while we learn from experience, experience is not enough. Reflection is what brings experience into the learning process. It does so by:

1. **Forcing us to notice our implicit and explicit assumptions, and to explain to ourselves why we did what we did and why things happened the way they did. This makes the experience *meaningful*.**
2. **Linking the past with the future, encouraging us to think what we can do next time, to reach a different result. This makes the learning *dynamic*.**
3. **Engaging the theory with the practice, particularly with respect to a professional role, encouraging us to think about the profession and our role within the profession. This makes the learning *critical*.**

[43] Adrian Evans et al, 'Reflective Practice: The Essence of Clinical Legal Education' in Adrian Evans et al (eds), *Australian Clinical Legal Education: Designing and Operating a Best Practice Clinical Program in an Australian Law School* (ANU Press 2017) 153, 165.

[44] Ibid 166; also Colin James, 'Seeing Things As They Are: Emotional Intelligence and Clinical Legal Education' (2005) 8 Journal of Clinical Legal Education 123.

[45] Ibid.

[46] Rachel Spencer, 'Private Lives: Confronting the Inherent Difficulties of Reflective Writing in Clinical Legal Education' (2014) 21 International Journal of Clinical Legal Education 177.

[47] Marjorie Silver, 'Emotional Intelligence and Legal Education' (1999) 5 Psychology, Public Policy and the Law 1173, 1174.

[48] Jennie Gibbons, 'How Is Reflection "Framed" for Legal Professional Identity? Using Bernstein and Leering to Understand the Potential for Reflection in Our Curriculum as Written, Experienced and Assessed' (2019) 53 The Law Teacher 401, 410.

6.2 **What Is Reflection?**

So far, we have discussed the importance of reflection assuming that, as a reader, you have a general, intuitive sense of what the concept means. Before moving further, however, it is useful to offer a clearer and more precise definition of reflection. As might be expected with such an abstract concept and varied practice, there is no single universally accepted definition. However, here are some of the definitions that many writers and scholars rely on:

- Reconstruction and reorganisation of experience which adds to the meaning of experience.[49]
- A generic term for those intellectual and affective activities in which individuals engage to explore their experiences in order to lead to a new understanding and appreciation.[50]
- Active, persistent and careful consideration of any belief or supposed form of knowledge in the light of the grounds that support it and the further conclusions to which it leads.[51]
- A form of mental processing with a purpose and/or anticipated outcome that is applied to relatively complex or unstructured ideas for which there is no obvious solution.[52]

Rather than choosing between these definitions, or attempting to create a new one, it may be more useful to identify the key elements they share. This will allow us, as we move forward, to 'check in' and see whether what we are doing truly counts as reflection. These elements will also feature prominently in the reflection models discussed in the next section. And so, the features of reflection are: reconstruction and reorganization of the experience; intellectual and affective activities; active, persistent, and careful reconsideration of beliefs and forms of knowledge. At first glance, these categories may seem broad or even a little abstract. However, they refer to aspects of reflection that you likely already grasp on an intuitive level. Let's explore each of them in more detail.

6.2.1 **Reconstruction and Reorganization of the Experience**

It is natural, and reasonable, that much of the discussion about reflection focuses on analysing experiences and planning future actions. However, focusing only on analysis risks overlooking the challenges of revisiting and describing the experience itself. As we will see in the models below, deciding which 'facts' from an encounter are 'relevant' requires deliberation,

[49] John Dewey, *Democracy and Education: An Introduction to the Philosophy of Education* (The Free Press 1944) 74.

[50] David Boud, Rosemary Keogh, and David Walker, 'What Is Reflection in Learning' in David Boud, Rosemary Keogh, and David Walker (eds), *Reflection: Turning Experience into Learning* (Kogan Page 1985).

[51] John Dewey, *How We Think: A Restatement of the Relation of Reflective Thinking to the Educative Process* (Heath and Co 1933) 9.

[52] Jenny Moon, *Reflection in Learning and Professional Development* (Kogan 1999) 23.

judgement, and even some theory. As one writer observed, 'we theorise every time we look at the world'.[53]

Donald Schön, a leading thinker on reflection, noted that in 'real world practice, problems do not present themselves to the practitioner as givens . . . [the practitioner] must make sense of an uncertain situation that initially makes no sense'.[54] This insight creates a surprising but meaningful link between legal realism and reflective practice. 'Surprising', because why would a dense legal theory have anything to do with a method designed to help individuals become better practitioners? But on further reflection, the strong, inherent connections become clear. Legal realism teaches that the world is made up of a vast range of facts, from which we consciously choose those we consider relevant to assessing a situation and deciding how to act. But while legal realism focused on identifying the facts relevant to deciding a case, a similar approach can, and arguably should, be applied to other experiences. If that is true, reflection helps improve our practice by prompting questions such as: Was it significant that the meeting was held early in the morning? That I arrived late? That the client was a gay man? That my partner came unprepared? That the supervising practitioner was a young, Black, female solicitor? Organizing and reconstructing the events is, therefore, an essential part of the reflective process. It also prompts us to ask: Did we make the best choices? Could we have done better? Reflecting on our work 'might prove something thought to be vital to be insignificant, or lead to insight about something unnoticed at the time'.[55]

6.2.2 'Intellectual and Affective Activities', 'Mental Processing'

Academics, especially those who teach, are generally skilled in intellectual processes. Reflection is one such process, relying on conceptualization and theorization to deepen our understanding of questions such as 'what just happened here?' and 'why was that important?'. Yet many academics are less comfortable writing in the first person, a discomfort often passed on to their students:

> The requirement to abandon the traditional third-person discourse is confronting to most law students and indeed also to law academics. The use of the third person (e.g. 'the writer found, the writer is of the view') and the passive voice (e.g. 'the literature was analysed') which form the basis of scientific scholarship style—personal involvement must be eschewed at all costs—are anathema to reflective writing.[56]

This goes beyond mere style. Academics often suppress—and teach students to suppress—their emotions, personal motivations, and instinctive reactions to a judicial decision ('can you *believe* that?') or to a piece of scholarship. Instead, they cloak their own agenda in

[53] JW von Goethe, *Goethe's Way of Science: A Phenomenology of Nature* (D Seamon and A Zajonc eds, SUNY Press 1998), cited in Gillie Bolton, 'Taking Responsibility for Our Stories: In Reflective Practice, Action Learning and Socratic Dialogue' (2005) 10 Teaching in Higher Education 271, 279.

[54] Donald Schön, *The Reflective Practitioner: How Professionals Think in Action* (Basic Books 1992) 40.

[55] Bolton and Delderfield (n 34) 9.

[56] Rachel Spencer, 'Holding Up the Mirror: A Theoretical and Practical Analysis of the Role of Reflection in Clinical Legal Education' (2012) 18 International Journal of Clinical Legal Education 181, 185.

intellectual and academic jargon. As Caroline Maughan notes, in higher education, 'the role of emotions in learning has largely been ignored and certainly under theorised'. In particular,

> the affective domain has traditionally been ignored at the curriculum design level. When we come to look at the formal design of our programmes we seek in vain for mention of those aspects of humanity which are not in the realm of understanding and manipulating propositional reasoning.[57]

Maughan goes on to explain why: emotions are hard to integrate into a learning programme, difficult to categorize as clear learning outcomes, and challenging to measure or assess. Bringing emotions into teaching also changes the tutor's role, often requiring them to handle issues they may feel unprepared for.

Despite these challenges, emotions are linked to thinking in the same way theory connects to practice. They are, in effect, intertwined—one feeds (on) the other. Emotions can be the starting point ('how I felt when the supervisor said my work wasn't good enough'), or they can emerge later when reflecting on what to do next ('I know I need to work on my interpersonal skills, but I don't have the bandwidth right now'). We need to *understand* why a specific event triggered such strong feelings, especially when others didn't react the same way, for example. Often, these intense reactions are linked to past experiences that resurface unexpectedly during the present situation. For example, one of us conducted a seminar in which a student became overwhelmed by complex feelings towards a client with severe depression, which stopped the client from attending meetings or replying to emails. In discussion, she realized that her reaction was linked to unresolved feelings about her mother, who was in a similar condition.

So how can we connect with our deeper emotions? We'll look at this in more detail in the next section, but for now, it's helpful to pause and consider this poetic reminder:

> Reflexivity is the near-impossible adventure of making aspects of the self strange: attempting to stand back from belief and value systems and observe habitual ways of thinking and relating to others, structures of understanding ourselves, our relationship to the world, and the way we are experienced and perceived by others and their assumptions about the way that the world impinges upon them.[58]

'Making the self strange' is not an easy thing to do. It means, perhaps (well, what do *you* think it means?), stepping back and looking at yourself, and what you did, from a distance. But it is also deeply important. In what is arguably one of the greatest works of legal fiction, lawyer Atticus Finch tells his daughter: 'if you can learn a simple trick, Scout, you'll get along

[57] Caroline Maughan, 'Why Study Emotion' in Paul Maharg and Caroline Maughan (eds), *Affect and Legal Education: Emotion in Learning and Teaching the Law* (Ashgate Publishing 2011). For a similar argument, that the 'traditional dominance and continuing significance of the doctrinal tradition has arguably led to a continuing disregard for, and suppression of, emotions within undergraduate legal education in England & Wales', see Emma Jones, 'Transforming Legal Education through Emotions' (2018) 38 Legal Studies 450, 453; Emma Jones, *Emotions in the Law School: Transforming Legal Education through the Passions* (Routledge 2019).

[58] Bolton and Delderfield (n 34) 10.

better with all kinds of folks. You never really understand a person until you consider things from his point of view.'[59] And the writer Amos Oz declared that 'Imagining the other is . . . a major moral imperative'.[60] So perhaps that is exactly what we should do: think about how others see us. Stephen Brookfield suggests that teachers can challenge ingrained assumptions by deploying four 'critical lenses'.[61] With minor tweaks to transfer them to the CLE context, these may be:

1. The practitioner who is reflecting autobiographically.
2. The client's/supervisor's perspective (in the case of CLE).
3. A colleague's/peer's perspective.
4. The perspective of detached theoretical, philosophical, or professional theory.

REFLECTION POINT

'Making the self strange'

To practice these perspectives, write an account of an event from your own perspective, and then from each of the other perspectives (the client/supervisor; the colleague/peer; the theoretical perspective).

Here are some possible scenarios (but, of course, these are just suggestions):

a. A meeting with a client in which the client was upset or hostile.
b. A meeting with a supervisor in which you felt insecure or unprepared.
c. A meeting with a partner in which tension developed regarding allocation of work and responsibility.

6.2.3 Active, Persistent, and Careful Consideration of Any Belief or Supposed Form of Knowledge

This feature of reflection should not be surprising at this stage, given the discussion above. We noted that reflection is only effective when it challenges our predispositions and assumptions—our 'supposed forms of knowledge'. Moreover, as this feature suggests, 'careful consideration' should be dynamic: both active and persistent. We saw this visualized in the circular model of the reflective process (Figure 6.1). Even when challenging a specific but long-held mistaken assumption, it cannot be erased in one clean sweep. It is a gradual process, slowly chipping away.

59 Harper Lee, *To Kill a Mockingbird* (50th anniversary edition, Arrow Books 1960, 2010) 36.
60 Judith Shulevitz, 'Why write while Israel burns?' Slate (6 April 2009).
61 Brookfield (n 11) 61–77.

The first step is to identify the belief. This stage can be trickier than it may seem. At times, our stated, explicit values—our 'espoused beliefs'—differ from our implicit values, which show up in practice. Espoused values are the ones we declare to others, and often to ourselves. But sometimes they are the values that we *wish we believed in*, if that makes sense. For example: 'I consider myself a "true feminist", but when I think of my behaviour in social or domestic situations, I'm not sure that my actions align with that belief.' Close reflection on our practice may reveal that, at least in part, we live by different beliefs—or that we do not hold our espoused beliefs as strongly as we assumed. What might be the consequence of such a realization? Two obvious options arise: we can try to adjust our practice to align with our espoused beliefs, or we can revisit those beliefs and accept that our true beliefs are actually different.[62]

Moreover, the process can and is expected to evolve over the years. Focusing on different aspects of one's behaviour and practice 'may develop the lifelong learning skills of the reflective practitioner'.[63]

A wide range of issues discussed in the previous two sections is captured in the insights from Vivien Gambing of Kent Law School, below.

A View from Clinical Practice

Vivien Gambling, Kent Law School

One of the joys of being a clinic supervisor lies in reading and discussing students' written reflections; some of these linger in my mind long after the event.

I suggest that reflection should begin by encouraging students to write a reflection soon after an 'event' (for example a client meeting or reading a case file) to 'capture the moment'. Starting with a non-assessed reflection, as a formative activity, is more likely to result in a reflection in the student's own voice (rather than writing what they think the supervisor wants), prompting expression of thoughts that might otherwise not be heard.

Students who question what is to be gained by doing a non-assessed piece of work may be advised that such a reflection will very likely help them to develop their thoughts, and thus benefit their subsequent assessed work (such as a critical reflection essay).

Interactions with clients provide rich opportunities for reflection at all levels.

After his first meeting with a client, one student, who aspired to high academic achievement, wrote: 'as soon as our client entered the room, I realised that it was not about me.' The student's focus had shifted from themselves and their 'academic performance' towards a focus on our client; they recognized the importance of human interaction and empathy in the lawyer/client relationship.

Another case involved a client who had experienced a relationship breakdown; their female partner had been arrested after threatening their child with a knife. After the first meeting with our male client, a student reflected that she had 'expected more drama in the person we

[62] Bolton and Delderfield (n 34) 27. [63] Newman and Nicolson (n 24).

met'; she had imagined someone more 'messy or troubled'. The student reflected upon her preconceptions, which she felt were linked to people she had 'grown up around'. The student also questioned her emotional response to the events relayed by our client, and went on to reflect more deeply about contrasting attitudes in society towards people of different genders in the context of domestic abuse.

When students and their supervisor have contrasting views of a client or the morality of a client's position, this can lead to a rich dialogue. After meeting a client who had failed to move out of a house where she had been allowed to stay temporarily by a charitable organization, a student, who in her own words 'came from a third world country where my family clawed their way through life with no days off', wrote that our client, who had a mental health condition, was 'wrapped up in emotions, making things worse for herself and exploiting the help she was getting'. The student went on to explore and question the reasons for her strong reactions and what might seem harsh judgement. A dialogue ensued between the student and myself, while we learned more about the client's background and health condition and investigated the limitations of the law. The student brought interesting perspectives to the discussion, and although our respective views did not converge, each shifted and was enriched through this process.

These examples illustrate that reflecting on their clinical legal experience facilitates students' understanding of key aspects of 'lawyering', including the uncertainty of facts and of the application of the law, and an appreciation of the emotional and ethical dimensions and responsibilities towards clients. It can also help students to identify wider socio-political issues, and to explore questions regarding inequality and justice.

REFLECTION POINT

My values

Complete the following (write as many as you like):

I am . . .

I believe . . .

I want . . .

I know . . .

I need . . .

I wish . . .

I hope . . .

I imagine . . .

I dream . . .

If I were not (a student?) I would be . . .

TAKING STOCK

This section drew on a number of accepted definitions of reflection, and identified the main features of the practice. They include:

1. The importance of accounting for the facts that are regarded as relevant for reflection, and the organization of those facts into a narrative that is useful for engagement.
2. The analysis, which is composed of intellectual and emotional (or 'affective') parts.
3. The active and persistent nature of the reflection, which requires constant engagement, and re-evaluation, of our explicit and implicit beliefs.

6.3 How to Reflect

Rudyard Kipling wrote:

> I keep six honest serving men
> (They taught me all I know)
> Their names are What and Why and When
> And How and Where and Who.

6.3.1 Introductory Points

It is now time to move from the theory of reflection, which addressed the 'what' (what reflection is) and the 'why' (why we reflect), to the practice—the 'how' of reflection. This step is essential; without it, the reader may be left thinking, 'You've convinced me to reflect, but I have no idea how to do it effectively'. Happily, there is no shortage of models to guide the process, and this section outlines four excellent examples or 'types' of reflective models. Before discussing them, a few introductory notes will help clarify the scope of this section.

First, while structured reflection of the type we discuss in this section is usually written, *oral* reflection or simple 'debriefing' can and should happen regularly. For example, you might use it to review an experience such as a client interview or a court appearance.[64] This informal method can start the process of making sense of the experience—collecting and storing details: *What actually happened? Was it effective? If so, what worked well? Where did it go wrong, and what could be improved? How do I feel about it?* This process can, of course, be internal, simply sitting with your own thoughts, but there is value in articulating them aloud, even to a friend or peer rather than a supervisor. Ledvinka gives the example of a student who 'prepared diligently prior to representing a client at an Employment Tribunal hearing but, despite

[64] Spencer (n 46); William Berman, 'When Will They Ever Learn? Learning and Teaching from Mistakes in the Clinical Context' (2006) 13 Clinical Law Review 115, 118.

her best efforts, the hearing was a disaster'. She explains that in such a situation, we can encourage the student to reflect on this intense learning experience immediately after the event:

> The reflection could take place in a small group setting with the student's peers and tutor, where the student could discuss her perceptions of what went wrong and how she felt about it. Other students could be encouraged to offer constructive comments. *In addition*, the student could make a written record of her reflection.[65]

Second, reflections can also take the form of journal entries, written soon after the event, kept private, and drafted in a manner that is completely *un*structured. Despite their potentially chaotic form, journal reflections are highly recommended. They are valuable both inherently, as an important way to process events, and instrumentally, as records of immediate feelings that can later inform a structured reflection.

Third, we should note an important distinction, attributed to Donald Schön, between *reflection-in-action* and *reflection-on-action*. According to Schön,

> [R]eflection-in-action is the process by which a new response is generated in the situation, in response to surprise and under conditions of uncertainty, in a way that involves on-the-spot experimentation and that does not necessarily take place in words ... [R]eflection-on-action is an attempt to describe the knowledge that was generated and the conditions under which it was generated and the on-the-spot experimentation was carried out.[66]

Despite the distinction, however, there is a strong link between the two. The better you become at reviewing what happened, why it happened, and how to respond more effectively next time, the more likely reflection-on-action will inform live situations, becoming reflection-in-action. This allows 'explicit knowledge' (eg *I'm not as good as others at making clients feel at ease; next time I'll do what my partner did and offer a cup of tea*) to become tacit knowledge, 'implicit in our patterns of action and in our feel for the stuff with which we are dealing'.[67] It also means we are more likely to improve by first focusing on reflection-on-action. This stage gives us time to consider, seek advice, theorize, and plan. So that is where we begin.

Finally, the aim of introducing you to a number of models is not to persuade you to choose one of them and follow it slavishly. Indeed, as some have suggested, 'all models are wrong, but some are useful'.[68] Less cynically, reflection models are not 'recipes or instructions for making a thing'.[69] Students sometimes 'pick and choose' stages within models that suit their thinking and worldview. Moreover, we encourage students to experiment, using one model (or a hybrid) for one reflection and another for the next, to see what works best.

65 Ledvinka (n 20) 39 (emphasis added).

66 Donald Schön, 'Educating the Reflective Legal Practitioner' (1995) 2 Clinical Law Review 231, 247.

67 Ibid 49.

68 George Box and Norman Draper, *Empirical Model-Building and Response Surfaces* (John Wiley and Sons 1984) 424; cited in Casey (n 26).

69 Stephen Rowland, *The Enquiring University Teacher* (Society for Research Into Higher Education, 2000) 51.

With this background in mind, it is worth noting that not all reflections are equally valuable or probing. Preferences vary regarding which models suit particular cases. and their suitability in particular cases. So it is, perhaps, best at the outset to clarify five components that *we* believe should be included in any reflection (but feel free to disagree!):

a. Reflections should be written.
b. The factual background for the reflection should be clearly set out.
c. There should be a clear section for conceptualization and analysis.
d. The cyclical nature of the reflection should be clear.
e. A reflection should include an action plan.

We now turn to expand on each of these elements.

First, while it is valuable to reflect in various contexts—on a run, staring at the clouds, in the garden—a significant part of reflection should take place in writing. 'Reflective writing *is* the reflective process, rather than recording what has been thought.'[70] Something intriguing happens when you put pen to paper (or, less romantically but often more efficiently, type on a keyboard). Writing connects feelings and values with rational thought, helping to make 'sense of the muddle of stuff in our minds'.[71]

Second, it is necessary to make a concrete observation outlining what happened, for the reasons noted above. Every experience contains countless data points. Which details do you value and why? Sometimes, practitioners move too quickly to analysis, assuming the facts are clear, uncontested, and obvious. But often this is not the case. As has been observed, 'memories and information are not just stored. They are *storied*.'[72]

Third, then, there is a need to analyse, conceptualize, and/or theorize. This involves gaining distance from the experience, perhaps by referencing academic or professional literature.

Fourth, reflective practice models should be cyclical in nature. Reflection is not obsessed with past occurrences, or rushing to plan ahead. Instead, like Janus, it faces both the past and the future. The cyclical nature indicates the move from the experience in the past, through the plan for the future, and on to new experiences. In fact, a more precise portrayal of the reflection process would be a three-dimensional spiral. The reason for this is evident from Heraclitus, who taught that you cannot step twice into the same river. Why? For the same reason that there is no second 'first impression'. Once you step into the river, the experience becomes part of you. The second time, there is familiarity, a memory, an experience you carry with you. You already know what to expect. Moreover, not only you have changed; the river too is not the same. It may be a different time of day, the sunlight may fall differently, different creatures may be scampering around, and so on. As TS Eliot beautifully put

[70] Bolton and Delderfield (n 34) 135. [71] Ibid 136.

[72] Gillie Bolton, 'Taking Responsibility for Our Stories: In Reflective Practice, Action Learning and Socratic Dialogue' (2005) 10 Teaching in Higher Education 271, 271.

it: 'the end of our exploring will be to arrive where we started, and know the place for the first time.'[73] Returning to the learning process, Dewey offers further insights:

> the principle of continuity of experience means that every experience both takes up something from those which have gone before and modifies in some way the quality of those which come after . . . As an individual passes from one situation to another, his world, his environment, expands or contracts . . . He does not find himself living in another world but in a different part or aspect of one and the same world. What he has learned in the way of knowledge and skill in one situation becomes an instrument of understanding and dealing effectively with the situations which follow. The process goes on as long as life and learning continue.[74]

Lessons from the past matter because they guide future actions. This leads us nicely to the fifth and final feature. The reflection should always conclude with an *action plan*. You observed, analysed, and concluded. Now what? 'Reflection in isolation can become retroflection, a turning in on itself that isolates the learners in their own self-confirming world unable to reach conclusions or test them in action.'[75] If you have not thought out what to do with the valuable insights gained about yourself and your actions, why did you do it? Reflection may be a fascinating theoretical exercise, but it is also deeply practical, firmly rooted in real-world experience.

Before turning to the reflection models, we add one final general point: reflections can have different levels of depth. Moon suggests three such levels, which are interrelated but also distinct from one another:

> **Descriptive reflection**: There is basically a description of events, but the account shows some evidence of deeper consideration in relatively descriptive language. There is no real evidence of the notion of alternative viewpoints in use.
>
> **Dialogic reflection**: This writing suggests that there is a 'stepping back' from the events and actions which leads to a different level of discourse. There is a sense of 'mulling about', discourse with self, and an exploration of the role of self in events and actions. There is consideration of the qualities of judgements and of possible alternatives for explaining and hypothesizing. The reflection is analytical or integrative, linking factors and perspectives.
>
> **Critical reflection**: This form of reflection, in addition to dialogic reflection, shows evidence that the learner is aware that the same actions and events may be seen in different contexts with different explanations associated with the contexts. They are influenced by 'multiple historical and socio-political contexts', for example.[76]

Helpfully, Moon illustrates three levels of reflection using one example: a 22-year-old in her first job, reflecting on a presentation she delivered. Because they clearly demonstrate basic (descriptive), good (dialogic), and excellent (critical) reflection, we offer them below in detail. Moreover, we would recommend reading Moon's text in full.[77]

[73] TS Eliot, 'Little Gidding' in *Four Quartets* (Faber and Faber 1943).
[74] John Dewey (n 1) 35, 44. [75] Kolb (n 4) 57.
[76] Jennifer Moon, *Reflection in Higher Education Learning* (PDP Working Paper 4, LTSN, 2001) 13.
[77] Ibid, Appendix 2.

First the descriptive reflection:

I had to take an agenda item to the weekly team meeting in my third week of working at PIGG PLC. I had to talk about the project that I am on (creating a new database for the management information system). I had done a presentation before and then I relied on my acting skills. Despite the acting, I spent quite a bit of time preparing it in the way that I have seen others make similar presentations. The presentation at the last team meeting, given by my colleague, went well—she used PowerPoint and I decided to use it. I spent a long time in the preparation and I went in feeling confident . . . Early on, I noticed that people seemed not to understand what I was saying despite the PowerPoint . . . I noticed that Mrs Shaw (my boss) repeated bits of what I had said several times and once or twice answered questions for me. This made me feel uncomfortable. I felt it was quite patronising and I was upset. Later my colleagues said that she always does it. I was disappointed that my presentation did not seem to have gone well. I thought about the presentation for several days and then talked with Mrs Shaw about the presentation (there was no-one else). She gave me a list of points for improvement next time . . . She suggested that I should do a presentation to several of the team sometime next week so that I can improve my performance.

Second, the dialogic reflection:

I had to take an agenda item to the weekly team meeting in my third week of working at PIGG PLC . . . I had given a presentation before and that time I relied on my acting skills . . . I was confident but I did spend quite a bit of time preparing. Because everyone else here uses PowerPoint, I felt I had better use it . . . When I think back on the preparation that I did, I realise that I was desperately trying to prove that I could make a presentation as well as my colleague, who did the last one. I wanted to impress everyone. I had not realised there was so much to learn about presenting, and how much I needed to know about PowerPoint to use it properly . . . Early on the PowerPoint went wrong and I began to panic. Trying to pretend that I was cool and confident made the situation worse because I did not admit my difficulties and ask for help. The more I spoke, the more my voice went wobbly. I realised, from the kinds of questions that the others asked, that they did not understand what I was saying . . . I felt worse when Mrs Shaw, my boss, started to answer questions for me. I felt flustered and even less able to cope. As a result of this poor presentation, my self esteem is low at work now. . . After a few days, I went to see Mrs Shaw and we talked it over. I still feel that her interventions did not help me. Interestingly several of my colleagues commented that she always does that . . . Partly through talking over the presentation and the things that went wrong . . . I can see several areas that I could get better . . . I recognise, also, that my old acting skills might have given me initial confidence, but I needed more than a clear voice, especially when I lost my way with PowerPoint. Relying on a mass of figures was not right either . . . I am hoping to have a chance to try with a presentation, practicing with some of the team.

And, finally, the critical reflection:

I am writing this back in my office. It all happened 2 days ago.

Three weeks after I started at PIGG PLC had to take an agenda item to the team meeting . . . I was immediately worried. I was scared about not saying the right things and not being able to answer questions properly. I did a presentation in my course at university and felt the same about it initially. I was thinking then, like this time, I could use my acting skills . . .

I decided to use PowerPoint. I was not very easy about its use because I have seen it go wrong so often. However, I have not seen anyone else give a presentation here without using it . . . I was not sure, when it came to the session, whether I really knew enough about running PowerPoint. (How do you know when you know enough about something?) . . .

In the event, the session was a disaster and has left me feeling uncomfortable in my work and I even worry about it at home. I need to think about why a simple presentation could have such an effect on me. The PowerPoint went wrong . . . My efforts to be calm and 'cool' failed and my voice went wobbly—that was, anyway, how it felt to me. My colleague actually said afterwards that I looked quite calm despite what I was feeling (I am not sure whether she meant it or was trying to help me). When I think back to that moment, if I had thought that I still looked calm (despite what I felt), I could have regained the situation. As it was, it went from bad to worse and I know that my state became obvious because Mrs Shaw, my boss, began to answer the questions that people were asking for me.

I am thinking about the awful presentation again—it was this time last week. I am reading what I wrote earlier about it. Now I return to it, I do have a slightly different perspective. I think that it was not as bad as it felt at the time. Several of my colleagues told me afterwards that Mrs Shaw always steps in to answer questions like that . . . I need to do some thinking about how to act next time to prevent this interruption from happening or to deal with the situation when she starts*. I might look in the library for that book on assertiveness.

I have talked to Mrs Shaw now too. I notice that my confidence in her is not all that great while I am still feeling a bit cross. However, I am feeling more positive generally and I can begin to analyse what I could do better in the presentation. It is interesting to see the change in my attitude after a week . . . I am not sure how helpful was my reliance on my acting skills* . . .

I probably will use PowerPoint again. I have had a look in the manual and it suggests that you treat it as a tool—not let it dominate and not use it as a means of presenting myself . . .*.

As I am writing this, I am noticing how useful it is to go back over things I have written about before. I seem to be able to see the situation differently . . . I realised that there were things I did not know at the time . . . I also recognise some of the areas in which I went wrong. At the time I could not see that. It was as if my low self esteem got in the way. Knowing where I went wrong, and admitting the errors to myself gives me a chance to improve next time—and perhaps to help Mrs Shaw to improve in her behaviour towards us!

* I have asterisked the points that I need to address in order to improve.

We now turn to an overview of four carefully selected models of reflection. Each offers a distinct perspective, enabling the reflective student or practitioner to choose one that aligns with their way of thinking or fits the specific event being reflected upon.

Practical Exercise 6.1

Read through the three descriptions and outline what makes the first 'descriptive', the second 'dialogic', and the third 'critical'. Which suits your 'natural' style of writing? Have a look at a reflective piece that you've written—which style does it fit? Can you add dialogic and critical layers to it?

6.3.2 The Three-step Model—Driscoll

This model,[78] originally developed for healthcare practitioners but later adopted more widely, is perhaps the simplest you will encounter. As you can see from Figure 6.2, it consists of only three stages, which offer a concise and memorable combination: What? So What? Now What?

This model may seem simple at first glance, but its apparent simplicity can be deceptive. While it is appealing that the model condenses the event, analysis, and action plan into just three monosyllabic titles, each stage actually requires careful unpacking and deeper elaboration.

Figure 6.2 Driscoll's three-step model

What?

This first stage captures everything that happened: the physical, social, and emotional dimensions of the experience. However, it is limited because it focuses only on description, without moving into analysis or suggesting what should change.

Helpful prompts that you might ask yourself at this stage include:

- What happened (including when did it happen, and who was there)?
- What were my thoughts when it happened?

[78] John Driscoll, 'Supported Reflective Learning: The Essence of Clinical Supervision?' in John Driscoll (ed), *Practising Clinical Supervision* (2nd ed, Elsevier 2007) 27.

- What was my reaction?
- What knowledge or skills did I use when it happened?
- What knowledge or skills did I feel were lacking during the event?
- What did other people do who were involved in this?

You can, of course, add your own questions depending on the event—whether it was a client meeting, a discussion with a supervisor, drafting advice, or participating in mediation or litigation.

So What?

This is the heart of the model: the reflection itself. Here, you place the facts that you've described into context and start making sense of them. For example, you might note you were late to a meeting and felt embarrassed. Now you explore why: how do you view punctuality? Is it a recurring challenge for you, or just a one-off? Driscoll[79] suggests revisiting your feelings during the event, then moving to a deeper, more analytical stage by asking:

- Were my feelings different from those of other people who were involved?
- Have my feelings changed since the event?
- Do I still feel troubled? If so, in what way?
- What were the effects of what I did (or did not do)?
- What positive aspects can I now see in what happened?
- What have I learned about my behaviour by taking a more measured look at it?
- What observations has another person made of the way I acted at the time?

Or perhaps, instead of answering questions, you may find the types of prompts presented in Figure 6.3 more useful.

Now What?

Welcome to your first (?) 'action plan'. As we noted earlier, this stage is crucial because it completes the circle. It moves you from the previous stage of analysis—which can sometimes be painful, time-consuming, and hard to process—into the practical and, hopefully, more optimistic stage of planning change. However, for this to work, your action plan needs to be carefully thought through and realistically achievable. Driscoll again suggests a series of questions. The first question bridges the gap between the analysis stage and this one. From there, the prompts should help you decide on concrete next steps.

- What are the implications for me and others in clinical practice based on what I have described and analysed?
- What difference would it make if I choose to do nothing?

[79] Ibid.

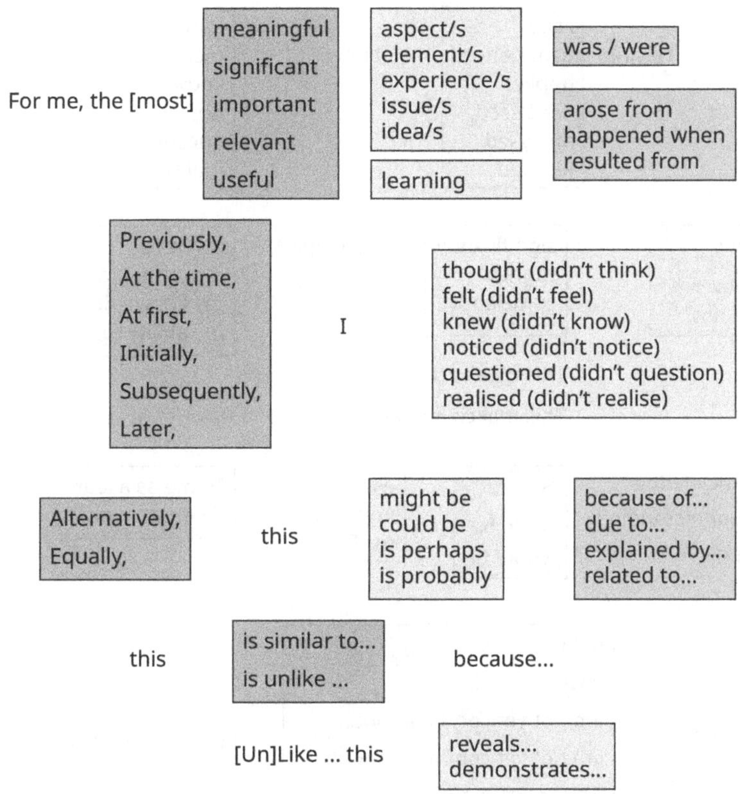

Figure 6.3 Prompts for reflection 1

- Where can I get more information to better handle a similar situation in the future?
- How could I modify my practice if a similar situation happened again?
- What help or support do I need to put my reflections into action?
- Which aspect should I tackle first? How will I know if I'm acting differently in future practice?
- What is the main learning that I take from reflecting on my practice in this way?

Again, some may prefer to use a different format of prompts, as offered in Figure 6.4, depending on what feels most natural for their reflection.

Other models also include a form of an action plan. But as this is the first model we're introducing, it is useful to explain the parameters of a good action plan. These are often captured in the acronym SMART: Specific, Measurable, Achievable, Relevant, and Time-bound. A vague resolution such as 'I'll try to do better next time' is unlikely to lead to meaningful change, because it lacks focus and accountability. Instead, a SMART action plan clearly defines *what* you will do, *how* you will know it has been achieved, and *when* it should be completed. For example, rather than simply aiming to 'improve client communication', a SMART plan would be: 'Before my next client meeting, I will prepare a structured list of open-ended questions to encourage discussion, and I will ask for feedback from my supervisor within

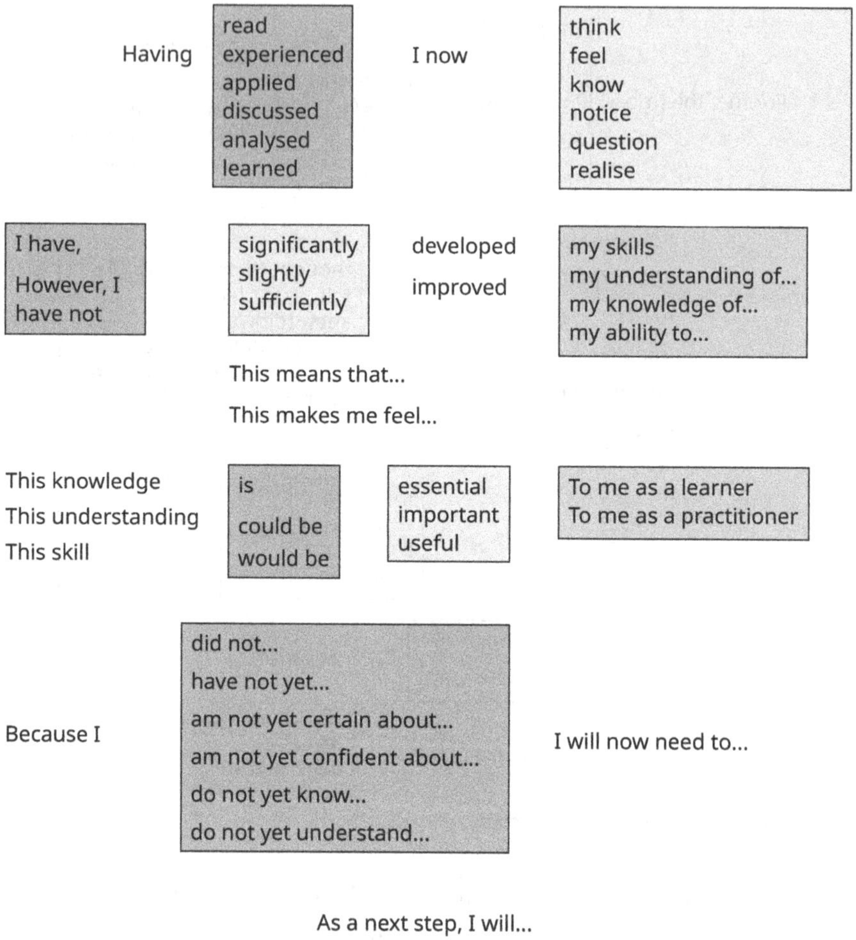

Figure 6.4 Prompts for reflection 2

24 hours of the meeting.' This level of clarity transforms reflection from an abstract exercise into a concrete pathway for personal and professional growth.

6.3.3 **The Four-stage Model—Kolb**

David Kolb offers an intermediate model, in terms of both the number of stages and the level of detail involved, between the relatively simple Driscoll model and the six-stage models that follow.[80] The model consists of four stages: concrete experience, reflective observation, abstract conceptualization, and active experimentation. One fascinating aspect of Kolb's model is how it not only connects each stage to the next, but also links stages across the entire cycle, as portrayed in Figure 6.5 below.

[80] Kolb (n 4). Incidentally, this model is repeatedly referred to in texts on reflection in legal education: eg Karen Hinett, *Developing Reflective Practice in Legal Education* (UK Centre for Legal Education 2002) 2; Adrian Evans et al, 'Reflective Practice: The Essence of Clinical Legal Education' in *Australian Clinical Legal Education: Designing and Operating a Best Practice Clinical Program in an Australian Law School* (ANU Press 2017) 153, 170. Kibble (n 30) 94*ff*.

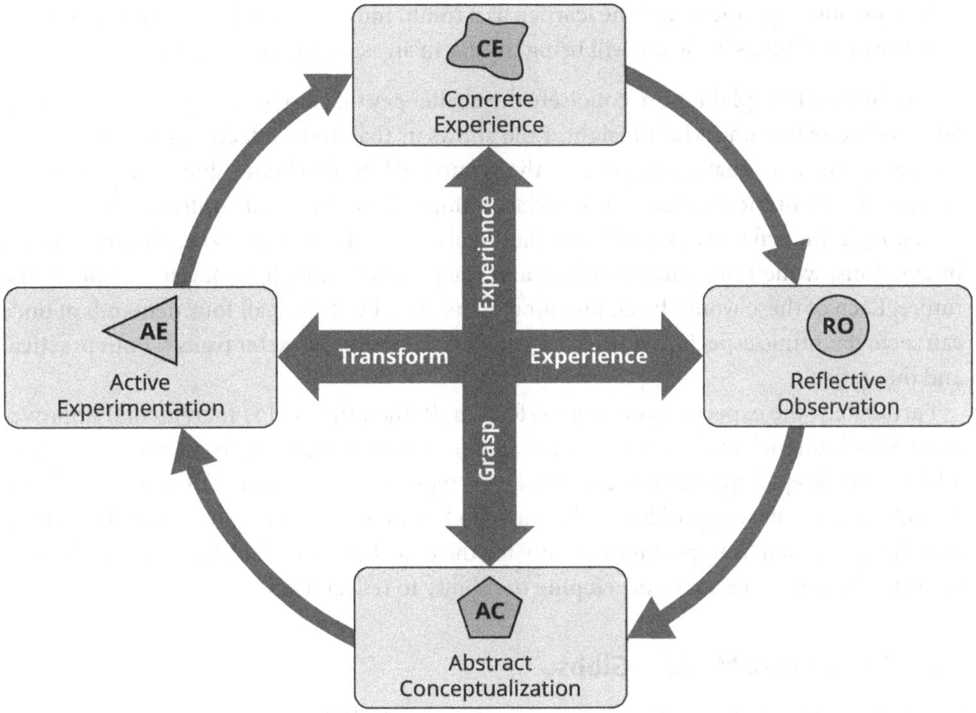

Figure 6.5 Kolb's four-step model

Kolb describes these links—the vertical *Grasp Experience* and the horizontal *Transform Experience*—as dialectics that highlight both the strong connection and the inherent tension between observation and action.[81] They can be seen as a bridge between theory and practice. He explains that these are 'two primary dimensions to the learning process. The first dimension [the vertical link] represents the concrete experiencing of events at one end and abstract conceptualization at the other. The other dimension [the horizontal link] has active experimentation at one extreme and reflective observation at the other.'[82]

This ambivalent view of the relationship between the two extremes—showing that their combination is both complementary and challenging—is a crucial insight. According to Kolb:

> Learners, if they are to be effective, need four different kinds of abilities—*concrete experience* abilities (CE), *reflective observation* abilities (RO), *abstract conceptualization* abilities (AC), and *active experimentation* (AE) abilities. That is, they must be able to involve themselves fully, openly and without bias in new experiences (CE). They must be able to create concepts that integrate their observations into logically sound theories (AC), and they must be able to use these theories to make decisions and solve problems (AE). Yet this is difficult to achieve. How can one act and reflect at the same time? How can one be concrete and immediate and still be theoretical? Learning requires abilities

[81] Kolb (n 4) 40. [82] Ibid 42.

that are polar opposites, and the learner, as a result, must continually choose which set of learning abilities he or she will bring to bear in any specific learning situation.[83]

It is difficult to explain more concisely the challenges that a reflective practitioner faces. So, to reiterate this important insight: Kolb shows us that, to be effective, one must have a clear awareness of 'what's going on, on the ground' while also being able to step back and identify the theoretical aspects of the relationships, dynamics, and context. And if that is not enough, the reflective practitioner should also have the capacity to probe and analyse interactions, while remaining practical and imaginative enough to devise a plan for the future. Each of these would be challenging on its own, but facing all four demands at once can seem daunting, especially as they rely on very different character traits—both practical and theoretical.

Fortunately, the expectation is not perfection. Rather, the goal is incremental improvement, ideally on each of these fronts. This can be achieved by learning from others or seeking advice: 'This keeps happening to me, but I can't figure out why it doesn't happen to others'; 'I think I know what my problem is, but how do I overcome it—or even manage it?' Setting realistic goals, then, is important not only for the object of reflection (for example, 'how to interview better') but also for developing the ability to reflect itself.

6.3.4 **The Six-step Model—Gibbs**

This highly influential model has much in common with Driscoll's, and perhaps it is no coincidence that it contains exactly twice the number of stages.[84] To an extent, it breaks down each of Driscoll's stages into two separate components, as you can see from Figure 6.6.

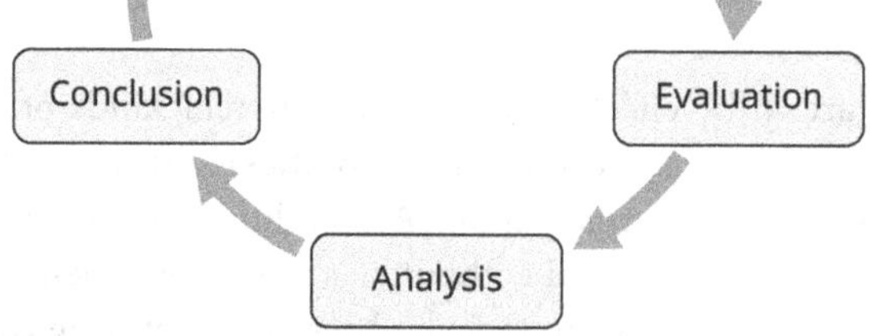

Figure 6.6 Gibbs' six-step model

[83] Ibid. [84] Graham Gibbs, *Learning by Doing* (Oxford Brookes University 2013).

Therefore, we do not need to repeat the details outlined above. For example, Driscoll's 'What' stage above can be seen as two parts: the 'objective reality', detailed in the *Description* stage here, and the emotional side of the experience, addressed under *Feeling*. If you prefer to separate factual descriptions from emotional ones, this model may suit you better. So, for the Description stage, you might write something like:

> We received the brief from the solicitor. The subject matter was unfamiliar, so I worked hard on my own (I did not make much effort to contact my partner) for three days straight to produce a timely, high-quality first draft.

And then, for Feeling, you may add:

> I was quite stressed about the matter. I really wanted to impress the supervising solicitor. I felt quite competitive with respect to my partner and didn't want them to take credit for my work. I now feel somewhat guilty about that, but also a bit satisfied.

A similar parallel applies to the next two stages, as Driscoll's 'So What?' stage can be seen as comprising both the objective reality ('*Evaluation*') and the critical assessment ('*Analysis*'). To simplify matters, we can suggest that the Evaluation stage involves asking 'what' questions—evaluative rather than factual in nature—such as:

- What went well during this experience?
- What didn't go well?
- What was your contribution to the positive aspects of the event?
- What was your contribution (or lack of contribution) that led to negative aspects?
- What were other people's contributions that led to positive or negative implications?

In contrast, the Analysis stage focuses on making sense of the situation, often through 'why' questions, such as 'Why did things go well?' and 'Why did something not go well?' Gibbs suggests enriching the analysis by drawing on 'ideas from outside the experience to help you. What was really going on?'[85] This is a 'dedicated space' for analysis, distinct from the emotional aspects. For the Evaluation stage, it would be good practice to consult research and academic literature that address the issues you were facing. To revert to the example above: you recognized that issues of competitive behaviour and (lack of) cooperation came up—be curious about this, and dip into insights from management theory, or even from literature about the legal profession itself. For example, it may highlight that while collaboration is a crucial skill for lawyers, you were expected to work with others without ever being taught how to do so (of course, now you can consult Chapter 10 of this book!).[86] Or perhaps you found that the event you're reflecting on involved issues of race or gender that made you uncomfortable, both generally and in terms of your own role in that context. This is perfectly normal. Engaging with issues of human rights, equality, and discrimination is often fraught

[85] Ibid 49.

[86] Susan Bryant, 'Collaboration in Law Practice: A Satisfying and Productive Process for a Diverse Profession' (1993) 17 Vermont Law Review 459.

with ethical and moral dilemmas. Confronting such issues directly can be overwhelming, and consulting relevant literature can help you better understand the subject matter and support both emotional and professional reflection.[87]

For the Conclusion, the Gibbs model asks you to consider the process in two ways: one general and one specific. First, consider what general lessons can be drawn from these experiences and analyses. Then, reflect on what can be concluded about your own specific, personal situation or way of working. Answering these two questions lays the foundation for the final stage: the Action Plan. The prompts outlined earlier in the third stage of the Driscoll model serve this purpose perfectly.

6.3.5 **The Six-step Model—Casey**

The final model we outline here is something of an outlier in several respects. It is designed by a law professor, Timothy Casey, and published in a journal that is dedicated to clinical legal scholarship.[88] In that sense, it is truly path-breaking. As mentioned earlier, lawyers, including legal academics, have only recently begun to familiarize themselves with and use reflective practices, including models. Therefore, finding a reflective model *designed* by a legal academic is particularly exciting within this field. Moreover, the structure, emphasis, and language of the model are often described as offering an almost natural fit for law teachers and students. For example, Stage 1 is based on the idea that there are objective truths in the world (eg 'the speed limit on this road is 30mph'), whereas Stage 2 involves choice and discretion (eg in assigning sanctions or compensation). This combination resonates with the law student's (and lawyer's) view of the world as consisting of a core of certainty (Stage 1) surrounded by a penumbra of vagueness (Stage 2).[89] The subsequent stages, which focus on individual and social biases, are equally familiar to lawyers' education and practice.

However, this divergence from mainstream reflective models can be challenging, as for some, Casey's model may stray *too* far from established approaches. Two aspects highlight this divergence. First, the model is not cyclical. The end of one process is not integrally linked to the beginning of another. Second, related but not identical, the model does not include an 'action plan' as its final feature. For these reasons, some law students who find that Casey's model resonates with their analytical style choose to add an action plan, creating a cyclical element and essentially developing a hybrid model of their own.

We can now outline the six stages of Casey's model.

Stage One: Competence

As noted above, this stage refers to the 'objective' phase of development. Just as a child initially learns that some problems (eg 2×3) have a single correct solution, and that 'wadder' is an incorrect spelling of 'water', we can similarly identify areas in which there are right and

[87] Hinett (n 80) 18–19. [88] Casey (n 26).

[89] The source for these two stages is found in the Reflective Judgment Model, developed by the educational psychologists Patricia King and Karen Kitchener, and imported into the world of (clinical) legal education by Laurie Morin and Louise Howells, 'The Reflective Judgement Project' (2002) 9 Clinical Law Review 623.

wrong ways to conduct ourselves professionally. In the legal profession, this task is guided by regulators such as the Solicitors Regulation Authority (SRA) and the Bar Standards Board (BSB), which set minimum expectations below which conduct is deemed to fall short of the required standard of competence. You will find discussion of these skills in Chapter 9 of this book. This is important because, by analogy, a student's work in the clinic can be assessed against these standards. So Casey suggests that a student can ask themselves to

> describe the standard of competence and then to apply that standard to her performance. Specific prompts could be any of the following: What would a competent lawyer do in this situation? What would be necessary to achieve a basic level of competence in the performance? Did you meet the standard of competence?[90]

Note that these standards are referred to as the *minimum expectations for competence*. A student in the early stages of professional development may fall below that standard, or they may meet the minimum bar yet still recognize that they expect more of themselves. This type of reflection is valuable in itself, as it reveals one's professional identity and values, such as integrity, proficiency, and communication.

Stage Two: Difference and Choice

Continuing the analogy with a child's educational development, at this stage a child discovers that there is more than one way to reach a predetermined goal, whether walking to school, playing a game, or building a treehouse. Although all routes lead to the same destination, some are better than others, some are more enjoyable, others are more efficient. In adult learning, it is not always obvious to the learner that they made a choice or that they could have chosen differently. For example, could they have offered the client a drink before the interview began? What would the implications of that choice have been? And would it have changed the dynamics in the room, if at all? So relevant prompts would be: Was there more than one way to have accomplished your objective? At what point did you make a choice? Could a different choice have led to different results?

Stage Three: Internal Context

For Casey, Stages Three, Four, and Five all build on Stage Two, which focused on choices made during the interaction, and prompt the student or practitioner to ask *why* that choice was made. In particular, these stages require them to engage with the biases—internal, external, and social—that impacted that choice. It is here that the student becomes 'more self-aware'.[91] This is where true learning begins, as knowledge is 'the result of the transaction between social knowledge and personal knowledge . . . between these objective and subjective experiences in a process called learning'.[92]

Stage Three focuses on the internal context, meaning the 'preferences, experiences, biases and characteristics owned by each of us that shape the decisions we make'.[93] It can be difficult, even unsettling, especially for those new to reflection and self-awareness, even to *acknowledge*

[90] Casey (n 26) 334. [91] Ibid 339. [92] Kolb (n 4) 48. [93] Casey (n 26) 339.

one's own biases, let alone discuss them with others. Discussion of preferences may be an option that is less taxing emotionally, and yet extremely conducive for reflection. This is because, just like biases, preferences directly influence decision-making. You might, for example, process situations quickly and 'cut to the chase' to save time. You might avoid conflict, making others feel that you agree with them. You may feel uncomfortable when people overshare. Or you may prefer to take risks, or to avoid them entirely. Can you see how such traits could affect client interactions, and how being aware of them helps manage their impact?

Stage Four: External Context

This stage focuses on something similar, yet crucially different, to the previous one: the 'preferences, experiences, biases and characteristics *of other people*'[94] with whom we engage in the experience. In the clinical context, this might include clients, practitioners, academic supervisors, or other stakeholders. As we note in Chapter 10 ('Working with Others'), law is not a solitary enterprise carried out in isolation. It requires engagement, communication, interaction, and negotiation. In the previous stage, we referred to preferences and characteristics that each person carries with them wherever they go. Here, the focus shifts to our responses and counter-responses to other people's styles, characteristics, and experiences. For example, your easy-going style may seem approachable and accommodating but could also create tensions for you or others. One student—a young, white, female native English speaker who was not British—described an uncomfortable interaction with an elderly British client of Asian descent. The interview was conducted under the supervision of a very senior male solicitor. The student felt that, despite being well prepared and ready to lead the interview, the client completely ignored her and responded only to the solicitor—even when he merely repeated her questions and comments. She was visibly distraught and tried to understand what drove that interaction. Was it her slight lack of confidence when facing older men in positions of authority? Or her understandable difficulty in calling out subtle bias in a complex situation? Whatever the explanation, it clearly reflected an interaction between the student's background, characteristics, and biases and those of the client, at the very least.

Stage Five: Social Context

In Stage Five, the practitioner examines how structural forces—political, economic, and social—shape their decisions. Because this context is often less intuitive and less accessible than personal biases, reflection may be supported by literature that explores power dynamics—including race, gender, and class—and their lasting influence not only on decision making but also on language, identity, and relationships. These forces are woven into daily life in ways that make them seem invisible, presenting the existing reality as 'normal' rather than simply one of many possible alternatives. Does this feel too abstract or theoretical? Let's break it down, then.

[94] Ibid 341.

In a different era, when same sex couples were not recognized as 'real' couples, a student in a law clinic found that he could not persuade a hospital to grant his gay client visiting rights for his partner. The experience revealed to him 'how his unawareness of his own heterosexuality affects his vision, reinforces the status quo and can heighten his client's pain'.[95] A similar moment might occur when a curious male student realizes, perhaps for the first time, his natural sense of safety after hearing how female students feel walking home late at night; or when white students genuinely listen to the complex realities of their racially minoritized peers. This recognition is aptly called a 'disorienting moment', as it can shake one's worldview and create a need to pause, step back, and reconsider 'truths' once seen as obvious but now needing to be questioned.[96]

It is worth noting that this social context underpins dialogic and critical reflection (section 4.1 in this chapter). Students often find this the most challenging aspect, and one way to address it is to view the experience from other perspectives (section 3.2).[97]

Practical Exercise 6.2

Clearly, 'I'm not racist/sexist/homophobic/ageist/ableist'. To which the answer is: you probably aren't, but many people who are not '-ist' have biases, for the simple reasons that everyone has their own background and experience which has, consciously or subconsciously, shaped the way we view the world. It is the unfortunate reality that because we are so frightened, or ashamed, of the possibility that we carry biases towards some groups of people, we are less likely to face them and mitigate their effects. So, the more we are aware of our biases, the better we can be at addressing them. Where are you in that respect? How can you test a bias that is, by definition, hidden?

Psychologists at Harvard, the University of Virginia, and the University of Washington created 'Project Implicit' to develop Hidden Bias Tests—called Implicit Association Tests, or IATs, in the academic world—to measure unconscious bias. Try it yourself: https://implicit.harvard.edu/implicit/takeatest.html

Stage Six: Metacognition

Casey's final stage refers to 'thinking about thinking'.[98] It can be a fascinating stage if given proper focus, though it may feel too advanced for students still developing their reflective skills. It encourages, or perhaps simply allows, the student to reflect on the process of reflection itself. Was it uncomfortable? Did it feel like a weight was lifted? Or did you simply shrug? Was it confusing? Do you see this as the start of an ongoing journey of reflection, or have you had enough, at least for now? Reflection can be emotionally demanding, and as we will see below, it becomes even more complex when part of an academic setting, especially

[95] Jane Aiken, 'Striving to Teach "Justice, Fairness and Morality"' (1997) 4 Clinical Law Review 1, 3.
[96] Quigley (n 18) 51. [97] Spencer, 'Private Lives' (n 46). [98] Casey (n 26) 346.

if submitted for assessment. Such feelings can be acknowledged at this stage, helping the student recentre and contemplate the process itself.

TAKING STOCK

This section provided an overview of four popular and helpful models for reflection, which could assist in structuring a reflection. Before describing those models, we made some important caveats, which can be emphasized here as well. First, there are quite a few, non-structured ways to reflect, such as orally, to a friend, to oneself, with a journal. These have immense value in their own right, and also as a way to supporting a structured reflection. Second, models are only as useful as you would like them to be. You may decide to mix and match, or not to use them at all. In any case, it would be a good idea to discuss your preferred model with your supervisor or project lead, and receive feedback before adopting a particular model, or a hybrid form.

And yet, with that in mind, there is a reason that these four models have been found to be useful to millions of people over the years. They guide our thinking, suggest question prompts, and (hopefully) ensure that we don't skip steps or miss important and relevant connections.

6.4 **Why We Don't Reflect**

If reflection was easy, we'd all be doing it regularly. But it is not easy, and at times it can be quite hard. To address the barriers and resistance to reflection, we must understand not only why we should reflect in theory but also why we often fail to do so in practice. These barriers are broadly defined as 'those factors which inhibit or block learners' preparedness for the experience, their active engagement in it, and their ability to reflect rationally on it with a view to learning from it'.[99] Boud and Walker compiled an extensive 'brainstormed list of barriers to working with experience':[100]

- Presuppositions about what is and is not possible for us to do.
- Not being in touch with one's own assumptions and what one is able to do.
- Past negative experiences.
- Expectations of others: society, peer group, figures of authority, family.
- Threats to the self, one's world view, or to ways of behaving.
- Lack of self-awareness about one's place in the world.
- Inadequate preparation.

[99] Boud and Walker (n 16) 80. [100] Ibid 79.

- Hostile or impoverished environments.
- Lack of opportunity to step aside from tasks.
- Lack of time.
- External pressures and demands.
- Lack of support from others.
- Lack of skills: in noticing, intervening.
- Intent which is unclear or unfocused.
- Established patterns of thought and behaviour.
- Inability to conceive of the possibility of learning from experience: 'this is not learning', 'this is not possible'.
- Stereotypes about how we learn.
- Obstructive feelings: lack of confidence or self-esteem, fear of failure or the response of others, unexpressed grief about lost opportunities.

Practical Exercise 6.3

Have another look at this list and identify which three resonate most clearly as a relevant barrier for you. Now think: are they part of the same group (eg 'feelings' or 'time'), or are they different? Now choose one such barrier and expand on the way it impedes your ability to learn from experience.

Following this exercise, we will take the same approach: rather than addressing each barrier individually, we will focus on their shared traits and effects as a group. Of course, these groups are not isolated; there are strong interrelations between them, some more obvious than others. For example, a clear distinction can be drawn between 'external' and 'internal' barriers. Indeed, there seems to be a clear difference between someone telling me that I cannot do something and my decision to prioritize other activities. Or is there?

> Many of the supposedly external barriers only begin to have real force when we take them on ourselves and think and act as if they were true. Often self-imposed censorship is more pernicious than anything imposed by others . . . There is a strong dynamic whereby learners are tricked, or trick themselves, into thinking barriers are external when they are not—'no one from my background could possibly aspire to a job like that' . . . When we were treated as working class boys who 'should' have low expectations of life [for example], rather than as the particular individuals whom we were, we internalized the external oppression and censored our own aspirations.[101]

With this caveat in mind, we now move from the most internal group of barriers to those commonly seen as 'beyond our control'.

[101] Boud and Walker (n 16) 80–1.

6.4.1 **Reluctance to Face the Self**

Reflection can be difficult for many reasons, but a key one is that it forces us to confront aspects of ourselves that may be deeply uncomfortable to recognize or admit:

> the reflective process is a complex one in which both feelings and cognition are closely interrelated and interactive. Negative feelings, particularly about oneself, can form major barriers towards learning. They can distort perceptions, lead to false interpretations of events, and can undermine the will to persist.[102]

Boud set a clear expectation, stating that 'Unless [my students] feel sufficiently free to write things in their journals that they would be embarrassed for me to read, then they are probably not using their journals sufficiently well for them to be good examples of reflection.'[103] It should be emphasized that Boud was explicitly referring to reflective *journals*, not the reflective portfolios often submitted to tutors. Yet this distinction may be overstated. While the written outputs may differ, the emotional process behind both is equally real. This process matters because it connects to 'the pedagogy of discomfort, the deliberate attempt to create moments of dissonance that disturb students in a productive way and opens them up to new ways of thinking . . . but not so much that they step back in fear from new learning.'[104]

A student on a teaching course explained how challenging the process felt for her:

> [Writing reflections is] unbelievably difficult. Writing it on the page. It makes it permanent somehow. I don't know. I find it really, really difficult. And we have actually discussed at PGCE whether oral reflections would be allowed as part of our coursework because they would be so much easier to do . . . if you reflect on a lesson that's gone really badly, by putting it on paper there's a record of it. It's saved on my disk, saved on the computer, and my mentor, who just happens to be my boss as well, could look at it and go, 'Oh God, that didn't really happen did it?' And I just think it's like emails rather than having a telephone conversation with someone. [As with] email, it's written down and it's a piece of written evidence I suppose.[105]

In law, this challenge is even sharper. As we saw, students are trained to value emotional detachment as a professional virtue, avoiding emotional involvement. So it can feel disorienting when they are suddenly asked—or required—to engage directly with their emotions.[106] Such feelings create two types of barriers. First, they may discourage students from engaging in the reflective process at all. For those unfamiliar with this kind of exercise, there can be a strong reluctance to even 'give it a go' and leave their comfort zone. Second, an 'affective

[102] David Boud, Rosemary Keogh, and David Walker, 'What Is Reflection in Learning' in Boud, Keogh, and Walker (n 50).

[103] David Boud, 'Using Journal Writing to Enhance Reflective Practice' in LM English and MA Gillen (eds), *Promoting Journal Writing in Adult Education* (Jossey-Bass 2001) 9, 16.

[104] Stephen Brookfield, *The Skilful Teacher: On Technique, Trust and Responsiveness in the Classroom* (3rd ed, Wiley 2015) 157.

[105] Jonathan Tummons, '"It sort of feels uncomfortable": Problematising the Assessment of Reflective Practice' (2011) 36 Studies in Higher Education 471, 475–6.

[106] Spencer (n 46).

barrier'[107] restricts flexible and creative thinking, temporarily stalling or blocking deeper reflection. Emotional factors 'can isolate and impoverish the new experience; they can make it difficult to integrate new learning with past knowledge, and to make judgements and draw conclusions from it'.[108] It is thus revealing that 'there is evidence in the literature on reflection that reflection at the practical or technical level is more likely than reflection at the emancipatory or ethical level'.[109] In CLE, for instance, it is easy to imagine a student or practitioner focusing their reflection narrowly on issues like tardiness, note-taking quality, or promptness in communication. But . . .

> The theme of technique has always been an element of the clinical movement, and properly so, just as it has for law schools generally . . . Technique is a powerful and highly focussed lens that reveals a tiny piece of legal skills or legal process with great clarity. But the magnification . . . blinds the observer to the larger framework in which technique is only a single element.[110]

6.4.2 **Fear of Change**

By now it should be clear that reflection is pointless without a genuine willingness to improve and change one's approach. However, the prospect of deep-seated 'change' may be threatening, for many reasons. Two can be noted here. First, consider Adam, who sees himself as engaging and stimulating but, through reflection, realizes he dominates conversations and leaves little space for others. The thing is that Adam actually *likes* to be engaging, exuberant, and stimulating, and, if it wasn't for the cost and effect of this behaviour, would never consider it a problem, let alone try to change it. Indeed, 'a change in self-perception is threatening, and that makes the process of reflection . . . threatening'.[111] Second, it is not only Adam's *subjective* reluctance to change—he may be right, at least initially. If he adopts a less dominant communication style, he may initially feel less confident, less intuitive, and less effective as a communicator, teacher, or confidant. Unsurprisingly, when 'people first set out to improve their performance through reflective learning, they notice a distinct drop-off in performance once their habitual level of skill is disrupted'.[112]

6.4.3 **What Will *They* Think of *Me*?**

As a preface to this subsection, let's make explicit what has so far been implicit. Contrary to common belief, reflection is not only about what you did wrong or how you should improve. As noted throughout, reflection must also recognize and understand what went well.

[107] David Boud, Rosemary Keogh, and David Walker, 'Promoting Reflection in Learning: A Model' in Boud, Keogh, and Walker (n 50).

[108] Boud and Walker (n 16) 80. [109] Kibble (n 30).

[110] David Barnhizer, 'The University Ideal and Clinical Legal Education' (1990) 35 New York University Law School Law Review 87.

[111] Neil Kibble, 'Reflection and Supervision in Clinical Legal Education: Do Work Placements Have a Role in Undergraduate Legal Education?' (1998) 5 International Journal of the Legal Profession 83.

[112] Philip Candy, Sheila Harri-Augstein, and Laurie Thomas, 'Reflection and the Self-Organised Learner: A Model of Learning Conversations' in David Boud, Rosemary Keogh, and David Walker (eds), *Reflection: Turning Experience into Learning* (Kogan Page 1985) 100, 102.

And yet, of course, few interviews, letters, meetings, or presentations are *perfect*. More often than not, there is room to ask what could have been done differently. But when reflection is shared with others—through discussion or writing—rather than kept in a private journal, it introduces an element of exposure. In a competitive environment where performance is routinely assessed, why would anyone volunteer information that could be 'not all positive' to their managers or assessors?

6.4.4 **No Time, No Energy**

Despite the importance of reflective practice, its value is not always immediately apparent. Learning, especially when it addresses deep-seated issues, takes time. There may be no immediate chance to test new insights, and even when we do, we may not succeed in changing ingrained instincts. Therefore, there is an understandable preference to clean one's (metaphorical or real) desk and to prioritize tasks that include a clear, hard deadline. In today's climate of strained work–life balance, fatigue, lack of energy, and study or work-related anxiety all create real barriers to reflection.

6.4.5 **How to Address These Barriers?**

As always, we can only address an issue if we recognize its existence, origins, and nature. For example, with negative feelings, the first step is to acknowledge not only the uncomfortable traits but also the feelings about having those traits.[113] How do we recognize them? Boud and Walker suggest that 'Comparing one's thoughts, feelings and behaviour with those of others can indicate that we are experiencing differently, which can prompt us to ask why . . . Hearing them tell their story, and telling our story to them, can help us to see ourselves and how we experience and learn.'[114] In other words, normalizing and even celebrating change by sharing and hearing experiences helps us approach it with curiosity and enthusiasm rather than fear.

And what of the second, more practical, fear that 'I'll not be as good as I was before'? Here, anyone who has played a sport or instrument can relate: you may have developed a habit—a swim stroke, a kick, or a finger placement—that was simply 'wrong'. Practice did not make your performance 'perfect'. Quite the opposite. It made it 'permanent': changing to a better posture feels harder and less comfortable at first. But staying as you were would have created a glass ceiling you can only break by accepting short-term discomfort for long-term improvement.

What about lack of time and energy? As Gandhi is (perhaps apocryphally) quoted as saying: 'if you don't have half an hour a day to do yoga, then do an hour.' By analogy, the busier we are, the more vital reflection becomes. And yet, it is acknowledged that some of these aspects may be partly outside our control. Work or study environments, standards, and priorities may not support effective reflection. Beyond making the best of limited resources (reflecting orally with friends or using downtime for self-awareness, for example) there may be opportunities to persuade others to build reflection into their structures, benefiting not only you rself but others as well.

[113] Boud, Keogh, and Walker (n 102) 37.

[114] Boud and Walker (n 16) 81.

TAKING STOCK

This section identified some of the barriers to reflection. Some of these barriers may be viewed as driven by our internal limitations, such as our belief in our abilities, our lack of motivation, or our fears. Others may be clearly impacted by external factors, such as what people will think of me if I reveal my inadequacies. We noted that the two groups are closer than what may seem: if people are more accepting and supportive, I may feel that I can achieve more. And yet, at times it is useful to identify each barrier separately, so as not to be overwhelmed.

We identified four such barriers or, perhaps, groups of barriers: the reluctance to face the self; fear of change; the worry of what others will think; lack of time and energy.

Each of these barriers may be significant and cannot be understated. But they are also familiar, and there are mechanisms, structures, and suggestions to deal with them.

6.5 Reflecting on Reflection: Ethical, Practical, and Critical Issues

As this chapter draws to a close, it is time to turn the critical lens of the reflective process onto . . . the reflective process itself. If taken seriously, reflection can be powerful, even transformative. But for that reason, the process must be approached with care. Ethical, pedagogical, and philosophical issues can arise for students and others, and it would be misguided to ignore them.

6.5.1 A Requirement to Reveal?

We have discussed the emotional demands of reflection and the difficulty of sharing such experiences with others. If these challenges already create *barriers* to reflection, what should we make of the ethics of *requiring* students to submit deeply personal material, or even share it with the class? One student nurse wrote during her studies:

> My feelings are private—yet I am expected to frame them in prose and submit them to my university. I don't know my lecturers or personal tutor intimately. What right has anyone to ask for such personal information, let alone ask that it be graded by a faceless lecturer? As nurses we respect patients' rights not to disclose their personal feelings. Yet no such right is afforded to students . . . I have had reflections returned with requests for more details about my feelings. I comply but completely resent being asked to do so.[115]

[115] Arabella Sinclair-Penwarden, 'Listen up: We should not be made to disclose our personal feelings in reflection assignments' Nursing Times 102(37) 12.

In the CLE context: we tell *clients* that they have a right to share as they wish, while explaining sometimes that withholding information may limit our ability to advise or represent them effectively. But what about students? They are expected to share negative feelings and experiences they might otherwise keep private, often with peers in a competitive environment and tutors who may also be assessing their work.

We also know that relying on formal consent from students can only go so far. For this reason, students should not be required to reveal anything they are uncomfortable sharing. As one clinical professor explained, 'Coercing personal disclosure from students is a nasty idea that could be expected to taint any method it touched'.[116] And yet, she went on to explain:

> virtually every request we make of students has coercive potential. This potential lies in the power imbalance between teacher and student, and more particularly, in students' perception of the teacher's greater power. Even our willingness to spend time in a one-on-one conversation with a student may be rare enough in law school to push students toward exchanging disclosure for more attention.[117]

In addressing this quandary, it is important to respect students' expectation of privacy and their understandable and justifiable nervousness about sharing vulnerabilities or low points.[118] There are ways to balance the benefits of reflection while still protecting that principle. For example, journal writing can include details never intended for others to see, let alone a tutor. There can also be intermediate levels of sharing, such as inviting (but not requiring!) students to share reflections with a trusted peer.

It can also help to create a supportive environment by starting with positive reflections, focusing on what went well. Recognizing what went well, whether in an interview, meeting, or supervision, helps solidify good practices for the future. Acknowledging that you felt good working independently, collaborating, or leading is an important and sometimes crucial aspect of self-awareness.

Reflection can also be more general, focusing on life goals, expectations, and future professional aspirations. Students may also share reflections privately with a tutor rather than the whole group, and tutors could allow anonymous submissions. Finally, students should be encouraged to choose what to share in each format and be reminded that reflection quality is not tied to how personal their disclosure is.

But, ultimately, the ethical dilemma cannot be avoided. We already drew the analogy with the client: the more a tutor knows about a student's background, character, and biases, the more effective the reflective process can be.[119] How can a tutor help a student manage anxieties if they do not know that the student is struggling? How can a tutor turn a problematic relationship between two students into a teaching moment if its nature remains hidden? This issue brings us full circle to why academics have often shied away from this challenge. Clearly, it feels 'safer' not to mix the emotional with the intellectual. However, as

[116] Ibid 221. [117] Ibid. [118] Spencer (n 46) 191, 195.

[119] Jennifer Lyman, 'Getting Personal in Supervision: Looking for That Fine Line Essay on Clinical Supervision' (1995) 2 Clinical Law Review 211, 218.

noted above, this approach has costs, including social and personal isolation and reduced well-being. Conversely, exposure to these reflections is a reminder of

> the privileged position that the clinical teacher occupies. To be privy to students' private reflections about their hopes and dreams and their personal recognition of the backgrounds that have shaped their personalities is indeed a rare and special one. It is critical that clinical educators respect this privilege.[120]

6.5.2 **How Much for That Reflection?**

A related, but not identical, matter is that the incentives built into reflective practice can 'encourage exaggeration or even prevarication'.[121] It has even been suggested that reflective practices risk resembling television reality shows, where 'participants' are rewarded for exposing deep emotions, showing remorse, appearing to embark on a journey, and ultimately conforming to a narrative of growth—reducing reflection to 'little more than a mantra'.[122]

The broader pedagogical and ethical question is whether students should be assessed on their reflections. Assessment imposes external criteria that may interfere with the personal, internal process of reflection. Some students may feel driven to exaggerate their 'journey' because the real process seems insufficiently impressive. One law student described the exercise as 'navel gazing . . . [in] . . . self-indulgent proportions'.[123] Another candidly admitted, 'Rather than being reflective, I care more about the marks that I will get. I give out what I think the lecturers will want rather than being reflective of my personal strengths/weakness'.[124]

Conversely, some may downplay the impact of personal characteristics (such as race, sexual identity, or disability), fearing that their analysis will not be welcomed by the tutor. Thus, students may see assessed reflections as 'mandated disclosures focused on eliciting the *right kind* of revelations'.[125] The reverse also causes problems: when an honest reflection receives a disappointing mark, the effect can be more demoralising than when 'only' knowledge is assessed. This problem is worsened if students feel that the feedback and marks are subjective, and that another assessor would have awarded a higher mark.[126]

Another issue concerns students' capacity to improve and, relatedly, legal academics' ability to teach effective reflection. These are connected. We assume most legal academics can teach subjects like contract, tort, and criminal law well, and that committed students can

[120] Spencer (n 46). [121] Ibid 224.

[122] Judith Kuit, Gill Reay, and Richard Freeman, 'Experiences of Reflective Teaching' (2001) Active Learning in Higher Education 128, 129; Bruce MacFarlane and Lesley Gourlay, 'The Reflection Game: Enacting the Penitent Self' (2009) 14 Teaching in Higher Education 455.

[123] Spencer (n 46).

[124] Rachel Spencer, '"First they tell us to ignore our emotions, then they tell us to reflect": The Development of a Reflective Writing Pedagogy in Clinical Legal Education through an Analysis of Student Perceptions of Reflective Writing' (2014) 21 International Journal of Clinical Legal Education 33.

[125] Stephen Brookfield, *Becoming a Critically Reflective Teacher* (Jossey-Bass 1995) 100, cited in Bolton and Delderfield (n 34).

[126] Tummons (n 105) 477, 481.

improve without inherent barriers. But can the same be said for reflection? Many students encounter reflective practice for the first time in clinical legal education, making the learning curve steep, even though legal study progresses incrementally.[127] Some students reach their final year with emotional maturity that allows them to excel at reflection, unrelated to the module itself, while others struggle despite genuine effort.[128] More broadly, some argue reflection cannot truly be taught, or that law teachers are ill-equipped to teach it.[129]

At this stage, it is worth remembering that reflective practices were developed in fields of education and medicine by professionals with subject expertise (ie not in reflection), training students who often had no more prior experience with reflection than today's law students. It is true that, since then, reflective practice has become embedded in these professions, leaving their students better prepared than law students for advanced, consistent practice. However, this only means legal education, with its professional training elements, should expand and develop reflective training earlier.

But this does not fully answer the argument that reflection should be included in legal education yet excluded from assessment—in other words, that it should remain a purely formative element of study.[130] However, our experience—which is shared by others—is that despite numerous invitations, 'very few students avail themselves' of opportunities for this formative assessment.[131] This often remains true even when the module includes an *additional* assessed reflective element. Perhaps regrettably for some, marking appears to send a signal in both directions. Students and teachers alike view the weight of an assessment—whether reflective, clinical, or doctrinal—as a currency signalling its value.[132]

What about concerns that reflection raises issues of parity, validity, subjectivity, and consistency?[133] First, despite its subjective elements, Rachel Spencer notes that subjectivity is not unique to assessing reflective writing, since

> there are a number of elements that are required for good writing of any kind. Grammatical correctness, syntax, sentence construction, appropriately organised paragraphs and the idea of a beginning, a middle and an end are arguably good basic building blocks for any kind of writing in any discipline.[134]

Second, as Jennifer Moon explains, all assessed work involves some subjectivity, which is managed through professional criteria and assessor moderation, making the assessment of reflective writing 'no more difficult than those involved in the assessment of anything'.[135] A recurring theme worth stressing is the need to clarify—both for assessors and students—whether assessment targets the content of reflective learning (eg managing authority) or

[127] Spencer (n 46) 195 (to clarify: Spencer addresses this argument, but does not support it).

[128] Jennifer Moon, *Reflection and Employability* (Learning and Teaching Support Network 2004) 13.

[129] Ledvinka (n 20) 36.

[130] Tummons (n 105) 481; Simon Rice, 'Assessing—But Not Grading—Clinical Legal Education' (2007) Macquarie Law WP 16 (arguing that CLE as a whole, not only reflection within CLE, should not be marked).

[131] Spencer (n 46) 199.

[132] Ross Hyams, 'Assessing Insight: Grading Reflective Journals in Clinical Legal Education' (2010) 17 James Cook University Law Review 25, 34–5.

[133] Ledvinka (n 20) 40, referring to the UK Centre for Legal Education's concerns.

[134] Spencer (n 46).

[135] Moon (n 52) 15.

the reflective process itself. How should we evaluate an excellent practitioner who reflects poorly, or a poor practitioner who reflects brilliantly on their shortcomings? Often there is overlap between clinical work and reflection, but not always; clarity is therefore welcome, if not even crucial.

Practical Exercise 6.4

Consider three points in favour and three against the following statement:

'Reflection should not constitute an assessed part of legal education.'

Taking account of both sides, do you agree or disagree with the statement?

6.5.3 Ethical Commitments at Cross Purposes

We noted that creating an environment of trust is conducive, perhaps essential, for fruitful reflection. Moreover, this is a unique form of trust. Here, participants feel safe sharing controversial feelings, missteps, and even serious errors of judgement. Creating such an environment within an educational setting means relinquishing familiar features such as distance, formality, hierarchy, and even power, replacing them with a close relationship, which some have characterized as intimacy (very distinct, of course, from personal intimacy).[136] Because some students form closer working relationships with tutors than others, there may be real or perceived bias and unfairness.[137]

However, towards the end of the term or year the power dynamic reasserts itself, as tutors must assess student performance, complicating the relationship and potentially undermining the trust built.[138] One student reflected on her clinic experience after developing a personal relationship with her supervisor and relying heavily on her approval.[139] She described her reaction to her supervisor's critical feedback, which noted that she 'worked compulsively and that my behavior made it difficult for others to work with me'.[140] The student's response included feeling 'a self-esteem [so] low [that] I could not ever remember feeling'.[141]
Reflecting on this episode, Jennifer Lyman observes:

> Students may generalize from the result on an anonymously graded exam, but that grade cannot approach the impact of face-to-face evaluation by a person on whose approval the student has hung her incipient career. Nor will the student so affected stop to ask herself whether to read a lawyer's evaluation as an assessment of her mental

[136] Kathleen Sullivan, 'Self-disclosure, Separation, and Students: Intimacy in the Clinical Relationship' (1993) 27 Indiana Law Review 115.

[137] Ledvinka (n 20) 45.

[138] Ibid 123–7.

[139] Jennifer Howard, 'Learning to Think Like a Lawyer through Experience: Essay on Clinical Supervision' (1995) 2 Clinical Law Review 167.

[140] Ibid 206.

[141] Ibid.

> health. The student's exposure of her personal self burdens the teacher with far greater responsibilities for predicting the impact of her evaluation, anticipating the student will perceive it as a broad assessment of her 'worth'.

If that is not enough, creating a close, intimate environment between clinic students and tutors can create tensions with formal and informal duties to third parties, especially clients. Gillie Bolton notes that medical professionals sometimes cope with the horrors of daily practice through dark, macabre humour.[142] If overheard by others, this humour can seem utterly disrespectful to patients and those in their care. Many legal practitioners also engage in similar humour, often after hours in pubs or bars.[143] Clinical legal education usually benefits from a slower pace and lower-risk environment. And yet, encouraging students to share doubts about a case or even distaste for clients as a way to process feelings treads a fine line.

6.5.4 **Reflection as a Neoliberal Process**

Finally, a more principled ideological or philosophical critique can target the reflective process. It may be argued that focusing on individual improvement aligns with a neoliberal paradigm that ignores structural economic, social, and cultural barriers. According to this view, the theory behind experiential learning is 'highly individualizing, and its psychological perspective . . . ignores or downgrades the social context'.[144] It may even echo new-age coaching clichés promoting the idea that 'anyone can do' this, that, or the other. This approach emphasizes individual responsibility, which runs counter to social justice aspirations and seems a peculiar platform for clinical legal education. Thankfully, it need not.

A possible escape—which some may view as elegant and others as narrow—is to explain that while reflective practice and experiential learning stem from a belief in *individuality*, they need not align with *individualism*. Embracing individuality means recognizing that each person brings background, experience, knowledge, biases, and character to each event, and while these cannot be easily discarded, they can be acknowledged, recognized, and at times addressed. It can also support a more ambitious claim: our past *does not necessarily dictate* our future. Indeed, as noted earlier in this chapter, reflective practice is deeply concerned with background and history, which shape character and biases—quite the opposite of an 'individualistic', let alone a neoliberal, approach.

> We are embedded and enmeshed within the stories and story structures we have created, and which have been created around us: some we are aware of, some very much not . . . My success as a person, or more correctly perhaps my happiness, rests on my ability to juggle this complexity; and my flexibility in response to the volatility and constant change created by my own behaviour, that of other individuals, and of my society (social, political and professional).[145]

[142] Bolton and Delderfield (n 36) 208–10.
[143] Daniel Newman, 'Are Lawyers Neurotic?' (2018) 25 International Journal of the Legal Profession 3.
[144] Michael Reynolds, 'Learning Styles: A Critique' (1997) 28 Management Learning 115, 128.
[145] Bolton (n 53) 273.

This suggests that the path out of unwanted traits, and the structures that enable them, begins with awareness of their power. Ultimately, this process is directed by the practitioner towards themselves, not towards others. It does not attribute blame or assign condemnation.

TAKING STOCK

This final section addressed a number of possible critiques regarding the reflective process, which relate to ethical, practical, and ideological concerns.

If the reflective process is such an important one (as we saw in section 1) and if it is sometimes quite difficult (as we saw in section 4), how can we require, in an educational setting, students to reveal their reflections? Moreover, how can we assess and mark students' reflections? There are, perhaps, persuasive responses, but they do not render the questions moot.

Similarly, the dynamic that facilitates the creation of an atmosphere of trust, flattening hierarchy, can lead to tensions with the power dynamics that necessarily exist between teacher and student, and with the ethical and professional commitments towards clients. These must be navigated with care.

Conclusion

This chapter has explored reflection as both a deeply personal and pedagogically vital process within clinical legal education. We began by asking *why reflect*, recognizing that it is essential for meaningful, dynamic, and critical learning. Reflection allows students to connect theory with practice, to challenge assumptions, and to build resilience and self-awareness. These are all qualities that are crucial not only for their development as lawyers but also for their lifelong learning journey. By engaging in reflection, students can begin to appreciate the complexity, uncertainty, and human dimensions of law that are obscured by a purely doctrinal or Langdellian approach.

We then sought to clarify *what reflection is*, acknowledging that no single definition can capture its multifaceted nature. Instead, we identified its key features: reconstructing and reorganizing experience, combining intellectual and affective engagement, persistently reconsidering one's beliefs, and translating insight into action. These elements highlight that reflection is neither linear nor passive but instead an active dialogue with oneself, others, and the broader social context.

The chapter also addressed *how to reflect*, introducing four models—Driscoll, Kolb, Gibbs, and Casey—each offering a different framework to suit different events, personalities, and learning styles. These models show that reflection can be structured and purposeful, yet flexible and adaptable. Importantly, each model underscores the need for an action plan, ensuring that reflection is not an exercise in introspection alone but a tool for growth and change.

Finally, we confronted the *barriers to reflection*: the reluctance to face discomfort, the fear of change, time and energy constraints, and the ethical dilemmas of sharing vulnerable insights in assessed settings. Reflecting on reflection itself reminded us that while the process can be unsettling, it is also liberating, fostering resilience, empathy, and a deeper sense of professional identity.

Ultimately, reflection is not an optional extra but a core dimension of clinical legal education. It invites students to see law not as a fixed body of rules, but as a living, relational practice shaped by human experience. By embracing reflection, with its challenges and rewards, students and educators alike can transform legal education into a more humane, self-aware, and socially engaged enterprise.

Further Reading

Gillie Bolton and Russell Delderfield, *Reflective Practice: Writing and Professional Development* (5th ed, Sage 2017).

Karen Hinett, *Developing Reflective Practice in Legal Education* (UK Centre for Legal Education 2002).

David Kolb, *Experiential Learning: Experience as the Source of Learning and Development* (2nd ed, Pearson 2015).

Professional Legal Ethics

7

Ethics is knowing the difference between what is right to do and what you have a right to do.

Potter Stewart

Chapter Overview

This chapter will introduce you to the nature and purpose of professional legal ethics. It sets out and interrogates the underlying principles and relevant ethical frameworks that regulate professional conduct. By the end of this chapter, you should be able to:

- Understand the values that underpin professional legal practice;
- Consider the relationship between moral character and ethical conduct;
- Interrogate the relationship between professional values and the codes of practice that govern the provision of legal advice and representation;
- Identify ethical issues as they might arise in the context of clinical legal education;
- Understand the different types of disciplinary action that might be taken when ethical rules are breached.

Introduction

The importance of legal ethics to legal practice, and to clinical legal education, cannot be overstated. The principles and rules that govern the ethical conduct of lawyers aim to ensure the honesty and integrity of the profession. Professional legal ethics regulate the relationship between lawyers and their clients, the courts, fellow professionals, and other people. The purpose of regulation is to ensure that members of the public are protected and that the rule of law is not undermined. The importance of professional legal ethics has been asserted not only at a national level but also in the international sphere. Principle 26 of the UN's Basic Principles on the Role of Lawyers states that codes of professional conduct must be established 'through appropriate organs, or by legislation, in accordance with national law and customs and recognised international standards and norms'.[1] Each national bar association (or similar) drafts and adopts its own rules and procedures. For the purposes of this chapter, we are predominantly guided by the ethical standards set out by the Solicitors Regulation Authority (SRA), which regulates solicitors in England and Wales.

Why do legal ethics matter to clinical legal education? First, the majority of law school clinics provide legal services to members of the public. Those members of the public deserve to be given legal advice in an ethical and competent way. In the UK, some clinics might be supervised by non-practising lawyers where the legal services provided are unregulated by formal legal services regulation. This means that the law does not require a *practising* solicitor or barrister to undertake the work because it is not 'reserved' as an area of legal work. Reserved areas for solicitors include, for example, exercising a right of audience and the conduct of litigation.[2] However, even where law school clinics do not undertake reserved work, they will generally aim to follow appropriate ethical rules as set down by professional legal regulators to ensure good levels of service provision, and help to better acquaint students with the operation of those rules in practice.

Second, developing an awareness of good professional conduct and learning how to identify professional misconduct are vital legal skills. As explored in this chapter, even among lawyers, perspectives can vary on the interpretation of ethical rules in individual cases; it is therefore important to take the time to actively reflect on what they might mean in the context of day-to-day legal practice. Third, the rules that lawyers must comply with have the potential to govern aspects of both professional *and* personal life. In that sense, we might conceive of legal ethics as a subset of ethics more generally. At a basic level, ethical principles ask us to interrogate what is morally right or wrong and help us to decide how to act. Learning and reflecting upon legal ethics during law school therefore provides a valuable opportunity to consider the interplay between professional rules of conduct and wider personally held moral, political, or social values.

It is important to note that while rules exist to guide the ethical choices of lawyers in practice, those rules can only take a lawyer so far in determining the right course of action. Herring points to the fact that the approach taken to an ethical issue may lead to a different answer: a *rule-based approach* will seek to simply follow the relevant rules and not look outside them; an *outcome-based approach* aims to determine simply how to get the best outcome; and a *character-based approach* will seek to make a decision based on values such as honesty and integrity.[3] Context matters and will dictate the best approach. However, people often disagree on which of these approaches to take, meaning that conclusions as to 'what to do' in any given ethical quandary can differ. Clinical legal education provides an excellent opportunity to explore what courses of action might be appropriate (or not) in any given scenario.

Commentators have highlighted the importance of ethical training and awareness in the realistic context of decisions as they might arise day-to-day as a lawyer against the wider background of social justice issues such as climate change, poverty, or ill-health, and across

[1] UN Basic Principles on the Role of Lawyers (adopted 7th September 1980).

[2] Legal Services Act 2007, s 12.

[3] Jonathan Herring, *Legal Ethics* (2nd ed, OUP 2017) 6.

all areas of legal practice (ie not simply those working in human rights and areas of social welfare law broadly conceived, but also those in the corporate legal sector for example).[4] It is also increasingly clear that well-being, such as the experience of stress in the workplace, has a bearing upon ethical practice. Therefore, considering the ethical issues in client cases in the context of personal, social, cultural, and socio-economic issues can be said to be intrinsically connected to the best interests of clients in a broader sense.

We acknowledge that ethical decision-making for lawyers can at times be inconsistent or even contradictory: quite often, there is no one 'right answer' to an ethical issue faced by a clinical law student or a lawyer in practice. Ethical decision-making requires some independent exercise of judgement on a case-by-case basis. By way of example, in England and Wales, the SRA has set down seven key principles that also operate as rules that can lead to sanctions should they be breached. As we explore, these principles are designed to help guide and determine decision-making in searching for what the 'right' answer might be.

This chapter considers each of these principles of ethical legal practice in turn. As outlined above, we are predominantly concerned with those principles that apply to solicitors; however, at times we also reference separate rules for barristers where they might be relevant to clinical casework, or draw comparisons with other jurisdictions where relevant. We use the SRA Principles as a guide but note that, while international jurisdictions of course differ, many will have some equivalent principles set out in relevant codes of conduct or professional legal rules of practice. The principles include the rule of law and the proper administration of justice; maintaining trust and confidence in the profession; lawyer independence; honesty and integrity; equality and diversity; and, finally, the duty to act in the best interests of clients. We will explore both the theories that underlie the principles and their application in practice. The chapter finally considers the role of professional legal regulation in fostering good ethical practice.

7.1 Ethical Principles in Practice

The values that underpin legal practice have developed over centuries. Nicolson and Webb point to how these values allow lawyers to hold the authority and standing they need to perform their professional functions in society.[5] From a more cynical perspective, they might be seen as self-serving, as they maintain the power structures needed to preserve professional status. An emphasis on, for example, legal knowledge and skill, trust, and collegiality means that lawyers can 'uphold an image of the professions as highly educated, highly skilled, independent yet socially responsible "communities within a community"'.[6] This professional status might be viewed as simply perpetuating elitism and power imbalance in society. Historically, it was often said that lawyers strike a deal with society to perform their functions:

[4] See eg Steven Vaughan, 'Existential Ethics: Thinking Hard About Lawyer Responsibility for Clients' Environmental Harms' (2023) 76(1) Current Legal Problems 1–34.

[5] Donald Nicolson and Julian Webb, *Professional Legal Ethics: Critical Interrogations* (OUP 2000).

[6] Nicolson and Webb (n 5) 53.

by putting the public good before their own self-interest they maintain their status and prestige.[7] However, in a cyclical sense, upholding the public good is of course vital for ensuring public confidence in the profession.

REFLECTION POINT

Consider whether as a law student you consider yourself to have any particular status? As you acquire legal knowledge, do you think it has changed how others (eg friends, family, academics, professionals) view you?

Has it changed how you view yourself?

Do you think it affects your choices and behaviour? If so, in what way?

Legal professional values relate to the rules that have developed in the Codes of Conduct and ethical rules that govern legal practice. In England and Wales, the Legal Services Act 2007 describes the values, or 'professional principles', with which we are broadly concerned.

The 'professional principles' are:

(a) that authorised persons should act with **independence and integrity**,

(b) that authorised persons should maintain **proper standards of work**,

(c) that authorised persons should act in the **best interests of their clients**,

(d) that persons who exercise before any court a right of audience, or conduct litigation in relation to proceedings in any court, by virtue of being authorised persons should comply with their duty to the court to **act with independence in the interests of justice**, and

(e) that the affairs of clients should be kept confidential.[8]

The SRA Principles further embody the standards we might expect by setting out the way in which solicitors must approach their work. These principles inform the SRA Code of Conduct, which sets out the standards of professionalism expected of solicitors. The Seven Mandatory Principles state that a solicitor must act:

1. in a way that upholds the constitutional principle of the rule of law, and the proper administration of justice;
2. in a way that upholds public trust and confidence in the solicitors' profession and in legal services provided by authorized persons;
3. with independence;

[7] Alan Paterson, *Lawyers and the Public Good* (Cambridge University Press 2012).
[8] Legal Services Act 2007, s 1(3).

4. with honesty;
5. with integrity;
6. in a way that encourages equality, diversity, and inclusion; and
7. in the best interests of each client.

7.1.1 The Rule of Law and Proper Administration of Justice

In many common law jurisdictions, lawyers are required to uphold the proper administration of justice. This intersects with the desire to maintain public confidence in the legal profession and aims to ensure that lawyers are trusted to perform their role in society. On some occasions, it could be that this duty clashes with the client's interests. The 'client's interests' refer to the legal entitlements that a client holds or could have. Or it might be that it clashes with the client's instructions on any given case. For example, the client might ask you to lie to the judge. What do you think you should do in such a case? This is one of the instances where the answer to the ethical quandary is clear. The duty to safeguard the wider public interest takes precedence over an individual client's interests (which we discuss further below). That said, what may or may not be in the public interest can be contentious and lawyers might disagree strongly on what it means on a case-by-case basis. This impacts lawyering 'identity', and the lawyer's conception, as well as that of others, on their own role in society.

We discussed the rule of law in Chapter 2 and considered its relationship to access to justice. There is some ambiguity about the breadth of what the rule of law encompasses but it is nonetheless well accepted as being critical to legal ethics given its concern with, for example, the independence of the court, transparency of decision-making, and government accountability. The rule of law requires that the law is clear, accessible, and predictable; that no one is above the law; and that everyone should have equal access to the protection of the law. The relevant ethical rules do not necessarily spell out exactly what upholding the rule of law means in terms of the behaviour expected of lawyers; however, there is naturally some overlap with other values such as integrity and honesty and maintaining confidence in the profession. A commitment to the rule of law includes promoting respect for the law, as well as helping clients to resolve disputes in a way that upholds the interests of justice.[9]

What might it look like to fail to uphold the rule of law and the proper administration of justice? For example, in the course of a dispute a lawyer might make allegations without merit, pursue litigation for an improper purpose, take unfair advantage, mislead the court, or conduct excessive or aggressive litigation.[10] Other examples include lawyers acting as 'professional enablers' of corruption[11] or protecting those engaged in sexual harassment.[12] It might be tempting for a lawyer to adopt such practices in the zealous pursuit of a 'win'

[9] Richard Moorhead et al, *What Does It Mean for Lawyers to Uphold the Rule of Law?* (Legal Services Board2023). Available at https://legalservicesboard.org.uk/wp-content/uploads/2023/11/FINAL-LSB-Lawyers-and-ROL-Report-2023.pdf

[10] SRA guidance. Available at https://www.sra.org.uk/solicitors/guidance/conduct-disputes/

[11] Moorhead et al (n 9) 31. [12] Ibid 35.

for a client; however, their duty to the public administration of justice is designed to ensure conduct of this nature is limited. The pursuit of profit at all costs may also make it more likely that such aggressive tactics will be pursued. A reflective practitioner will consider the impact of their actions more widely on the administration of justice and be alive to their duties in ensuring the rule of law is not undermined. A lawyer's duty to uphold the rule of law should be widely construed and it is important to remember that it is a duty not only to clients but also to legal institutions and, more broadly, to society.

7.1.2 **Trust and Confidence in the Profession**

A number of matters relate to upholding trust and confidence in the legal profession. For example, it is important that lawyers do not unfairly discriminate in their service provision. It would not be appropriate for a lawyer to refuse to offer services to clients of a particular religion, sexual orientation, or any other protected characteristic. Likewise, lawyers must not abuse their position or mislead others. Let us consider further two wider principles that fall under the duty to ensure trust and confidence, which are particularly relevant for clinic work: the duty to provide diligent and competent service, and client confidentiality. For solicitors in England and Wales, these duties can be found in the SRA Code of Conduct;[13] however, for barristers, or indeed for other regulated lawyers either in the UK or in other jurisdictions, similar duties can be found in relevant professional rules.

Diligence and Competence

Lawyers are required to have the skill to carry out their work. They must be competent to provide the services they hold themselves out as being able to provide and do so in a timely manner. This is usually clear from relevant professional codes and is also required more generally by law.[14] Liability for poor service provision can extend, in very limited circumstances, to third parties who might be negatively impacted by negligent actions or advice.[15] The requirements of the SRA Code of Conduct in relation to service and competence are as follows:

SRA Code of Conduct – Service and Competence

3.1 You only act for *clients* on instructions from the *client*, or from someone properly authorised to provide instructions on their behalf. If you have reason to suspect that the instructions do not represent your *client's* wishes, you do not act unless you have satisfied yourself that they do. However, in circumstances where you have legal authority to act notwithstanding that it is not possible to obtain or ascertain the instructions of your *client*, then you are subject to the overriding obligation to protect your *client's* best interests.

[13] SRA Code of Conduct paras 3.1–3.6 and 6.3–6.5.

[14] See eg SRA Code of Conduct, para 3.1; BSB Professional Statement for Barristers, paras 1.2–1.3: 'Barristers must have the "knowledge and understanding of the key concepts and principles of public and private law" as well as "knowledge and understanding of the law and procedure relevant to their area(s) of practice".'

[15] See eg *White v Jones* [1995] 2 WLR 187.

3.2 You ensure that the service you provide to *clients* is competent and delivered in a timely manner.

3.3 You maintain your competence to carry out your role and keep your professional knowledge and skills up to date.

3.4 You consider and take account of your *client's* attributes, needs and circumstances.

3.5 Where you supervise or manage others providing legal services; (a) you remain accountable for the work carried out through them; and (b) you effectively supervise work being done for *clients*.

3.6 You ensure that the individuals you manage are competent to carry out their role, and keep their professional knowledge and skills, as well as understanding of their legal, ethical and regulatory obligations, up to date.

What, practically speaking, does competence require? By way of example, the SRA's statement of competence rests upon a broad definition of competence, which is 'the ability to perform the roles and tasks required by one's job to the expected standard'.[16] This envisages that the requirements might themselves change, depending on the nature of the role and that a holistic approach should be adopted. As a starting point, of course, comes knowledge of the law. This is acquired through legal education and training but also, in a constantly changing field, lawyers are expected to stay up to date and have 'current awareness' of developing legislation (or wider overarching rules and frameworks) and case law. Therefore, legal knowledge must not only be acquired but needs to be reviewed and maintained. In view of that knowledge, as Cranston notes, 'clients must be advised of the legal consequences of any step which they propose to take, about the alternative remedies available, and that any particular step ought to be taken without delay'.[17]

Imagine that a client asks for advice in a housing law matter and a lawyer agrees to provide representation despite having no knowledge of housing law and not ever having acted in that area. The lawyer would obviously not be considered competent to provide the advice. Another example might be where a client is required to lodge an appeal on a matter within 28 days but their lawyer neglects to tell them. In another, a client must gather particular types of evidence in support of their case, but their lawyer doesn't know what types of evidence, in what form, are needed and by when.

Any such failure to advise a client in relation to procedural and evidential matters could have considerable adverse impacts financially and personally (including on organizations and other entities as legal persons) and may result in disciplinary action or legal challenge by the client themselves.[18] As such, the old adage 'you don't know what you don't know' is critically relevant in legal practice. Without the knowledge in the first place, it is almost impossible to know what you might be missing in terms of applicable rules and relevant

[16] SRA, Statement of Solicitor Competence (last updated 9 August 2022) quoting Michael Eraut and Benedict Du Boulay, Developing the Attributes of Medical Professional Judgement and Competence (University of Sussex 2001). Available at http://users.sussex.ac.uk/~bend/doh/reporthtml.html

[17] Ross Cranston, *Legal Ethics and Professional Responsibility* (OUP 1996) 10.

[18] *Otter v Church, Adams, Thatam & Co* [1953] Ch 280.

deadlines; and lawyers can be held responsible for this lack of knowledge where they fail to advise their clients correctly. Importantly, lawyers should not misrepresent themselves as having specialist legal knowledge they do not have. They should not exaggerate their skill, given the clear duty to only act within one's skill and competence. In the clinical context, it is the duty of supervisors to ensure this knowledge is passed on to clinical students as necessary and appropriate[19] and the duty of students to ensure that they take all reasonable steps to acquire and apply relevant knowledge to their cases, and that they don't suggest that they are proficient in areas in which they lack knowledge or experience. Clinical supervisors must ensure not only that the client receives the best possible representation, but also that students receive the best possible training, which may involve pushing a student to the limit of their ability—or even just beyond. Arguably, the best and deepest student learning comes from making mistakes. However, the supervisor must carefully manage those mistakes in a way that ensures the client is not harmed.

REFLECTION POINT

At a drop-in clinic session, a man attends saying he has a family law matter and he needs help. He has been going through a difficult separation and has been unable to have contact with his children. A friend has just told him that his ex-wife is going to take the children to live in Canada, where she has citizenship, in the next few days. You know that your clinic doesn't offer legal advice in family law and that none of the supervising lawyers are qualified or experienced in that area. You have been working with a more senior student in their final year who insists that because it is a general advice session you can take the client on. The other student says you cannot wait for your supervisor (who is with a student on another case) as it is an urgent matter and it is your duty to act for the client in a timely manner. You are sent away to look up some legislation on international child abduction and the student says you can both give 'on the spot' advice and help them with next steps in their case.

What would you do next in this situation? What steps might you take in relation to:

(i) your supervisor;
(ii) the other student;
(iii) the client?

Resting closely alongside knowledge of law and relevant procedure, competence requires that a lawyer acts with reasonable care and skill in the conduct of their work. It is a rule that applies to almost all professionals and ensures that members of the public get the standard of service they might reasonably expect of someone with relevant professional qualifications, and therefore upholds trust and confidence in the profession itself. The professional codes of

[19] For example, solicitors in England and Wales remain accountable for the work carried out through them where they supervise or manage others providing legal services. They also have a duty to ensure that those they manage are competent to carry out their role and that they keep their professional knowledge and skills up to date (SRA Code of Conduct, paras 3.5–3.6).

conduct consider any lack of reasonable care of skill as 'professional misconduct', as we discuss further below. In general terms, lawyers have a duty to act with care and skill, to exercise proper diligence, to act promptly, and to keep clients properly informed.

It is especially worth noting that the rise in the use of generative AI has raised questions about the proper conduct of lawyers and, in some cases, has resulted in false information being put before the court and subsequent investigation by regulatory bodies. As we mentioned in Chapter 4, such false information usually involves AI 'hallucination', for example, fake case citations or quotations, which can have adverse consequences when relied upon by parties and the court. In one recent case in England and Wales, a pupil barrister was instructed by a law centre in London on a housing matter. She included five fake cases in her pleadings, which led to the defendant local authority making a wasted costs application against the law centre. When questioned about the cases, the barrister said they were merely 'cosmetic errors'; however, the judge at the wasted costs hearing found her conduct, and that of the law centre, to be 'improper, unreasonable and negligent'.[20] The matter was referred to the High Court under its inherent powers to help enforce duties owed by lawyers to the courts. The judgment of the High Court generally noted:

> In the context of legal research, the risks of using artificial intelligence are now well known. Freely available generative artificial intelligence tools, trained on a large language model such as ChatGPT are not capable of conducting reliable legal research . . .
>
> Those who use artificial intelligence to conduct legal research notwithstanding these risks have a professional duty therefore to check the accuracy of such research by reference to authoritative sources, before using it in the course of their professional work (to advise clients or before a court, for example) . . .
>
> This duty rests on lawyers who use artificial intelligence to conduct research themselves or rely on the work of others who have done so. This is no different from the responsibility of a lawyer who relies on the work of a trainee solicitor or a pupil barrister for example, or on information obtained from an internet search . . .
>
> We would go further however. There are serious implications for the administration of justice and public confidence in the justice system if artificial intelligence is misused. In those circumstances, practical and effective measures must now be taken by those within the legal profession with individual leadership responsibilities (such as heads of chambers and managing partners) and by those with the responsibility for regulating the provision of legal services.[21]

The Court went on to outline the relevant rules that apply when AI is used, finding that reliance on AI, without sufficient checking and verification, could constitute a breach of a lawyer's duty not to mislead the Court.[22] It also outlined the range of sanctions the Court could impose on lawyers in these circumstances, including 'public admonition of the lawyer, the imposition of a costs order, the imposition of a wasted costs order, striking out a case, referral to a regulator, the initiation of contempt proceedings, and referral to

[20] *R (on the application of Frederick Ayinde) v London Borough of Haringey* [2025] EWHC 1383 (Admin) [48].

[21] Ibid [6–9].

[22] Ibid. The Court discusses the relevant rules for barristers at [17]–[18] and the duties for solicitors at [22].

the police'.[23] In this matter, they found that while the threshold for contempt proceedings had been met, it was more appropriate to refer the case to the appropriate regulators to consider what sanction to impose.[24]

The case raises a number of important questions about professional legal ethics and AI use. It is clear that the public administration of justice is undermined where overreliance on AI results in potentially misleading opposing parties in a case, and the court itself. It is also clear that supervisors of trainee lawyers have a role to play in checking work to ensure it is accurate. In this case, the law centre had argued they were an 'overstretched charity providing an important service to vulnerable members of society with limited resources'.[25] The Court noted however that, in these circumstances, it is all the more important that standards are maintained.[26] Likewise, in a clinical setting, it is imperative that any reliance on AI is responsible, and any such reliance is communicated clearly to clinical supervisors so they can check the veracity of legal research sources.

Practical Exercise 7.1

Read the case of *R (on the application of Frederick Ayinde) v The London Borough of Haringey* [2025] EWHC 1383 (Admin) paras [1]–[72]. Consider the following questions:

1. What information did the barrister, Ms Sarah Forey, submit in her grounds for judicial review that was false?
2. When the fake cases were identified, what is your impression of the response she drafted to the opposing party (at [42])?
3. What is your impression of the justification she gave for the reliance on fake cases?
4. Do you think the court came to the right conclusion in not initiating contempt of court proceedings (at [63] to [69])?
5. The case was referred to the regulators—what do you think the appropriate sanction might be?

The Duty of Confidentiality

The duty of confidentiality is arguably one of the most important in professional legal life. In fact, it is considered the 'cornerstone' of the lawyer–client relationship, given that it is intrinsically connected to so many other ethical values. Naturally, confidentiality helps to facilitate the *confidence* that a client places in their lawyer and facilitates the sharing of information. In general, the lawyer–client relationship implies a duty to keep the client's affairs confidential and not to disclose such affairs, unless required or permitted by law or when the client consents. In addition to being regulated in terms of professional conduct,[27] it is an implied term in contracts between lawyers and their clients. A lawyer will have breached confidence

[23] Ibid [23]. [24] Ibid [68]–[69]. [25] Ibid [71]. [26] Ibid.

[27] See SRA CD6: you 'must keep the affairs of each client confidential'.

where they wrongfully (ie the exceptions discussed below do not apply) disclose confidential information to others.

In the clinic context, it is crucial to note that the duty of confidentiality extends to staff working on a case and to students and administrative staff working on clinical casework. Likewise, it is sometimes overlooked that the duty of confidentiality exists even after a case has ended and must be maintained after a legal matter reaches resolution (or not). Notwithstanding the importance of the general principle, there are some exceptions to the duty to keep clients' information confidential. Before reading on, can you think when you would be entitled, or perhaps even required, to disclose something your client told you? And to whom would you be entitled to disclose?

A disclosure might be permitted where it is required by law (even without the client's consent) or when the client gives informed consent.[28] The key examples usually relate to public protection and safeguarding. For example, these would apply to prevent the commission of a criminal offence, where a client has indicated an intention to commit suicide or commit self-harm, or for the protection of vulnerable children or adults. In these circumstances, a breach of confidentiality will usually be *justified* even though it is technically still a breach. There are also requirements to disclose information to the court in relation to legal proceedings. Where informed consent has been given, a client would have to waive confidentiality in clear terms and in possession of full knowledge in relation to the purpose (ie to whom, where, and when) of the disclosure. In relation to third party disclosure it is useful to ask the following questions:

1. What is the purpose of the third party access to the information and can the purpose be achieved in other ways?
2. Should there be any limitations on the access?
3. Are you satisfied that seeking the client's consent to disclosure would not harm the client's best interests?[29]

Alongside the general duty to keep a client's information confidential, there are further safeguards that seek to enhance *confidence* in the relationship that stem from the general principle of client confidentiality but relate to situations which are beyond breach of confidence. Thus, some communications between lawyers and their clients are subject to what is known as *legal professional privilege*. This could relate to a situation in which someone overheard a discussion between a client and a lawyer, or an email was sent to the wrong person. In such cases, as the information is subject to legal privilege, it cannot be used in legal proceedings. The underpinning rationale is to promote trust between lawyer and client, such that the client will provide the lawyer with all the information that might be relevant to the representation of the client. There are some exceptions to the protection offered by lawyer–client privilege. For example, it does not cover matters that are irrelevant to the legal case, nor any

[28] BSB Handbook Rule C15.5; SRA Code of Conduct (4.1). Notably, in some jurisdictions duties of disclosure are not as onerous. For example, in the US the only required disclosure is to prevent false testimony to the court, and even then the lawyer must exhaust other options before revealing the information.

[29] SRA guidance. Available at https://www.sra.org.uk/solicitors/guidance/confidentiality-client-information/

communication that might result in or relate to the commission of a crime or the perpetration of fraud.

REFLECTION POINT

A barrister leaves court and gets on a train home. It is rush hour and the train carriage is full. He sits at a table and takes out his laptop and begins writing an attendance note about what happened in court that day. He then answers a phone call from another barrister and proceeds to describe the day in court. He details the evidence given by the witnesses in a sensitive sexual harassment case, including referencing the names of the victims and making derogatory comments about them, as well as giving his views on the experts in the case. He expresses his own feelings of pride at his successful cross-examination.

(i) How has this lawyer breached confidentiality? If so, at what point?

(ii) What do you think would be appropriate in terms of disciplinary sanction?

There are two types of privilege: *legal advice privilege* and *litigation privilege*. Legal advice privilege extends to all communication between a lawyer and client in relation to the giving and receiving of legal advice. The context of either giving or receiving advice is important and communications outside of that would not be subject to privilege. Litigation privilege extends to all communication between a lawyer and any third party (for example, an expert witness) in connection with litigation. For litigation privilege to be relevant, the communication must be in progress or in contemplation and the litigation must be adversarial rather than inquisitorial or investigative in nature (as discussed further below).[30] It is important to recognize the circumstances under which legal professional privilege might be engaged. For example, open court proceedings or meetings where members of the public might be in attendance and some types of correspondence between lawyers may not be subject to privilege. Crucially, privilege may be lost or waived where it is disclosed, as it only attaches to *confidential* communications.

The complex nature of privilege, especially the concept of waiver, requires that lawyers explain privilege to clients in a way that ensures the client understands the concept and can avoid actions that might waive the privilege. For example, privilege would be lost if information is disclosed and made publicly available. It is not always the case that privilege might be lost if a document is disclosed to a third party, if disclosed for a limited purpose and on a confidential basis. It is good practice, where limited disclosure to a third party is required, to ask the third party to acknowledge that it is sent to them on a limited basis, that the communication does not amount to a waiver of privilege, and that the documents should be held in confidence and not be disclosed further without consent from the disclosing party. In a clinical setting, supervising lawyers must make specific efforts to instruct students about confidentiality, lawyer–client privilege, and the deleterious effect of disclosure.

[30] *Three Rivers District Council v Bank of England (No. 6)* [2004] UKHL 48, [102].

It is worth noting the interaction between confidentiality and the ethical duty not to mislead the court. Imagine a situation in which, during a pre-trial meeting, the client tells her lawyer that she had knowingly dismissed the claimant when she discovered that the claimant is gay. The lawyer devised a strategy that focused on the competence of the claimant, seeking to evade the matter of discrimination. But when the client was cross-examined, she explicitly denied that she ever knew that the claimant is gay. What should the lawyer do? Their obligation to maintain confidentiality is in conflict with their duty not to mislead the court (which they do, indirectly, by knowingly allowing an untrue statement to go into the record unchallenged). In such a case, the lawyer's ethical obligations to the court supersede those that they have towards the client.

A View from Clinical Practice

Professor Tim Casey, Professor from Practice and Director of Curricular Administration, UCLA Law

A deeper dive into the example above shows the complexity of this dilemma. In this example, it appears the only basis of the lawyer's knowledge about the client's knowledge that the claimant is gay is the statement from the client to the lawyer. Her statement to the lawyer contradicts her sworn testimony. Which of her statements is true?

Does a single statement (from a client to a lawyer) provide enough justification to destroy the lawyer–client relationship through the lawyer's action in telling the court about a prior inconsistent statement? Or are we biased toward believing that the client's first statement (to the lawyer) is the 'true' statement?

We would not be alone in our belief that a statement against one's interest holds more veracity than a statement in support of innocence (or against liability). In the US, rules of evidence support the notion that statements 'against penal interest' are more believable and more trustworthy. But what is the basis for that rule?

Is it possible that our long-held religious notions of penance, reconciliation, confession, and atonement provide this basis? And should we challenge these deeply held beliefs? (The history of the Inquisition might help.) Reflections on our biases and the root causes of those biases might cause us to challenge the notion that a statement of guilt is truthful. Empirical evidence would support this challenge. In a review of cases of exonerations through DNA evidence, the Innocence Project compiled statistics on the underlying causes of the wrongful conviction. An astounding 25 per cent of those cases involved false confessions.

Returning to our ethics problem, might the first question for the lawyer be one targeting the basis and degree of the lawyer's knowledge? Does the lawyer 'know' the client is lying in her testimony? Or does the lawyer have a 'reasonable belief' that the testimony is false? In many jurisdictions, the rules governing a lawyer's disclosure obligations are different where the lawyer knows evidence is false, and when a lawyer has a reasonable belief that the evidence presented to the court is false.

What if we change the problem slightly to include an initial interview with the client where she states she did not know the claimant is gay? Now we have two statements that she did not know, and one statement that she knew. In fact, it's common for clients to present the best possible version of their situation at their initial interview.

But, in some situations, a client might not reveal relevant information to the lawyer, and that information might make a huge difference in the case. For example, a victim of domestic violence might be reluctant to disclose the past history of her relationship with her abuser. However, these details might provide important information to support a battered victim's defence.

It is therefore important to be alive to the different motivations that clients have for both what they say and what they fail to say. The complex nature of these scenarios confirms the importance of developing and honing client interviewing skills.

Usually, the lawyer must seek the client's consent to ensure that the court is not misled (for example, by correcting an otherwise misleading statement or withdrawing evidence). Should the client refuse to consent, the lawyer is usually required to entirely withdraw from the case. This is often described as having to withdraw on the grounds of being 'professionally embarrassed'. A common example in practice is where a client changes their instructions (eg their account in relation to facts or issues in the case) and to continue in view of those changed instructions would be impossible without misleading the court. However, it is important to note that when a lawyer withdraws from a case, the purpose of underlying rules might be frustrated. A client may simply instruct a new lawyer who does not have a basis to evaluate whether the client's testimony is false. The client may not also trust the new lawyer with the truth, so all statements would be in support of the lie. The new lawyer would stand behind the false testimony and the harm that the first lawyer sought to avoid—the presentation of false statements to the court—would nonetheless occur. Arguably, withdrawing from a case also impacts the lawyer–client relationship more generally. The rationale for the rule of confidentiality rests on the sanctity of trust between the lawyer and the client. However, if the client learns not to trust the lawyer, over time, other clients may do the same. The effect of withdrawal therefore may be the erosion of trust between lawyer and client, thus undermining the principle of confidentiality.

REFLECTION POINT

A client at your clinic has recently instructed you on a housing matter. You have arranged to meet with the client to gather some information about her case and give some early general advice. The client comes to the meeting with you in an agitated state. She is not happy about the allegations her landlord has been making in relation to her behaviour and gives an alternative version of events. When you advise her about the strength of her case she becomes verbally aggressive. She shows you a knife in her pocket and tells you that she is going to find her landlord. She says that she knows where he lives and she wants to hurt him, and then leaves abruptly.

(i) Should you tell someone about this incident? If so, who?

(ii) What ethical considerations might there be in disclosing information about the client's case?

(iii) What steps might you take to ensure you are complying with relevant rules and procedures?

Finally, rules in relation to confidentiality and legal privilege interact with rules in relation to data protection. As a clinical law student or lawyer, certain obligations apply. Information must be processed lawfully and fairly and all data must be processed in a way that protects the person it relates to (the 'data subject'). We see here the importance of good file management, given that the rules in relation to data protection require that the right systems are used and that data protection rights of data subjects are upheld. These include having the right to see any information that is held and to request that data is deleted or that it is not used for certain purposes. These rules equally apply to law school clinics and there should usually be a data protection officer who is responsible for ensuring data protection rules are followed. In addition to confidentiality duties, these rules protect the more general right to privacy for all those engaging with the clinic and extends beyond the client relationship. We set out in Chapter 9 how data protection rules will apply in practice in clinical casework.

7.1.3 Independence

Lawyer independence is necessary to preserve the lawyer's role and function. It is usual, except for limited exceptions, that lawyers be required to be independent in relation to 'the courts, public authorities, economic powers, professional colleagues and the client, as well as the lawyer's own interest'.[31] Examples of a threat to independence might be where the client of a firm brings in high levels of revenue but becomes overbearing or even aggressive in their demands, thus compromising the lawyer's ability to give independent advice. Extreme examples might include situations where the client demands that the lawyer take action without a basis in law or fact, or demands that the lawyer take action that violates professional ethics for the personal or political benefit of the client. Independence may also be called into question where a lawyer accepts an expensive gift from a client for a job well done, or where a lawyer and client become overly friendly. Where independence is compromised, it is likely to also have a negative bearing on the administration of justice and the rule of law.

However, like best interests, lawyer independence is a somewhat elusive concept in terms of recognition and definition, especially as compared to how we might understand judicial independence. Green notes:

> We have a much better sense of what we mean when we talk about 'judicial independence', although even there, understandings have evolved over time and leave room for debate. In contrast, it may not even be clear into what category lawyers' independence falls. Is

[31] International Association of Lawyers, *Core Principles of the Legal Profession* (Resolution, ratified 30 October 2018). Available at https://www.uianet.org/sites/default/files/core_principles_of_the_legal_profession_-_final_porto.pdf

> it an attribute of character, like 'professional integrity', a state of mind like objectivity or detachment, or a standard of conduct like avoidance of conflicts of interest or preserving client confidences? Is it an aspiration like 'professional excellence' or an obligation like 'professional competence'? Is it a collective trait or an individual trait (or both)?[32]

Lawyer independence means acting in an unbiased way without consideration of one's own interests or those of others. The SRA, in outlining the importance of independence in its annual survey of challenges and risks, made clear its interrelationship between independence and other principles of professional legal ethics:

> Solicitors must put their ethical obligations first and keep their independence. This means that they must not and should not put their own, or their clients', interests above their wider professional obligations to the administration of justice, the rule of law and the courts. Given their professional responsibilities, this means that they should be prepared to decline instructions that would conflict with their obligations.[33]

Lawyer independence is therefore central not only to relationships with clients but also to how a lawyer should more generally act and conduct themselves in their day-to-day practice. Do we consider that it is *always* feasible in practice? In a large-scale empirical study of lawyer independence among corporate lawyers in England and Wales, Oakley and Vaughan stress the 'vulnerabilities of lawyers to clients in a global corporate marketplace'.[34] They raise questions about the prevalent narrative that clients should be protected *from* lawyers when, in fact, corporate clients hold so much power:

> Corporate lawyers may be powerful people working in powerful organisations but they are significantly less powerful than the corporate clients and institutions they serve. They create and facilitate on behalf of their powerful clients a wide array of products, transactions and arrangements that structure and inform almost all aspects of everyday life. In return for this, they are richly rewarded, both financially and in terms of social status. It is their relative power that makes their vulnerabilities to clients and market pressures, and their position as a source of vulnerability and harm to others, so serious.[35]

Oakley and Vaughan highlight the 'interdependence and interconnectedness' of relationships in the globalized corporate sphere.[36] Their research asks us to consider how rules and ethical practices are understood, indeed negotiated through, the interests of powerful clients such as banks and companies worth millions of pounds. While this landscape is obviously markedly different from that of law school clinics, it nonetheless raises important questions

[32] Bruce Green, 'Lawyers' Professional Independence: Overrated or Undervalued?' (2013) 46 Akron Law Review 599, 599–600.

[33] SRA, Risk Outlook 2018/19 (25th July 2018). Available at https://www.sra.org.uk/sra/research-publications/risk-outlook-2018-2019/

[34] Emma Oakley and Steven Vaughan, 'In Dependence: The Paradox of Professional Independence and Taking Seriously the Vulnerabilities of Lawyers in Large Corporate Law Firms' (2019) 46(1) Journal of Law and Society 83–111, 85.

[35] Ibid 96. [36] Ibid 109.

about the nature of independence in different types of legal practice and the different types of power relationships that might bring lawyer independence into question. It also encourages us to reflect upon whether there is an air of unreality to the assertion that lawyers will *always* be able to put their professional obligations ahead of the interests of their clients.

In terms of compliance with the duty of independence, some lawyers may, in practice, go beyond what is required to minimize all possible risk to their independence, while others might toe the line close to (or even beyond) what is permissible. Interestingly, lawyer independence is often said to be best maintained where lawyers govern themselves and regulate their own professional disciplinary proceedings. Some scholars have argued that where regulatory measures are instead aimed at consumer protection (such as in England and Wales), this serves to undermine independence.[37] Conversely, professional bodies that regulate themselves might also lack transparency and serve to protect their own interests rather than the public interest. Others argue that more attention should be paid to lawyers' independence from the courts, for example, the freedom to criticize judges or resolve ethical dilemmas 'as a matter of professional conscience.'[38]

Conflict of Interest

Another challenge to lawyer independence in any given case might be where a conflict of interest arises. The ethical foundations of conflicts of interest are so self-evident that they are deemed to be part of 'natural justice'. In this respect, it is prescribed that a person cannot be a judge in their own case. This is considered 'natural' because the vast majority of people, with or without a legal education, would probably agree to such a basic principle of the delivery of justice. There is always a risk that, even if one is not entitled to win the case, their own interest would cloud their judgment, or at the very least, the aggrieved party could legitimately argue that this was the case. A lawyer is not a judge, and yet must make decisions that are based on the merits of the case, the interests of the clients, and the interests of justice more broadly. Here, we might also consider the concept of loyalty: a lawyer must be loyal to a client and to a client's cause. The lawyer must be able to provide representation that is not challenged or limited by the interests of the lawyer herself, or by the interests of any other client.

The move from the conflict of interest that relates to a judge to one that relates to a lawyer rests on the same principle, but unsurprisingly also becomes more complex. A lawyer may actually face two types of conflict: an **own interest conflict** and a **client interest conflict**. First, imagine a situation in which a lawyer is asked to advise a client who seeks to claim sexual harassment against their employer, a start-up company. What the client does not know, however, is that the lawyer has invested in the start-up company, and the claim may significantly undermine their prospects of attracting further investments, and thus endanger the future of the company. It is easy to see that the lawyer's advice (for example, whether to accept a settlement offer from the employer) would be deemed tainted by their financial interest. Similarly, think of a client who seeks advice from a lawyer about the future of his

[37] Gordon Turriff, 'The Consumption of Lawyer Independence' (2010) 17(3) International Journal of the Legal Profession 283–305.

[38] Green (n 32) 602.

marriage because he suspects that his wife is unfaithful to him. As luck would have it, he is right, and the 'other man' is actually the lawyer himself. Here, while the lawyer's interest is not financial, it is clearly personal.

In both those cases, the lawyer faces an 'own interest conflict'. If a lawyer finds themself in such a conflict, they cannot act, and there are no exceptions. This means that even the client's express and informed consent would not allow the lawyer to act. Note that this situation extends to a conflict between a client and a close member of the lawyer's family, or the lawyer's employer. So, for example, an employment law clinic at a university, which is funded by the university (even if only partly) cannot represent an aggrieved member of staff in a claim against the university. If there is a significant risk that the duty to act in the best interests of a client may conflict with a lawyer's own interest (or someone sufficiently close to them)[39] in relation to that (or a related matter), they must cease to act.[40] This is in order to avoid not only actual conflicts of interest but also *perceived* conflicts of interest, thus serving to uphold the integrity of the profession. Case law makes clear that there does not need to be an actual breach of confidentiality for conflict rules to apply.[41]

The second type of conflict of interest is 'client conflicts'. These happen when a lawyer represents (or is asked to represent) two or more clients, and the duties towards each of the clients are in conflict. Classic examples may include representing a buyer and a seller in a commercial contract, or representing two clients competing for the same contract or business opportunity. In such situations, a lawyer should refuse to act for at least one of the parties, even when they are asked to do so (for example, because both parties trust the lawyer, or wish to save money). However, unlike the 'own interest conflict' situation, there are exceptions to the rule that a lawyer should not act when clients' interests are involved. Thus, for example, a criminal lawyer may act for two clients charged with assaulting a third person, if both deny (or accept) their guilt, and do not accuse each other. However, if matters become complicated, and the parties turn on each other, the lawyer will have to cease representing one or, most likely, both (because the lawyer would have information from both clients). In civil cases, a lawyer may represent two or more clients who have a substantially common interest, such as setting up a business together, and a consensus as to what might be achieved.[42] In this situation, a lawyer must explain the risks associated with joint representation, including the effect on confidentiality. After informing the clients of the risks, good practice includes obtaining written consent from each affected client.

It is important to stress the role that good case management plays in both avoiding and identifying conflicts of interest. Lawyers and clinics need to be aware of potential conflicts of interest from the first time they meet with a client. A 'conflict check' should be done before any confidential information is taken. In practice, a conflict of interest may also arise as a case progresses or during the course of proceedings. When the lawyer becomes aware of a conflict during the representation, action is required. The specific action will depend on

[39] *Richards v Law Society* [2009] EWHC 2087 (Admin). [40] See SRA Code of Conduct, para 6.1.
[41] *Bolkian v KPMG* [1999] 2 AC 222, 234. [42] SRA Code of Conduct, para 6.2(a).

the circumstances but may include, at a minimum, informing the client of the change of circumstances, and perhaps withdrawing from the case. The SRA Code of Conduct makes this clear by requiring that 'systems and controls for identifying own interest conflict' to 'enable you to assess all the relevant circumstances'.[43] These systems and controls must identify conflicts that might exist across the firm (or law school clinic) so that the best interests of the client will not be impaired by any financial interest, personal or commercial relationship, or appointment to public office, or the lawyer's own employment.[44]

It is sometimes appropriate to put an 'information barrier or ethical screen'[45] in place to manage conflicts of interest. This enables a law firm (usually larger organizations) to separate out particular employees so they might still be able to work on a matter that might otherwise involve a conflict. Herring identifies four elements which make up the 'informational barrier' in these circumstances: physical separation, separating out records (ie access to files), restrictions on communication, and management control.[46] It might be challenging in practice to maintain these barriers permanently but they would need to be in place for as long as a firm (or counsel in a self-employed capacity in the same set of chambers) is acting for two clients where a conflict might arise. In any event, the long-term nature of the duty of confidentiality (ie even after ceasing to act) also needs to be adhered to. For clinic purposes, as well as for future engagement, the rules concerning conflict of interests remain in place even after the engagement with the client has ended and even after the client's death.

Finally, for barristers, the BSB Handbook also prohibits accepting instructions (ie taking on a client) where there is a conflict of interest.[47] It is worth noting that the rules for barristers add another requirement in relation to independence colloquially known as the 'cab-rank rule', which demands that they cannot refuse to act for a client except in limited circumstances.[48] The rule is designed to maintain the independence of the profession and ensure that all individuals, regardless of the issue or facts relevant to their case, receive representation. As Sir Igor Judge explains in the case of *R v Uclay*: 'Counsel cannot choose his clients, or more accurately, cannot refuse to accept the instructions of a solicitor to act on behalf of an individual because of the nature of the charge he faces, or because of his character and reputation.'[49]

Another justification for the rule is the need to protect barristers from any negative consequences that might arise from representing certain clients and to allow them to take on cases regardless of the opinion of others.

By way of example, consider a barrister who is instructed by a private landlord to evict a tenant. The barrister knows this landlord to be unscrupulous: he has a large property portfolio with a reputation for failing to undertake necessary repairs, aggressive tendencies, and racist treatment of prospective tenants. The cab-rank rule would not permit the barrister to

[43] SRA Code of Conduct, para 3.2. [44] Ibid. [45] Herring (n 3) 193. [46] Ibid 194.
[47] Bar Standards Board Handbook, Part 2, Rule CD4. [48] Rules C29 and C30.
[49] [2007] EWCA Crim 2379, para 39.

refuse instructions and she must take the case if it is within her area of expertise and no other rule, such as conflict of interest, prohibits her from representing the landlord.

Consider also the barrister who holds deeply held views about the importance of climate action. She dedicates a considerable amount of time undertaking pro bono work on environmental cases and research on law and policy reform in relation to climate justice. She is instructed by the Crown to prosecute a group of climate action protesters. Can she refuse the case? A strict application of the rule, where no other exceptions apply, would not allow the barrister to refuse instructions. It is worth noting, however, that several barristers in the UK have recently signed a Declaration of Conscience stating that they will 'withhold services' in respect of support for new fossil fuel projects or action against climate protesters exercising their democratic right to protest.[50]

The cab-rank rule is therefore not without controversy, and whether it achieves its stated aims has been a matter of some debate.[51] One study found that the rule did not in fact influence behaviour or promote transparency in practice and concluded that it 'seems at best a statement of principle masquerading as a rule in order to make it appear to have more teeth than it does'.[52] Another study suggests that lawyers themselves can feel conflicted about the application of the rule in their own practice and may find ways to justify their failure to strictly comply with it (for example, simply refusing instructions on the basis of time constraints or a diary clash).[53] On the other hand, abolishing the rule might have adverse access to justice consequences. We consider further in Chapter 8 the extent to which different types of lawyering, for example so-called activist or cause lawyering, might serve to challenge the notion of lawyer independence.

REFLECTION POINT

You are reading through some initial documents on a new case you are working on that has come to the clinic. It concerns a claim for unfair dismissal against the owner of a large local retail store. You recognize the name of the business owner because he came to the clinic for advice on a business-related matter a few months ago. The business clinic runs separately to the general advice clinic and with different lawyers supervising the students. You haven't seen any of the documents in the other case but you do recognize the name from discussions about the case with another student.

(i) Do you think the clinic can continue to act for the new client?

(ii) What steps might you take next to decide the best course of action?

[50] See Lawyers Are Responsible (last accessed 30 November 2025). Available at https://www.lar.earth/

[51] Danielle Viall, *Reflections on the Cab Rank Rule* (Bar Standards Board 2023). Available at https://legalservicesboard.org.uk/wp-content/uploads/2023/10/08.-Paper-23-58-Reflections-on-the-cab-rank-rule.pdf

[52] John Flood and Morten Hviid, *The Cab Rank Rule: Its Meaning and Purpose in the New Legal Services Market* (Legal Services Board 2013) 38. Available at https://legalservicesboard.org.uk/wp-content/media/Cab-Rank-Rule_final-copy.pdf

[53] Jacqueline Kinghan, *Lawyers, Networks and Progressive Social Change* (Hart 2021) 129–46.

TAKING STOCK

In the preceding sections, we have considered some important rules of professional legal ethics. First, we looked at how lawyers are required to uphold the rule of law and the proper administration of justice. Second, we discussed the need for the public to have confidence in the legal profession. In that respect, we addressed the diligence and competence of lawyers and considered different examples that might mean that lawyers are not acting with the appropriate level of knowledge and expertise expected of them, and what the consequences might be.

Third, we considered the principle of independence. We saw that lawyer independence is central not only to relationships with clients but also to how lawyers conduct themselves more generally in day-to-day practice. With respect to independence, we looked at the important issue of conflict of interest and identified two main types of conflict of interest: 'own interest conflict' and 'client conflict'. We saw that there are different ways of effectively managing potential conflicts of interest, as well as the importance of proper file management in ensuring conflicts of interest can be monitored and identified.

7.1.4 **Honesty and Integrity**

The extent to which legal professional ethics should involve adherence to moral values, for example honesty and integrity, has long been debated. It is regretfully true that we do not have to look far to find examples of poor ethical practice by lawyers; and ethical rules in this area have been said to serve to protect the legal profession itself rather than being concerned with the public interest.[54] Nonetheless, there is a core legal requirement for lawyers to be honest and have integrity in professional practice.

The principles of honesty and integrity interact with other ethical principles. Naturally, being an honest person and acting with integrity ensures that members of the public can have confidence in the legal profession. The connection between law and morality in practice can sometimes be overlooked in legal education. Nicolson and Webb have argued that the discipline of professional legal ethics has largely failed to take adequate account of practical realities, such that the dominance of formalism and adherence to rules acts to 'anaesthetise the moral conscience of lawyers'.[55] It is clear that the demands placed on lawyers in relation to their honesty and integrity in their professional and wider personal lives pose a number of questions: Should lawyers be held to a higher moral standard in their personal lives by virtue of their professional standing? Can a good lawyer be a bad person?[56]

The requirement for lawyers to act with honesty and integrity can be expressed in different ways. The SRA Code of Conduct refers to 'maintaining trust and acting fairly', which

[54] Cranston (n 17) 1. [55] Nicolson and Webb (n 5) vii.

[56] David Luban (ed), *The Good Lawyer: Lawyers' Roles and Lawyers' Ethics* (Rowman and Littlefield 1983); Charles Fried, 'The Lawyer as Friend: The Moral Foundations of the Lawyer–Client Relation' (1976) 85 Yale Law Journal 1060. See also Abbe Smith, 'Can You Be a Good Person and a Good Prosecutor?' (2001) 14 Georgetown Journal of Legal Ethics 355–400.

means, for example, ensuring that no position is abused by taking unfair advantage of clients or misleading (or attempting to mislead) clients, the court, or others.[57] For example, the Post Office Horizon Scandal resulted in hundreds of sub-postmasters being wrongfully convicted of fraud due to faulty IT systems. By 'looking the other way' in the face of evidence to the contrary, many lawyers in the case arguably failed to act with integrity. In the Post Office case, Moorhead notes, 'harms directly arose from the way legal work was managed and conducted: people were threatened, sued, fired, and prosecuted via legal work. Denials, non-disclosure, and delay were enabled, at least in part, by legal work.'[58] In Moorhead's 2024 Hamlyn Lectures, he noted that the scandal shows that lawyers 'have to do more than say sorry half-heartedly' in being accountable for their actions and observed:

> We have to change the way lawyers think and behave, we have to put complete integrity and particular care not to mislead at the front of our thinking, not at the back. We should turn away from lauding amorality and guard against harm.[59]

Properly guarding against harm goes beyond strict interpretation of ethical rules imposed by regulators. For example, some forms of non-disclosure may not be a strict breach of conduct rules but nonetheless lack integrity. Other failures to disclose information can be dishonest and amount to misconduct. For example, Phil Shiner, an English human rights lawyer, was struck off the solicitor's role for false allegations of torture made against British troops. He had made 'unsolicited direct approaches to potential clients' in Iraq and was found guilty of professional misconduct by the Solicitors Disciplinary Tribunal, including dishonesty and lack of integrity.[60]

REFLECTION POINT

In a speech to graduating law students at Washington College of Law, Duncan Kennedy gave the following challenge:

> If I asked each of you to swear an oath to try to avoid doing harm with your lawyer skills, I bet most of you would say, 'Why object? All right, boss, you're the graduation speaker, sounds harmless, even obvious, to me, I hereby pledge myself to avoid doing harm with my lawyer skills.' . . .
>
> I want to go a step further . . . While it's true no one should blame you for refusing to represent a client whose activity you disapprove of, that's not enough. You should feel guilty, and we should disapprove of you, if you go ahead and argue a cause you think will do more

[57] SRA Code of Conduct, para 1.

[58] See John Hyde, 'New call for lawyers to be probed in Post Office Inquiry' *Law Society Gazette* (2 November 2021).

[59] Richard Moorhead, Hamlyn Lecture III at UCL Faculty of Laws, 13 November 2024. Available at https://law.exeter.ac.uk/about/thehamlyntrust/lectures/

[60] Owen Bowcott, 'Lawyer ignored rules in claims against soldiers in Iraq, tribunal hears' *The Guardian*, (2 February 2017).

harm than good. You shouldn't take the case if you think it would be better for society, or more moral, for the client to lose. You shouldn't take the case if you think the client shouldn't be in court in the first place, for example, because the client should morally have made recompense even though he has a technically good legal defence. You shouldn't take the case if your client is enforcing his legal rights, but is using his legal rights in a bad cause.

This is the tough meaning of the vacuous piety that you should avoid doing harm with your lawyer skills. Most lawyers don't agree with it at all. They believe that you are not tarred morally by your clients' underlying intentions, or character, or by the outcome, as long as you don't participate in law breaking yourself. Maybe they make an exception and condemn Mafia lawyers, even when they aren't involved directly in criminal activity. But that's about it. I think you are tarred with bad actions of clients that you facilitate in your work as a lawyer.

To the extent this is right, it is wrong to represent an abortion clinic that's trying to lease a new building to expand its operations, if you are pro-life. And it's wrong to represent a landlord who has been intimidated into trying to evict an abortion clinic if you are pro-choice . . . It's wrong to lobby for the postponement of environmental controls if you think they should be imposed right now; and wrong to do antitrust work against a corporate merger, if you believe mergers are good for the economy . . . I'm saying you should turn down the client even though she isn't trying to get you to do anything illegal, and even though she isn't doing anything illegal herself.'[61]

To what extent do you agree with Kennedy's position, and why?

Do you think this approach is workable in practice?

There may, of course, be wide-ranging implications to drawing in one's own perspective and moral judgement on issues. Kennedy notes in the reflective exercise above that a subjective view of what is 'right' in any given case is in fact important. Related to the discussion above about independence, we see here the contestation that exists around the idea that a lawyer should maintain objectivity and independence at *all* costs. Kennedy asserts that the maxim 'do no harm' as a lawyer means being true to oneself and one's own beliefs. He broadly discusses the issue of case selection and decisions to accept or reject particular clients, which is relevant to acting with integrity. Taking this argument to its logical conclusion, he critiques the lawyer who acts contrary to their own values, raising the question of whether such hypocrisy should be tolerated by society, or the profession itself, because of the absence of a moral touchstone for what is the right course of action in any given case. Others might view this tension between personal morality and professional ethics as an expected aspect of working life. Is it any different, for example, from a chef who is required to cook a meal for an unpleasant person? Or a doctor who must provide life-saving treatment for a patient who has committed heinous crimes? Just as the doctor might need to focus on the professional value of healing, even where the doctor does not like the recipient of the doctor's services, so too lawyers must be able to represent clients they disagree with or, in criminal cases, defend individuals who have committed heinous acts. Just as the doctor preserves life, the lawyer preserves the higher principle of the rule of law and the fundamental right of the accused to have a lawyer. In many professional roles the need to move beyond one's

[61] Duncan Kennedy, 'The Responsibility of Lawyers for the Justice of Their Causes' (1987) 18 Texas Tech Law Review 1157.

personal ethics—especially where it might otherwise discriminate against clients in service provision—is inevitable. Vaughan observes as follows:

> Having integrity as a solicitor means, on the one hand, being able to justify to the wider world things that would seem wrong or bad or immoral if done by other people . . . What some might call in one context dishonesty, prevarication, and a lack of moral courage others might call—in some legal professional contexts—the consequences of client confidentiality and professional privilege.[62]

Kennedy's approach perhaps also fails to appreciate how difficult it might be for lawyers starting out in their careers to challenge the status quo, especially in hierarchical workplaces.[63] His provocation nonetheless forces us to acknowledge the extent to which lawyers are acting as agents with influence within the environments in which they work. In that sense, again relevant to our discussion about independence above, lawyers may not actually be independent of those environments but rather influenced by different power relationships and interactions within them. Studies of in-house lawyers, for example, have highlighted issues in respect of different layers of influence and how that impacts upon legal risk management.[64] In considering honesty and integrity in clinical legal education, it is similarly important to reflectively consider what it might mean in the realistic context everyday relationships, for example with fellow students, supervisors, clients, and institutions themselves.

7.1.5 **Equality, Diversity, and Inclusion**

The legal profession has had a longstanding issue with diversity. For example, recent research in relation to solicitors in England and Wales shows that while there has been an increase in the proportion of women in the profession in recent years, there is still a large gap at more senior levels. There is still significant under-representation of disabled lawyers compared to the wider workforce and a lack of partners from diverse ethnic groups in larger law firms. Solicitors are still more likely to come from professional socio-economic backgrounds (determined by parental occupation at age 14) or to have attended independent school as compared to the general population.[65] Likewise, at the Bar, a disproportionately high number of barristers attended independent school (19.3 per cent of barristers as compared to 7 per cent of the general population).[66] Women are less likely to become KCs and those from minority ethnic backgrounds still experience barriers entering the profession.[67] Herring notes that

[62] Steven Vaughan, *Moral Remainders: What Is the Price of Professional Integrity?* (The Master's Lecture, City of London, 3 June 2024) 2. Available at https://papers.ssrn.com/sol3/papers.cfm?abstract_id=4856109

[63] Robert Granfield and Thomas Koenig, 'It's Hard to Be a Human Being and a Lawyer: Young Attorneys and the Confrontation with Ethical Ambiguity in Legal Practice' (2002) 105 West Virginia Law Review 495.

[64] Richard Moorhead, Steven Vaughan et al, *In-House Lawyers' Ethics: Institutional Logics, Legal Risk and the Tournament of Influence* (Hart 2019).

[65] SRA, 'How Diverse Is the Legal Profession?' https://www.sra.org.uk/sra/equality-diversity/diversity-profession/diverse-legal-profession/ (22 April 2022).

[66] Bar Standards Board, *Diversity at the Bar: A Summary of the Latest Available Diversity Data for the Bar* (January 2022) 6.

[67] Ibid 4.

'prejudicial stereotypes have proved hard to change and the ingrained legal culture creates barriers that are hard to shift'.[68]

Why is this important? A more diverse profession can better meet the needs of a diverse population, and will better ensure respect and dignity in the workplace. Legal regulators have identified the need to 'promote' diversity so as to ensure, for example, that barriers to entry are broken down, and prevent issues relevant to discrimination escalating.[69] Research shows that one in five lawyers have experienced bullying or discrimination in the workplace and that this adversely affects well-being.[70] Those who have been subject to bullying or harassment in the workplace are more likely to experience burnout, have lower levels of autonomy and psychological safety, and experience higher levels of work intensity.[71]

Those working in law firms and in regulated law clinics have an obligation to carry out their roles in a way that 'encourages equality of opportunity and respect for diversity'.[72] Equality means ensuring people are treated fairly; diversity means valuing people from different backgrounds with different knowledge, skills, and experience; and inclusion relates to ensuring everyone can be accepted in order to participate and contribute fully in the workplace. Other relevant legal requirements, for example in the UK context in the Equality Act 2010, ensure that people do not discriminate against clients or colleagues, directly or indirectly, in relation to any of the protected characteristics (age, disability, gender reassignment, marriage and civil partnership, pregnancy and maternity, race, religion or belief, sex, and sexual orientation) and make reasonable adjustments as required.

Relevant policies and practices must be in place at an organizational level to ensure the equitable provision of legal services and an inclusive workplace. However, to practically achieve inclusive places of work and study, it is important to promote respectful interactions with others beyond the minimum standards set. This extends to all those that clinical students come into contact with, from clients and opposing parties to supervisors, fellow students and court staff. For example, as we discussed in Chapter 3, the decimation of legal aid has led to a significant increase in the number of litigants who are not represented. While popular legal culture is rife with examples of lawyers taking advantage of their knowledge and skills, solicitors and barristers in England and Wales must not abuse their position in such circumstances. An inclusive, diverse workforce that does not discriminate in its service provision is also vital in terms of upholding public confidence in the profession.

Respect for equality and diversity also helps to achieve a workplace environment that promotes well-being and embraces learning from mistakes. It is positive that legal regulators are beginning to recognize the importance of well-being and its relationship to sound ethical practice. The SRA, for example, has proposed a change to its Code of Conduct which would include a positive obligation to treat colleagues fairly and also call out behaviour which does not meet appropriate standards. Such a change would certainly reflect a wider conception of ethical responsibility. As we discuss in Chapter 10, it is imperative that students and trainees

68 Herring (n 3) 413.

69 Solicitors Regulation Authority, *Benefits of Diversity in the Profession* (SRA 2016) 5.

70 Lawcare, *Life in the Law* (Lawcare 2021) 45. Available at https://www.lawcare.org.uk/media/14vhquzz/lawcare-lifeinthelaw-v6-final.pdf

71 Ibid.

72 SRA Code of Conduct, principle 6.

feel able to learn from mistakes, rather than seek to cover them up, which can usually relate to high levels of pressure, workplace bullying, a fear of failure, and/or stress in the workplace. One of the less obvious missions of clinical legal education is to create a baseline for student-lawyers where they feel supported on both personal and professional levels, and where they can openly identify mistakes and learn collectively. New lawyers may not always encounter the same nurturing environment when they enter practice, but they will at least know there is a better manner of operating. On the whole, promoting inclusion and fostering well-being will also create a 'supportive, ethical practice where confession of mistakes is welcomed'.[73]

A View from Clinical Practice

Professor Tim Casey, Professor from Practice and Director of Curricular Administration, UCLA Law

I'll make two claims, both of which might face some resistance.

Legal ethics is the most important subject in legal education.

Simultaneously, legal ethics is the most difficult subject to teach and learn.

As to the first claim, legal ethics is important because the subject defines the legal profession and all of those who practice within it. Ethics can be said to be the unifying field of law: all lawyers must adhere to ethical rules. And while a lapse in interpreting a contract or property conveyance might result in liability for malpractice, an ethical lapse could result in expulsion from the profession.

Ethics is difficult to teach because we often don't adequately define what it is we are teaching. One might focus on positive law—rules or statutes that regulate lawyer behaviour. But legal ethics involves more than just law; it also involves values and norms of behaviour. Determining values—even professional values—requires significant work, and often leads to unsatisfying results. While lawyers might agree on the importance of 'professional values', it is exceedingly hard to find agreement on what exactly those values are or how they should be articulated. And when it comes to applying those values to a course of action in a given situation, there will be even less agreement. Thus, we have the task of teaching something that is almost universally agreed to be important, and simultaneously about which there is almost universal disagreement in terms of application.

Ethics also includes norms of behaviour—unwritten expectations about the way lawyers should act. These norms can include everything from appropriate dress, to forms of professional greeting, to limits of tactics in negotiation. The ethical norms or behaviour can be difficult to ascertain. Experienced lawyers might say 'I know it when I see it', but that refrain falls mute on the ears of law students and new lawyers. Newbies might learn from observation, but here too, pitfalls remain. Most lawyers act ethically, but some do not. And there is no quick reference guide to discern proper and acceptable behaviour from improper and unacceptable actions.

Most attempts to teach legal ethics in a traditional classroom setting are not effective. A series of lectures might help students understand the law, but little attention can and will be

[73] Jane Ching, Graham Ferris et al, '"To act is to be committed, and to be committed is to be in danger": The Vulnerability of the Young Lawyer in Ethical Crisis' (2002) *Legal Ethics*, online.

paid to the values and norms that fully comprise the topic of legal ethics. The only effective way to teach legal ethics is through guided experience.

Fortunately, we have law clinics. The clinic is the ideal location to truly learn legal ethics. First, clinics place the student in the role of the lawyer. Second, the clinic can present dilemmas that challenge students, even to the point of disorientation. Third, clinical supervision provides not only the necessary backstop to prevent harm to the client, but also effective role modeling and guidance about acceptable norms of behaviour. Finally, clinics provide opportunities for reflection, which enables the student to explore and define her own personal sense of morality, and how to integrate that morality into a professional identity.

7.1.6 **Best Interests of the Client**

The exercise of knowledge, care, and skill should be in furtherance of the best interests of the client. It is not altogether easy to define what 'best interests' might be in any given case and it will require an exercise of judgement, which draws upon expertise and experience. As a clinical student, this involves paying close attention to what a supervisor determines to be in the best interests of the client, while also respecting client autonomy. Following the principle of client autonomy, lawyers should not substitute their own view as to what client best interests might be. Rather, clients should be given independent advice and information on all the factors relevant to their case and be empowered to make their own decisions and choices. The best interests of the client therefore depend on the client exercising their own free will and making informed decisions.[74]

Nicolson and Webb note that there can be fundamental tensions between lawyer and client autonomy in practice. They identify three scenarios: 'where lawyers use their control over clients in their own self-interest; where they use their control (as they see it) in the interests of clients; and conversely where clients seek to exercise control over lawyers.'[75] Following a standard conception of ethics, it might be assumed that the second of these tensions is largely positive. However, this may lead to a paternalistic legal practice that overrides a client's own decision-making. There are of course times when this is appropriate, for example in the exercise of power of attorney. Nicolson and Webb assert that instances of 'soft paternalism' can be justified to an extent. An example might be to simply progress a case on an uncontroversial or previously agreed matter in order to meet a deadline, when failing to do so could have adverse consequences for the client. They also describe 'moral activism'—that is to say restricting autonomy to 'protect others or uphold fundamental moral values'—but distinguish it from paternalism as it is 'no longer the "material" interests of the client which come first' when moral values are being prioritized.[76]

Of course, it may be the case that these moral imperatives align with the client's best interests, broadly conceived, but questions would nonetheless remain about the proper role and value of autonomy in the decision-making processes. Ensuring that advice and information has been reasonably understood and that clients can make decisions in light of it, as well as taking wider considerations about capacity and safeguarding into account, is therefore a fundamental aspect of the duty to uphold best interests.

[74] Andrew Boon and Jennifer Levin, *The Ethics and Conduct of Lawyers in England and Wales* (Hart 2008) 184.
[75] Nicolson and Webb (n 5) 123. [76] Ibid 130.

The principle of acting in the best interests of the client is underpinned by the so-called standard conception of legal ethics. Together with the notion of 'zealous advocacy', the standard conception is closely connected to, and indeed relies upon, the existence of the adversarial system. This system, prevalent in common law jurisdictions, means that advocates represent parties on either side of a case before an impartial person (or group of people such as a jury) in an attempt to reach the truth as to the facts and the application of the law to those facts. The decision makers then reach a conclusion, or judgment, in the case based on this determination. The adversarial system can be contrasted with an inquisitorial system, more common in civil law jurisdictions, where the court itself is actively involved in investigating the facts of the case. The adversarial system is said to be attractive because it (supposedly) discovers the truth in any given case, as well as fostering the correct interpretation of the law.

The standard conception of the lawyer's role in the adversarial system consists of three main principles. The first is the principle of *partisanship*, where a lawyer has an obligation to zealously defend the client according to their best interests and within relevant boundaries prescribed by law.[77] The second is *neutrality*, which maintains that the lawyer is neutral and it is not for them to interfere or determine whether the ends that a client may want to achieve are valid or not, thus suspending rather than exercising their own moral judgement. The third is the principle of *non-accountability*, that is to say that a lawyer is not accountable for the actions of their client, nor for the outcomes of the trial process in relation to a client's case.[78]

We see aspects of this standard conception in the ethical rules across many different legal jurisdictions. Some aspects are expressed more strongly, and clearly, than others. For example, reflecting the principle of partisanship, the promotion of the best interests of the client is at the forefront of a solicitor's ethical responsibilities.[79] The Bar Standards Board Handbook, which regulates barristers in England and Wales, also contains a clear overview: as a barrister, you 'must observe your duty to the court in the administration of justice'[80] and 'must act in the best interests of each client'.[81] The BSB Handbook elaborates further on the duties to the client (emphasis added):

1. you must **promote fearlessly** and by all proper and lawful means **the *client's* best interests**;
2. you must do so without regard to your own interests or to any consequences to you (which may include, for the avoidance of doubt, you being required to take reasonable steps to mitigate the effects of any breach of this *Handbook*);
3. you must do so **without regard to the consequences to any other person** (whether to your *professional client*, *employer* or any other person);
4. you must not permit your *professional client*, *employer* or any other person to limit your discretion.[82]

The standard conception therefore provides protection for individual rights and the lawyer's role is understood within that prism. It also promotes zealous advocacy: a model where lawyers advocate for their clients with a 'partisan' zeal and with the aim of their client winning.

[77] David Luban, *Lawyers and Justice: An Ethical Study* (Princeton University Press 1988).
[78] Ibid. [79] Solicitors Regulation Authority (SRA), Outcome 1.2. [80] Rule CD1.
[81] Rule CD2. [82] Rule C15.

The problem with this approach, critics argue, is that it breeds competitiveness and 'encourages manipulation and tactical abuses of the system'.[83] They stress that lawyers adhering to the standard conception might exploit loopholes or even promote unjust outcomes in the interests of their clients. On this interpretation, it is arguably even acceptable for a lawyer to be a morally 'bad' person. It is said that the standard conception and associated practice of zealous advocacy create a market for legal services, which is distorted by those who can afford to pay for the 'better' lawyer to win and therefore leads to disparities in the quality of representation that clients receive.[84] Of course, it could also be argued that the market itself perpetuates the notion by demanding that a 'good' lawyer is a zealous defender of their client no matter the cost. The lack of inherent accountability risks creating 'apathetic' lawyers and, in the corporate legal context, has been shown to result in a lack of 'ethical infrastructure' and 'ethical leadership' to appropriately guide decision-making.[85]

Unsurprisingly, other models have emerged that seek to challenge and provide an alternative to the standard conception. Some scholars have argued that ethical lawyering must surely involve greater exercise of moral judgement, less confined to rules in professional codes and more to professional moral character.[86] Other work, as discussed above, encourages us to ask whether lawyers *should* justify their conduct simply on the basis that it is in their client's best interests, even though such a course is permissible. It is important to interrogate whether a lawyer's own moral values should have a bearing on their professional decision-making. Herring observes that 'what someone is and what someone does are closely related', noting that 'you cannot really claim to *be* brave if you *do* not do brave things'.[87] For example, what about when a lawyer who claims to always act with integrity but in pursuing the best interests of their client regularly lacks integrity in their interaction with others and with the court?

In this regard, Rhode firmly asserts that lawyers must 'take personal moral responsibility for the consequences of their professional acts'.[88] At times, even where the rules are unclear, Rhode's position would be that lawyers need to be both personally and professionally accountable. Indeed, she would say, the two are closely interlinked. Another leading proponent of the consideration of a lawyer's 'good' character in wider public life is Kronman, who stresses the importance of deliberation and articulates the role of the ideal 'lawyer statesman'. A lawyer statesman, he says, 'has a keener sense than others do of the risks and opportunities that each choice presents for the preservation of those bonds of fellow-feeling on which the existence of their community depends'.[89] There are arguably many areas where a lawyer

[83] Nicolson and Webb (n 5) 54; see also Shai Agmon, 'Undercutting Justice—Why Legal Representation Should Not Be Allocated by the Market' (2021) Politics, Philosophy & Economics 20(1) 99–123.

[84] Gillian Hadfield, 'The Price of the Law: How the Market for Lawyers Distorts the Justice System' (2000) 98(4) Michigan Law Review 953–1006.

[85] Steven Vaughan and Emma Oakley, '"Gorilla Exceptions" and the Ethically Apathetic Corporate Lawyer' (2016) 19(1) Legal Ethics 50–75.

[86] Donald Nicolson, 'Making Lawyers Moral? Ethical Codes and Moral Character' (2005) 25(4) Legal Studies 601–26; Richard Zitrin and Carol M Langford, *The Moral Compass of the American Lawyer: Truth, Justice, Power, and Greed* (Random House 2000).

[87] Herring (n 3) 9.

[88] Deborah Rhode, *In the Interests of Justice: Reforming the Legal Profession* (OUP 2000) 17.

[89] Anthony Kronman, *The Lost Lawyer: Failing Ideals of the Legal Profession* (Harvard University Press 1995) 98.

can exercise good judgement and make a positive, rather than negative, impact on the development of a case; for example, when a client seeks advice in clarifying their goals[90] or even in advising as to the prospects of success and the merits of a claim. Even outside of the boundaries of legal casework, those 'bonds of fellow-feeling' between practitioners and others perhaps demand a deeper understanding of the myriad factors that might have a bearing upon acting in the client's best interests.

It is worth noting that some believe that a moderate version of the standard conception is acceptable, arguing that the courts have frameworks for dealing with so-called hyper-zeal and that there are forms of legitimate 'mere-zeal' advocacy that the courts can already properly regulate.[91] Still others go further, however, and argue that ethical lawyering requires an entirely new 'theory of moral character' and that the institutions and structures within which lawyers work need to pay more attention to integrity, which includes resisting the prioritization of profit at all costs.[92] In that respect, it is perhaps not difficult to see the connection between the pursuit of profit (ie assuring clients they will get the 'best' representation for significant sums) and the standard conception of ethics.

A View from Clinical Practice

Professor Donald Nicolson, Law Clinic Director, University of Essex

For those intending to uphold high ethical standards when they enter legal practice (and why would you not?), it is crucial to realize that you will not find the relevant professional rules remotely capable of resolving, or even alerting you to, the ethical issues which arise on a regular basis in practice. Perhaps the most ubiquitous of these is how to act in clients' best interests while respecting their autonomy, which hardly features in the professional codes at all. In fact, problems of respecting client autonomy also arise whenever you offer clients the option of waiving conflicts of interest or raise issues of morality relating to client ends, means to their ends, or suggesting that they disclose confidential information to prevent harm to others. This is because power imbalances and knowledge asymmetries between you and clients raise the risk of them deferring to your perceived authority or being led by subconscious and sometimes imagined messages you might convey.

At the same time, not engaging clients in such dialogue may also impinge on clients' autonomy in that they might presume that issues not discussed are off the table, and hence never raise their own moral doubts or perspectives on their problems. Here, as with so much of professional ethics, lawyers—at least if they are aware of the relevant issues—are faced with fiendishly difficult choices and the constant risk of doing the wrong thing. As Michel Foucault once said: 'My point is not that everything is bad, but that everything is dangerous.'[93]

[90] Ibid 129.

[91] Tim Dare, 'Mere-Zeal, Hyper-Zeal and the Ethical Obligations of Lawyers' (2004) 7(1) Legal Ethics 24–38.

[92] Sharon Dolovich, 'Ethical Lawyering and the Possibility of Integrity' (2002) 70(5) Fordham Law Review 1629, 1630.

[93] Hubert Dreyfus and Paul Rabinow, *Michel Foucault: Beyond Structuralism and Hermeneutics* (2nd ed, University of Chicago Press 1983) 232.

But then again, postmodernist ethics argues that being moral involves a constant state of anxiety about whether or not you have done the right thing.

One answer to this challenge is to stay constantly vigilant to ethical issues so that you do not become heavily embroiled in problems like conflict of interest without even realizing it and you give yourself enough time to make the best possible decision. Another is to immerse yourself in the ethics literature in order to gain a comprehensive idea of the range of issues which might arise in practice and the pros and cons of various suggested solutions to these issues. Finally, you should draw on this literature and your clinical experiences to think through the possible ethical challenges which arise in various areas of practices and whether you will be comfortable grappling with them and sometimes doing things that are ethically uncomfortable. Choice of career is perhaps the most momentous ethical choice you will make. Fortunately, clinics provide ideal opportunities to try out different forms of legal practice while also developing legal skills and, most importantly in my view, serving those in need of legal assistance—itself an ethical obligation.

7.2 **Fostering Good Ethical Practice**

So far, the discussion in this chapter has highlighted the extent to which principles interact with, and indeed rely upon, one another. For example, to act in the best interests of a client, a lawyer arguably needs to also maintain diligent standards of work and keep the affairs of clients confidential. To uphold the rule of law and the proper administration of justice, lawyers need to act with honesty and integrity while also ensuring trust and confidence in the profession.

These legal professional values, as reflected in the principles outlined in this chapter, form a critical part of clinical legal practice as a law student. It is imperative that knowledge and understanding of ethical rules is developed to 'see' ethical issues as they might arise in casework and that, together with casework supervisors, students engage in reflective problem solving in response. When considering the professional principles and applying them to realistic situations in practice, the *context* of the decision-making is important. As Nicolson and Webb observe in arguing for a contextual approach to legal ethics:

> As we have repeatedly argued, in contrast to the current narrow and categorical approach to ethics, lawyers should be required to take into account the real life situation of their clients, including all their needs, desires and interests, and the possible impact of their actions on third parties, the general public and the environment.[94]

As we have seen from our discussion above, the type of legal education a lawyer has had, the structure and culture of the law firm or organization where a lawyer works, the area of law and the types of clients they represent, and their own professional and wider social networks can all influence decisions and actions. Research tells us that lawyers tend to take

[94] Nicolson and Webb (n 5) 280.

'ethical cues' from those around them.[95] It has been noted that lawyers also have a tendency to believe themselves to be more ethical than other lawyers[96] and compare, indeed justify, their own ethical choices with reference to other lawyers within their own areas of legal practice.[97] We also know that camaraderie can be strong among certain groups of lawyers, and so they often look within their own sub-groups and networks of practice to guide their decision-making.

A matter of key importance is to ensure that clinical law students and trainee practitioners consult with those with more experience of ethical issues about what the right course of action might be. Finding a trusted 'ethical compass' among more senior lawyers (and also more experienced students) in a clinic or law firm is critical to ensuring one feels comfortable about the approach taken in the early years of training and practice, and with the outcomes of decisions made. The following step-by-step model has also been articulated and asserts that in order to take 'self-conscious ethical action', an individual must:

(i) see the ethical aspect of the situation they are in;
(ii) understand what the ethical response is in this situation;
(iii) care enough to wish to act ethically; and
(iv) be able to find some effective way to act ethically (despite potential opposition or risk).[98]

Recognizing the different constraining or facilitating factors, which may either neglect or foster good ethical practice, is an important part of professional life. As a first step, and to identify the ethical aspects of the situation one is in, it is necessary to understand and apply the ethical values and related rules of practice. Chapters 9 and 10 provide further examples of ethical decision-making in relation to managing oneself and one's relationships in the workplace.

7.3 **Professional Discipline**

Consideration of professional legal ethics would not be complete without mention of enforcement strategies. This means that lawyers can be disciplined for any breach of the rules in the delivery of legal services. Notably, any liability for breach extends to practising solicitors acting as supervisors to students who may breach regulatory rules. As Cranston notes, professional rules and related disciplinary procedures exist to ensure the standing of the profession in the eyes of the public (ie public confidence) and also to protect the public from 'the unscrupulous or incompetent'.[99] Acknowledging that professional discipline may well

[95] Leslie Levin and Lynn Mather (eds), *Lawyers in Practice: Ethical Decision Making in Context* (University of Chicago Press 2012).
[96] Jennifer Robbennolt and Jean Sternlight, 'Behavioral Legal Ethics' (2014) 45 Arizona State Law Journal 1107.
[97] Kinghan (n 53). [98] Ching et al (n 73) 45. [99] Cranston (n 17) 3.

result in negative impacts on the practice of the lawyer in question, 'the power of discipline is protective in purpose, rather than punitive'.[100] That said, there are wide-ranging sanctions available where there has been a serious breach of conduct. Sanctions might include a fine or a rebuke, or both. Reflecting Cranston's observation, the SRA makes clear that sanctions 'are broadly intended to discipline the person to prevent similar behaviour by them or others, maintain standards and uphold public confidence in the profession'.[101] The level of sanction imposed will depend on the type of firm and the work that they do or that the individual lawyer does. For some types of behaviour a financial penalty is not appropriate:

> We [the SRA] consider that some behaviours demonstrated by individuals—such as those relating to sexual misconduct, discrimination, and non-sexual harassment—are unsuitable for a financial penalty, except in exceptional circumstances. This is because the underlying attitudes and behaviours displayed present such a risk to the public or to colleagues that they are incompatible with continued unrestricted right to practise, and/or because suspension or removal from the profession is necessary to maintain public confidence in the solicitors' profession and in legal services. It is also often the case that the level of harm cannot be financially quantified and it is not appropriate to do so.[102]

A solicitor may therefore be suspended or disbarred for a serious breach of the principles set out in this chapter. Similarly, for barristers, breaches of the BSB Handbook could result in a range of sanctions, from a warning or a fine to removal of the authorization to conduct litigation, disbarment, or suspension from practice.[103] Aggravating and mitigating factors, as well as personal or other circumstances, will be taken into account. Aggravating factors might include taking advantage of a person's vulnerability, repeated acts of misconduct, or showing a reckless disregard for the obligations of professional practice. The threat of disciplinary action gives bite to the ethical rules, which might otherwise not have force in day-to-day professional practice.

Disciplinary investigation, and relevant sanctions, are aimed at ensuring adherence and public confidence in the system. It is important that lawyers report actual and potential serious breaches to the appropriate regulatory body. The SRA requires that 'any facts or matters which you reasonably believe are capable of amounting to a serious breach' be reported to them. Even where a solicitor might not have sufficient information about whether a serious breach has occurred, there is a freestanding obligation to bring any facts or matters that might cause you to 'reasonably believe' they should be brought to the attention of the SRA. This helps facilitate early investigation and regulatory action where appropriate. We note that the SRA does not necessarily define what a 'serious breach' of the rules might be;

[100] Ibid.

[101] SRA guidance on sanctions. Available at https://www.sra.org.uk/consumers/solicitor-check/sanctions/#:~:text=Disciplinary%20sanctions%20include%20a%20fine,public%20confidence%20in%20the%20profession

[102] SRA, *Changes to Enforcement Strategy* (July 2022) para 2.2. Available at https://www.sra.org.uk/globalassets/documents/sra/consultations/annex-3---enforcement-strategy.pdf?version=4a45c1

[103] The Bar Tribunals and Adjudication Service, *Sanctions Guidance: Breaches of the BSB Handbook* (Inns of Court, 15 October 2019) 16–17.

however, it has made clear in its enforcement strategy that the following types of allegations are considered to be particularly serious:

- Abuse of trust
- Dishonesty
- Taking unfair advantage of clients or others
- Misuse of client money
- Sexual or violent misconduct
- Criminal behaviour

Conclusion

Compliance with ethical principles requires an ability first to identify when an ethical issue arises, and then to consider how the principles might be engaged to resolve or guide decision-making. We considered the seven key ethical principles in relation to the provision of legal advice and representation: upholding the rule of law and the proper administration of justice; trust and confidence in the profession; honesty; integrity; independence; equality, diversity, and inclusion; and upholding the best interests of the client. We established that often these principles can interrelate and that undermining one may in fact undermine others. Finally, we explored the ways in which the principles might be encountered in day-to-day practice through a number of reflective exercises. We also considered the potential consequences of breaching ethical rules in terms of disciplinary action.

It is imperative that knowledge and awareness of professional legal ethics is fostered in clinical legal education in order to adequately protect the needs of clients and ensure public confidence in advice provision. Even if such provision is in a 'lay' student capacity, rather than being officially supervised by a regulated practising legal professional, adherence to the appropriate principles as set out in this chapter is highly recommended. Likewise, it is never too early in one's journey as a legal professional to begin to think about the ways in which ethical values can underpin the development of relationships with clients, with others, and with a range of relevant institutions such as the courts, and to practice good ethical decision-making as a law student.

Further Reading

Jonathan Herring, *Legal Ethics* (3rd ed, OUP 2023).

Barbara Mescher, *Legal Ethics for Lawyers: A New Model* (Routledge 2023).

Donald Nicolson and Julian Webb, *Professional Legal Ethics: Critical Interrogations* (OUP 2000).

Julian Webb (ed), *Leading Works in Legal Ethics* (Routledge 2024).

Lawyers and Social Justice

8

Fight for the things that you care about but do it in a way that will lead others to join you.

Ruth Bader Ginsburg

Chapter Overview

This chapter will introduce you to the ways in which social justice lawyers seek to make a positive social impact through their work. It explores the different types of work that social justice lawyers do, including exploring their relationships with others and the networks and collaborations that make their work possible. The role of pro bono in society is also considered, for example, by interrogating the motivations of lawyers undertaking pro bono work and critical considerations around whether—especially in times of access to justice crisis—pro bono work for lawyers should be made a mandatory requirement of legal practice. By the end of this chapter, you will be able to:

- Understand the different theories that relate to lawyers working in the not-for-profit sector
- Compare and contrast different theories that seek to understand the motivation and impact of lawyers working to advance social justice
- Critically evaluate the role of pro bono in society
- Consider the ways in which law school clinics seek to make positive change
- Reflect upon the impact of different uses of law in the public interest.

Introduction

The context of social justice lawyering has changed considerably over time and yet has a deeply embedded history. As we explored in Chapter 2, lawyers have a unique role to play in the access to justice landscape by helping others to enforce their rights and resolve legal disputes. This is important when working with individual clients, as well as when lawyers work collectively with others to create strategic or systemic change. In the UK context we know, from the successful abolition of slavery in the 1800s to the miscarriages of justice cases in the 1970s, that the law has long had a potentially transformative power in society.[1] Similarly,

[1] See eg Carol Harlow and Richard Rawlings, *Pressure through Law* (Routledge 1992).

law school clinics make meaningful impacts in meeting access to justice needs and promoting social justice locally, nationally, and internationally. For example, students might equip individuals to access housing, welfare benefits, or citizenship in frontline legal advice clinics; they might empower communities to know their rights through public legal education; or they might support policy and law reform projects in discrete areas such as environmental rights or children's rights before international courts and tribunals. Regardless of the area of clinical casework, or the type of activity and legal forum relied upon, there can be wide-ranging positive social justice impacts from a decision to deploy legal tools to create change.

Underpinning these activities are a range of theories that seek to explain the work that lawyers do in the pursuit of social justice. This body of scholarly work aims to address questions that interrogate the '*why*' and '*how*' of legal action. In Chapter 7, we discussed the notion that lawyers should take personal moral responsibility for their professional conduct. We saw that some scholars have asserted that lawyers need to ensure they 'do justice' to their own personal convictions, even though this might serve to challenge traditional conceptions of legal ethics. Other scholars have tried to interrogate and understand the work of lawyers motivated by particular 'causes' in relation to their work, and to situate this within a lawyer's duty to uphold justice more widely in society. In Clinical Legal Education, the label of 'scholar activist' might even be apt to describe some clinical legal practitioners who situate their clinical practice against the backdrop of wider movements for change. Indeed, the practice sites in which theories of community and movement lawyering have developed have often been in the context of Clinical Legal Education, especially in the US.

In this chapter we will bring together relevant theories to help explain and better understand the practice of lawyers who connect their work to wider ideals of advancing social justice. We will reflect on the ways in which personally held beliefs might motivate lawyers to pursue practice in certain areas, and the connection between that motivation and the tools they use in their everyday work. Alongside different theories of lawyering for change we will also address some of their critiques. For example, does reliance on the law displace other, more effective methods of creating social change? Do lawyers tend to take a 'law-centric' approach that imposes legal strategies on communities and movements for change? In addressing these critical questions and considering what we know about the importance of reflection from our reading in Chapter 6, we can then meaningfully ask whether social justice lawyering is an appropriate path we might wish to pursue in the future. We might otherwise also reflect on whether there are other ways in which we might seek to contribute to meeting access to justice needs in society, for example through pro bono provision. Against that backdrop, we will also critically consider the role of pro bono in modern society and its relationship to access to justice.

8.1 Lawyers and Tools for Change—Why?

Lawyers working in the public interest undertake a variety of activities to make a positive contribution to society, often in relation to distinct social justice issues. Examples include ensuring fairer treatment of women in the workplace; advancing children's right to voice, empowerment, and participation in education; challenging corporations for failing to meet climate justice targets; or fighting to abolish the death penalty. A body of work investigating lawyers working in this way has termed them 'cause lawyers', which involves 'using legal skills to pursue ends and ideals that transcend client service'.[2] This field acknowledges the importance of better understanding why and how lawyers use the law to advance wider missions and interests. Cause lawyers seek to 'use the law as a vehicle through which to build a better society' and this commitment usually means that they look outside the law (ie to social, moral, economic, or political goals) in their day-to-day work.[3] The work of lawyers in law centres, and in some law school clinics, may well fall within this framing:

> Although they may not identify as 'cause lawyers', the work of lawyers affiliated to UK law centres (who routinely provide their services free) and other organised pro bono institutions resonates strongly with our notion of a commitment to broader social and political causes.[4]

In Chapter 5, we discussed the development of Legal Realism and its implications for clinical legal education. Legal Realists argued that the everyday practice of the law should be incorporated into legal education and stressed the importance of the impact of legal decisions on, for example, the rights of workers, minority groups, and those more generally experiencing discrimination and disadvantage. The Legal Realists also observed that the law itself should not be divorced from the real world in which it operates, nor from the relevant (often unfair) processes and systems that govern legal practice. Relatedly, for cause lawyers, the realistic context of the relationship between law and politics, as well as socio-economic conditions in society, is critical. While there are many different types of cause lawyering, from moderate to more radical approaches, most cause lawyers are highly attuned to the socio-political landscape in which they work and are motivated to use the law in a way that positively impacts upon that landscape.

This aligns with Sarat and Scheingold's analysis which captures the 'democratic aspirations' of progressive cause lawyers. In comparing a body of case studies globally in the early 2000s, they surmised that there are two distinct 'visions of democracy' represented by different types of cause lawyering: one focused on 'securing political accountability, basic human rights and the rule of law' and another focused on 'a more expansive vision of social and economic democracy'.[5] In pursuit of these democratic visions, there exists a range of motivations for cause lawyers. Some scholars argue that cause lawyering rests on 'altruism' and

[2] Austin Sarat and Stuart Scheingold (eds), *Cause Lawyers: Political Commitments and Professional Responsibilities* (OUP 2004) 3–6.

[3] Kieran McEvoy and Rachel Rebouche, 'Mobilizing the Professions: Lawyers, Politics and the Collective Legal Conscience' in John Morison et al (eds), *Judges, Transition and Human Rights* (OUP 2007) 275–314.

[4] Anna Bryson et al, 'Cause Lawyering in Conflicted, Authoritarian and Transnational Societies' in Richard Abel et al (eds), *Lawyers in 21st Century Societies: Volume 2, Comparisons and Theories* (Hart 2022) 328–9.

[5] Austin Sarat and Stuart Scheingold, 'Cause Lawyering and Democracy in Transnational Perspective: A Postscript' in Austin Sarat and Stuart Scheingold (eds), *Cause Lawyering and the State in a Global Era* (OUP 2001) 382–401, 383.

ideologies that seek to enhance the well-being of others.[6] For others, such as Halliday, cause lawyering is an expression of 'civic professionalism' related to the lawyer's elite role in society.[7] Similarly, Hilbink's typology of cause lawyers describes a distinct set of 'elite/vanguard' lawyers motivated to use the law because they view it as a superior form of politics. These lawyers will be more likely, for example, to pursue change by seeking changes to substantive law or to use litigation strategies, given their faith in legal processes.[8]

Alongside altruism and civic professionalism rests a third conception of cause lawyering motivation, which is arguably the most prolific, and relies on political ideology.[9] The interplay between politics and associated values and beliefs cannot be underestimated when considering how lawyers use the law to create change. For example, research has shown that lawyers working on progressive causes often connect their role as lawyers in society to long-standing, personally held, liberal political values. For such progressive lawyers, money tends rarely to be described as a motivating factor; rather, they intimate in various ways a desire to pursue justice (in different forms) or, otherwise, an anger at injustice which they seek to remedy through their work.[10] The role of state power, and the desire to hold the government to account for the unlawful or unfair exercise of power, also features strongly for progressive lawyers. In Etienne's study of criminal cause lawyers, for example, a 'shared ideology or worldview combined with skepticism of government action' commonly motivated lawyers in the study in their representation of clients.[11]

At the other end of the political spectrum, lawyers on the conservative right are motivated to use the law to advance considerations of justice related to socially conservative causes, libertarian beliefs, and business advocacy.[12] In Southworth's extensive study of conservative cause lawyers in the US, she found that restricting access to abortion services, defending 'traditional social arrangements and working to reshape the balance between religious and secular values in public life' were at the heart of the strategies of religious lawyers.[13] Libertarians were motivated to 'bolster property rights and personal liberty and generally resist government regulation' while business leaders 'pursued favorable trade policies, tort reform, tax cuts and restrictions on union activity'.[14] Across both the left and the right of the political

[6] Carrie Menkel-Meadow, 'The Causes of Cause Lawyering: Toward an Understanding of the Motivation and Commitment of Social Justice Lawyers' in Austin Sarat and Stuart Scheingold (eds), *Cause Lawyering: Political Commitments and Professional Responsibilities* (OUP 1998) 31–68.

[7] Terrence Halliday, 'Politics and Civic Professionalism: Legal Elites and Cause Lawyers' (1999) 24(4) Law and Social Inquiry 1013–60.

[8] Thomas Hilbink, 'You Know the Type: Categories of Cause Lawyering' (2004) 29(3) Law and Social Inquiry 657–98. See also Steven Berenson, 'Government Lawyer as Cause Lawyer: A Study of Three High Profile Government Law Suits' (2009) 86(2) Denver University Law Review 457.

[9] Austin Sarat and Stuart Scheingold, 'Cause Lawyering and the Reproduction of Professional Authority: An Introduction' in Austin Sarat and Stuart Scheingold (eds), *Cause Lawyering: Political Commitments and Professional Responsibilities* (OUP 1998) 431–52.

[10] Jacqueline Kinghan, *Lawyers' Networks and Progressive Social Change: Lawyers Changing Lives* (Hart 2021) 82.

[11] Margaret Etienne, 'The Ethics of Cause Lawyering: An Empirical Examination of Criminal Defence Lawyers as Cause Lawyers' (2005) 95 Journal of Criminal Law and Criminology 1195, 1209.

[12] Ann Southworth, *Lawyers of the Right: Professionalizing the Conservative Coalition* (University of Chicago Press 2008).

[13] Ibid 2. [14] Ibid 2.

spectrum, however, lawyers hold in common the use of highly effective networks and diverse coalitions and alliances to successfully use legal tools for change.

Of course, there will always be tensions where the cause lawyer chooses to rely on political rather than legal strategies. It is perhaps unsurprising that in pursuing purely legal approaches the cause lawyer can continue to situate themselves in the mainstream legal profession because such approaches tend to uphold the ethical ideal of 'neutral partisanship' which we explored in Chapter 7. Indeed, research has shown that *legally* engaged cause lawyers work on behalf of entrenched legal rights and the rule of law, and are indeed more likely to deny that any 'cause' other than the higher cause of the law motivates them in their work.[15] These lawyers also tend to enjoy greater professional success and are viewed as being within, rather than outside, the legal profession itself:

> On the whole . . . legally engaged cause lawyering may actually embellish an attorney's professional reputation . . . In contrast, to politicize one's legal practice is to test and probably to violate the nethermost boundaries of mainstream professionalism.[16]

Lawyers working more overtly in a political way might be viewed as 'on the edge' of the profession itself.[17] For some political cause lawyers, the client and the cause may even be one and the same:

> In contrast to the liberal-legal version of cause lawyering, politicization is all about solidarity with clients and/or their causes. This means overt identification with and commitment to the political agenda of one side in conflicts over constitutional rights, public policy, regime structure, etc.—rather than identification with rights, legality, and constitutionality as ends in themselves. Solidarity is a marker of political cause lawyering, in part, because cause lawyers who thus become enmeshed in their clients' agendas do so in order to make a political statement and are ordinarily perceived as doing so by outsiders.[18]

Of course, lawyers will often use a combination of legal, political, and wider strategies for change, as we explore further below. The lawyer's relationship with the state in this regard is one that often must be delicately managed. For the independent barrister, they might one day represent an individual against the state in a high-profile human rights matter and the next represent the government, or an arm of government, in defending an action against it. It has been noted that immigration lawyers often work closely with campaigners and advocacy groups and use different strategies depending on the forum in which they operate and the goal they are trying to achieve (for example, obtaining citizenship on behalf of a client in an immigration tribunal as opposed to advocating for law reform with parliamentarians).[19]

[15] Hilbink (n 8). [16] Sarat and Scheingold (n 5) 386.

[17] Andrew Francis, *At the Edge of Law: Emergent and Divergent Models of Legal Professionalism* (Routledge 2011).

[18] Sarat and Scheingold (n 5) 386.

[19] Susan Cotin, 'Cause Lawyering in the Shadow of the State: A US Immigration Example' in Austin Sarat and Stuart Scheingold (eds), *Cause Lawyering: Political Commitments and Professional Responsibilities* (OUP 1998) 117–40.

It might be that a delicate balance must be sought to maintain both proximity (ie to achieve positive outcomes) and distance (ie to enable challenge) with the state. As Sarat and Scheingold observe, 'even those cause lawyers who are committed to fundamental political transformation and pursue a confrontational mode are, at least implicitly and contradictorily, dependent on the state that they wish to transform.'[20] They offer the following observations about the strategic choices that lawyers might make in this respect:

> As for strategic choice, two core questions that confront virtually all cause lawyers emerge over and over again in the research record. The more familiar of these questions is whether and to what extent cause lawyers should privilege legal as opposed to political strategies. Secondly, cause lawyers must decide how to position themselves between maintaining their distance from the state and operating in close proximity to it. What emerges from the evidence is that, contrary to the conventional wisdom, the former choice is more fraught with professional than policy consequences while the latter choice has decisive consequences for what cause lawyers can hope to accomplish.[21]

The suggestion therefore is that those lawyers working more closely with the state, or at least within the confines of 'legal' approaches, may be able to accomplish more in traditional legal forums. For those lawyers who privilege political strategies, success may look different and could indeed rely on one's motivation to engage with non-legal platforms such as the media or campaigning in the wider public sphere. In so doing, they distance themselves from the law, and some might even argue that they cease to be lawyers (in the traditional sense) the more politically engaged they become.

REFLECTION POINT

In thinking about your future career as a lawyer, would you prefer to work 'within the law' or 'outside the law'? Why?

Notably, theories of cause lawyering have been underdeveloped in the UK context and tend to receive more attention in other jurisdictions. There are several possible explanations for this comparative lack of study. For example, Boon describes a 'cold climate' for cause lawyering in the UK linked to what he terms a 'quiet conservativism.' Others observe the negative portrayal of so-called activist lawyers working on progressive causes, even from government actors and particularly in the immigration context, and thus a fearful reluctance to be identified as such.[22] There appears to be a cultural constraint related to professional legal

[20] Sarat and Scheingold (n 5) 390. [21] Sarat and Scheingold (n 5) 38.

[22] Andrew Boon, 'Cause Lawyers in a Cold Climate: The Impact of Globalization on the United Kingdom' in Austin Sarat and Stuart Scheingold (eds), *Cause Lawyering: Political Commitments and Professional Responsibilities* (OUP 1998) 143–85.

ethics, as well as professional legal culture, which tends to more readily preserve traditional conceptions of lawyering in the UK as compared to some other jurisdictions. Likewise, law schools have been comparatively slow to develop research to better understand the motivations of law students who may wish to pursue social justice legal practice in future. However, it is worth noting that other jurisdictions have paid considerable attention to such issues by, for example, tracing the motivations of law students during law school and then longitudinally tracking their future careers.[23] It is certainly worth exploring the types of motivations that might underpin one's clinical casework and future legal practice in order to reflect upon the type of lawyer you wish to be in future, and the values that will underpin your professional life.

A View from Clinical Practice

Dr Lucy Welsh, Reader in Law and Director of Clinical Legal Education, University of Sussex

The criminal process is designed to deter people from committing individual and social harms, as well as to identify and punish those who do. This means that the whole system is important to our social fabric. But—as is noted in this chapter—the justice system often also perpetuates inequalities for already marginalized groups; we are all aware of the racialized nature of policing and problems of sexism and misogyny in the police, which feed into the criminal process. All criminal justice lawyering has, therefore, social justice issues at play.

Any defence lawyer will tell you that they could have made lots of money if they were paid for how many times they were asked how they could defend someone they knew to be guilty. As someone who is still asked those questions, it is important to do three things: break down what that question asks, think about the lawyer's role, and think about personal motivation. My reflection on this, as a lawyer who has aligned practice, teaching, and research along the same ideals, is as follows.

First, the question asks about knowing someone is guilty. The only way I can know a client is guilty is if they tell me so. If that happens, I have professional conduct rules to follow about the advice I give and limitations in my role. Aside from that, my opinion of the client's guilt or otherwise is pretty meaningless, though it might cause personal conflict on occasion.

Second, I have always believed myself to be a due process lawyer (even though I didn't necessarily know that until quite far into my career). This means that I see my role as very much about doing my best to equalize the power of the state against the individual, and hold the state to account when things are not done properly. Whether that is the right approach, or if conviction of the guilty at any cost is a better moral approach, is a matter of debate.

That brings me to my third reflection about personal motivation. I still do not know why (though it is probably connected to my politically left-leaning family and study of sociology at A level), but my concern has consistently been power imbalances, and I am suspicious

[23] See eg Ronit Dinovitzer et al, *After the JD III: Third Results from a National Study of Legal Careers* (American Bar Association 2014).

about placing boundless trust in the powerful. If that were not a personal motivation of mine, maybe I would be more focused on the crime control model of criminal process, which trusts the accuracy of the process in obtaining conviction.

None of these reflections are ones with which I expect anyone to necessarily agree, but I offer them as one approach to a view of social justice lawyering. My own motivations have enabled me to engage in work that aims to assist people who believe they have been wrongfully convicted, to support charitable work advising people who have family members in prison, and to work with organizations to help people understand their legal rights and try to empower them when navigating the criminal process.

Through your own clinical experiences, I encourage you to look for where the balance of power lies, at the resources and routes available to parties; to consider what your role is or should be, and to reflect on your own motivation for your response to the cases that you experience.

TAKING STOCK

Some lawyers in society expressly aim to make a positive impact through their work. To explain why lawyers might use different tools, such as campaigning or activism, alongside their casework it is important to understand the connection between professional and personal identity and to consider why lawyers are motivated to use the law in a particular way on behalf of their clients. Likewise, in the clinical context, both students and clinical legal educators may wish to interrogate the 'why' of using the law for social change as part of their own reflective practice.

8.2 Lawyers and Tools for Change—How?

A variety of legal tools might be used by lawyers to achieve positive change: the law can be mobilized to **empower**, **inform, and persuade** or to **challenge and enforce**.[24] Examples of activities include collective campaigns, grassroots activism, rights awareness, specialist legal advice, developing and coordinating legal research, policy advocacy, engaging in networks and coalitions, frontline legal representation, and strategic litigation.[25]

Let us consider first the notion of **legal empowerment**, especially given its relationship to access to justice, which we explored in Chapter 2. Legal empowerment is a term that has developed over the past two decades and is said to refer to 'the use of law to specifically

[24] Lisa Vanhala and Jacqueline Kinghan, *Revised Framework for Effective Use of Law* (The Baring Foundation 2024).

[25] Lisa Vanhala and Jacqueline Kinghan, *Literature Review on the Use and Impact of Litigation* (The Public Law Project 2018).

strengthen the disadvantaged'.[26] Legal activities aimed at empowering might exist at multiple levels, including locally, nationally, and internationally, and might also be aimed at creating wider systemic change (ie challenging systems that operate unfairly for certain groups of people). The UN Secretary General describes legal empowerment as 'the process of systemic change through which the poor are protected and enabled to use the law to advance their rights and their interests as citizens and economic actors'.[27]

Do law school clinics empower individuals and communities? It is certainly true that clinical casework and related pro bono projects could be said to be aimed at legal empowerment. Empowering others using law might include the provision of legal training, offering general legal advice and representation to raise awareness of rights, or raising awareness of related duties of public authorities or private corporations. The delivery of training and other forms of public legal education might empower frontline service providers and those seeking to achieve better outcomes on behalf of their clients. As Vanhala and Kinghan note, 'representing claimants and supporting others involved in legal action can also help to *build power*' (emphasis added).[28] Legal empowerment can operate on multiple levels, both in terms of building a sense of identity (as individuals and as organizations) and in terms of strengthening positions in relation to other powerholders. This is especially the case where clinics are embedded in local communities or work in close partnership with civil society organizations.

Using the law to **inform and persuade** might involve, for example, specialist legal education and training, engaging with law reform processes, or the provision of early legal help and representation. The work of 'informing' seeks to 'address a lack of awareness among, for example, individuals facing discrimination or who are disadvantaged, service providers, public authorities and businesses of their responsibilities and the rights of those who engage with them'.[29] As a step further, the work of 'persuading' suggests that 'there is more than a knowledge gap that needs to be addressed and that underlying beliefs and attitudes need to shift'.[30] Examples for law school clinics include the provision of specialist legal advice in discrete areas of law or students working on consultation responses to influence law reform.

Finally, using the law to **challenge and enforce** relates to directly challenging stakeholders who fail to live up to their legal obligations. This might include legal representation in the courts and tribunals and strategic litigation efforts, as well as representing individual or group interests in public inquiries. The 'enforcement' of law may of course be the result (or remedy) in a legal challenge, leading to the 'just outcome' in the case or helping to create long-term change. Examples in a clinical context include students working under supervision on strategic litigation, including third party interventions, or enforcing international rights and obligations in UN Committees. See Figure 8.1.

[26] Stephen Golub, 'What Is Legal Empowerment? An Introduction' in Stephen Golub (ed), *Legal Empowerment: Practioners' Perspectives* (International Development Law Organization 2010).

[27] United Nations, *Legal Empowerment of the Poor and Eradication of Poverty*. Report of the Secretary-General (UN Doc A/64/133) (United Nations 2009).

[28] Vanhala and Kinghan (n 24) 11. [29] Vanhala and Kinghan (n 24) 11. [30] Ibid.

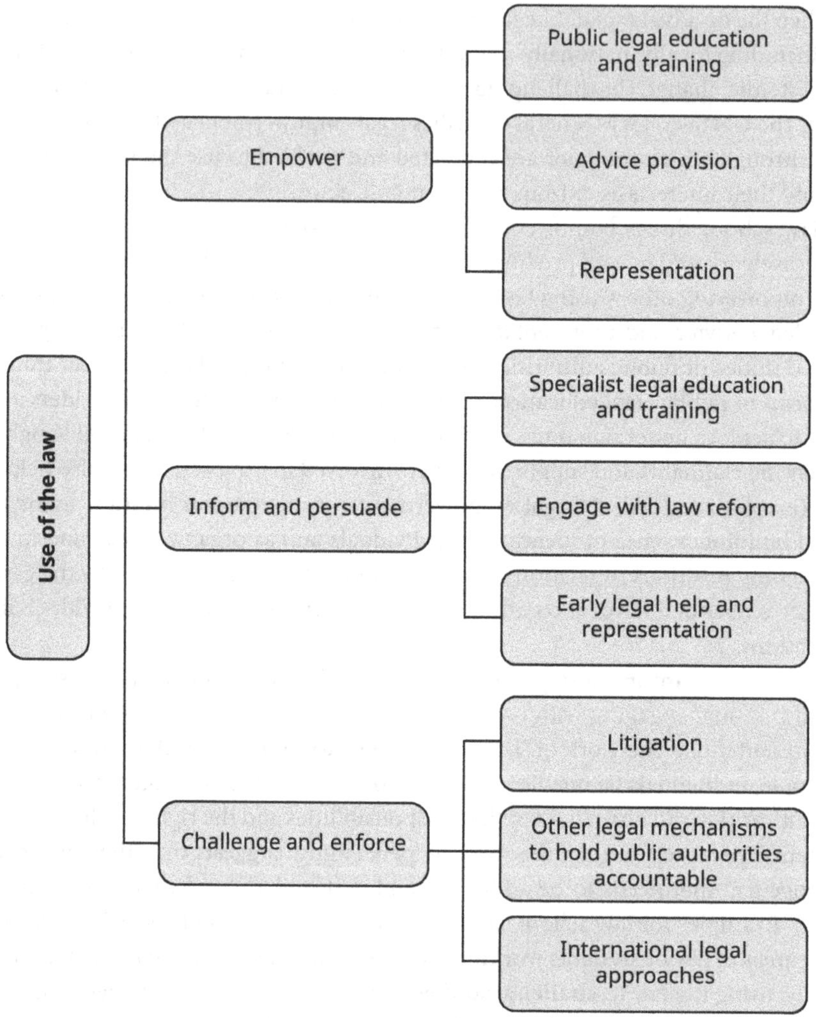

Figure 8.1 Framework on use of law[31]

Related to the 'how' of social justice lawyering is the question of 'where'? While it is often clear in the corporate context what types of firms exist or what roles are available in an 'in house' capacity, it can be difficult for students to ascertain where social justice lawyering takes place, including in the UK context those lawyers who work on legal aid cases, as we explored in Chapter 3. Social justice lawyers most commonly work in a variety of not-for-profit settings such as law centres, charities, NGOs and some law school clinics. However, they might also work at the independent Bar, in legal aid law firms or in the pro bono department of large corporate law firms. Again, what appears to be critical is the extent to which they move within and across their networks to create change. Lawyers often rely on partnerships either with other lawyers in similarly situated organizations or with frontline charities

[31] Ibid.

engaged in service provision (for example, supporting survivors of sexual or domestic abuse, homeless shelters, or youth centres) to identify the most common legal issues and to collectively harness resources and expertise to appropriately respond. These types of partnerships and collaborations are of crucial importance as they can strengthen the depth and breadth of potential impacts achieved when using legal tools. Several theories have also been developed to capture different types of approaches, all of which are relevant in the context of clinical legal education, which we explore further below.

8.2.1 **Community and Movement Lawyering**

Some law school clinics adopt a community lawyering approach where advice, representation, and other legal activities are delivered in partnership with local communities. This might be considered a sub-set of cause lawyering given that the provision of legal services aims to help those facing economic, cultural, or social disadvantage and to generally make access to justice more equitable. It is possible to trace the origins of community lawyering approaches to the US Neighbourhood Law Offices in the 1960s and 1970s. A number of US scholars captured this approach in a variety of ways, including labelling it political lawyering,[32] rebellious lawyering,[33] or collaborative lawyering.[34] In 1993, Angelo Ancheta developed Gerald Lopez's conception of 'rebellious lawyering' and termed it 'community lawyering'.[35] Notably, Lopez had sought to expose the domineering ('regnant') progressive lawyering models emerging in the US at the time and proposed an alternative model of shared partnership together with communities. Lopez was highly critical of 'regnant' progressive lawyers and observed:

> Lawyers understand their profession as an honourable calling and see themselves as aesthetic if not political heroes, working largely alone to make statements through their (more than their clients') cases about society's injustices.[36]

Lopez identified an issue of concern in this area, which is the extent to which the lawyer becomes the 'hero' and thereafter loses sight of the individuals and communities they represent. For example, consider a lawyer who represents a group of low-income clients against a private landlord. Having succeeded in a case challenging prospective eviction and improving the conditions of their tenancies, the case is used as part of a marketing campaign to advertise the services of the lawyer. The win is showcased in the press and then the lawyer moves on to represent clients elsewhere rather than ensuring longer-term change for others who are similarly affected in the first community. As Freeman notes, even the most dedicated of public interest lawyers can engage in 'drive-by lawyering', where they move too quickly from one case to the next. He observes that such lawyers might be 'willing to address some discrete need for a grassroots campaign but then leave without ever engaging deeply enough

[32] Gary Bellow, 'Steady Work: A Practitioner's Reflection on Political Lawyering' (1996) 31 Harvard Civil Rights-Civil Liberties Law Review 297; Gary Bellow, 'Legal Aid in the United States' (1980) 14 Clearinghouse Review 337.

[33] Gerald Lopez, *Rebellious Lawyering: One Chicano's Vision of Progressive Law Practice* (Westview Press 1992).

[34] Lucie E. White, 'Collaborative Lawyering in the Field? On Mapping the Paths from Rhetoric to Practice' [1994] Clinical Law Review 154, 608.

[35] Angelo N Ancheta, 'Community Lawyering' (1993) 83 California Law Review 1363.

[36] Lopez (n 33) 24.

with the community to create a meaningful difference'.[37] Community lawyering seeks to highlight the participatory, rather than hierarchical, approach that lawyers should take. Jennifer Gordon similarly identifies this problem in her seminal article where she stresses that 'the lawyer is not the protagonist' in any story for social change. Gordon argues that lawyers are in fact 'supporting players' rather than 'main characters'.[38] It is this underlying participatory, shared approach that has come to characterize community lawyering. As such, community lawyering aims to minimize the traditional roles of lawyers and clients. Notably, in the context of clinical legal education, Tokarz defines community lawyering as follows:

> An approach to the practice of law and advocacy that centers on building and sustaining relationships with clients, over time, in context, as a part of and in conjunction with communities. It incorporates a respect for clients that empowers them and assists them in the larger economic, political, and social contexts of their lives, beyond their immediate legal problems.[39]

Following this approach, as discussed above, it is important to consider the ways in which clients and communities might be empowered. To ensure long-term change rather than a short-term fix, community lawyers often work closely with community organizers and other civil society organizations to identify the ways in which the law, or knowledge of law and legal tools, might make a difference. Moreover, Lucie White observes that community lawyering has the potential to not only transform communities, but also transform universities by moving beyond the traditional 'sites of privilege' of professional and academic worlds:

> Clinics can educate other law school faculty about the realities of poverty in their own communities, particularly when those faculty are recruited to work on clinic projects. Clinics can also help redirect the universities' research agendas, as the complexities of systematic poverty and the challenges of poverty advocacy are subjected to sustained, practically-grounded reflection . . . the potential for clinical legal education to transform the people that they touch and the institutions in which they are embedded—that potential is great indeed.[40]

Movement lawyering is related to community lawyering in many respects but tends to refer more explicitly to the ways in which lawyers work together with social movements to achieve their goals. It is aimed at democratic transformation that shifts power towards social movements and away from traditional power holders, which are often elite groups. The goal of using the law is to help movements gain power and change structural conditions that may otherwise serve to create disadvantage.[41] Movement lawyering therefore tends to describe

[37] Jim Freeman, 'Supporting Social Movements: A Brief Guide for Lawyers and Law Students' (2015) 12 Hastings Race & Poverty Law Journal 191, 196.

[38] Jennifer Gordon, 'The Lawyer Is Not the Protagonist: Community Campaigns, Law and Social Change' (2007) 95 California Law Review 2133.

[39] Karen Tokarz et al, 'Conversations on "Community Lawyering": The Newest (Oldest) Wave in Clinical Legal Education' (2008) 28 Washington University Journal of Law and Policy 359, 364.

[40] Lucie E. White, 'The Transformative Potential of Clinical Legal Education' (1997) 35 Osgoode Hall Law Journal 603, 604.

[41] See eg, Austin Sarat and Stuart Scheingold (eds), *Cause Lawyers and Social Movements* (Stanford University Press 2006).

practices which pursue structural and legal reform. Cummings sets out the core features of movement lawyering and offers the following definition:

> A model of practice in which lawyers, accountable to marginalized constituencies, mobilize law to build power to produce enduring social change through deliberate strategies of linked legal and political advocacy.[42]

In his survey of the relevant literature, Cummings categorizes work in this field as 'input' and 'output' campaigns. The former model addresses the factors that cause activists to turn to law as a tool for reform in the first place. The latter addresses the extent to which mobilizing the law advances movement goals in practice. He summarizes the complexity of these often competing understandings of what the law can achieve as follows:

> Law, in its multiple forms, is viewed as both power and peril: constituting justice while instantiating inequality, a tool to resist oppression but also its main instrument, a force for progress yet defender of the status quo. At bottom, these competing visions reflect the gap between what law is and what it aspires to be—a gap that justifies pessimistic appraisals of legal change, but also creates opportunities for transformation by allowing challengers to hold those in power to their promise of fidelity to law.[43]

There is no doubt that lawyers play a role in shaping disputes, and often in helping to design strategies in which movements might create change. From legal challenges in relation to Brexit, access to abortion, freedom of speech, and privacy to medical interventions and the right to life, one cannot underestimate the allure of the law in advancing campaigns. Related to our discussion above, Cummings also finds that the relationship between legal mobilization strategies and political power, as well as the relationship between lawyers and clients and wider strategies for change, is extremely complex. However, in his consideration of 'output' campaigns he highlights the considerable challenge of evaluating the success or failure of different types of legal intervention—for example, whether background conditions have been adequately considered or whether counterfactual analysis has taken place (ie are there alternative explanations for the outcomes achieved?).[44]

The extent to which the law is effective in creating social change has long been a puzzle. Let us consider the 1954 US case of *Brown v Board of Education*, which found that racial segregation in schools was unconstitutional. It was heralded as a great success at the time and is considered by some constitutional scholars as the most important case in US legal history in terms of advancing the civil rights movement. Yet, others have argued that the success of the case has been exaggerated. Klarman suggests that the ruling, and others that followed, in fact did little to alter the prevalence of racial oppression in the US and may even have encouraged extremism.[45] He draws attention to the role of activism, rather than the case itself, in bringing about social change in the decade that followed *Brown* and warns against

[42] Scott Cummings, 'Movement Lawyering' (2017) University of Illinois Law Review 1645, 1653.

[43] Scott Cummings, 'Empirical Studies of Law and Social Change: What Is the Field? What Are the Questions?' (2013) Wisconsin Law Review 171, 174.

[44] Ibid 187–99.

[45] Michael Klarman, *From Jim Crow to Civil Rights: The Supreme Court and the Struggle for Racial Equality* (OUP 2004) 385.

putting too much faith in litigation.[46] He also notes the risks of litigation in failing to help those most in need:

> Litigation is unlikely to help those most desperately in need. We have already seen that the justices, reflecting broader social mores, are unlikely to side with litigants who lack significant social standing. Even once litigants secure Court victories, they must have a certain amount of power in order to enforce them . . . Litigation requires lawyers, economic resources, and some security from physical danger.[47]

Rosenberg similarly highlights examples of other cases, from marriage equality to access to abortion, where the courts themselves cannot be said to be the main drivers of change. He describes both a 'Dynamic' and a 'Constrained' view of the role of the US Supreme Court in society.[48] The former suggests that the Court exerts important influence while the latter sets out the limitations of the Court's power which, Rosenberg argues, means that it has minimal influence in terms of creating social reform. He notes the 'limited nature of constitutional rights', the 'lack of judicial independence', and the 'judiciary's inability to develop inappropriate policies and its lack of powers of implementation'.[49] Rosenberg points to the many actors that play a role in ensuring that change happens in practice including, for example, in passing new legislation or changes to policy at local level, to ensure court decisions have an impact. His overall thesis might even be summarized as: 'people, not courts, make social movements.'[50]

There is no doubt that the 'legacy' phase of a legal intervention can be critical in movement lawyering; that is to say, the years following the case wherein the decision is embedded by way of policy change or strengthening a social movement through related campaigning and awareness raising. By engaging and participating in legacy activities, often over many years, a court decision may be more likely to achieve lasting change.[51]

Before moving to consider another subset of social justice lawyering, we must acknowledge the ethical tensions that arise in movement lawyering. In these instances, the lawyer acts in such a way as to be accountable to the movement itself and its goals, and acts in service to the movement. This can obviously create an ethical quandary—as does cause lawyering more widely—where the lawyer may, for example, put the social movement (or its cause) above the interests of an individual client. What does the lawyer do when those interests might come into conflict? As we explored in Chapter 7, the ethical rules governing professional legal life would demand that a client's best interests be upheld and that the lawyer does not act in such a way as to undermine them. Take, for example, a case where the legal issue in question may serve the wider movement with respect to a potential change in the law that could impact a wide number of people in terms of accessing a particular resource such as

[46] Ibid 381. [47] Ibid 463.

[48] Gerald Rosenberg, *The Hollow Hope: Can Courts Bring About Social Change?* (University of Chicago Press 2008) 1–7.

[49] Ibid 10.

[50] Stephen Carter, 'Do Courts Matter?' (1992) 90 Michigan Law Review 1216, 1220.

[51] Michael McCann, *Rights at Work: Pay Equity Reform and the Politics of Legal Mobilization* (University of Chicago Press 1994).

housing or education. However, let us imagine that the individual client is particularly vulnerable and does not want adverse publicity, or that the outcome in the case, while beneficial to the movement, will not give them the remedy they desire. In these circumstances, if the interests of the client and wider movement cannot be reconciled, it is strictly incumbent upon the lawyer not to pursue the litigation and to find alternative means of redress on behalf of the client. This may, however, have the knock-on impact of losing the faith of the wider movement. As we know from our discussion of legal ethics, there may be no resolute and clear answer to these ethical problems. Of course, different lawyers will deal with such an issue in different ways.

CASE STUDY **Immigration and the Right to Education**

R (on the Application of Tigere) v The Secretary of State for Business, Innovation and Skills [2015] UKSC 57

Those with unsettled immigration status did not have access to student loan entitlements to allow them to access higher education in the UK. Therefore, young people who may have been in the UK from a very young age found themselves unable to complete their university undergraduate degree studies. One young woman, who had been in the UK since the age of 6 and achieved good grades at school, found herself unable to take up a university place. She decided to challenge the blanket ban on student loans. The issue went all the way to the UK Supreme Court, where the court considered whether the ban infringed the right to education (Article 2 of the First Protocol of the European Convention on Human Rights) and unjustifiable discrimination linked to national origin (contrary to Article 14 ECHR). The charity Just for Kids Law, together with the UCL Centre for Access to Justice Clinic, intervened in the case. This meant that they assisted the court, as an independent third party, to better understand the wider impact of the case. UCL students gathered witness statements in support of the intervention by interviewing young people affected by the provisions, and conducted background legal research. Their work, together with that of others involved in the case, assisted the court to find that the policy discriminated based on immigration status and was therefore unlawful. The court case, and the wider campaign, mobilized a movement of young people in the UK inspired by the 'US Dreamers', called 'Let us Learn'. This later became a youth-led organization called 'We Belong', which engages in awareness raising, leadership programmes, and wider campaigns to advocate for a fairer immigration system.

8.2.2 **Anti-racist Lawyering**

Closely related to community and movement lawyering, indeed often embedded within it, is anti-racist lawyering. It has been widely observed that the law itself serves to advantage some while disadvantaging others, all while perpetuating racial hierarchies.[52] Law schools

[52] See eg Danielle Conway, 'Antiracist Lawyering in Practice Begins with the Practice of Teaching and Learning Antiracism in Law School' (2002) 4 Utah Law Review 723.

have also been cited as institutions that have long embedded such racial hierarchies and when they seek to replicate, rather than challenge, them, they risk becoming sites of exclusion and oppression.[53] In the clinical context, scholars have noted the need to reflect upon longstanding approaches and make change:

> We may be too quick to cast aspersions onto the 'old school' methodologies and histories of the rest of the school while avoiding critique of our own clinics and programs. Sometimes, we even perpetuate racial hierarchies in how we operate, unconsciously (or consciously) preferring the status quo to more substantive change . . . if we want anti-racist law schools, we must 'clean up our own houses', or make change in our own clinics, first.[54]

So, what is anti-racist lawyering and what does an anti-racist law school clinic look like? As a starting point, racism can exist and persist at multiple levels, including *individual, institutional*, and *systemic*. The centrality of racism at institutional and systemic levels can especially adversely impact the opportunities available to racialized groups.[55] Racial injustice is also closely embedded and intertwined in societal structures due to the historical consequences of slavery and colonialism, which should be confronted in appropriate ways. Let us take, by way of example, the areas of policing and criminal justice. The 2017 Lammy Review examined the treatment of Black, Asian, and Minority Ethnic (BAME) groups by the criminal justice system and made 35 recommendations including improved data sharing, greater transparency, and evidence-based explanations for disparities between ethnic groups. However, it has been argued that the very approach of the review obfuscated systemic and institutional racism, for example by using terms such as 'unconscious' bias and only implicitly referencing racism. It has been further argued that such an approach seeks to remove blame from criminal justice agencies and practitioners, whereas an explicit anti-racist approach would seek to identify, challenge, and tackle racism at multiple levels.[56]

Anti-racist lawyering therefore aims to surface and respond to the needs and perspectives of those who experience, and are most affected by, racism. For example, a study comprising close engagement with the views and experiences of organizations, movements, and collectives expressly sought to inform potential litigation and other strategies for change at the intersection of racial, social, and economic injustice.[57] A key finding of the study was the interconnectedness of wide-ranging justice issues and racism, for example, the relationship between climate change and other systemic harms related to 'Islamophobia, Afrophobia and anti-Blackness, as well as anti-gypsy and anti-Roma attitudes in laws and policies'.[58]

[53] Peter Goodrich and Linda G Mills, 'The Law of White Spaces: Race, Culture, and Legal Education' (2001) 51 Journal of Legal Education 15, 19. See also Foluke Adebisi, 'Seeking the University That Is Ours: Understanding, Unpacking and Unsettling Black Student Racialised (Un)belonging in UK Law Schools' (2025) 1 The Law Teacher 1–17.

[54] Anne Gordon, 'Cleaning Up Our Own Houses: Creating Anti-racist Clinical Programs' [2022] Clinical Law Review 49–109, 50.

[55] Coretta Phillips, 'Institutional Racism and Ethnic Inequalities: An Expanded Multilevel Framework Journal of Social Policy' (2011) 40(1) Journal of Social Policy 173–92.

[56] See eg Lee Bridges, 'Lammy Review: Will it Change Outcomes in the Criminal Justice System?' (2017) 59(3) Race and Class 80–90.

[57] Patrick Williams et al, *Surfacing Systemic (In)justice: A Community View* (Systemic Justice 2023). Available at https://systemicjustice.ngo/wp-content/uploads/2022/09/SystemicJusticeACommunityView.pdf

[58] Ibid 17.

Likewise, in the access to justice context an inability to enforce rights or access entitlements (such as eg employment, housing, healthcare, or education) could be connected to the denial of citizenship or nationality based on oppressive systemic policies and practices.[59] Participants also expressed frustration at 'the absence of protective laws on one hand, and the absence of protection from laws on the other' (eg absence of adequate anti-discrimination and anti-hate speech law).[60] Such insights derived directly from affected individuals and communities reflects an anti-racist lawyering approach, which can help to better develop collaborative anti-racist strategies for change.

In the criminal justice context, Cox found that UK lawyers need to generally be more proactive in identifying, calling out, and challenging racism in their everyday practice.[61] In focus groups with practitioners, lawyers observed that relevant authorities and key decision makers tended to rely on 'colour-blind' or 'race-neutral' ideologies. Notably, such an approach risks perpetuating systemic harm 'by neglecting to understand the ways that racialised dynamics shape the construction of laws, legal decision-making, and patterns of criminalization'.[62] Cox recommends that lawyers 'summon the courage to have difficult conversations with their clients about their experiences of racism, classism and sexism before the law'.[63] Malkani similarly sets out four key principles for anti-racist lawyering: **reflection**, **creativity**, **collaboration**, and **accountability**. For lawyers to pursue racial justice, they must engage in processes of reflection, adopt creative approaches in their work, collaborate with others, and remain accountable to their clients.[64]

Clinical legal education, especially in view of the centrality of reflective practice, has been said to be an ideal forum for embedding anti-racist law and championing and adopting new approaches. For example, Malna suggests exploration of the following key themes in a clinical context against the background of critical race theory:

1. Understanding autonomy, paternalism, racialised paternalism, and white saviourism, and reflecting on one's own assumptions and actions and working to deconstruct them.
2. Considering whether favourable outcomes for clinical clients are only reached when student and client interests converge.
3. Considering whether student/client interest convergence with a client of colour influences the extent to which lawyering is paternalistic.
4. Considering interest convergence and racialized paternalism in relation to government-granted legal aid.
5. Considering whether law clinics can contribute to racial equity or whether they are perpetuating it by the very provision of pro bono support.[65]

[59] Ibid 20. [60] Ibid 21.

[61] Alexandra Cox, *Race Consciousness and the Law: Criminal Defence Practitioners' Perspectives* (Howard League for Penal Reform 2023).

[62] Ibid 3. See also Michelle Alexander, *The New Jim Crow: Mass Incarceration in the Age of Colorblindness* (The New Press 2010).

[63] Cox (n 61) 9.

[64] Bharat Malkani, *Antiracist Lawyering in Racial Justice and the Limits of the Law* (Bristol University Press 2021) 121–35.

[65] Sumayyah Malna, 'Inspiring Antiracist Lawyers through Clinical Legal Education' in Foluke Adebisi et al (eds), *Decolonisation, Antiracism and Legal Pedagogy: Strategies, Successes and Challenges* (Routledge 2023) 223–38, 232.

Paternalism assumes that people cannot decide for themselves what is good for them and so, whether consciously or not, involves making decisions on behalf of other people. Racialized paternalism makes this assumption about others based on their race. It has been noted that when white lawyers see whiteness as the 'baseline' or 'norm' they view racial identity as something that belongs to others rather than also to themselves.[66] Racialized paternalism might also assume, for example, that certain groups are unable to speak for themselves. Malna observes the importance of understanding and recognizing 'white saviourism' in clinical legal education, which refers to instances when white people might act from a position of superiority, seeing themselves in the best position to help racialized groups. Malna notes that 'intrinsic paternalism' involves offers of help which can ignore the socio-economic, political, and geographical reasons for oppression.[67]

Similar to community lawyering advocated by Lopez above, an anti-racist approach rejects the notion of the 'saviour' lawyer and ensures collaboration, empowerment, and voice. In her seminal article 'Notes on the Hearing of Mrs G', White reflects upon what *meaningful* participation looks like in a legal environment where a client is subordinated by race, gender, and class. White concludes that overcoming systemic bureaucratic barriers will only come from 'diverse, localized institution-building activities' where clients undertake change for themselves and 'on their own ground' rather than having solutions imposed by others.[68] Effective clinical practice, as we explored in Chapter 6, involves constantly engaging and re-evaluating our implicit and explicit assumptions to review, and reconsider, our actions and what might be required at multiple levels to create positive change. This includes reconsidering what meaningful participation looks like and how our own actions as lawyers can serve to promote it.

REFLECTION POINT

Read the extract from Alexandra Cox's report on the reality of trying to take a race-conscious approach in day-to-day criminal legal practice and answer the questions that follow:

> The practitioners who participated in the focus groups were overwhelmingly aware of the racial and ethnic disparities that exist in the justice system in England and Wales, which they witness in their daily work. However, practitioners faced opposition in the courts in their efforts to highlight the roles that race and ethnicity may have played in key decision-making by legal authorities, particularly the police. A number of the practitioners explained that their efforts at being race conscious in their work were often stymied by legal authorities' demands, both explicit and implied, that they be race neutral in their presentation of the facts of the case . . .

[66] Russell Pearce, 'White Lawyering: Rethinking Race, Lawyer Identity and Rule of Law' (2005) 73(5) Fordham Law Review 2081.

[67] Malna (n 65) 50.

[68] Lucie White, 'Subordination, Rhetorical Survival Skills and Sunday Shoes: Notes on the Hearing of Mrs G' (1990) 38 Buffalo Law Review 1–58, 58.

[They] spoke about the challenges of practicing in an environment where they knew that their clients' lives had been negatively affected by racism, but where they felt that they had few avenues to raise those matters as relevant to the criminal case. They talked about facing people in positions of authority in the legal system who would invoke the language of neutrality and colour blindness in the face of stark racial disparities.

. . . Jennifer argued that the only way to face the racism was to address it openly. However, other lawyers felt that it was more challenging to openly address those disparities, particularly in court contexts where they may not be understood by a predominately white judiciary.

(i) What is the difference between a 'race-neutral' and a 'race-conscious' approach?

(ii) Can you think of an example form of words or a set of questions you might ask to illustrate how you might openly address racism:

a. with a fellow student in a client consultation;

b. with a supervising lawyer; and

c. in front of a judge?

A View from Clinical Practice

Cameron Wong McDermott, Lecturer in Social Change and Clinical Legal Education, University of Glasgow

Racial inequality remains embedded across virtually every aspect of UK society. Yet our legal system, through its structures, processes, and the actors that uphold it, operates under the illusion that it is immune from this injustice. Cloaked in values of fairness and equal treatment, the system often defaults to 'colour-blind' policies and practices, despite decades of social psychological research showing that we all harbour bias.[69]

In a survey of 373 legal professionals in England and Wales, 95 per cent of respondents said that racial bias plays some role in the processes or outcomes of the justice system.[70] It is fair to say, however, that racial bias in the law remains something of an uncomfortable subject of discussion among lawyers.

This chapter sets out a case for why we need lawyers and the wider legal system to adopt antiracist approaches. But the more difficult question is *how*.[71] As actors working within structures that often disempower, what can we do to help achieve fairer, more just outcomes for marginalized communities?

[69] Pragya Agarwal, *Sway: Unravelling Unconscious Bias* (Bloomsbury 2020).

[70] The University of Manchester, 'Racial Bias and the Bench: A Response to the Judicial Diversity and Inclusion Strategy (2020–2025)', November 2022.

[71] See The Howard League, *Making Black Lives Matter in the Criminal Justice System: A Guide for Antiracist Lawyers* (The Howard League 2021).

In legal education, the answer begins with how we train future lawyers. While, however, there is growing interest in developing anti-racist pedagogies in UK higher education, what we teach (particularly the sources of knowledge we prioritize) and how we teach it remains steeped in tradition.[72]

Clinical legal education, I believe, offers an underexplored site of possibility to critique the power structures that sustain racial injustice, and the role of law not just as a tool for justice, but as a system that is often complicit in oppression. Through pedagogies rooted in reflection and ethics, clinic provides a foundation through which students can analyse legal frameworks through an anti-racist and intersectional lens, while confronting complex (uncomfortable) questions about systemic and judicial racism, personal bias, and positionality.

Anne Gordon reminds us that if we are serious about antiracist lawyering, we need to critically evaluate our own clinic programmes.[73] So how can we do that?

First, there is a need for more scholarship and examples of practice connecting critical race theory and decolonial research with the everyday work of law clinics: from client relationships and community partnerships to the development of case strategy. Indeed, the growing number of clinical initiatives in the UK supporting racialised and marginalised communities bring into sharp focus the tensions surrounding the role of clinics in advancing social change, and the need to embed antiracist values and methods more explicitly into clinical legal education.

Second, and reflecting on the values that underpin social justice work, we must think more expansively about the pedagogies we use in clinic. The potential of arts, humanities, and cultural methods to inform and transform how we understand and challenge systemic injustice remains underexplored in clinical practice in the UK. Creative expression and activism have long been central to racial justice movements, from the US civil rights movement, to contemporary campaigns in the UK against police brutality, state violence, and institutional racism. Law clinics are well placed to integrate these approaches when exploring the limits of formal legal responses in addressing racial harms.

Third, and finally, we must not shy away from the reality that this work is unfolding in a political climate increasingly marked by backlash. Clinical legal education must respond by not only working to protect and maintain progress, but reimagining how legal education can equip students to challenge power and injustice.

In this respect, Betty Hung describes movement lawyering as a practice of 'love in action' that combines humility, love, and courage.[74] For me, courage lies at the heart of anti-racist lawyering: courage to reform curricula; courage to talk openly with our clients about their experiences of racism; courage to challenge bias in courtrooms; and most of all, courage to look inward, examine our own biases, and reflect critically on our own positionality.

[72] In the context of US legal education, see eg Kimberley Crenshaw, 'Towards a Race-Conscious Pedagogy in Legal Education' (1988) 11(1) National Black Law Journal 1–14, 2.

[73] Anne Gordon, 'Cleaning Up Our Own Houses: Creating Anti-Racist Clinical Programs' (2022) 29 Clinical Law Review 49–109.

[74] Betty Hung, 'Movement Lawyering as Rebellious Lawyering: Advocating with Humility, Love and Courage' (2017) 23 Clinical Law Review 663, 664.

8.2.3 Trauma-Informed Lawyering

In Chapter 6, we considered the importance of reflection in helping to understand clinical experience and, crucially, the role of emotion in clinical legal education. We discussed how it can be challenging to understand why a particular event makes us feel a particular way, especially if we observe that it may not have a similar effect on others. This relates to experiences of trauma, which we might have experienced ourselves or observed in the experience of others (for example, fellow students, clients, or supervising lawyers). In recent years, trauma-informed lawyering approaches have been considered important to empower clients and therefore advance social justice.

Trauma has been defined in different ways and there is some contestation as to what should be included (or not) both in the definition of trauma and in what we mean by 'trauma-informed'. For the purposes of our discussion, we define trauma as resulting from 'an event, series of events, or set of circumstances that is experienced by an individual as harmful or life threatening'.[75]

Importantly, trauma affects different people in different ways. Indeed, whether an event is traumatic depends not only on our individual experience of that event, but also on how it negatively impacts on our emotional, social, spiritual, and physical well-being.[76]

Trauma-informed approaches typically embed six commonly agreed principles:

Safety: the physical, psychological, and emotional safety of service users and staff is prioritized.

Trustworthiness: transparency exists in an organization's policies and procedures, with the objective of building trust among staff, service users, and the wider community.

Choice: service users are supported in shared decision-making, choice, and goal setting to determine the plan of action they need to heal and move forward.

Collaboration: the value of staff and service user experience is recognized in overcoming challenges and improving the system as a whole.

Empowerment: efforts are made to share power and give service users and staff a strong voice in decision-making, at both individual and organizational level.

Cultural consideration: move past cultural stereotypes and biases based on, for example, gender, sexual orientation, age, religion, disability, geography, race, or ethnicity.[77]

It is well recognized that being 'trauma-informed' is necessary but not sufficient depending on the type of trauma and other needs presented by clients or cases. For example, working in the field of legal representation for victim-survivors of sexual violence or asylum

[75] UK Government, *Working Definition of Trauma-Informed Practice* (UK Government Office for Health Improvement and Disparities, 22 November 2022). Available at https://www.gov.uk/government/publications/working-definition-of-trauma-informed-practice/working-definition-of-trauma-informed-practice#:~:text=Trauma%20results%20from%20an%20event,emotional%20or%20spiritual%20well%2Dbeing

[76] NHS Education for Scotland, *Transforming Psychological Trauma: National Trauma Training Programme* (NES 2020).

[77] UK Government (n 75).

seekers who may have suffered torture often requires specialist skills, as well as knowledge of appropriate referral mechanisms and bespoke interventions. A trauma-informed lawyering approach will aim to create a safe environment, reduce stress, and give clients sensitive awareness of choices available to them. From an access to justice perspective, the goal is to ensure that the experience of trauma is not a barrier to effective participation in the justice process. As such, the 'four Rs' of trauma-informed approaches are often relied upon to this end: **realize** the prevalence of traumatic experience; **recognize** the impact of these experiences; **resist** re-traumatization; and **respond** in ways that support recovery.

Many law school clinics have sought to embed trauma-informed approaches and to provide opportunities for students to reflect upon the impact of trauma in clinical casework. Importantly, a trauma-informed approach is also cognisant of the impact of vicarious trauma and seeks to adequately respond, as well as anticipating and minimizing the risk of vicarious trauma where possible.[78] This refers to the negative reaction one might have when working with survivors of trauma. It might include, for example, a response to face-to-face interactions with clients or when reviewing case files and evidence relevant to a traumatic event. We explore the issue of vicarious trauma in clinical legal education in greater depth in Chapter 10.

It is important to recognize that the development of trauma-informed approaches has not been without criticism and debate. Some argue that 'a predominant focus on trauma may construct the kinds of psychological conditions it professes to respond to'.[79] While a trauma-informed approach should be strengths-based and promote resilience, there is perhaps a risk that such approaches limit empowerment by framing traumatized people as needing saving. Some argue, for example, that the identification of marginalized people as traumatized simply constructs and replicates hierarchical power relationships that rely on 'shock and awe'. Others have identified the risk of over-reliance on generalist trauma-informed approaches where specialist intervention, usually by trained expert psychologists in the field, is required. In resource-constrained times, there is a risk that public service providers will favour the former over the latter even where it does not meet the needs of service users. Problems also arise in view of the lack of commonly agreed definitions for both trauma and trauma-informed, which means that it is difficult to both implement and evaluate appropriate interventions.

8.3 Critical Perspectives on Using the Law as a Tool for Change

The academic field of legal mobilization studies has sought to better understand why organizations, communities, and movements might turn to law in pursuit of their goals. Definitions of legal mobilization can vary, but a commonly cited interpretation is that the law is

[78] Joanna Fleck, *Vicarious Trauma in the Legal Profession: A Practical Guide to Trauma, Burnout and Collective Care* (Legal Action Group 2021).

[79] Mark Smith and Sebastian Monteux, 'Trauma Informed Approaches: A Critical Overview of What They Offer to Social Work and Social Care' Iriss Insights (8 March 2023). Available at https://www.iriss.org.uk/resources/insights/trauma-informed-approaches-critical-overview-what-they-offer-social-work-and-social-care#:~:text=The%20Scottish%20Government%20defines%20psychological,physically%20harmful%20or%20life%20threatening

mobilized 'when a desire or want is translated into an assertion of right or lawful claim'.[80] Research in this field has sought to identify the barriers to, and challenges of, using the law. We have already discussed above the issue of lawyers assuming hierarchical roles that may serve to disempower, rather than empower, communities. Other critiques include that limited resources are diverted away from communities and their campaigns towards using costly legal approaches; or that an over-emphasis on litigation and court-centred approaches leads to a misunderstanding of the lawyer's role in promoting social change.[81] It is also clear that challenges that involve political dimensions may not always be suited to the use of the law: they may lead to a mythologizing of rights-based approaches,[82] which can result in reshaping social movements and diverting progress they might have made had they not sought to rely on legal tools.[83] Other scholars have noted that reliance on the law can lead to a focus on individual rights rather than collective action. Regarding human rights-based approaches, they may pose a risk of offering false redemption and solidarity[84] or re-victimization of clients.[85]

The way in which we view transformational change and the role of the law, and lawyers, in creating it might also be potentially problematic. White explains in her reflections below her changing perspective in terms of understanding the phrase 'transformation':

> First, there was the assumption that those other institutions and individuals were indeed in need of 'transformation'. Second, there was the assumption that legal clinics are in a position to determine what 'transformations' are needed, and endowed with the social power to carry out the transformations that they have first prescribed. Third, there was the assumption that clinical educators and their students are an appropriate social agent to execute those transformations. When these assumptions are spelled out, they are quite clearly contestable; indeed, they sound somewhat obnoxious. Particularly in contexts where clinics work with poor people, their institutions, and their communities, it is hard to say exactly why lawyers and legal clinics should designate ourselves to be the privileged agents of other people's social and political change. From where does our knowledge, power, and normative claim to assume their role purport to come?[86]

In Chapter 7, we touched upon the notion of the privilege that comes with having professional legal status as a lawyer. In reflecting on transformation, White observes that instead of asking law school clinics how much potential they have to create change, we might alternatively 'transform who we are, how we see ourselves, what we do in our own practices as to open those practices to the knowledge, power, and human agency of the people with

[80] Francis Zemans, 'Legal Mobilization: The Neglected Role of Law in the Political System' (1983) American Political Science Review 77, 690–703.

[81] Eduardo Capulong, 'Client Activism in Progressive Lawyering Theory' (2009) 16 Clinical Law Review 109.

[82] Stuart Scheingold, *The Politics of Rights: Lawyers, Public Policy and Political Change* (University of Michigan Press 1974).

[83] Catherine Albiston, 'The Dark Side of Litigation as a Social Movement Strategy' (2010) 96 Iowa Law Review 61.

[84] David Kennedy, 'The International Human Rights Movement: Part of the Problem?' (2002) 15 Harvard Human Rights Journal 101.

[85] Dina Francesca Haynes, 'Client-Centered Human Rights Advocacy' (2006) 13 Clinical Law Review 379.

[86] White (n 34) 608.

whom we work'.[87] Indeed, in answer to the question posed above as to whether a lawyer ceases to be a lawyer when they become engaged in politics (or, relatedly, the work of communities and movements), White suggests that we can only answer such a question when we 'stretch the boundaries of the lawyer role through new, less lawyer-dominated advocacy practices'.[88] She reflects on Lopez's work in the context of law school clinics seeking to create change:

> [Lopez's] work suggests that lawyers who seek to transform the world for their clients, or to transform their clients to change the world, risk producing a very different result. For the paradigm within which legal clinics transform others pictures 'the client' or the 'community' as the entity with the 'problem' that needs the help of lawyers in order to 'change'. This paradigm attributes to lawyers the insight to translate those problems into the symptoms of political and economic subordination. It then authorizes lawyers to prescribe the practices—be they impact litigation or community organizing—that will reverse those pathologies. Within this paradigm, it is the lawyers but not the clients, who are called upon to act in the roles of fully human beings. In contrast, the clients are called upon to respond to the lawyer's questions, and to comply with the lawyers' instructions . . . The era of vanguard visions is over. The theories which grounded those visions are in crisis. The violence which those visions has supported is finally getting exposed in every area of social and political life. We can no longer repress this insight and return to a complacent practice which positions us to draw the blueprints for changing other people's lives. Rather, we have no morally consistent option except to confront and embrace the tension between our aspirations to 'fix' the blatant injustices of poverty, and the poverty of our claims to undertake that task.[89]

Notably, legal education itself is often perceived to be a barrier to developing community and movement lawyering. Even in the US context, where the practice is arguably more established in the UK and has greater prevalence in law school curricula, the following has been observed:

> First, we must recognize that most legal education and training does not prepare one for effective movement lawyering. On the contrary, in many respects it produces or reinforces a set of traits that we must recognize and resist if we are to successfully support social movements. Instead, we must enhance and expand upon our training by adopting different approaches to addressing legal or social problems, embracing a broader collection of advocacy strategies and tactics, acquiring new skill sets, and being willing to discard those aspects of our formative legal education that hinder our efforts.[90]

[87] White (n 34) 608.
[88] White (n 34) 609.
[89] White (n 34) 610–11.
[90] Freeman (n 37) 194.

Freeman identifies five essential elements for movement lawyering:

(i) Dedication to building the capacity and power of oppressed communities;
(ii) Willingness to address the root causes of structural disempowerment and oppression;
(iii) Use of knowledge, skills and connections to support community organising and movement building;
(iv) Commitment to meeting the full array of the on the ground advocacy needs; and
(v) Professional humility.[91]

Again, we come to the importance of reflection for maximizing opportunities for learning. This can begin at law school by asking questions about the possibilities, and limitations, of using the law in the areas in which clinics might work and considering whether service delivery fosters community participation and empowerment or, conversely, might serve to limit it.

TAKING STOCK

We have considered the 'how' of lawyers using the law for social change. The law might be used to empower, inform, and persuade or to challenge and enforce. Different theories have developed in recent years to guide the work of lawyers working in the public interest to overcome the main critiques of using the law as a tool for social change. These theories include, for example, community and movement lawyering, anti-racist lawyering, and trauma-informed lawyering. Taken together, we can see that they collectively aim to promote equality, challenge the traditional hierarchical role of the lawyer in society, and create long-term systemic, rather than symptomatic, change.

8.4 The Role of Pro Bono

We have considered the ways in which lawyers use different legal tools in partnership with communities and movements to advance particular social justice goals. This work, for some lawyers, may be undertaken in a pro bono capacity somewhat to the side of their usual day-to-day legal practice. For others, pro bono work is undertaken as a more discrete activity relevant to their area of practice; for example, volunteering in a local law centre to provide advice to small businesses or on employment matters. In this section we will consider different types of pro bono provision, which often form part of a law firm's corporate social responsibility or sustainability agenda.

[91] Freeman (n 37) 195–203.

Pro bono comes from the Latin phrase *pro bono publico*, which means 'for the public good'. It generally refers to legal work that is done voluntarily and without payment in the public interest. Clinical legal education and pro bono often serve to complement one another in the delivery of services and projects. The Pro Bono Protocol designed by the charity Law Works in England and Wales gives the following definition of pro bono:

> 1.1 When we refer to Pro Bono Legal Work we mean legal advice or representation provided by lawyers in the public interest including to individuals, charities and community groups who cannot afford to pay for that advice or representation and where public and alternative means of funding are not available.
>
> 1.2 Legal work is Pro Bono Legal Work only if it is free to the client, without payment to the lawyer or law firm (regardless of the outcome) and provided voluntarily either by the lawyer or his or her firm.
>
> 1.3 Pro Bono Legal Work is always only an adjunct to, and not a substitute for, a proper system of publicly funded legal services.

The definition includes that pro bono should always be free to the client and it will only be pro bono work if that is the case. It is also important to note that the definition incorporates the assumption that pro bono should rest alongside, rather than being a substitute for, a proper system of publicly funded legal services (ie legal aid). The protocol therefore seeks to codify a rule that has developed over many years in the UK context, which is that the availability of publicly funded advice or representation should *always* be considered before a lawyer undertakes pro bono work.[92] This rule is intended to minimize the potential for pro bono work to undermine the provision of legal aid, as well as ensuring that expert lawyers are relied upon where possible within particular areas of law.[93] We saw in Chapter 3 how, in resource-constrained times, it may be tempting for the state to cut back publicly funded provision and make the argument that lawyers should be providing services on a pro bono basis to meet access to justice needs instead. Such arguments are often directed at large commercial law firms averaging revenues of billions of pounds, with profits per equity partner of several millions of pounds a year.[94]

We discussed in Chapter 2 the importance of access to justice, and in Chapter 3 we considered the many areas of law where it is not possible to obtain state-funded legal support either because the area of law is not in 'scope' for legal aid funding or because eligibility requirements are not met. We discussed the rising 'justice gap' in the UK context, where people may not be eligible for legal aid due to their income but otherwise cannot afford legal advice and representation. Pro bono has an important role to play in meeting these legal needs, for example, through the provision of free legal advice clinics. Indeed, some law school clinics

[92] Lawworks, Joint Pro Bono protocol, section 2.2.

[93] Robert Abbey and Andy Boon, 'The Provision of Free Legal Services by Solicitors: A Review of the Report of the Law Society's Pro Bono Working Party' (1995) 2 International Journal of the Legal Profession 261, 265.

[94] See eg Clifford Chance, 'Revenues surpass £2bn with profit per equity partner maintained at £2mn' (19 July 2023).

run only through the commitment of time pro bono by lawyers who act in a supervisory capacity. Another important example of pro bono work relates to representation in courts and tribunals. It can be extremely daunting to have a date for a court hearing and no legal representation, nor the means to pay for it. Organizations such as the Free Representation Unit, Advocate, and the Free Legal Services Unit (FLSU) will provide supervised volunteer students or barristers/advocates at hearings provided certain criterion have been met. For example, if legal aid is available, it is unlikely that free representation will be provided. A similar conclusion will be reached if a client has legal expenses insurance or the court hearing is less than three weeks away. Such services, especially in, for example, welfare benefits and employment tribunals, where large numbers of individuals are likely to otherwise appear as litigants in person, are extremely valuable. For early career lawyers, there can be strong motivations to do pro bono work, not only to put legal skills to good use but also to support one's own training and development.[95] Engaging in pro bono work might even allow for more opportunities to do more complex work at a higher court level than otherwise offered during training.

Arguments in favour of lawyers plugging the access to justice gap in society also relate to questions of whether pro bono provision should be mandatory. There is no doubt that pro bono work has become an important part of professional legal identity for lawyers. In some jurisdictions, it is compulsory either at the stage of legal education and training, during legal practice, or both. For example, in 2012 the New York State Court of Appeals adopted a rule requiring that all applicants to the New York State Bar had to complete at least 50 hours of pro bono. Such mandatory requirements also exist in other jurisdictions, such as Indonesia, Japan, and the Philippines. As we explored in Chapter 7, this aligns with the notion that lawyers have a heightened moral obligation by virtue of their role as lawyers in society. Some argue that the moral duty placed on lawyers can be understood as a duty to help those who do not otherwise have access to the law.[96] However, it is not necessarily clear that lawyers 'should' provide pro bono services and there may well be negative unintended consequences in the mandatory delivery of pro bono. In his article 'The Paradoxes of Pro Bono', Richard Abel considers the way in which volunteerism in the provision of legal services is problematic.[97] Again, we begin to see why motivation can be so important. For example, if a commercial law firm engaging in pro bono activity is more focused on the 'gains', there may well be negative unintended consequences; for example, delivering advice in areas of law that lawyers may not have sufficient experience in, or lacking the skills needed to represent clients who have experienced vulnerability and trauma. A law firm might ignore these issues in favour of, for example, positive publicity, casework training for trainees, or aligning itself with an issue it knows might lead to more commercial work due to those aligned interests.

95 Lisa Webley, 'Pro Bono and Young Solicitors: Views from the Front Line' (2001) 3 Legal Ethics 152–68, 157.

96 Reed Elizabeth Loder, 'Tending the Generous Heart: Mandatory Pro Bono and Moral Development' (2001) 14 Georgetown Journal of Legal Ethics 459, 463.

97 Richard Abel, 'The Paradoxes of Pro Bono' (2010) 78 Fordham Law Review 2443.

REFLECTION POINT

Consider the extract below from Richard Abel's article 'The Paradoxes of Pro Bono':

> Pro bono is a puzzle. It provides high quality legal services to large numbers of clients who would otherwise go unrepresented, thereby helping to fulfil our legal system's promise of 'Equal Justice under Law'. But what a bizarre way to address a foundational element of liberal legalism. Could we imagine relying on volunteerism to perform other core governmental functions: police (the deputy sheriffs of the frontier are a distant memory), national security (privateers), foreign relations (honorary consuls), education (volunteer parents as the only teachers), or transportation (hitchhiking)? There is something very strange about having privileged lawyers—who earn huge incomes by acting for large corporations and wealthy individuals—constitute a major source of legal representation for the poor and subordinated.[98]

- Do you think that delivering legal services to those who cannot otherwise afford it through voluntary pro bono work is problematic?
- What might the negative consequences of pro bono work be?
- What are the advantages of delivering legal advice and representation in this way?

Relatedly, Cummings describes an 'institutionalization' of pro bono work by large law firms in recent years. Almost all large corporate firms have pro bono departments, which have become 'centralized and streamlined, distributed through an elaborate institutional structure by private lawyers acting out of professional duty'.[99] Large law firms started to be ranked for their pro bono work from around the 2000s, leading to new management structures, allocation of resource and the opportunity to gain public prestige. Many firms view the development of pro bono as a way to help 'sell' the firm in terms of attracting the best recruits.[100] As law students request information about pro bono from prospective firms, so the firms increasingly feature pro bono in their marketing materials.[101] In large corporate law firms, evidence also tends to suggest that engaging in pro bono work elevates the status of early career lawyers and is pursued as an 'elite strategy' towards success.[102] Pro bono is now heavily managed such that individual lawyers have responsibility for running comprehensive, often international, pro bono programmes together with large teams of coordinators and specialists. Some lawyers act as managers and oversee pro bono work, and some firms even have a

[98] Ibid 2443.

[99] Scott Cummings, 'The Politics of Pro Bono' (2004) 52 UCLA Law Review 1.

[100] Marc Galanter and Thomas Palay, 'Public Service Implications of Evolving Law Firm Size and Structure' in Robert Katzman (ed), *The Law Firm and the Public Good* (Brookings Institute Press 1995) 19–58.

[101] Esther Lardent, 'Structuring Law Firm Pro Bono Programs: A Community Service Typology' in Robert Katzman (ed), *The Law Firm and the Public Good* (Brookings Institute Press 1995) 59–89.

[102] Ronit Dinovitzer and Bryant Garth, 'Pro Bono as an Elite Strategy in Early Lawyer Careers' in Robert Granfield and Lynn Mather (eds), *Private Lawyers and the Public Interest: The Evolving Role of Pro Bono in the Legal Profession* (OUP 2009) 115–34.

'pro bono partner'. It has been observed that this may result in a struggle in terms of being perceived as a manager rather than a 'real lawyer', and most pro bono managers work to ensure they still practise law in addition to their management or training roles.[103] Research has also shown gender differences in relation to pro bono work: a US study demonstrates that men are more likely to engage in impact litigation, criminal representation, or multiple areas of practice, whereas women are more likely to work on family law, immigration, or human rights.[104]

Practical Exercise 8.1

Together with another student from your class, choose a side and think of at least three arguments for and against the statement below. Each present your arguments and debate the proposition:

'Pro bono is so important in the access to justice landscape that all lawyers should be required to undertake a minimum amount of pro bono hours each year.'

When pro bono is heavily managed in this way in large firms, it arguably begins to change its shape and ethos. Rhode observes that such lawyers may not necessarily be giving time as *volunteers* to pro bono, given that the firm itself compensates them—or allows them—to work in a pro bono capacity in addition to their billable targets.[105] It has been suggested that despite lawyers' altruistic intentions and desire to undertake pro bono, this would be difficult in large law firms without the support structure offered by the firm.[106] As such, in order to provide pro bono at scale, such bureaucracy and high levels of management are inevitable. Research also shows some divergence in terms of what lawyers consider might count as pro bono activity.[107] For example, and in a very different professional context to large corporate firms, there is naturally some reluctance to term the finishing of legal aid cases 'for free' when funding runs out.[108] Webley offers some observations on early career lawyers' motivation and commitment to pro bono below:

> All levels of the young profession considered that a commitment to pro bono would improve the profession's image, even though those approaching senior status are more likely to consider pro bono to be a public relations exercise rather than a duty. Seniority appears to diminish the view that pro bono is part of a solicitor's professional and ethical obligations. This does not, however, extinguish an acceptance of the merit of pro bono to the community. Whilst many were convinced that the service that pro

[103] Atinuke Adediran, 'Negotiating Status: Pro Bono Partners and Counsels in Large Law Firms' (2022) 47(2) Law and Social Inquiry 635–68.

[104] Ibid 637.

[105] Deborah Rhode, 'Pro Bono in Principle and Practice' (2003) 53(3) Journal of Legal Education 413–64.

[106] Andrew Boon and Avis Whyte, 'Charity Begins at Home: The Aetiology of the New Culture of Pro bono Publico' (1999) Legal Ethics 169.

[107] Webley (n 95). [108] Ibid 154.

> bono clients received was of a good standard, others were more sceptical and some very critical. And yet young solicitors are concerned about their ability to carry out the work, to spend sufficient time on cases for pro bono clients and, understandably also, that they will progress in their careers.[109]

A key point raised by the sample in Webley's study was the extent to which pro bono is consistently of a good standard. Notably, it can be difficult to measure pro bono when definitions vary and there is a lack of consistency in terms of reporting.[110] However, large law firms have not been without criticism for failing to properly measure the impact of their pro bono work, and generally being more likely to showcase it rather than evaluating it.[111] In order to ensure good standards of pro bono work are adhered to, many jurisdictions have adopted rules and guidance to govern pro bono activity. For example, in England and Wales, the charity LawWorks developed a protocol to promote greater clarity about the purpose of pro bono and set out expected standards of work. Reflecting on one's own motivation for doing pro bono work, following relevant protocols, and engaging in effective monitoring and evaluation processes can all go some way to ensuring the pro bono contribution made leads to a positive social justice impact.

REFLECTION POINT

Consider the motivations below which might relate to why you have chosen to participate in clinical casework or a pro bono project at law school.

- Opportunity to help those facing economic, cultural, or social disadvantage
- Opportunity to make access to justice more equitable
- Opportunity to enable social change
- Opportunity to have a positive impact on society
- Opportunity to improve access to justice
- Opportunity to change or make better laws
- Opportunity to hold government accountable
- Opportunity to make a fairer society
- Opportunity to make a difference to my community
- Shared values
- Opportunity to gain experience
- Opportunity to develop legal skills

[109] Webley (n 95) 168.

[110] Fiona Mcleay, 'The Legal Profession's Beautiful Myth: Surveying the Justifications for the Lawyer's Obligation to Perform Pro Bono Work' (2008) 15(3) International Journal of the Legal Profession 249–71, 251.

[111] Steven Vaughan et al, 'Symbolism over Substance? Large Law Firms and Corporate Social Responsibility' (2015) 18(2) Legal Ethics 138–63.

- Sense of professional obligation
- Opportunity to apply my skills to help others
- Opportunity to network and meet lawyers in the field.[112]
  - (i) Which of these motivations, if any, apply to you?
  - (ii) Can you choose what your top three motivations are?
  - (iii) For those that don't apply, why do you not consider them relevant?

Conclusion

This chapter engaged with a range of issues raised by the work that lawyers do in the pursuit of social justice. The concept of legal empowerment was introduced both with respect to providing individuals with legal information, advice, and representation, and concerning building power more widely for organizations and communities. We saw that some lawyers in society are explicit about the extent to which they use the law to further particular causes, challenge the unlawful use of state power, and help individuals who might not otherwise be able to enforce their rights. We were introduced to subsets of 'cause lawyering', which developed over the past 50 years, especially interrogating the way in which lawyers can work together with communities and movements to use the law in pursuit of shared goals. We also considered the role of anti-racist and trauma-informed approaches in terms of addressing unequal power relationships, ensuring safety, and maximizing participation.

Large law firm pro bono provision has exponentially expanded and institutionalized since the early 2000s. Pro bono is an important way in which access to justice needs in society can be met. While it should never be a substitute for properly funded legal advice by the state, in times of access to justice crisis the availability of pro bono is a lifeline for those who would otherwise not have legal advice and representation. We saw that it is important to interrogate the way in which pro bono is managed and delivered, and especially to ensure it is properly measured and improved. There can perhaps sometimes be an assumption that if a service is provided for free it is 'better than nothing'; yet, legal interventions made without appropriate training and expertise, and under effective supervision, regrettably risk doing more harm than good.

Developments in the arena of law and social justice have received much scholarly attention. There have been longstanding debates about whether lawyers are effective allies for grassroots organizations and community groups, or simply elite players whose professional status and privilege can limit the chances of success and displace other more effective strategies for change. It seems clear that under certain conditions, and accounting for different drivers and consequences of legal action, impactful social change is possible when using the law. As with so many other issues raised by clinical legal practice, it is critically important

[112] Adapted from Catrina Denvir et al, *Legal Aid and the Future of Access to Justice* (Hart 2023).

that law students and lawyers take a reflexive approach, mindful of both their own motivations and the impact of their interventions and the lived and learned experience of those they represent.

Further reading

Frank S Bloch (ed), *The Global Clinical Movement: Educating Lawyers for Social Justice* (OUP 2011).

Faith Gordon and Daniel Newman (eds), *Leading Works in Law and Social Justice* (Routledge 2021).

Bharat Malkani, *Racial Justice and the Limits of the Law* (Bristol University Press 2024).

William P Quigley, 'Letter to a Law Student Interested in Social Justice' (2007) 1(1) DePaul Journal for Social Justice 7–22.

SECTION THREE

Legal Skills for Clinical Legal Education

Core Skills: Getting Started in a Clinical Legal Setting

9

Chapter Overview

This chapter looks at three core skills that will underpin all your work in a clinical legal setting. We begin with some practical advice and tips on the importance of communication skills in any legal setting. We go on to provide advice on how to manage a legal file: keeping your files organized and following the rules associated with your setting provide the foundations for ensuring that professional codes of practice are adhered to. It is likely that you will find the pace and workload of experiential learning in a clinical setting different to that of other law courses, and the final section of this chapter offers advice and guidance on how to manage your time in the clinic effectively.

Having read the chapter and engaged with the exercises, you will be able to:

- Describe different types of verbal and non-verbal communication
- Recognize the need for different tone and register of language depending on the intended recipient
- Explain the importance of good file management to comply with professional and ethical standards expected of practising lawyers
- Identify practical examples of how to keep clear records of client work and record time accurately
- Reflect on different techniques to manage your time effectively

Introduction

Communication is the foundation of working with other people and maintaining relationships with peers, supervisors, and clients. Up to this point in your legal studies it is likely that the majority of your work will have been produced for the sole purpose of achieving a mark. Whether giving an oral presentation, producing a poster, writing an essay, or sitting an exam, you may not have thought about your work as a form of communication. However, whether your law clinic work is part of an assessed module or an extra-curricular project, you may need to change how you think about your work. A client letter may be assessed and awarded a grade, but the letter has another purpose, which is to communicate with the client in a way that is clear. You may produce file notes because you have been told you have to or because your file is being marked, but you are also writing them so that supervisors and peers can find out what work has been done on the file. This is extremely important in terms of progressing legal casework. In Chapters 11 and 12 we will look at the practicalities involved in interviewing clients, drafting letters and other documents, advocacy, and negotiation. This chapter begins by exploring the different types of communication that provide a foundation for the practical legal skills in the following three chapters.

In Chapter 7 we discussed the professional conduct rules and ethical obligations that underpin legal practice. Good file management is part of the practical application of those rules. Keeping accurate records of work done and work to be done creates an audit trail that protects you and your supervisor if complaints are made. It also enables teamwork and efficient supervision as records can easily be found and reviewed. There are different ways of organizing files and most firms will have house rules, but there are core principles that apply to all file management, whether you use a case management system or still work with paper-based files. The section on file management in this chapter will take you through the basics of file management and there are downloadable templates for file notes on the companion website.

Learning to manage time comes more naturally to some people than others. Being able to plan your work forms a part of the SRA competence statement because legal work normally involves working to multiple deadlines and the consequences of missing deadlines can be serious for the client. In a student law clinic you are likely to have a limited number of cases, and work will be paced to allow supervisors time to check your work before sending it to clients. You will probably have to work to shorter deadlines than the usual university timescales. This may suit you as it may help you to focus, or you may find it difficult to fit clinic work into your normal week. This chapter will take you through some different ways of organizing time and help you to reflect on time management strategies. We would encourage you to use your time in a law clinic setting to explore ways of organizing your work so that you can find out what works for you.

9.1 Communicating Clearly and Effectively

Below (Table 9.1) is an extract from the SRA Statement of Solicitor Competence. Refer to the companion website to this book to find a downloadable template to audit your skills and help you reflect on your development.

9.1.1 Why Communication Skills?

Humans are highly social animals. We usually learn to communicate at an early age, so you may think, having practised communication for so long, that you are already a good communicator. However, not all communicating is the same and most of us have weak spots. You might be very confident at getting up and giving a presentation in front of a large group of people, but not consider yourself confident in listening or reading other people's body

Table 9.1[1] Statement of solicitor competence on communication

C1 Communicate clearly and effectively, orally and in writing, including:	Questions to Consider
a. Ensuring that communication achieves its intended objective	
b. Responding to and addressing individual characteristics effectively and sensitively	Do you have experience in these competencies?
c. Using the most appropriate method and style of communication for the situation and the recipient(s)	How would you rate your competence?
d. Using clear, succinct and accurate language avoiding unnecessary technical terms	Do you need more experience?
e. Using formalities appropriate to the context and purpose of the communication	How could you gain experience?
f. Maintaining the confidentiality and security of communications	
g. Imparting any difficult or unwelcome news clearly and sensitively	

language. You might be very shy and find it hard to contribute to a seminar discussion, but communicate well in writing. Your ability to communicate well is context-specific. In a new situation, it is not unusual to feel anxious and find it harder to communicate. Sometimes you may have to deal with a difficult person and this could throw you, leaving you feeling unable to manage the situation you find yourself in.

On a law degree, students' time is spent learning about rules, cases, and relevant theory. It is therefore common to lose sight of the fact that the legal profession is a client-focused profession. Law in practice involves communicating with clients, other lawyers, professional experts, legal administrators, and often the judiciary. A trainee solicitor in a large commercial or corporate firm may have little direct contact with clients in person, but will communicate with them in letters and emails. Lawyers working in legal aid law firms or in the voluntary sector often find they have to use a range of different communication methods, depending on client needs. In a university law clinic, it is extremely likely that students will be involved in interviewing a client and writing a letter of advice. They may also attend court or tribunal hearings. It is likely they will work with other students, a supervisor, an administrator, other lawyers, and possibly court staff or judges. Some encounters will be very formal, others quite informal, and finding the right tone between formality and informality is not easy.

[1] https://www.sra.org.uk/solicitors/resources/continuing-competence/cpd/competence-statement/ (last accessed 27 November 2025).

The ability to communicate is one of the competencies expected in a qualified solicitor, yet 20 per cent of complaints about solicitors that were upheld by the Legal Ombudsman in 2020–21 were about poor communication. Another 17 per cent were about delay and failure to progress a case, which often comes down to poor communication.[2] Clinical legal experience provides opportunities to identify different ways of communicating in a work environment and to reflect on your strengths and weaknesses in communication.

9.1.2 What Do We Mean When We Talk about Communication?

Communication is about an exchange of information between two or more people. It is easy to forget this and focus energy on the way we are transmitting information, without thinking about or analysing the information coming from the other person or people or the audience for which the information is intended. An important part of communication is noticing and understanding what is being communicated.

Communication is not just about speaking. Different kinds of communication include:[3]

- Language (speech, sign language, and writing)
- Paralanguage—intonation, accent, and tone of voice
- Facial expressions
- Gestures
- Body movement and posture
- Choice of medium (eg telephone, email, video call, letter, etc)
- Personal appearance and clothing
- Decoration or design of the environment
- Audio-visual aid (eg PowerPoint)

All of these channels might be used at once and few people are skilled at processing all of this information all of the time.

REFLECTION POINT

Buildings and their surroundings communicate messages to visitors before they engage with the people inside. Think about your law clinic. What is your building like? Is it part of a modern glass building on the university campus, or do you have dedicated premises for the clinic? Some universities have law clinic spaces in shopping centres or on local high streets. What messages do you think your building gives to your client group? Do you think that the clients feel welcomed or intimidated by the building?

[2] Legal Ombudsman's Annual Report for year ending 31st July 2021 at page 8, https://www.legalombudsman.org.uk/media/f5xfeyd5/olc-annual-report-20-21-final.pdf (last accessed 27 November 2025).

[3] Marie Reid and Richard Hammersley, *Communicating Successfully in Groups* (Routledge 2000) 13.

Non-verbal Communication

There are seven basic types of non-verbal communication and it is normal for them all to be used at once.[4] Most will vary according to context and culture so can be hard to read:

1. Proximity—how close we stand to someone, and how often we touch them (if at all).
2. Posture—how people sit, stand, or walk.
3. Body behaviour—fiddling, twitching, doodling.
4. Facial expressions and gestures—some facial expressions are universal, such as anger, disgust, happiness, sadness, and fear.
5. Gaze and eye contact—too much or too little eye contact can be awkward.
6. Quality of speech—tone, pitch, volume, pace, and hesitancies.
7. Self-presentation—appearance and dress.

The social rules or norms governing non-verbal means of communication vary depending on context and culture. For example, standing very close to someone and touching their arm as you speak could be disrespectful or it could be friendly. The same gesture can mean completely different things in different cultures. For example, nodding your head can signal agreement or disagreement depending on the culture. We often don't analyse non-verbal communication carefully, but use it to create an impression of the type of person we have just met. This impression could be quite wrong if we have misread the signals. A first step to improving communication skills is to start noticing non-verbal cues in yourself and in others and take time to think about what they might mean or how they might be construed by others.

Non-verbal Communication and People on the Autistic Spectrum

People on the autistic spectrum communicate differently.[5] In particular, they may find it very difficult to understand non-verbal communication. It can also be difficult for an autistic person to make eye contact and they may find it very uncomfortable if you stand too close to them. To a neurotypical person someone on the autistic spectrum may appear rude because they don't make eye contact or because they misread non-verbal signals.

If you work with someone or have a client who does not look at you and does not make small talk, they may not intend to be rude; they may simply be communicating in a different way.

If you have a client or colleague who you know is on the autistic spectrum, find out how you can adapt your communication.

[4] Marie Reid and Richard Hammersley, *Communicating Successfully in Groups* (Routledge 2000) chapter 3.

[5] Rob George, Laura Crane, and Anna Remington, 'Our Normal is Different: Autistic Adults' Experiences of the Family Courts' (2020) 42 Journal of Social Welfare and Family Law 2.

Emotions and Communication

As law students starting out in a law clinic, you may be thinking about communication in terms of sharing knowledge and information, but problems with communication often arise because a listener has failed to deal with emotions. Thinking like a lawyer and being objective does not mean that emotions need to be ignored or suppressed. Failing to recognize and deal with emotions when communicating with others can lead to conflict or breakdown in relationships.

Effective Listening

Listening effectively is an important first step to recognizing another person's emotions.

1. Pay attention to what the other person is saying, both verbally and non-verbally.
2. Demonstrate that you are paying attention with verbal and non-verbal cues such as nodding in agreement.
3. Reflect back to the speaker by summarizing content and feelings:
   a. 'So, you have three pieces of coursework due next week.'
   b. 'You seem quite worried about how you are going to manage to get all this done.'

Acknowledging emotion enables both people to continue a conversation in a constructive way and avoid misunderstanding or conflict.[6] In the examples above, acknowledging the worry about how to manage the deadlines may make it possible to agree how and when the clinic work can get done. This conversation might go very differently if the first response was 'You must prioritize your clinic work, as clients depend on you and these deadlines are non-negotiable'.

REFLECTION POINT

Law clinic work is often very different from other learning at university. Students starting in the clinic can feel anxious or worried about the experience.

How did you feel when you started in the clinic? How about the other students? Did you feel able to share what you were thinking with a supervisor or other students? What advice would you give to new students starting a clinic project or module?

9.1.3 The Purpose of Written Communication

Who are you communicating with and why?

For most of your education, you will have produced written work for assessments. There is often a focus on using language creatively, avoiding short and simple sentences. In a law

[6] Marie Reid and Richard Hammersley, *Communicating Successfully in Groups* (Routledge 2000) chapter 4.

clinic setting you may need to re-learn some of your writing habits. It is helpful to think of each file note, letter, or email as a form of communication. You need to think about the purpose of the communication:

- Who will read it and why?
- What does the reader need to know?
- If you are sending an email to a lawyer acting for your opponent, have you introduced yourself and explained who your client is and why you are contacting them?

Keep your language simple. State who you are and why you are writing. For example:

- If you need information, ask a clear question or series of questions: 'Could you confirm whether you would like to attend your meeting in person or by video call?'
- If you are answering an email or a letter, say so—for example: 'I am writing in response to your email of 23rd February.'
- If you need to send a reminder say: 'I am writing to remind you that . . . '
- Or you may be sending an email to follow up on a conversation: 'Following our telephone conversation this afternoon, I am writing to confirm that . . . '

9.1.4 **Culture and Communication**

Be aware of cultural differences. Accept them and adapt how you communicate. Be careful not to make assumptions about culture and communication that are based on stereotypes. Start by thinking and reflecting on your own culture. Culture is not something that other people have; we all have culture and often don't stop to think about the social rules that we take for granted. It is important that you don't assume that you know what the rules of someone else's culture are and take care not to assume that you know what someone's cultural background might be from their ethnicity.

If you are worried that you have offended someone, for example by standing too close or by being overly familiar, just ask and apologize. It is not your fault if you do not understand the rules, but it is poor communication if you don't notice that something is wrong, or neglect to do something about it. Similarly, if someone offends you with a gesture that you find rude or insensitive, find a way to tell them that does not lead to a confrontation or further offence. You could say: 'I don't know if you realize, but the gesture you just made can be considered rude. I am just asking if you are annoyed with me, or was it a mistake?'[7]

It is not only non-verbal communication that varies according to culture. Many of the rules and norms around digital communication vary according to regions and cultures. For example, emojis have different meanings in different countries.[8] Social norms and expectations around the culture of written communication vary in different cultures. Starting emails

[7] Peter Washer, *Clinical Communication Skills* (OUP 2009) chapter 8.

[8] Alex Rawlings, 'Why emoji mean different things in different cultures' (2008) BBC Futures, https://www.bbc.com/future/article/20181211-why-emoji-mean-different-things-in-different-cultures (last accessed 27 November 2025).

with 'dear' or 'hi', referring to the recipient on a first-name basis on the first interaction, or starting with no salutation (Dear Dr Smith) can be seen as overly formal or inappropriately informal depending on culture.[9] If you are not sure about email etiquette, seek guidance from a supervisor.

9.1.5 **Tone and Register**

Dividing communication into categories of formal and informal is often too simplistic. When you communicate with your supervisor, you may do this by text, by email, or face to face. This may impact on the level of formality you use. There may be a difference in the way that you communicate with your supervisor if they are also a lecturer at your university or rather a supervisor from an external law firm who is reviewing your letter of advice. If you are contacting a lawyer representing the other side, you may start out very formal, but become less formal over a period of time. You can follow the cue of the person you are corresponding with. For example, you may want to write to another lawyer and address them as Ms Jones, but if when they reply they sign as Katy, when you reply, address them as 'Dear Katy'. Even when you are writing a formal letter, keep your grammar and your language structure clear and simple.

Practical Exercise 9.1

In Table 9.2 below, look at the different messages and decide which one you think is appropriate given the context.

Table 9.2

Communication	Formal	Less formal	Informal
A text to your client	Dear Mr Smith, We are writing to confirm that we can offer you an appointment at 5pm on Tuesday 27th February. Please advise us whether this appointment time is convenient for you. Yours sincerely, Law Clinic Admin	Hi John, we have an appointment at 5pm on Friday. Please text back to tell us if that time is OK for you. Thanks, Law Clinic Admin	Hey John, Can you come and see us at 5pm on Tuesday 27th Feb? Let us know if that's OK.

[9] Erica Dhawan, *Digital Body Language: How to Build Trust and Connection No Matter the Distance* (Harper Collins 2021), 212–18. This text gives a helpful summary of some of the common pitfalls of communicating by email across cultures.

Table 9.2 (Continued)

Communication	Formal	Less formal	Informal
Email to external supervisor, a volunteer solicitor from a local firm who is providing feedback on your draft advice letter	Dear Mrs Singh, I am just writing to ask whether you received my draft letter last week. I would be grateful if you could give me an indication of when I will be receiving feedback. Thank you for your time. Yours sincerely, Ade	Dear Jyoti, I hope you don't mind me contacting you, but did you get my draft letter? I am keen to get it finished, so could you let me know when I'm likely to get feedback. Many thanks, Ade.	Hi Jyoti, I hope my draft letter is OK. I need to finish it off so can you send me any feedback soon. ☺ Cheers, Ade
WhatsApp to your student group	Dear All, I am writing to let you know that I have booked a meeting room for 3pm on Wednesday 14th March. It is really important that we all meet to finalize the client letter. Please confirm by return that you can attend at that time. Yours sincerely, Beth	Hi All, I am just writing to confirm that I've booked a meeting room for 3pm on Weds this week. Can you all come? We need to get the letter finished. Best, Beth	Meeting room booked for 3pm on Weds. Everyone needs to come. Letter nearly finished. Beth
Teams chat message to your tutor	Dear Dr Kaminski, I am writing to inform you that I will be unable to attend my case supervision meeting tomorrow as I have a clashing commitment. I have let the other students in my group know about this and they will update me on Friday. Apologies for the inconvenience. Yours sincerely, Charlie	Hi Jakub, I'm really sorry, but I have a job interview tomorrow so won't be able to come to the case supervision meeting. The others know and have said they'll let me know what I've missed. Charlie	Hey Jakub, I won't be around tomorrow as I've got a job interview! Wish me luck. I'll catch up with the others on Friday. See you next week, Charlie.

9.1.6 **Improving Communication Skills**

The first step to improving your communication skills is to be able to analyse and reflect on them. You can then practice improving your communication in the areas where you have less confidence or strength.

Complete the skills audit below in Table 9.3 below and use the action plan to help you improve your communication skills. There is a downloadable version of this on the companion website.

Practical Exercise 9.2 —Communication Audit

Table 9.3

Aspect of Communication	Give yourself a score out of 5, which 5 being excellent and 1 being weak	Give a reason for your score	Set out a plan to improve this
Awareness of your own non-verbal communication			
Ability to analyse non-verbal communication in others			
Ability to recognize and acknowledge emotion in others			
Willingness to express an opinion in a group setting			
Confidence speaking to strangers			
Ability to write emails to professionals			
Ability to explain legal terms in plain English			

TAKING STOCK

In this section of Chapter 9 we have looked at the importance of good communication skills in legal practice. Communication skills form an important part of the SRA Competence Statement for solicitors. Lawyers need to communicate clearly with clients, colleagues, and other legal professionals. Your tone and register need to change depending on who you are communicating with and what you are communicating about.

It is easy to underestimate the need to learn about and practise good communication. It may seem obvious to you that you know how to communicate. But most of us have strengths and weaknesses in different areas of communication and it is worth bearing in mind that one of the most common complaints upheld against solicitors is related to poor communication.

Communication is a two-way process and includes both verbal and non-verbal information. We can become overly focused on how we are transmitting information—listening and receiving information is equally important. Whether you are advising clients or negotiating with another lawyer, you need to learn to understand what their goals are, and this can only be achieved by observing and listening.

Clinical legal education provides a wide range of opportunities to reflect on your communication skills and practise different styles of communication. Whether you are engaging with group work, interviewing a client, or seeking advice from a supervisor, you will find yourself communicating about the law in new ways, so start by noticing all the different aspects of communication and thinking about how your communication skills change and develop during your time in the clinic.

9.2 File Management

Table 9.4 is an extract from the SRA Statement of Solicitor Competence. Refer to the companion website to this book to find a downloadable template to audit your skills and help you reflect on your development.

Table 9.4 Statement of solicitor competence on maintaining accurate records

D2 Keep, use and maintain accurate, complete and clear records, including	Do you have experience in these competencies?
a. Making effective use of information management systems (whether electronic or hard copy), including storing and retrieving information	How would you rate your competence?
b. Complying with confidentiality, security, data protection and file retention and destruction requirements	Do you need more experience? How could you gain experience?

9.2.1 **Key Rules of File Management**

Keeping a full, accurate, and up-to-date client case file is a key feature of legal practice. At any time, your colleagues and supervisors should be able to access your files and to understand exactly what is happening on your case. Most legal practices now use an online case management system and it is likely that you will have access to a case management system in your clinical experience. If you don't have a case management system, there will be a secure system for storing confidential client documents and records.

A key aspect of keeping a file up to date is creating a written record of all work that you do. These written records are generally referred to as attendance notes or case notes. As a solicitor/legal advisor there are four reasons why you need to write up an attendance note after any work done:

1. As a record for yourself, so that you can remember the details of the case when you come to work on the file.
2. As a record of the work done and the time spent so that you can bill for the work.
3. As a record for colleagues or other people who may need to work on the case.
4. As a record of what the client told you, the advice you gave to them, and the work that you have done, in case the client makes a complaint about you. This enables a supervisor to assess whether there is any reason for the complaint.

In a clinical legal education setting, you also need you to keep clear records of the work you do, so that your supervisors can review your work and give you feedback.

In addition to recording all the work you do, you should also record the amount of time spent on the task.

STOP and THINK: CODE OF CONDUCT

In Chapter 7 we looked at professional legal ethics and related rules of professional conduct. Good file management helps you to follow codes of conduct. In particular, good file management protects client confidentiality and evidences procedures that have been followed, client instructions, and advice given. It is important to follow the rules set by your clinical setting as this will protect you and the client.

9.2.2 **Time Recording**

Traditionally, lawyers charge by the hour, and time recording is an essential part of file management. If the time has not been recorded, you cannot charge for the work. Many solicitors' salaries are based on the amount they have billed and most solicitors will have billing targets. Time recording is therefore a part of the job. Fixed fees are now a common part of the legal charging landscape and for some areas of work the Legal Aid Agency pays fixed fees rather than hourly rates, but time recording is still a common feature of legal practice.

Why Time-record Free Work?

In a clinical setting, it is likely that you will be providing free advice or representation and your clients will not be billed. You may therefore think that time recording is not important and question whether it is necessary.

Time recording:

1. Helps you to manage your own time

   We often underestimate how long it takes to complete a task. When you start in a clinical setting you will be working in new ways and doing new things. All of this is likely to take longer than you anticipate. Recording your time helps you to think about how to plan your time and allow enough time to complete work on your files.

2. Helps to make your work visible to your group

   If you are working in a group or a pair on your files, keeping clear records of the time spent can help to allay worries about different members of the team not pulling their weight. If group work marks are allocated for assessed clinical work, accurate time recording can help resolve any disagreements around fairness.

3. Helps your supervisor review your work

   Accurate time recording makes it possible for a supervisor to review your work and gives them a clear idea as to how challenging you might be finding the work. It also helps the supervisor to resolve any disputes about fair distribution of work.

4. Helps you to evidence work done

   If you are planning to qualify in England and Wales, you may want to claim qualifying work experience[10] for the time spent in a clinical setting. Unlike a work placement in a firm, the amount of time you spend on client work in an educational setting may not be immediately clear, as you spend different amounts of time each week on your casework. Accurate time recording will allow you to show how much time you have spent and enable your supervisor to sign off an accurate amount of work. Always seek advice from your clinical setting about claiming qualifying work experience. You can only claim for a maximum of four placements and the hours spent in a university law clinic may only add up to two or three weeks.

5. Helps your organization evidence the work done

   Organizations that provide free services need funding. An internal law clinic may be funded by the university. Your law school will need to demonstrate the benefit of the law clinic to senior management and one way it can do this is through the hours given to the community by staff and students. Charitable organizations are normally funded by grants. They need to provide evidence of the services they provide to apply for grants and to report to funders. One way of doing this is by reporting on the number of hours given.

[10] https://www.sra.org.uk/become-solicitor/sqe/qualifying-work-experience-candidates/ (last accessed 27 November 2025).

In commercial practice, some firms will expect their lawyers to commit to a certain number of pro bono hours a year. Recording pro bono hours can be one way in which commercial firms demonstrate corporate social responsibility.

6. Helps you with employability

   Learning to time-record in a clinical setting will help you to develop good habits. If you then go on a work placement or get a job as a paralegal you should find that time recording is second nature to you, which is likely to be noted and appreciated by employers.

How Do You Time-record?

Your clinical setting will almost certainly have a house rule on time recording. Traditionally lawyers work in units of six minutes, so you may be asked to record units, or to round up or down to the nearest multiple of six. For example, you spend 20 mins in a team meeting, which might be recorded as 3 units or 18 minutes. One hour is 10 units.

If you are working with a case management system, time recording may take place automatically. Take care not to leave the timer running while you chat with friends or go for a tea break.

If you are working without a case management system, each file will have a time-recording sheet. This may be an Excel spreadsheet or it may be a Word document. You will need to remember to keep an eye on the time and record time spent on tasks.

Time recording should be broken down into time spent on individual tasks. Look at the two examples in Table 9.5, with respect to the following questions:

1. Consider them from the point of view of the student recording the time. Which one would have been quicker and easier to fill in?
2. Consider them from the point of view of the supervisor. Which one gives a clear record of exactly what work the student has done and how they have managed their time?
3. Consider them from the point of view of a costs draftsman (someone who prepares bills at the end of a case). Which one would enable the costs draftsman to prepare an accurate bill for the client or the Legal Aid Agency?

9.2.3 GDPR and Client Confidentiality

In a clinical setting you will need to follow procedures and rules to protect client data. In Chapter 7 we set out the professional conduct rules in relation to client confidentiality and data protection. One of the key aspects of good file management is that systems should be in place to protect client data.[11] Most organizations that handle sensitive data have strict rules about how that information is to be stored and protected. If they make a mistake and

[11] SRA Guidance on Client Confidentiality, https://www.sra.org.uk/solicitors/guidance/confidentiality-client-information/ (last accessed July 2022).

Table 9.5 Examples of time recording

Date	Student name	Work done	Time spent in mins	No of units	Running total (in units)
Time-Recording Sheet File number AB12345					
5/03/22	Jo Carter	Reviewing file in preparation for interview, attending client, clarifying points with supervisor, and typing up interview notes	1hr 45	18	18
7/03/22	Jo Carter	Researching law and drafting relevant section of advice letter	3hrs	30	48
Time-Recording Sheet File number AB54321					
Date	Student name	Work done	Time spent in mins	No of Units	Running total (in units)
7/03/22	Kemi Adejayo	Reviewing file in preparation for interview	20 mins	3	3
7/03/22	Kemi Adejayo	Attending client interview	45 mins	9	11
7/03/22	Kemi Adejayo	Supervision meeting—discussing interview with supervisor	12 mins	2	13
7/03/22	Kemi Adejayo	Casework—writing up interview summary	24 mins	4	17
9/03/22	Kemi Adejayo	Research—researching caselaw on LA duties re homelessness	2hrs	20	37
9/03/22	Kemi Adejayo	Drafting—first draft of advice on LA duties re homelessness	1hr	10	47

disclose confidential client information to the wrong person, any supervisor regulated by the SRA or the BSB will need to report themselves to their professional body. Their organization (university or voluntary sector organization) may also need to report themselves to the Information Commissioner. In other words, the consequences of a data breach are serious, not just for you and your future career, but also for the law clinic or advice centre where you are working. It is important that you understand and follow the rules in relation to file management and file storage. Some common file management rules on client data are:

- Any paper files or documents are kept in a locked filing cabinet.
- Paper files or documents are not to be removed from the office.
- All notes must be typed directly onto the case management system.
- Handwritten notes must be scanned in and then shredded.
- Documents must not be downloaded from the case management system onto personal laptops or devices.
- If documents are downloaded they must be deleted as soon as possible.
- Case management systems can only be accessed from certain computers or from certain rooms.
- Documents are not to be emailed from personal email accounts.
- Only certain dedicated email accounts can be used for client work.
- Client files are password protected.
- Students are only permitted to print client documents from specified printers.

The rules will depend to a certain extent on the type of work done and the availability of a case management system. Rules about data storage are important and need to be taken seriously.

STOP and THINK: CLIENT CONFIDENTIALITY

EVERY TIME you do any work on a client file make sure you are following the rules to protect client confidentiality. ALWAYS tell your supervisor if you make a mistake and save something in the wrong place. NEVER try to cover up a mistake.

9.2.4 **Attendance Notes**

When you work on a client file you will create attendance notes for the following different types of work:

- Research
- Team meeting
- General work on the file

- File checklist
- Supervisor meeting
- Client interview summary
- Client interview
- Drafting
- Phone calls

You can find templates to download for all of these on the website that accompanies this book.

An attendance note is a relatively informal document. Keep the language simple. Using bullet points and abbreviations is normally acceptable and welcomed in attendance notes, as long as they aid understanding for the reader. Follow guidance given by your supervisor on house style.

It is a common convention to use people's initials when keeping records on a file. For example, Lucy Yeatman, Jacqui Kinghan, and Amir Paz-Fuchs would be LY, JK, and APF.

An attendance note should always provide answers to the following four questions:

1. When?

   When did the work take place? All attendance notes need a date. Case management systems will make a record of the time you created the case note. Sometimes you write up a note after the event. If this is the case, make sure the note records the time and date on which the work took place as well as the time and date on which the note was recorded.

2. Who?

   Case management systems will automatically provide the name of the person creating the attendance note. If more than one person is involved you need to include this in the note. Make a clear list of all the people who did the work, for example:

   - names of students;
   - name of supervising solicitor who sits in on a client interview;
   - name of the client and anyone else who attended a client interview with them—clients will often bring a friend or relative to provide support;
   - name of supervisor if it was a supervision meeting.

3. What?

   What work did you do? Before describing work always give a case note a title, for example 'supervision meeting' or 'planning'. Using appropriate templates will help with this. Your clinical setting may have templates. There are templates that can be downloaded on the companion website.

4. How long?

   Always record the time spent on a task. This should be recorded on the attendance note as well as on a time-recording sheet if you have one.

Client Interview

During a client interview you need to take detailed notes. This is difficult and it is a good idea to practise before your first interview.

Do not paraphrase what your client says but write down their words as accurately as possible. There are real risks that if you paraphrase what your client says, you will misrepresent their words and change their meaning. You may think that it would be easier to just record an interview, but this is not always practical: you may not have recording equipment; your client may not feel happy about being recorded; there may be data protection issues about where the recordings should be saved and how long they should be saved for; you need to be able to review your notes and use them as a reminder of what was said in the interview; other students and your supervisor may also need to review the notes and do not want to have to listen back through a recorded interview to clarify a fact. Normally, it does not matter if interview notes are a bit messy or have typing errors. This shows that they are probably contemporaneous. You can concentrate on accurate spelling and grammar when you write up a summary after the interview.

In addition to keeping a detailed note of everything the client says, you need to keep a note of advice given, and of other information given to the client during the interview. For example, notes should clearly record:

- Any oral explanation of the service, limits of the service and any charges (client care)
- Any documents handed over by the client in the interview (including a record of whether these were copies or originals)
- Any documents signed by the client during the interview (eg consent to make a referral or signing the client care agreement)
- What you have said to the client about the steps you will take next and how long this is likely to take (eg We will send you a letter setting out our advice within two weeks of the date of this meeting).

Interview Summary

You need to write up a summary of your client interview as soon as possible. If you attended the interview with another student, both of you can create one joint note.

The aim of the summary is to create a record of the client interview that is easy for a supervisor or student colleague to read through to understand the key points of the case. It should act as a reference point for the work that you are going to do on the file. It is unlikely that your client will have given you the facts of their case in chronological order. If a solicitor gives verbal advice in an interview, this is likely to take place at different points in the interview. When you write up your summary you are going to reorganize all the information into a clear and logical order, divided into different sections. The means you can come back to the file and quickly remind yourself of the key facts and issues.

An interview summary of a first client meeting should include the following information:

1. Events

   Dates, times, places, people involved, the cause and course of events, people affected, property affected, incident that led to visit to solicitor—these should be set out in chronological order.

2. What the client wants

   The main problem, the desired outcome, difficulties in achieving the outcome, people who might be affected by the outcome.

3. Previous advice or assistance

   Anyone else consulted—when; what advice was given.

4. Existing legal proceedings

   Nature of proceedings, parties, stage in process, past/future hearing dates.

5. Advice given (where relevant)

   Advice given on both law and procedure and likely outcome.

6. Next client–lawyer contact

   When and what will this involve—eg phone call, letter, etc.

7. Work to be done by lawyer

   Next steps to be taken and in what timescale.

8. Work to be done by client

   For example, bringing documents in, attending medical appointment, arranging mediation.

A summary of a client meeting mid-way through the case work should include:

1. Events

   An update on what has occurred since the last meeting/contact.

2. What the client wants

   The main purpose of the meeting and why it has been arranged.

3. Advice given (where relevant)

   Advice given on both law and procedure and likely outcome.

4. Next client–lawyer contact

   When and what will this involve—eg phone call, letter, etc.

5. Work to be done by lawyer

   Next steps to be taken and in what timescale.

6. Work to be done by client

   For example, bringing documents in, attending medical appointment, arranging mediation.

STOP and THINK: GDPR

Your client is entitled to a copy of their own file. File notes refer to the client in the third person, but it is still their file. Take care to be respectful in the way you write about the client and their case. If you were the client, would you be happy with the records made? Take care to write with respect.

Research Record

We discuss how to conduct practical legal research in detail in Chapter 11. Where research is directly relevant to the client's case, you will need to keep a record of this on the client file. Research records on the file need to be concise and specific so they can be used to help write an advice letter or draft a document.

Accurate research records on a file are important for showing why you have advised a client in any given way. A practising lawyer needs to be able to justify decisions made and advice given. Accurate research records provide evidence of your decision-making process.

Team Meetings

Making an accurate record of a meeting is a useful skill in most professional jobs. Meetings are used in work environments to share information, brainstorm problems, and make decisions about who is doing what and when. In a clinical setting, it is likely that you will have team meetings to plan case strategies, share research findings, plan how to allocate work, and set deadlines.

Records of meetings are usually referred to as minutes and should record the following:

1. Date and time of the meeting.
2. Who was present, absent and sent apologies.
3. Summary of points discussed.
4. List of action points.
5. Who is responsible for completing action points.
6. Date and time of next meeting.

It is common practice to have an agenda with a numbered list of items to organize the minutes around the agenda items. See Table 9.6 for an example.

STOP and THINK: CLIENT CONFIDENTIALITY

Did you discuss more than one client case in your team meeting? Do not put a record of work relating to Client 1 on Client 2's file. Make separate notes for separate files.

Table 9.6 Record of a team meeting

Agenda item	Topic	Summary of discussion	Action points
1	Research for client 2	Reviewed client interview and research done for client 1—agreed that we were not at all clear on a number of issues. We need to look again at a. procedure in child arrangement cases with a focus on when and why there might be a fact-finding hearing, b. law in relation to children's wishes, c. rules around evidence of domestic abuse for legal aid applications	JF to do procedure AP to do children's wishes SS to do legal aid All research records to be on the file by 9am on Monday

Supervisor Meetings

Keeping a record of meetings with your supervisor is very important, as you need a clear record of what you have been told to do. In addition to all the obvious practical reasons for making a note of what you are expected to do, there are important professional conduct reasons for this. The supervisor is professionally responsible for all your work. If you make a mistake because you did not follow instructions, you will be responsible for that mistake and could face disciplinary action. If you followed your supervisor's instructions, you will be better protected from any consequences.

Some clinical settings have open-door access to supervisors and you may often have short informal meetings with them, to clarify a point or ask a question. You must keep a record of all these meetings and conversations on your file. This might be a short note, but you need to record it.

For example:

> LY spoke to JK about how much advice on legal aid should go into the letter. JK said to keep it brief as this area of law is out of scope so legal aid not available.

Organizing Paper Files

Legal work is increasingly done through case management systems and the demise of paper files was hastened by the pandemic and the practicalities of working from home for most lawyers. However, in some settings you may be expected to work with paper files. For long-running cases where your clinical setting works on appeals or provides full representation, this could involve a large number of documents and papers. A criminal appeals case (Innocence Project) for example may have several lever-arch files of documents.

The convention in legal files is to keep correspondence and attendance notes in reverse chronological order, so that the most recent document is at the top of the file. Documents are usually kept in a separate file from correspondence and attendance notes. Documents need to be kept in order so that they are easy to find. The order will depend on the type of case and you should seek advice from your supervisor—it is likely that you will have your documents organized in sections. For example:

- statements;
- court documents including directions and applications;
- medical reports.

Within each section the documents need to be in date order. Keep an index at the front of the file so that it is easy to see what documents you have and where to find them.

STOP and THINK: CLIENT CONFIDENTIALITY

What are the rules about paper files? Do not remove them from the clinic without permission. If you take documents out of the file, put them back in the correct place. If you are the last to leave the room, check the filing cabinet or store cupboard is locked.

TAKING STOCK

In this section we have looked at the importance of file management and provided examples of how to use file management systems to help you comply with professional conduct rules.

File management systems are an essential part of legal practice. Each organization has its own systems and rules, but there are common features on all file management systems. All work should be recorded on a file to provide an accurate record that is accessible to supervisors and colleagues. Work done on files is recorded in attendance notes. All attendance notes should record *when*, *who*, *what*, and *how long*.

Time is normally recorded in units of six minutes. Accurate time recording is essential for billing and can also be important evidence of pro bono commitments.

Following rules on file management protects client confidentiality and is an important part of GDPR compliance.

9.3 Planning and Prioritizing

Table 9.7 is an extract from the SRA Statement of Solicitor Competence. Refer to the companion website to the book to find a downloadable template to audit your skills and help you reflect on your development.

9.3.1 Time Management

As a student, time management is important. Study at university tends to require independent study, with perhaps only 8 or 10 hours in a week spent in lectures or seminars. Even full-time students tend to have jobs and may have other responsibilities at home. Students can find it very difficult to manage and organize their time so that they study effectively over the whole academic year. Not everyone has the same experience with managing their studies. There are students who spend hours reading every case and every article but may lose track of key issues because they have not focused on core materials, and there are students who find themselves working all night to finish coursework because they left it all to the last minute. In order to manage your time, you need to know yourself and understand your own strengths and weaknesses.

Managing time in a law clinic setting can present new challenges for students:

- The pace of the work can be quite fast—your client needs their advice now, not at the end of term when assessments are due.
- You may need to work in a small group or pair, which means finding time when you can meet and work together.

Table 9.7 Statement of solicitor competence on planning and managing work

D1 Initiate, plan, prioritise and manage work activities and projects to ensure that they are completed efficiently, on time and to an appropriate standard, both in relation to their own work and work that they lead or supervise, including	Do you have experience in these competencies? How would you rate your competence?
a. Clarifying instructions so as to agree the scope and objectives of the work	
b. Taking into account the availability of resources in initiating work activities	Do you need more experience?
c. Meeting timescales, resource requirements and budgets	How could you gain experience?
d. Monitoring, and keeping other people informed of, progress	
e. Dealing effectively with unforeseen circumstances	
f. Paying appropriate attention to detail	

- You may need to come in to do your work in the clinic or at your placement, which may not be open 24 hours a day like some university libraries.
- You need to allow time for your supervisor to read your work and give you feedback, and for you to redraft it before the deadline.

Meeting deadlines and managing time is important in many jobs and professions, but the combination of professional conduct rules and the type of work make time management particularly important in the legal profession.

- The Code of Conduct for Solicitors states that the service you provide to clients must be 'competent and provided in a timely manner'.
- It is normal to provide your client with clear timeframes in which work will be done. For example, in a first appointment you may say that you will send an advice letter within two weeks. Professional obligations mean that you need to stick to that timeframe or update your client if you cannot do so.
- Delay is one of the biggest areas of complaint to the Legal Ombudsman, accounting for 17 per cent of all complaints upheld.
- Many types of legal cases have strict time limits. Missing deadlines can lead to losses for your client and potentially a negligence claim against you. For example, employment cases have to be issued within three months of a claim arising. But a client may not have come to see you until a month or more has already passed, and a case needs to be investigated and prepared before tribunal proceedings can be started. Even a personal injury case, with a time limit of six years to issue a claim, may involve a client who has come to see you late, where the case needs to be dealt with swiftly to ensure the time limit is not to be missed.
- If you work in litigation, deadlines and hearing dates are set by courts and you have to comply with the timetable set by the court. Delays can lead to cost penalties or to a case being dismissed.
- If you work in a commercial environment, you may not be subject to court deadlines, but delays in completing documents can lead to delays in contracts being completed and subsequent financial loss for commercial clients.
- If you take instructions on drafting a will from a young and healthy person, this may not seem urgent, but if your client dies suddenly and unexpectedly there may be serious consequences.
- Even small jobs that might not seem urgent should not be left unattended. For example, after a client interview you should write up a summary of your notes promptly, while they are still fresh in your mind and in case someone else needs to do work on the file.

In other words, the work of a lawyer is often urgent and most lawyers work to tight deadlines. The pace of work in a university law clinic is often slower than in a law firm as time is built in for supervision and feedback and you won't have as many cases to deal with at once. It is however often swifter than the pace of academic study, and you will need to fit this into your week around other studies, jobs, caring responsibilities, other commitments, and having fun.

9.3.2 **Use a Calendar to Organize Your Time**

Time needs to be planned in both the long and short term. An overview of the whole semester and an overview for each week will help you to work to deadlines effectively.

Use a wall planner or term planner to put in coursework deadlines, lectures, and seminars to give you an overview of your term. Find out what the expectations are for seminar and lecture preparation and clinic so that you can plan your weeks.

For each week, map out your time. Allow time for breaks, meals, socializing, and study. Block out regular time on your calendar for seminar preparation. If you use an electronic calendar such as Outlook, you can colour-code different types of activity and set them to recur, so that the calendar is populated with regular commitments for the whole term. You may need to work with other students, so once you have a clear plan of your own weekly commitments you will need to compare diaries with your team in order to find times for meeting and working together.

9.3.3 **Set Realistic Goals**

Think about how and where you like to study, but be prepared to experiment. If you normally study at night, it might not work if you suddenly decide to be in the clinic at 9am every morning because you think this looks efficient. You may be setting yourself up to fail. You might need to change your habits slightly to fit in with clinic opening times, but aim to come to the clinic in the afternoon if you are not a morning person.

When planning your time, plan breaks. If you have a free day with no work or teaching commitments, blocking this out for seven hours of EU seminar preparation is not realistic. Try organizing the day into study blocks and breaks.

Practical Exercise 9.3

Look at the time-planning charts in Tables 9.7 and 9.8 and Figure 9.1. Which one appeals to you? Do you ever plan your time in this way? Do you build in time for meals and meeting up with friends? Do you think it is helpful to spend time creating planning documents, or can this just become another form of procrastination?

Table 9.8 Planning time using a diary

9am	10am`	11am	12noon	1pm	2pm	3pm	4pm	5pm	6pm
Get up, have breakfast, and faff about	Human Rights lecture	Human Rights lecture	Lunch with Sam then to library at 12.30 and start prep for medical seminar	Seminar prep for medical law—read one article	15-minute break (go to café in the library) then team meeting in Clinic at 2.15pm	Clinic work—research law for client 1	30-min break at student social space in Law building Followed by more research in clinic	Go swimming	Go home—20-min walk then another hour of medical law reading

Table 9.9 Planning time by prioritizing tasks

Task	Priority
Medical law seminar prep	Urgent
Attend employability talk—2pm	Medium
Clinic research for client 2	Urgent
Human Rights lecture	Medium (can watch recording later)
Shopping for food for the next two days	Urgent
Meet J (friend) for tea and chat	Low
Take library books back—due tomorrow	Medium
Meet International Law tutor in office hours for feedback on assessment 1 (2pm today or 10am on Friday)	Medium

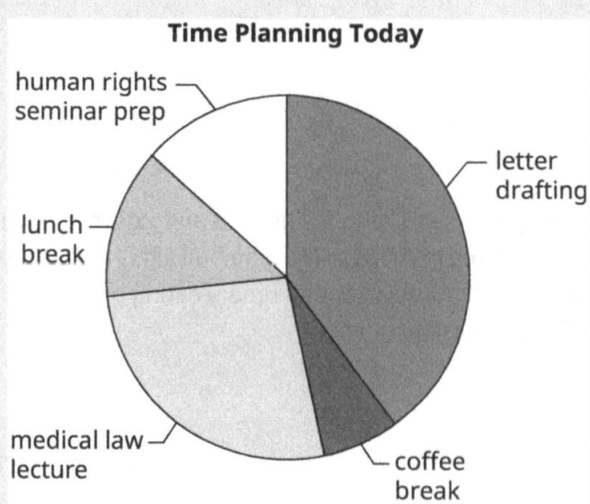

Figure 9.1 Time planning wheel

9.3.4 **Distractions and Procrastination**

Modern life can make it hard to focus. TV streaming services, games, and social media all provide 24-hour distractions that can make it very difficult to manage your time. There is no easy solution to these types of distractions, but you do need to find a way to focus on work and study.

Pomodoro is a popular technique for helping with focus. Developed by Francesco Cirillo,[12] pomodoro is the Italian word for tomato and is called this as Cirillo used a tomato-shaped kitchen timer when developing the technique. The basic idea behind the pomodoro technique is to work in short bursts and take regular breaks. Setting a timer for 35 or 40 minutes can help you to get down to work. Decide on a task—for example draft the first part of a client letter—set a timer to 35 minutes, turn off notifications on your phone for the 35 minutes, and start working. At the end of the 35 minutes, take a break, and then do the whole exercise again.

You might want to try Shut Up and Write (SUAW) as a way of working with another person to focus. Arrange to meet someone for two hours. You can do this in person or online. Allow five minutes to discuss what work you plan to achieve in the two hours. Break the two hours up into shorter blocks using pomodoro timing. Set the timer for 35 minutes, switch off phone notifications, and do some writing. At the end of the 35 minutes take a break, compare notes with your friend on how much you have got done, set the timer, and start again. This might not work for everyone, as the presence of someone else might just distract you even more, but being accountable to another person might help you to get started.

Another popular method of dealing with procrastination is known as Eat That Frog.[13] The basic idea behind this is that if you tackle the thing you want to do least at the beginning of the day then the rest of the day will be easier. This might not work for you.

Ultimately, whatever technique you use, you need to learn how to turn off distractions and focus on the work you need to do. You need to learn what works for you. This means understanding yourself and what motivates you.

Practical Exercise 9.4

Your student days are a good time for you to experiment with different ways of managing your time. Try a different way of planning your time each week for four weeks. Keep a reflective diary for each week. At the end of the period review the diary and think about which method worked best for you.

9.3.5 **Too Much to Do Is Too Much to Do**

No amount of good time management will help you to get through your workload if you simply have too much work to do. All workloads can reach a tipping point where it becomes impossible to achieve everything expected. If you simply cannot get everything done, good time management should help you to recognize the problem before it becomes

[12] https://www.pomodorotechnique.com/ (last accessed November 2025).

[13] Brian Tracey and Anna Leinberger, *Eat That Frog for Students* (Hodder & Stoughton 2021).

unmanageable and help you to develop strategies for prioritizing. If you simply keep going when you can't manage your workload, you are likely to suffer from stress and burn out. Identifying stress and burnout, and their consequences, are discussed in Chapter 10. It is important to seek help if you feel unable to manage your workload.

REFLECTION POINT

Do you think it is ever reasonable to be expected to work evenings and weekends?

If you were told to work weekends and evenings in order to get through your workload, would you think this was fair?

If you were put under pressure to meet targets so that you were required to work at weekends, would you be tempted to start falsifying documents? This is what happened to a newly qualified solicitor, Sovani James, who worked at McMillan Williams in the clinical negligence department.

Over the course of more than one year, she falsified documents on a file and made misleading statements to the client and her supervisor about progress on the file. After she handed in her resignation, she wrote four backdated letters suggesting that progress was being made on the file, when no work had been done. After she left, her dishonesty came to light and she was reported to the SRA. Ms James gave evidence that she had been under extreme pressure to meet high billing targets and the stress and anxiety had caused her to behave in the way that she did. The Solicitors Disciplinary Tribunal (SDT)

> found that the firm was a challenging place to work. It was seeking external investment which would bring time recording and billing under scrutiny. The senior management sought to pass pressure on to junior staff such as Ms James, with monthly publication of league tables to create competition between fee-earners. The SDT was particularly critical of an email from a senior manager in July 2012 complaining about a shortfall of Ms James' billed hours as against her target and a letter from the senior partner to Ms James in April 2013 requiring her to work evenings, weekends and bank holidays to make up chargeable hours. The SDT found this was a 'notable example of bad, ineffective and inappropriate management.' (para 8)

The SDT accepted Ms James' evidence that she was under pressure and that she was terrified and had suffered hair loss. Her getting behind on the file (described by the STD as a small issue) became magnified and she anticipated dire consequences. She lost her confidence and believed that she was not able to do her job well.

The SDT found that Ms James had been dishonest but, because of the pressure on her at the time, that these were exceptional circumstances. Since leaving McMillan Williams she had continued to practise as a solicitor at a different firm, which provided her with positive references to say that they had no concerns about her work. Despite the finding of dishonesty she was not struck off but was suspended for two years.

However, the SRA appealed the decision (along with two other decisions) and the High Court overturned the decision of the SDT.[14] Ms James was struck off the roll as a practising solicitor:

> This was not isolated dishonesty or a moment of madness but repeated dishonesty over a sustained period of time. It caused harm to the client. As I have said, the toxicity of her working environment may go some way towards explaining the dishonesty although it cannot excuse it, so that it may be said to reduce her culpability, but the difficulty is that the SDT has not engaged in the balancing exercise which the case law requires. Had it done so, it should have concluded that this was not a case within the narrow category of 'exceptional circumstances' justifying a lesser sanction, so that striking Ms James off the Roll was the appropriate sanction and only that would properly and adequately protect the public and the reputation of the profession [114].

9.3.6 **Putting It All in Context with the Statement of Solicitor Competence**

Table 9.10 sets out a summary of action points from the topics covered in the chapter, placing them in context with the statement of solicitor competence.

Table 9.10 Putting it all in context with statement of solicitor competency

Clarifying instructions so as to agree the scope and objectives of the work	It is hard to plan your time if you are not completely clear about what needs to be done. In the client interview you need to identify: • What the client needs/wants • What action you can take to help the client achieve this • What further information the client needs to provide you with—for example you might need copies of documents or correspondence to be sent • Whether there are key dates for the client, such a deadline for filing a statement, or a time limit for starting proceedings • What steps you are going to take for the client • When you will next contact the client After a client interview you need to clarify with your supervisor: • What work you need to do • When each step needs to be done by—for example research report to be shared with supervisor for feedback, draft letter to be shared with supervisor for feedback • What the final deadline is for sending advice letter to the client is If you work in a pair or a team you need to clarify • Who is going to complete each task • When the work will be done

(*Continued*)

[14] *SRA v James* [2018] EWHC 3058 (Admin).

Table 9.10 (Continued)

	Once you have all this information you can plan your time accordingly. When you plan your time in the law clinic, you need to also take account of time commitments of other people with whom you are working.
Taking into account the availability of resources	When planning clinical legal work you need to be aware of where you can work and when. Your clinical setting may have rules about working in the clinic or using clinic computers to do your work. These may only be available at certain times of day, or you may need to book rooms and laptops in advance.
Meeting timescales, resource requirements, and budgets	It is unlikely that you will need to manage a budget in your clinical setting. You will need to meet timescales. Clarifying the work that needs to be done and identifying deadlines will help you to meet timescales. You need to allow time for other people to review your work when planning your time.
Monitoring, and keeping other people informed of, progress	To monitor your progress you need to be able to keep track of what you need to do and what you have done. Using a planner or to do list of some kind makes this possible. You can keep handwritten lists, make timetables or use an electronic diary as suggested above. It is likely that in a student clinical setting you will only have one or two client cases to work on at a time. In legal practice you will have lots of cases with varying deadlines. You need to keep track of the work that you have done and of what you need to do next. Use your time as a law clinic student to explore different ways of doing this. 'Other people' includes: • Your client • Your supervisor • Your peers. Often you will be working in a team in a law clinic setting. Make sure you keep your team members informed about where you are up to with your work. Your supervisor will need to review your work. Make sure you keep them informed about what you have done. Don't leave them to search through files looking for work that needs checking. Sometimes even the most well-organized person can fall behind with a deadline because of illness or accident. If this happens you need to keep the relevant people informed. Let your supervisor and peers know if you are ill. If you have made a commitment to a client to do a piece of work within a certain time frame, it is important that you contact them with a revised time frame if there is a delay. Managing expectations and keeping your client informed about progress on their case is an important part of professional obligations and commitments.
Dealing effectively with unforeseen circumstances	Unforeseen circumstances can be very stressful. Section 3 of this chapter explored management of stress and well-being in more depth. You are likely to have to deal with unforeseen circumstances during your time in a law clinic setting. For example, your client may cancel their appointment at short notice; one of your team members or your supervisor might get ill; your client's circumstances might change suddenly, meaning the case either settles or becomes more complex. Some unforeseen circumstances may be small and only affect you and a few other people at most.

Table 9.10 (Continued)

	One of the best ways to do this is to build some flexibility into your time management. Don't cram your day with activities so that there is no slack at all. Don't plan to complete work five minutes before a deadline. Then if something unexpected happens to delay you, you have time to deal with this. If you do miss a deadline, or know you are going to miss a deadline—contact your supervisor. When you plan your time, prioritize activities, and be prepared to re-prioritize if circumstances change.
Paying appropriate attention to detail	Managing time well does not mean that you always get work done quickly; it means you do the work well. This can take time. The practice of law involves attention to detail. Good time management means allowing time to do work with care. It also means being able to focus and concentrate. Think about distractions, turn your phone off, and consider using techniques such as a pomodoro timer so that you can pay attention and work effectively.

TAKING STOCK

In this section of the chapter we have looked at the importance of organization and planning in legal practice and considered how overwork can have a negative impact on someone's ability to carry out their job in a safe and competent way. Time management in a clinical setting can present new challenges as you may have to work to much shorter deadlines than other study and you may have to be physically present in a clinic to do your work.

Sometimes, however organized you are, you may find yourself in a position where you simply have too much to do. Developing techniques for managing your time and your workload can help you to recognize what you can achieve and to know when you need to ask for help. Overwork can lead to stress and burnout. It is important to seek help if you cannot manage your workload. Stress and anxiety are not excuses for dishonesty and solicitors who cover up mistakes can be struck off for dishonesty regardless of overwork and pressure.

Managing and organizing your time and meeting deadlines are important aspects of most jobs, but for those of you who want to qualify as lawyers, meeting deadlines and managing multiple deadlines is critical. Your time in a law clinic setting provides you with a valuable opportunity to reflect on different techniques for managing yourself and your time.

Conclusion

This chapter has considered some of the core skills that underpin legal practice. These skills are not unique to legal practice; good communication and good time management are the grease that oil the wheels of most jobs, whether you work in a bar, a shop, or an office. Clinical legal education provides time and space to reflect on these core skills and to find ways to manage yourself and build relationships with both peers and clients.

The importance of good communication skills in legal practice cannot be underestimated, and the general guidance on communication in this chapter forms the foundation for the clinical legal skills in the following chapters, including working with peers, communicating with clients, interviewing, advising, drafting, negotiation, and advocacy. Good communication skills are essential to good legal practice. Lawyers work with clients, colleagues, and other professionals constantly, so getting communication right is an important aspect of the job. A student law clinic is a good environment to reflect on your own communication skills and experiment with different ways of communicating. Good communication also underpins professional conduct and can prevent problems or complaints arising.

Learning good file management will help you to practise safely within the rules, work in partnership with other students, and work with your supervisor. The specific rules for each organization will vary, but most law files are organized along the same principles. File management systems are designed to ensure that everyone working in an organization complies with the rules and codes of conduct for the legal professions. The rules are there to protect you, your supervisor, your peers, and your client, so take them seriously and keep a record of everything that you do.

Studying and practising law can be very rewarding, but it can also be quite stressful and demanding. Lawyers often have to work to strict deadlines and the consequences of missing dates for filing documents or issuing proceedings can lead to adverse outcomes for clients. Time in a clinical legal setting can give you the opportunity to learn how to manage tight deadlines and multiple demands on your time in a safe environment. The pace and nature of the work in a clinical setting tends to be different to that of studying on other courses and you may need to work to short deadlines in order to research the law. Working in a law clinic can also teach you some good practical habits for keeping work organized and keeping regular written records. That said, it is important to remember that too much work is too much work. Sometimes even the best time-management techniques will not make it possible to get work done, and doing work well is as important as doing it quickly. Always ask for help if you need it. Communicate with your supervisor and your peers if you think you can't meet deadlines.

A View From Clinical Legal Practice

Professor Jeff Giddings, Clinical Director, Monash Law School

I have recently finished editing a book on Global Clinical Legal Education with contributions from 65 authors from 44 countries. There is great diversity in the approaches taken to 'learning by doing and reflecting' of clinical legal education approaches, framed by what your supervisor-teacher is encouraging you to learn, who manages the clinical program, and the resources available.

I encourage you to think about how your supervisor can most effectively help you to make the most of your clinic experience. Think about what you really want to learn through your time in the clinic. Without an effective supervisor to support and appropriately challenge you and your fellow students, at least some of the learning potential of the legal workplace is likely to be lost.

In 2014, I completed an Australian National Teaching Fellowship looking at how to make supervision arrangements as effective as possible for all concerned—students, supervisors and clients. As a result of that project, I developed the following advice for students who are working with a supervisor in a clinic:

Prepare in a professional manner. You should expect to receive clear instructions on the task at hand rather than your supervisor providing you with answers to research issues. Always check your work before consulting your supervisor and anticipate and address issues the supervisor may raise. This can be usefully summarized as 'make it easy for your supervisor to guide and support you'.

Consider the relationship from the supervisor's perspective. Mutual respect is a key to any relationship. It is also helpful for you to appreciate that good supervision is time-consuming.

Receive feedback in a constructive manner. The United States Best Practices in Legal Education guide calls on students to 'listen to the critique with care and an open mind'.

Take a problem-solving approach. This is as important in the student–supervisor relationship as it is in the student–client relationship.

Take a reflective approach. You should appraise their own performance and be honest about whether they have performed well. I have found the 'What? So What? Now What?' process developed by Rolfe, Freshwater and Jasper to be particularly helpful. These three questions support your learning through the stages of describing an event, analysing its implications and considering future actions building on the description and analysis. I find this structure easy to remember and useful for students and practitioners alike.

Always remember the client. Students need to appreciate the central significance of their client in whatever work they do. Working with and on behalf of the client is central to professional work.

Further Reading

Stella Cottrell, *Study Skills Handbook*, (5th ed., Bloomsbury Academic 2019) chapters 6 and 7.

Erica Dhawan, *Digital Body Language: How to Build Trust and Connection No Matter the Distance* (Harper Collins 2021).

Marie Reid and Richard Hammersley, *Communicating Successfully in Groups* (Routledge 2000).

Kate Williams, *Time Management Pocket Study Skills* (Palgrave 2011).

10 Working with Others

Chapter Overview

This chapter starts by looking at risk factors in both legal education and the legal profession that can impact negatively on mental well-being of law students and practising lawyers, and explores how a clinical legal setting can support students. An important part of self-care is the ability to build relationships of trust with peers and supervisors, and the chapter goes on to provide advice and guidance on how to build collaborative working relationships with your peers in the clinic. The final section of the chapter builds on the advice in Chapter 9 on general communication skills, to explore key communication skills needed to build a good working relationship with clients.

Having read this chapter and engaged with the exercises, you will be able to:

- Describe some of the mental health risk factors associated with the study and practice of law
- Analyse some recent disciplinary cases that have been connected to high levels of stress and anxiety in the legal profession
- Identify strategies to protect your own mental well-being as law students and as legal professionals
- Recognize the advantages of collaborative working
- Develop strategies for successful collaborative working
- Explore strategies for communicating complex legal issues to lay clients
- Identify appropriate ways of communicating with vulnerable clients

Introduction

We start this chapter by exploring connections between mental well-being and the study of law. Regrettably, law students and lawyers frequently report high levels of stress, anxiety, and depression. In this chapter we will look at some of the risk factors and consider how these might impact on clinical legal education. Although universities are increasingly aware of the need to support students' mental health, most institutional responses place responsibility on the individual to manage their difficulties. Poor well-being can be overly medicalized, with an emphasis on counselling or medication. Some mental health problems and mental illnesses do require appropriate medical support or treatment, but in this chapter we will look at how the structure and support systems available in law clinics might help develop protective factors and create a support network for all students. It is common for law students to believe that being stressed is normal, and that they need to just persevere and keep going. We contend that reflection, a personal connection with human problems, belonging to a community, and an approach to legal study based in legal realism in clinical legal education can help to address some of the structural risk factors in place that impact on law students' mental well-being.

Group work, or pair work, is a common feature in university law clinics. Students frequently work in small teams of six or more students to progress cases regardless of whether their work is assessed or on a voluntary basis. Working with other students can support your learning, as well as your mental health. Making connections and feeling part of a community can give students a sense of belonging and there is extensive research that shows that students' academic performance and well-being can be improved through working together in groups. Being able to work in a team is a key employability skill and most job applications will ask you to give examples of your ability to work in a team. However, the reality for many students is that group work can be stressful and difficult. A lack of trust in each other can make it hard for students to collaborate and help one another with their work. In this chapter we therefore provide advice and guidance on how to navigate group work to get the most out of it, both for yourself and for the other students that you are working with.

Having explored ways to make the most of working with your peers, this chapter goes on to look at some of the key communication skills needed to build successful relationships with clients. Law is a service industry, meaning that your relationship with your client is a key aspect of the role of a practising lawyer. In commercial practice, keeping clients is fundamental to the business practice. Without the clients the firm will not make money. In a clinical setting most of your work will be provided for free to clients who cannot afford to pay. The client's best interests are still your priority when providing free legal services, and developing a relationship with your client forms the foundation on which you are able to provide those services. This is a complicated relationship. It is important that a client trusts you and believes that you have the knowledge and skills needed to provide advice and representation. The relationship needs to be friendly, but also the lawyer needs to maintain a professional distance and maintain their independence from the client in order to give advice. This chapter provides an introduction to communicating with clients. In Chapter 11 we look in greater depth at the particular skills needed for interviewing and advising your clients.

10.1 **Care of Self and Others**

Well-being is defined in the Oxford Dictionary as the state of being healthy, happy, or prosperous; physical, psychological, or moral welfare. In this chapter we are concerned more with the second part of that definition and, in particular, with the psychological welfare of law students. It is not the responsibility of law schools or law clinics to ensure that all of our students are happy, but the psychological well-being of lawyers and law students can have an impact on how you learn. Stress and anxiety brought about by pressures in the workplace can also have a professional impact and can affect ethical decisions and compromise client care.[1]

10.1.1 **Well-being of Law Students**

There is an increasing body of evidence showing that a significant number of university students in the UK face poor well-being and that law students in particular have issues with well-being.[2] Concern about well-being and high levels of mental distress among law students in the US dates back to the 1980s[3] and later studies in Australia[4] made similar findings.

The mental health of students and the well-being of the student population in general was already a concern for senior leadership in universities before the COVID-19 pandemic,[5] which only increased the focus on the questions of psychological well-being for young people in general, and law students in particular.[6]

When support and services are put in place by universities, there is often an emphasis on the individual student and their responsibility to access support to solve their problems. However, it is well documented that law students experience more psychological distress than the student population as a whole, which indicates that structural factors in law school are part of the cause. Later in this chapter, in section 10.4.3, we look at vulnerability theory as a more inclusive way of looking at a client's needs. Vulnerability theory recognizes that as individuals we are affected by events and circumstances and that vulnerability is a societal issue can help to shift perspective away from identifying individuals or their behaviour as a problem to be solved and instead help us to see structural issues that can be tackled. Graham Ferris has argued that 'vulnerability theory is a powerful heuristic that helps us to analyse the problems of student well-being as a system problem and avoid an inappropriate contemporary tendency to seek the causes for problems in individual choices and character'.[7] The causes of law student psychological distress are complex and not fully understood, but the literature suggests a number of contributory risk factors connected to the traditional structure of law schools and the way in which the subject is taught. Both physically and pedagogically, law clinics tend to sit outside or on the edge of law schools. They often occupy their own physical

[1] Margaret Castles and Carol Boothby, 'Which Hat Shall I Wear Today?' in Caroline Strevens and Rachael Field (eds), *Educating for Well-being in Law, Positive Professional Identities and Practice* (Routledge 2020) 126.

[2] Caroline Strevens and Emma Jones, 'Legal Education for Wellbeing: Design, Delivery and Evaluation' (2022) 56(1) The Law Teacher 1–4.

[3] GAH Benjamin, A Kaszniak, B Sales, and SB Shanfield, 'The Role of Legal Education in Producing Psychological Distress among Law Students and Lawyers' (1986) 11(2) Law & Social Inquiry, 225–52.

[4] Norman Kelk et al, *Courting the Blues: Attitudes towards Depression in Australian Law Students and Lawyers* (Brain and Mind Research Institute 2009).

[5] The University Mental Health Charter was published in 2019 by Student Minds, following extensive consultation across the university sector, https://universitymentalhealthcharter.org.uk/ (last accessed 8 November 2022).

[6] Michael Faye and Yvonne Skipper, '"I was able to ask for help when I became stressed rather than sitting alone and struggling": Psychology and Law Students' Views of the Impact of Identity and Community on Mental Wellbeing' (2022) 56(1) The Law Teacher 20–36.

[7] Graham Ferris, 'Law Students' Wellbeing and Vulnerability' (2022) 56(1) The Law Teacher 5–19, 18.

space in a separate building. The approach to teaching, with an emphasis on reflection, ethics, client work, and a bridge between the worlds of theory and practice, means that the clinic may ideally be situated to dismantle some of the structural risk factors that are contributing to psychological distress among law students.[8]

Learning to Think Like a Lawyer

Part of studying law involves learning to apply legal rules to practical problems in an objective way. In other words, students must learn to put aside emotional responses to human problems. 'The world-view generated by learning to think "legally" creates the expectancy that problems are soluble by the mere application of legal reasoning, and that human need and its complexity can be filtered out.'[9] As we saw in Chapter 5, traditional legal education based on doctrinal analysis is based on the assumption that law is a science that can be learned in a library with no engagement with people. This disconnect between law as a rational reason-based discipline and the messy, emotional factual complexity of human lives demands that law students switch off their emotional engagement with the subject. This may lead law students to lose a connection with their personal values and sense of moral development.[10] Krieger describes thinking like a lawyer as 'fundamentally negative; it is critical, pessimistic and depersonalising. It is a damaging paradigm in law schools as it is usually conveyed and understood as a new and superior way of thinking, rather than an important but strictly limited legal tool.'[11]

The clinical legal setting may be your first experience of law in practice where you will be faced with the messiness and complexity of people's lives. The objective doctrinal approach to law divided into discrete categories that tends to dominate in an undergraduate law programme does not fit neatly into the way that people live their lives and experience legal problems. As we discussed in Chapter 5, clinical legal education takes a very different approach to the law. When you first arrive in a clinical setting this can be unsettling, and may cause students to feel quite stressed by the new and different way of looking at law. As most clinical settings provide access to justice services to members of the community who are often characterized as vulnerable, a focus on the client's needs and an understanding of a client will nearly always require an emotional response of some sort. This does not mean that law students are expected to throw away all objectivity or professionalism, but in order to connect with your client, obtain instructions, and engage with their problems, a level of empathy or emotional labour is required.

[8] Castles and Boothby (n 1) 129.

[9] Tony Foley and Stephen Tang, 'Being, Not Just Thinking Like, a Lawyer' in Rachel Field, James Duffy, and Colin James (eds), *Promoting Law Student and Lawyer Well-being in Australia and Beyond* (Routledge 2016).

[10] Emma Jones, *Emotions in the Law School: Transforming Legal Education through the Passions* (Routledge 2020) 132.

[11] Lawrence S Krieger, 'Institutional Denial about the Dark Side of Law School and Fresh Empirical Guidance for Constructively Breaking the Silence' (2002) 52(1) Journal of Legal Education 112–29, 117.

REFLECTION POINT

What does the phrase 'thinking like a lawyer' mean to you? Do you think that you have changed the way that you think through studying law? Do you agree with the idea that lawyers need to set aside their emotions in order to apply logic and rules?

Fear of Failure

Law students often compare themselves unfavourably to others and can be concerned that they are not as clever as the other law students.[12] Fear of failure or not wanting to look stupid can prevent students from asking for support from peers or staff. Bleasdale and Humphreys found that students tended to believe that resilience meant showing grit or perseverance and just keeping going. Bleasdale and Humphreys were troubled by this understanding of resilience, partly because 'a "resilient" individual is arguably one who can reflect upon the need to alter one's approach, and perhaps to accept that an alternative course of action is required. "Persevering" or "keeping going" do not imply that such reflection is taking place, but rather imply that there is a need to run through a metaphorical brick wall in order to demonstrate "resilience".'[13]

The approach to learning law in a clinical setting may be unsettling to students when they first join. Clinical legal education is based on experiential learning and reflection plays a key role in this style of learning. In Chapter 6 we explored how reflection can aid learning and help to develop autonomous self-directed learning. The rationale for experiential learning is that you learn through trial and error, reflection and feedback. A clinical setting provides you with a safe environment to learn how to manage mistakes. You may find the transition to experiential learning in a law clinic setting unsettling to start with, but support from peers and supervisors and learning to reflect should help you to develop the strategies needed to navigate a world where there is rarely one right answer.

REFLECTION POINT

Do you worry about making mistakes or 'looking stupid' in front of other students? Are you afraid of asking a stupid question?

Think about a class or seminar where you have taken part in a discussion or activity that you found interesting and helped you to clarify your understanding of the subject matter Now think about a seminar or tutorial where no one wanted to speak and no discussions took place.

What do you think the factors were that led to students' willingness to engage in a discussion?

[12] Stella Coyle and Hannah Gibbons-Jones, '"Make glorious mistakes!" Fostering Growth and Wellbeing in HE Transition' (2022) 56(1) The Law Teacher 37–53, 38.

[13] Lydia Bleasdale and Sarah Humphreys, *Undergraduate Resilience Research Project: Project Report* (Leeds Institute for Teaching Excellence 2018) https://teachingexcellence.leeds.ac.uk/wp-content/uploads/sites/89/2018/01/LITEbleasdalehumphreys_fullreport_online.pdf at page 64 (last accessed 27 November 2025).

Identity and Belonging to Community

Another factor for law students is possibly the lack of a sense of belonging to a community. Law students are more likely to see their peers as competitors, to dislike group work, and perhaps to form instrumental relationships with peers, viewing them in terms of networking and potential career advancement. This lack of social connectedness may impact on law students' sense of well-being.[14] One study found that students with a strong sense of identity as a lawyer 'appeared to behave in line with competitive and adversarial norms, which may lead to decreased well-being as it may diminish peer support opportunities'.[15] While psychology students found peer support from other students helped them with stress, particularly around coursework, law students in the study were less likely to turn to other students for support, believing that stress was a normal part of studying law and that they should just be able to deal with it.

Group work, or pair work, in a law clinic setting is common. In this chapter we discuss some of the ways in which you can work collaboratively with other students. Working for a client who needs legal advice or representation can help to shift the focus of the group away from competition to a more collaborative environment. The simple fact that clinic work often must be done in a clinic setting to protect confidentiality can help students to develop a sense of community. Social connection and meaningful group memberships can have a positive impact on mental well-being and participating in a law clinic can provide students with a sense of belonging to a community within the law school that may have hitherto presented a hostile and competitive environment.

REFLECTION POINT

Do you recognise this description of law students as competitive? Do you think you have become more competitive since studying law? Has your experience in a law clinic been different when it comes to relationships with other law students?

Motivation

It is not uncommon for law students to be extrinsically motivated to study law—for example, by the desire to get a good job, please parents, or have professional status, rather than simply the love of the subject. Engaging with your learning beyond just seeking the quickest route to good grades can have a positive impact on your mental well-being. This is the distinction between deep and surface learning, and students who engage in deep learning are focused on improving their understanding of their subject matter and are more likely to get a sense of fulfilment from academic work. Finding an emotional connection with your studies can

[14] Massimilliano Tani and Prue Vines, 'Law Students' Attitudes to Legal Education: Pointers to Depression in the Legal Academy and Profession?' (2009) 19(1) Legal Education Review 3.

[15] Faye and Skipper (n 6) 34.

help you to become a deep learner. Surface learners are more likely to be concerned about how to get a good grade without developing an interest in the subject matter. Surface learners are more prone to anxiety and burnout and tend to be less satisfied overall with their time at university.[16] This is not to say that grades are not important: getting a good degree result can improve your employability and give you a sense of achievement. Understanding marking criteria and what you need to do to achieve good marks is part of studying, however, finding a connection or motivation to study beyond the desire for a good grade can actually help you to achieve more academically and improve your mental well-being.

Working in a clinic setting can change the emphasis in student motivation. Students may join a clinic to get experience for their CV and see the clinic as a stepping stone to help them with their career, but once faced with a client and the client's problem, some of the focus and motivation tends to change. Students want to produce good work, not just to get good grades, but to provide useful advice and help to their clients. A change in emphasis away from 'what do I have to do to get a first' to 'what do I have to do to provide high-quality advice to my client' may make learning more meaningful and bring the subject to life in new ways.

As we saw above, law students are more likely to be motivated by grades than by an intrinsic interest in the subject. Often there are few optional choices on a law degree, which can be dominated by the study of core subjects. Time in a law clinic setting provides an opportunity for you to evaluate your priorities and your motivation. Putting a client first can change your focus and may help you to engage in the subject matter in a different way.

REFLECTION POINT

Why did you decide to study law? Has your motivation changed since you started? Were you partly or wholly influenced by the wishes of your parents? Has the study of law been different to how you imagined? What advice would you give your younger self about the decision to study law?

Vicarious Trauma

'We bear witness to the pain of our clients, to the suffering that humans inflict upon each other, and to the incredible strength of survivors of violence, torture and abuse of all kinds.'[17]

Most of the literature about stress and burnout in the legal profession is concerned with workloads and the workplace culture in many law firms (see below for a summary Life in

[16] Gareth Hughes, *Be Well, Learn Well: Improve Your Wellbeing and Academic Performance* (Macmillan 2020) 41–42.

[17] Joanna Fleck and Rachel Francis,Joanna Fleck and Rachel Francis, *Vicarious Trauma in the Legal Profession: A Practical Guide to Trauma, Burnout and Collective Care* (Legal Action Group 2021) 4.

the Law). However, for social justice and legal aid lawyers, the nature of the work itself may be distressing. Vicarious trauma occurs when a professional working with traumatized clients experiences symptoms of stress or depression similar to those caused by experiencing trauma directly.

In this chapter we have looked at how clinical legal settings may provide a structure that supports student mental well-being and mitigate against some of the factors that can negatively impact law students. There is however one aspect of a law clinic experience that you could find difficult or distressing. In a law clinic setting you may interview clients who have experienced very traumatic life experiences, or you may be involved in a project where you have to read documents that recount violent events in detail. For example, you may need to interview a client who has experienced sexual abuse, or you may need to read witness statements detailing an asylum seeker's experience of torture. Even if you are prepared for this, you may be surprised by your emotional response. If you are affected by the work, speak to your supervisor.

Feeling upset or distressed by a client's story or circumstances is normal and does not mean that you have experienced vicarious trauma, but understanding your emotional responses now will help you to develop awareness and self-care if you decide to work in the social justice or legal aid sector. Research on vicarious trauma in the legal profession suggests that lawyers working with traumatized clients are more often affected than professionals working in other sectors, such as mental health and social work.[18] It is not necessarily clear *why* this is the case; however, it seems likely that one factor is the fact that there is little discussion or recognition of the emotional work involved in being a lawyer. The emphasis in training and supervision of lawyers is on problem-solving and legal reasoning, leaving lawyers to manage their emotional response and exposure to trauma alone.

Fleck and Francis identify some key factors that can help protect social justice lawyers from experiencing vicarious trauma from their work. These include recognition that the work is emotionally demanding, training, support from peers in the workplace, and reflective practice. They argue that training and supervision for legal aid lawyers needs to include training in working with traumatized clients and on the impact that working with traumatized clients can have on the lawyers. Supervision should consider the legal and procedural issues arising in cases, but also the emotional impact that the work may have on practitioners.

In your time in a law clinic, you may find the work emotionally demanding or even distressing. Being upset by listening to another person's experiences is a human response. Your experience in the law clinic can help you to develop an understanding of the emotional impact of legal work and to develop some of the tools to protect yourself. Peer support and reflection can be key to developing a workplace culture that is trauma-informed. You may find work in the clinical setting very rewarding, but do not be afraid to speak to other students or your supervisor if you feel distressed. You will probably find that you are not alone, and sharing your experience will enable you to find strategies to manage.

[18] Andrew Levin and Scott Greisberg, 'Vicarious Trauma in Attorneys' (2003) 24(1) Pace Law Review 245–847.

A View from Clinical Legal Practice

Student Well-being in Legal Clinical Settings

AMANDA THURSTON, DIRECTOR, HERTFORDSHIRE LAW CLINIC, AND DIANA KIRSCH, LEGAL CLINIC DIRECTOR, LSE LAW SCHOOL

Having both been in practice as solicitors for many years before moving over to teach at universities, we know how stressful being a legal professional can be. There are the practical considerations, such as deadlines, meeting billing targets, working long hours, and ensuring you give the correct advice; and also issues affecting mental health, such as stress, emotional clients, distressing cases, and office politics.

The legal profession has woken up to how pressurized the life of a lawyer can be, and changes are being made to improve the working life of both solicitors and barristers—which is good timing for those of you planning a career in law. At the same time, universities have recognized the need to protect the well-being of their students—and particularly those of you volunteering in law clinics and other pro bono projects. These activities are a great opportunity to gain practical experience and enhance relevant skills—all of which improve your chance of getting a job in the highly competitive legal graduate market. However, taking part in these projects, particularly as part of extra-curricular work, can take its toll on you.

There are the practical issues, such as fitting the work around your studies and other commitments, working well with your peers, and ensuring you adhere to deadlines and regulations. There are also the emotional considerations—particularly if you are dealing with distressed clients explaining upsetting or traumatic events. While the client themselves can find discussing their situation triggering, any student working on these sensitive cases can be at risk of stress, burnout and/or secondary trauma.

At the University of Hertfordshire, we have taken steps to ensure students working on our pro bono projects feel supported—these include:

Peer support—students work in pairs, so they have someone to talk to about the case without the risk of breaching client confidentiality.

Trauma-informed training—a compulsory session which has expanded from supporting vulnerable clients to avoid triggering them to covering how students can protect their own well-being.

Supervision—regular, informal drop-in sessions to encourage students to get in touch with a member of the clinic team if they need support.

Restricted contact—ensuring clients never have personal contact details for student advisers, so all communications are through the clinic coordinator.

Culture change and resources—being open about well-being and providing easy access to useful resources and links to the university's specialist mental health team. Most recently an extra resource was added allowing students to anonymously post questions and concerns, as well as share their own coping strategies.

Reflection/Debriefing—an online well-being session each semester facilitated by clinic staff, but student-led to allow an informal discussion of issues and solutions.

We undertook research in 2020 after noticing a correlation between students working in the clinic and students who access School well-being support. It was unclear whether the students undertaking clinical work were being adversely affected by their experiences (despite the efforts to protect them), or if students who had already experienced or witnessed trauma of some kind in their own lives were more likely to volunteer to help others, as they appreciate how much it is needed.

An anonymous survey of students working in the clinic was undertaken to try to find the answer, but there were no definitive results. The vast majority confirmed they suffered no negative impact from their clinic work and all found the online well-being sessions useful.

Some of the 'Top Tips' and personal coping strategies that have come out of our student well-being sessions include:

- compartmentalizing your clinic work by organizing it on specific days and times so it doesn't take over your life;
- taking a complete break if possible after a difficult client meeting, by going to the gym or meeting up with a friend, or even just going out for a walk;
- keeping yourself detached from your client by recognizing that you did not cause their problem and it is not your responsibility to solve it;
- talking to someone else about a difficult case (taking into account confidentiality issues), which can 'lessen the load'; and
- recognizing the need to protect yourself and avoid any triggering or retraumatizing—so if you need to, ask to be removed from a case.

Mental Well-being in the Legal Profession

Along with growing concerns about the mental health of law students, there are also growing concerns about the mental health and well-being of the profession.

In 2021, Law Care published *Life in the Law*,[19] a report into the mental health of the legal profession. They found that 20 per cent of respondents reported bullying, harassment, and discrimination in the workplace and 69 per cent of respondents reported mental health problems in the previous 12 months. As we saw in the case of *SRA v James* [2018] EWHC 3058 (Admin) in Chapter 9, the impact of a toxic work environment can have disastrous consequences on an individual's career.

REFLECTION POINT

In 2018 Claire Matthews, a junior solicitor who had just started a new job, left a briefcase full of confidential client documents on a train. She panicked and, instead of telling her supervisor, spent a week trying to retrieve the briefcase while lying to the firm about what

[19] *Life in the Law*, https://www.lawcare.org.uk/media/14vhquzz/lawcare-lifeinthelaw-v6-final.pdf (last accessed 8 June 2023).

had happened to the files, before finally admitting to what had really happened. The SRA brought a disciplinary action. At the hearing before the SDT Claire Matthews represented herself and did not produce any medical evidence. She gave evidence that she was overwhelmed with panic when she realized her mistake. She was struck off by the SDT, but following wide publicity about her case, a team of pro bono lawyers assisted her to lodge an appeal with supporting medical evidence about her mental health at the time. It was initially agreed that her case should go to a re-hearing but in April 2020 the case was withdrawn and Claire Matthews was free to practise again.[20] The case received widespread publicity due in part to fact that she was unrepresented and did not produce medical evidence, and neither the SRA nor the SDT saw it as part of their role to identify the need for medical evidence. Both the SRA and the SDT have now introduced guidelines on medical evidence which make it clear that although it should normally be the responsibility of the individual being investigated to produce medical evidence, this can also be requested by the SRA. Furthermore, if the Tribunal is concerned that mental health of the individual is relevant to the proceedings, it can encourage the SRA to obtain medical evidence.[21]

- Have you ever made a mistake or done something wrong that led you to panic?
- If you left confidential papers on a train, what would be your first reaction?
- If your first instinct would be to get them back, at what point would you decide to own up to the mistake?
- What factors might make it easier for you to tell someone?

Life in the Law identified three main factors in law firms that had a negative impact on the mental health of lawyers:

- *Low Autonomy*—respondents who had less control over the type or work they did were more likely to experience symptoms of depression or anxiety.
- *Lack of Psychological Safety*—respondents who did not feel able to speak up with ideas, ask questions, or raise concerns about mistakes had higher rates of burnout.
- *High Levels of Workload*—working long and intense hours meant that even in environments with high autonomy and psychological safety, symptoms of burnout were more likely.

The report makes recommendations for changes in working culture which include more management training and regular catch-ups that are supportive. The report also calls for an end to stigma around mental health and well-being. A common reason for not reporting stress at work was fear of stigma attached to disclosing mental health problems and of a negative impact on career and reputation. There is a need to recognize that well-being is not just the responsibility of the individual, but a collective responsibility.[22]

[20] 'Struck-off junior Matthews free to practise after two-year ordeal', Law Gazette (accessed 14 July 2025).

[21] Solicitors Disciplinary Tribunal. Guidance Note: Health Issues, https://www.solicitorstribunal.org.uk/sites/default/files-sdt/Guidance%20Note%20%28Health%20Issues%29.pdf (last accessed 8 November 2022).

[22] *Life in the Law*, https://www.lawcare.org.uk/media/14vhquzz/lawcare-lifeinthelaw-v6-final.pdf (last accessed 8 June 2023).

Following the *Life in the Law* report, the SRA published updated Guidance called 'Workplace Environment: risks of failing to protect and support colleagues'. This Guidance makes the responsibilities on firms and individuals in relation to fair treatment at work more explicit, and in particular places an obligation on firms to

> do everything they reasonably can to look after the well-being of those who work in and with the firm. And protect them from bullying, harassment, discrimination and victimisation, while supporting them so they can work safely and effectively.
>
> This means taking steps such as:
>
> - Having effective systems and controls to supervise work, and monitor concerns which may affect individuals' well-being and competence.
> - Providing a safe environment for people to raise concerns and addressing them promptly and in a constructive manner. Firms should also be aware that poor performance by an individual could be a warning sign that an individual is working under stress or duress.
> - Treating people with dignity and respect to create an ethical workplace and an engaged workforce that provides a better client experience.
> - Having in place and implementing policies on bullying, harassment, discrimination and victimisation as well as disciplinary procedures for breach of those policies.[23]

This guidance is relatively new, and it remains to be seen whether this will lead to a change in culture across the profession.

Recognizing Stress and Burnout

So far in this chapter we have explored some of the structures that can cause stress and anxiety in law students and the legal profession. This does not mean that as a law student you have no control and can do nothing if you are struggling. Where possible, you need to try and take control of a situation and to recognize when you need help. The examples of disciplinary proceedings relating to junior lawyers experiencing mental health problems had a common theme, which was that they panicked about a mistake that was serious but not fatal, and then took steps to hide the mistake. It was the dishonesty attached to the cover-up that led to the disciplinary proceedings, not the mistake itself.

Studying law is challenging, but can be interesting and rewarding. You may also face challenges in your personal life. Negative emotions are not always bad; they are a normal response to difficult or upsetting situations. Sometimes negative emotions overwhelm you or prevent you from achieving your goals, and this is when poor well-being or mental health problems begin. Learning to recognize your emotions and understand them is an important step towards maintaining perspective and staying in control. It is helpful to learn the

[23] 'Workplace environment: risks of failing to protect and support colleagues', Solicitors Regulation Authority (accessed 14 July 2025).

difference between stretch and stress.[24] Being stretched means that you are challenged to do something difficult, but you feel able and motivated to achieve. Learning anything new can be challenging, but if you are stressed the negative emotions can prevent you from making progress or learning. Learning to recognize the difference is important. As law students, you do not need to be stressed all the time, but you should be stretched.

If you are feeling overwhelmed with work, seek help. You may simply have too much to do and need help deciding on priorities. You may be panicking or worried about something that can be dealt with. Learn about basic self-care and take it seriously. Good starting points are the *Student Minds* website, which has practical advice on self-care, or the *Law Care* website.

Some Tips on Self-Care

Keep active

Take a break

Get enough sleep

Prioritize social relationships

Talk about emotions and feelings

Eat well and drink in moderation

Volunteer or get involved in student societies

Ask for help

10.1.2 Self-care in a Law Clinic Setting

As law students, time in a clinic setting can be challenging; you may find this stressful, or you may find it stimulating. The structure of clinic may protect against some of the risk factors for law students and it might help you to reflect on this when you are in a clinic setting. When you start in a law clinic setting it can all feel new and different, which may be hard to start with. Think about whether you are feeling stretched or stressed. If you feel confused, ask for help. You probably won't be the only one.

File Management

File management will help you to recognize what work you need to do, and to organize your time. If you feel overwhelmed with the amount of work you need to do, speak to your supervisor or your peers and decide whether you have too much work to do and, if so, whether some of the work can be shared with another person. Keeping records of work done and clarifying instructions will help you to prioritize and organize your time.

[24] Hughes (n 16) 26.

Working with Others

Working with other students will help you to build a support network. In this chapter we look at how to have a positive experience in group work. Feeling supported and socially connected can improve well-being and protect against burnout and anxiety. Use your time in the clinic to build relationships with other students and share your experiences.

Working with Clients

In a clinical setting you will experience the human side of law. A shift away from doctrinal analysis and theoretical application of rules may bring the law to life for you and make the subject more interesting. It may also increase your anxiety levels as you may be worried about getting things right for the client. If you feel anxious about having responsibility for your client, speak to a supervisor. It is unlikely that your work will go out unchecked.

Reflection

Use your time in clinic to learn to reflect. Whether your experience goes well or not, reflecting will help you to understand your own strengths and weaknesses.

Making Mistakes

Every year, students in law clinic settings make mistakes, some of which might compromise client confidentiality or have serious professional consequences. Your clinical setting will have procedures on how to deal with mistakes and breaches of the rules. It is normal to worry about this. In fact, as aspiring lawyers you should worry about ethics, conduct, and client confidentiality. But you do need to report mistakes. If you make a mistake and don't know what to do, speak to someone. The longer the mistake is left, the worse you will feel, but also the more serious the consequences.

TAKING STOCK

In this section of the chapter we have explored some of the factors that may have an impact on the mental health and well-being of both law students and people working in the legal professions. Research tells us that law students are more likely to suffer from poor mental health compared to other student cohorts. It is likely that there are structural factors in law programmes that impact on student mental health and law clinic settings may have a mitigating effect on some of these factors. Use your time in a clinical legal setting to build connections with other law students so that you can support one another.

Reflection is a tool that can help individuals to understand the causes of stress and seek help if needed. You can use your time in the clinic to develop the habit of reflection, which will help you to continue learning and developing skills when you leave education.

There is a difference between stretch and stress. Learning is challenging and stretch can be an important part of learning. Stress can impact negatively on your capacity to learn or do your job well. Try to learn the difference between the two and ask for help if you are experiencing high levels of stress.

Finally, everyone makes mistakes. It is important to report mistakes to a supervisor quickly. Trying to cover up mistakes can have serious consequences for a career in the law and is also likely to have an adverse effect on your mental health.

A View From Clinical Legal Practice

Imposter Syndrome

Francine Ryan, Director, Open Justice Centre, Open University

Have you ever doubted your own abilities; questioned whether you are clever or academic enough? If, so, you might be surprised to learn that you are not alone. These are classic signs of imposter syndrome, which is a common experience, particularly among high-achieving individuals, where, despite evidence of success, they feel like they are not good enough and worry about others finding this out.

Before I moved into academia, I worked as a practising lawyer. In that role, I was confident: I understood the job, knew how to advise clients, and felt secure in my professional abilities. But transitioning into academia was challenging. Many aspects of the role were unfamiliar, and I found myself questioning whether I was capable or good enough. My confidence wavered, and like many people, I began to struggle with imposter syndrome.

Over time, I have learned to manage those feelings. When I feel self-doubt creeping in, I remind myself that I am competent and capable, and that almost everyone struggles with these feelings at some point. I now try to use imposter syndrome to challenge myself, to step outside of my comfort zone, and as a way to grow and develop myself.

It is important to address imposter syndrome because it can hold you back from pursuing opportunities or achieving your goals. It is also important to remember that self-doubt is entirely normal. You are not alone in feeling this way.

One of the most helpful things you can do is talk to someone you trust—that could be a friend, your tutor, or a family member. Often, simply acknowledging those feelings and hearing someone else's perspective can really help. It also helps to focus on your own achievements: What have you done well? What are you proud of? Use those successes to challenge the negative beliefs that imposter syndrome can create.

And finally, reframe the voice in your head. Remember self-doubt is not a sign of weakness, and challenge that self-doubt by encouraging yourself to take a chance and try something new. The more you practise stepping outside of your comfort zone, the better you will be at managing imposter syndrome, and the more confident you will become in your own ability.

10.2 **Working with Others**

Table 10.1 presents an extract from the SRA Statement of Solicitor Competence. Refer to the companion website to this book to find a downloadable template to audit your skills and help you reflect on your development.

In most clinical legal settings students work in small groups or pairs. These can be groups that you choose, or you may find yourself placed in a group with students you don't know at all. This can be quite daunting and it is common for students to report that they don't like group work.

There is extensive evidence that group work can help students academically and that it can support well-being and self-esteem across all social groups.[25] Group work can help develop a sense of belonging or group identity and this can then help motivate students. But for group work to have these benefits, the group has to function well. Part of the responsibility for making sure that happens falls on your lecturers to set clear expectations for you about why you are doing group work and how that will contribute to a good outcome for the clients and

Table 10.1 Statement of solicitor competence on working with other people

C3 Establish and maintain effective and professional relations with other people, including	Questions to Consider
1. Treating others with courtesy and respect 2. Delegating tasks when appropriate to do so 3. Supervising the work of others effectively 4. Keeping colleagues informed of progress of work, including any risks or problems 5. Acknowledging and engaging with others' expertise when appropriate 6. Being supportive of colleagues and offering advice and assistance when required 7. Being clear about expectations 8. Identifying, selecting and, where appropriate, managing external experts or consultants	Do you have experience in these competencies? How would you rate your competence? Do you need more experience? How could you gain this experience?

[25] David W Johnson and Roger T Johnson, 'An Educational Psychology Success Story: Social Interdependence Theory and Cooperative Learning' (2009) 38(5) Educational Researcher 365–79 at 372; Jana M Hanson, Teniell L Trolian, Michael B Paulsen, and Ernest T Pascarella, 'Evaluating the Influence of Peer Learning on Psychological Well-being' (2016) 21(2) Teaching in Higher Education 191–206; Yi-Fang Luo, Shu-Ching Yang, Rueywei Gong, and Chia-Mei Lu, 'Learning Performance of University Students from the Perspective of Positive Psychology' (2019) 47(3) Social Behavior and Personality: An International Journal 1–10.

a positive experience for you.[26] The other half of the responsibility for making this work falls on you, as students. This section of the chapter will set out some of the ways in which you as students can make the group work for you.

10.2.1 Why Do So Many Students Resist Group Work?

There tend to be two barriers in students' mind to engaging with group work.

- Myths about how you learn
- Worries about perceived fairness.

10.2.2 Myths about How You Learn

There are many myths about how you learn that can prevent you from wanting to engage in work with other students.

Myth 1: The lecturer is there to impart knowledge and students are there to receive it

The way you learn in law clinics tends to be very different from the way you learn in the rest of your law degree. Working with real clients shifts your thinking away from marking criteria and grade expectations, and clinical legal education is a form of experiential learning. The emphasis is on you, the students, working things out for yourself through trial and error. The role of your teachers is not to impart factual information through lectures, but to help you to develop the skills to find answers and evaluate your own work. You need to develop the ability to judge the standard of your own work. This is difficult but necessary and is likely to form a central role in your clinical legal education experience. For many law students, this can be challenging.

REFLECTION POINT

Judging the standard of your own work

- Are you confident you have found the correct law?
- Are you confident you have understood the statutory provisions you have found?
- If you are not confident, do you know when or how to ask for help?
- Have you applied the law to your client's situation?
- Have you explained the law clearly?
- Have you focused on the relevant issues?

How do you know that you have done all of the above? If you are not confident that you judge the standard of your work, how do you think you can develop this ability?

[26] Hannah Leopold and Ann Smith, 'Implementing Reflective Group Work Activities in a Large Chemistry Lab to Support Collaborative Learning' (2020) 10(1) Education Sciences 7; Timothy J Nokes-Malach, J Elizabeth Richey, and Soniya Gadgil, 'When Is It Better to Learn Together? Insights from Research on Collaborative Learning' (2015) 27 Educational Psychology Review 649.

It is likely that in your core modules you have been given lectures about the law, and these lectures are recorded so you can review the content more than once. Lectures will be accompanied by PowerPoint slides or handouts, referring you to key cases and statutory provisions, with brief summaries identifying the main points. Although you are expected to read articles, textbooks, or cases, the lecture and its accompanying slides gives you a safety net of core knowledge to rely on. In contrast, in a law clinic, while your lecturers hold expertise and may well give you introductory lectures on the law, there will be an emphasis on working things out for yourself and learning to judge your own work. If you are the sort of student who believes that studying law is about learning facts, and that it is the job of a lecturer to tell you the facts, then it can be hard to see the value in group work. You may see group work as a waste of time, as you want to learn from your lecturer and not from other students.[27]

As we saw in Chapter 5, experiential learning is grounded in theories that view knowledge as something that has to be constructed by a student, not imparted by a lecturer. You may see this referred to as a social model or a constructivist model. To learn and understand the subject you need to do more than passively receive knowledge from you tutors. You need to make sense of the subject matter by making connections between legal materials, your life experience, and the experience of your client.

Working in groups can help you with this process. This does not mean that your fellow students are replacing the lecturer, but discussing and researching problems together can help you to make sense of the subject matter.[28]

Myth 2: You can't rely on other students' work as they may have got it wrong

If you are put in a group to work together, but believe that the lecturer is the only one with the answers, then you do not want to rely on other students to give you the answers.[29] This is closely related to Myth 1. Working in groups does not necessarily mean that you have to rely on other students to give you the right answer. Discussing problems together can help you make sense of the law. It might be time-consuming and even lead to some confusion, but the process of thinking and talking about the problem together can help you to a much deeper and more nuanced understanding of the legal issues involved.[30]

Myth 3: There is only one right answer

In most cases, there is more than one way of resolving a legal problem. Believing that there is only one right answer, or one way of going about solving a problem, will often lead to a belief that only the lecturer has the right answer. If you believe this, then spending time working with other students can seem like a waste of time.

[27] Sheri Stover and Cindra Holland, 'Student Resistance to Collaborative Learning' (2018) 12(2) International Journal for the Scholarship of Teaching and Learning, Article 8.

[28] David Boud, 'Making the Move to Peer Learning' in D Boud, R Cohen, and J Sampson (eds), *Peer Learning in Higher Education: Learning From and With Each Other* (Kogan Page 2001) 1–20.

[29] Naomi E Winstone et al, 'Supporting Learners' Agentic Engagement with Feedback: A Systemic Review and a Taxonomy of Recipience Processes' (2017) 52 Educational Psychologist 17.

[30] Kristi Lundstrom and Wendy Baker, 'To Give Is Better Than to Receive: The Benefits of Peer Review to the Reviewer's Own Writing' (2009) 18(1) Journal of Second Language Writing 30–43.

There is never only one right answer, and this is even more true in the law clinic than in some traditionally taught law courses. For example, when you study principles of criminal law in the first or second year of your degree, you will probably be set short problem questions based on fictional scenarios for coursework or exams. It is likely that the person setting the question has a clear idea about how the answer should be structured and what advice should be given. In a law clinic setting, you are exploring legal problems in a very different way, and a client's case is unlikely to fit neatly into a particular area of law.

Working with other students in groups can help you to develop your ability to see a problem from different perspectives. You are not relying on other students to give you the right answer, nor is group work delaying you in getting the right answer from your lecturer. Working with other students should help to develop your ability to see things from different perspectives. In a law clinic setting:

- There are different ways to draft a letter. Much of that might be to do with house style or the type of client that you are writing to.
- There are different ways to organize research records and different ideas and theories about how best to interview a client.
- Different experts may differ in the advice they give on the merits of a case, or on what evidence is needed to support your client's case. One lawyer may place much more emphasis on mediation or ADR than another lawyer.

Myth 4: Giving peer feedback is about criticizing someone else's work

As part of group work, you may be asked to give feedback on other students' work in the clinic. Giving feedback is difficult and students often report that they do not want to do this. Some research in this area suggests that student feedback can be superficial and overly positive. Students are nervous of criticizing someone else for fear of being criticized in return.[31] Giving feedback is difficult and takes practice.

Research into feedback and peer feedback suggests that it is most valuable when there is dialogue or conversation around the feedback.[32] It might help you to think of feedback as a process whereby you reflect on what is good about a piece of work and how it might be improved. Even an outstanding piece of work can be changed or improved or approached in a different way.

Moreover, when students engage in peer feedback, it is the student giving the feedback who benefits the most.[33] This is because the process of giving feedback helps you to think critically about a piece of work and to really understand what is good or needs improving.

[31] Ina Blau, Tamar Shamir Inbal, and Orit Avediel, 'How Does the Pedagogical Design of a Technology-enhanced Collaborative Academic Course Promote Digital Literacies, Self-regulation and Perceived Learning of Students?' (2020) 45 The Internet and Higher Education, 100722 p.6.

[32] David Boud, Ruth Cohen, and Jane Sampson (eds), *Peer Learning in Higher Education: Learning From and With Each Other* (Routledge 2014).

[33] Qiyun Zhu and David Carless, 'Dialogue within Peer Feedback Processes: Clarification and Negotiation of Meaning' (2018) 37 Higher Education Research & Development 883, 893.

If you are going to engage in peer feedback or review of your peers' work, you will need input from your supervisor. Peer feedback does not replace feedback from your supervisor; it supports that feedback and helps you to develop your own ability to judge the quality of your own work as well as others'.[34]

REFLECTION POINT

Have you ever been asked to give peer feedback, perhaps on a student presentation or on a draft answer in class? How did you feel about doing this? Were you confident that you could make sense of what you were looking at? What might have made that experience better for you?

10.2.3 **Fairness**

Is group work inherently unfair because not everyone will pull their weight? This is certainly how many students feel, and it can cause problems for everyone in a group. Often the stress of getting the group to work together is exacerbated by assessment. If you are going to get a group mark for the work, it can feel very unjust if some people in the group do all the work but everyone gets the same mark. It can also feel very unfair if you think that the quality of the work would have been better if you had done the work alone and therefore achieved a higher mark.

In a law clinic you may be worried about producing a high standard of work for your client and you may be under pressure to work to quite tight deadlines, which can lead to stress about managing the group and being sure that work is distributed fairly.

REFLECTION POINT

Can you give an example of a negative experience of group work at university?

- What was it about that experience that made it negative?
- What do you think you could have done differently to improve the experience?

Can you think of an example of a positive experience of group work at university?

- What factors influenced the positive experience to make it work for you?
- If you had to do group work again, could you recreate those circumstances to make the experience positive for you?

[34] David Nicol, Avril Thomson, and Caroline Breslin, 'Rethinking Feedback Practices in Higher Education: A Peer Review Perspective' (2014) 39 Assessment & Evaluation in Higher Education 102, 120.

Group dynamics can be very difficult and teamwork could go wrong at many different points in your professional life. The possible negative consequences of poor teamwork in a university law clinic are not as serious as they might be in the workplace. Your work will be closely supervised in the clinic and advice to clients will be checked by a supervisor. If collaborative working in the law clinic is difficult, you have an opportunity to reflect on this and talk about how it might have gone differently. You will have had a valuable learning experience which will stand you in good stead later in your working life.

Students can be very quick to judge one another in a group setting.[35] The worries about fairness can quickly translate into assumptions that someone is not pulling their weight or will be a burden on the group. Often the 'loafer' or 'free rider' feels excluded. They don't contribute in a meeting or they miss deadlines because they feel judged or excluded, and a vicious circle is created. The best way to prevent this from happening is to address group communication from the very start. Don't approach group work presuming that this will be a barrier to your success or that working with other students might cause you problems. It will help you to get more out of the experience if you think of this as an opportunity to learn about how to manage teamwork and to develop strategies and skills for working with others.

REFLECTION POINT

Consider the following scenario:

Dev and Ellie have joined the law clinic. They have been put into a pair by the clinic administrator to work on a case together. They are both in their final year and have never met before. Dev is from a middle-class professional family. He was privately educated and his mother is a judge. He is socially confident and has done lots of legal work experience, which was arranged for him by his parents.

Ellie is the first person in her family to attend university. She lives at home with her mother and her sister. Her sister has a serious disability so Ellie helps her mother to care for her sister. She also works three days a week in a local supermarket, which makes it hard for her to commit to any extra-curricular activities.

Dev is used to doing well in assessments. He knows that his parents expect him to get a first-class degree and secure a training contract in a top commercial firm. He is not sure that this is what he wants for himself but is afraid of letting his parents down. He is very anxious and has not been sleeping well.

Ellie has not done as well on her law degree as she wanted to. She often struggles to get as much reading done as she would like to, because she has to fit this around her job and her caring responsibilities. She is very worried about finding enough time to commit to the law clinic, but she knows she really needs to get some practical experience. She is worried that she will not have the skills to do the work well and that students like Dev will think she is stupid because she does not have any legal work experience.

[35] Cinnamon Hillyard, Diane Gillespie, and Peter Littig, 'University Students' Attitudes about Learning in Small Groups after Frequent Participation' (2010) 11(1) Active Learning in Higher Education 9–20.

Ellie and Dev have been allocated a client with an employment law problem. They need to conduct a fact-finding interview and then prepare a letter of advice, which needs to be approved by the supervisor and sent the client within three weeks of the appointment. They are meeting today for the first time to plan the interview.

- What problems with communication could arise for these two?
- What steps could they take in this first meeting?
- Both students are worried about doing well. Do you think they are likely to share this with one another in their first meeting?
- What different strengths might they have?
- When you are paired with someone new, do you take time to get to know them a bit, or do you prefer to just get on with the work?

10.3 Getting Started with Group Work

The basic building blocks of group work are trust and communication. You don't have to be friends with everyone you work with, but putting some effort into getting to know your colleagues can help to build trust and communication. If you are going to be in a group for the whole academic year, make some time at the start of the year to go for a coffee or a drink, or do something social together. If your group is online, you can still take time to get to know each other. In virtual meetings make sure you allow five minutes at the start of meetings to check in on how you all are and how your week has been.

Practical Exercise 10.1

One way to help break the ice and help set some ground rules is to think about personality types and traits so that you can adapt how you work to suit other people in the group. It can also help you to get to know one another. You need to have a basic level of trust to do this, and may want to wait until you have known one another for a week or two before trying this activity:

Take this online test at https://www.16personalities.com/free-personality-test and share your strengths and weaknesses. Use this exercise to decide how to organize work in the first few weeks of term. Then agree to challenge yourselves by changing roles and seeing what it is like to work on your weaknesses. For example, someone who is extroverted with a high empathy score is probably a good person to do the first client interview. In the first set of pairings work with someone who has opposite traits to you. Then try changing pairs and work with someone who is your opposite. Which was more productive? As you work together, try to remember who has a high introvert score and who has a high extrovert score. Extroverts, you need to make sure you give introverts space to speak up and contribute in meetings. Introverts, you need to find ways to contribute that work for you.

Another useful online resource is the Belbin site at https://www.belbin.com/about/belbin-team-roles. An assessment of your type has to be paid for, but you can look at the different team roles and think about which one you fit most closely. Share this with the group and use it to help set ground rules.

Remember, if you use these resources, that traits are not fixed and you may find you respond differently to stress or challenges for multiple reasons. These types of activities can help you to get to know one another and think about how you work together, but they should not define you or become a reason to limit your own or someone else's experience.

10.3.1 **Set Out Some Ground Rules**

For example, from the beginning you need to think about the following:

- How often are you going to have meetings?

  You may have regular timetabled or scheduled meetings with a supervisor, but it is likely that you will need to meet regularly without your supervisor in order to progress the work on your file. Take time to compare your timetables and agree on some times for meetings.
- Who will keep a note of the meetings?

  Keeping a record of meetings is important and is a good habit to get into. A record or a meeting should include who was there, any apologies (ie someone who could not come but who let you know they were not coming), a summary of what was discussed, a list of actions agreed with time scales, and a clear record of who is responsible for each action. This record will help you all to keep track of what is happening. If someone is ill, they can see what they have missed and can still be allocated work. Your supervisor can also keep an eye on what you are doing and can see if one person is not keeping up or doing their fair share.
- How will you divide the work?

  If you are going to work as a team over a number of cases, think about rotating roles as you work through your clients. If you only have one case together, think about how to share the work fairly. Where will you save your work?

  You may have a case management system where all your client work has to be saved. If you don't have a case management system, do you have shared files where you can all see one another's work. Make sure you agree from the beginning where work will be, so that it is easy for everyone to find.
- How will you notify one another when work is completed?

  Do you need to send each other messages to say when work is done? Or will you just rely on finding work in the file? You need to find a balance between overwhelming one another with messages and leaving people to keep checking to see if work is finished or ready.

- Who will be responsible for making sure that people stick to deadlines?
  This might be a role that you rotate. Or you could take shared responsibility for meeting deadlines. It is sensible to build in a system of ensuring that you meet deadlines. If it is your job to keep everyone on track, think about how to do this in a way that is not perceived as overbearing or bossy.

10.3.2 Dividing Work

If working in a team is going to be worthwhile, you need to find ways to divide the work in a way that is useful. To do this you need to divide the tasks so that each individual on the team is contributing to the final piece of work. A common error is duplication of effort. You agree that you all need to do some research, head off and do the research, then come back and find you have all researched the same area of law and created duplicate research records. Another error is to split the work into sections without thinking about what the final product needs to look like.

For example: you have to write a letter of advice on a family law case where the client is about to issue an application for a child arrangements order. There are six of you in the group. You split into pairs. Pair 1 will research and write about procedure. Pair 2 will research and write about the relevance of domestic abuse allegations in an child contact case. Pair 3 will research and write about the availability of legal aid for this client. Each pair goes away and does their work and the three sections of the letter are cut and pasted together for the supervisor to approve. The letter is disjointed and written in three completely different styles. There is repetition of some issues and some points don't make sense as they contradict what was said in another section. None of you were thinking about the client when you did this. What's more, your learning is limited to your part of the letter. You have no overview. For example, you were in pair 1. You never reviewed or thought about the research or section of the advice letter written by pair 2. At a later date you have to complete an assessment on child arrangement orders and domestic abuse. Although you were on a team that wrote a letter of advice on this issue, you know absolutely nothing about the topic because you did not do any work on this part of the letter and have to start from scratch. Or perhaps you are asked about your clinic experience during a job interview, but you find yourself floundering as you clearly know little about the relevant law.

The benefit of the group was that it reduced your workload as you only had to research and write one part of the letter, but that was all. Saving time and energy meant that you did not have to get to know the other four students in your team and you only learned about a small area of law.

When you divide the work, you need to think about how each individual component will contribute to the whole. One way you can do this is to split the research and the letter writing in a different way. For example, pair 1 will research procedure, but will write the section of the letter explaining the substantive law. Pair 2 will research the substantive law, but write the section of the letter on procedure. Pair 3 will be responsible for the final overall letter and running the file, so they will need to make sure that work has been time-recorded, chair meetings, and check that everyone is keeping to agreed time limits. If you are writing a research record for someone else to use, you need to understand the law in depth and highlight the most relevant points. If you are writing advice based on someone else's research, you need to be able to ask them questions to clarify points and feel confident that you can use their work to explain the issues to your client. This probably means that you need to meet up and work together on the letter to make sure you have got it right. Working like this is more complicated than the first scenario but it means you need to keep communicating and the final letter is likely to be much more coherent. You will also come out with an understanding of how all the law and procedure for this one case fit together.

10.3.3 **Confidentiality and Teamwork**

When you are organizing meetings or thinking about communication among your team, you need to think about confidentiality. If your clinic has a dedicated space for students to work in then you can be confident that your discussions will not be overheard. If you don't have a confidential workspace, check the rules about meetings and think about meeting in a place where your discussions can't be overheard—for example, you can often book a meeting room in the library. If you are working remotely, where will you be when you join on online meeting? Can anyone overhear your conversation? Do you have headphones to help protect confidentiality?

Think about how you will communicate. You might want to set up a social media chat group (for example on What'sApp) to keep in touch about meetings, but this is probably not a suitable channel for sharing client information.[36] Set some ground rules from the start about how you want to communicate about work. Keeping good file notes is the best way of making sure that everyone in the group knows what is going on. Good file management, with records of meetings, research, drafts of letters, interview notes, and so on saved in one place, means you only have to send short confidential messages to one another—such as 'I finished a first draft of the letter for client PN. It's in the file labelled draft 2.'

A View From Clinical Legal Practice

Valuing Collaboration in Legal Clinics

Catherine F. Klein, Professor, The Families and Law Clinic, The Catholic University of America and Erin M. Scheick, Faculty, The Families and Law Clinic, The Catholic University of America

Collaboration in legal practice is both challenging and rewarding. It requires active listening, open-mindedness, patience, and creativity. It also brings fresh perspectives, shared successes, and a sense of collective purpose to legal representation. In clinic, students collaborate not only with peers, supervisors, and other professionals, but also with clients—working together to understand their needs and build trust, while developing effective legal strategies to advance their clients' interests. In turn, teamwork strengthens advocacy, makes problem-solving more dynamic, and produces the joy of achieving meaningful outcomes together.

[36] Don't forget to check the rules about communication. You may not be permitted to use What'sApp. You may have to use secure clinic software to communicate as a group.

Like any skill, effective collaboration requires thoughtful planning and consistent practice. In the clinical setting, this begins with the design of the course syllabus and learning objectives, and is practised through in-class exercises and direct client representation. Clinicians can be creative about including collaboration skills-building in the clinical setting, including by incorporating the following:

- **Learning Objectives in Course Syllabi**: Including learning objectives in course syllabi supports student focus on learning goals while ensuring that course activities are designed in furtherance of purported aims. A suggested learning objective pertaining to collaboration may be that students enrolled in the course will 'Develop the tools necessary to effectively collaborate with your peers and legal system actors, by engaging in meaningful teamwork, providing and responding to constructive feedback, and reflecting on ways to strengthen and integrate collaboration in direct client representation'.
- **Peer Editing to Encourage Critical Reflection and Constructive Feedback**: Peer editing, by which students review one another's written or oral work product and provide feedback, can be an effective method for practising compassionate collaboration and the healthy exchange of constructive suggestions aimed at skill improvement. One exercise that can be employed is having students first work independently to draft written legal work product, such as an intake memo, complaint, direct examination, or closing argument. Scaffold the exercise by providing students with evaluation criteria that not only explain the stated goals of the written assignment, but also include benchmarks for assessing whether the student has satisfied those targets (e.g. Does the writing include a clear articulation of the theory of the case, by weaving together the facts and applicable law?) During class, students can pair up and exchange drafts, provide feedback alongside the evaluation criteria, and then deliver that feedback to the other person. The key is to provide thoughtful feedback that both improves the draft writing and builds trust and open communication between partners.
- **Incorporating Honest Self-Assessment into the Collaborative Partnership Model**: Within the clinic, students generally work in pairs, where they practice teamwork and collaboration in representing their clients and working on clinic-related projects. In order to facilitate communication and planning, during the first week of class students will fill out a 'Human User Guide' or 'HUG' that asks for an assessment of one's work style, schedule, communication preferences, and workplace values. This honest reflection is used as the foundation of our first supervisory meeting, where students are encouraged to share from their HUG and speak openly about how they will collaboratively approach work tasks. One way they put this in practice immediately is in drafting, and maintaining, weekly supervision agendas. Teams are asked to prepare one agenda, and also lead the supervision meetings. In this way, students are able to take ownership of the collaborative process—sharing in who presents on what topic from the agenda; discussing in advance which items require supervisor input; and transparently recording a work plan for the week based on next steps and tasks identified by the students and/or supervisor.

The practice of law is an inherently collaborative process, whereby lawyers, clients, experts, and other professionals share information and input in order to advance interests and direct just outcomes. Developing effective collaboration skills during law school—and through the law school clinic—primes students for carrying these skills into their careers, building a fruitful foundation for future success.

10.3.4 **Common Problems**

Someone Taking Control

> 'There is one person in the group who is really controlling and she just takes over. It really gets on my nerves. She tells everyone what to do and then takes all the credit for everything when we meet with our supervisor.'

First, it is probably helpful to step back and think about why they are behaving in this way. This person may have had a bad experience in groups before. They may be anxious about doing well. The rest of you may have been slow to get started, giving them the impression that you would not be reliable in getting work done.

At the start of the term, did you discuss roles within the group? Did you decide that you would take it in turns to be responsible for leading each case, or each week? If you did, perhaps you could tackle the situation by going back to that initial plan and gently pointing out that it is X's turn to take responsibility for managing the group. If you did not have any discussions about allocating roles, this might be a good time to do it. You don't necessarily need a group leader. If you have a meeting and allocate work to individuals with clear deadlines then each individual can be responsible for their own work.

When you have meetings, allocate a chair to run the meeting and make sure that everyone is given an opportunity to contribute. The chair can directly ask people who have not contributed if they want to say something. Or the chair can set ground rules at the start of the meeting to make sure that everyone gets a chance to speak. Rotate the role of chair so that the same person is not always in charge of the meeting. If you are the chair, be respectful while controlling the meeting—for example, if there is one person who won't stop talking, thank them for their contribution before saying that it is someone else's turn to speak.

If work is being recorded accurately on the file, your supervisor will be able to see who has done the work, even if one person is trying to take credit for everything.

Meeting Times Taken Up with Chat

> 'I just want to get on with work on the file, but when we have meetings everyone spends the time chatting and then we don't have time to get anything done.'

Some chat at the beginning of a meeting is OK. Friendly relationships in groups can help you to work well together. But too much time spent chatting can mean that work does not get done. Perhaps look at the time that you have set aside for meetings. Do you need to just have a longer meeting? Or can you change the time of the meeting so that you don't have something else to get to afterwards?

Talk to the group about priorities and agree a time limit for chat at the start of meetings. Try allocating the role of meeting chair to someone so that they are responsible for setting an agenda and for timekeeping so that you are able to get through the work. Agree that you will all go for a coffee after the team meeting so that there is time to chat later.

Fear of Looking Stupid

> 'I feel like everyone in the group knows more than me. I don't want to share my work with them in case it is all wrong and I look stupid.'

This is best overcome through building trust within the group. If you trust your colleagues you will be less worried about sharing your work with them. It is likely that you are not the only person in the group who feels this way. Working in a clinical setting is a new and different way of learning for everyone.

Look at ways to build a culture of respect within the group. If there are five or six of you in the group, split into pairs to do some work. Sharing your work with just one person is less intimidating than sharing it with five. Make sure you get feedback from your supervisor early on. If this is helpful and constructive it should help to build your confidence.

Even highly experienced and successful lawyers and academics worry about making mistakes or producing poor work. This is completely normal, but in order to produce good work or improve the quality of your work, you need to get feedback. The more feedback you get, the more you learn. Take a leap of faith and remember that it is better to make mistakes and learn from them in the relative safety of the clinic, where your work is closely supervised.

Fear of Making Someone Else Feel Bad

> 'When we shared our legal research on the client's case I thought that someone in my group had got the law all wrong, but I did not want to make them feel bad so did not say anything.'

It is normal to be afraid of hurting someone else's feelings. Start by putting yourself in the shoes of the other person. If you had gone completely wrong in your research, would you want someone to point this out to you? How would you want this done? Giving constructive feedback takes practice and you won't always get it right:

- Frame your feedback as a question—how did you go about doing the research? What resources did you use? How did you check this was the right source?
- Give positive feedback—if you are going to give feedback on someone's work, start with the positives.
- Give feedback sensitively—comment on the work and not the person.
- Give constructive feedback—rather than thinking about what is 'wrong' or 'right' try to focus on how a piece of work can be improved.
- Give accurate feedback—if you think the research is wrong, where has it gone wrong? Is it out of date? Missing a key case? Not relevant to the client's problem?
- Be helpful with your feedback—could you offer to help your colleague do a bit more research to find more information?
- Be kind—think about your tone of voice and body language.
- Ask for feedback on your feedback—ask your peers to tell you how they felt about your feedback.

Feedback is not a one-way process. A conversation around feedback that explores where the mistakes might be and how work can be improved is helpful for both the giver and the receiver of feedback. Learning to give constructive feedback can help you improve your own work as it helps you to form judgements on the quality of a piece of work.

Someone in the Group Has Gone Missing

> 'One person in my group has not done any work on the file for two weeks. They don't seem to care and have not answered my messages demanding to know where they are.'

Don't presume the worst. This student may be ill or involved in a family crisis. They may be worried about letting the group down or embarrassed about something. If you have been chasing them with 'demands', they might not feel able to tell you what has gone wrong. Instead of demanding to know where they are, try asking if they are OK or if they need any help. If you still don't get a response, let your supervisor know. The student either needs to be called in to explain themselves, or they need help. You need to know what to do about the outstanding work for the client. Better to contact your supervisor than struggle on alone.

One Person Is Always Late

> 'There is one person in the group who is late for every single meeting. It's really annoying.'

This is annoying. But don't allow your annoyance about the lateness colour your whole relationship with your colleague. They may be late because they have something else directly before the team meeting. It does not mean that they are lazy or lack commitment to the work. Address this issue by asking if you need to try and find a different time for the meeting, or discuss a strategy that means the lateness does not disrupt the meeting. For example, if they are late, you won't go back over what they have missed; they can catch up later by reading the minutes of the meeting.

Missing a Meeting Because You Were Ill

> 'I missed the team meeting last week because I was ill and now I don't know what I am supposed to be doing this week.'

Everyone is ill sometimes and it is likely that there will be occasions throughout your career when you will have to miss or rearrange something. This should only cause you and other people problems if you don't communicate about it.

- If you are ill, make sure you let everyone know in advance that you will miss a meeting.
- Keep your team informed about how long you are likely to be off and whether you will be able to complete work on time.
- If your absence is likely to be short, ask them to allocate you work in the meeting. If you are going to be ill for a while, make sure that your team know this, so they can cover your work.

- There should be a clear note on the file of the meeting that you missed, so you can look at what was discussed and what work you need to do.
- If there is no note on the file and you don't have a group chat then it's probably a good idea to contact your supervisor to let them know you were ill and don't know what work you need to do next.
- With groups that work together for a whole term or a whole academic year, there is plenty of time for some give and take. If you were ill in November you can make sure that you offer to do some extra work in the second term to make up for time missed.

Troubleshooting

Sometimes you will run into real difficulties when working with other people. Even if you usually get on well in groups and like working with other people, a relationship can go wrong and the experience can be upsetting. The best way to avoid problems is to:

- build some trust;
- communicate regularly;
- be clear about who is doing what and when;
- don't make assumptions;
- be flexible;
- be kind; and
- keep good file records.

If you have all this in place and you are still struggling, tell your supervisor and ask for help.

Practical Exercise 10.2

When the work for your first client is complete, take 2–3 mins to reflect on the questions below individually. Once everyone has reflected individually, take turns sharing your answers with other group members. As a group, agree on something you will change and how you will do it for the next client.

1. What is the one change your group will make to improve your performance?
2. What is your group going to do to solve the problem or improve?

After your second client, review your improvement plan:

1. What did you do to implement your improvement plan?
2. If you implemented the plan:

   (a) What specific effect did this have? Can you give examples? Are there any additional changes you think your group needs to make?

(b) If you did not follow through with the plan, why not? How will you change this for the next client? Think of some clear actionable steps.

If you will only work on one client case with your group you can adapt this exercise and consider an improvement plan at the end of the first week.[37]

TAKING STOCK

In this section of the chapter we have explored some of the potential benefits of group work and considered ways in which you can create some ground rules to help you overcome resistance or problems. Being able to work in a team can support learning and help to build resilience, and is an important employability skill. Time spent in a law clinic can be a good opportunity to develop teamwork skills.

There are two major barriers to group work: myths about how you learn and worries about fairness. Clinical legal education is based on theories of experiential learning. Students learn through trial and error. The role of the supervisor/lecturer is not to impart knowledge, but to provide feedback on student work. Giving and receiving peer feedback and sharing work on files, such as research and drafting, can help students to develop the skills needed to form judgements on the quality of their own work.

Distribution of work in groups can be unfair, but good communication and sensible ground rules about expectations can prevent disagreements about workload. Working in groups can be challenging, but when the conditions are right it can support learning and well-being.

10.4 Communicating with Clients

As a student adviser in a law clinic, you are likely to meet a client in a client interview. You may have an ongoing relationship with your client through casework. It is likely that some of the communication will go through a supervisor. Chapter 11 contains guidance on conducting a client interview and writing letters to clients. This section of the chapter explores some more general themes about communication and relationships with clients.

Below (Table 10.2) is an extract from the SRA Statement of Solicitor Competence. Refer to the companion website to this book to find a downloadable template to audit your skills and help you reflect on your development.

[37] This exercise is adapted from an activity described in H Leopold and A Smith, 'Implementing Reflective Group Work Activities in a Large Chemistry Lab to Support Collaborative Learning' (2020) 10(1) Education Sciences 27.

Table 10.2 Statement of solicitor competence on maintaining effective relations with clients

C2 Establish and maintain effective and professional relations with clients, including:[38]	Questions to consider
1. Treating clients with courtesy and respect 2. Providing information in a way that clients can understand, taking into account their personal circumstances and any particular vulnerability 3. Understanding and responding effectively to clients' particular needs, objectives, priorities and constraints 4. Identifying and taking reasonable steps to meet the particular service needs of all clients including those in vulnerable circumstances 5. Identifying possible courses of action and their consequences and assisting clients in reaching a decision 6. Managing clients' expectations regarding options, the range of possible outcomes, risk and timescales 7. Agreeing the services that are being provided and a clear basis for charging 8. Explaining the ethical framework within which the solicitor works 9. Informing clients in a timely way of key facts and issues including risks, progress towards objectives, and costs 10. Responding appropriately to clients' concerns and complaints	Do you have experience in these competencies? How would you rate your competence? Do you need more experience? How could you gain this experience?

10.4.1 **Treating Clients with Courtesy and Respect**

Being in a clinical legal setting provides you with an excellent opportunity to learn and develop new skills. It can help you to make important decisions about your future career and it can provide you with valuable experience to put on your CV. This means that sometimes students lose sight of the fact that the client is not there to serve their needs and help them gain experience. The client is there because they need legal services and it is your job to provide them. A core principle in the way in which lawyers are regulated around the world is that lawyers have a duty to act in their client's best interests (see Chapter 8: Professional Legal Ethics).

It is likely that your clients in the law clinic will be accessing your service because it is free or affordable. They may have a problem that is personal and difficult to talk about with anyone, let alone a stranger. They may be coming to see you at a time in their life when they are particularly vulnerable and emotional. It may be hard for a client to trust you. At times,

[38] https://www.sra.org.uk/solicitors/resources/continuing-competence/cpd/competence-statement/ (last accessed 27 November 2025).

you may feel annoyed or frustrated with your client. They may not answer emails, may miss appointments, or may not bring you the important documents you asked them for. You may also find your client's story very distressing and find it hard to maintain a professional distance because of your desire to help your client. Whatever your experience is, you need to remind yourself that you are there to provide a service to the client; the client is not there to provide you with experience for your CV. Whatever problem the client has, you have a duty to put their interests first, and this means treating them with courtesy and respect, not only when you communicate directly with them but also when you speak about them with your peers.

Try to put yourself in the client's shoes and treat them in the way that you would like to be treated. Basic rules around respect and courtesy include:

- Follow your law clinic's protocols on using first names. Age, culture, and context can make a difference to whether it is better to use first names or address people using their title.
- Check your file before you meet with a client for the first time, so that you are clear about their name and the key elements of their case.
- If you are not sure how to pronounce a name, ask.
- If you are in a hurry to get to your next appointment and the client is telling a long story, don't keep looking at the clock.
- Answer emails and phone calls promptly.

10.4.2 **Legalese**

It is common for lawyers to use language and terms that lay people do not understand. There are abbreviations, names for documents, names for types of hearings, and expressions that we use without thinking. For example, a person at court without a lawyer is a litigant in person. They might be asked on arrival at court: 'Are you in person?' This might be a confusing question, because they don't realize the question means 'Do you have a lawyer representing you today?'

REFLECTION POINT

In your law clinic, have you supported someone through court or tribunal proceedings? Did you understand everything that happened? Did you have to explain to the client what the judge had said? Have you ever observed a hearing? Could you follow everything that happened? What could have been done differently to help you understand?

It is important that clients understand what you are telling them. Part of your role as a lawyer is to enable your client to make informed decisions about what they can do. As a student lawyer you are in a good position to judge communication, as much of the language is new to you as well. However, lack of experience can make it tempting to hide behind difficult language to give an impression of expertise.

Practical Exercise 10.3

Look at these three extracts from a letter explaining exceptional case funding for legal aid to a client. Which one would you hand in as a piece of coursework? Which one would you send to a client? Why?

Example 1

What is ECF?

Exceptional Case Funding (ECF) is legal aid which falls outside the usual scope and is dealt with by a team within the Legal Aid Agency (LAA).

The case law sets out that funding may be available for vulnerable parties where a European Convention Right issue comes up, under LASPO 2012, s10(3).

What are the requirements for ECF?

The test for legal aid must be met but the applicant otherwise must not be eligible for legal aid.

The government guidelines set out the requirements for ECF, asking:

1. Does the case involve the determination of civil rights or obligations?
2. Will withholding of legal aid mean the applicant will be unable to present his or her case effectively, or lead to an obvious unfairness in the proceedings?

There is no requirement to provide legal aid to ensure complete equality between the parties, just as long as one side does not face a substantial disadvantage compared to the other party (as per *De Haes and Gijsles v Belgium* [1998] 25 EHRR 1).

Example 2

Exceptional Case Funding

If your case does not fall within the scope of legal aid, you may still be able to secure funding for your case through Exceptional Case Funding (ECF). Provided that your EU or convention rights will be breached if you do not receive funding for a lawyer, ECF should be available to you. In other words, if you cannot present your case effectively and without obvious unfairness, then you should be eligible for ECF. Based on our discussions so far, it is clear that your case is very complex, making it difficult for you to represent yourself. You also informed us of your issues surrounding your mental health, which further indicates that it may be hard for you to present your case effectively. Both of these factors suggest that you may be eligible for ECF and I would recommend that you consider it as an option. If you do wish to apply for ECF, we will need to check that you meet the financial eligibility and merit criteria. Provided that you do, you will need to complete and email a CIV ECF1 form to the ECF team at ContactECC@justice.gov.uk.

Example 3

Legal aid—Exceptional Case Funding

I explained to you, this morning, that legal aid is not normally available for this type of case. I cannot grant legal aid in your case.

However, there is a scheme called 'Exceptional Case Funding' (ECF). Through this, we can make an application to the Legal Aid Agency and ask them to allow you to have legal aid. We need to explain what it is about your case that makes it 'exceptional'.

The Legal Aid Agency will look at three things to decide if you should get legal aid.

1. How important are the issues?

   The issues in your case are very important. This case involves your family and your future together with them.

2. Complexity

   Your case is quite complicated. There is more than one legal problem and the issues are all interconnected. The facts are also complicated as this has been going on for a long time and there is a lot of information to organize and present to the court.

3. How able are you to deal with the case yourself?

   You were very upset when you came to see me this morning. There is a lot of emotion in this case and that would make it more difficult for you to deal with it yourself. You also explained to me that you have problems with your mental health and this makes it very hard for you to manage the case without help.

Discussion

When you write a piece of coursework, you need to demonstrate to the marker that you understand the law and that you have used relevant and reliable sources. The marker already knows about and understands the law, and your coursework is therefore written using language and terms that the marker will already be familiar with. The purpose of your writing is essentially to impress the marker with the range and depth of your expert knowledge. In contrast, when you write a letter to a client you need to be sure that they understand what the law or legal procedures mean for them. You are explaining how this is relevant to them. You want to be sure they understand what the law means, rather than impressing them with your legal knowledge and jargon. These are quite different aims and adjusting to the idea that you need to remove many legal terms and references from your writing can be challenging to students when they start in law clinics. The first example above is much more like a piece of coursework than a clear piece of communication to a client. The second example is a clearer attempt to explain the issue in client-friendly terms, but the solid paragraph is hard to digest and the explanation is still phrased in legal terms—for example '*If your case does not fall within the scope of legal aid*' or '*Provided that your EU or convention rights will be breached if you do not receive funding*'. The third example avoids legal terminology, breaks the issue down into small digestible points and applies the law to the client's own personal circumstances.

10.4.3 **Vulnerability**

According to the Guidance of the Law Society of England and Wales, 'The terms "vulnerable" and "vulnerability" cover a range of situations that could affect any client who is at a disadvantage because of factors that affect their access to, and use of, legal services'.[39] The Guidance focuses on three broad categories of vulnerable clients:

- clients who have capacity to make decisions and give you instructions, but need extra support to do this because of mental and/or physical disabilities;
- clients who lack mental capacity to make decisions and provide you with instructions, for whom you must follow a range of statutory and other safeguards;
- clients who are vulnerable to undue influence, undue pressure or duress and who may or may not have mental capacity to make decisions and provide you with instructions.

As student advisers in a law clinic, you are most likely to encounter the first of these three categories. If, at any point, you suspect that the client has been put under pressure or are unsure if your client has capacity, you must seek advice from a supervisor as quickly as possible.

The Law Society provides a list of risk factors that indicate a client may be vulnerable:

- advanced age
- young age
- physical disabilities
- ill health
- cognitive impairment, such as dementia
- mental health problems
- learning disabilities
- sensory impairment
- acquired brain injury, caused for example by a stroke or head injury
- behavioural disorder, such as attention deficit hyperactivity disorder
- neurodiversity, such as autism spectrum disorder
- psychological or emotional factors, such as stress
- communication difficulties, including no or limited speech, English as a foreign language, limited ability to read or write, trouble with reading and writing accuracy and comprehension, and illiteracy
- experience of domestic violence or sexual abuse
- heavy reliance on others (family or friends) for care, support, or accommodation
- long-term alcohol or drug abuse
- exposure to financial abuse

[39] *Meeting the Needs of Vulnerable Clients* (2020) Law Society Guide, https://www.lawsociety.org.uk/en/topics/client-care/meeting-the-needs-of-vulnerable-clients (last accessed 21 February 2022).

- poor financial literacy
- lack of a social network
- living alone
- living in poverty
- adverse life events, such as bereavement
- dependence on a care provider.

This list of factors does not necessarily mean that someone is vulnerable, but these might all be indicators that suggest a client is vulnerable and that extra care should be taken to ensure that they understand advice given to them and that they are able to make informed decisions about the best course of action available to them. The Law Society encourages lawyers to be alert to vulnerability to protect themselves from complaints or claims of discrimination. Rather than focusing on the circumstances of different individuals and their response to adverse circumstances, vulnerability can be seen as systemic and something that affects all of us at some point in our lifetime. Vulnerability theory provides a tool for analysing society that recognizes that we are all vulnerable at different points in our lives, and we are all at risk of vulnerability through the possibility of illness, accident, or adverse event. Understanding the 'significance, universality and constancy of vulnerability'[40] allows us to shift our attention away from the negative associations with victimhood and dependency. Rather than looking at each client to determine whether or not they are vulnerable, it is more inclusive and realistic to take account of potential vulnerabilities in all our interactions with others. Prioritizing clear and timely communication which sets out what you want to say and why will help you to communicate with all your clients, not just those who are deemed vulnerable. The requirement to treat all clients with respect and courtesy will include your vulnerable clients.

There may be particular circumstances which mean that you have to adapt your communication, and in some cases you will need to ask the client what steps they would like you to take. For example:

- If you know your client can't read (not everyone will admit to this in the first instance), ask them how they would like to receive letters. They may want to come to the clinic to collect a letter and have someone read through it with them. They may prefer receiving it in the post so that it is easy for a support worker or relative to read it with them. Consider—could you ask all clients whether they would like to have a letter explained to them, meaning that clients with reading difficulties would not need to identify themselves?
- If your client has a disability that affects communication, seek advice, but also ask them. Some deaf people will need a sign language interpreter, whereas others can lip-read.
- If your client is visually impaired, speak to them about how they want to receive written communication. In particular, you may need to use certain types of software when writing letters that is compatible with programmes for reading text out.

[40] Martha Fineman, 'The Vulnerable Subject: Anchoring Equality in the Human Condition' (2008) 21(1) Yale Journal of Law and Feminism 10.

- If you use an interpreter, speak directly to your client and not to the interpreter, and allow plenty of time for your interview. Agree with your client how you will communicate with them outside the interview. Are texts and emails better than phone calls? Do you need to get letters translated?
- If you know your client has mental health problems, consider whether they need a supporter with them in a client interview. Some clients with mental ill-health conditions struggle with particular forms of digital communication, for example Zoom, while others feel comfortable using them. You should consider carefully what might work best for each individual client.

Practical Exercise 10.4

In each of the following scenarios, A and B are students who do not know each other well but are working together in the law clinic. Consider all of the different possible responses by Student B. How might Student A feel in each of these situations? Might B have responded differently had they known the full situation?

Casework situation	Student A says	Student B says
Two students are working on an advice letter for a family law client. Student B comments on the fact that it is sad that the children have not seen their father for two years.	'Actually I have not seen my father since I was 2 years old, but my mother married again when I was 5 and I have always called my step-father Dad.'	'But you shouldn't call him Dad because he is not really your father.' 'What happened to your real father?' 'How do you feel about that? Would you like to have contact with your other father?' 'That is sad. Why did you lose contact?'
A group of students are discussing a recent client interview and planning the work that needs to be done. The client is homeless as a result of domestic abuse and disclosed in the interview that she is considering returning to her abusive partner.	'I think it can be very difficult for someone with children to leave a violent partner'. Unknown to others in the class A's father was very violent and he spent periods of time as a child and teenager living in refuges and temporary accommodation as a result.	'I think it is hard to imagine how you might behave in that situation unless it has happened to you.' 'There is plenty of support out there for women. Anyone who stays with a violent man is a bad mother.' 'Lots of women just exaggerate violence to get attention and stop fathers from seeing their children.' 'I know it's not really OK to hit people but really some women bring it on themselves.'

Casework situation	Student A says	Student B says
Two students on a welfare benefits project are preparing to meet a client to assist with an application for PIP (a type of benefit for people with a disability). They don't have much advance information other than that the client has mental health problems.	'We need to really plan how to manage this interview so that the client feels safe to speak to us about how their mental health problems affect them'. Unknown to Student B, Student A spent a year in hospital with anorexia when she was 15.	'I don't know why people with mental health problems are entitled to disability benefit. It's not the same as being in a wheelchair.' 'I agree, let's think about how to start the interview so that they feel comfortable.' 'OK—but we only have 45 mins because I have a seminar at 1pm so we need to make sure we get through all the questions quickly.' 'I don't know how we can do that. I've never really had to talk to someone who is mentally ill before.'
A group of students are planning research following a client interview in an employment law case. The client believes they have been discriminated against on the grounds of sexual orientation.	Student A is gay but he is not out to other students in the law clinic. He says 'I am always so shocked by how often you encounter homophobia. It makes me really angry.'	'My sister's a lesbian – she came out in year 9. My parents were totally cool with it, but some of the girls at her school were horrible. It was really a distressing time for all of us.' 'I don't think there is that much homophobia, gay people can get married and everything now. I think gay people are a bit over-sensitive.' 'Really I think this client brought it on himself. He was so flamboyant and over the top. Maybe not everyone in the office needs to know about his private life.' 'I agree. It's awful—I can't imagine how horrible it must be to be treated differently just because of who you love.'
A group of students on an innocence project have just been given their first case. They are looking through the file and discussing the facts.	'Prison is bad enough for anyone, but imagine being stuck inside for all that time if you did not even do it.' Unknown to the group, Student A has a brother who is serving a 5-year prison term for drugs offences.	'Well, prison's not that bad really. Modern prisons are quite comfortable and prisoners get access to all sorts of education and support.' 'OK, but looking at this file so far, I would say that guy is guilty anyway, so deserves to be locked away.' 'I think we should reserve judgement until we really understand the case and why he is claiming innocence.' 'There's no smoke without fire. Even if he's not guilty, the fact that he lied to the police and tried to cover his tracks led to him ending up inside, so it's kind of his fault anyway.'

10.4.4 **Trauma-Informed Lawyering**

There is a growing recognition that trauma-informed practice for lawyers can help to develop services that put the client at the centre of their work, and can also protect the lawyers from the effects of vicarious trauma.[41] Katz and Haldar advocate developing trauma-informed practice in law clinics to help place the client at the centre of our practice and to train future lawyers to understand the need for trauma-informed practice.[42] They identify three steps to developing trauma-informed lawyers:

1. understanding trauma
2. understanding vicarious trauma
3. understanding trauma-informed practice.

Large numbers of people experience trauma at some point in their lives, and many of the clients helped by law clinics and their partner organizations have suffered trauma. A client may not be seeking advice directly related to a mental health problem, or even identify as someone who has survived trauma, but if they have recently experienced the breakdown of relationship, domestic abuse, discrimination at work, housing difficulties, forced migration, or other adverse life circumstances they may be experiencing trauma. The impact of trauma can affect people's behaviour in different ways, rendering it hard for them to manage their circumstances. For example, it may lead to disassociation, anger, depression, sleep disorders, substance abuse, or self-harm. A trauma survivor may be trapped in semi-permanent flight-or-fight mode, interacting with the world around them as if the traumatic event was still happening. [43] Understanding the impact that trauma can have on people can help law students in their communication with clients. Law students can become frustrated with clients, for example, because they are not forthcoming with information; they are angry with the legal system; they have unrealistic expectations; or they miss appointments. They may blame the client for the problems encountered. Trauma training can help students to 'focus on seeing the client as an individual' needing support, with a 'recognition that providing support to a legal client is a holistic and incremental process'.[44]

Professionals who work with trauma victims may suffer from forms of vicarious trauma, sometimes referred to as 'secondary PTSD', burnout, or compassion fatigue. There is little research on the impact of vicarious trauma on the legal professions, but poor mental health in the legal profession is well documented.[45] Colin James suggests that the 'legal profession

[41] Colin James, 'Towards Trauma-Informed Legal Practice: A Review' (2020) 27(2) Psychiatry, Psychology and Law 275–99.

[42] Sarah Katz and Deeya Haldar, 'The Pedagogy of Trauma-Informed Lawyering' (2016) 22 Clinical Law Review 359–93.

[43] Bessell van de Kolk, *The Body Keeps the Score: Mind, Brain and Body in the Transformation of Trauma* (Penguin 2014).

[44] Gemma Smyth, Dusty Johnstone, and Jillian Rongin, 'Trauma-Informed Lawyering in the Student Legal Clinic Setting: Increasing Competence in Trauma Informed Practice' (2021) 28(1) International Journal of Clinical Legal Education 149–94, 175.

[45] For example, the Law Society UK Junior Lawyers Division Resilience and Wellbeing survey in 2019 found that 48 per cent of lawyers in a survey of 1,800 reported poor mental health in the past month. https://communities.lawsociety.org.uk/Uploads/b/y/k/resilience-wellbeing-survey-report-2019.pdf (last accessed 27 November 2025).

may be the last of the human services to acknowledge that its members face risks of indirect trauma'[46] and that 'competition in the legal profession and the adversarial nature of legal practice may have fuelled the denial of the risk of indirect trauma to lawyers and hindered recognition of their vulnerability'. James makes the case for adopting trauma-informed policies of supervision and management in legal practice, suggesting that lawyers need 'to recognise that self-care habits will not only enhance their well-being and help protect them for work-related trauma but also improve the productivity and efficacy at work'.[47]

Models of trauma-informed practice can be found in therapeutic and social work professions and normally involve a systemic approach that includes everyone in the organization having training and embedding understanding of trauma and its impact across all structures. This includes recognizing the impact of vicarious trauma on professionals and developing a culture of self-care and openness in the workplace. In addition to the benefits to client care and well-being of staff, Katz and Halder's pedagogy of trauma-informed clinics provides rich opportunities for exploring the social justice and the limits of the law as a problem-solving tool.[48] When students understand the impact of trauma on their clients, they can begin to understand how legal solutions will not necessarily change the impact of trauma and may in fact re-traumatize someone by expecting them to relive their experiences through legal proceedings.

10.4.5 **Professional Conduct and Communication with Clients**

As a lawyer you need to be sure that your communication with clients enables you to fulfil your role. Client care letters that set out the terms of a service are important documents and the client needs to understand these. It is likely that there is a standard letter or document given to all clients and checking that this has been received and understood is often the job of students. The documents need to be in a format clients can understand and, if needed, adaptations should be made for accessibility.[49]

Any advice given to clients that recommends one course of conduct over another needs to explain clearly why that advice is being given so that the client can make their own informed decision. Chapter 11 addresses writing letters of advice in detail. The principles set out in this chapter on how to communicate clearly underpin the section on writing and client interviews.

Any organization offering a service to the public will have a complaints procedure. As a student, if a client is not happy with you it is important to take this to a supervisor quickly, even if you are not sure whether it constitutes a 'formal' complaint.

Legal communication is confidential so it is important to be aware of security when emailing, phoning, or using messaging services such as WhatsApp or Teams. Make sure you follow the rules of your organization.

[46] James (n 41) 284. [47] Ibid 290.

[48] Sarah Katz and Deeya Haldar, *Teaching Trauma-Informed Lawyering through Family Law Clinics* (2016) Paper from the Association of American Law Schools Conference, https://www.aals.org/wp-content/uploads/2015/06/Katz-Haldar.pdf (last accessed 27 November 2025).

[49] SRA Guidance on Client Care Letters, https://www.sra.org.uk/solicitors/guidance/client-care-letters/ (last accessed 27 November 2025).

TAKING STOCK

Building a relationship with your client is an important part of the job of a lawyer. Lawyers have professional duties towards their clients and a relationship of trust is fundamental to providing good advice and representation.

You need to learn to explain legal principles in non-legal terms. For example, a letter of advice to a client has a very different purpose to a piece of coursework. The letter is not a test of your understanding of legal knowledge; it is an explanation of the law and procedure for your client to assess their own options.

Your clients may have particular vulnerabilities that affect the way in which you need to communicate with them; for example, they may have a disability, need an interpreter, or have experienced trauma. It might be helpful to remember that we can all have life experiences that make us vulnerable at different points in our lives. Remembering that we can all be vulnerable is a useful tool to help understand clients' needs.

Conclusion

Studying law and practising law can be stressful at times due to the volume and pace of work, but it should not be so stressful that your mental health or well-being is put at risk. Building relationships of trust with your supervisor and your peers so that you feel able to seek help or admit mistakes when you need to is crucial. Learning to understand the difference in your studies between feeling stretched, which helps you learn, and feeling stressed, which can hinder your learning, is important. Your time in a clinical legal setting can provide you with an ideal opportunity to develop the habit of reflecting on your learning, which in turn can help you to identify causes of stress or overwork. Try to use the tips and advice in this chapter to develop strategies to take care of yourself and of others.

Building connections and feeling that you are part of a community can help to improve the mental well-being of students, and clinical settings often provide an environment that encourages students to collaborate and work together. Most law clinics will expect students to work in groups of pairs. When this goes well it can provide a rich and stimulating learning experience, but group work can be fraught with difficulty and poor communication can lead to breakdown in relationships. Finding ways to work with others and build strong team relationships is a useful life skill that will be required in most professional jobs. Co-operative groups don't form without some work and reflection into how the group will communicate and organize itself, and a student law clinic provides an ideal opportunity to explore some of the ways in which groups can work well.

In addition to developing relationships with your peers, a university law clinic may be the first time that you work with a client. The legal profession is a service industry, and the lawyer–client relationship underpins legal practice. Building a good relationship with a client, be they corporate or individual, is crucial to providing the relevant and appropriate service. Experience in a student law clinic provides an opportunity to begin developing the core skills needed to establish and maintain client relationships. Reflecting on communication with clients and the way in which this forms the basis of a client–lawyer relationship enables law students to build on their own strengths and weaknesses and find their own voice as professionals.

Further Reading

Stella Cottrell, *The Study Skills Handbook* (Chapter 8) (Macmillan 2019).

Joanna Fleck and Rachel Francis, *Vicarious Trauma in the Legal Profession* (Legal Action Group 2021).

Gareth Hughes, *Be Well, Learn Well* (Red Globe Press 2020).

Bessell van de Kolk, *The Body Keeps the Score: Mind, Brain and Body in the Transformation of Trauma* (Penguin 2014).

Law Care, Life in the Law 2020/21, https://www.lawcare.org.uk/media/14vhquzz/lawcare-lifeinthelaw-v6-final.pdf

Kathyn Mannix, *Listen: How to Find the Words for Tender Conversations* (Collins 2021).

Interviewing and Advising

11

We're paying the highest tribute you can pay a man. We trust him to do right. It's that simple.

Harper Lee, *To Kill a Mockingbird*

Chapter Overview

In Chapter 10 we looked at the importance of a lawyer–client relationship. A first interview with a client creates the foundation that the lawyer–client relationship is built on. This chapter contains advice and guidance on how to conduct a client interview before considering how to analyse their case, conduct practical research, and write a letter of advice.

Having read and engaged with the exercises in this chapter, you will be able to:

- Plan a client interview
- Analyse the facts and circumstances in order to pinpoint the issues raised
- Identify the questions of law that need to be investigated
- Create and maintain a record of practical legal research
- Evaluate the merits of the client's case to offer reasoned views on strengths and weaknesses
- Recognize the features of a good advice letter.

Introduction

As a law student you have likely been given problem questions to solve, with neatly organized facts that fit around a legal issue. Problem questions will give you all the relevant facts you need to answer the question and, in most cases, will not present you with facts that you don't need. Things are very different when you meet with a client. In Chapter 5 we looked at legal realism and considered the idea that law is about experience, not logic, which underpins clinical legal education. A client interview is the point at which the theory of legal realism meets the real world of legal practice. As lawyers we want to try and organize factual information in neat and tidy categories so that we can follow through some logical reasoning and solve a legal problem. The reality of law in practice is not that simple. Legal problems do not come neatly packaged for us to advise on, and sometimes social reality and legal reality don't come together with a good solution for your client. For example, you may see a client with a clear social problem, such as the fact that they are facing homelessness, but there is no neat legal solution for them as there are no grounds for them to defend a possession order. As we discussed in relation to access to justice, in social welfare law, clients often present with a cluster of problems. Your client may have come to see you about a family problem, but they also need advice on welfare benefits, education, and housing. Studying law through the case method often leads law students to see the law through the process of litigation and the appeal courts. In reality, most legal work does not involve court proceedings, let alone cases in the Court of Appeal. Advising clients on both contentious and transactional work involves finding solutions to the client's problem, not rushing to court to win a point against the other side.

In this chapter we will look at the practicalities of interviewing and advising clients. When you first interview a client, you may feel frustrated as the interview might not go to plan. This is because your client will be a person who comes to the interview with their own thoughts and feelings and their experience will not necessarily fit neatly around a point of law for you to advise on. In addition, you will need to take time to build a relationship with your client so they can trust you. No one interview is the same as the next and it will take time for you to develop the skills needed to conduct a client interview and advise your client. After an interview you need to take time to analyse your case and identify the relevant legal issues before setting out your advice in a letter. Throughout this process you will put to use all the communication skills and file management skills explored in Chapters 9 and 10.

One case study has been used throughout this chapter to provide examples and practical exercises. The case study has been used to illustrate how a case can develop from an initial enquiry to a letter of advice. However, all of the examples and skills are relevant and transferable to other areas of law.

As the skills needed to interview and advise take time to develop, it is unlikely that your first interview will go according to plan, so this is also where you will need to start practising reflection. There is no single right way to conduct a client interview or to write an advice letter, but there are better or worse ways to do so. Each case will depend on the relationship between the adviser and the advisee. As law students this can be a hard task to master. You have often come through the education system focused on how to achieve a high grade, which is often best done by following a set structure or working to a model answer. The uncertainty of working with clients can feel unnerving to start with, but if you use reflection as a tool to help you learn from each experience, you will develop the confidence to approach each new case ready for the unexpected situations that will arise in law in practice.

Table 11.1 contains an extract from the SRA Statement of Solicitor Competence. Refer to the companion website to this book to find a downloadable template to audit your skills and reflect on your development.

Table 11.1 Purpose of a client interview

B1 Obtain relevant facts, including: a. Obtaining relevant information through effective use of questioning and active listening b. Finding, analysing and assessing documents to extract relevant information c. Recognising when additional information is needed d. Interpreting and evaluating information obtained e. Recording and presenting information accurately and clearly.	**Questions to consider** Do you have experience in these competencies? How would you rate your competence? Do you need more experience? How could you gain this experience?

11.1 Client Interviews

On a clinical placement it is very likely that you will take part in a client interview. Client interviews are an important part of the client–solicitor relationship and have a number of important functions. Sometimes an initial interview may be conducted in two or three steps—for example, an interview may take place to find out about the factual background to the client problem. A follow-up interview may be conducted to give advice once research has been carried out. A further interview might discuss the client's understanding of the advice given, and options and next steps available.

11.1.1 Purpose of a Client Interview

The multiple functions of a client interview mean that the skill of conducting a *good* client interview can take time to master. Books and guides (including this chapter) lay out strategies and stages for the interview. However, all of the best planning and researching cannot fully prepare you as a student for the reality of taking instructions from a client for the first time.

Client interviews have a number of different purposes, including:

1. Building (or maintaining) a relationship of trust with a client
2. Clarifying the client care agreement
3. Checking and confirming key information and details
4. Taking a detailed factual history
5. Exploring the client's concerns and objectives
6. Setting out next steps
7. Giving advice

Client interviews have different purposes, but as shown in Figure 11.1 the relationship with the client is central to every step in the interview. If you forget to ask a question, or you don't

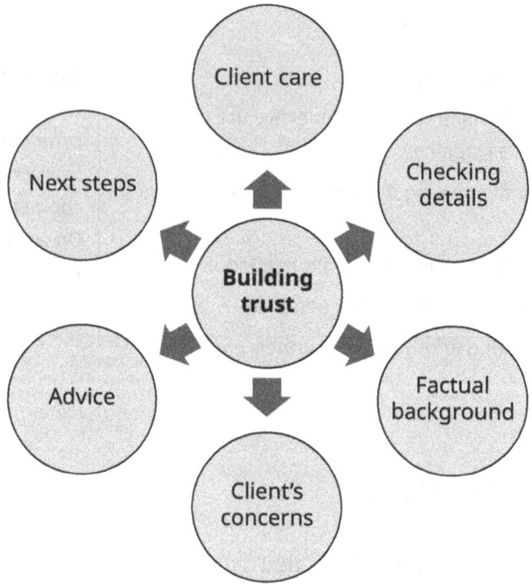

Figure 11.1 Purpose of a client interview

have time to explain next steps, you can follow up later with a phone call or an email. However, if your client does not trust you, or gets the impression that you are judging them in some way, this is not something that can be easily rectified with a phone call or a letter. It is important therefore to think carefully about how you will build a relationship with the client.

Building a Relationship with the Client

When you are new to conducting client interviews it can be hard to focus on the importance of your relationship with your client, because you are worried about remembering everything you need to ask or check. People come to see lawyers for advice and assistance because they need expert help on an issue that is important to them. But it is crucial to remember that, perhaps even as a precondition to developing this professional relationship, clients need to trust the lawyer and feel respected by the lawyer. It may be useful to spell this out: within moments of meeting you for the first time, a client is expected to share very personal information about what may be the worst moment in their lives: why they lost their job; the fact that they are homeless; that they are in a failed, and perhaps abusive, relationship.

Developing a relationship with your client, so that they feel comfortable to tell you about their problem and trust you to help them achieve their goals, is hard to prepare for by writing a checklist or presupposing what the issues are. You will need the communication skills explored in Chapter 10 to conduct a good interview. There is no one technique for doing this, as much will depend on your own personality and communication skills as well as on your clients and their situation. Law in practice often involves complex factual situations and not all lawyers approach client interviews in the same way. With the rapid development of technology and artificial intelligence, the human ability to build a relationship with your client and bring a personal element to the service provided will become ever more central to the role of a practising lawyer in the future.

For aspiring solicitors in England and Wales, it is worth considering the assessment brief for the client interviewing assessment in the Solicitors Qualifying Exam. The interview itself is assessed against the following criteria:

- Listen to the client and use questioning effectively to enable the client to tell the solicitor what is important to them.
- Communicate and explain in a way that is suitable for the client to understand.
- Conduct themselves in a professional manner and treat the client with courtesy, respect, and politeness, including respecting diversity where relevant.
- Demonstrate client focus in their approach to the client and the issues (ie demonstrate an understanding of the problem from the client's point of view and that of what the client wants to achieve, not just from a legal perspective).
- Establish and maintain an effective relationship with the client so as to build trust and confidence.[1]

You will note that the assessment criteria do not place great weight on expert knowledge of the law. While general knowledge of the law is important if you are to know what questions to ask, and perhaps even offer very initial advice, the assessment emphasizes the relationship developed and the communication skills of the interviewer.

Clarifying the Client Care Agreement

Clients need to be given clear information about the service that you offer.[2] Client care information provided to clients should include information about the limits of the service, costs, complaints procedures, and responsibility and regulation.

This information is normally sent to a client before a first appointment, and if the service is provided by regulated solicitors this is referred to as the client care letter. Often clients are asked to sign an agreement before their first appointment, or your setting may ask clients to sign the agreement in the initial interview. Even when the agreement has been sent and signed before the first appointment, it is good practice to go over this agreement in a first interview and check that the client understands the service being offered.

Checking Details

How much detail you have before an interview will depend on your clinical setting's approach to collecting information from clients before a first appointment. If you are interviewing at a drop-in service, you may start with no details at all. In most cases you will have a client's name and address, details of any opponent or party, and some information about

[1] https://sqe.sra.org.uk/exam-arrangements/assessment-information/sqe2-assessment-specification (last accessed 27 November 2025).

[2] https://www.sra.org.uk/solicitors/guidance/client-care-letters/ (last accessed 27 November 2025).

the area of law in question. You may have a record of a phone call or initial enquiry providing some background information about the case and why the client is seeking advice.

It is very easy for mistakes to be made when initial details are taken from a client. Phone numbers, email addresses, dates of birth, spellings of names can all be entered on a client database erroneously, even if the client themselves filled in an enquiry form. When meeting a client for the first time, it is therefore important to check that these details have been correctly recorded. You do not want to send emails or letters to the wrong address or leave messages on the wrong voicemail. Quite apart from the inconvenience of the client not receiving your communication, this has serious implications for conduct and client care. An advice letter sent to the wrong person is a serious breach of client confidentiality and will almost definitely need to be reported to the regulator. Your first interview with a client gives you an important opportunity to go through some of those key details and check that you have them down correctly.

Taking a Detailed Factual History

This will take up most of the time in the interview and is the aspect of interviewing that you are likely to spend most of your time preparing for. In order to give advice, you need to find out what has happened. Some clients will be very forthcoming, come well prepared, and give you a vast amount of detail in response to one question. Other clients will be reticent and give you short, limited answers to questions, and it can be hard to find out everything you need to know.

Exploring the Client's Concerns

Before you can give legal advice, you need to understand what it is that your client wants to achieve. This may seem obvious, but often a client will be booked in to see you about a housing problem, which is in fact also a family law problem, because the housing problem has been caused by the breakdown in a relationship. Or they may have come to see you with a family problem when the most pressing need is welfare benefits advice, as a recent relationship breakdown may have led to financial difficulties.

Exploring options with your client means that you need to understand the problem from your client's perspective. As a law student you are likely to be thinking about any issue from a legal perspective, but your client is a person and their perspective on their legal issue will depend on their circumstances.

Setting Out Next Steps for the Client and the Lawyer

Before your client leaves, you need to clarify what will happen next and set a timescale for this. For example, you may wish to communicate some of the following information:

- You will have a look for the documents we discussed and send them to me before the end of the week.
- Within two days of receiving the documents I will review them and send you an email confirming whether I need to see anything else.

- I will write to you within two weeks of this meeting confirming the advice I have given you and setting out your options.
- Once you have received my letter you can contact me if you decide to take further action.

Giving Advice to the Client

Clients will often attend an interview with an expectation that they will get detailed advice providing them with a solution to their problem. In reality, it is likely that advice in a first interview will be limited, as the lawyer may need to review documents before giving advice or conduct further legal research. In any issue that is contested, everything will depend on the other party. Something that seems straightforward in an interview can turn out to be much less certain when you contact the other side to start negotiations.

Therefore, advice given in a first interview is likely to be quite general and contingent. If there are options open to a client, then they will need to have those options explained and given time to make a decision. This might mean a follow-up phone call or appointment.

In many university law clinics, students do not give verbal advice to their clients in an interview but put the advice in a letter. This allows time to research the law and discuss the advice with a supervisor before it goes out.

11.1.2 **Planning an Interview**

It is important to keep in mind all the different purposes that an interview serves and consider how you will manage each one. As law students you are likely to be focused on asking the right questions and gathering relevant factual information, but it is important to plan for the whole interview.

Time and Space

Before you start planning, find out where the interview will take place and how much time you have.

If the interview takes place on campus, can you try and choose a room that is sufficiently discreet? If it's not a dedicated 'clinic interview room', consider posting a 'Do not disturb' sign on the door.

If you are not familiar with the interview room, try to visit this before the interview and focus on everything you know about non-verbal communication. Approach the room as if you were the client: Is it easy to find? What does the building feel like? You may not have control over the space, but if you try to view it through the client's eyes before they arrive you can plan some ways to mitigate difficulties. For example, if you know the building is hard to find, you can check in advance that the client has clear instructions; you may be able to meet them at the entrance to the building; you can be prepared for them to arrive a little late or a little flustered and you can start your greetings with some chat about finding the building such as 'I hope you managed to find us without too much difficulty'.

Consider the layout of the interview room and decide how you want to sit. Do you want to sit across the desk from your client or next to them? Sitting across the desk makes it easy to make eye contact and observe your client's body posture but might feel intimidating and formal to the client. Sitting beside them might feel less intimidating and can make it easier to read through documents that have been shared or check that contact details are entered correctly on the file. Try to make a decision about seating arrangements before the interview so that you are ready to invite everyone to sit down at the start. You can also make sure that you have enough chairs in the room. A client will often bring a friend or relative to an interview and you don't want to start by having to leave the clients alone while you search for a spare chair in another room.

For an online interview, take time to plan where this will happen. Do you have an interview room to conduct online interviews, or can you do the interview in a place of your own choosing? If you can choose, you need to plan carefully for a confidential space where you won't be interrupted. What about background? If you are interviewing someone from your bedroom, how professional does this look, and what can you do to mitigate this? If you are going to do the interview with another student, do you want to be in the same room or join the meeting from separate computers?

Know how much time you have for your interview when planning. If you only have one hour, and you need to be the other side of the campus at the end of that hour, you need to plan to finish in plenty of time. Think about how to manage this. You don't want to be looking at your watch every few minutes when the client is telling their story. If you know you have to finish at a certain time, tell the client at the start and remind them 10 minutes before you need to finish, so that you have time to complete the interview. The client may also have limited time and you don't want them to leave when you are only halfway through your planned interview. If you don't have to finish at a certain time, the client might. Ask them at the start of the interview if they have to leave at a certain time to limit the risk of them rushing off when you are only halfway through your interview.

When you check the room, remember to plan how you will take notes. If you are going to type notes directly into the case management system, allow time to log into your laptop and get the file open before you start. If you are making handwritten notes, check that you have plenty of paper and pens before you start.

Check What You Already Know

The amount of information you have before a client interview will vary depending on the setting and the circumstances. In some settings there may have been a screening or triage call with quite a bit of background information before the first appointment. In most settings you will have some key details, such as names, prior to your first appointment. At a drop-in service you may have no information at all and have to start by asking the client's name.

CASE STUDY

The case study introduced below will be developed through the Interviewing and Case Analysis sections of this chapter.
You receive the following email from clinic administrators on 18 November:

> Dear Alice and Ben
> Your client, PG, is booked in for an appointment at 10am on 22 November. I have booked Interview room 2 for you from 9.30am to 11.30am. The file number is 6543.
> If you have any questions or problems accessing the file, let me know.
> Elizabeth

When you look at the file you find the following note of a phone call:

> Client phoned wanting an appointment for advice about custody and access for his children. He seemed to think it was quite urgent. I didn't get the details as he said he could not talk, but he said there is a hearing coming up. I offered him the first available slot.

What other information might be available on the file? These are some of the things you might want to look for:

1. Is the appointment in person, online, or on the phone?
2. Has a client care letter been sent explaining the terms of the service offered?
3. Do we have the names and ages of the children?
4. Are the details of the other parent on the file? Has a conflict check been carried out?
5. Is there any information about PG's financial situation?
6. Does your clinic routinely monitor clients in relation to Equality Act protected characteristics? Is any of this information relevant for your client interview?

Once you have reviewed the file, you have the following information:

Client's name:	*Pawel Gronowski*
Address:	*23 The Close, The Town, TO23 6PL*
Email:	Pawelg123@gmail.com
Children:	*Kalina, aged 10 and Liv, aged 12*
Other parent:	*Hannah Ingals, 42 The Street, The Village, VI12 5TP*
Client care:	*letter sent by email*
Key dates:	*hearing on 6 December 11am (FHDRA)*

Equality data:

• *Age*	*36*
• *Ethnicity*	*white British*
• *Sexual orientation*	*straight*
• *Gender*	*male*
• *Religion*	*atheist*
• *Marital status*	*married*
• *Disability*	*is disabled, chose not to specify*
• *Employment status*	*unemployed*
• *Income*	*welfare benefits—universal credit and personal independence payment*

Planning Fact Gathering

In order to plan the interview, you may need to start by researching the law. You need an understanding of the law to know what factual information is important and relevant. For example, when advising parents, it is important to know whether they have parental responsibility. This will depend on certain factual information such as whether they are married or named on the birth certificate.

Having reviewed the file and researched the law, the temptation for an inexperienced interviewer is to write out a list of questions you want to ask. This approach can lead to three problems with the interview:

1. First, you are making an assumption regarding the problem the client is coming to see you about. Even where a detailed note of a phone call has been prepared, once an interview is under way it can become clear that the issues are not quite what you thought they would be.
2. Second, it prevents you from responding to what the client is saying, thus potentially creating a stilted atmosphere. Moreover, the interview can become more like an interrogation. This in turn can make it hard to build a relationship and prevents you from really listening to the client and understanding what it is they want to achieve.
3. Finally, you can miss important information if it is not on your list of questions.

An alternative to a list of questions is a checklist of key topics that you want to cover in the interview to ensure you cover all the relevant facts. Putting your checklist in diagram or circle form can be a useful strategy and allows you to respond to the client rather than imposing your structure on the interview.[3]

[3] Julian Webb et al, *Lawyers' Skills* (22nd ed, OUP 2019) 16.

Practical Exercise 11.1

Consider the following scenarios:

Students Anna and Bisha have looked at Pawel's file and prepared the following list of questions for the interview.

1. Can you tell us about why you want legal advice?
2. Please explain why you separated from your wife?
3. Are you now divorced?
4. Are you named on the children's birth certificates?
5. What are the current contact arrangements?
6. What are the children's wishes and feelings?
7. How would you like these arrangements to be changed?
8. How long have the current arrangements been in place?
9. When is the court hearing?

Students Chyou and Dani have decided to use a checklist to help them remember topics that need to be covered. They have the following list prepared:

1. Current living arrangements
2. Current contact arrangements
3. Timeline of breakdown in relationship and arrangements
4. Safeguarding issues
5. Other relevant people (grandparents, new partners, etc)
6. Previous court proceedings
7. Details about mediation and court case (including date of next hearing)
8. Children's wishes and feelings

Students Enzo and Femi have the same checklist and have put it in a diagram form (Figure 11.2).

What do you think the pros and cons of these different interview plans might be? Which do you prefer?

When Pawel arrives, the students meet and greet him and, once introductions are over, they ask: 'Can you tell us about why you want advice today?' Pawel replies: 'It's all about arrangements for the children. You see, my wife and I split up six years ago and divorced quite quickly. The children were still very young when we split up. Kalina is 10 now, so she must have been about 4 at the time. She hadn't quite started school and Liv was in year 2. At first it was OK, and the children were back and forth. There was never a problem and the children were happy, but since Jamal's been around, it's just been a nightmare. I've really had enough. We can't go on like this.'

Students Anna and Bisha look down at their list of questions.

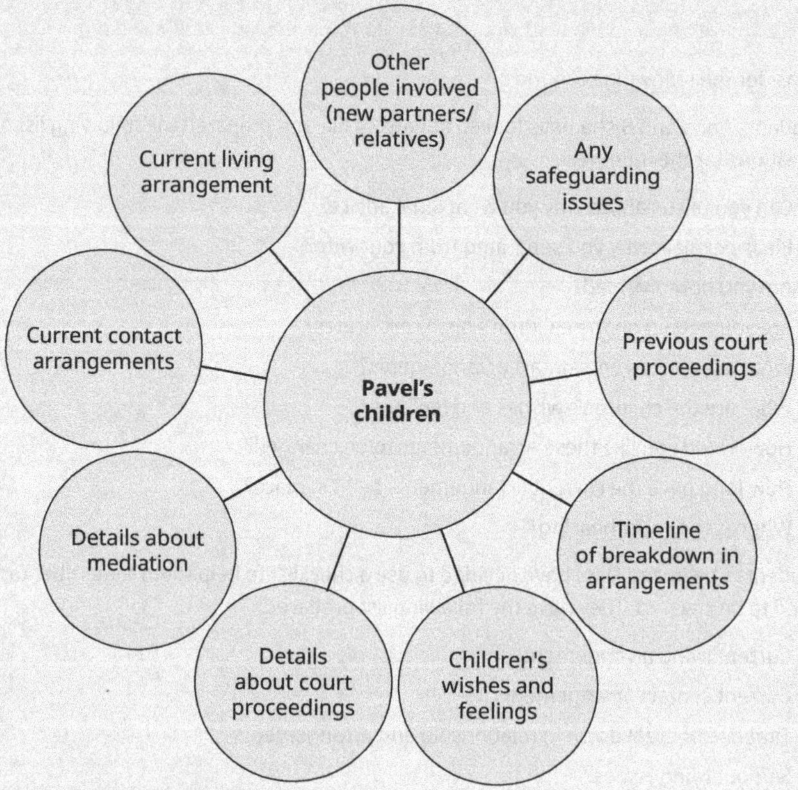

Figure 11.2 Interview planning diagram

- What is the next question? Do they need to ask this? How do you think Anna and Bisha feel at this point?
- There is a pause while they look down the list. Anna then asks question 4 (Are you named on the children's birth certificate?) as this is the first question she comes to that hasn't been answered yet.
- How do you think the client feels? What question would be more appropriate at this point?
- If you were using a checklist, do you think it would be easier to respond to the client if you had a diagram or a list?
- Students Chyou and Dani look down the checklist, make a note of Jamal's name next to item 5 (other relevant people), and then ask a question seeking more detail about the current arrangements for the children, as these are the first issues on the list. They plan to ask for more details about Jamal when they get to item 5 again. How do you think the client will feel/respond?
- Enzo and Femi have the key areas set out in a circle. Enzo notes down Jamal's name next to the box 'other people involved' and asks: 'Can you tell us who Jamal is and why he has caused so many problems?'
- Of the three different approaches to the plan and the interview, which one is most responsive to the client and his story?

Client Care

When planning an interview you need to know what information has been sent to the client and familiarize yourself with procedures for your clinical setting. For example, you may need to ask the client to sign an agreement in the interview, but this may have been signed in advance, in which case you only need to summarize the agreement and check they have understood it. You should go over the following points with your client during the interview:

1. The limitations of the service—eg advice only, representation up to a certain point, etc
2. Costs—including any possible disbursements or fees
3. Timescales
4. Expectations for the client
5. Expectations for the lawyer
6. Contact details
7. Information about regulation and responsibility for the case
8. Information about complaints procedures.

Some guidance on interviews recommends leaving this to the end of the meeting. A client is often anxious at the start of an interview and may want to get on with explaining their story. Starting with formalities and an explanation of complaint procedures might put them off their stride.[4] On the other hand, some recommend going through these issues at the start of an interview.[5] There are advantages to both approaches, but if you are new to interviewing it is safer to include this at the start of the interview. This information is important and you do not want to run out of time or forget to cover some of these points.

If you are new to client interviews and feel nervous, you could write yourself a short script for this section of the interview. It is not ideal, as reading something aloud can be stilted and awkward, but if you are nervous about meeting a client for the first time, it might help you to get started if you write down what you want to say at the beginning of the interview.

Checking Details

This is also best done at the start of an interview, but can be left to the end if you are confident you will not run out of time or forget. The advantage of leaving this to the end is that there may be information from the interview that you want to clarify.

These are some of the details you will need to check:

- Client's full name (check the spelling)
- Client's date of birth

[4] Kevin Kerrigan and Victoria Murray, *A Student Guide to Clinical Legal Education and Pro Bono* (Palgrave Macmillan 2011) 113.

[5] See for example Webb et al (n 3), Katherine Blow and Jacqueline Kempton, *Oral Skills for Lawyers* (University of Law 2023).

- Client's address, phone number, and email address
- Names and contact details of other people involved in the case. Who is relevant will depend on the type of case. For example, a partnership agreement for a small business might require details of all the partners, a case about children would require details of children's names and dates of birth, and so on
- Important dates (this includes past and future dates).

You need to have this information to hand, either on a printed sheet or easily accessible on the electronic file, so that you can check that you have the correct details.

Equality and Inclusion

When you plan your interview consider whether there are any equality issues that may be relevant. For example, does your client need an interpreter? Do they have a disability? What pronouns does your client use? These questions are important. In Chapter 8, we considered the legal and ethical frameworks governing equality and diversity for lawyers in England and Wales. Most jurisdictions have similar provisions. You have a legal and ethical duty to treat people equally when you provide a service to your client.

It cannot be stated often enough that an essential aspect of a client interview is to build a relationship of trust with your client. The way in which you approach equality and inclusion will have an impact on your relationship with your client. If your client arrives for an interview and they can't get into the building, or they can't understand what you are saying to them, or you presume they are heterosexual when they are not, they will probably not trust you and the relationship that you are trying to build with them will not have started well.

If you know that your client has a disability, find out what adjustments, if any, they need so that they are able to participate fully in the interview and give you instructions.

If English is not your client's first language, find out if they need an interpreter. Consider how long you will need for the interview. If you are using an interpreter, you will need to allow more time for the interview.

REFLECTION POINT

In the example of Pawel Gronowski, the file notes state that the client has a disability. He has not specified what his disability is and there is not any information on the file about the need for adjustments.

What steps might you take before the interview?

Sometimes people feel awkward or uncomfortable speaking to another person about a disability. How do you feel about discussing a disability? On the other hand, some people can be quite insensitive or intrusive when asking about a disability. Have you ever made assumptions about what someone else can do because of a disability? How do you think you can avoid making assumptions or offending a person with a disability?

Giving Advice

If you are going to give advice and information in an interview, you do need to be prepared. Take care not to pre-empt the interview by presuming you know the client's concerns, but make sure you do some research and have some notes with key legal principles to hand. This will enable you to give advice and information if you need to.

The amount of preparation that you can do will always depend on the circumstances—sometimes you may be taking instructions on something very specific such as a bail application or a housing repossession case. In these circumstances you can prepare quite thoroughly and have detailed notes ready to explain key legal principles and advise the client. At a general advice drop-in, there is limited preparation that can be done. Most cases fall somewhere between these two examples. It is likely you will have some information, but not enough detail to prepare full advice before the appointment.

Putting It All Together

Having considered all the different aspects of the interview, now is the time to make a checklist. Keep it brief so that it is easy to follow. If you are going to conduct the interview with another student, plan who is going to take notes and who is going to do the talking.

Example

Student Enzo and Femi have made a plan set out below in Table 11.2. The plan is brief so it is easy for them to refer to during the interview without having to search through their notes for information. It clearly identifies who is doing what and reminds them of key points.

Table 11.2 Interview Checklist

Checklist for Pawel's interview DON'T FORGET WE DON'T HAVE TO DO IT IN THIS ORDER—BUT WE DO NEED TO COVER THESE POINTS. KEEP AN EYE ON THE TIME—WE NEED TO FINISH AT 12.45		
Meet and Greet	Welcome client Introduce both of us Show him where to sit Say how long we have (got to finish at 12.45) DON'T FORGET SMALL TALK—BE FRIENDLY!	Enzo
Go over client care	There's a script for this on the next page	Femi
Checking details	There's a printed list of key info we need to check	Enzo
Clarify adjustments needed	Client has ADHD—don't rush, remind him we will put advice in writing so he doesn't have to remember everything today. Make sure we break things down into clear steps. ASK client what he needs from us—Don't assume	Femi

(*Continued*)

Table 11.2 (*Continued*)

Checklist for Pawel's interview DON'T FORGET WE DON'T HAVE TO DO IT IN THIS ORDER—BUT WE DO NEED TO COVER THESE POINTS. KEEP AN EYE ON THE TIME—WE NEED TO FINISH AT 12.45		
Going over facts and clarifying instructions	Use the diagram over the page to help remember everything Find out what Pawel wants to achieve	Both of us—taking it in turns
Advice	Keep it very simple and general—detailed advice will be in the advice letter	Femi on law—welfare principle Enzo on procedure—purpose of hearings and timescales
Next steps for client	Remember to ask him for any documents or updates Let him know he can email if he thinks of anything later that he forgot to tell us	Enzo
Next steps for us	Give a date for advice letter to be sent- Don't forget hearing is on 6 Dec—say letter by 3rd?	Femi

A View From Clinical Legal Practice

How to Teach Trauma-Informed Lawyering in a Non-Harmful Way?

Mariia Tsypiashchuk, attorney-at-law, legal clinical supervisor (2009–2022), and Board Member of the Association of Legal Clinics of Ukraine (2017–2024)

Trauma-informed legal practice was not common in Ukraine until Russia's war in 2014, which brought a surge of traumatized individuals—victims of hostilities, internally displaced persons, veterans, and their families—seeking legal aid for increasingly complex issues. The need intensified following the full-scale invasion in 2022.

Importantly, trauma isn't limited to wartime contexts. Lawyers working in areas like domestic violence, human trafficking, car accidents, and so on must also be equipped to recognize and respond to trauma appropriately.

It soon became clear that legal clinical faculty and students needed training in trauma-informed practices—yet few experts understood how to teach these concepts in the context of legal clinics without causing further distress.

Here, I share a tool that has proven both effective and sensitive in its approach.

In 2022, American lawyer and educator Marcia Levy invited me to join the faculty of the Summer School *Legal Skills in a Time of War*, initially launched through her Fulbright scheme and since then hosted with ongoing support from the CEELI Institute in Prague—held for the fourth time in 2025.

As part of the agenda, we included a trauma-informed lawyering and self-care (TIA) block led by Olivia Wilson-Bushell, pro bono attorney at Skadden UK. In 2024, Olivia introduced an interactive bingo game to help students identify constructive and harmful behaviours in trauma-sensitive client interviews.

And it worked brilliantly.

This game was subsequently tested after the Summer School in 2024 at the 10th ENCLE/21st IJCLE Conference in Amsterdam, the Netherlands, where it received enthusiastic feedback. The training was piloted again in April 2025 during the workshop *Human Rights-Based Legal Assistance for Ukrainian Refugees and IDPs* held in Lund, Sweden.

So, how does the game actually work?

Students first attend a presentation by faculty, where they learn key recommendations on how to conduct interviews with clients who may have experienced trauma. The presentation highlights specific 'dos', 'don'ts' and potential triggers that trauma-informed lawyers should be mindful of.

Afterwards, each student receives two bingo cards—one featuring positive statements, and one with negative ones. Examples include: 'Encouraging feedback', 'Clarifying why a question is relevant to the case', and on the negative side 'Victim-blaming questions' and 'Pushing for details when the client shows discomfort'. Each card contains 12 statements.

Students then observe a simulated client interview performed by faculty. As they recognize a statement being demonstrated, they mark it off on the card. As in traditional bingo, students call out 'Bingo' upon completing a horizontal line or the full card and receive candies or other treats as prizes.

This tool is remarkably versatile—it can be adapted to different learning content, group types, and case scenarios.

In a playful, low-pressure setting, students learn to avoid behaviours that may retraumatize clients and instead gain practical strategies that foster empathetic and effective communication.

11.1.3 **Conducting the Interview**

With a plan in place, it is time to meet the client.

If you are new to interviews, it is normal to be nervous. Remember, the most important aspect of the interview is to build a relationship with your client. They are a person, not a case. They are probably nervous too. It may have taken time for them to pluck up the courage to seek legal advice. They do not want to talk about their personal problems with a stranger and may appear defensive, angry, or tearful. They may be very forthcoming, or very withdrawn. You need to use your communication skills to build a rapport with the client. The more you practice, the easier it will become.

Asking Questions

In the section on planning, we advised against writing a list of pre-prepared questions. However, if you are new to interviewing, you need to think about the type of questions you need to ask, and how you will ask them. Often you need to ask clients about emotional and private matters that you would normally only discuss with a close friend. Each lawyer tends to develop their own style of asking questions and some of this approach will naturally be based on your own personality and on the client's responses. For example, the question 'How did you feel about that?' could elicit a five-minute monologue about different incidents with a description of how the client felt about each one, or it could elicit a shrug and 'Not great, really'.

It is worth considering the types of questions you are going to ask. There are two broad categories of questions: **open** and **closed**.

An open question is hard to answer with a single word. Open questions invite the respondent to answer in their own words. They normally start with why, how, what, where, or when. For example,

- Why did the children come to live with you?
- How do the children feel?
- What happened on 6 October?
- Where were the children living before the current arrangement?
- When did you realize there was a problem?

Another form of open question may not be phrased as a question at all, but rather as an invitation to speak. For example:

- Please tell me about the reasons you are here.
- I'd like to hear more about the events leading up to the police being called.

Closed questions, on the other hand, can normally be answered in one word, such as yes or no. For example:

- Did your daughter phone you on 6 October?
- Are you able to manage the school run around your work commitments?

Leading questions are a form of closed question that presupposes a certain response. We discuss leading questions in more detail in Chapter 12 (Advocacy). For example:

- You don't want the children to have contact with their mother, do you?
- You had already planned to stop the contact before the incident with the police, hadn't you?

Open questions allow the client to tell the story in their own words. One open question can lead to a full and lengthy answer. For an example, see Practical Exercise 11.1 above. The students asked one open question at the start, 'can you tell us about why you want legal advice today', and the client started telling his story. But he might have said 'because I've got a court hearing in two weeks'. Remember that a client could give a short and limited response for several reasons:

- The client does not feel comfortable talking about very personal and difficult problem with strangers.
- The client does not understand why you have asked the question, so gives the answer they think you want.

- The question was asked in a tone that was abrupt and firm, which made the client feel nervous.
- The client has already told the administrator that he needs an appointment for advice about his children, so is frustrated to be asked to repeat himself.

Asking the right questions is important, but the question is only one part of the communication that is happening. Think carefully about listening to the client and being alert to non-verbal communication. The dynamic between the interviewer and the client means that each interview will be different. The lawyer needs to be flexible and respond to the client. Most interviews involve a mixture of open and closed questions, but how many of each and the order they go in will depend on you, your client, and their circumstances.

Interview guidance tends to suggest that questions should progress from open to closed questions, and the closed questions should be used to clarify details.[6] However, the order in which questions come will often simply depend on the client and the circumstances. There are no fixed rules. The key is to avoid interrogating your client, and rather to approach the interview as a conversation.

> We have both observed interviews where the interviewer has continued with closed questioning for ten or fifteen minutes before it becomes apparent what the client's real concern or objective is . . . Such behaviour, so students frequently tell us, helps them to feel in control of the interaction. However, the effect is to convert the interview process from one of interaction into an interrogation. Many's the time we have observed client interviews with the feeling that we were sitting in a police station! In an interrogation, the agenda is controlled by one participant and the other does not participate willingly. In a free-flowing conversation, on the other hand, both participants want to communicate and to do so openly. The closer to a conversation your interview is, the more likely you are to build rapport and get the information you need.[7]

Practical Exercise 11.2

Table 11.3 shows examples of different ways students might ask the client, Pawel Gronowski, questions in his interview. It has been established that Jamal is the mother's new partner and there was an incident of domestic abuse which led to the police being called by the children. The girls are now living with their father and have not seen their mother for two months. The mother has applied for an order for the children to live with her. Jamal is no longer living in her house, but she is still seeing him.

Read the questions and consider how Pawel might feel or respond in each scenario.

[6] Blow and Kempton suggest a T-shape with open questions at the top and closed questions at the bottom. Webb et al describe this as a funnel.

[7] Caroline Maughan and Julian Webb, *Lawyering Skills and the Legal Process* (2nd ed, Cambridge University Press 2005).

Table 11.3 Asking Questions in an Interview

Students Anna and Bisha	Students Chyou and Dani	Students Enzo and Femi
Please explain what happened when you separated from your wife? What was the cause of the separation?	Can we go back in time a little? We'd like to ask you about the breakdown of your marriage and how this affected the children. Could you tell us about what happened? In particular, we'd like you to tell us about whether the breakdown was amicable, how you went about organizing arrangements for the children, and what those arrangements were.	I understand the current situation is very difficult, but you said it has not always been like this. Could you tell us a bit more about how you agreed arrangements for the children at the time of your separation?
Kalina is of an age where her wishes carry weight. What will she say to Cafcass if she is interviewed?	Do you know what the children's wishes are? Are they likely to say they want to live with you? You have told us that there are problems with Jamal—what is their relationship with him like? How about their mother? How do they feel about her after what has happened?	The children have not seen their mother for some weeks now. How do you think Liv and Kalina feel about that?
Please describe what happened on the day the children called the police.	You've told us that the children called the police because of domestic abuse between Jamal and Hannah. Could you tell us a bit more about what happened? Did the children directly witness abusive behaviour? What did they see? Or did they just hear it? Was it more than one incident?	You told us that the children called the police on 4 October. Could you tell us what you know about the incident that led to the police being called to Hannah's house?
Was Jamal ever violent to either of the children?	I understand this is probably difficult to talk about, but we need to ask you about Jamal's relationship with the children. Do you think that he was ever violent towards them, or was it just with Hannah?	You have told us that the children are frightened of Jamal. Can you tell us a bit more about what they experienced?
Was there any domestic abuse between you and Hannah?	Please don't be offended by this question, but we need to ask you, were you ever violent to Hannah or was your relationship with her abusive in any way?	The court routinely ask all parents about risks of harm or abuse. Do you think Hannah will say that you were abusive?

(Continued)

Table 11.3 (Continued)

Students Anna and Bisha	Students Chyou and Dani	Students Enzo and Femi
At the hearing, the judge and Cafcass will try to narrow the issues. You need to make a clear proposal for future arrangements. What is your proposal?	At the hearing, the judge will see if you are able to agree anything with Hannah, even if it's just temporary. Do you think you could agree to some contact between the children and their mother? What if she gave a promise to the court not to let Jamal in the house while the children are there? Or perhaps a relative could help? What about grandparents? Could the children see their mum at their grandparents' house?	At the first hearing, the judge will try and find out if there is any possibility of an agreement, but only if this is safe for the children. If there was a guarantee that Jamal would not be present, how do you feel about the idea of the girls seeing Hannah?

Checking and Clarifying

In addition to asking questions, it is important to check and clarify the facts at regular intervals. You can do this by **summarizing** and **recapping**. This is important for three reasons:

1. It shows the client that you are paying attention and listening to them.
2. It helps you to check that you have understood them correctly and gives you time to make a note.
3. It helps the client to remember and to rule out inconsistencies in their story. Timelines and events can easily become muddled in someone's memory, so recapping back to the client can help them to remember clearly.

At regular intervals through the interview, recap before moving on to the next question. For example, you might say 'So, just to be sure I have this noted down right, you separated in 2018 and got divorced in 2019. Things were relatively friendly between you until 2022, when your ex-wife met her new partner, Jamal. He moved into her house in the spring of 2023.' At this point, it is not unusual for a client to realize that they have made a mistake in the information they have provided, and this gives them a good opportunity to correct it.

Taking Notes

It is important to take detailed contemporaneous notes during a client interview. Details and dates can be quickly forgotten or confused. A clear record of any advice you have given, or alternatively a record that you explained you cannot give advice during the interview, is also extremely important.

How you take notes will depend on the rules in your clinical setting. It may be that you are required to take notes on a laptop directly into a case management system, as this is the best way to protect client confidentiality and protect against data breaches. You may prefer the idea of typing notes rather than handwriting them. However, it is worth considering handwritten notes if they are permitted. A laptop creates a barrier between you and your client and the tapping on the keyboard can feel distracting. Handwritten notes create a more open physical space between you and your client and can be less distracting. Taking notes with a digital pen might be another option.

When taking notes in an interview, take them verbatim. You won't manage to get every single word down, but don't paraphrase. For example, if the client uses a swear word, write it down. Anyone reading the file later needs a clear understanding of the client and their concerns. Use the first person—if the client says 'I don't want my children to stay the night at her house' write down his actual words, rather than writing down 'he doesn't want the children to stay at mother's house'. It is easier for you to take verbatim notes as you are just noting down what is being said without having to process it and change it. The verbatim note provides an accurate record of the interview.

In some settings a client interview might be recorded for supervision purposes, so it may be tempting not to try to take notes, but instead to concentrate fully on all the other aspects of the interview. Always seek guidance from a supervisor and consider the risks of not taking notes. There is a possibility that the recording won't work or will get deleted before you have a chance to make notes. If the interview is an hour or more long, you will need to find an hour or two to listen back and take notes. It is safer to take notes in the interview, even if it is being recorded.

Try not to worry too much about spelling mistakes, and use abbreviations where you can. A file note is a relatively informal document so grammar and spelling are not as important as in formal documents. As long as it is relatively easy for the reader to decipher what you have written, a spelling or typing error can remain in the notes. It is more important that you get as much down as possible and that you reflect as accurately as possible what the client has said. A helpful way of keeping notes in an interview is to have two columns or a table with the lawyer on one side and the client on the other. This saves time as you will not have to write down who is speaking. There is a template for this which can be downloaded from the companion website.

Interview Structure

It is tempting to approach an interview with a plan for a linear structure which moves through the following phases sequentially:

However, an interview often follows more of a circular or spiral structure than a linear one. You may start with meeting and greeting, but a nervous client, anxious to get things off their chest, might start telling you their story before you have even sat down or had a chance to go over the client care agreement. Remember, however, that practicalities and formalities are important, so you will need to decide whether to interrupt them and deal with client care, or to let the client talk and come back to some of the formalities later. Alternatively, you may have a client who is very reticent, so you need to ask lots of questions in order to get a full picture.

Compare Figures 11.3 and 11.4, which both show stages of an interview. Rather than attempting to follow a rigid structure that moves in set stages like Figure 11.3, it is more helpful and realistic to see the interview structure as a series of interlocking parts which you can move through in multiple different directions, always keeping the client at the centre, as in Figure 11.4.

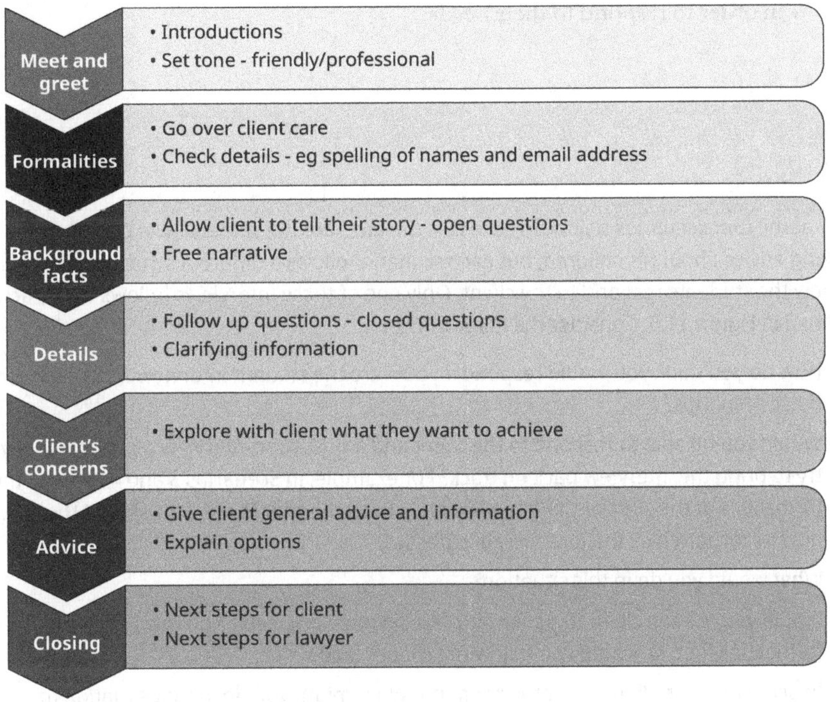

Figure 11.3 Stages of an interview 1

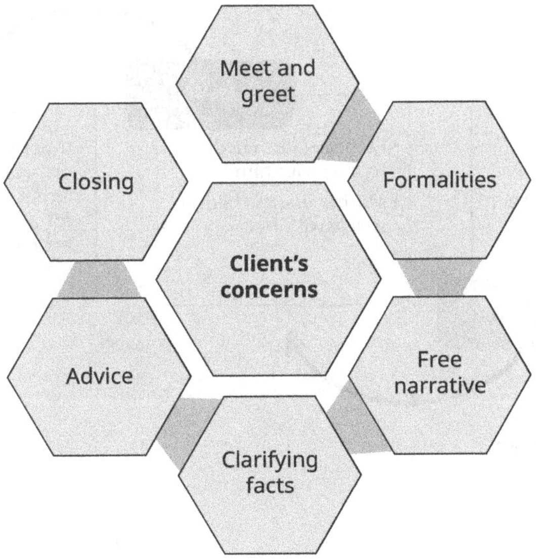

Figure 11.4 Stages of an interview 2

By keeping your focus on the client and responding to their needs and concerns, you will build a relationship of trust. Following a rigid structure is likely to put barriers in the way of the relationship and lead to a stilted interview that feels more like an interrogation than a conversation. You need a framework and a plan to help you remember everything while also keeping the framework open and flexible in order to keep the client at the centre of the interview in order to respond to their needs.

Practical Exercise 11.3

Look at the four scenarios below. In each one the facts are the same. Pawel Gronowski is seeking advice about his children, but each scenario follows a different structure depending on how the students respond to the client. Only one of these interviews follows the structure outlined in Figure 11.5. Consider the following:

(i) How do you think you would respond if you were the student interviewers in each of these scenarios?

(ii) Would you be able to respond to the client and adjust your interview plan, or would you try to bring the interview back on track? For example, in Scenarios 3 and 4 some of the formalities at the start of the interview have been missed. There is a risk that these might now be forgotten as the interview progresses.

(iii) What would you do in this situation?

(iv) Would you ask the client to pause and explain that you need to go through some formalities first, or would you follow the client's lead?

(v) In Scenario 2 the client is not forthcoming. What might you do in that situation to encourage him to tell you more?

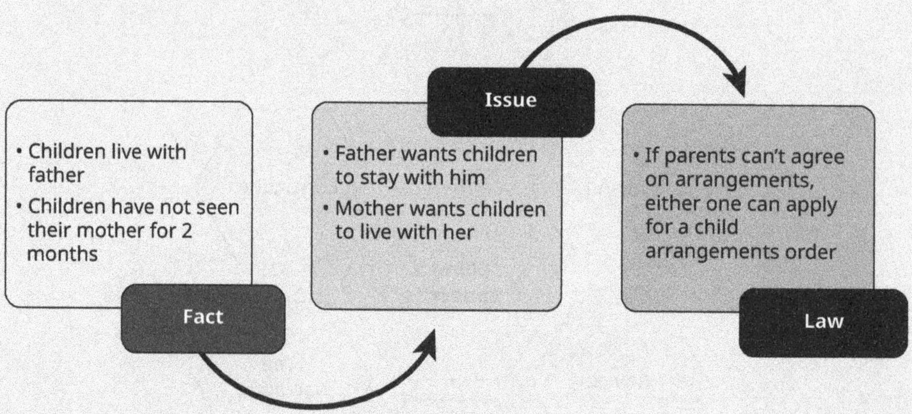

Figure 11.5 Case analysis

Scenario 1

The students introduce themselves, explain client care, check details, and then ask:

Can you tell us about why you want advice today?

This is a simple open question, designed to elicit a narrative response from the client.

Pawel replies:

It's all about arrangements for the children. You see my wife and I split up six years ago and divorced quite quickly. The children were still very young when we split up. Kalina is 10 now, so she must have been about 4 at the time. She hadn't quite started school and Liv was in year 2. At first it was OK, and the children were back and forth. There was never a problem and the children were happy, but since Jamal's been around, it's just been a nightmare. I've really had enough. We can't go on like this.

The client has given a full answer giving some key facts.

The students then ask:

'I see, so the problems started with Jamal. Could you explain a bit more about who Jamal is and why he has caused so many problems?'

The students have checked understanding and then asked another open question.

Pawel explains:

'Jamal is Hannah's new partner. They met about a year ago and he moved in with her very quickly. I can't remember when exactly but he's been there for at least six months. I never liked him and the atmosphere changed completely. Hannah didn't want me coming to the house to pick up the girls or phoning her about arrangements. I thought the girls were quite withdrawn and they kept asking if they could spend more time at mine. Kalina started getting into trouble at school for being cheeky and it was more than just normal behaviour. Then on 6 October, the police turned up on my doorstep with the girls at about 10 o'clock at night. It turned out Jamal is violent and there had been an incident where he'd attacked Hannah and so Kalina called the police. Jamal had been arrested but the girls were terrified and did not want to stay in their mother's house in case the police had let him out. I spoke to social services the next day and the girls have been living with me ever since.'

The client responds to the open question with another full narrative answer.

The students say:

'That must have been very difficult and upsetting for you and the children. Was Jamal charged with the assault?'

The students respond by acknowledging the emotionally distressing incident and follow up with closed questions to clarify some detail.

Scenario 2

The students introduce themselves, explain client care, check details and then ask:

'Can you tell us about why you want advice today?'

Unlike scenario 1, this open question does not elicit a narrative response, but rather a very short answer.

Pawel replies:

> 'Like I told the lady on the phone. I've got a hearing in two weeks.'

The students ask:

> 'Do you have a copy of the documents the court sent you? Could we see them so we can see what type of hearing it is, please?'
>
> The students ask a follow-up closed question to try and find out more about the client's situation.

Scenario 3

The students introduce themselves and invite the client to take a seat. Before they have a chance to explain the client care agreement or discuss the purpose of the interview, Pawel starts getting out all his papers and says:

> 'I'm so worried about what is going to happen. I can't believe my ex-wife is taking me to court after all that has happened. I really need to know what is going to happen at the hearing. I don't understand any of this. Look, it says the court can make an order without me if I don't turn up. What will happen? Will they take my children away from me? The children are terrified. They don't want to go. What will the judge do?'
>
> The client has told us quite a bit of important information about the facts and his concerns here, but there are also a number of questions that he wants answered.

As he talks, he is handing the students various documents.

The students say:

> 'I can see that the hearing is a FHDRA. This means the First Hearing and Dispute Resolution Appointment. The purpose of the hearing is to see if there is any possibility of an agreement, and to decide what steps the court should take next. The children's welfare is the court's paramount concern, so the judge will need to find out what the problem is and why they are afraid. We need to know a bit more about what has happened before we can really discuss what is likely to happen at the hearing. Could we go back in time a bit, please, so you can tell us about what has gone wrong and why your ex-wife has started court proceedings?'
>
> The client is very worried about the hearing, so the students start the interview by giving some advice about the purpose of the hearing. They then ask an open question to try and find out more about the factual background.

Scenario 4

The interview begins in the same way as Scenario 3, but in this clinical setting students are not authorized to give verbal advice in interviews. The purpose of the interview is to take instructions. The advice is sent in a letter of advice at a later date.

The students introduce themselves and invite the client to take a seat. Before they have a chance to explain the client care agreement or discuss the purpose of the interview, Pawel starts getting out all his papers and says:

> 'I'm so worried about what is going to happen. I can't believe my ex-wife is taking me to court after all that has happened. I really need to know what is going to happen at the hearing. I don't understand any of this. Look, it says the court can make an order without me if I don't turn up. What will happen. Will they take my children away from me. The children are terrified. They don't want to go. What will the judge do?'

As he talks, he is handing the students various documents.

> The client has told us quite a bit of important information about the facts and his concerns here, but he also asks a number of questions.

The students say:

> 'Thank you for sharing all these documents. We will make a copy and give the originals back to you before you leave. We sent you a letter before the meeting explaining that we can't give you advice in the meeting today but will put our advice in writing after the meeting. This way a supervisor can check that our advice is correct and you can have something in writing to help you remember everything. We are going to write down all of your questions, but we also need to ask you for some more information about the problems with your ex-wife that led to these court proceedings before we can advise you about what is likely to happen at the hearing. Could we go back in time a bit, please, so you can tell us about what has gone wrong and why your ex-wife has started court proceedings.'

> The client is very worried about the hearing. The students are not able to advise him, so need to explain this and then ask an open question to try and find out more about the factual background. They have responded to the client's needs and questions so will need to go through the client care agreement and check details for the file later in the interview.

Ending the Interview

Keep an eye on the time. Allow yourself plenty of time to finish the interview and remember that it is common for a client to ask several questions at the end of an interview. Give the client a clear signal that you need to finish. For example, 'Mr Gronowski, it's nearly 2pm now, and as we explained at the start, we only have the room booked until 2pm. We just want to make sure we are clear about what you would like to happen. I'm going to recap the main points and then we will go over what will happen next.'

It may be that the case is more complicated than you anticipated and you are not able to get through everything in one meeting because the client has a lot to say. Don't be afraid to end the appointment and arrange a second meeting if that is what is needed.

Finish your interview by stating clearly what you will do next and what the client needs to do next.

For example:

> We can see from the documents you showed us that Cafcass have to send you a safeguarding letter by 4pm on 26 November. Please send this on to the law clinic as soon as you receive it.
>
> You have a hearing on 6 December at 11am. You should arrive at court by 10am.
>
> We will write you a letter setting out the advice we have given you today in detail. We won't finish the letter and send it to you until after we have received the safeguarding letter as we need to consider the contents of this letter when we give our advice. We will send you an advice letter by email before 4 December.
>
> We will meet you at court at 10am on 6 December. As we have explained already, this is for support and note taking; we can't represent you.

Common Problems

1. 'I am fairly sure the client is lying to me. They are evasive and won't answer my direct questions. The story does not add up.'

Always be careful not to make assumptions. Sometime people might simply feel embarrassed or just want to present themselves to you in the best light possible.

Consider whether you really need the information you are asking for and if it is not strictly relevant don't pursue it. You can always follow up later with a phone call or an email.

Try explaining why you need this information—it may help the client to open up: 'The court routinely carry out safeguarding checks, which include making enquiries with the police, so it is important that you tell us about anything now so that we can advise you about whether the court will take this into account or consider it relevant.'

Try presenting the case back to the client to get them to justify their position: 'You have told us that you were arrested for domestic abuse four years ago, but there was no reason for this and it was just a mistake. When you go to court, the judge will want to hear your side of the story and may need to make a decision about who is telling the truth, you or your ex-wife. The little information that you have told us might not sound convincing to the judge. We do need you to explain in more detail what happened and why the police were called so that we can advise you on how relevant this is.'

2. 'Our client wouldn't stop talking and did not stick to the relevant facts or answer questions directly. We did not get through everything and don't have the information we need to advise them.'

This can be difficult; however, remember that the client will be telling you things that matter to them. The most important function of the interview is to get to know your client and find out what they want to achieve. If you keep interrupting the client or tell them that information is not relevant, they will not feel listened to. You can try and narrow their answers by asking closed questions, but this could lead to you missing something important or misunderstanding the priority for the client. Sometimes you need to finish the interview—go through your notes before you decide how to proceed. You might need to arrange a follow-up interview, or perhaps send some questions in an email asking for clarification.

3 'I don't like my client. They are a bit arrogant and pushy. They are not my type of person at all. I don't really want to work with them.'

It is not your job to like your client. Although the relationship that a lawyer has with their client is very important, this is not a friendship, it is a professional relationship. The client needs to trust you and have confidence in your professional ability, but you don't need to like them. You have a professional responsibility to provide a competent service regardless of your personal like or dislike of your client.

4. 'I don't like my client. He made me feel very uncomfortable. He made several very personal comments about my appearance. When I did not give him my phone number he said he would contact me on social media so he could ask me out for a drink to say thank you.'

This is very different from the previous situation. If you feel uncomfortable, unsafe, or discriminated against in a client interview, find a way to pause the interview and speak to a supervisor. You can say something along the lines of: 'Please excuse me for a moment, I need to check something with my supervisor.' Or if the client has documents, you can excuse yourself to go and scan the documents and take a pause. While you are out of the room you can find a supervisor and explain the situation. You are entitled to protection from discrimination or harassment in your clinical setting in just the same way that your clients are entitled to protection.

5. 'I was very upset by my client's story. I was not prepared for the emotional impact and my eyes filled with tears while they were talking. I feel embarrassed as this was not professional.'

It is better to have a human response than to be unmoved by your client's situation. We explored some of the risks and rewards of emotional responses to a client's situation in Chapter 10. Lawyers need to objectively analyse a case, but this does not mean that they need to suppress their emotions or distance themselves from a client's distress. An emotional response is a normal response. If you are very upset during an interview, take a moment and pause. Sometimes getting a drink of water provides a reason to pause and regroup when you or the client is upset. Acknowledge your distress to the client: 'This must have been very hard for you, as you can see, just hearing about it has made me feel quite upset.' After the interview, speak to your supervisor about what happened.

6. 'The client would not stop shouting. Although he was not directly angry with me, he was very angry about his case and I felt scared.'

Often people who are going through a stressful experience are angry and intimidating. Telling someone to 'calm down' is not helpful and can aggravate the situation. Often the person just wants to be heard, and if you show that you are listening and sympathetic they may well calm down. You need to use your communication skills to defuse the situation. However, if you feel intimidated or unsafe, always leave. When you plan your interview, think about the seating arrangements and how you could leave the room quickly should the need arise. Your clinical setting should have risk assessments in place and it is important that you know what the procedures are if a client is threatening or abusive. Always seek help if you need it.

7. 'My client asked me to lie in their statement.'

This is a relatively straightforward issue regarding professional ethics. You have a duty to the court as well as to the client and you cannot lie to the court, or act in a way that is dishonest. These issues are discussed in full in Chapter 7. You need to explain to the client that you cannot do this. If they insist, then you cannot continue representing them. However, it can be quite daunting in an interview to refuse to do as the client asks. It may feel confrontational for you to do this. Never agree to do something unethical. If you feel unable to manage the situation yourself, tell the client you need to seek advice and find a supervisor.

8. 'My client did not want to follow my advice and has said they will do completely the opposite.'

As long as the client is not planning to do something unlawful or asking you to do something unethical, they do not have to follow your advice. In fact, your role when giving advice should be to present the client with options so that they can make an informed decision about what they can do. (See section 11.3 of this chapter for a full discussion of how to give advice.) If you have set out the options available to them and your client decides to choose the least appropriate option in your opinion, then that is their choice. You need to accept their instructions. Seek advice from a supervisor and make sure that your advice is clearly recorded in the interview notes and set out in your advice letter.

9. 'It was really hard getting any instructions. My client was almost monosyllabic and answered every question with just one or two words. I tried everything.'

This can happen. The client may be shy, may be neurodiverse, or may just feel very uncomfortable explaining their problem to strangers. If they are unresponsive, try not to put them under too much pressure and simply try to get as much as you can out of the interview. Afterwards you can analyse what you have and give advice, if possible, while also explaining that you need more information to give more specific advice. The client may feel more comfortable answering questions in writing as it is less personal, so you could send a list of questions in an email. Or you could try arranging a follow-up phone call, perhaps sending out some questions in advance for the client to think about.

TAKING STOCK

This section of the chapter looked at client interviewing and considered the purpose of an interview, how to plan an interview, how to conduct an interview, and finally how to deal with some common problems.

- A client interview can serve many different purposes, from getting information, to clarifying details, to giving advice. The aims of the interview all centre on building trust with your client.
- An interview needs a plan, but this should be flexible so that you can respond to your client's needs.
- You need to listen carefully to your client and take note of all the non-verbal communication that is taking place.
- An interview should be more like a conversation than an interrogation.
- Be prepared to pause the interview and seek advice from a supervisor if there is a problem.

11.2 Case Analysis and Research

As soon as possible following the interview, go through your notes and write up a summary of the interview. As we have seen, it is unlikely that your client will present you with all the relevant facts in a clear and logical order. As you write up your summary you can analyse the facts and the issues so that the information you have is organized in a way that allows you to evaluate the case and develop a strategy.

Start by putting the facts in chronological order. This will help you to organize the information that you have and to see if anything is missing. Some of the factual information may be contained in documents or an initial phone call, as well as coming from the interview itself. Try to think of your supervisor or another student reading your factual summary. They need to be able to understand the client's story clearly from reading this note.

Next, go over the notes again and identify what it is that the client wants to achieve. Set this out in the client's words. At this point you are looking at the problem from the client's perspective. Once you are clear about what the client wants to achieve, you can then identify legal and non-legal solutions or options.

Practical Exercise 11.4

In relation to Pawel Gronowski, which of the following summaries do you think most closely reflects the client's objectives?

In the second example, the client's concerns are expressed as legal issues. Sometimes clients have some legal knowledge before their interview. They may have been through proceedings before or they might have looked up some of the terminology online before their meeting. What are the risks in expressing the client's objectives in legal terms? Could this close down the options or limit the range of advice that you give?

Example 1

- Client wants the children to remain living with him.
- He wants them to be able to see their mother *but* he wants to be sure they won't come into contact with Jamal. He wants an independent assessment from social services or something to be sure that the children won't see any more domestic abuse.
- He does not want to have any direct communication with his ex-wife and wants someone neutral to be involved in the arrangements.
- He wants the court proceedings over as quickly as possible, as he is finding the current situation very stressful.
- He is very upset about allegations his ex-wife has made about him and wants her to withdraw these as he says they are not true.
- He is very worried about what will happen at the hearing on 6 December.

Example 2

- Client wants a child arrangements order, setting out that the children live with him and spend time with their mother.
- He wants Cafcass to prepare a section 7 report to consider safety.
- He wants contact with the mother to be organized through a contact centre.
- Although he wants the proceedings over quickly, he wants the court to hold a fact-finding hearing to establish whether the allegations against him are true or not.

When you analyse your case, you need to analyse the factual and legal issues. These two types of analysis go hand in hand, but separating them out will help you to identify the issues and give advice that reflects the client's concerns. In the examples in Practical Exercise 11.4, by jumping straight to a summary of possible legal outcomes rather than a summary of the client's objectives based on the facts, the emphasis has shifted to the way in which legal proceedings might be conducted, which may not necessarily reflect the client's desired outcome.

When you analyse your case by linking the facts to the legal issues you will be able to identify any gaps in your factual information that you might need to follow up on. Figure 11.6 shows how the facts, issues, and law can be separated out for one simple point. This pattern then needs to be repeated to break down the client's problem in order to then apply the law and offer advice on possible solutions.

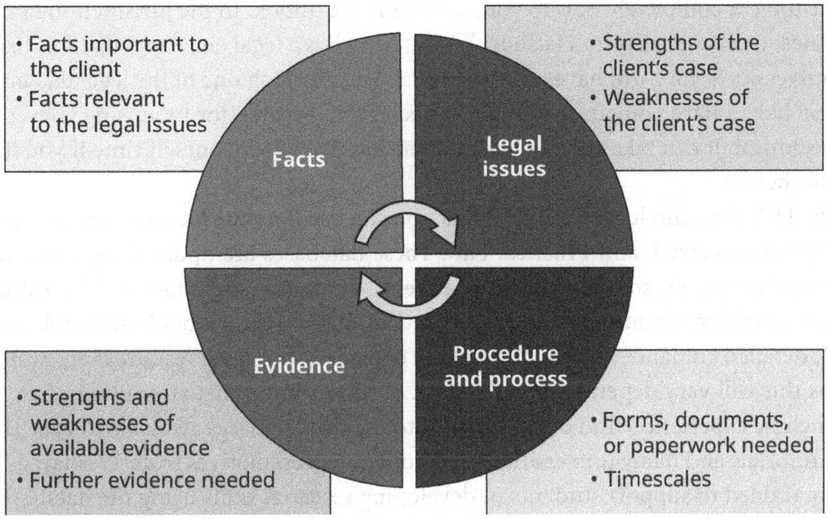

Figure 11.6 Analysis of factual legal and procedural issues

As a lawyer, the tem the ptation is to view the client's issues through the lens of the legal issues. This is after all what you have been trained to do. Your research and advice will be clearer and more specific if you keep breaking down the information you have into factual and legal issues.

As you begin to analyse your case, you need to start planning your research. Sometimes you might not have to do much research at all as you have seen more than one client with a similar problem.

Your research will be more useful to you and your colleagues if you focus on your client's problem and find the relevant law and procedure that you need to give advice. Think about:

1. What courses of action are possible for the client?
2. Which course of action is the best option for the client?
3. How can they achieve this?

You then need to identify:

1. What do you already know?
2. What are the gaps in your knowledge?
3. How are you going to fill those gaps?

You are going to give legal advice to real clients. This is not just an academic exercise. You need to be confident that you have the right law and the right procedure. This means using primary sources, not just relying on articles, websites, or even textbooks.

If the topic is completely new to you, start with a textbook. In the jurisdiction of England and Wales, you could also try Halsbury's Laws, which is a legal encyclopedia. It is likely that your university library will have access to Halsbury's through one of the legal databases and may als6 have a hard copy in the library. Halsbury's is written for practising lawyers and is quite technical. It can take time to learn to navigate, so allow yourself time if you have not used this before.

In the UK, the main legal databases that you can use for your practical legal research are Lexis, Westlaw, Lawtel, and Practical Law. These databases are updated regularly and give you access to caselaw, statutes, practitioner texts, guidance, and analysis. The features and tools for searching are added to and improved annually. This textbook does not, therefore, include detailed guidance on how to use these databases, nor what resources are available on each, as this will vary depending on the level of subscription that your library has. As part of your clinic experience, find out about how to use the databases available to you. There are online tutorials and many universities have student representatives from Westlaw and Lexis who are trained to support students in developing research skills using the databases. Find out if your university has reps or if your university library has tutorials and guidance on using the legal databases. Take the time to learn how to use them. A textbook, or your lecturer's PowerPoint slides, are not primary sources; they are just one person's interpretation and summary of the law. They are invaluable for getting an overview but they are not enough to give advice to a client in a law clinic.

A View From Clinical Legal Practice

Reflections on Learning and Teaching Lawyering Skills

Professor Richard Grimes, former Director of Clinical Programmes, University of York, UK now independent legal education and access to justice consultant

In their seminal report back in 1992 the ABA Taskforce, under the leadership of Robert MacCrate, highlighted the need for a joined-up approach to legal education in which doctrinal knowledge, lawyering skills, and professional values and attributes are studied in a holistic and practically applicable way. As those familiar with clinical legal education will know and, judging by the exponential growth of experiential learning in law schools, as many others are discovering, clinics in their various guises are an ideal vehicle for such an approach to study. Subsequent legal education reviews in the UK and abroad have overwhelmingly endorsed this view.

Of course, what the purpose of any particular clinic is will depend on its rationale, for example addressing unmet legal needs and serving social justice ends. If the clinic is part of a law school offering then it will also surely have clear learning outcomes for those clinic students who participate, and these may variously address the appropriate knowledge, skills, and/or values implicit in the clinic's work.

For understandable reasons, the skills component is often stressed as being a key element of the anticipated learning outcomes—where else in the law school curriculum can a student gain both a theoretical and an applied understanding of the range of skills a lawyer needs to be able to do his, her, or their work effectively? This may include specifically 'legal' skills such as interviewing, drafting, and perhaps advocacy, depending on the exact extent of the clinic's activity and permissible legal practice rules. In addition, there are a host of other skill-related activities that are central to effective lawyering but are transferable to other working contexts, such as time management, teamwork, critical thinking, problem-solving, reflective practice, and, increasingly relevant, IT and e-competency.

While none of this should be taken as undermining the role of clinic in the intellectual understanding of the law, the learning and teaching of the skills dimension, in all its scope, is inevitably a major part of the clinic's function.

Much has been usefully said in this volume about legal and related skills which one can only agree with. But in all of my clinic work, which goes back a very long time, there are two things that to me seem to be of fundamental importance.

First is the need to be able to conduct research in a comprehensive way and then to be able to apply the findings critically. It is so easy to 'Google it' and accept the results without question. We have, I am sure, all been guilty of that temptation. Technology clearly has its considerable value, but we must remain vigilant—can you be sure that what you have found is both up to date and applicable? You must be able to locate the relevant legal authority, not someone's (with the initials AI, perhaps?) account of it.

The second, linked to the first, is the need to prepare thoroughly for whatever task lies ahead, be that the research you conduct, the correspondence you draft, or the submission or presentation you intend to make. Again, modern technology can provide us with short-cuts, but we must ensure that our preparation is robust and has been tested, at least to the extent of critical scrutiny (by ourselves and/or others—remember that teamwork dimension), and, most importantly, before final application.

Of the many benefits, even joys, that the clinic can provide, developing one's skills base is clearly a major component, and one that will be picked up on at any subsequent job interview. Couple that with the identification and application of legal principles alongside a growing appreciation of matters ethical and professional, and we see clinical legal education as an exemplar for effective and socially relevant learning.

It is little wonder that the clinic—be that an in-house advice service, a full-representation model, a *Street Law* option, an externship programme, a policy/law reform module, or even a simulated offering—is now a familiar feature across civil, common, Sharia, and customary law jurisdictions. Long may that continue. Experience suggests that it is a win/win situation for all.

Let us return to Pawel Gronowski. The record of the initial phone call from the client refers to the fact that he wants advice in relation to custody and access. It may be tempting to start your research with the terms custody and access. What you may not know, if you have not studied family law before, is that custody and access are terms that are rarely used in the Family Court in England and Wales. Starting your search with the terms custody and access could lead you in the wrong direction completely, and you may find yourself looking at laws relating to child abduction. Across many different areas of law, often a client will use legal terms when they come to see you, but they may not be using these correctly. Relying on your client's knowledge of the law to start your research may not be the best place to start. Whatever area of law you are working in, you are likely to come across legal terms that are used by lay people inaccurately or that have a specific meaning in relation to a legal issue. The best advice is to start with a textbook or seek some guidance from a supervisor if you are researching a completely new area of law.

11.2.1 **Developing a Research Plan**

When you start to plan your research:

1. Use the client's objectives as your starting point.
2. Make a list of questions that you think need to be answered to advise the client.
3. Decide which sources you are going to use to conduct your research.
4. Make a list of search terms or phrases.

Table 11.4 shows an example of how students might break down research in relation to the type of hearing in the Pawel Gronowski case study.

In Table 11.4 the students have used Google as one of their resources for research. Sometimes a search on the web can be a useful starting point. In this case, we have a very specific search term, which is the name of the hearing. It is quite possible that a web search will take you to a reliable source that might give you an overview or description of what these letters stand for. Searching free, easily digestible sources on the web can be a useful way of getting an overview of a new subject. However, as lawyers giving professional advice this must

Table 11.4 Research Plan

Client concern	Research questions	Possible sources	Search terms
Client is very worried about what will happen at the hearing on 6 December	Hearing is listed for a FHDRA. What does FHDRA stand for? What is the purpose of a FHDRA? What documents are normally filed before a FHDRA? Who attends a FHDRA? What happens after a FHDRA? What is the likely outcome of a FHDRA?	Practitioner text on family procedures Practical law Lexis Google or other web search engines	FHDRA 'Family court hearings' 'First hearings' 'Family court procedure'

always be your starting point, not your end point. Once you have an overview you need to go to the primary legal sources and use reliable practitioner texts that give links to cases, statutes, and procedure rules. In addition to a general search of the web using Google or other search engines, you may start your research by using an AI research tool. If you do, this must always be a starting point, and you must check all of your sources properly. The responsibility for doing this lies with you and, as we saw in Chapter 8, the consequences of not checking your research with reliable primary sources can be very serious for both you and your client.[8]

11.2.2 **Keep Records of Each Stage of Your Research**

You need to keep an audit trail of your research with clear records that break down the research done into clear digestible sections. The client's file should have a research record for every point of law and procedure that is relevant to your client's case, in the same way as a piece of coursework will have a footnote to support each point made. Table 11.5 has an example of a research record relating to one of the research questions identified in the Pawel Gronowski case study.

Example Research Record

A template for research records is available for downloading on the companion website to the book.

This process of breaking down the research into questions and keeping a short research record for each question can feel slow and laborious. But the more accurate your research records are, the easier it is to give the client advice that is relevant to their issue.

In Table 11.5, the information about the purpose of the hearing came from a document called Practice Direction 12B (relevant to England and Wales). While it might seem tempting to copy out the whole of this Practice Direction, or at least copy over all 13 paragraphs in relation to FHDRAs, it is worth reminding yourself why you are doing the research. You are conducting research, not to find the relevant document, but to understand the procedure in the court in order to explain it to your client and advise him of the likely outcome in his case. By breaking the research down and recording answers to research questions in this way, you are keeping the focus on the client and creating a record that you can come back to and use again. Keeping your research on the file in this way also facilitates supervision and collaboration. Your supervisor can quickly identify errors or confusion and your peers can use your research and build on it.

Don't stop once you have found the relevant point of law or procedure. Go back to your client, remind yourself why you are researching this point, and then apply your research to the client's problem. At this point, it is helpful to explain your research finding in your own words. This gives you an opportunity to check your own understanding and it will help you put the research findings together into advice for your client.

[8] *R (on the application of Frederick Ayinde) v London Borough of Haringey* [2025] EWHC 1383 (Admin).

Table 11.5 Analysis of factual, legal, and procedural issues

Research Question:	What is the purpose of a FHDRA (First Hearing Directions Resolution Appointment)
Search Terms	FHDRA, Family Court Hearings
Sources	Practical Law and Westlaw
Results	Westlaw—76 cases, 2 journal articles, and 1 overview—journal articles and overview were not specifically about FHDRA so not helpful for this question and overview was about reports—too many cases to read through looking for purpose of FHDRA **Practical Law—38 hits for FHDRA** The 4th item is a guide to child arrangement proceedings—explains whole process—most of the procedure comes from Practice Direction 12B—followed up by looking at PD 12B online and Practice Direction 12J—Practice Direction 12B has a whole section on FHDRAs—relevant paragraphs are copied below https://www.justice.gov.uk/courts/procedure-rules/family/practice_directions/pd_part_12b **14.8** The FHDRA provides an opportunity for the parties to be helped to an understanding of the issues which divide them, and to reach agreement. If agreement is reached— (1) The Court will be able to make an order (which in many cases will be a final order) reflecting that agreement (2) The Court will assist the parties (so far as it is able) in putting into effect the agreement/order in a co-operative way **14.11** At the FHDRA the judge, working with the Cafcass Officer, or WFPO, will seek to assist the parties in conciliation and in resolution of all or any of the issues between them. Any remaining issues will be identified, the Cafcass Officer or WFPO will advise the court of any recommended means of resolving such issues, and directions will be given for the future resolution of such issues. At all times the decisions of the court and the work of the Cafcass Officer or WFPO will take account of any risk or safeguarding issues that have been identified
How does this apply to my client?	The hearing seems to have 3 purposes—to try and reach an agreement, to identify outstanding issues and give directions The client wants to know what will happen at the hearing—it seems this will not be the final hearing—unless he can reach an agreement with his ex-wife (does not look likely from the interview, but we need to explore this possibility with him) and if no agreement, court will give directions
Next research question	What are directions? Or what directions are likely in a case about children?

11.2.3 **Law, Process, and Procedure**

As your research progresses, try to separate substantive law from process and procedure. Most undergraduate law programmes focus on the substantive law so, depending on where you are in your studies, you may not be used to researching or applying procedure. If you are advising your client in relation to any form of litigation, the relevant court or tribunal will have a set of rules about how cases are to be conducted. You will need to find out what these rules are and where to find them. In transactional work you may not need to learn procedural rules, but you still need to understand the processes involved in achieving the client's goal. There is a difference between understanding that there are certain elements that make up a legally enforceable contract and actually agreeing terms so that the contract can be drafted. Keep the initial three research questions in mind:

What courses of action are available to my client?—*Substantive law*

Which is the best course of action?—*Application of substantive law (facts and law)*

How can they achieve this?—*Process and procedure*

For example, advice to a client about welfare benefits could be summarized and broken down as follows:

What benefits is my client entitled to? As a person with a disability they could receive

a) Employment Support Allowance (ESA) or

b) Universal Credit (UC)

c) Personal Independence Payment (PIP)

Which is the better option? This client has savings and is working part-time. Therefore they are

a) not eligible for UC or ESA but

b) can claim PIP as it is not means tested

How can they claim PIP?

a) They need to start the claim by phoning the PIP New Claims Phone Line and then fill in the form that will be sent to them.

11.2.4 **Putting It All Together**

Analysis and research is not a linear process but more circular as you keep adding to your understanding of the facts and the issues, as shown in Figure 11.6. You need to break down the information that you have, but keep connecting it back to the client and their objectives.

As your research and analysis progresses, your understanding of the law and procedure will deepen. You will need to keep returning to the facts to reassess what is relevant and what is not. You may find that some facts that seemed irrelevant at the start are more significant than you first realized. As you categorize and organize facts, it is helpful to keep in mind what is important and relevant to the client and what is relevant to the legal issues. If something is important to the client but unlikely to be relevant to the legal issue, you will need to explain this in your advice. You might find it helpful to create a diagram of the facts and the legal issues to help you visualize how the different elements might all fit together. In Figure 11.7 the facts that are important to the client are set out in the circles and the key legal and procedural issues are listed in the box in the centre. A diagram like this might help you to better understand how to fit different factual issues around the law and procedure.

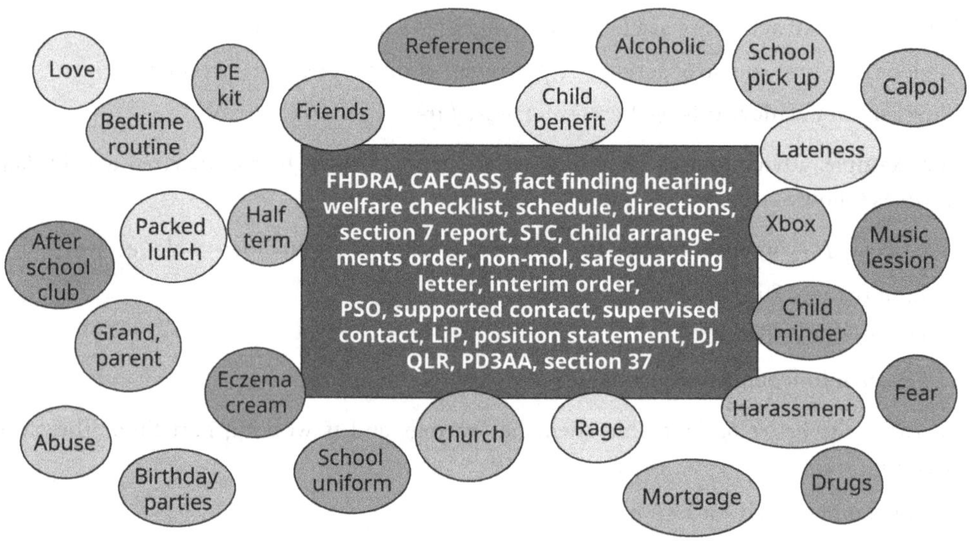

Figure 11.7 Connecting facts to legal issues

You will also need to consider whether the best option for the client is to find an alternative solution. Court proceedings, legal action, and legal processes are not always the quickest or cheapest way for a client to achieve what they want to achieve. In the example of our client Pawel Gronowski, even though his ex-wife has now issued court proceedings, it is worth bearing in mind that they were able to agree arrangements for several years. Some form of mediation or negotiation may still be a possibility and could bring the court proceedings to a close more quickly. One of the client's clear objectives is to get the court proceedings over quickly, as he feels very stressed by them. As a lawyer it is sometimes tempting to just keep ploughing along the route to court, but court is stressful, slow, confusing, and uncertain. Finding a compromise and reaching an agreement is nearly always the best solution. This applies equally to transactional work. You might negotiate the best possible terms on a contract, but if your client will have an ongoing business relationship with the other party for some years to come, goodwill and mutual trust might be worth more in the long term than a long drawn-out negotiation over a particular clause in the contract.

TAKING STOCK

This section of the chapter looked at analysing and researching your case in order to give legal advice to your client. Like the interview itself, this is not a linear process but one in which you need to link facts, law, and process while maintaining a focus on your client's objective. Start by writing up a case summary with facts in chronological order and listing the client's concerns.

If this is a new area of law for you, begin with a textbook or guide to get an overview. Keep an audit trail of your research on your client file. Research records are like footnotes. Your supervisor and your colleagues should be able to follow them through to the primary source.

Focus your research on what the client needs to know. Stick to the relevant points. Remember to research procedure as well as law. Be practical in your research. Your client does not want or need to know about the academic journal articles critiquing the law that is relevant to them; they want to know what the relevant legal principles are and why they are relevant.

11.3 Letters of Advice

The essence of legal advice is to evaluate the merits of the client's case and set out the options available to them, so that they can make an informed decision as to what steps they should take next. Giving advice is not the same as providing information.

Practical Exercise 11.5

Look at the following two extracts from an advice letter. Which would you describe as legal information and which legal advice? Imagine you are the client. Which one would you find most helpful?

Extract 1

You have a hearing next week which is called a FHDRA. There are several purposes to a FHDRA.

a) To help you reach an agreement. If an agreement is reached the court will make a final order and the case will be over.

b) If you cannot reach an agreement, the judge will identify what the key areas of disagreement are and what evidence is needed to resolve the case.

c) The court will set a timetable for the next stage of the proceedings and set out clearly what evidence needs to be filed, when it needs to be filed, and when the next hearing will be.

Typical directions are a report from Cafcass or social services, letters from the children's school, police disclosure, statements from parents with schedules of allegations, or drug and alcohol testing. Proceedings can take between six months and a year to reach a conclusion depending on the issues and the evidence available.

Extract 2

The hearing that you have coming up is a possession hearing. The Housing Association have applied for a possession order because you fell behind with your rent payments. There are three possible orders that the court can make:

a) A possession order, which will give you notice that you need to leave your home by a fixed date—normally in four weeks' time.

b) A suspended possession order. If this order is made, the court will set conditions for you to pay your rent and the £5 a week that you have agreed with your housing officer. If you then fail to stick to the agreement, a possession order will be made.

c) No order at all.

You have now sorted out your benefits payments so your rent is being paid and you have reached an agreement with the housing officer to pay your arrears off at a rate of £5 a week. It is therefore very unlikely that the court will make a possession order in your case. You have been a tenant for 20 years and have never fallen behind with the rent before. You can ask the court to consider your history and ask the judge to make no order at all. However, the most likely outcome is a suspended possession order, as the amount of money that you owe the housing association is quite high.

Remember, the client needs to make an informed decision. If you tell the client 'in my opinion you should do x, not y' without giving reasons, they are not able to understand why you are giving that advice, or make their own choice as to whether to follow your recommendation. This means that when you give advice you need to include the following elements:

1. Identify the options available (sometimes there is only one option).
2. Explain the relevant law or procedure to the client.
3. Explain the options.
4. Evaluate the strengths and weaknesses of the client's position in relation to each option.

5. Make a recommendation on what option is best for them.
6. Set out clearly what the client needs to do next and what you will do next.
7. Advise the client on funding and costs—you may provide a free service, but there may be costs associated with the recommended course of action or they may be able to get financial support or qualify for legal aid.

11.3.1 Style

Keep your language simple. Remember, this is not coursework, so you are not trying to demonstrate your knowledge of the law, or your ability to critique the law. You are checking that you have the facts right and you are helping the client to understand how the law applies to their personal set of circumstances. Always keep the client in mind when you are writing a letter.

Short sentences are clearer and easier to understand. Long sentences often contain several ideas, which can be confusing. If you have a list of points to make, consider using a bullet point list or a table. For example:

> Before starting court proceedings, there are a number of steps you need to take. First, you need to attend a meeting with a mediator; second, you need a certificate from the mediator confirming they met with you. Third, you need to complete a form called an EX160 to apply for a fee exemption. Once you have taken all these steps you can complete the online form called the C100.

Or

> Before starting court proceedings, there are a number of steps you need to take:
>
> 1. Attend a meeting with a mediator.
> 2. Ask the mediator to provide a certificate.
> 3. Complete fee exemption form EX160 online.
> 4. Complete form C100 online. You will need the mediation certificate and code from EX160 to complete and submit this form.

Too many lists, tables, subheadings, and bullet points can make a text feel disjointed. On the other hand, long sentences or long paragraphs can be hard to follow.

Think about the number of words you use. Are they all necessary? Students often use a phrase when a single word will do. Common examples include the following:

- At this point in time — Now
- In order to — To
- In recent weeks — Recently

Avoid the Passive Voice

In coursework and academic writing, the passive is often used to create a sense of formality and to avoid the use of the first person. Writing an advice letter is personal, and you need to be clear about who needs to do what and when.

- When all of the documents have been received and collated, your application will be submitted to the Home Office.
- You need to send us the remaining documents on the list. When we have all the documents needed we will organise them and submit your application to the Home Office.

In the first sentence it is not clear who is going to send the documents, who will collate them, and who will send them to the Home Office. In the second example, there is a clear instruction for the client to send in the remaining documents and that the clinic will collate them and submit the application.

Explain Legal Terms, Acronyms, and Abbreviations

Write out names of institutions in full when you first name them. You can use an acronym in a letter once you have introduced it. You might write: 'Her Majesty's Revenue and Customs ("HMRC")'. You can then use HMRC throughout the letter.

As you become familiar with a particular area of law, you will begin using new terms with confidence and forget that they are still new to the client. Keep reviewing your letters and check that you have explained all legal terms used.

Formalities

There are certain formalities in writing a letter. Make sure you know what your clinical setting's rules are. The letter should include:

- The date it was written
- The client's address
- Your file reference number
- A salutation—ie Dear Mrs Khan or Dear Zainab. Your clinical setting may have guidance on using first names in the salutation. Keeping the formality of titles and surnames can set the tone of your letter as a formal letter, or a first name can feel more personal
- A subject line—Re your daughter's education
- A signature line with the name of the letter writer printed alongside the signature.

11.3.2 **Structure of an Advice Letter**

It is likely that your clinic will have a template for writing letters of advice. Each organization will have slightly different guidance on how letters should be set out and you should familiarize yourself with the 'house style'. Although templates and house style may vary from one organization to the next, most advice letters will include the following sections:

- A clear record of the facts that are relevant to the legal issues
- A summary of the client's concerns or objectives
- Advice which includes an explanation of the relevant law and procedure and an evaluation on the merits of the different options available (including do nothing if relevant)
- Recommendations on what the client should do in order to pursue their chosen option
- A clear summary of any action that you (the lawyer) have agreed to take, and any action the client has agreed to take, with timings/time limits
- Costs and funding.

Background Information

You need to include all the factual information that is relevant to the legal issues at the start of your letter. This can seem strange when you begin writing advice letters, as you are telling the client something that they know already. For example, you might start the letter by saying 'You explained to me that you live at 65 High St, New Town, Old County. This is a four-bedroom property owned by you and your wife, Hannah, in joint names.'

It is good practice to repeat this information back to the client for three reasons. First, you are checking that you have the facts right. Second, it helps you and the client to identify facts that are unclear, unsure, or unsupported by any evidence. Finally, you are helping the client to identify and organize the relevant information for themselves. This is particularly important if your clinical setting offers advice only, as the letter will be used by the client to go on and take action for themselves. As you move through the letter explaining the law and giving advice, you need to be able to refer back to the relevant factual information set out at the start of the letter.

Set out the background facts in chronological order and make it personal. Identify key people by name at the start of the letter and then use those names throughout the letter. Keep in mind that you are writing to the client about a problem in their life and that is important to them. Getting the facts right and using names shows that you have taken time to listen to them and are taking time with their case. Use clear, simple language with short sentences so that it is easy to follow the story and the timeline. If the factual background is particularly long or complex, it can be helpful to set the chronology out in columns or in a table.

Follow the client's lead when deciding what terms to use to talk about something sensitive or difficult. For example, you may need to advise someone about a situation where a family member has died. A good rule of thumb is to use the words they themselves have used. For example, if the client talks about their relative 'passing away', then use this phrase in the letter. If they use the word 'died' then don't be afraid to also use the word died.

If the client has given you any documents, you should include a list of the documents that you have in the letter. For example, you may have bank statements, copies of passports or birth certificates, contracts of employment, or court documents. State clearly whether you have the original documents or copies. If you need more documents, it is helpful to create a table listing the documents that you have and the documents that you need the client to supply.

Practical Exercise 11.6

Look at the following examples or extracts from an advice letter and consider which wording is the most appropriate in each case. Which summaries set out the facts in chronological order? How do you think the client would feel receiving Letter A and Letter B?

Letter A	Letter B
You explained to me that you have two children, Kehinde and Taiwo. You do not have a job because one of the children is disabled and you are therefore reliant on benefits. Following a mistake with your benefits, you have accumulated rent arrears. Your landlord, the Housing Association, is seeking a possession order because it took you two months to resolve your benefits problem, meaning that you failed to pay your rent.	You explained to me that you have three-year old twins, Kehinde and Taiwo. Kehinde has a disability and you care for Kehinde and Taiwo full time. You have not been able to work outside the home since the twins were born. In May this year, there was an error at the DWP and your benefits were stopped for a period of two months. This has led to your falling behind with your rent. You rent your property from the Housing Association, and have found your housing officer, Abigail Jones, to be very unhelpful.
You explained that your two grandchildren came to live with you six months ago after their mother (your daughter) died of cancer. They are 8 and 10 years old.	You have two grandchildren, Aisha, who is 8 years old, and Hassan who is 10 years old. You are their maternal grandmother and you told us that you very sadly lost your daughter, Sara, to cancer six months ago. The children now live with you.
You explained to us that you resigned from your job last week after working for the same organization for eight years. You have made allegations of bullying by a colleague but these allegations were not upheld by your manager or by HR when you made a complaint. You believe you have been treated unfairly and that you were forced out.	You explained to us that you started work for the Company approximately eight years ago. In June last year, a new colleague, John, joined your team and from the start the relationship with him was difficult. You spoke to your boss several times, but she said you needed to make the relationship work. You felt that John's attitude towards you was unacceptable. After two attempts at informal resolution you made a formal complaint of bullying. You found the complaint process very difficult and had to take some time off with stress. You received confirmation last week that HR had upheld your complaint. You have now handed in your notice.

Client's Concerns or Objectives

You should already have a clear list of the client's concerns and objectives in your case analysis. This can be copied into the letter. A list is helpful here. You need to make sure that you address each of these concerns in the letter.

Advice

An initial advice letter is likely to be limited by the information that you have available. It is possible that you are waiting for documents from the client or you may not yet know the position of the other parties. The advice section of your letter should state clearly what the advice is based on. For example:

> Please note that this advice is based on the information that you gave to us in the client appointment. Once we have received the documents set out below and established the other party's position the advice may change.

Break the advice down into sections so that it is easy for the client to follow. At each stage of the letter, identify, explain, and apply relevant law and procedure and evaluate the merits of your client's case.

Identifying the law:

> Tell the client what the law relevant to their case is. You do not need to cite statutes and cases, but you do need to set out legal rules that are relevant to your client's situation.

Explaining the law:

> Using your own words, tell the client how the law works. If you use legal terminology, you need to explain the terms used. Remember, the purpose of the letter is for the client to understand what their options are so that they can make an informed decision about what steps to take.

Applying the law:

> In your client's situation, how will the law affect them. Make explicit connections between the law and the client's situation. You should always refer back to the facts set out at the start of the letter, and not introduce new facts at this point.

Example:

Your case has been listed for a hearing on 12 December called a First Hearing Directions Resolution Appointment (FHDRA).	The letter identifies a point of procedure.
The purpose of this hearing is to help you reach an agreement. If no agreement is reached, the judge will decide what evidence is needed to progress the case.	The letter explains the purpose of the hearing.
You have told us that your daughter does not want to stay overnight in her mother's house. It is therefore likely the court will ask for a report from Cafcass to find out more about your daughter's wishes and feelings.	The letter applies this to the client's case.

Evaluate the merits of the client's case.

In other words, you need to tell the client how likely it is that they will succeed in achieving their desired outcome and set out the strengths and weaknesses of their position.

This is the essence of legal advice and is the difference between advice and information. Sometimes the advice might be very qualified as there are many uncertainties; however, in most cases you can give clear advice about likely outcomes.

Example:
Depending on the facts, you might advise on merits in any one of the following ways.

a) Your child is a British national and you do not have to make an application for citizenship for them. You can apply directly for a passport.
b) Your child is entitled to apply for British citizenship. Your application will be successful if you complete the forms correctly and provide all the necessary documents.
c) Your child can apply for British citizenship, but there is a possibility that the application will not be successful.
d) Your child can apply for British citizenship but it is very unlikely this will be granted.

It should be clear from the analysis of the facts and the application of the law why you have reached this conclusion.

When you begin giving advice, do not slip into overly formal legal language. Continue to keep the letter personal throughout.

Avoid legal jargon and think about who is going to read the letter. Make it personal to the client. Remember this advice is about the client's life and is important to them. Put yourself in the client's shoes when thinking about whether the tone and style of the letter is appropriate.

Compare the two styles below:

Example A
Children with a disability are entitled to support at school and a parent can request an assessment under the Children and Families Act 2014. As your child has autism and is failing to achieve at school, a request for an assessment can be made by you.

Example B
You explained to us that Josie is finding it very difficult to keep up at school. She has autism and this means she needs some extra help with instructions and with social interaction. As a parent, you can write to the local authority to make a formal request for an assessment of Josie's needs.

Next Steps

The advice letter should set out clearly what the client should do next and what you will do next.

This can include practical steps that are not legal steps, such as signposting your client to relevant support services.

Provide links to online resources such as application forms. Don't leave the client to find these for themselves.

If there are important time limits for your client, make sure that you spell these out in the next steps. Be precise with time limits: use actual dates where you can and consider whether a date is inclusive or not. If you say that a document must be filed by 10 January, does this mean on 10 January or before 10 January? If the client needs to file a document within 14 days, look at the calendar and work out the date for the client.

If your next steps are dependent on the client providing information, make this clear. For example, 'When we receive all the documents set out above, we will prepare your application and send it to the Home Office. We aim to do this within seven days of receiving the documents. If we do not receive everything on the list we cannot complete the application.'

Costs and Funding

Even if your service is free, you must always advise the client about potential costs. They may need to pay for evidence, for example obtaining an expert report. They may need to pay a fee to the court or tribunal service. If they are going to start litigation, they must be advised about the risks of costs orders being made against them.

Your client may be able to get help with costs, from insurance or legal aid, or fee exemption procedures. Your advice letter should include clear guidance on any financial support available.

Closing

Finish your letter with a closing paragraph. You may find that your setting has a standard closing paragraph. Don't forget to sign the letter.

TAKING STOCK

This section of the chapter looked at writing letters of advice, including the style of an advice letter, how to structure an advice letter, key points to include, and the importance of explaining reasons for advice:

- **Make the letter personal. Use names of people.**
- **Use clear simple language with short sentences and avoid the passive voice.**
- **Set out the facts that are relevant to the law and procedure in chronological order.**
- **Explain the law and apply it to the client's situation.**
- **Give clear advice on the options and prospects of success.**
- **Set out the next steps for both the client and the clinic.**
- **Don't forget to include information about costs and any possible funding routes.**

Conclusion

Interviewing and advising clients is the core work of the legal profession. Whether you do contentious or non-contentious work, the role of the lawyer is to give advice and either assist the client to achieve their goal or explain to them why the goal may be unachievable. In this chapter we have focused on an initial interview and advice as this point marks the start of the relationship between a lawyer and a client. In reality, if you represent a client over a long period of time, you will interview and advise them on many occasions. The first interview will set the tone of that relationship. Advice will change over time as the facts will change and the client's objectives may also change.

Many university law clinics offer advice-only services, so you will not go on to represent the client. The initial interview will form the basis of the advice given, so it is crucial that you get it right. This can feel quite daunting to law students. It is important for you to remember that you are beginners, and it will take more than one attempt at a client interview to find out what works best for you. Each client is different and even experienced lawyers will sometimes find it hard to build a rapport or establish what it is that their client wants to achieve. At this stage, all you can do is to take the time to prepare for an interview and take the time afterwards to reflect on what went well and how you might do things differently next time. The transition from law in books to law in the real world can be a shock to some law students and a relief to others. Just remember that your clients are people like you, are nervous like you, and have come to you for help. You can always arrange a follow-up phone call or ask to email some follow-up questions if you come to analyse your case and realize that you have a crucial piece of information missing. Be kind to yourselves and your clients, seek advice from your supervisor, and allow yourself time to develop these skills.

Further Reading

Katherine Blow and Jacqueline Kempton, *Oral Skills for Lawyers* (University of Law 2023).

Elaine Heslop, *Giving Legal Advice* (Legal Action Group 2014).

Caroline Maughan and Julian Webb, *Lawyering Skills and the Legal Process* (2nd ed, Cambridge University Press 2005).

Julian Webb, Caroline Maughan, Mike Maughan, Marcus Keppel-Palmer, and Andrew Boon, *Lawyers' Skills* (OUP 2019).

Representing Your Client

12

Chapter Overview

In Chapter 10 we looked at the core skills of interviewing and advising clients. In this chapter we go on to look at the work involved in representing a client, which, depending on the nature of the work, will include drafting documents, conducting negotiations, and advocacy.

Having read and engaged with the exercises in this chapter, you will be able to:

- Describe common features of legal documents
- Recognize the need to adapt precedents to the circumstances of your client's case
- Identify different approaches to negotiation
- Analyse a case to plan a negotiation
- Analyse a case to prepare submissions for a hearing
- Describe techniques for handling witnesses
- Understand rules of court etiquette

Introduction

In the previous chapter we looked at giving legal advice. Many university clinical legal settings provide advice-only services, but in some settings you may go on to represent your client. In the popular imagination, representing a client means going to court and advocating for them in a contested hearing. However, in reality, there is much more to representation than court hearings. Many lawyers do transactional or non-contentious work, meaning that litigation plays no part in their role as a lawyer. If you represent a client, you may prepare documents for them, correspond with the other party, instruct experts, carry out negotiations on behalf of your client, advocate on behalf of your client in a court or tribunal, or do all of the above.

This chapter is divided into three sections: drafting, negotiation, and advocacy. The guidance given in this chapter is general and aims to provide an overview of common practice across a wide range of legal practice. In other words, it offers an introduction to the key skills needed when representing clients, all of which are underpinned by the importance of good communication and an understanding of your client's instructions. When faced with complex facts, law, and procedure, much of which may be new to you, it is important not to lose sight of the fundamental purpose of your role: to achieve the best possible outcome for your client.

12.1 Legal Drafting

Most lawyers spend a considerable amount of their working life writing. They write letters; draft minutes of meetings, contracts, leases, wills, witness statements, letters of instruction to experts, briefs to counsel, indexes to bundles, application forms, pleadings, defence, skeleton arguments, and draft orders; and the list goes on. Most of these documents follow set structures and there are rules about the way in which they are set out and written. There will usually be examples to draw upon, often referred to as a 'bank of precedents'. These are typically standard documents with standard clauses, which are then adapted and added to according to the needs and circumstances of the client and their case. The way in which lawyers use precedent and draft documents has changed rapidly in recent years with the introduction of large language model artificial intelligence systems (also known as LLM and AI, respectively) and will likely continue to do so. However, the work of the lawyer will always still involve preparing written legal documents in one form or another. Knowing what needs to be included, understanding the conventions and formalities, and being able to adapt all documents to the needs of your client will remain key legal skills. However much the computer produces the text and wording of your documents, the lawyer is still responsible for the final product. It is beyond the scope of this book and this chapter to consider all of the different conventions and formalities associated with different types of documents. We will however consider some of the basic rules and concepts associated with legal writing.

Table 12.1 contains an extract from the SRA Statement of Solicitor Competence. Refer to the companion website to this book to find a downloadable template to audit your skills and reflect on your development.

As we have established, most legal documents follow a prescribed format and many law firms and advice agencies have templates and precedents to help with drafting and preparing

Table 12.1 Statement of solicitor competence on legal drafting

B4 Draft documents which are legally effective and accurately reflect the client's instructions including a. Being able to draft documents from scratch as well as making appropriate use of precedents b. Addressing all relevant legal and factual issues c. Complying with appropriate formalities d. Using clear, accurate and succinct language	Questions to consider Do you have experience in these competencies? How would you rate your competence? Do you need more experience? How could you gain this experience?

documents. Each area of law and each type of document follow different rules and customs, which can seem bewildering to someone who is new to this type of work. Even an experienced lawyer can find themselves confused when encountering new areas of law or practice. However, there are some common features and rules that underpin legal drafting across all disciplines, which we consider here in this chapter.

In section 4.1 of Chapter 11 we identified some key principles relating to the use of clear language when writing advice letters. These rules also apply to legal drafting. It is tempting to think that a formal legal document should be written in complex language, but this is not the case. The use of complex sentences, the passive voice, and long paragraphs or multiple clauses can often obscure meaning and leave the document open to dispute or disagreement. Whatever document you are drafting, it is important to think about clarity. As a lawyer, learning how to summarize and present large amounts of information succinctly and clearly is a critically important skill.

The different types of document you may have to draft in your legal career include:

- Correspondence (eg with clients, the opposing side, and third parties)
- Application forms
- Pleadings
- Contracts
- Settlements
- Submissions
- Statements
- Skeleton arguments
- Instructions (eg to counsel or to an expert)
- Legal research notes (eg for supervisors)

You can find examples of precedents for all of these different types of documents and your clinical legal setting is likely to have a house style. The precedent will usually have standard clauses and a set structure. The risk, when you rely on precedent, is that you can put together a document that you do not fully understand. This can then lead to unnecessary or irrelevant material being included, or to meanings becoming obscured by the use of 'legalese'. The same risks will apply when using generative AI, which is becoming increasingly common in legal practice. There are, for example, numerous programmes that generate contracts, but the final decision about how the contract is worded and which clauses are included is down to the lawyers who draft and negotiate the contract, not the computer programme that generated it.

12.1.1 **Planning Your Document**

The first step in any drafting task must be to have a good grasp of the facts, the issues, what the client wants, and the possible courses of action available. In other words, you need to analyse your case and understand what you are trying to achieve before putting pen to paper (or fingers to keyboard). If you do not understand the purpose of the document or the reason why you are drafting it, you will not be in a position to make decisions about what needs to be included in your document. Learning how to use precedent effectively is a skill. Precedents should not be seen as a shortcut, as this can lead to poorly drafted documents that do not address the needs of the specific case you are dealing with. Adler and Perry recommend starting by thinking about what you need to say, rather than relying on precedent from the start:

> Many lawyers skip the thought stage and rely on hand-me-downs. They expect a precedent—or just their favoured form of words—to work, not only in general but for the case in hand. They are often under pressure and do not have time to check the detail each time; that responsibility is delegated silently, retrospectively, and ineffectively to whoever developed the precedent.[1]

Step 1
Review your file, analyse your case, and make sure you understand the relevant facts, the legal issues, and the client's instructions.

Step 2
Understand the purpose of your document and consider the intended audience.

For example:

- If you are preparing submissions you need to focus on the legal argument.
- For pleadings you need to focus on the issues in the case.
- For witness statements you need to focus on the factual details.
- For a contract, you need to understand the nature of the commercial agreement being entered into, and the relationship between the parties.
- For correspondence, consider the person who will receive the letter and what they need to know.

Step 3
Make sure you have all the relevant information. Often, you will need to fill in forms which require specific information. They can be time-consuming to complete. Read through a blank version of the form to see what is needed. You may need to go back to your client for information such as a National Insurance number or a child's date of birth.

Step 4
Identify templates that are available. Most legal documents are set out in a particular format with headings. These formalities are important.

Step 5
Find out if there is an example of a similar document drafted on another case. This is not the same as having access to a set or precedents. You should never copy paragraphs or sections from a completed document on another file. This is a quick and easy route to mistakes being

[1] Mark Adler and Daphne Perry, *Clarity for Lawyers: Effective Legal Language* (3rd ed, The Law Society 2017) 55.

made with names and dates. At worst, this can lead to a breach of confidentiality. It can also lead to the client losing trust as this looks to them as if you have not taken care with their case, which is important to them. It is also likely that the facts and issues will not be exactly the same for both clients, so your document may not be appropriately tailored for this case. The purpose of using an example document from another case is to give you an idea of the length, style, and potential content of the document that you are now planning to draft.

Step 6
Find out whether your clinic has a set of precedents or standard documents for you to use. Identify clauses that might be relevant for the document you are drafting and consider whether they need changing or can be used as they are. Standard clauses for documents are often referred to as boilerplate clauses. Choose the paragraphs or clauses you actually need, but resist the temptation to just import everything.

You are now ready to start drafting.

Practical Exercise 12.1

Leighton Coleman is a 53-year-old man who suffers from severe anxiety and depression. He worked as an electrician since leaving school but has been unable to work due to breathing problems and lower back pain. He has been diagnosed with chronic obstructive pulmonary disease (COPD) and arthritis.

Mr Coleman has called your organization and requested support in completing an application for welfare benefits. He wants to apply for Personal Independence Payment (PIP). You explain that he needs to complete what is known as the 'PIP2' form. The deadline for submitting the form is one month from receipt. However, he wasn't aware of the deadline and only has two weeks left to submit it. He can attend an initial appointment with you at 2pm the next day.

You are going to meet with Mr Coleman to interview him to assist with the PIP application. You will be completing the application form for him after the appointment. What steps might you need to take to prepare for the interview? Where might you look for the information that you need?

12.1.2 Features of a Legal Document

Each type of document has its own particular format and formalities and it is important to know what these are. There are common features to most legal documents regardless of the particular rules about layout and it is helpful to bear these in mind when you are drafting:

1. The document needs a title and will often have a heading in a particular format.
2. The document needs to include a reference number. In litigation this will be the court reference number; in correspondence or non-contentious work this will be a clinic or firm reference number.

3. The document starts with the names of the parties. This may be in the title, or in the opening pages of the document, or both.
4. The document will state its purpose at the beginning, some examples might include:
   - This is the defence to claim no LV24C234 . . .
   - I am writing to you on behalf of my client Joe Bloggs in response to your letter dated 5th May 2024.
   - I am writing this statement in accordance with directions made by DJ Smith on 2nd July 2024.
   - This is a contract between X and Y . . .
5. Pages and paragraphs should be numbered.
6. The document should be signed and dated. There are formalities which need to be observed for signing and dating depending on the document. You should always check precedents or templates to find the correct wording.
7. Legal documents often repeat facts and issues that are already contained in another document. This is partly convention, but mainly because it assists with the clarity of the document. For the drafter it helps to focus on the purpose of the document and for the reader it helps to make the purpose of the document clear.

Practical Exercise 12.2

You supported Mr Coleman with his PIP application, and submitted it on his behalf. However, three months later, he has received a letter from the Department for Work and Pensions (DWP) to say the application had been refused. In particular, the client is very unhappy with the assessment that he is able to walk unaided. On a good day, he can walk without his walking frame, but these days this only occurs once a month, at most, and he does not feel safe to walk outside the house without his frame. He also needs to use an oxygen tank. When he had his PIP interview he walked along his kitchen, which was only 5 metres, and he was never out away from the wall. He considers that if the points had been awarded differently for being able to walk unaided, he would qualify for the mobility element of the benefit.

You agreed to help him ask the DWP to look at this decision again. You explain that this process is called a 'mandatory reconsideration' and that you can help him to draft a letter.

Review the opening paragraphs below and consider which one sets issues out most clearly.

1. My name is Leighton Coleman and my national insurance number is LC12 34 56 H.

   I have received a letter refusing my application for PIP.

   I would be grateful if you could reconsider my claim. I think the refusal letter is full of mistakes. For example, you have not fully understood my difficulty with walking. I explained this in question 6 of the application form. I really can't walk that far without help.

2. I am writing to appeal the refusal of PIP.

   I cannot walk 20 metres unaided. I explained the reasons in my application form. Please read this again.

3. My name is Leighton Coleman and my national insurance number is LC 12 34 56 H
   I am writing to ask for a reconsideration of my application for PIP.

   My application was submitted on 1 September 2024 and I have received a refusal dated 28 October 2024.

   The refusal letter gave the following reasons for refusal:

   First, that I can walk 20 metres unaided. This is not correct. On question 6 of the form I stated clearly that I am not able to walk 20 metres due to the pain in my back and shortness of breath caused by my COPD. I have an oxygen tank and I require a walking frame to walk. It is not possible to move the oxygen tank and my walking frame at the same time. I can move around inside my house, but am unable to walk any distance outside the house.

   Imagine that you are the officer from the DWP who is reviewing the application. Which one would you prefer to receive and why?

- Example 1 starts clearly, setting out who the letter is from, with the national insurance reference number so that the file can be identified. It also states the purpose of the letter. But to understand the point that Leighton is appealing, the caseworker has to go back and cross-reference this letter with the application form.
- Example 2 is not at all clear. The letter states that Leighton wishes to have his claim reconsidered, but does not explain clearly who he is or what the original application said.
- Example 3 is much clearer. The reader knows who the letter is from and why the letter is being written. The point that Leighton wishes to have reconsidered is clearly explained. This third example includes most of the features that you would expect in a legal document.

A View From Clinical Legal Practice

Getting the Most out of Feedback in Your Clinical Legal Setting

Louise Hewitt, Associate Professor in Law, University of Greenwich; Director of Innocence Project London

I could talk *a lot* about feedback practice in a clinic environment, because for me it's framed around discussion, and students taking control of their learning. The approach students take to the work produced in clinic is nearly always fundamentally different to that found on traditionally taught modules with lectures and seminars. It is my view that this is attributable to the combination of: highly motivated students who want to work on real cases for real people; the need to produce documents to a professional standard, requiring a number of drafts to 'get it right'; and the collaborative way that students work in small groups where they reflect on what they have done and what they have learnt. These factors are unique to the clinical legal education environment.

When I think about the feedback on case work for the Innocence Project London law clinic, it takes the form of conversations. Students often draft letters to clients, and they need to be drafted clearly and using language they will understand. If the language is too convoluted or complicated, the letter has to be re-drafted. Similarly, if a letter to a law firm is too colloquial and does not have sufficient detail, it will need to be re-drafted. When letters need to be changed, we have a conversation about why and how. Making changes is not perceived to indicate failure by the students who wrote the letters; far from it, it's seen as part of the process in terms of ensuring that the client benefits from the best possible standard of work. We have group discussions about what has been done and how it can be made better, because the outcome is much more than simply them achieving a high grade. Students see the benefit of having engaged with the feedback when they receive a letter back from their client answering all their questions and providing them with information, or the law firm replies sending them the documents they need.

In the clinic environment, feedback is not passive; it is pro-active, and students develop a sense of agency in how they use it. The discussions in clinic break down power dynamics between me and the students, because we are all working on the same case with a shared goal of assisting the client. The feedback loop is underpinned by communication and trust in how I give feedback and how the students I work with in clinic receive it.

Conversations in law clinics seem to happen naturally and you as students start to develop skills relating to effective communication almost without knowing you are doing it. Feedback is one part of those discussions, so it's worthwhile pausing every now and then to identify what you have heard and how you have used it. I guarantee that in some small way you will be acting on that feedback and in doing so, taking control of your learning.

12.1.3 **Putting It All Together**

Once you have considered the purpose of your document and gathered all the information you need to draft you can start writing:

- Allow yourself time, as writing something new can take longer than expected.
- Keep in mind the purpose of the document and carefully consider any standard clauses from templates and precedents. Include them only if needed.
- Keep your reader in mind. Who needs to understand this document?
- Write short sentences.
- Avoid the passive voice.
- Make it clear who needs to do what and when.
- Use sub-headings and numbered lists where appropriate.
- Be prepared to review and redraft more than once.

Practical Exercise 12.3

You can now try to draft your own version of the letter at Practical Exercise 12.2 above using the template of your own university clinic. *What else might you add to make the mandatory reconsideration letter as persuasive as possible?*

TAKING STOCK

In this section we reviewed some of the common features and rules in legal writing and drafting. The work of most lawyers involves writing documents and correspondence on a regular basis. Technology will change the way in which we write and produce documents, but lawyers will still need to be able to check, amend, and redraft documents that are generated by AI models, just as they already manipulate precedents and templates to produce documents tailored to their client's needs.

Before you start writing, check that you understand the purpose of your document before you start writing. Analyse the facts and issues so that you know what you are trying to achieve on behalf of your client.

Consider your reader and don't presume they have read or remembered the contents of other documents associated with your piece of writing. Try to set out clearly what has come before and what you want to achieve. If they need to look at other documents, assist them by summarizing what they need to read and why.

There are formalities associated with most legal documents and you will need to use templates or precedents. Use precedent judiciously and don't be afraid to leave out irrelevant clauses. It is your document and the precedent is just there to guide you.

Finally, keep your language simple and be prepared to listen to feedback and redraft more than once until you are satisfied with the final version.

12.2 Legal Negotiation

Most lawyers will undertake negotiation. Whether you litigate or undertake non-contentious work, negotiation is at the heart of what many lawyers do. Negotiation can take place through correspondence, over the phone, on a video call, or in person at a meeting. Negotiations can be quite formal or relatively informal. We hope that by the time you have reached this point in the book, and by the time you have reached the point of negotiating an agreement, you will have realized that people's personalities and communication skills have an impact on nearly everything that lawyers do in practice. Negotiation is no different—after all, negotiators are people first.

> A basic fact about negotiation, easy to forget in corporate and international transactions, is that you are dealing not with abstract representatives of the 'other side' but with human beings. They have emotions, deeply held values, and different background and viewpoints; and they are unpredictable. They are prone to cognitive biases, partisan perceptions, blind spots and leaps of illogic. So are we.[2]

In other words, like client interviewing, negotiation does not always follow the same structure or go to plan, and you will need all your communication skills to conduct a successful negotiation. In this chapter, we explore some of the different ways in which you can approach a negotiation and offer some practical advice on how to manage a negotiation.

[2] Roger Fisher, William Ury, and Bruce Patton, *Getting to Yes* (3rd ed, Penguin Books 2011) 20.

Table 12.2 Statement of solicitor competence on negotiation and case progression

B6 Negotiate solutions to clients' issues, including	Questions to consider
a. Identifying all parties' interests, objectives and limits b. Developing and formulating best options for meeting parties' objectives c. Presenting options for compromise persuasively d. Responding to options presented by the other side e. Developing compromises between options or parties B7 Plan, manage and progress legal cases and transactions, including a. Applying relevant processes and procedures to progress the matter effectively b. Assessing, communicating and managing risk c. Bringing the transaction or case to a conclusion	Do you have experience in these competencies? How would you rate your competence? Do you need more experience? How could you gain this experience?

'Everyone negotiates something everyday . . . Negotiation is a basic means of getting what you want from others. It is a back-and-forth communication designed to reach an agreement when you and the other side have some interests that are shared and others that are opposed.'[3] Nearly all legal work involves an element of negotiation. Whether you litigate or conduct non-contentious work, your role is to help your client find a solution to their problem. Settling the case is often the best way to resolve the problem. Advising a client on transactional work, such as agreeing terms of a contract, will involve a negotiation of some description with the other party to the contract.

Table 12.2 contains an extract from the SRA Statement of Solicitor Competence. Refer to the companion website to this book to find a downloadable template to audit your skills and reflect on your development.

12.2.1 **What Is a Negotiation?**

Negotiation can be described as having the following features:

1. There are two or more parties who need the involvement of the other, creating a common interest.
2. The parties have different objectives or opinions which has prevented an agreement being reached.
3. The parties believe or accept that negotiation is an appropriate route to reaching a solution.
4. Each party thinks that they will be able to persuade the other to change their position.
5. Both parties believe that an agreement is possible.

[3] Ibid xxvii.

6. Each has some influence (if one party is completely powerless, negotiation is not an option).
7. Negotiation involves interaction between people.[4]

These seven factors revolve around two core elements: conceptual and behavioural. The conceptual element consists of analysing the problem to identify what is at stake. The behavioural aspect refers to the process of making choices about the actions you will take when negotiating.[5] It is this complex interplay between human behaviour and the factual matrix that makes the skill of negotiation hard to master.

Lawyer negotiation has an added layer of complexity. Lawyers are engaged in representative negotiation. Each step of the way, the lawyer needs to make sure that they are still acting on their client's instructions. When you are close to reaching an agreement, you need to take care not to go beyond what your client has agreed to. Lawyers are also bound by codes of professional conduct that will affect the way in which they negotiate. A lawyer cannot mislead the court or behave in a manner that is dishonest when dealing with the other party as this may well breach ethical standards.

In addition to agreements negotiated directly between the lawyers, there are a number of forms of alternative dispute resolution (ADR) that can be used to assist with reaching agreements. The three most common are:

Mediation: In mediation an impartial expert will speak to both parties, either together or separately, to help them to reach an agreement. Mediation is widely used in some areas, such as family disputes, where parties are required to meet with a mediator before issuing court proceedings.

Conciliation: This is similar to mediation, but is used more to resolve a more narrow and specific issue than mediation. Conciliation is often used in employment disputes.

Arbitration: In arbitration a neutral expert makes a decision about the dispute, which a conciliator or mediator will not do. Arbitration is often used in disputes with a number of parties, or with complex issues. Before arbitration, the parties will agree whether to be bound by the decision of the arbitrator.

Neutral Evaluation Hearings: These are judge-led discussions to try and settle a dispute early on in litigation. The meeting takes place in a courtroom, but the aim of the hearing is for the judge to assist the parties to reach an agreement. If an agreement is reached a consent order can be drafted, and if agreement is not reached, the case is then heard by a different judge.

12.2.2 **Analysis of the Facts**

Before you can begin to plan a negotiation strategy you need to decide on the 'stakes'. What exactly is it that you are negotiating and what are the parameters? Is this a one-off transaction or an ongoing relationship? Are you creating something new—for example setting up

[4] Alan Fowler, *Negotiation Skills and Strategies* (Chartered Institute of Personnel and Development 1996).
[5] Carrie Menkel-Meadow, *Negotiation: A Very Short Introduction* (OUP 2022).

a new company, or dividing an existing asset such as dissolving a business and deciding on the distribution of the assets? Once you have a clear understanding of what the possibilities are, your client needs to understand the options and you need to know what their priorities are. For example:

- In an employment dispute, there is no point negotiating a good payout for your client if what they really wanted was to have their job back.
- In a housing dispute, your client may well be willing to move out of a property, but may need more time to do so. In such a case, negotiating for them to keep their tenancy may feel like a win to you, but may not be the best result for the client.
- In a case involving children, your client may be willing to have less than half the summer holidays because of work commitments, but would rather have an extra weekend with their children every month.
- In a contract negotiation, your client may be willing to accept a lower price if there is a promise of future contracts. You may want to hold out for the highest price, but in doing so you could damage the long-term relationship between the parties. If your client comes across as unreasonable or difficult the other party may not want to do business with them again in the future.

It is therefore crucial to understand both what all the possible solutions are and what your client's preferred options might be, before you plan a strategy. Often, there are underlying motivations or ambitions in a negotiation, and it is worth trying to understand what these are in order to find creative ways to reach a settlement.

Once you have identified your options, you need to work out your best alternative to a negotiated agreement (BATNA) so that you can set parameters to your negotiation. For lawyers who are involved in litigation, the BATNA will normally be to allow a judge to decide. Litigation involves a series of negotiations over both procedure and substantive issues—so much so that modern litigation has been described as 'litigotiation'.[6] Negotiation is not an alternative to litigation, it is part of the process. If you are involved in transactional work, the BATNA may be to leave the deal completely, or to find a third party to invest in the product.

The traditional view of a negotiation is that of two competitive parties battling it out until one party wins, or both parties give a little and they meet in the middle. However, there is a different way of approaching negotiation, which is to see it as a problem-solving process. Rather than focusing on your position and what your client wants to achieve, you can try to identify the underlying ambitions of all the parties and work towards a solution that works for both sides. This approach developed by Fisher and Ury relies on four basic rules: separate the people from the problem; focus on interests not positions; invent options for mutual gain; and insist on using objective criteria.

[6] Marc Galanter, 'Worlds of Deals: Using Negotiation to Teach about Legal Process' (1984) 34(2) Journal of Legal Education 268–76.

12.2.3 **Separate the People from the Problem**

As mentioned, negotiators are people first, and relationships between negotiators can affect the process both negatively and positively. And relationships can change from trust to distrust quickly, sometimes based on misunderstandings. A negotiation can get stuck in a cycle of point-scoring which can lead to the negotiation failing. It is, therefore, important to try and separate the human responses from the problem the negotiation is attempting to solve. There are three aspects to understanding the people problem: perceptions, emotion, and communication.

> Conflict lies not in objective reality, but in people's heads. Truth is simply one more argument—perhaps a good one, perhaps not—for dealing with the difference. For difference itself exists because it exists in their thinking. Fears, even if ill-founded, are real fears and need to be dealt with. Hopes, even if unrealistic, may cause a war. Facts, even if established, may do nothing to solve the problem. Both parties may agree that one lost the watch and the other found it, but still disagree over who should get it.[7]

It is important to try and understand both your perception and that of the other party. By putting yourself in their shoes and understanding how they see the issue, you can find a way to reduce conflict and present solutions. You don't have to agree with the other party's point of view, and you need to take care not to project your fears onto them, but if you try to see things from their perspective you may find a way to reduce conflict. The aim of the negotiation is to find a solution, after all. As a lawyer, it is your job to bring a case to a conclusion, not to get a 'win' at all costs.

CASE STUDY

You have been advising a parent, Kate, who has a child with autism and ADHD. The child, Lilly, is 12 years old and is finding school so stressful that she is refusing to attend. The parents have been told by the school, Green Street Academy, that they will be fined if they do not send Lilly to school. Lilly's mother believes that the school environment is wrong for Lilly and wants her to go to a specialist school, The Grove, that can support her properly. Lilly finds noisy, busy environments very difficult so some aspects of the school environment are very hard for her, particularly the congestion in corridors between lessons. She also finds it very difficult to organize herself or plan ahead, so frequently misses hand-in dates for homework and gets very upset if she gets detention for missed homework. She finds any change in routine difficult to manage and a high number of supply teachers due to staff sickness and shortages led to an increase in her levels of anxiety. Lilly's needs have been assessed, and an education health care plan (EHCP) has now been issued. This is a document setting out Lilly's needs and naming her school. The EHCP does not name the school that the parents want. The plan names Lilly's current school, Green Street Academy, but puts in place a high level of support to help her manage her day.

[7] Fisher, Ury, and Patton (n 2) 25.

The parents have the right to challenge the contents of the EHCP and the school at the Special Educational Needs Tribunal. The waiting times for hearings are between 10 months and 1 year. Before going to tribunal, the parents also have the option of mediation, which could take place within a couple of weeks. Depending on the circumstances, they may also have the option of judicial review if the local authority is failing in its duty to provide an education to Lilly.

Your law school clinic has agreed to the following action:

1. To conduct some written negotiations with the local authority on behalf of Kate to try and get the plan amended without the need for tribunal proceedings.
2. To assist the parents to prepare for mediation and attend mediation with them.

Table 12.3 sets out the perceptions of both parties.

Table 12.3 Perceptions of both parties

Kate's Perceptions	Local Authority's Perceptions
The Grove is perfect for Lilly's needs. It is worth investing in her education now so that she is able to thrive as an adult, which will save the government money in the long term.	The parents' choice of The Grove is very expensive and this is a disproportionate expense for one child.
The Green Street Academy doesn't care about Lilly. That attitude won't change just because there is some funding in place to support her.	The Green Street Academy did not try to put support in place when Lilly's anxiety started making it hard for her to manage. So, with some support, things might change.
We tried so hard to speak to Green Street and they never answered our calls; they just threatened us with fines. They made us feel like it was our fault.	The parents did not try to work with Green Street Academy to get support in place to help Lilly attend.
Lilly was top of her class at primary school and had outstanding scores in her SATS. She is now achieving lower than average and is being moved down a set in maths and in English. 'Average' is not good enough when she has the ability to achieve more.	Lilly is doing well academically despite her poor attendance so she does not need a special school.
Lilly has been on the waiting list for mental health support for two years and still—nothing. It is all government money, whether therapy is paid for by the NHS or by the local authority. She needs help and she needs it now.	The Grove includes a high level of therapeutic support and Lilly should be receiving therapy from children's mental health services at the NHS. It is not the role of the local authority to pay for therapy at school.

Table 12.3 *(Continued)*

Kate's Perceptions	Local Authority's Perceptions
The Grove is close to our work, so we can manage taking Lilly to school and collecting her; therefore the journey is not a problem.	The Grove is several miles away. Lilly will not be able to get there by herself and will need expensive transport.
Lilly's best friend at school has moved to a new school and she is socially isolated because of all her absences.	Lilly has a friendship group at Green Street Academy and will suffer socially if moved away. She needs to stay with her peer group.
We don't believe that the local authority plan will work and think they are only delaying the inevitable.	We don't think the parents have tried hard enough to support Lilly at her current school, and we think it is worth trying to make it work with some support in place before giving up completely.

Understanding the perception of the other side can help you identify issues that might be resolved quickly or remove them from the negotiation immediately. You can discuss the perceptions openly and invite the other side to come up with solutions. For example, in the case study above, the issue of transport could be dealt with quickly because a solution is offered by the parents.

But negotiation is not only about understanding the factual, or even the legal, context. **Emotions** play an important part in most negotiations. Whether you are dealing with a disputed parking fine or a multi-party merger and acquisition deal, the people involved want the issue to be resolved, and either personal or professional pride can influence their approach to a negotiation. In a law clinic, it is likely that you will work on cases where the outcome may have a major impact on the individual client you are representing. Emotions can therefore run high. Your own emotions can also affect the way you approach a negotiation. You may want to get a good result for your client, or feel angry on their behalf about the situation they find themselves in. There is no single solution to dealing with emotion in a negotiation, but a starting point is to try and step back to recognize and acknowledge the emotions of both the parties and the negotiators.

Finally, as a reminder and to (almost) state the obvious, **communication** is at the heart of all negotiations. You need all of your communication skills to conduct a successful negotiation. We explored key communication skills in Chapter 9. Non-verbal communication and listening skills are crucial in negotiation.

REFLECTION POINT

Look at the perceptions of the parents and the local authority in Table 12.3.

- What emotions do you think Lilly's parents might be feeling? How could those emotions impact on their ability to negotiate an agreement about Lilly's education?
- What about the local authority caseworker? How might the caseworker feel about this situation?
- How could acknowledging and discussing the different perceptions of the parents and the local authority help to narrow the areas of disagreement?

12.2.4 **Focus on Interests, Not Positions**

Your position in a negotiation is driven by your interests. Before you start negotiating, you need to understand what the positions are, and separate them from interests. The position that a person takes is phrased in terms of a desired outcome or starting point for a negotiation. For example, on a commercial transaction or property sale, your position might be 'I won't accept less that £300,000 for the sale of the house' but your interest may be that your client needs to complete a sale by a certain date to facilitate a move to a new area and to start a new job.

The position taken by Kate in the case study is: 'We want Lilly to go to the special school.' The position taken by the local authority is: 'We are only willing to fund a place at the mainstream school.' If we assume the best, and not the worst, on both sides (and we must be aware that we don't always do that!), then both parties have, in fact, a shared interest: they both want Lilly to be receiving education that is right for her and her needs. The local authority also has an interest in providing this education with the least cost to the SEN budget. They have a responsibility to cater for the needs of all the children in the area. The parents do not have an interest in the education of other children; they are only concerned about securing an education and support for their child. It may be that the parents are right that the school they have identified is the only provision that can meet her needs, but by starting the negotiation with a focus on the interests of the parties, which is to find a way to support Lilly so that she can engage in education, you have a better chance of narrowing the differences between them to find a solution.

12.2.5 **Invent Options for Mutual Gain**

This is the heart of the problem-solving approach to negotiation. Once you have looked at perceptions and identified the underlying interests of the parties, you can begin to explore ideas to resolve the case.

Practical Exercise 12.4

Split into pairs or small groups. Allocate the groups the role of local authority or parents.

In your groups, brainstorm as many ideas as possible for ways in which Lilly's access to education could be supported. Try to think of pros and cons for each possible solution.

You do not need knowledge of education structures or education law to do this. All you need is basic familiarity with the way schools operate, which you should have as part of your personal background. After all, you've been to school. The purpose of the exercise is to just imagine how to find a way to support Lilly. Remember that she is academically able, but can't manage noisy, busy environments; struggles to organize herself; and needs a high level of predictability and structure in her day. Try to think of different creative solutions to addressing these difficulties so that she can continue to get an education.

- When you have finished brainstorming, pair up with one of the groups brainstorming for the other side. Compare your suggested solutions. Are any of them the same?
- Once you have compared your list of possible solutions, put them together in one list, but keep a note of which team proposed each solution. In other words, was this a parent solution, a local authority solution, or did both sides come up with the same idea?
- Now join up with another group and compare ideas again. How many of your solutions are the same? Put your two lists of solutions together into a total list.
- Continue with this process until everyone in the room has shared their ideas.
- How many different ideas for supporting Lilly have you come up with? How many of those ideas were proposed by both parents and local authority?

It may be that none of the solutions you have come up with are practical or affordable, but by approaching the problem by looking at the interests rather than the positions, which were school X or school Y, you may have found some ways in which Lilly can be helped to continue in education, either in the short term or the longer term. Remember, one of the problems facing the parents is that they could be waiting for a year to get a tribunal hearing, as by then Lilly may not be able to access school at all.

Having identified interests and possible solutions, you can plan your negotiation strategy. Focusing on interests, not positions, does not mean that you must then compromise. The aim of the negotiation is still to get the best solution for your client. It is just that you are approaching the negotiation from a position of principle. You need to defend your interests hard. Lilly needs to be in school and needs support to access education. Once you have this clear, rather than focusing on the preferred school, you can approach the negotiation by asking the local authority to explain how they think that their solution will provide for Lilly. The goal of your negotiation may still be for Lilly to go to the school identified by her parents, but the local authority may have other solutions or schools that could meet her needs, so prepare to consider alternative suggestions. Don't dismiss options out of hand without taking time to take your client's instructions. Allow the clients time to inform themselves about other schools suggested. Ask questions. If the option suggested is not suitable or viable, then go back to the negotiations to pursue the option of The Grove again.

12.2.6 **Insist on Using Objective Criteria**

When looking at the possible solutions to the negotiation, you need to find objective criteria to then decide and explain your position. The way in which you establish objective criteria will depend on what you are negotiating. For example, you may want to look at:

- Market value
- Industry standards
- Regulatory frameworks
- Precedent
- Procedural rules
- Independent expert reports

By referring back to objective standards, you can negotiate from a position of principle rather than pressure or will power: 'Concentrate on the merits of the problem, not the mettle of the parties. Be open to reason, but closed to threats.'[8]

REFLECTION POINT

Think of a situation where you have had to engage in a negotiation in your life. This could be a personal negotiation or a professional one.

How did you approach the negotiation? Did you think of it in terms of win or lose? Were you aware of different techniques for negotiation? Having read this chapter so far, would you have done things differently if you had to conduct that negotiation again?

CASE STUDY

Consider these two extracts of letters in Table 12.4. These are draft letters to the local authority on behalf of Kate, Lilly's mother. Which one has used the framework set out above? If you were working for the local authority, how would you feel on receiving these two letters? How would you respond to each one? Which one would you describe as based on a competitive position-based approach? Which one would you describe as based on an interests-based approach based on objective criteria?

[8] Fisher, Ury, and Patton (n 2) 84.

Table 12.4 Comparison of negotiation styles

Letter A	Letter B
The parents are not willing to accept the proposal that Lilly remain at her current school, Green Street Academy, as they do not accept that it is possible to provide the support she needs in a mainstream environment. Even if the right support could be put in place, the parents have no confidence that the school would have the will or capability to provide what is needed. It has been clear, up to now, that they are not interested in working with the family to support Lilly so without a fundamental shift in the entire approach to meeting needs of disabled students from the senior leadership team, our clients will not accept the option of Lilly remaining at her current school. The local authority and the school have so far failed Lilly and she is entitled to an education like any other child. We are therefore writing to you to say that the EHCP must be amended to name the Special School forthwith. You will be fully aware that the parents have the right to name the school of their choosing in an EHCP and if we do not receive an amended plan within seven days of the date of this letter our clients will make an application to the Special Educational Needs Tribunal, which they will no doubt win.	Our clients have some questions and concerns regarding the decision to name Lilly's current school, Green Street Academy, on the EHCP. The educational psychologist's report prepared as part of the EHCP assessment made the following specific recommendations: • Lilly needs to be taught in small classes of no more than 12 students. • Lilly needs support with developing relationships with her peers with a specific programme of social skills activities and support—for example, a circle of friends or similar programme. • Lilly needs a high level of certainty and predictability in her school day. The recommendation is that she should have access to a timetable with only three lessons in each day, to limit the number of transitions between classes. We would be grateful if you could confirm how you think the current EHCP and proposed school will address these specific recommendations. Even with the level of 1:1 support that you are proposing, the structure of the school day at mainstream will remain at 7 lessons a day with classes of 30 or more students. Furthermore, the school have stated very clearly that there is no capacity for social skills support within the day and they would not be able to support a circle of friends programme. We would remind you that you have a legal duty to provide all children in the borough, including Lilly, with appropriate education. Lilly has already missed 60 days of school in the past 4 months and there is a serious risk that if the current EHCP remains unchanged she will continue to struggle to access any education, thus falling further behind, which may lead to a need to greater intervention and support in future. Please could you respond to this letter setting out a clear proposal of how you intend to provide the educational structure set out in the educational psychologist's report, within the next seven days.

12.2.7 Lawyer Negotiation

So far this chapter has considered some ideas about how to negotiate that apply to all negotiations, from buying a car to international border disputes. While these concepts all apply to lawyer negotiations, there are certain factors that add a layer of complexity to negotiations that are driven by lawyers. When you negotiate as a lawyer, there are certain features to the negotiation that are different to negotiating as an individual. Maughan and Webb identify four distinctive attributes to a lawyer-led negotiation:[9]

1. *Facilitative or settlement negotiations*—Lawyers negotiate deals on non-litigious cases or negotiate settlements in disputes, often within the context of ongoing litigation. These two types of litigation require different skills and knowledge.
2. *Representative negotiations*—You are not negotiating for yourself, but on behalf of your client. You have professional duties and responsibilities in relation to your client.
3. *Inter and intra-party negotiations*—Lawyer negotiations are complex because you must negotiate not only with the other side, but also with your own client.
4. *Negotiating in the shadow of the law*—Negotiation takes place within the context of legal rules which sets parameters and shapes the way in which negotiations take place.

We would add a fifth distinctive attribute to this list:

5. *Ethical framework and professional code of conduct*—Lawyers in all jurisdictions operate within the context of strict codes of conduct and ethical standards. The standards of honesty and integrity apply as much to lawyer negotiations as any other area practice, along with duties to the court as well as duties to the client.

These five features mean that as a lawyer negotiator you must have a thorough understanding of:

a. your client's aims and objectives;
b. the relevant facts;
c. the relevant law and procedure;
d. the ethical framework within which you are operating.

It is only when you have a grasp of all four of the above that you are ready to start planning and conduction a negotiation.

12.2.8 Ethics and Lawyer-led Negotiations

The fact that lawyers are leading the negotiation has additional implications. In particular, there are tactics and strategies that could be deemed acceptable in other forms of negotiation, but would not be tolerated when done by lawyers. Your position as a lawyer in relation

[9] Caroline Maughan and Julian Webb, *Lawyering Skills and the Legal Process* (2nd ed, Cambridge University Press 2005) 317.

to ethics is complicated by the rules governing lawyer ethics. Some of these rules can be in conflict with each other. As a lawyer you have a duty of confidentiality to your client but you also have a duty to disclose material information in a dispute, particularly if you are involved in litigation. You have a duty to act in your client's best interests and to act on your client's instructions, but you also have a duty to act with integrity and to uphold the rule of law. In lawyer-led negotiations there are two ethical rules in particular that you need to consider when planning or conducting negotiations: the duty to act with honesty and integrity, and the duty not to use threats or abuse superior bargaining power.

Unethical behaviour from lawyers can take a number of different forms, including:[10]

1. Lying intentionally about the relevant or material facts.
2. Giving misleading information about the material facts.
3. Lying or making misleading statements about the issues, for example the party's bottom line or mandate.
4. Non-disclosure of information.
5. Use of threats.
6. Abuse of superior bargaining power.

Is It Permissible to Lie When You Are Negotiating?

There is some acceptance that, when negotiating, you do not have to disclose everything from the start. But does that mean that the seller must disclose that there is a new estate planned on the park next to the house, or that they cannot say that theirs is the 'best car in the world'? The traditional common law position of *caveat emptor* (buyer beware) has been restricted by legislation in different ways in different jurisdictions. For example, consumer protection legislation and rules regarding sale and purchase of houses place duties of disclosure on the seller, but these duties may vary from one jurisdiction to another. However, the standards of acceptable 'puff' vary according to industry standards and also according to jurisdictions.

Research suggests that competitive negotiators are more likely to lie and that the higher the stakes, the greater the temptation to lie or act dishonestly.[11] However, lying and deceit can lead to a deal being reversed at a later date, if the buyer relied on fraudulent misrepresentations. It can also lead to a breakdown of trust and therefore a breakdown in negotiations if exposed before a deal is made. Before you plan any negotiation, it is, therefore, important to carefully consider how much you need to disclose and when. Acting ethically does not mean that you have to put all your cards on the table from the start, but you do need to decide whether you are crossing a line if you suggest something that is not true or even if you are not disclosing a substantial fact that you are required to disclose. On the other hand, in addition to thinking carefully in advance about the limitations on the information you might disclose

[10] Barney Jordaan, *Negotiation and Dispute Resolution for Lawyers* (Edward Elgar 2022) 232.
[11] Ibid 233.

while still upholding honesty and integrity, you need to be aware that your opponent in a negotiation may not be completely truthful.

Carrie Menkel-Meadow advises that 'important things to do in all negotiations are to ask lots of questions and investigate facts, personnel and conditions. Asking questions persistently and demanding answers, in writing where possible, is one way to protect against deception or at least get it on the record'.[12]

REFLECTION POINT

Do you ever watch legal dramas on TV?

Think about a legal drama that you have enjoyed.

How were the lawyers' ethics portrayed in the drama? Did they sometimes lie or break the rules to win their case? Lawyers are often portrayed as highly competitive and as people who like to win. Has working in a clinical setting or reading some of the chapters about ethics and legal practice changed the way that you think about the role of honesty, integrity, and emotional intelligence in legal practice? If so, how?

Threats or Abuse of Superior Bargaining Power

Often in a legal negotiation, whether in negotiating with the state in a matter of regulation or compliance or in negotiating in a commercial context, one party has significantly more power than the other. For the lawyer representing the stronger party, there may be a temptation to use this position to intimidate the weaker side. In a clinical setting, it is likely that you will be advising or representing the weaker party. It is therefore important to recognize when the other side is crossing a line and using intimidatory practices, as this may well be unethical and a breach of the regulations. For example, in the case study of Lilly, the local authority is the more powerful party, but they still need to operate within the law. The caseworker cannot make a false statement to the parents, such as telling them that they do not have a right of appeal to the tribunal, or threaten them with repeated fines for non-attendance if they don't accept the local authority proposal. A solution can and should be found without intimidating the parents. Part of your role as an adviser and negotiator is to ensure that the parents are fully informed as to their rights and their options and to point out to the local authority what the expectations are in terms of negotiating honestly.

One area of abuse of power that has come under the spotlight in the UK is the use of threats of legal action to prevent stories being published. These are known as SLAPPs (Strategic Lawsuits Against Public Participation). These are defined by the SRA as a

> misuse of the legal system, through bringing or threatening claims that are unmeritorious or characterised by abusive tactics, in order to stifle lawful scrutiny and publication, including on matters of corruption or wrongdoing.

[12] Menkel-Meadow (n 5) 30.

Our key messages for solicitors and law firms are:

- you must not bring or threaten unmeritorious claims or engage in tactics that are intimidatory or otherwise oppressive
- your duty to act in your client's interest must be balanced with your wider professional obligations, including your duty to the courts and to uphold the rule of law, which take precedence should these come into conflict
- you should identify proposed causes of action or behaviours which comprise a SLAPP or abuse of the litigation process, and decline to act in this way
- particular care is required where a publication ventilates a matter that is likely to engage the public interest.[13]

Sometimes it may be completely appropriate to threaten legal action against an individual or an organization, and this is often an important part of negotiations. But what the SLAPP rules prevent is the threat of initiating litigation when in fact you know you have no grounds for issuing proceedings. This is a misuse of power.

If you are involved in negotiations and you think that the other party is behaving unethically, one way of dealing with this can be to remind them of their ethical obligations and to point out the consequences of breaching the rules. If the behaviour is not serious enough to risk sanctions from a regulator, loss of reputation or future business is also a deterrent to unethical practice.

REFLECTION POINT

In December 2024, Ashley Hurst, a solicitor acting for the former Chancellor of the Exchequer, Nadim Zahawi, was fined £50,000 and ordered to pay £260,000 in costs by the Solicitors Disciplinary Tribunal in relation to the use of 'without prejudice' on email correspondence. Without prejudice correspondence allows lawyers to negotiate a settlement. The 'without prejudice' label means that correspondence cannot later be disclosed in court, so it allows negotiators to make offers to try and settle a dispute without later being held to that offer if no settlement is reached.

The case related to allegations about the former Chancellor's tax affairs. A lawyer and investigative journalist, Dan Neidle, stated publicly on social media that Mr Zahawi had lied. Mr Hurst did not want correspondence with Mr Neidle to be published, and said that the 'without prejudice' heading meant that the correspondence could not be disclosed save for the purposes of obtaining legal advice. The SDT did not find that Mr Hurst's correspondence amounted to SLAPP, but they did find that he had 'improperly attempted to restrict Mr Neidle'. The SDT went on to find that he had breached principles 2 and 5 of the SRA Principles, namely the duties to uphold public trust and confidence in the profession and to act with integrity.[14]

Does this outcome surprise you? The lawyer concerned was acting to protect his client's interests. Do you think that lawyers should be able to threaten litigation or use legal correspondence to prevent individuals from publishing damaging material, even if the allegations are true?

[13] SRA, 'Strategic Lawsuits against Public Participation (SLAPPs)—Warning Notice' Solicitors Regulation Authority (last accessed 25 March 2025).

[14] *SRA v Hurst* [2024] SDT 12612.

12.2.9 **Planning Your Negotiation**

1. Analyse your case and make sure you have a good grasp of the facts.
2. Research the law carefully so you fully understand the realistic options for the case.
3. Discuss the negotiation with the client. Make sure that you understand their objectives and priorities. Consider their underlying interests and explore ideas for alternative solutions with them before entering negotiations. You do not want to reach an agreement which your client subsequently rejects, forcing you back into the negotiation with a loss of good faith.
4. Try to think about the other side's interests and put yourself in their shoes to try and imagine what their perceptions might be. Remember, both parties can agree on the facts, but still differ in their idea of what a fair outcome might look like.
5. Work out what your BATNA is and agree this with the client.
6. Get your ethics right. Make sure the client understands your ethical position. They cannot ask you to lie on their behalf or mislead the court if you are involved in litigation. Nor can they ask you to threaten court action which you would not actually have grounds to issue.
7. Be clear about the timescales involved and the manner in which you will negotiate. Are you arranging a face-to-face meeting, a phone call, or a video call, or entering correspondence?
8. Find out who the legal representative for the other party is, and consider what you know about them and their style of negotiation. Often, lawyers in practice negotiate regularly with the same people. You will therefore have an idea about how they will approach a negotiation, which will help you prepare. In a university law clinic you may be entering into a legal negotiation for the first time, so you are less likely to know your opponent. Speak to your supervisor—they may be able to give you some guidance on what to expect.
9. Organize your notes and documents so that you can find your way around them easily.

12.2.10 **Conducting Your Negotiation**

Here are some final tips for conducting your negotiation:

- Negotiations can be conducted in writing or in a meeting. Make sure that you are clear about the venue and format for the negotiations and agree an agenda in advance. Don't allow the other party to take you by surprise. If they phone you at 4pm on a Friday and say 'shall we just try and agree some of the preliminaries now?' don't be afraid to say that this is not a convenient time and arrange to speak at a later date when you are ready. Similarly, if something comes up in the negotiation that you were not expecting, ask for time to discuss this with your client before responding.
- Set and agree an agenda with the other parties. If you are meeting to negotiate, agree objectives for the meeting and keep to the agenda.

- Throughout your negotiations, keep in mind the goal, which is to settle your client's case. Focus on underlying interests, not positions, and ask the other side questions rather than making demands.
- Negotiation is about communicating, so use all of your communication skills. Listen carefully and pay attention to non-verbal clues.
- If you need a break, take a break. It is normal for people to have emotional responses to a negotiation and if your client gets distressed or frustrated then you can ask for a break.
- When you reach an agreement, make sure you record it in writing.
- Remember, there is nothing wrong with compromise. The purpose of negotiation is to reach an agreement. This does not mean you have to meet in the middle, but you do need to be prepared to compromise.

TAKING STOCK

In this section of the chapter, we looked at some of the skills needed for negotiation. Most lawyers conduct negotiations regularly, whether involved in transactional work or litigation. The key skill needed in negotiation is communication.

The key to successful negotiation is to have a good understanding of not only your own client's objectives, but also those of the other side. Lawyer negotiation has an added layer of complexity, due to the fact that you are negotiating on behalf of someone else, so you will need to agree strategies and possible outcomes with your own client before reaching an agreement with the other side.

Lawyers are bound by professional ethics and must take account of this when negotiating. In particular, lawyer negotiators must take care not to abuse a position of power or threaten litigation which they do not have grounds to bring.

Finally, don't lose sight of the purpose of negotiation, which is to reach an agreement—so be prepared to compromise.

12.3 **Advocacy**

As a clinical student, your opportunities for advocacy may be limited by regulatory rules that only give rights of audience in court to practising lawyers, or by the complexity of the issues that might arise in any given case. However, in some law school clinics, students have the opportunity to work on tribunal cases or to act as a lay representative on behalf of a client in court. There are, of course, other environments where having good advocacy skills can be important. This could include, for example, a job interview or simply contributing to discussion in classes at law school.

Of course, the art of advocacy is about more than standing up in a courtroom and making a clever argument. Good advocacy is about thorough preparation, well-organized and well-drafted documents, and the ability to know when to stop as well as when to start

Table 12.5 Statement of Solicitor Competence on Negotiation and Case Progression

B5 Undertake effective spoken and written advocacy, including	Questions to consider
a. Preparing effectively by identifying and mastering relevant facts and legal principles b. Organising facts to support the argument or position c. Presenting a reasoned argument in a clear, logical, succinct and persuasive way d. Making appropriate reference to legal authority e. Complying with formalities f. Dealing with witnesses appropriately g. Responding effectively to questions or opposing arguments h. Identifying strengths and weaknesses from different parties' perspectives	Do you have experience in these competencies? How would you rate your competence? Do you need more experience? How could you gain this experience?

speaking. The '5 P's of performance'—proper preparation prevents poor performance—could not be more apt in the context of legal advocacy. When it comes to preparation you should make sure that you familiarize yourself not only with your own case and that of the other side, but also with the relevant rules and procedure of the court or tribunal in which you are appearing.

Perhaps paradoxically, while it is important to prepare, it is also important to be flexible. For example, some tribunals may be more informal than you initially expect. A case might be held around a table as if it is a meeting rather than a more formal courtroom setting. Even in more formal courtrooms, judges can vary in terms of what they might expect and the approach they take to the case and to the advocates appearing in front of them. Effective advocacy therefore demands careful preparation, as well as expecting the unexpected.

Table 12.5 contains an extract from the SRA Statement of Solicitor Competence. Refer to the companion website to this book to find a downloadable template to audit your skills and reflect on your development.

12.3.1 Preparing Submissions

Your oral submissions will often follow written submissions that you may have already submitted to the court or tribunal in relation to the legal issues in the case. For other matters, such as in a preliminary hearing, you will be required to make submissions 'on your feet' either in response to judicial questioning or to deal with matters that arise in the course of the hearing itself. As explained above, you should always be guided by the rules and relevant procedure of the court or tribunal in which you are appearing. Your submissions must comply with the relevant rules so it is important to acquaint yourself with them before (rather than after!) you begin drafting. In England and Wales, by way of example, this would be set out in what is known as the 'White Book', which contains the civil procedure rules and practice directions relevant to different areas of civil law.

In preparing your submissions, you should also consider the following questions:

1. What are you asking for?
2. Does the court or tribunal have the authority to decide or direct what you're asking for?
3. If so, how can you persuade them to decide in your favour?

In relation to the first question, it goes without saying that you need to know your own case to know what you're asking for. You also need to be familiar with your opponent's case—the key strengths of their case will be the weaknesses in yours, and vice versa. As Scalia and Garner observe:

> No general engages the enemy without a battle plan based in large part on what the enemy is expected to do. Your case must take into account the points the other side is likely to make. You must have a clear notion of what ones can be swallowed (accepted but shown to be irrelevant) and which must be vigorously countered on the merits.[15]

You should therefore try to ask yourself how you might argue the case if you were on the opposing side. Acquaint yourself with what their 'case theory' might be, as well as carefully considering your own. The case theory essentially refers to your story of the case: it is the version of the facts, and the relevant legal principles, that support your client's position. It is on the basis of this case theory that you must be sure to properly justify and explain, so that the judge will be able to decide in your favour.

The SRA has developed the following questions as a useful way to begin developing your case theory. Consider how you might answer them with respect to one of your clinic cases:

- What are your client's objectives?
- What decision or order are you asking for?
- What law and legal practice is relevant to your case?
- What is the evidence supporting and undermining your client's case?
- What is the evidence supporting and undermining the case of the other side?
- What facts or issues do you need to try to prove and what facts or issues do you need to try to disprove?
- What are the facts or issues which the parties have agreed?
- What witnesses do you need to call to support your case and/or challenge the case of the other side?
- Are there any evidence gaps or issues of admissibility? If there are evidence gaps, can you do anything to fill them?

[15] Antonin Scalia and Bryan Garner, *Making Your Case: The Art of Persuading Judges* (West Publishing Company 2008) 10.

- What points are not relevant or important to your case? Putting minor points to the court could create the perception that your case is weaker than it actually is.
- What themes do you want to bring out in your advocacy? For example, if you were seeking a care order, the themes for your advocacy could be domestic abuse, drug use, and refusal to cooperate with professionals.[16]

In order for the judge to accept your case theory over that of your opponent, it must be presented clearly. So, how best can you persuade a judge to decide in your favour? We discussed the '5 Ps of performance', and they should be considered alongside the '5 Cs of communication': clear, concise, coherent, compelling, and complete. Always try to think about how you can present your submissions in the most concise way, while also trying to tell a compelling story (ie your case theory) about your client's position.

Another aspect of persuasion that is often overlooked in the early years of practice is to remember to never overstate your case. Having worked closely on a case on behalf of a client, you may in fact be persuaded of it. It is important to remember to persuade the court of the merits of the case, rather than your own opinion (which, in fact, is not relevant at all). Stretching an argument too far, or using language which overstates it, will only undermine it. Hyperbole is not your friend.

Finally, when preparing oral submissions, never underestimate the importance of signposting the judge: think about your submission as if you are taking the judge on a journey. You want to tell them where you're going and why you're going there, and then guide them through each of the important points along the way. In your conclusions, you might want to remind them of where you've been. For this reason, paying close attention to the structure of your submissions is critically important. Prepare your submissions in a logical order so you can also guide the judge through them—if you're confused and jumping from one issue to the next and back again, it is highly unlikely that they will be well understood by the judge and you are only likely to cause frustration. At the beginning of your submissions, you want to be sure to explain the main argument that you are making. Having structured your submissions into key points, you should outline from the outset what those points are and then move through them in turn. Some turns of phrase that can help you to signpost your advocacy include:

When presenting your overall submissions:

- I have three key points in relation to X . . .
- There are four issues in this appeal and I will deal with each of them in turn . . .
- In relation to the factual matters in this case, I have three submissions. These are x, y, and z.

[16] Solicitors Regulation Authority, 'Developing an Effective Case Theory' (SRA, 22 August 2022). Available at https://www.sra.org.uk/solicitors/resources/specific-areas-of-practice/developing-effective-case-theory (last accessed 27 November 2025).

When moving on to consider a new point:

- Turning to the issue of X, my main submission is . . .
- Having dealt with the issues of X, I will now turn to issue Y . . .
- Judge, I would now like to consider the issue of . . .
- Moving on, my main argument in relation to X is . . .

When summarizing or concluding a point:

- To reiterate, the prescient point is . . .
- In conclusion, I submit that . . .
- In summary, our key points are that . . .
- We have established that . . .

When turning up documents or introducing evidence:

- I would like to refer the court to the chronology at bundle X, tab Y.
- The evidence, as presented in the witness statement of X, demonstrates that . . .
- I now draw the court's attention to . . .
- It is clear from the testimony of X that . . .

12.3.2 **Your Day at Court—Preparing for the Hearing**

Make sure you have identified the correct term of address for the judge and others in the courtroom (whether in person or online) so you can prepare your submissions with the appropriate address in mind. For example, Tribunal judges and District judges (in England and Wales) are simply addressed as 'Judge' whereas a magistrate is addressed as 'Your Worship' or 'Sir or Madam'. More senior judges are usually referred to as 'My Lord' or 'My Lady'.

Consider your attire and ensure you will be dressed appropriately to help make a good first impression—business dress is appropriate in most courts and tribunals (with the exception of some hearings involving children). Leave plenty of time to get to court and be sure to check where it is, and the best transport options, the day before. It is good practice to aim to arrive at least an hour before the time for the hearing so you can meet with your client and discuss matters with the opposing party. It goes without saying that you should try not to arrive at court late or flustered. Having time goes a long way in terms of minimizing anxiety, both for you as the advocate in the case and also for your client.

For online hearings, you should always ensure your internet connection is secure and that your computer (or other electronic device) is fully charged or otherwise plugged in. Think carefully about your screen background—it should be tidy and professional. You should ideally try to book a space in your law school to have the online meeting for the hearing (your supervisors will be able to advise on where is appropriate). If, for any reason, you do need to conduct the online hearing at home, remember that either blurring the background, using a virtual background, or otherwise having a blank wall or bookcase is best. You should avoid having online hearings in a kitchen or bedroom, if possible, and if you live in a shared space, try to ensure that your housemates know in advance that you have an important hearing and will need there to be quiet and minimal disruption. Even for an online hearing, ensure that your appearance is smart.

Before your hearing, try to meet with your opponent and talk through any anticipated issues and applications there might be. If you can, work towards agreement so that you can present this agreement to the judge. For an online hearing, this might involve setting up a call prior to the hearing. Remember that the judge, or Tribunal panel members, will thank you for anything you have done to make the hearing move quickly and efficiently. You might also want to talk to your opponent about agreeing an order for your submissions.

12.3.3 **During the Hearing**

If you are first to speak, you should introduce yourself and make clear which party you represent. In some courts, it is also appropriate to introduce the advocate on the other side (again, if you are first to speak). Even experienced advocates often find it useful to have the introduction and first few lines of submissions memorized. This can help to get into the flow of advocacy, especially if you're feeling nervous, and will ground you as you develop your submissions.

It is also good practice to check at the beginning of your submissions that the judge has had a chance to read all the relevant documents. You want to avoid making submissions on issues that the judge already knows about but, equally, you want to make sure they have all the relevant information they need to make their decision. One way of ensuring this is the case is to simply ask a question such as, for example, 'Judge, do you require a summary of the facts and issues in the case?' In any event, you want to use your opening address to succinctly familiarize the judge with the key documents in the case. Always be led by the judge during your submissions—if it looks like they're reading and need more time to consult the documents then you will probably need to pause.

While there are different approaches depending on the type of hearing and the case, the following three aspects tend to feature in most submissions:

1. Drawing out the facts relevant to your client's case.
2. Clearly setting out the legal issues.
3. Making clear the legal propositions you are inviting the court to draw.

In terms of advocacy style, experienced advocates are conversational but not overly familiar with the judge. This takes time and experience, so remember that it is probably best to err on the side of respectful formality rather than disrespectful familiarity. Try to maintain eye contact and connect with the judge where possible. This is obviously more difficult in an online hearing, but this, again, is where preparation is key. Particularly in online hearings, it is less compelling and much harder to engage with the judge if you are unprepared and always looking down at notes or reading verbatim from another screen than if you can look directly into the camera when speaking. In any event, where there is more than one judge be sure to address the panel as a whole, and not just the Chair, as the decision will ultimately made by all the judges.

It is natural that you will feel nervous, so have strategies in place for dealing with nerves. Some advocates find it useful to simply pause and take a sip of water. Other tips for oral advocacy include 'treasuring simplicity', 'presenting your arguments as truth rather than your own opinion', 'never speaking over the judge', 'welcoming judicial questions (and asking for clarification if necessary)', 'being cautious about humour', and 'not biting your fingernails'![17] Think of your advocacy as a conversation with the court and remember that when the judge starts to speak, you should immediately stop speaking. Finally, remember that throughout any legal hearing you need to be actively listening. For example, questions will be asked by the judge and by other parties or new issues might even come to light, and you don't want to miss anything.

Opening Statement

In many types of legal proceedings, both civil and criminal, it is common for there to be an opening speech. This is an important opportunity for you to show that you are well prepared and understand the factual and legal points relevant to your case, and also sets the tone in terms of how you engage with the judge. Be clear and precise: knowing how to condense large and often complex amounts of information is a critical legal skill, and perhaps especially so in oral advocacy. This will involve being on top of your papers—you need to reference important documents where necessary and also assist the judges, if needed, to find them. It might be appropriate to give the judge a written chronology that you guide them through in the opening statement. Keep your opening statement engaging and interesting. Hensler (amended in italics) suggests the following structure, which can be adapted depending on the case.

a) Start with a short statement of two or three sentences setting out the nature of the case;
b) Outline who the parties are, the main events and the participants in those events. This may take the form of, or be augmented by, a chronology;
c) explain the pleadings (*eg the statement or particulars of the claim or defence*);
d) list the issues;
e) briefly outline the main legal propositions, and identify the main authorities and statutes;
f) give a short analysis of the case;
g) identify the witnesses to be called and briefly outline the evidence that they will give; and
h) attend to any practical matters such as how documents are to be tendered, or whether any witness has to be interposed or give evidence by video link.[18]

Witness Handling

Oral examination of witnesses usually involves examination-in-chief (of your own witness) and cross-examination (of your witness by the opposing side, or by you of witnesses for the opposing side). The approach to witness handling varies considerably depending on the

[17] Scalia and Garner (n 15) xii.
[18] Elspeth Hemsler, 'Opening and Closing Statements' (2015) 126 Precedent 11.

nature of the proceedings and the area of law concerned. In civil matters, there may only be a brief examination-in-chief to confirm evidence that has been submitted in the written statement. Regardless, the aim of examination-in-chief is to get your own witness to tell their story and present evidence to the court. Note that you cannot use leading questions when examining your own witnesses. Instead, you can only use open questions, which are designed to let the witness tell their story in their own words rather than leading them to give an answer. Open questions tend to begin with words like 'what, where, why, when, and how'. For example:

- What time of day did you leave your house?
- Where did you go?
- How did you travel?
- What route did you take?
- Why did you take that route?
- When did you arrive at the law school?
- What happened when you arrived?

The exception to not asking leading questions during examination-in-chief is where you might have agreed facts with the opposing side. You could then present those facts and ask a leading question (eg 'You left your house at 11am, didn't you?').

To prepare for an examination-in-chief you should closely work through your case and determine the information you need to elicit. Write down the main issues you want to cover and think carefully about some questions you might ask to get that information, including follow-up questions in case the witness is vague in their answers. You will not necessarily know what they might say in open court and responding appropriately, including the careful use of follow-up questions to provide clarification and direction, is important. Try not to talk too quickly or rush witnesses when they are giving evidence. It may take time for them to turn up pages in the bundles of documents should they need to consult them.

After examination-in-chief, your witness may be cross-examined by the opposing side and you may also cross-examine their witnesses. According to the SRA, cross-examination has two key aims:

- First, to advance your case by putting it to witnesses from the other side and getting them to say things which support your case. If you fail to put your case on a particular issue it may be assumed that you accept the other side's account of that issue and you will not be able to put your account of it in your closing speech.
- Second, to undermine the case of the other side by exposing weaknesses in the reliability and credibility of its evidence. This usually means attempting to show that a witness' account is mistaken, inconsistent, or deceitful.[19]

[19] Solicitors Regulation Authority, 'How to Cross-examine a Witness' (31 August, 2022), https://www.sra.org.uk/solicitors/resources/specific-areas-of-practice/conducting-cross-examination/ (last accessed 27 November 2025).

Cross-examination is often thought of as one of the most difficult advocacy skills, given that it requires an ability to think on your feet and be persuasive. You should carefully prepare for your cross-examination while building in enough flexibility to respond to what the witness might say. A general rule is to try not to ask questions you don't know the answer to—ideally, you don't want the witness on the other side to give evidence that might not be favourable to your client in such a way that it takes you by surprise! Think about what you want the witness to say that will support your case or harm the case of the other side and prepare questions accordingly.

Generally, cross-examination questions can and should be leading questions that provide closed answers. For example: You travelled by the law school by bus, didn't you? It was rainy that morning, wasn't it? The SRA provides the following top ten tips for cross-examination:

1. Prepare thoroughly but don't write a script.
2. Keep the two aims of cross-examination in mind: putting your case and undermining the case of the other side.
3. Carefully consider whether a leading or open question is more likely to generate valuable evidence on a particular factual matter.
4. Keep questions short and clear by limiting them to one issue or query at a time.
5. Make sure your questions are relevant and support your case theory.
6. Make sure that every accusation is founded on evidence.
7. Start and finish with strong points.
8. Remain fair, calm and composed at all times.
9. Be firm and robust but never raise your voice, bully, harass or intimidate a witness.
10. Move on from unhelpful answers which weaken your case.[20]

Finally, it is important that there are ethical rules for both solicitors and barristers, which prohibit the coaching of witnesses. You are allowed to familiarize the witness with the court process and what they might expect. However, expressly telling them what to say or how to answer questions or otherwise influencing the evidence they might give is strictly prohibited.

Closing Statement

Your closing statement should summarize your case but also give an account of the points that have arisen on the evidence that has been presented by the other side. If your opposing party has made further points during the hearing itself, make it clear whether you agree or disagree with them and why. Remember, this is likely to be your last chance

[20] Ibid.

to remind the judge of what is important about your case and to persuade them that your side should win. It therefore brings together the evidence that has been presented with your case theory. It is also an opportunity for you to draw attention to the relief you seek (this might be, for example, damages, specific performance, an injunction, or reconsideration of an earlier administrative decision). Whatever way you structure it, try to work through your key points methodically, again recognizing the importance of signposting. Always ask yourself whether the point you're making is strictly necessary. Factors that might weigh in favour of including it would be whether the point is needed in order to correct or clarify a misconception or misunderstanding in the case, whether it directly relates to the facts, or whether it is key to the legal arguments you have presented.

Hensler suggests identifying the following issues in order to prepare for a closing statement:

a) the evidence for and against your client's case;
b) how to minimize the impact of what is against your client's case;
c) how to maximize the impact of what is helpful to your client's case.

This will require a consideration of:

a) the oral evidence adduced for your client;
b) the oral evidence adduced by other parties;
c) exhibits (documentary and otherwise)—to the extent that they really are relevant;
d) questions and comments from the court—these can be a very useful indication of what is on the court's mind or what is troubling the court. These indications from the court enable the advocate to target their closing statement accordingly;
e) statements by other advocates (particularly any concessions or any statements that suggest that another party has had to change its position—these should be noted so that closing statements can inform the court of what is no longer in issue and what is unclear, incoherent, or perhaps recently invented on the part of other parties);
f) pleadings and particulars—in case it is necessary to confine other parties to their case;
g) answers to interrogatories; and common sense (but only if it is supported by the evidence).[21]

Taken together, your closing statement should aim to present the judge with a roadmap and give clear directions so they can make decisions that will lead to a favourable outcome for your client.

[21] Hemsler (n 17) 12.

TAKING STOCK

Developing advocacy skills takes time and experience. We have considered here some of the key points to consider in developing your own advocacy skills. It is important to recognize the purpose of the different stages of the hearing or court process and plan accordingly. The distinctions between opening statements, witness handling, and closing statements have been set out in this chapter. However, the procedural approach will depend on the type of case and stage of proceedings in which you are involved. We have also outlined the importance of knowing your own case and being on top of your 'case theory' so you can advance this during the hearing and always be guided by it when you have to think on your feet. Different advocates have different styles in practice, as well as wide-ranging techniques for engaging the judge (or jury). Aside from clinical opportunities, going to your local court and observing either civil or criminal trials in action is a great way to start learning what effective advocacy looks like.

Conclusion

In this final chapter we have looked at some of the key skills needed to represent your client. Representing a client requires a commitment to progress their case and bring it to a conclusion, whether that is by way of a negotiated agreement or through tribunal or court proceedings. All of the skills explored in this chapter are underpinned by the skills discussed in the previous chapters.

Communication:

Drafting, negotiation, and advocacy are all underpinned by communication skills. You need to be able to communicate with your client, your colleagues, and the other parties involved in the case.

File Management:

Keeping on top of the work and keeping to deadlines is crucial to progressing a case. You need to make careful notes of all the work you do and keep all the correspondence on the file. Having a good grasp of the facts and the issues is essential for drafting, negotiation, and advocacy. You need to be able to navigate documents quickly and easily, as do your colleagues if you are working in a team.

Client Interviewing:

In order to represent your client, you must be clear about their instructions. Your client needs to trust you and you need to understand their objectives and priorities.

Practical Legal Research:

In order to give clear advice and understand the risks and benefits associated with different courses of action, you need to be confident in your understanding of law and procedure. Relying on lecture handouts, search engines, or AI search tools will not be enough if you want to be confident that you are right. If you represent your client in a tribunal or negotiate with lawyers for the other party, you cannot quote your tutor's notes as a reliable source.

Advice:

Your need to give your client clear advice from the outset so that they understand what their options are. You cannot develop a strategy based on client objectives if their objectives are unrealistic.

Ethics:

All of the work you do in a clinical legal setting has an ethical underpinning. This does not just mean that you must follow the codes of conduct; more than that, you need to learn to exercise your own judgement about whether your behaviour meets the highest standards of honesty and integrity and whether you are upholding the rule of law. Sometimes this will create conflict between your duty to act on your client's instructions and your duty to the professional standards.

Reflection:

The work of a lawyer is complex and none of these skills can be learned in one case. They take practice and the art of being a good lawyer is something that is developed over years of practice. We have encouraged you throughout this book to reflect at regular intervals. Each new client and each new case presents you with an opportunity to reflect on what you have done, whether you could have done things differently, and how you might do things differently next time. Developing the habit of reflection now, while you are a law student, will stand you in good stead whatever career path you choose.

Further Reading

Mark Adler and Daphne Perry, *Clarity for Lawyers. Effective Legal Language* (The Law Society 2017).

Roger Fisher, William Ury, and Bruce Patton, *Getting to Yes: Negotiating Agreement Without Giving In* (2nd ed, Penguin 2011).

Caroline Maughan and Julian Webb, *Lawyering Skills and the Legal Process* (2nd ed, Cambridge University Press 2005).

Carrie Menkel-Meadow, *Negotiation: A Very Short Introduction* (OUP 2022).

Julian Webb, Caroline Maughan, Mike Maughan, Marcus Keppel-Palmer and Andrew Boon, *Lawyers' Skills* (22nd ed, OUP 2017) chapters 4 and 7.

Index

B

C

R

Z